Economic Stabilization
in Developing Countries

WILLIAM R. CLINE *and* SIDNEY WEINTRAUB
Editors

Economic Stabilization in Developing Countries

WILLIAM R. CLINE *and* SIDNEY WEINTRAUB

STANLEY W. BLACK

ANNE O. KRUEGER

CARLOS F. DIAZ-ALEJANDRO

MONTEK S. AHLUWALIA *and* FRANK J. LYSY

ALEJANDRO FOXLEY

IRVING S. FRIEDMAN

JAMES H. WEAVER *and* ARNE ANDERSON

STEPHEN E. GUISINGER

ROGER D. NORTON *and* SEUNG YOON RHEE

LANCE TAYLOR

THE BROOKINGS INSTITUTION
Washington, D.C.

Library of Congress Cataloging in Publication Data:

Main entry under title:

Economic stabilization in developing countries.

  Includes bibliographical references and index.
    1. Underdeveloped areas—Economic policy.
2. Economic stabilization.   I. Cline, William R.
II. Weintraub, Sidney, 1914–
HC59.7.E313   338.9'009172'4   80-26363
ISBN 0-8157-1466-1
ISBN 0-8157-1465-3 (pbk.)

9 8 7 6 5 4 3 2 1

THE BROOKINGS INSTITUTION is an independent organization devoted to nonpartisan research, education, and publication in economics, government, foreign policy, and the social sciences generally. Its principal purposes are to aid in the development of sound public policies and to promote public understanding of issues of national importance.

The Institution was founded on December 8, 1927, to merge the activities of the Institute for Government Research, founded in 1916, the Institute of Economics, founded in 1922, and the Robert Brookings Graduate School of Economics and Government, founded in 1924.

The Board of Trustees is responsible for the general administration of the Institution, while the immediate direction of the policies, program, and staff is vested in the President, assisted by an advisory committee of the officers and staff. The by-laws of the Institution state: "It is the function of the Trustees to make possible the conduct of scientific research, and publication, under the most favorable conditions, and to safeguard the independence of the research staff in the pursuit of their studies and in the publication of the results of such studies. It is not a part of their function to determine, control, or influence the conduct of particular investigations or the conclusions reached."

The President bears final responsibility for the decision to publish a manuscript as a Brookings book. In reaching his judgment on the competence, accuracy, and objectivity of each study, the President is advised by the director of the appropriate research program and weighs the views of a panel of expert outside readers who report to him in confidence on the quality of the work. Publication of a work signifies that it is deemed a competent treatment worthy of public consideration but does not imply endorsement of conclusions or recommendations.

The Institution maintains its position of neutrality on issues of public policy in order to safeguard the intellectual freedom of the staff. Hence interpretations or conclusions in Brookings publications should be understood to be solely those of the authors and should not be attributed to the Institution, to its trustees, officers, or other staff members, or to the organizations that support its research.

Foreword

IN SEVERAL Latin American countries in the 1950s and 1960s, persistent inflation and balance-of-payments difficulties called forth a variety of policies for economic stabilization. More recently, in the 1970s, major international economic disruptions renewed the quest for economic stability as global inflation and the oil price shocks spread inflation and balance-of-payments deficits to virtually all developing regions. At the same time, many developing nations embarked on domestic programs that in themselves added further instability.

By the turn of the decade economic stabilization policies in developing countries had become a highly charged political issue. Were orthodox stabilization policies harmful to national economies, especially to the poorer segments of society? Had the international community failed to provide adequate financing to facilitate adjustment to problems that were international in origin? Was the International Monetary Fund, the main international agency responsible for external financing for stabilization programs, too narrowly focused in its program requirements? Had private banks extended excessive international credit, facilitating lax policies in some countries and necessitating a "bail-out" by public lending?

Fundamental questions have also been raised concerning the theory of economic stabilization. Do the traditional remedies of fiscal and monetary restraint and devaluation take account of the special circumstances of developing countries? Can these or other measures be carried out in ways that avoid prolonged loss of output, and undue concentration of hardship on the poor? Are gradualist programs more effective than shock treatment? How are the purely technical answers changed by considering the limits of tolerance of the political system?

In 1979 the Office of External Research of the U.S. Department of State commissioned the Brookings Institution to organize a conference of experts to analyze the foregoing questions and policy issues. The papers and proceedings of that conference, held on October 25–26, 1979, constitute the text of this volume, which was edited by the conference coordinators, William R. Cline, a senior fellow in the Brookings Foreign Policy Studies program, and Sidney Weintraub, also a Brookings senior fellow at the time of the conference and currently professor of international affairs at the Lyndon B. Johnson School of Public Affairs of the University of Texas. The editors have provided an introduction and summary of the volume. A list of the other contributors with their affiliations at the time of the conference follows the text.

In addition to the individual acknowledgments in the various chapters, the editors acknowledge their indebtedness to many experts in the U.S. Departments of State and Treasury and in the International Monetary Fund for comments, and to Julia Sternberg for typing and logistical administration of the conference. The index was prepared by Patricia Foreman.

The views expressed in this volume are those of its editors and contributors and should not be ascribed to the institutions or individuals whose assistance is acknowledged here and in the various chapters, or to the trustees, officers, or other staff members of the Brookings Institution.

BRUCE K. MAC LAURY
President

January 1981
Washington, D.C.

Contents

1. Introduction and Overview   1
   William R. Cline and Sidney Weintraub
   The Economic Setting   *1*
   The Policy Setting   *4*
   Design of the Volume   *8*
   Highlights of the Studies   *8*
   Major Findings and Issues   *31*

2. The Impact of Changes in the World Economy
   on Stabilization Policies in the 1970s   43
   Stanley W. Black
   Sources of Macroeconomic Fluctuations   *46*
   Global Economic Conditions and Domestic Economic Conditions   *53*
   External and Internal Factors in Stabilization Problems   *62*
   Policy Issues   *71*
   Appendix A: Discriminant Analysis   *73*
   Appendix B: Data   *75*
   Comments by Sidney Dell   *77*
   Discussion   *81*

3. Interactions between Inflation and Trade Regime
   Objectives in Stabilization Programs   83
   Anne O. Krueger
   The Price Level/Exchange Rate/Trade Regime Relationship   *84*
   Interactions between Inflation and the Trade Regime   *93*
   Stabilization Programs and Long-Term Development   *100*
   Trade-Offs in Stabilization Programs   *110*
   Implications for Donor Countries   *113*
   Comments by Hollis B. Chenery   *114*
   Discussion   *116*

4. Southern Cone Stabilization Plans   119
   Carlos F. Diaz-Alejandro
   Historical Background and Initial Conditions   *120*
   The Scorecard   *124*

Some Additional Complications of the Late 1970s *128*
Are These Hardships Really Necessary? *133*
The International Framework *138*
Comments by Ronald McKinnon *141*
Discussion *146*

5. Employment, Income Distribution, and Programs
   to Remedy Balance-of-Payments Difficulties   149
   Montek S. Ahluwalia and Frank J. Lysy
   A Summary of Received Theory *152*
   A One-Sector Model *156*
   A Five-Sector Model *175*
   Conclusions *186*
   Discussion *188*

6. Stabilization Policies and Their Effects
   on Employment and Income Distribution:
   A Latin American Perspective   191
   Alejandro Foxley
   Historical Perspective *192*
   The "New" Stabilization Policies of the 1970s *196*
   The Policies and Their Employment and Distributive Effects *198*
   Adjustment Processes for Economic Stabilization *205*
   Conclusions *221*
   Comments by Arnold C. Harberger *226*
   Comments by Albert Fishlow *229*
   Discussion *232*

7. The Role of Private Banks in Stabilization Programs   235
   Irving S. Friedman
   Growth of Private Bank Lending to Developing Countries *235*
   Relationships between Private Banks and the International
       Monetary Fund *243*
   Conclusions and Suggestions for Private Bank Participation
       in Stabilization Programs *250*
   Conclusions *254*
   Appendix: Case Studies *256*
   Comments by H. Robert Heller *265*
   Discussion *268*

8. Case Study of Economic Stabilization: Mexico   271
   Sidney Weintraub
   The Buildup to the Crisis *272*
   The Stabilization Period *284*
   Conclusions *291*
   Comments by Saúl Trejo Reyes *292*
   Discussion *295*

9. Economic Stabilization in Peru, 1975–78   297
William R. Cline
Origins of the Economic Crisis *298*
Special Factors *301*
The Stabilization Programs *305*
Role of the Banks *309*
Evaluation of the Stabilization Experience *310*
Future Prospects *322*
Lessons from the Peruvian Case *324*
Comments by Daniel M. Schydlowsky *326*
Discussion *332*

10. Stabilization and Development of the
Tanzanian Economy in the 1970s   335
James H. Weaver and Arne Anderson
Background *335*
The Crisis *338*
The Government's Response *346*
Critiques *354*
Conclusions *367*
Comments by G. K. Helleiner *369*
Discussion *374*

11. Stabilization Policies in Pakistan:
The 1970–77 Experience   375
Stephen E. Guisinger
Pakistan's Development, 1950–70   *376*
The Stabilization Problem *377*
Sources of Destabilization *379*
Fiscal Policy *387*
Monetary Policy *393*
Stabilization Policies: An Evaluation *398*
Comments by Gustav F. Papanek *399*

12. A Macroeconometric Model of Inflation
and Growth in South Korea   407
Roger D. Norton and Seung Yoon Rhee
The Equations of the Model *411*
Sample Period Performance of the Model *425*
Historical Experiments with the Model *438*
Concluding Remarks *447*
Appendix: Dynamic Simulation Results for Additional Variables *450*
Comments by Larry E. Westphal *457*
Discussion *462*

13. IS/LM in the Tropics: Diagrammatics
of the New Structuralist Macro Critique   465
Lance Taylor
Economic Structure *466*
Structure in Equation Form *469*
Savings-Investment Balance: Keynesian and Fisherian Investment
Demand, and Contractionary Devaluation Effects *475*
The Market for Loans: Substitution and Wealth Effects in Interest
Rate Response *481*
Comparative Statics *484*
A Complication: Inflationary Pressures from Nontraded Goods *490*
Long-Term Trade-offs among Inflation, Income Distribution,
and Growth *493*
Monetarist Approaches *497*
Possibilities for the Medium Term *501*
Comments by Kemal Dervis *503*
Discussion *506*

Conference Participants   507

Index   509

Tables

1-1. Consumer Price Inflation   2

2-1. Shock to Real GNP in Industrialized Countries   49
2-2. Deficit Finance in Non-Oil-Producing Developing Countries   52
2-3. Cyclical and Secular Changes in Growth and Trade   54
2-4. Balance of Payments of Non-Oil-Producing Developing
Countries   56
2-5. Growth of Reserves, Money, and Prices   60
2-6. Coefficient of Variation of Developing Country Export Volume
and Unit Values   61
2-7. Group Size and Missing Values   65
2-8. Estimated Discriminant Functions   67
2-9. Percentage of Observations Correctly Classified   69
2-10. Contribution to Distance between Groups   70

3-1. Characterization of Alternative Market Interactions   85
3-2. Financial Programs as a Component of Stabilization Programs,
Seventy-nine Countries, 1963–72   107

5-1. The One-Sector Model   159
5-2. Base Data, Malaysia, 1970   160
5-3. Effects of a 10 Percent Devaluation   164
5-4. Effects of Increased Export Demand or Reduced
Investment Demand   170

Contents xiii

5-5. Effects of Combined Policies   174

5-6. Devalue Malaysia's Foreign Exchange Rate 5 Percent,
with Base Data   180

5-7. Devalue Malaysia's Foreign Exchange Rate 5 Percent,
with Expected Profitability Kept Constant   181

5-8. Raise World Price of Exports 5 Percent   182

6-1. Variation in GDP and Consumer Prices   200

6-2. Unemployment Rate   201

6-3. Real Wage Index   202

6-4. Income Distribution in Brazil and Uruguay (Montevideo)
and Consumption Distribution in Chile (Santiago)
by Household   203

6-5. Prices, Money Supply, and Exchange Rate Increases, Argentina   207

6-6. Prices, Money Supply, and Exchange Rate Increases, Chile   207

6-7. Fiscal Deficit as a Percentage of Gross Domestic Product   219

6-8. Percentage Increase in Money Supply   228

7-1. Estimate of Disbursed External Term Debt Outstanding
in Developing Countries, 1970–80   236

7-2. Debt Service Ratios   238

7-3. Modified Debt Service Ratios   239

8-1. Growth of Mexican Gross Domestic Product
and Its Components, 1950–78   273

8-2. Estimated Distribution of Family Income in Mexico, 1950,
1968, 1975, and 1977   275

8-3. Financing Granted by the Banking System, 1965–72
and 1970–76   278

8-4. Allocation of Total Credit, Selected Years, 1970–76   279

8-5. Wholesale Price Indexes, United States and Mexico City,
1954–70 and 1954–76   281

8-6. Elements of Mexico's Balance of Payments, 1965–77   282

8-7. Mexican Economic Growth, Inflation, and Balance-of-Payments
Indicators, 1975–78   285

9-1. Peru: Selected Economic Indicators, 1967–78   298

9-2. Selected Data on the Peruvian Economy, 1955–76   300

9-3. Imports of Arms, 1968–77   303

9-4. Impact of Exogenous Shocks and Military Exports on Peru's
Trade Balance, 1974–77   304

9-5. Trade Performance and Exchange Rates, 1959–78   313

9-6. Central Government Revenues and Expenditures, 1972–77   317

9-7. Real Wages in Lima, 1970–78   318

10-1. GDP by Industrial Origin, 1970–78   340

10-2. Indices of Value, Volume, and Prices of Six Major Agricultural
Exports, 1970–78   342

10-3. Yearly Percentage Changes in Unit Export Prices, 1971–78   343
10-4. Total Production of Five Major Export Crops, 1964–78   343
10-5. Balance-of-Payments Estimates   344
10-6. Domestic Price Indices   350
10-7. Annual Percentage Increase in Dar es Salaam Prices   374

11-1. Inflation, National Income, and the Balance of Trade, 1970–77   378
11-2. Components of National Expenditure   380
11-3. Simulation for Pakistan   386
11-4. Consolidated Public Revenues and Expenditures   388
11-5. Expenditures on National Product   390
11-6. Planned and Actual Increases in Money and Credit, 1971–76   394
11-7. Estimate of the Stock of Money and Its Velocity   396
11-8. Growth, Inflation, and Real Wages   400
11-9. Factors Related to Changes in Wages   402

12-1. List of Variables in the Model   408
12-2. Static Simulation Error Analysis   426
12-3. Dynamic Simulation Error Analysis   427
12-4. Exogenous Values for the Oil Shock Experiments   439
12-5. Oil Shock Experiments   442
12-6. Export Push Policy Experiment   443
12-7. Monetary Policy Experiments   446
12-8. Dynamic Simulation Results: *YC*, GDP in Current Prices   450
12-9. Dynamic Simulation Results: *PY*, GDP Deflator   451
12-10. Dynamic Simulation Results: *CGC*, Government Consumption
       in Current Prices   452
12-11. Dynamic Simulation Results: *PCP*, Private Consumption
       Price Deflator   453
12-12. Dynamic Simulation Results: *PIF*, Gross Fixed Investment
       Deflator   454
12-13. Dynamic Simulation Results: *IVC*, Inventory Investment
       in Current Prices   455
12-14. Dynamic Simulation Results: *SC*, Total Savings
       in Current Prices   456
12-15. Dynamic Simulation Results: *BPCW*, Balance of Payments
       in Current Won   457
12-16. Average Annual Rates of Change, 1956–77   459

13-1. Balance Sheets for Major Economic Agents   474
13-2. Impacts of Stabilization Policies under Various Regimes   490

Figures

2-1. Plot of Groups versus Functions A (Horizontal)
     and B (Vertical)   68
2-2. Separation by Discriminant Function: The Two-Group Case   74

Contents

5-1. Form of the CES Supply Function 158
5-2. Supply-Demand Curves in the Five-Sector Model 177

6-1. Chile, Selected Indicators (Quarterly Variations and Index) 211
6-2. Argentina, Selected Indicators (Quarterly Variations and Index) 212

12-1. Annual Growth Rate of Nonagricultural GDP (DYN), 1963–77 428
12-2. Annual Inflation in the Nonagricultural GDP Price Index ($DPYN$), 1963–77 429
12-3. Annual Percentage Rate of Change in Commodity Imports (in dollars, $DIMPO$), 1963–77 430
12-4. $DYNC$: Actual Path and Static and Dynamic Simulations, 1963–77 431
12-5. DYN: Actual Path and Static and Dynamic Simulations, 1963–77 432
12-6. $DPYN$: Actual Path and Static and Dynamic Simulations, 1963–77 433
12-7. $DCPC$: Actual Path and Static and Dynamic Simulations, 1963–77 434
12-8. DCP: Actual Path and Static and Dynamic Simulations, 1963–77 435
12-9. CP: Actual Path and Dynamic Simulation, 1963–77 436
12-10. $DPCP$: Actual Path and Static and Dynamic Simulations, 1963–77 437

13-1. The Usual IS Model: Effects of an Increase in Output on the Interest Rate (i) and Price Level (P) 476
13-2. The IS Model When the Price Level Depends on the Interest Rate 477
13-3. The IS Model When Devaluation Improves the Trade Deficit in Domestic Prices or a Price Increase Makes the Deficit Grow 478
13-4. The Effects on Price Level and Interest Rate of an Output Increase in the Contractionary Devaluation Case 480
13-5. The IS Curve in the (X, P) Plane under Different Assumptions about Savings-Investment Response and the Impacts of Devaluation 481
13-6. Determination of the LM Curve in Response to Output Shifts 482
13-7. Comparative Statics of the LM Curve 484
13-8. Impacts of Policy Changes in the Keynesian IS Case 485
13-9. Impacts of Policy Changes in the Fisherian IS Case 487
13-10. Impacts of Policy Changes in the Contractionary Devaluation IS Case 489
13-11. A Two-Sector Model 492
13-12. Long-Term Trade-offs between Inflation and the Growth Rate of Capital Stock 497
13-13. Alternative Adjustment Paths under Economic Stabilization 504

CHAPTER ONE

Introduction and Overview

WILLIAM R. CLINE *and* SIDNEY WEINTRAUB

ECONOMIC stabilization in developing countries concerns attempts to correct excessive or unsustainable balance-of-payments deficits, reduce the rate of domestic inflation, or (usually) both. Frequently, stabilization efforts also involve exchange rate reform and changes in the systems of import protection and export incentives. A country may make these efforts on its own, in conjunction with a supporting financial program from the International Monetary Fund (for example, a standby loan with policy performance conditions), or with financial support from other international or bilateral financial sources.

The Economic Setting

In the 1970s, economic stabilization became a central policy issue for many developing countries and for international agencies. In Latin America, heated controversy over appropriate stabilization policy dates back to the 1950s. In the 1970s, stabilization also became a priority issue for countries in Asia, Africa, and the Middle East, as worldwide inflation and the balance-of-payments pressures associated with higher oil prices affected developing (and developed) countries in all regions.

Table 1-1 shows the sharp acceleration of inflation in developing countries in the 1970s compared with historical levels. The major surge in inflation occurred in 1973 and 1974, when the worldwide economic boom and commodity price increases, and then higher oil prices, led to domestic inflation on a global scale.[1] As table 1-1 shows, inflation rose in all continents, not just in Latin America where an inflationary tradition already

1. For an analysis of the impact of worldwide inflation, see William R. Cline and Associates, *World Inflation and the Developing Countries* (Brookings Institution, forthcoming).

1

Table 1-1. *Consumer Price Inflation*

Average annual percentage

Country	1967–72	1973–74	1975–78
Africa	4.8	14.0	19.8
Asia	5.4	21.4	7.0
Latin America	15.9	35.8	52.9 (27.7[a])
Middle East	4.3	17.2	20.4 (12.0[b])

Source: International Monetary Fund, *Annual Report 1979*, p. 11.
a. Excluding Argentina, Chile, and Uruguay.
b. Excluding Israel.

existed. Table 1-1 also shows that only national governments in Asia succeeded in bringing inflation down to moderate levels by the late 1970s; elsewhere, developing countries generally had little success in regaining price stability. Moreover, growth in GDP in both middle- and low-income countries in Asia was higher (relative to historical rates) than in other regions over this period, suggesting that successful control of inflation does not necessarily imply a sacrifice of growth in the medium term.[2]

Balance-of-payments problems also plagued developing countries in the 1970s. Following unusual strength in current account balances in 1972 and 1973, the non-oil-exporting developing countries suffered an unprecedented deterioration in external accounts in 1974 and 1975, primarily as the result of higher oil prices and (in many cases) higher real import volumes and sluggish demand for their exports due to economic slowdown in the industrial countries. The aggregate current account deficit of non-oil-exporting developing countries rose from $11 billion in 1973 to an average of $34 billion in 1974 and 1975, representing a rise from approximately 16 percent to 35 percent of export earnings. In contrast to their general inability to recover price stability, in the realm of external accounts developing countries managed to adjust substantially (with the help of recovering terms of trade), and by 1976 and 1977 they had reduced their aggregate current account deficit to $23.5 billion, or approximately 19 percent of export earnings.[3] Even for the relatively benign period of 1976–78, however, the aggregates mask individual cases of particular difficulty. Countries such as Peru, Sudan, Turkey, Zaire, and Zambia experienced "significant problems of debt management" even

2. For growth data, see World Bank, *World Development Report, 1979* (World Bank, 1979), p. 11.

3. International Monetary Fund, *Annual Report, 1979*, p. 23, and *International Financial Statistics*, selected issues.

though developing countries as a whole experienced satisfactory external account performance after 1975.[4]

Beginning in 1979, the international economic setting turned much worse for the non-oil-exporting developing countries. The prices of oil charged by OPEC members rose by approximately 135 percent from the end of 1978 to mid-1980. Primarily because of higher oil prices, the combined current account deficit of the non-oil-exporting developing countries rose from $36 billion in 1978 to $55 billion in 1979, an expected $68 billion in 1980, and was forecast to rise to $78 billion by 1981.[5]

Slow growth in industrial countries, led by the U.S. recession in 1980, limits the prospects for adjustment through rapid expansion of exports by developing countries. To make matters worse, the strength of the fabric of the international monetary mechanism for recycling funds from OPEC countries in surplus to developing countries in deficit stands open to question. Already carrying heavy exposures in developing countries as the result of massive lending following the 1974 oil price increase, the major international banks seem unlikely to be able to repeat their earlier lead role in financial recycling in this second round of oil price increases. Many major American banks are reaching legal ceilings on the ratio of their lending in individual developing countries to their capital. At the end of 1977, U.S. bank loans to non-oil-exporting developing countries already stood at 130 percent of bank capital, and the nine largest American banks had loans to Brazil and Mexico alone amounting to 48 and 38 percent of their capital, respectively.[6] While some scope exists for European, Japanese, and U.S. regional banks to replace the largest U.S. banks in expanding new loans to developing countries, the prospects are that the private banking sector's ready solution to the financial recycling problem of the mid-1970s will no longer be available in the early 1980s. Instead, greater reliance on official lending is likely, as well as a greater role for direct lending from OPEC countries to non-oil-exporting developing countries.

Despite their inflationary and balance-of-payments problems, the developing countries managed to sustain economic growth relatively well

4. *World Development Report, 1979*, p. 29.
5. International Monetary Fund, *World Economic Outlook* (May 1980), pp. 5, 95.
6. Jane D'Arista, "Private Overseas Lending: Too Far, Too Fast?" in Jonathan D. Aronson, ed., *Debt and the Less Developed Countries* (Westview Press, 1979), p. 67.

during the 1970s. Comparing 1970–77 with 1960–70, annual average GDP growth rates fell moderately, from 3.9 percent to 3.2 percent for low-income countries and from 6.2 percent to 6.1 percent for middle-income countries. By contrast, industrial country growth fell from 5.1 percent to 3.1 percent.[7] Whether this relatively strong performance of developing countries will continue into the 1980s remains to be seen. One factor that will influence the outcome is whether the international mechanisms for financial recycling, both private and public, prove to be fragile or robust. One of the most important of those mechanisms is the conditional lending by the International Monetary Fund in support of economic stabilization programs.

The Policy Setting

The question of how to deal with inflation and balance-of-payments difficulties raises policy issues at both international and national levels. The International Monetary Fund (IMF) is the international agency charged with helping member nations carry out stabilization programs. Many spokesmen from developing nations have criticized the IMF's performance of this role, however. They maintain that its criteria of loan "conditionality" have been too rigid.[8] One influential analysis maintained that external factors, especially deteriorating terms of trade and recession in industrial country markets, had been primarily responsible for stabilization problems in developing countries in the 1970s, and that stabilization programs under international auspices should accordingly increase the amount and flexibility of balance-of-payments support.[9] Journalistic accounts often painted the IMF as the heavy-handed villain in stabilization efforts that resulted in rioting in Egypt and Peru.

The IMF has sought to review its approach to stabilization programs. One staff analysis of past conditional lending (standby programs) concluded that the purposes of the programs had been achieved in 72 percent of the cases, that there was no evidence that the programs decreased

7. *World Development Report, 1979*, pp. 128–29.

8. Thus, at the 1978 annual IMF-World Bank meetings, the developing country Group of 24 stated concern about "the multiplicity of performance criteria and some other forms of conditionality that inhibit access to Fund resources." *IMF Survey*, October 2, 1978, p. 307.

9. Sidney Dell and Roger Lawrence, *The Balance of Payments Adjustment Process in Developing Countries* (London: Pergamon Press, 1980).

growth rates (or increased them), that external accounts improved in three-fourths of the cases (but only one-fourth in statistically significant terms), and that the programs generally neither worsened nor reduced inflation.[10] Another IMF study focused on income distributional consequences of stabilization programs.[11] It concluded that changes in the income distribution inevitably result from stabilization measures, although the proper base for comparison is not the actual distribution under unsustainable prestabilization conditions. The study emphasizes the rise in the price of traded goods relative to those of nontraded goods as the key to successful stabilization. This change in internal terms of trade has distributional consequences, as in the case of Ghana (1966–70) where it benefited small holder agricultural exporters. The direct distributional effects of fiscal measures (such as food subsidy cutbacks) are also important, and they are determined mainly by political strength of different groups. The study is optimistic about generally equitable results of stabilization programs because their typical elimination of exchange controls ends windfall gains to privileged interests, and their stimulus to exports expands employment. Both of these studies by IMF staff are on balance sanguine about the effects of past IMF stabilization programs, in contrast to the implicit or explicit critiques of some of the chapters in this volume (in particular those by Diaz-Alejandro, Foxley, and Taylor). But the two IMF studies usefully show that it is difficult to generalize about the growth and equity effects of these programs, and that country-specific circumstances heavily affect the outcomes.

Largely in response to pressure from the developing countries, the IMF has issued new and apparently more flexible rules of lending conditionality.[12] It has also expanded its lending limits and liberalized the terms on which it makes resources available. In the fall of 1980 the IMF sharply increased the maximum amount of borrowing permissible for member countries, to 600 percent of a country's quota (up to 200 percent each

---

10. Thomas Reichmann and Richard Stillson, "Experience with Programs of Balance of Payments Adjustment: Stand-by Arrangements in the Higher Credit Tranches, 1963–72," *IMF Staff Papers,* vol. 25 (June 1978), pp. 293–309.

11. Omotunde Johnson and Joanne Salop, "Distributional Aspects of Stabilization Programs in Developing Countries," *IMF Staff Papers,* vol. 27 (March 1980), pp. 1–23.

12. "New Guidelines Issued on Fund Conditionality," *IMF Survey,* March 19, 1979, pp. 82–83. In addition, the maximum period for repayment under the Extended Fund Facility was increased at the end of 1979 from eight to ten years. *IMF Survey,* December 10, 1979, p. 381.

year for a maximum of three years).[13] The IMF's policy revisions and on-going reviews are timely, because in 1978 and 1979 it was taking in more funds than it was lending out; total IMF credits outstanding fell from 16 billion SDR (special drawing rights) in August 1977 to 10 billion SDR in April 1979, as loans through the oil facility and credit tranche borrowings declined sharply. These reductions primarily reflect repayments by in-dustrial countries. For the non-oil-exporting developing countries also, however, repayments exceeded new borrowing in 1978 by 700.8 million SDR (and while borrowing exceeded repayments in 1979, the net amount was a minimal 154.0 million SDR).[14] In coming years the IMF will have even more resources to lend because of the new Witteveen facility and the recent increase in member quotas. To the extent that IMF resources go relatively underused by developing countries because of disagreement over appropriate stabilization measures, a potentially serious problem will exist in the functioning of the international payments system.

For its part the World Bank plans to provide more fast-disbursing loans to facilitate structural adjustment, in light of severe balance-of-payments pressures brought on by the oil price increase of 1979. The operations of the private international banking system also affect stabili-zation in developing countries. Whether the banks are lending too much or too little, whether they are too cautious or incautious, and how their lending will evolve in the future are questions that directly affect devel-oping country stabilization. Answers to these questions indirectly affect an assessment of the IMF's role, because banks and the IMF can be either substitutes or complementary sources of funds for stabilization efforts.

This volume focuses primarily on policies adopted by developing coun-tries rather than on international policies. While it is well to reiterate the need for greater concessional resource transfers from North to South and for adequate and well-functioning financing at market-related terms, each developing country must act on inflation or external imbalance within the external context it faces; therefore, the relevant policy issue for a devel-oping country is the design of its own appropriate stabilization policy. Clearly, country policy matters vitally, despite external shocks. Thus, table 1-1 suggests that domestic stabilization policies had greater success

13. *IMF Survey,* October 13, 1980, p. 1. The 600 percent of quota ceiling com-pares with a previous maximum of 260 percent of quota, taking into account normal credit tranches, the supplementary financing facility, and the extended Fund facility.

14. International Monetary Fund, *Annual Report, 1979,* p. 71, and *IMF Survey,* February 4, 1980, p. 45.

in Asia than in Latin America or Africa in the 1970s, even though all these regions faced similar worldwide disturbances.

Concentration on developing country policies does not mean that this conference was an exercise in which economists of the North admonished policy makers in the South. The authors in this volume include experts from developing countries for both the thematic studies and the country chapters. Even policy analyses strictly concerned with internal economic policies of developing countries have direct implications for international and bilateral lending agencies, because these institutions usually apply some form of conditionality or evaluation of country performance in their lending operations. More fundamentally, the objective of these studies is to analyze, theoretically and empirically, the most desirable means of economic stabilization; neither North nor South has a monopoly on the required skills for this scientific task.

Some policy issues in developing country stabilization are part of an old debate dating to controversy over policies in Latin America in the 1950s and 1960s. The first basic issue is how to design a stabilization policy that minimizes the sacrifice of economic growth in the short term and maximizes economic growth results in the long term. The long-standing controversy between structuralists and monetarists recurs in the writings in this volume, particularly among those on Latin America. Structuralists tend to oppose primary reliance on orthodox policies such as devaluation and monetary and fiscal restraint on grounds that foreign trade elasticities are low and the root causes of inflation are structural bottlenecks requiring still more investment. Monetarists emphasize more orthodox solutions, but disagree on whether to apply these solutions gradually or as shock treatments.

The consequences of stabilization programs for income distribution are a second major policy area. In recent years, development economists, international institutions and bilateral donors, and policy makers in many developing countries have been increasing their attention to income distribution and absolute poverty in the development process. Many economic stabilization programs appear to have been implemented at the expense of the poor, as governments reduced subsidies on basic consumer goods and social spending, held back wages in the face of inflation (causing real wage declines), and took other measures that may have concentrated income. Therefore, stabilization programs must consider not only growth effects but also effects on the distribution of income and the incidence of absolute poverty.

Design of the Volume

The papers in this volume cover the range of issues discussed above. Chapter 2 reviews the international economic setting for economic stabilization in developing countries. Chapters 3 and 4 examine alternative aspects of the traditional issue of the trade-offs involved between economic growth and stabilization. Chapters 5 and 6 concern the more recent policy focus on income distributional consequences of alternative stabilization strategies. Chapter 7 examines the role of the foreign private banks in the stabilization process. Following these six thematic analyses, chapters 8 through 12 are five country studies (Mexico, Peru, Tanzania, Pakistan, and South Korea) that review specific country experience in pursuit of general analytical and policy lessons. Chapter 13 presents a theoretical study that pertains to trade-offs between stabilization and growth, income distributional implications, and analytical techniques used in some of the country studies.

Highlights of the Studies

The major implications of these studies, and the unanswered questions they raise, are explored later in this chapter. Before turning to that synthesis, the following discussion presents a précis of the individual studies and the critiques made of them.

International Environment

Stanley Black's analysis (chapter 2) of the influence of the international economic environment distinguishes between the internal and external origins of instability in the 1970s. Monetary disturbance from abroad was transmitted through increased developing country reserves and induced domestic monetary expansion in the early 1970s. Commodity price fluctuation rose in the 1970s. Terms of trade fell for non-oil-exporting developing countries because of higher oil prices. Boom and recession in industrial countries caused less growth disturbance for developing countries than generally thought, according to LINK model simulations. Developing country growth fell by less than would have been expected from declining import capacity because of high capital inflows.

The oil price increases of 1979 again seemed manageable through external financing.

Internal sources of instability included monetary expansion caused by asymmetrical sterilization policy: nonsterilization of reserve inflows in 1972–73 but sterilization of outflows in 1974–75. That is, increased reserves were not offset by restrictive monetary policies, but decreased reserves were offset by expansionary monetary policies that kept reserve contraction from reducing the money supply. Excessive domestic credit expansion was common and frequently was caused by government deficits (which, in turn, were often associated with food subsidy programs). Successful stabilization programs in several Asian countries, when contrasted with failures in most other developing areas, show the importance of internal policies: after the external source of inflation disappears, the domestic response determines whether inflation declines or continues.

The principal empirical analysis of the study applies discriminant analysis that separates developing countries into five ascending categories of implied stabilization success as measured by creditworthiness. The categories range from countries that defaulted on external debt to countries that successfully floated bonds internationally. (The creditworthiness standard limits the classification to the balance-of-payments dimension of stabilization, omitting the dimension of price stability.) The independent variables are inherent country characteristics (size, stage of development, openness, etc.), internal variables (consumer price inflation, monetary expansion, government deficits, real exchange rate, etc.), and external variables (import price inflation, terms of trade, change in reserves, and real export growth). Black found the following composition of sources of discrimination among the country groupings: inherent characteristics, 47 percent; internal factors, 35 percent; and external factors, 17 percent.

The overall implication of Black's study is that both internal and external factors caused heightened economic instability in the 1970s, but that the role of external factors was more limited than asserted by some analysts, who attributed most instability to external factors and accordingly advocated major expansion in international financing facilities and softening of their conditionality. Black commends recent expansion of IMF compensatory financing, but disagrees with softening conditionality, pointing out that the key role identified for internal policy argues for conditionality in IMF programs in order to enhance prospects of good domestic policies. He cites realistic exchange rates and appropriate monetary response to reserve changes as examples of desirable internal policies.

Sidney Dell, who questioned the applicability of discriminant analysis, contended that the predominant factor by far in the deficits of non-oil-developing countries had been the deterioration in their terms of trade combined with slackening import demand in the industrial countries. He argued that stabilization programs should take into account the degree of responsibility of developing countries for their own balance-of-payments difficulties.

Stabilization and Long-Term Growth

A crucial issue for stabilization policy is how to achieve price stability and balance-of-payments equilibrium with maximum benefit for long-term growth and minimum sacrifice of short-term growth. The studies by Anne Krueger (chapter 3) and Carlos Diaz-Alejandro (chapter 4) approach this issue from two vantage points: Krueger's approach is global, while Diaz focuses on the experience of Latin America's "Southern Cone" countries.

Krueger deals with the goals of correcting trade regime bias and reducing inflation. A major theme of this discussion is that by using a sliding-peg exchange rate, it is possible to separate efficient factor allocation through the trade regime from domestic inflation, because appropriate ongoing devaluation to offset domestic inflation can leave real variables unaltered. Unfortunately, developing countries more frequently respond to domestic inflation by imposing protective quotas on imports, export subsidies, and other devices that distort factor allocation. Sliding-peg regimes can eliminate a first dimension of factor misallocation—excessive price of home goods relative to tradables—caused by domestic inflation. Biased trade regimes are a second major source of inefficiency; trade regimes biased toward import substitution (where the domestic price ratio of importables to exportables is greater than their foreign price ratio) are typically more inefficient than export-biased regimes. The loss of growth from both dimensions of external bias—payments (exchange rate) and trade regime—probably exceeds the loss from inflation, for which there is little hard evidence of growth loss.

There are long-term and short-term costs of trade-regime-liberalizing stabilization. Research conducted for the National Bureau of Economic Research suggests that developing countries can expect to raise their long-term annual growth rate by two or three percentage points by eliminating the bias in their trade and payments regimes. The short-term cost is likely to be only 1 to 2 percent of GNP for a year to eighteen months. The short-term cost occurs because liberalization is recessionary: it immediately reduces demand for import substitutes (where the bias was toward import substitution), whereas a time lag occurs before investment and output rise in the new favored (export) sectors. The short-term cost is higher when the stabilization program is not "credible" because of past failures and political pressure; firms are skeptical about the permanence of the changes and accordingly are reluctant to make investments. In stabilization programs, nothing succeeds like success. The short-term cost can be reduced by a gradual instead of a shock treatment approach, but gradualism runs a greater risk of failure.

Reducing inflation is harder than correcting external imbalance and eliminating trade regime bias. Inflation and the trade regime interact. Import liberalization can be used to dampen inflation. The inflationary consequences of devaluation will be greater if the prior regime was one of repressed inflation/open trade deficit (adjustment through borrowing or reserve loss) than if it was one of open inflation/repressed trade deficit (adjustment through import quotas, in which case the inflationary penalty had already been paid, and a higher price of foreign exchange would be offset by elimination of protection).

Appropriate policy measures for developing countries typically involve correcting overly expansionary demand policies through deceleration of credit expansion and other measures (as in most IMF standby agreements), as well as reduction of tariffs, quotas, export subsidies, and other trade regime distortions. Borrowing abroad to maintain imports can help maintain income and growth, providing the stabilization program is maintained. Appropriate policies for industrial countries include foreign aid to support developing country imports during stabilization programs (foreign exchange can have a high marginal product). Creditors are not well advised to force developing countries into involuntary policies, for example, through debt rescheduling leverage; stabilization programs are more likely to succeed when domestic authorities voluntarily adopt them.

In his critique of chapter 3, Hollis Chenery argues that Krueger omits such crucial areas as future adjustment by developing countries to higher energy prices and the likelihood of slower growth and protectionism in developed countries.

In chapter 4, Carlos Diaz-Alejandro depicts the stylized facts of stabilization in Latin America's Southern Cone (Argentina, Uruguay, and Chile) as a framework for analysis. Citing the area's history of unsuccessful stabilization plans dating from the 1950s, he notes, as did Krueger, that unfavorable expectations mean less chance of successful stabilization. The political-economic scenario begins with a populist government that raises government spending without raising taxes, borrows from the central bank, and raises wages. These actions cause acceleration in chronic inflation and relative price distortions as the government freezes the exchange rate and other basic prices. The government then raises protection to control external disequilibrium. As inflation accelerates, sometimes aggravated by terms of trade or other shocks, conditions become unviable, more radical policies are proposed, and a military coup occurs.

The new regime, often with IMF help, aims at a balance-of-payments equilibrium, efficient real prices, and lower inflation. Typically, the policy package includes limits on bank credit, price adjustments (especially for foreign exchange), trade liberalization (especially in recent variants), and wage repression.

These orthodox measures result in an improved balance of payments, but they do little to lower inflation. Diaz also suggests that there has been "overkill" in the reduction of aggregate demand. The external account improves as the capital account turns around, and imports fall because of a decline in income and investment; in the medium term, exports respond to the crawling-peg exchange rate and export subsidies. Diaz states, "Evidence indicates a clear victory for export optimists." Inflation proves inexplicably stubborn. Excess demand explains inflation only at first, until excess capacity develops; repressed wages are hardly a cause, nor is money supply, as the deflated money supply falls. Import liberalization is disappointing as an anti-inflationary device because it is offset by faster-working devaluation. Collapse of output reflects an excessive cutback in aggregate demand through credit restrictions and wage repression. Income distribution follows no particular path in principle, but in practice the package concentrates income distribution.

Today's world economy complicates matters. The highly liquid international capital market produces an "embarrassment of riches." With high interest rates, generously indexed government bonds, and stable real exchange rates, foreign capital rushes in, causing increased reserves, increased money supply, and inflationary pressure. Preannouncing the schedule of the crawling peg worsens matters, because foreign capital has a sure bet on high interest rates and secure reconversion. A variant on the problem is that capital inflows make the exchange rate appreciate, frustrating export expansion. Moreover, the end result is high external debt at short maturities owed to foreign private banks.

The prescriptions Diaz offers for change in stabilization policies include (a) less severe reduction in aggregate demand; (b) government investment in bottleneck sectors to buoy stagnant investment (such as in Brazil); (c) price guidelines, for example, to force oligopolists to pass on import price savings; (d) more modest balance-of-payments targets; (e) less stringent credit policies, with lower interest rates and less capital inflow; and (f) greater use of tax measures for efficiency and equity. Diaz emphasizes that one recent Southern Cone measure, ending the bias toward import substitution and against exports, is correct and long overdue. With respect to the international framework, Diaz notes the developing countries' perception of "niggardly" IMF lending conditions and the low utilization of IMF funds, while approving recent IMF expansion of longer-term facilities and movement toward more sophisticated analysis. Nevertheless, Diaz suspects that the major semi-industrial developing countries will continue to bypass the IMF.

In his comment on chapter 4, Ronald McKinnon suggests that poor growth performance in Southern Cone stabilization programs is exaggerated. He believes that just as earlier industrial growth was overstated because of artificially high prices for protected products, new growth is understated because industrial prices are reverting to international levels. He also offers the principle that exchange rate indexation leads to destabilizing capital inflow after successful liberalization of financial, foreign exchange, and traded goods markets; and he suggests that exchange controls may be needed. In the discussion, Gustav Papanek noted that because of its regional bias, Diaz' study omitted important phenomena, such as the use of food grains imports for stabilization purposes in Asian countries.

Stabilization and Income Distribution

A common critique of stabilization programs is that they impose an unduly heavy burden on the poor, in practice if not in principle. Chapters 5 and 6 examine the relationship between income distribution and economic stabilization programs from alternative perspectives. Montek Ahluwalia and Frank Lysy (chapter 5) develop two economywide models and carry out a sensitivity analysis using data for Malaysia for their reference case. Alejandro Foxley (chapter 6) reviews experiences in Argentina, Brazil, Chile, and Uruguay to assess the distributional consequences of alternative stabilization strategies.

The central focus of the Ahluwalia-Lysy study is the possible recessionary consequence of devaluation. Their models also throw light on the distribution of income between capital and labor during stabilization. Following the recent literature by Cooper, Diaz, Taylor, and others, the authors criticize the standard stabilization package of devaluation combined with contractionary monetary and fiscal policies. The common critique in this literature is that because exports may fail to respond sufficiently to devaluation, the "normal" balance between stimulus and restraint will be missing from the standard package; instead, devaluation will itself be contractionary, as the rise in spending on imports exceeds the rise in export earnings (in local currency for both), causing a Keynesian aggregate demand reduction.[15] Accordingly, the result of the standard package can be highly recessionary.

Ahluwalia and Lysy explore the dimensions of the problem by simulating two macroeconomic models. The first is a one-sector model that assumes (a) imports in a fixed coefficient relationship to output (so devaluation cannot directly reduce imports), (b) export demand less than infinitely elastic (so the price received falls when the country expands exports), and (c) fixed capital with variable labor. A crucial feature of the model is that product price includes the cost of imported inputs and that after devaluation raises this price, the level of consumption declines in response, adding another source of Keynesian contraction. A central result from the model's equations is a critical value for the elasticity of foreign demand for exports, below which devaluation causes economic contraction instead of expansion. This elasticity weighs the expansionary effect of extra exports against the contractionary effects of higher import prices for both import spending and working through reduced consumption caused by higher product prices. Applying Malaysian data, the authors calculate the critical elasticity as approximately 0.5, and they maintain that export demand elasticities are frequently below this level

15. Although not explicitly stated, the argument hinges on a large initial trade deficit, low foreign demand elasticity for exports, and low elasticity of import demand. Note that starting at zero trade balance (exports = imports), if foreign demand elasticity is infinite, increases in import and export values in local currency would be identical when domestic elasticities are zero (causing no change in aggregate demand), and if domestic elasticities are not zero, increased export earnings would exceed increased import expenses (in local currency).

for developing countries. (This view contradicts the conclusion of both Krueger and Diaz that experience vindicates the "export optimists."[16]) With considerably higher export demand elasticities, the model gives economic expansion and trade balance correction as the result of devaluation. Simulation with Malaysian data brings out several nuances.

The model incorporates income distribution through neoclassical analysis of changes in labor and capital shares as the labor/capital ratio rises in expansion and falls in recession (because capital is fixed and labor is variable). If the degree of substitutability between capital and labor is high, recession reduces labor's share; if substitutability is low, recession increases labor's share. The authors are agnostic about any particular degree of substitutability, and in any event their simulations indicate that factor shares change very little in response to recession or expansion. Within the confines of the model, then, income distribution is insensitive to stabilization.

A second model uses five product sectors, allowing specification of an export supply elasticity and detail on investment behavior. This model allows for import substitution in response to devaluation, but counters this change by assuming a low supply elasticity for exports. Simulations with the model depend on elasticities assumed, but they bring out the important point that increased imports of capital goods are necessary to expand output in the export sector, justifying long-term financing to enable long-term benefits of devaluation to occur.

Ahluwalia and Lysy conclude that devaluation is a poor stabilization tool because it causes economic contraction and terms of trade loss, but this conclusion hinges on their pessimism about export demand elasticity. Based on favorable simulations that shift out export demand, the authors advocate special trade concessions by industrial countries to help developing countries in balance-of-payments difficulties; however, this proposal appears impractical and also would penalize developing countries with stable economic performance. The authors advocate longer-term financing to facilitate capital equipment imports so that exports can respond positively to devaluation in the longer term. Their policy conclusions do not focus on income distribution, but their analysis suggests that there is no inherent economic reason for stabilization effects to be in-

16. Ahluwalia and Lysy add the caveat that they are referring to the short-run elasticity, making a low value more likely but raising the more fundamental question of whether policy makers should avoid devaluation needed for long-term adjustment just because there may be short-term contractionary consequences.

equitable, and therefore any major inequity results probably stem from the specific way each program is applied.

Arnold Harberger criticizes the Ahluwalia-Lysy recommendations on trade policy, noting that such a system would tempt developing countries to get into even greater balance-of-payments problems. He also maintains that the model is relevant only for economies in which policy makers have followed erroneous and extreme import substitution policies, causing a severe foreign exchange constraint. Albert Fishlow notes the contribution of Ahluwalia and Lysy in demonstrating the possibility of perverse response to devaluation, but points out the model's limitations in assessing income distributional effects, in part because of its Malaysian base.

In chapter 6, Alejandro Foxley draws on Latin American experiences to show that income distributional consequences of stabilization depend on the policies adopted. Reviewing traditional monetarist and structural views, he notes the monetarist argument that inflation causes regressive income redistribution. Monetarist stabilization programs in the late 1950s and early 1960s generally failed, however, and were regressive as unemployment rose and wage share fell. For their part, subsequent structuralist programs in the 1960s and early 1970s raised labor's share but ended in persistent inflation.

The "new" stabilization programs of military governments in the 1970s went beyond orthodox monetarism, adding long-term structural change: they reduced the size of the public sector, reformed capital markets, and freed trade. Referring to Chile (1973–78), Argentina (1976–78), Uruguay (1974–78), and Brazil (1964–67), Foxley identifies the following profile of stabilization: (a) monetary and fiscal restraint, (b) higher prices for public utilities, (c) wage repression, (d) freeing of prices, (e) gradual elimination of import controls, (f) devaluation, (g) reducing public employment, (h) sale of public enterprises to the private sector, and (i) free market interest rates. The general results of these programs were (a) stubborn persistence of inflation (at 40 percent or more, and even 150 percent in Argentina), (b) prolonged economic stagnation (Chilean GDP fell by almost 17 percent in 1975), (c) higher unemployment (especially in Chile), (d) real wage reductions by 30 to 40 percent, and (e) a worsening size distribution of income (although data during stabilization periods are available only for Uruguay, longer period distributional data for Brazil and Chile are not inconsistent with the point).

Foxley examines the asymmetry between wage and price policy, noting that wage repression in the face of rising prices directly tends to worsen the income distribution (although he implicitly assumes organized wage labor is in the lower part of the distribution). He attempts to explain the puzzling persistence of inflation in terms of oligopoly structure, price overshooting by firms in the face of uncertainty, and output instead of price adjustment during recession. Financial markets are another central area affecting income distribution. Liberalizing interest rates led to exceptionally high rates (more than 40 percent per year in real terms in Chile). Noting the possible production cost impact through higher interest costs of working capital (as emphasized by Lance Taylor in chapter 13), Foxley suggests these effects may be only temporary. The more lasting effects are concentration of asset distribution as large firms (especially those with access to foreign funds) buy undervalued medium-sized and government enterprises. Asset concentration means future income concentration.

Reviewing the impact of devaluation, Foxley judges that the experience of several countries rejects the export pessimism underlying recent literature that holds that devaluation is contractionary; however, he considers devaluation to be definitely inflationary. Foxley then shows how fiscal policy was income concentrating in Chile, where the government sharply cut back investment in labor-intensive construction and social sectors while eliminating taxes on wealth, capital gains, and interest and instituting an indirect value-added tax (a shift from progressive direct to regressive indirect taxes). The government of Brazil, also recognizing the need for reduced fiscal deficits, raised taxes and cut current expenses but raised public investment considerably, including investment in public works and housing. Brazil's public investment helped dampen unemployment and recession.

For improved stabilization policy Foxley recommends that authorities act through a variety of instruments including price guidelines instead of relying solely on monetary contraction; that they recognize interdependent effects of devaluation, monetary contraction, and interest rate liberalization in provoking income concentration and recession; and that if cost-push inflation is their problem, they seek disinflationary shocks, which may require some monetary expansion. Foxley also notes that severe wage repression is feasible only under authoritarian rule, and he concludes that in a nonparticipatory political context the redistributive effects of stabilization are likely to be regressive.

Arnold Harberger criticizes the study for reviving old structuralist arguments he considers to be lacking in scientific content. Taking issue with Foxley on specific aspects of Chilean experience, Harberger makes a broader critique of attributing guilt by association to policies adopted by authoritarian regimes. Albert Fishlow notes that orthodox policies too have become radical and structural. He admonishes that it is insufficient for structuralist critics merely to chronicle the deterioration in income distribution under stabilization. Instead, they must offer a persuasive alternative to orthodoxy, and in particular they must confront the issue of whether real wages have become so high that they discourage investment and employment growth.

Role of Private Banks

From the perspective of an economist with experience in private banking as well as international agencies, Irving Friedman (chapter 7) examines commercial lending to developing countries, particularly when these countries are involved in stabilization efforts. His thesis is that private bank lending plays an essentially developmental role. Because banks expect to be lending to developing countries indefinitely, the long-term, not short-term, future of borrowing countries is most meaningful to the banks.

Friedman provides data on the growth of the term debt (that is, debt with original maturities of more than one year) of developing countries and the significant role commercial banks played in this growth. At the end of 1978, about 50 percent of the $300 billion term debt of 100 developing countries came from commercial banks. In 1978, term claims on developing countries of banks in the major industrial countries increased by $30 billion, compared with a flow of $18.3 billion in official development assistance. Friedman argues that the increase in term debt has not been excessive for the developing countries since 1970; when deflated for price changes, it increased by about 7 percent a year, or not much more than the increase in world trade.

This chapter provides an extensive list of criteria that banks use to determine their actions when a country undertakes a stabilization program. These criteria deal with the desire of banks to minimize their vulnerability as well as to look to business in the poststabilization period. Willingness of a country to undertake a stabilization program supported by the IMF weighs heavily in decisions that banks make.

Several of Friedman's points are controversial. First, he argues that to the best of his knowledge, no country avoided an IMF standby because

the program coincided with increased oil exports and the discovery of potentially vast reserves of oil and natural gas.

The burden of adjustment fell most heavily on wage earners. Real wages declined in 1977 and 1978 (from a base of substantial real increases in the previous fifteen years), but this decline is now being reversed. There is no evidence that the most underprivileged groups in Mexico, the jobless and the near jobless, were damaged by the stabilization program. In other words, the adjustments demanded by the stabilization program turned out not to be harsh. However, the longer-term problems of inequitable income distribution, joblessness and underemployment, and inadequate growth in agriculture inherited by Echeverría must still be faced.

Discussant Saul Trejo Reyes notes that Weintraub's study begins in the middle of the story and that, given earlier events and the existing political structure, Echeverría had no real alternatives. The destabilization was corrected less by policy measures than by the luck of oil and gas discoveries.

Peru

William Cline analyzes the experience of Peruvian economic stabilization in the latter half of the 1970s. Beginning in 1974, Peru's external sector had difficulties that culminated with near default on external debt in 1978. After aborted stabilization attempts in 1976 and 1977, Peru adopted an effective program with IMF participation in 1978, achieving external sector stabilization. However, per capita income declined by 8 percent (1976 to 1978) and inflation increased to over 50 percent. By 1979 Peru had achieved a major turnaround on its external accounts, in part because of higher export prices.

Peru's crisis originated in policies of the 1968 military revolution that allowed exports to decline, fostered economic mismanagement in the "reformed" industrial sector, pursued ambitious government investment plans without adequate taxation, allowed the exchange rate to become overvalued, and incurred excessive foreign debt. To make matters worse, the disappearance of anchovies, the collapse of copper prices, and higher oil import prices reduced Peru's potential of foreign exchange availability by approximately one-fourth, and heavy outlays on military imports meant additional foreign exchange losses of comparable size.

In 1976 Peru entered a stabilization program with private foreign banks, circumventing IMF participation for political reasons. By early 1977 the government's spending far exceeded the limits of the agreement, and the banks insisted on IMF approval of any future program. IMF-Central Bank negotiations in March 1977 collapsed in the face of budget spending pressure from other parts of the government. In November 1977 Peru signed a standby agreement with the IMF, but by February 1978 the IMF found Peru not to be observing the terms and suspended funding under the agreement. In retrospect many Peruvian analysts considered the terms impossibly hard to meet. Finally, in the face of near external bankruptcy in May 1978, the government accepted strong measures of a new economic team. These measures included a sharp devaluation, increased fuel and food prices, and reduced government spending. The measures prompted riots and even deaths, but they secured successful debt rescheduling and a new (and apparently "softer") IMF agreement, which Peru thereafter fully observed.

Critics have accused the IMF and Peru of a misguided stabilization program. Structuralists argue that devaluation was inappropriate because imports and exports are unresponsive to the exchange rate; some argue that imports are not responsive to aggregate demand. Critics also state that demand and credit restraint were too costly in terms of lost output, and one expert maintains that Peru did not have a problem of excess demand because excess industrial capacity existed, especially on a hypothetical triple-shift basis. Critics also fault the seeming heavy incidence of adjustment on the poor. However, statistical tests in chapter 9 showed a significant response of imports to the exchange rate and GNP level, as well as a significant response of exports to the exchange rate, casting doubt on the structuralist critique. Government deficits of 10 percent of GNP in the period from 1974 to 1977 indicated that large excess demand existed. The deficits were not attributable to a recessionary decline in revenue. Furthermore, indices of industrial output did not decline (and therefore provided no evidence of cyclical excess capacity) until 1977, well after the crisis began. Therefore, the diagnosis of excess demand appears to have been valid. In addition, the income-distributional impact of stabilization was not necessarily regressive. Real wages declined 28 percent for blue-collar and 38 percent for white-collar workers, but these workers were in the middle and upper-middle part of the income distribution; the overall wage share in GNP did not decline, terms of trade appeared to have improved for the impoverished countryside, and the termination of gasoline subsidies was progressive. Tax measures could have been much more progressive, however.

The chief valid criticism of the program is not that it was too orthodox but that it was not begun sooner, in 1975 instead of 1978; earlier adjustment could have had less severe output costs. The private foreign banks helped delay adjustment by excessive lending, in part because of their excessive optimism about oil prospects and because of abundant international liquidity. A central lesson to be learned from Peru's experience is the need for better coordination between the IMF and private foreign banks. Earlier IMF flexibility also would have helped, as would the presence of an international facility for converting private bank loans to debt with longer maturities.

In his comment, Daniel Schydlowsky maintains that Cline misdiagnoses the problem as being of excess demand. He cites documentation of extensive excess industrial capacity, especially if the possibility of moving to multiple shift operation is taken into account. Schydlowsky doubts the effectiveness of devaluation, disputes the appropriateness of Cline's statistical tests showing the influence of the exchange rate on imports and exports with other tests showing the contrary, and attempts to demonstrate that the large government deficits of 1977 and 1978 were due to stabilization policy rather than the cause for its need. As an alternative to the orthodox strategy finally adopted, Schydlowsky suggests the government should have used selective incentives to industrial exports in order to earn foreign exchange by using the existing excess capacity.[17]

Tanzania

Tanzania had several balance-of-payments crises in the 1970s: in 1970 and 1971; a more serious crisis in 1974 and 1975; and large deficits again in 1978 and 1979. James Weaver and Arne Anderson (chapter 10) deal primarily with the 1974–75 stabilization program. They state that although they tried to be objective in analyzing stabilization, their viewpoint is "sympathetic with the Tanzanian effort to build a socialist society."

Two distinct analyses of the causes of the crisis are presented. The first analysis, based on a UNDP study, attributes the 1974–75 crisis mainly to exogenous shocks: drought in 1973–74, which adversely affected production of food, especially corn, for domestic consumption and

17. For Cline's reply, see the discussion at the end of chapter 9.

of export crops, particularly cotton; and worldwide increases in import prices, with food leading the way. A second analysis portrays the crisis as policy induced and attributes the fall in agricultural production mainly to low producer prices and to the forced movement of people into the Ujamaa villages.

Government actions to meet the crisis were a combination of pragmatism and ideology. Agricultural producer prices were increased, communal farming was abandoned, import controls were instituted, and in late 1975 the Tanzanian shilling was devalued by 11 percent despite the government's belief that both import demand and the export supply response would be inelastic. Most of these measures were departures from past policies. However, Tanzania and the IMF were unable to reach agreement on a stabilization program. The chapter cites the Tanzanians as stating this lack of agreement was due to their refusal to deflate the economy at the expense of the poor. In their conclusion, Weaver and Anderson imply that the international system cannot help democratic socialist countries that experience balance-of-payments crises, yet they point out elsewhere in the chapter that external assistance to Tanzania, from the World Bank and bilateral donors, was substantial and predominantly on soft terms.

The analytic portion of the chapter provides several critiques of Tanzania's development model and stabilization program. The first, which comes from the left, is that the stabilization measures effectively meant the end of the earlier socialist model. Another critique holds that the stabilization policy was deficient in that although food crop production was encouraged, steps to stimulate export crops were not taken, a failure which resulted in a fall in export volume and led to the balance-of-payments crisis in 1978. Still another criticism is that not only were the agricultural policies mistaken, but also Tanzania's basic industry strategy emphasizing self-reliance by 1995 should have focused on efficiency, by minimizing the opportunity cost of factors of production and maximizing value-added cost measured by world prices. Finally, the UNDP argues that the government had a clear stabilization program and carried it out with considerable success. The authors agree to some extent with all of these views. They are not willing to concede the Tanzanian experiment has been a failure. In this respect, they point to the 2.6 percent annual growth in per capita product from 1960 to 1977, a rate that compares favorably with most low-income countries.

In his comment, G. K. Helleiner emphasizes the policy significance of what appears to have been a split between Tanzania and the IMF in 1974 and 1975 over income distributional issues. Helleiner believes that Tanzania's success in pursuing its own course without IMF support indicates a need to review IMF conditionality.

Pakistan

In chapter 11, Stephen Guisinger examines the experience of economic stabilization in Pakistan in the 1970s. After years of price stability, inflation rose to 30 percent in Pakistan in 1973–74 but fell to approximately 10 percent by 1976–77. Moreover, a large trade deficit emerged by 1974–75. Therefore, economic stabilization became a problem in the 1970s, adding to the traditional problem of the need for long-term growth.

Pakistan's development strategy in the 1950s and 1960s at first emphasized highly protected manufacturing but later stressed agriculture (in the "Green Revolution") and the subsidized export of manufactured products. In the 1970s, growth slowed and became more variable. Inflationary shocks came from drought in 1970–71 as well as war and separation from East Pakistan in 1971. A trade balance shock came from the sharp decline in terms of trade in 1974 due to higher oil prices following a period of buoyant cotton export prices. Higher foreign economic assistance, especially from OPEC, financed the larger trade gap, as aid doubled from 1972 to 1974.

In 1972 the Bhutto government devalued the rupee sharply and liberalized the trade regime at the same time. Critics charge that this devaluation caused inflation, but using a simulation model Guisinger finds that the devaluation probably had limited inflationary impact. More significant for inflation was the government's large increase in nominal wages while holding real wages relatively constant. Guisinger finds some contractionary effect from devaluation in the simulation, assuming low export elasticity, and concludes that higher wages were appropriate to offset the contractionary effects of devaluation.

On fiscal policy in the 1970s, the conventional wisdom is that expansionary government spending fueled inflation. Increased military spending and spending on social programs and wheat subsidies meant higher fiscal deficits. Guisinger contends that this policy was appropriate because autonomous demand for investment and exports was declining, and increased government spending was necessary to avoid Keynesian recession. He notes that real consumption rose, however. On monetary policy, Guisinger concludes that although some of the contradictory data suggest excessive monetary expansion driven by public deficits and increased credit to the public sector, on balance monetary policy was not the origin of inflation. Moreover, he considers monetary instruments to be rudimentary.

Overall, Guisinger approves of the government's handling of stabilization. Inflation fell from 30 percent to 10 percent. The 1972 devaluation was balanced by wage increases that raised demand and helped Pakistan keep a constant or slightly improving income distribution. A crucial feature of this unorthodox "success" was a large increase in foreign aid; therefore it may be dangerous to generalize from the case of Pakistan, a country that benefited atypically from new OPEC lending.

The comment by Gustav Papanek stresses the role of supply in explaining inflation. Buoyant supply growth contributed to price stability in the 1950s and 1960s; stagnant or declining per capita production, especially of foodstuffs, contributed to inflation in the 1970s. Citing the cases of Indonesia and Bangladesh, Papanek broadens the theme to emphasize the strategy of expansionary stabilization, whereby correction of prior distortions enables the country to raise output, facilitating stabilization of prices and the trade balance.

Korea

In the final country study, Roger D. Norton and Seung Yoon Rhee examine the case of Korea (chapter 12). Their analysis is unique in this volume because it applies a formal macroeconomic model to conduct policy simulations for assessing actual country experience in areas such as the oil price shock, export policy, and monetary policy. Because Korea has had persistent problems with inflation in the past five years despite anti-inflationary efforts variously involving price controls, import liberalization, monetary restraint, and proposals to limit export growth, the model's potential implications for reducing inflation have special relevance.

The model is demand-led. Output is a function of the money supply (under the hypothesis that credit for working capital influences output), the export target, and the past inflation rate (under the argument that higher prices mean more buoyant expectations). Thus the model is a short-term model in which normal supply-side production function constraints (capital stock, labor supply) do not enter. This fact means that caution must be used to apply the model within modest limits of changes; otherwise, for example, extreme increases in money supply would unrealistically predict extreme increases in output.

Output change determines investment change (by an accelerator relationship) and therefore savings; consumption is determined residually (so savings is not a constraint as it is in many models of the development process). Prices are determined by the excess of nominal money supply growth over real output growth and a price expectations (cost of holding money) variable (following Harberger) and by import prices (following Laidler). The price equation shows a low direct elasticity of inflation to nominal money supply growth (about 0.2). The model contains other equations for government consumption, investment, inventories, and so forth, although exports are exogenously stated as the annual government export target. Overall, the model obtains a high degree of accuracy in explaining what actually happened to output, prices, and other macroeconomic variables over the period 1963–77.

The first policy experiment simulates what would have happened in the absence of higher oil prices. The conclusion is that without the oil shock Korean inflation would have been lower by about seven percentage points; accordingly, the oil shock was the major reason Korean inflation has been higher in recent years than before. The oil shock also reduced GDP growth rate by 0.8 to 1.6 percentage points per year.

A second policy simulation reduces the exogenous export annual growth rate target by 5 percent. The results indicate that this lowering of export performance would have reduced annual GDP growth by almost one percentage point; it would have worsened the balance of payments markedly. Slower export growth would have meant higher inflation, not lower, casting doubt on recent recommendations to slow exports for antiinflationary reasons. The cause of this result is that lower growth would have meant lower real transactions demand for money and therefore more inflationary consequences of given money growth.

The third policy simulation reduces the annual growth rate of money supply by 5 percent (from its average 33 percent rate). The result is a one percentage point drop in the real GDP growth rate, given money supply's direct role in the "production function." More striking, slower monetary growth would have made inflation slightly higher instead of lower, according to the model. The reason is that money's influence on output swamps its direct influence on prices; lower monetary growth means lower

output and therefore a greater spillover of monetary expansion into inflation instead of real transactions demand. Norton and Rhee conclude that
monetary growth has been closely in line with demand for real money
balances for transactions (and for increasing monetization of the economy). They note that the role of money in their production function explains why these results differ from other results (such as those of Harberger and Vogel) that show a strong positive relationship between
money supply growth and inflation. Nevertheless, the authors caution that
large monetary changes could give different results by changing expectational parameters; thus, if monetary policy is to be used to combat inflation, it must be sharp and sustained, not marginal and temporary.

Concerning income distribution, the simulations suggest that actual
growth-oriented policies pursued by the Korean government have tended
to improve the distribution, as measured crudely by the wage-rental factor shares, while sacrificing current consumption in favor of future
generations.

Larry Westphal's comment suggests that the Norton-Rhee study pays
too much attention to statistical goodness of fit and too little to policy
meaningfulness. Westphal questions specific features of the model, such
as its absence of a capacity ceiling and its dependence on money supply.
With some others in the general discussion, he considers the model to be
of only limited utility for the purpose of simulating major alternative
policy strategies.

Modeling Stabilization

In the final chapter, Lance Taylor presents an analytical model of
stabilization in semi-industrial countries using an IS/LM framework (that
is, building on the standard Keynesian-monetary synthesis that sees
equilibrium interest rates and output as determined by their unique
combination where desired investment equals savings and money demand
equals money supply). The earlier chapters by Ahluwalia and Lysy,
Guisinger, and Norton and Rhee all involve models related to Taylor's
underlying analysis. Taylor's main purpose is to provide theoretical support for the structuralist critique that orthodox stabilization policies (devaluation, monetary contraction, and fiscal restraint) are both contractionary and inflationary. The most crucial feature of Taylor's model is
that interest costs enter directly into production costs and final price because of interest expenses for working capital. In addition, imports are

intermediate inputs that show little response to devaluation but cause higher prices when devaluation occurs; and devaluation can cause a contractionary decline in the trade balance stated in domestic currency.

Because of Taylor's central assumption that the interest rate is directly related to product cost and price, he is able to draw IS/LM curves relating price to national output (instead of the conventional diagram relating interest rate to national output). The IS curve has the normal downward slope in the Keynesian case but slopes upward in a "Fisherian" case, where a direct positive response of investment to higher profits at higher output (and a sluggish response of savings to output) means the interest rate must rise to hold investment back to equal savings at higher output levels. For its part, the LM curve has a normal zone (upward sloping) but an abnormal zone (downward sloping) as well, where the traditional portfolio shifting (between money and bonds) is weak and is dominated by the price-interest relationship.

A central result is that monetary restraint (leftward shift of LM curve) not only reduces output (as usual) but also increases prices (the surprise)[18] in the Taylor-modified "Keynesian" case. Thus Taylor maintains there is theoretical support for the structuralist argument that orthodox stabilization is stagflationary.

Taylor acknowledges that this perverse effect is short term, and that in the longer term monetary restraint causes a rightward shift of the LM curve and a downward shift of the IS curve as slower wage growth and lower inflationary expectations take hold; at that time, both output and inflation will fall, but before the long term, inflation will rise.

Similarly, Taylor argues that if the abnormal zone of the LM curve is relevant (a case he holds is common in developing countries), fiscal contraction will cause both higher prices and reduced output. For its part, devaluation can be stagflationary because it causes the LM curve to shift to the left (as higher import prices require higher working capital to finance intermediate inputs and thus higher excess demand for money) and the IS curve to shift upward (under the "normal" case where export increase exceeds import increase in domestic currency, raising demand and thus IS). This version of a stagflationary result from devaluation derives not from export elasticity pessimism but from the working capital

18. Standard IS/LM analysis would show a rise in the interest rate but not in prices. In the textbook case, monetary restraint causes prices to decline (not rise) if the economy is above full employment and to remain unchanged if it is below full employment.

requirement in the model. Taylor then explores other variant cases (the Fisherian IS curve and contractionary devaluation).

Taylor then formalizes the old structuralist argument of "sectoral bottlenecks" in a diagrammatic analysis. Next he constructs the long-term trade-off between growth and inflation, in which generally monetary policy that achieves higher long-term growth also causes more inflation; however, the inflationary impact can be lessened either by reducing wage response to inflation and growth (an inequitable solution) or by raising labor's savings propensity (for example, through financial mechanisms).

Taylor then reviews the Walrasian theory implied by orthodox stabilization policy as in the IMF's "financial programming." Monetary restraint amounts to causing excess demand in the stock (money) market in order to call forth excess supply in the flow (commodity) market so prices will fall, but structuralists argue the process will take too long and be too costly in lost output. Recognition of the high cost of such a "shock" is an element of wisdom of "gradualist" monetarists (whom Taylor nevertheless sees as less enlightened than structuralists). The main critique is that the economy is not in Walrasian equilibrium as assumed by orthodox approaches; it has excess potential demands that do not sum to zero.

Taylor's policy recommendations include a favorable word for gradualism; emphasis on export promotion and an appeal for industrial countries and international agencies to be broadminded about such devices as drawbacks, subsidized credit, and dual exchange rates; the hoary structuralist recommendation to modernize agriculture to remove a bottleneck; and financial mechanisms to increase savings from wages. Taylor's main policy recommendation is negative: avoid the orthodox package of fiscal stringency, credit contraction, devaluation, and wage repression because the results for semi-industrial countries are both increased inflation and reduced output. He closes with a warning that the IMF must learn less draconian measures or else risk a response from the South that may end the present international economic system. Taylor, however, neither documents draconian IMF measures and their negative results nor cites other references doing so, and in one footnote he acknowledges that "in some IMF stabilization exercises a good deal of non-model-based economic sophistication is brought to bear."

The main critique of discussant Kemal Dervis (as well as others in the general discussion) is that Taylor's model is short term. Although monetary restraint may be inflationary in the short term, a more normal anti-inflationary effect is likely to be achieved in the medium term. Dervis argues for greater attention to the full time path of adjustment.

Major Findings and Issues

The following discussion attempts to synthesize the overall results of the conference. The conference papers and discussants' comments revealed areas of both consensus and sharp controversy. There was consensus on several new patterns in stabilization.

Stylized Facts

These patterns amount to a new set of "stylized facts" of stabilization. One such pattern is that inflation has proved more difficult to deal with than balance-of-payments problems. Inflationary experience in the 1970s (table 1-1 above) shows a widespread inability among developing countries to reduce inflation back to earlier levels after the global shocks of 1973–74 (with the important exception of the Asian region). In contrast, the non-oil-exporting developing countries managed to reduce their real current account deficits substantially in 1976 and 1977, after massive deficits in 1974 and 1975 (chapter 2). The case studies of this volume, especially those of Mexico, Peru, and Korea, also bear out the greater difficulty in meeting anti-inflationary goals than in reducing balance-of-payments deficits. The reasons for the inability to control inflation vary from country to country, but it generally has been difficult to contract simultaneously real wages and public sector deficits. With respect to the balance of payments, export performance for most of the countries studied proved to be sensitive to exchange rate changes. Nor is the distinction between inflation and balance of payments necessarily caused by the fact that limits on borrowing inevitably constrain external deficits while there is no corresponding constraint on internal inflation. In the Southern Cone experience, where inflation was especially difficult to reduce, external current and especially capital transactions were buoyant to the point of excess. One major factor underlying the greater difficulty in reducing inflation seems to be the higher background level of international inflation than in the past.

A second stylized fact is that both international and domestic factors caused stabilization problems in the 1970s. By contrast, in the 1950s and

1960s the absence of severe global economic shocks meant that most stabilization difficulties were the result of domestic causes (or, if externally related, they were the consequence of deteriorating prices for specific export products). Stanley Black is right, however, in emphasizing that even in the 1970s not all or even necessarily the bulk of stabilization problems could be attributed to external shocks. In our view, the evidence from the country studies attributes greater weight to internal than to external causes for stabilization problems. By itself, this says nothing about the appropriate extent of IMF conditionality, but does argue for some conditionality linked to domestic policy measures.

Based on his UNCTAD-UNDP study, Sidney Dell argues that external forces were by far the predominant source of stabilization problems in the 1970s, and that accordingly IMF conditionality should be more lenient. But even based on the calculations of the UNCTAD-UNDP study, worldwide inflation in the prices of developing countries' imports accounted for only about half of the deterioration in the trade balances of non-oil-exporting developing countries from 1972 to 1975. Alternative analysis indicates that from 1972 to 1975 worldwide inflation and recession caused only one-fourth of the current account deterioration in middle-income non-oil countries, but as much as three-fourths of the deterioration for low-income countries.[19] These estimates suggest that in middle-income countries internal forces dominated balance-of-payments developments in this period while in low-income countries subject to more severe constraints because of their inability to borrow on private capital markets, external forces were dominant. In any event the new stylized fact remains: both internal and external factors caused stabilization problems in the 1970s, and external shocks played a larger role than in previous decades.

A third common pattern is that stabilization prospects are affected by the government's credibility and therefore by the success or failure of past attempts. Where economic actors are more skeptical because of past failure, stabilization is less likely to succeed and its costs are likely to be higher. False stabilization starts can thus be costly. The policy implication of this is that stabilization efforts must either be sudden or sustained if carried out gradually. The cases of Peru and Colombia illustrate the point. A pattern of repetitive, unsuccessful stabilization measures in Peru preceded an ultimately painful adjustment. By contrast, in Colombia,

19. Dell and Lawrence, *The Balance of Payments Adjustment Process,* and Cline and Associates, *World Inflation and the Developing Countries,* chap. 2.

the lack of policy credibility caused by a sequence of unsuccessful devaluations in the 1950s and early 1960s was reversed by the coherent and successful policies beginning in 1967 (chapter 3).

A fourth stylized fact is that early action is crucial to successful stabilization with minimum adjustment cost to real economic growth. A pervasive problem has been that countries wait too long before adopting stabilization measures, necessitating more painful adjustment when it finally comes (as in the case studies of Mexico and Peru). This is hardly a new or startling fact but is cited because delays in instituting stabilization measures are so frequent. The reason for this is not hard to find; stabilization measures normally involve unpopular political actions. Easy access to private bank lending may be another reason for this pattern, as discussed below.

A somewhat puzzling pattern in international experience is that Asian countries have shown a greater ability to deal with stabilization problems (especially inflation) than countries in other regions. We can give no simple explanation of this fact. Past structure is an inadequate explanation since the level of consumer price inflation before the 1973–74 upsurge was about the same in Africa, Asia, and the Middle East, rose to a higher level in Asia than in the other two regions, but then declined again in 1975–78 to a lower level in Asia (table 1-1). Past structure of inflation may be an explanatory factor in Latin America, which traditionally has had more inflation than other regions. Average inflation rates in Asia were only 1.6 percentage points higher in 1975–78 than in 1967–72, while the increase was 15 percentage points in Africa, 37 in Latin America, and 16.1 in the Middle East (table 1-1). This divergence holds at the country level. Among thirty developing countries (excluding those with traditionally high inflation), after a nearly universal surge in inflation during 1973–74, approximately half succeeded in reducing inflation in the period 1975–77 while the other half failed to do so. Of the sixteen successful countries, eight were Asian nations (India, Pakistan, Sri Lanka, Thailand, the Philippines, Korea, Malaysia, and Taiwan). There were no Asian nations among the fourteen countries unsuccessful in reducing inflation from 1973–74 levels.[20]

Another surprising new "stylized fact" is the problem of excessive capital inflow in the process of stabilization turnaround, particularly in Latin America's Southern Cone, with its consequences of excess buildup of reserves and domestic money supply (as discussed below).

20. Cline and Associates, *World Inflation and the Developing Countries*, chap. 8.

Structuralist Critique

Controversy is still flourishing in the debate between structuralists and advocates of orthodox (monetarist) policies. Current vintage structuralism seems to adhere to the old view that devaluation is not only inflationary but also ineffective in correcting the external balance because of unfavorable trade elasticities. Contemporary structuralists add the arguments that (a) devaluation therefore is contractionary, and (b) monetary restraint is inflationary because it raises product price through higher interest costs of working capital.

On devaluation, Ahluwalia-Lysy and Taylor devoted new modeling efforts based on the old export pessimism. However, more authors emphasized that "export optimism" is increasingly supported by the evidence (Krueger, Foxley, Cline, and especially Diaz, an early theorist of contractionary devaluation). It is possible that export optimism should be related to the stage of development; while middle-income countries of Latin America and Asia provide examples in its support, there is less evidence for low-income countries in Africa and Asia.

The specific Taylor formulation, which stresses perverse inflationary consequences of monetary restraint working through the assumed interest cost channel, is vulnerable to the charge that it is a short-term view, as emphasized by discussant Kemal Dervis and other participants. Moreover, both the antidevaluation and anti-monetary-restraint positions fail to distinguish between real and nominal values. Surely it is the real (purchasing parity adjusted) exchange rate and the real (inflation adjusted) interest rate Taylor and others must mean when they oppose devaluation and monetary restraint; otherwise (if specified in nominal terms), they are advocating real appreciation (fixed nominal exchange rate in the face of inflation) and negative real interest rates, hardly defensible stabilization strategies even to structuralists. Once this point is recognized, however, much ground is conceded by the structuralists already because orthodox analysts frequently find it difficult to convince governments to devalue and slow monetary growth enough to hold real exchange rates constant and real interest rates nonnegative.

The main contribution of the new structuralist critique is probably that it brings out the need for more careful attention to the time path and intensity of stabilization measures. By pointing out the risks of an intense combination of contractionary measures that may also be inflationary in the short term, they highlight that it may be overly costly to concentrate orthodox policies fully in the first few months or year of a stabilization program. Thus, cumulative net GDP gain over, for example, three to five years might be considerably higher under a gradual phasing in of corrective measures such as real devaluation, monetary restraint and real interest rate increase, and fiscal restraint, rather than through a joint and vigorous application of such measures immediately. The shortcoming of the gradualist approach is the uncertain staying power of governments in a political milieu. Dynamic modeling work will be needed that spells out the time sequence of these two approaches (essentially, "gradualist" versus "shock") in order to draw firmer conclusions, although the modeling will be unlikely to capture political change. Moreover, the more gradualist option may require greater availability of external financing.

Expansionary Stabilization?

Gustav Papanek suggested that the Asian experience shows the possibility of expansionary stabilization, essentially a supply-side economics approach, circumventing the whole structuralist-monetarist argument. Over certain periods, there is evidence of expansionary stabilization in Brazil as well. To the extent that theoretical substance can be developed for strategies of expansionary stabilization, this area is clearly one of high return to more research. Certainly the general "absorption approach" to balance-of-payments stabilization traditionally implies that at least some of the demand restriction required to reduce absorption is likely to spill over into reduced output as well. Krueger and Diaz spell out the reasons for recession as expansion in newly favored sectors lags behind downward adjustments in formerly favored sectors when a rationalization of the incentive structure occurs.

With regard to inflation, some macromodeling for developing countries incorporates a Phillips curve trade-off between inflation and expansion, but other analyses find little relationship or even a reverse relationship (higher inflation correlated with reduced levels of national output), suggesting dominance of the supply side in inflationary determination.[21] In

21. See, respectively, Antonio C. Lemgruber, "Inflation in Brazil," in Lawrence B. Krause and Walter S. Salant, eds., *Worldwide Inflation* (Brookings Institution, 1977), and Surjit S. Bhalla, "The Transmission of Inflation into Developing Economies," in Cline and Associates, *World Inflation and the Developing Countries*.

any case, more theory and evidence on expansionary stabilization is needed before it can be considered a policy alternative that can be generalized.

Crawling Peg

One policy approach on which there appears to be fairly wide consensus is the desirability of following a crawling-peg exchange rate policy where domestic inflation is high so that the real (purchasing power parity) exchange rate may be at least maintained, if not devalued. The structuralist analysts recognize the crawling peg's utility as an export stimulant, and the case for its beneficial resource allocational result is stated forcefully in Krueger's study. While beneficial for the trade account, the crawling peg may cause trouble on the capital account if the rate of crawl is preannounced. With high domestic inflation and correspondingly high nominal domestic interest rates, a preannounced crawl may provide a strong incentive for inflows of capital. As long as the domestic interest rate exceeds the rate of devaluation over time in the preannounced crawl by more than the level of the international interest rate, foreign capital can enter to take advantage of high domestic interest rates without risk to reconversion (except for the risk that the government will not honor the preannounced rate). The resulting capital inflow can cause an inflationary expansion in reserves and the monetary base. Broadly speaking, this inflationary consequence of preannouncing the crawl must be traded off against any anti-inflationary effect preannouncing may have through the reduction of inflationary expectations.

Sterilization

Another important finding is that capital inflows, reserve buildup, and monetary expansion can provide a source of inflationary destabilization. At a general level, Black cites this pattern as a source of transmission of external inflation in the early 1970s.[22] In the context of an "embarrassment of riches" of capital inflows shortly after stabilization has begun, the pattern is emphasized by Diaz for the Southern Cone and is mentioned by Cline for Peru.

The policy instrument that is lacking in this phenomenon appears to

22. Also see Cline and Associates, *World Inflation and the Developing Countries,* especially chap. 3.

be an adequate means of sterilization, so that capital inflows do not increase the domestic monetary base. The lack of well-developed open market operations is the primary example. In short, in the new international environment of high liquidity, it is increasingly important to develop means of sterilization of capital inflows. McKinnon formulates the problem in terms of premature liberalization of the external capital market, that is, in advance of liberalization of the goods market. Thus, if sterilization instruments remain difficult to develop, it may be necessary to apply controls on capital inflows (such as the mandatory deposits used in Brazil). One source of the problem seems to be clear: the preannounced crawling peg (as just discussed). Where sterilization is difficult and excessive reserve expansion is a problem, either the preannouncing should be suspended or capital inflow controls (or tax disincentives) should be applied, or both.

Income Distribution Theory

Studies in this volume (Ahluwalia-Lysy, Foxley, and to some extent Diaz and the country studies on Mexico, Peru, and Pakistan) indicate that there is no inherent analytical reason for the distribution of income to become more (or less) concentrated during stabilization. There is a need for more work on this subject, however. A fuller analysis of distribution over the business cycle is necessary. For example, the presumed greater variability of profits over the cycle might be expected to make labor share anticyclical, so that income distribution would become less concentrated during the stabilization phase of corrective recession. On the other hand, the increased incidence of unemployment means that greater inequality among workers would work against more equal functional distribution of income (between capital and labor) in affecting the size distribution of income among families.

Absolute poverty requires a separate analysis. It is possible and even probable (aside from political specifics) that the size distribution of income may become more nearly equal during a stabilization-induced recession (because profits are more variable than wages or because elasticity of substitution is as usual below unity in a neoclassical approach with fixed capital and variable labor) while the incidence of absolute poverty will rise. For absolute poverty, the crucial issue is whether temporary recession (from orthodox policies) and increased incidence of absolute poverty will enable faster long-term growth; if so, the entire time profile of poverty incidence will be more favorable if authorities accept the short-term losses of stabilization instead of trying to avoid them.[23] Thus, a poverty (as opposed to distributional) focus seems to lead right back to the issue of the trade-off between stabilization and growth.

Income Distribution Policy

These issues of abstract analysis, which suggest that distributional consequences of stabilization need not be regressive, must be supplemented with a wide review of distributional results of stabilization policies in practice, on which there is some evidence that they tend to be regressive. Foxley's view is that stabilization concentrated the distribution of income in Brazil and the Southern Cone. As Johnson and Salop emphasize, distributional effects of some sort are inevitable, and the particular outcome depends heavily on the relative political power of various groups. It is noteworthy that in its program to slow inflation in late 1979 the Brazilian government instituted new wage indexing policies that raise wages of low-income workers by more than the rate of inflation and raise wages of higher-income workers by less than the inflation rate.[24] These policies reflect growing pressures for populist measures on a military regime committed to transition to political liberalization and return to civilian rule. This example illustrates how the political context of a given stabilization program may affect its distributional consequences more than the technical economic imperatives of stabilization.

In practice some changes in stabilization strategies could have obvious equity benefits. Tax policy can rely more heavily on progressive taxes (usually direct rather than indirect taxes) in raising revenue for fiscal balance. Taxes on capital gains are especially relevant where reformed capital markets can produce enormous windfalls. Cuts in government expenditures can be designed so that they do not affect the poor disproportionately. For example, gasoline subsidies that benefit the middle and upper classes are better areas for cuts than are subsidies for basic foods (although even food subsidies should be harmonized with terms of trade

---

23. Although Foxley's study portrays the impact of Latin American stabilization programs on poverty and income distribution quite well, it does not demonstrate that alternative measures of gradualism or structuralist strategies would have guaranteed higher growth over a medium or long term, and therefore that such policies would have had more favorable total results for reducing absolute poverty.

24. *InfoBrazil*, vol. 1 (Johns Hopkins School of Advanced International Studies, March 1980).

that do not discriminate against small farmers). Government investment programs in construction and other labor intensive projects are areas to avoid spending cuts (Foxley and Diaz on Brazil). Wage policy is crucial for income distribution. Where wages have become grossly overstated, real wage declines may be necessary (Fishlow); otherwise, major declines in real wages through wage repression in the face of inflation should be avoided (except perhaps for privileged high-wage sectors enjoying monopoly rent). The contrast between the 30 to 40 percent real wage reductions in the Southern Cone and nominal wage increases to maintain real wages in Pakistan is striking, and success at reversing inflation was at least as great in Pakistan, although from a lower base. Nevertheless, it is also clear that complete protection of wages can be a recipe for continued wage-price spiral.

Chance

Several chapters refer to the intrusion of the unpredictable in successful or unsuccessful stabilization programs (Krueger; the Mexican, Peruvian, and Tanzanian case studies). Chance in this sense includes good or bad harvests, unexpected changes in terms of trade (such as oil-import costs, as specifically modeled in the Korean case), and discovery of resources (Mexican oil). To the extent that luck (good or bad) or expectations can be estimated, this factor may provide some guidance to the timing of stabilization programs.

Political Constraints

The conference discussion brought out the influence of political conditions on stabilization strategy, an old theme. Sharp erosion of real wages in the Southern Cone probably would have been impossible without authoritarian regimes, and the strategies chosen in Tanzania and Pakistan reflect socialist or populist political constraints. Dervis clearly spelled out the central point: a technically sound stabilization program is of no use if it is so harsh that before enough time can pass for the program to bear fruit, political upheaval will cause the program to abort, leading to worse economic instability than before. Recognizing political constraints is a particular challenge to the design of wise conditionality requirements in IMF standby loans; moreover, the IMF must balance the need for political reality against the need for comparability in its treatment of different countries and for credibility in the private banking sector. The case of Peru may be one where earlier IMF flexibility in light of political constraints would have reduced ultimate adjustment costs. However, recognition of political constraints cannot go so far as to make externally imposed conditions meaningless. In its bargaining over conditions with the IMF for access to what, after all, are funds at rates below those that would have to be paid in the private capital market, the government may exaggerate the political consequences of meeting more stringent conditions.

Papanek pointed out that the political constraint may be a question of trade-offs, for example, reducing subsidies to one group (such as government enterprises) and thereby raising some prices, or reducing import protection for some and expanding the choice for others. At one stage in the Peruvian case, the political problem was to reduce military expenditures. In other words, the political constraint may not be a macroproblem but one of choosing between different groups, and this is particularly hazardous territory for an international agency to enter.

International Banking System

The private banking system clearly has made a historic contribution to development by bridging the financial gap caused by the OPEC actions in the 1970s (Friedman, Heller). There is reason for concern, however, that the private banks are not exercising as much caution as they should (Wallich, Pelikan). Ample liquidity in world capital markets in the 1970s (as banks sought to place OPEC funds) appears to have led to some excesses. In some cases (Peru as analyzed in this volume; others include Turkey and Zaire), banks appear to have lent too much for too long, and then abruptly closed off new lending once the country had gone past a point where stabilization might have been relatively easy to a point of severe instability. The turnaround in bank lending adds to the external account crisis, meaning the country must cover not only a trade account deficit but a new capital account deficit. Ample bank lending before the final crisis may also discourage the country from going to the IMF (where there will be performance conditions) at an earlier stage.

A systemic problem may be that many banks assume the international institutions and OECD countries will act in a way that minimizes any real risk to the banks in the event of default or rescheduling. If so, then these banks are failing to "internalize" an "external diseconomy" of excessive lending. That is, if the full risk of each loan were internal to the bank, it would lend less; but because much of the risk is "externalized" to the international community, the bank lends too much relative to the underlying risk of the situation, causing the dynamic of delayed adjustment just outlined. This problem of externality is increased when, in addition, European, Japanese, and medium-sized U.S. banks seek to enter the international market at extremely low-risk spreads over LIBOR interest rates because of longer-term objectives of market penetration.

There are two major aspects to the problem of overlending by banks: internalizing risk and providing information. The issue of information is sensitive for the IMF because of the need to respect member confidentiality, but much of the tabular material in IMF country reports could be made public without jeopardizing member countries. Indeed, many countries could benefit from improved access to lending (where conditions warrant) because of increased information in the system. It would be less appropriate to make public IMF policy judgments. The publicly available debt-reporting system of the World Bank is an important source of information, and further efforts to expand the comprehensiveness of its coverage of private debt deserve high priority.

With respect to internalizing bank risk, it might be helpful to develop within the OECD standard policies that spell out more clearly what private banks can and cannot expect in rescheduling situations. In particular, clarification of the principle of "comparability"—that private banks will be expected to reschedule debt on criteria that are comparable to those for rescheduling by public entities—would help make banks perceive "sovereign risk" as internal to the firm.[25] This recommendation is precisely opposite to that made by Friedman.

International Financial Institutions

Finally, although the conference was not designed to evaluate operations of the IMF or the World Bank, several policy implications emerged. The recent pattern of amassing lending resources in the IMF with a dearth of clients, particularly for conditional funds, should be reversed. Higher

25. Although "comparability" would not necessarily mean that banks would accept lower interest rates on rescheduled debt comparable to those on rescheduled public loans, it would mean that private banks would be expected to postpone payment on a portion of their debt comparable to that postponed by public sources, and that interest rates on deferred debt would be subject to negotiation.

oil prices in 1979–80 may make this reversal automatic. Other factors are important, however, including revisions in bank lending (as discussed above) that would make it more unlikely that countries would bypass the IMF until severe crises had set in; and possibly more IMF flexibility in response to political constraints in borrowing countries. The structuralist critiques also raised the need for at least a review of IMF stabilization strategies, for example, with special attention to possible stagflationary effects in the short term where interest costs are a major component of production costs. The theory underlying IMF practice and the patterns of action of the IMF as an institution warrant detailed examination.

For the World Bank, the need to combine stabilization with long-term growth means that stabilization cannot be delegated wholly to the IMF. For example, the Brazilian experience of raising public investment (some of it labor intensive) during the stabilization process illustrates the desirability of coordinating growth and stabilization programs. The World Bank already has recognized this need and has instituted structural adjustment lending with fast disbursal.[26] The need for this approach will be all the greater if, because of considerable exposure already, the private banking system is unable to provide the same degree of financing to meet the impact of higher oil prices in the 1980s that it did in 1974 and 1975.

26. In his address to the 1979 annual meeting, World Bank president Robert McNamara indicated his intention to increase program lending for this purpose. *IMF Survey,* October 15, 1979, p. 328.

CHAPTER TWO

The Impact of Changes in the World Economy on Stabilization Policies in the 1970s

STANLEY W. BLACK

THE DECADE of the 1970s has seen a series of momentous events affecting the global economy: major exchange rate realignments in 1971 and 1973; the collapse of the Bretton Woods system and an associated drastic expansion of international liquidity during 1970–72; the adoption of floating exchange rates among most industrialized countries; and a worldwide inflationary boom in 1973 capped by massive oil price increases in early 1974, leading to the longest and deepest recession since the 1930s.

During most of this dramatic history, the non-oil-producing developing countries have not been major actors on the world stage. Instead, they have responded to the effects of the events occurring in the developed countries of the Organization for Economic Cooperation and Development (OECD) and in the Organization of Petroleum Exporting Countries (OPEC).

Reflecting this situation, most analyses of stabilization policies to cope with these major shocks to the world economy have dealt with the industrialized countries.[1] The developing countries, by contrast, have focused

The computations in the section on external and internal factors were ably performed by Hal McClure and Jon Wight.

I thank William Cline, Ronald Clapham, Jacob Dreyer, Rolf Hasse, and others from the Cologne group, Vanderbilt, and conference participants for useful comments.

1. See, for example, *Towards Full Employment and Price Stability* (Paris: OECD, 1977), or Stanley W. Black, "Policy Responses to Major Disturbances of the 1970's and Their Transmission Through International Goods and Capital Markets," *Weltwirtschaftliches Archiv,* vol. 114, no. 4 (1978), pp. 614–41.

much of their attention and efforts on the debate over their proposals for a New International Economic Order (NIEO).[2] As is well known, most of the NIEO proposals are directed toward long-range goals for changing the structure of international institutions and international commodity markets and the international structure of trade and production. Thus their relevance to the short-term problems of economic management of developing countries is limited, at best. Not surprisingly, the "North-South dialogue" over the original NIEO proposals has gradually become somewhat less intense. For example, the 1979 Manila Conference of UNCTAD was interpreted in the press as something of a failure in terms of advancing the original goals of NIEO.

At the same time, attention has been turning increasingly to macroeconomic, monetary, and stabilization issues affecting developing countries. Some of these issues have been discussed earlier.[3] But recent communiques of the Ministerial Group of 24, which meets in conjunction with the Interim Committee of the International Monetary Fund (IMF) and IMF/World Bank Annual Meetings, have brought these issues to the forefront of international debate. For example, their March 1979 communique expressed ". . . concern over the persistence of low rates of growth and substantial underutilization of capacity in a number of industrialized countries," together with ". . . the disquieting possibility of a further deterioration in world economic activity." The economic outlook appeared to them ". . . unfavorable for the developing countries, not only because of its adverse effect upon world trade, but also because it was likely to intensify the protectionist trends in the industrial countries."[4]

Other issues raised by the Group of 24 in recent meetings have included exchange rate instability among major currencies, the conditionality applying to the use of IMF resources by members borrowing in the upper credit tranches, and the need for greater transfer of real resources from developed to developing countries. Many of these issues have been dealt with in a recent UNCTAD report to the Group of 24 that offers a

2. As set forth in UNCTAD IV, "New Directions and New Structures for Trade and Development," Report by the Secretary General of UNCTAD to the Nairobi Conference, May 1976, and elsewhere.

3. See the papers in D. M. Leipziger, ed., *The International Monetary System and the Developing Nations* (Agency for International Development, 1976); also William R. Cline, *International Monetary Reform and the Developing Countries* (Brookings Institution, 1976).

4. *IMF Survey,* March 19, 1979, p. 87.

series of recommendations relating to the stabilization difficulties of developing countries.[5]

This chapter analyzes some of the major issues affecting stabilization policies of developing countries, both in the recent past and, by implication, in the near future. This chapter discusses the various possible internal and external sources of fluctuations and stabilization problems in developing countries. The transmission mechanism of each potential source of fluctuation is discussed briefly to indicate the appropriate data needed to analyze the developments in the 1970s, to be discussed later in the chapter.

Further, relatively aggregated data and other recent evidence on the external and internal economic developments affecting the non-oil-producing developing countries, both during the 1970s and as compared with the 1960s, are examined. An attempt is made to distinguish between cyclical and secular linkages between economic activity in developing countries and in industrialized countries, taking account of oil price changes affecting both.

This chapter then attempts a cross-sectional statistical analysis classifying the relative importance of various external and internal factors causing stabilization problems in a random sample of forty developing countries during the 1970s. The method used is a discriminant analysis of the need for countries to take drastic stabilization actions, such as a debt rescheduling or upper-tranche IMF standby loan agreement, versus their ability to borrow in international capital markets. This measure is probably somewhat biased toward finding external causes for stabilization problems, since it ignores instability that does not spill over into external payments difficulties. Nevertheless, this measure avoids the pitfall of simply equating inflation and/or low growth with instability.

In light of the available evidence on the relative importance of various factors causing stabilization problems, the most important policy issues are discussed from the point of view of stabilization policies affecting non-oil-producing developing countries. These issues include the behavior of the developed countries and of OPEC and IMF policies. They also include the domestic policy problems of the developing countries themselves.

5. Sidney Dell and others, "The Balance of Payments Adjustment Process in Developing Countries: Report to the Group of Twenty-four," UNDP/UNCTAD Project INT/75/015, January 2, 1979.

Sources of Macroeconomic Fluctuations

The major sources of macroeconomic fluctuations in developing countries, or indeed in any country, can be divided into external sources and internal sources, although there can be significant linkages between the two.[6] The most important external sources of fluctuations would appear to be externally generated changes in trade volumes or trade prices that can be transmitted to the domestic economy through changes in the ability to import essential intermediate inputs, through the Keynesian income generation process, or through direct price and cost effects of changes in prices of traded goods. Fluctuations in international capital flows motivated by changing profit prospects or interest rate differentials would a priori seem to be relatively less important as a cause of cyclical fluctuations for developing than for developed countries, primarily because of the lower degree of financial integration between domestic and foreign capital markets. When a country's access to foreign capital changes suddenly, this change can act as an external shock to the economy, either adding to or subtracting from the flow of imports. On the other hand, changes in capital flows to allow financing of cyclically induced trade imbalances can be an important means of adjustment to disturbances from other sources.

In the monetary area, failure to sterilize the domestic monetary implications of overall surpluses or deficits in the balance of payments can lead to excessive monetary expansion or contraction, an important source of cyclical fluctuations. Finally, failure to keep the nominal exchange rate adjusted for domestic inflation can lead to important fluctuations in the domestic incentives to export or import. Both of these monetary factors are, it will be seen, subject to control by the domestic monetary authorities, and in that sense have both internal and external aspects.

On the internal side, fluctuations may originate from domestic crop failures, from fluctuations in domestic monetary and fiscal policies, from politically motivated investment projects or consumption spending, or from politically inspired excessive wage increases supported by monetary expansion. Other sources of stabilization problems could lie in misguided

---

6. For a complete model see Jere R. Behrman, "Modeling Stabilization Policy for the LDCs in an International Setting," in Albert Ando, Richard Herring, and Richard Marston, eds., *International Aspects of Stabilization Policies,* Federal Reserve Bank of Boston Conference Series, no. 12 (Boston, 1974).

policies to subsidize the prices of either wage goods or goods produced by government-owned enterprises. Finally, domestic and foreign private investment may conceivably fluctuate significantly relative to saving and foreign borrowing, generating a private sector source of internal instability. Political instability is a noneconomic factor that may be very important in causing economic instability in specific countries at specific times. Political instability may also have either domestic or foreign origins.

Transmission Mechanisms for External Disturbances

The three types of externally generated disturbances to developing country economies may be transmitted to them by a variety of mechanisms, which are familiar from certain well-known economic models. Quantitative estimates are available from various sources for some of these transmission mechanisms.

The relationship between economic growth and trade in developed and developing countries is one of the key questions currently being debated by economists and policy makers alike.[7] The overall relationship includes not only the primary trade relationships between the two groups, but also supporting movements of capital, labor, technology, and money.

Most analyses put their emphasis on the "direct" trade linkage between growth in the industrialized group of developed countries and developing countries' exports.[8] For example, 65 percent of total exports of non-oil-exporting developing countries went to industrialized countries in 1978. Thus, there must be a clear relationship between industrialized countries' demand and developing countries' supply. Nevertheless, one must not ignore the "reverse linkage" between developing country growth and exports of the industrialized countries. It is true that industrialized countries trade primarily with each other, with trade among industrialized countries accounting for 63 percent of total industrialized countries' ex-

7. For some different approaches, see Wassily Leontief and others, *The Future of the World Economy* (New York: Oxford University Press, 1977); *World Development Report, 1978* (World Bank, 1978); Interfutures Report, "Facing the Future: Mastering the Probable and Managing the Unpredictable" (OECD, 1979); and the LINK exercise reported below.

8. As of 1979, the IMF classification of industrialized countries (ICs) included the United States, Canada, Japan, Austria, Belgium, Denmark, France, Germany, Italy, Luxembourg, Netherlands, Norway, Sweden, Switzerland, and the United Kingdom.

ports in 1978. But of the remaining industrialized country exports to the
rest of the world, non-oil-producing developing countries accounted for
40 percent, by far the largest fraction. Therefore, trade linkages in both
directions can be significant for each group.

A further distinction must be made between cyclical and secular relationships between trade and growth. While market shares do not change
rapidly from year to year, they can certainly change very significantly
over any extended period.[9] Thus, inferences based on cyclical relationships must not be allowed to obscure more fundamental long-term
changes that are taking place. As will be seen, this is particularly true of
the 1970s.

Changes in world trade volumes induced by cyclical fluctuations in
industrialized countries have been studied in the LINK system of econometric models, which includes both Keynesian models of the industrialized countries and supply-side determined models for developing geographical regions.[10] The main assumptions made by LINK are that export
volumes and prices of all traded goods are essentially exogenous to the
non-oil-producing developing countries, being determined primarily by
the real growth of industrialized countries and by international commodity markets. A fall in export volume or price or a rise in import prices will
be quickly reflected in a reduction in developing country import capacity
in real terms. The reduction in import capacity would quickly restrain
essential imported intermediate imports, reducing both domestic investment and production. Table 2-1 contains a quantitative estimate of this
mechanism based on a LINK simulation of fiscal stimulus amounting to 1
percent of real GNP in six large industrialized countries and 0.5 percent
in five other industrialized countries during the period 1978–80. It will
be seen that world trade volume changes by about 1.4 times the change
in industrialized country real GNP in each year. The value of world trade
changes by about 1.25 times the value of industrialized country GNP. The
value of developing country exports then changes by about 0.8 times the

9. For an illuminating analysis of world trade taking account of such factors,
see W. Arthur Lewis, "The Rate of Growth of World Trade, 1830–1973," presented
to the symposium, "The Past and the Prospects of the Economic World Order,"
Stockholm, Sweden, August 25–28, 1978.

10. See section 4 of "Models for Developing Countries," in R. J. Ball, ed., *The
International Linkage of National Economic Models* (Amsterdam: North-Holland
Publishing Co., 1973), and J. Waelbroek, ed., *The Models of Project LINK* (Am-
sterdam: North-Holland Publishing Co., 1976), chap. 17, on the structure of the
LDC models in the LINK system.

Table 2-1. *Shock to Real GNP in Industrialized Countries*
Percentage deviation from control

Item	1978	1979	1980
IC real GNP	1.1	2.5	3.5
IC GNP deflator	0.2	0.6	1.8
World trade value	1.6	3.9	6.6
World trade price	...	0.4	1.0
World trade volume	1.5	3.4	5.5
LDC export value	1.2	3.2	5.2
LDC real GDP growth (percentage points)	0.1	0.2	0.4

Source: H. G. Georgiadis and G. Tavlas, "Coordinated Expansion Policies in the Main Industrial Countries: Impact on Growth, Inflation, and International Trade," U.S. Department of State, Bureau of Intelligence and Research, Report no. 1013, June 27, 1978. One percent stimulus during 1978, 1979, and 1980 was applied to Belgium, France, Germany, Japan, the United Kingdom, and the United States, and 0.5 percent to Austria, Canada, Finland, Italy, and the Netherlands.

change in the value of world trade. This change in developing country exports is then passed very quickly into a matching change in developing country imports.[11] What may be surprising is the low estimated effect of the changes on developing country growth rates. The basic reason for this result is that real GDP in the developing countries was estimated to be less sensitive to short-term changes in import volumes than to the accumulated stock of capital, which changes only slowly.

Two alternative transmission mechanisms that may operate on a change in developing country export earnings are monetary and capital flow mechanisms, which operate only if imports do not fluctuate pari passu with exports. If the trade balance fluctuates sharply, the change in foreign exchange availability may be reflected either in changes in capital flows to the economy or in changes in monetary reserves. If capital flows offset the change in the trade balance, then the availability of credit from abroad offsets the monetary effect of a decline in foreign exchange earnings. Nevertheless, the domestic economy may still be affected significantly, because foreign lending finances a quite different pattern of domestic spending than do export earnings.

If neither imports nor capital flows offset a change in export earnings, then changes in international reserves and/or increased borrowing from foreign monetary sources must do so. Either of these is likely to result in changes in the domestic money supply, which are unlikely to be sterilized by offsetting domestic operations in most developing countries. For

11. For some independent evidence on this mechanism, see William L. Hemphill, "The Effect of Foreign Exchange Receipts on Imports of Less Developed Countries," *IMF Staff Papers,* vol. 21 (November 1974), pp. 637–77.

example, Surjit Bhalla has estimated equations of the form $\Delta M = a + b \Delta R$, where ΔM is annual change in money supply and ΔR is annual change in international reserves, for thirty developing countries over the period 1956–72.[12] The b coefficients were statistically significant in all but six cases, with a median value of 0.8. These results indicate a failure to sterilize reserve flows in most developing countries.[13]

The final apparently external source of disturbance is failure to maintain the "real" exchange rate, which is caused by allowing a pegged exchange rate to become overvalued through domestic inflation that is faster than foreign inflation and is not offset by devaluation. As a result, the prices of traded goods in domestic currency are held down relative to the prices of nontraded goods, resources are reallocated away from production of traded goods, and the economy begins to suffer from chronic foreign exchange shortages.[14] The response to this situation may take the form of protectionism or devaluation, either of which leads to serious disturbance in the economy, one gradual and the other abrupt. In any event, although this disturbance arises in the foreign trade sector, it should not really be called an external disturbance, since the origin is a misguided exchange rate policy, which is under control of the domestic authorities. Therefore, failure to maintain the real exchange rate will be treated as a domestic source of disturbance in this paper.

Transmission Mechanisms for Internal Disturbances

One of the most frequently occurring internal disturbances in primary-producing developing countries is fluctuation in production of crops, either food or nonfood export crops. The result will be a tendency for the domestic price of the crop to rise, limited, however, by the world price if the country is a small producer. At the same time exports would fall and/or imports would rise, compensating for the shortfall in production. These factors would then be transmitted to the economy by much the same mechanism as an externally generated fluctuation in trade volume.

12. Surjit S. Bhalla, "The Transmission of Inflation into Developing Economies," in William R. Cline and Associates, *World Inflation and the Developing Countries* (Brookings Institution, forthcoming). Complete sterilization implies $b = 0$.

13. For a contradictory finding for the Philippines, see Edmund J. Sheehey, "On the Measurement of Imported Inflation in Developing Countries," *Weltwirtschaftliches Archiv*, vol. 115, no. 1 (1979), pp. 68–79.

14. See Anne O. Krueger, *Foreign Trade Regimes and Economic Development. Liberalization Attempts and Consequences* (Ballinger, 1978), chap. 5 and pp. 229–39.

Changes in the availability of foreign exchange for intermediate imports and complementary capital goods would affect both domestic investment and production unless offset by capital flows or reserve changes. In the latter case, changes in the money supply would follow, in the absence of sterilization. Access to the IMF's Compensatory Finance Facility (CFF) and the European Community's STABEX facility has provided a growing capability to offset the domestic effects of such fluctuations by capital flows.

Domestic monetary policies furnish a major potential internal source of disturbances. In an open economy with an underdeveloped financial system typical of many developing countries, the transmission mechanism for monetary policy operates primarily through the availability of credit and the growth of the money supply and only in some countries through the interest rate mechanism. For in many developing countries, nominal interest rates are held below inflation rates, leading to negative real rates of interest. The resulting infinite demand for credit must be limited by credit restrictions on the banking system. These frequently take the form of selective quotas for rediscounting various types of loans at the central bank, specific ceilings on the expansion of various types of loans by banks, or advance deposits for imports, which are specifically targeted at control of an external imbalance.[15] On the other hand, where real interest rates are allowed to remain positive, changes in interest rates can furnish an additional channel for monetary policy, which has been used successfully in a growing number of countries.[16] Under the conditions prevailing in both sorts of economies, monetary disturbances can be transmitted either through significant negative real rates of interest leading to repressed demands for credit or through rapid growth in money supply and bank credit to the economy.

A major outlet for bank credit in developing countries and therefore a major contributor to monetary expansion is finance for the government budget deficit. For example, table 2-2 indicates that deficit finance in 1976 (or thereabouts) covered about 15 percent of government expendi-

15. See Andrew F. Brimmer, "Central Banking and Economic Development: The Record of Innovation," *Journal of Money, Credit, and Banking*, vol. 3 (November 1971), pp. 780–92; Y. C. Park, "The Role of Money in Stabilization Policy in Developing Countries," *IMF Staff Papers*, vol. 20 (July 1973), pp. 379–418; and Sergio Bortolani, *Central Banking in Africa* (Milan: Cassa di Risparmio delle Provincie Lombarda, 1975), chap. 4.

16. See Ronald I. McKinnon, *Money and Capital in Economic Development* (Brookings Institution, 1973), chap. 8, for the successful cases of Korea and Taiwan.

Table 2-2. *Deficit Finance in Non-Oil-Producing Developing Countries*

Area	Government deficit as percent of expenditure and net lending	Percent share financed by central bank
Latin America	8.8	50.1
Middle East	22.7	13.0
Asia	19.1	26.9
Africa	30.6	40.7
Total	14.6	39.2

Source: Calculated from IMF, *Government Finance Statistics Yearbook*, vol. 2 (1978), p. 14, using 1976 GNP weights from *1978 World Bank Atlas*. Data available for forty-three countries for left-hand column, twenty-four countries for right-hand column, usually for 1976 or adjacent year. Expenditure and net lending represent purchases of goods and financial claims from private sector.

tures and net lending on average in non-oil-producing developing countries, ranging from an average of 9 percent in Latin America to more than 30 percent in Africa. The weighted average share of these deficits financed directly by central bank credit was 39 percent, with the highest fractions of direct monetary finance observed in Latin America (50 percent) and Africa (41 percent). There seems little reason to doubt that excessive monetary financing of government deficits can be a significant domestic source of instability.

Furthermore, it has recently been documented that the inflationary process itself tends to enlarge the government deficit further in many developing countries, as nominal government spending rises more or less proportionally with prices while tax revenue lags behind. For example, Tanzi, Aghevli, and Khan, using different techniques, have estimated that tax revenues in various developing countries fall behind the growth in the nominal tax base by average lags varying from one and one-half quarters to six quarters.[17] The enlarged government deficit then requires additional monetary financing, thus accelerating the inflationary process.

Either a directly generated excessive monetary expansion or a fiscally generated expansion will be transmitted to the economy by an increase in credit and money growth and/or negative real rates of interest. A typical developing country economy would respond to these shocks through a variety of mechanisms, including rising domestic prices and a direct spillover of demand onto foreign goods and possibly exportables. Given a pegged exchange rate, both factors will tend to worsen the current account of the balance of payments, leading either toward protectionism,

17. See Vito Tanzi, "Inflation, Lags and the Real Value of Tax Revenue," *IMF Staff Papers*, vol. 24 (March 1977), pp. 154–67, and Bijan B. Aghevli and Mohsin S. Khan, "Government Deficits and the Inflationary Process in Developing Countries," *IMF Staff Papers*, vol. 25 (September 1978), pp. 383–416.

exchange controls, or falling international reserves. In the latter case, the money supply leaks abroad. If the nominal exchange rate is adjusted to maintain the real exchange rate by depreciating in line with inflation, an extra dose of inflation will be added to the economy through rising prices of importables and exportables, while the external deficit will be alleviated. Furthermore, the increased rate of inflation will reduce the demand to hold domestic nominal assets, leading to a process of financial disintermediation, overinvestment in real assets, and capital flight. This process is exacerbated if nominal interest rates are not allowed to rise, so that real rates of interest turn negative. The process can be ameliorated by indexation of financial assets.[18]

Politically induced excessive wage increases, financed by expansion of credit to private industry and government, offer another domestic source of instability. The impact of government wage increases is not much different from other rises in government expenditure, except that government wage increases tend to raise private wages more directly. On the other hand, private wage increases financed by credit expansion involve a somewhat different mechanism, which is exactly parallel to monetary expansion caused by financing of losses occurring in domestic industry due to price controls. In this case, government-mandated price ceilings on various types of goods are financed either through direct subsidies or through credit extended to the private sector at favorable interest rates. For example, Chu and Feltenstein have estimated that credit expansion to cover losses in industry in Argentina during the period 1965–76 averaged more than three times larger than direct government deficits during the same period.[19]

Global Economic Conditions and Domestic Economic Conditions

Global Economic Disturbances

The relationship between economic growth in industrialized countries, world trade growth, developing country exports, and developing country growth is examined in table 2-3, both in terms of cyclical relationships of

18. See Gustav D. Jud, *Inflation and the Use of Indexing in Developing Countries* (Praeger, 1978), for an account of the uses and limitations of indexation.

19. Ke-Young Chu and Andrew Feltenstein, "Relative Price Distortions and Inflation: The Case of Argentina, 1963–76," *IMF Staff Papers*, vol. 25 (September 1978), pp. 452–93.

Table 2-3. *Cyclical and Secular Changes in Growth and Trade*

Percent

Item	Secular changes		Cyclical changes					
	1962–72[a]	1972–78[a]	1973	1974	1975	1976	1977	1978
Real GNP, industrialized countries	4.6	3.0	6.1	0.1	−0.9	5.4	3.7	3.7
World trade volume	9.0	5.8	13.0	5.5	−5.0	12.0	5.0	5.1
Export volume, non-oil developing countries	6.5	6.9	8.0	5.0	1.0	13.5	6.5	8.0
Terms of trade, non-oil developing countries	−0.5	−1.8	10.0	−8.0	−13.0	5.0	3.0	−6.0
Real GDP, non-oil developing countries	5.5	5.3	7.3	5.3	4.1	4.8	4.9	n.a.

Sources: IMF, *Annual Report, 1978* and *1976*, and *International Financial Statistics*, July 1979.

n.a. Not available.

a. Compounded annual rates of change.

the type studied in the LINK system and in terms of longer-term secular trends. To begin with the cyclical developments in the 1970s, the 1973 boom in industrialized countries was followed by the 1974–75 recession, recovery in 1976, and then relatively slow growth averaging 3.7 percent per year in the industrialized countries since that time. World trade volume mirrors that development, much as the LINK exercise of table 2-1 suggested, although it is notable that world trade volume has actually responded *more* to changes in industrialized country GNP growth than predicted in table 2-1. For example, average world trade growth in the 1970s was reduced by twice the shortfall in industrialized country GNP growth, compared with the 1960s, while table 2-1 suggests a multiplier of only 1.4. One reason may be the large extent to which the 1973 boom and 1974–75 recession reflected speculative inventory accumulation and then reduction in industrialized countries. A second reason would be the depressing effect on world trade volume of the tripling of the price of oil in 1974, as the sharp deterioration in the terms of trade squeezed import volumes for many countries. Of the 8 percent decline in developing country terms of trade in 1974, virtually all is attributable to the higher price of oil.[20]

The slowdown in world trade volume had depressing effects on both the volume and price of developing country exports, just as the 1973 boom had stimulating effects. But it is interesting to note in this case that developing country export volume expanded and contracted less than proportionally to world trade volume, while their terms of trade fluctuated much more than proportionally. Thus non-oil-producing developing country import capacity, measured as the value of exports in terms of importables, increased 19 percent in 1973 and then fell 3.4 percent in 1974 and a further 12 percent in 1974, before rebounding 19 percent in 1978. Since then, developing country export volume has been increasing well, while terms of trade deteriorated in 1978 and again in 1979 due to the recent oil price increase.

To complete the analysis of external trade disturbances on the devel-

20. According to the 1978 IMF *Annual Report,* tables 3 and 4, non-oil developing countries' export prices rose 36.5 percent while import prices rose 48.5 percent in 1974, of which at least 30 percentage points are attributable to oil prices. This calculation is based on a 14 percent average share of oil imports in total non-oil developing countries' imports for 1973–74 and a 226 percent increase in the price of oil in 1974. If oil prices had risen less, both non-oil import and export prices would have risen less, but the non-oil terms of trade would almost certainly have improved further.

Table 2-4. *Balance of Payments of Non-Oil-Producing Developing Countries*

Billions of dollars

Item	1972	1973	1974	1975	1976	1977	1978	1979[a]
Current account	−6.0	−6.0	−23.5	−37.5	−25.5	−23.0	−35.0	−45.0
Capital account	11.0	13.5	25.0	34.5	35.0	35.5	50.5	58.0
Long-term[b]	8.2	12.5	15.5	18.5	19.8	21.7	26.0	34.5
Short-term[c]	2.8	1.0	9.5	16.0	15.2	13.8	24.5	23.5
Overall balance	4.8	7.5	1.5	−3.0	9.6	12.4	15.5	8.0
Official borrowing	1.0	0.1	1.3	1.8	2.0	−0.4	−0.5	−1.0
Increase in reserves	5.8	7.6	2.8	−1.1	11.6	12.0	15.0	7.0

Source: OECD, *Economic Outlook*, vol. 25 (July 1979), p. 142.

a. Estimated.

b. Includes direct and portfolio investment, aid, and other official flows.

c. Includes official export credits, other capital, Euroborrowing, and errors and omissions.

oping countries, it is necessary to examine the balance-of-payments adjustment process and its role in transmission of these disturbances. Before leaving table 2-3, however, it is worth noting that the slowdown in GDP growth of developing countries has been much milder than the reduction in growth of import capacity, just as forecast by the LINK simulation of table 2-1. In fact, the average growth rate of import capacity has slowed from 6 percent per year in the 1962–72 period to 5 percent a year in the 1972–78 period, while GDP growth in the aggregate has hardly been affected. The role foreign capital flows and domestic policies may have played in this development should be examined.

The balance-of-payments implications for non-oil-producing developing countries of the world trade developments discussed above are shown in table 2-4. The 1973 boom in export earnings, which the IMF estimates rose 34 percent above 1972, was apparently fully spent in 1973 on increased imports. Furthermore, the 1972–73 boom spurred a sharp increase in long-term capital flows, as direct and portfolio investment alone doubled from $3 billion to $6 billion between 1972 and 1973. As a result, the overall balance-of-payments surplus of developing countries rose sharply, generating a significant rise in their international reserves. It is noteworthy that this external monetary stimulus was *not* induced directly by an increased current account surplus but rather by increased capital inflow, no doubt stimulated in part by the temporarily optimistic outlook for developing country exports. At the same time real GNP growth was 7.3 percent in 1973, as the stimulative effects of the export boom raised production, imports, and incomes directly.

It seems clear that the high levels of spending set off in the 1973 boom continued into the 1974 recession year, as non-oil-exporting developing country export prices and volume continued to advance, despite the slowdown in industrialized countries. The rise in oil prices raised the cost of (gross) developing country oil imports by $17 billion in 1974, accounting for the entire deterioration in the current account. Official and private capital inflows rose sharply, however, allowing a further rise in international reserves.

As the recession deepened in 1975, export prices fell sharply and volumes stagnated. But the 12 percent decline in import capacity led to only a 6.5 percent decline in import volume, as both long-term official flows and short-term capital inflows accelerated and reserves were run down slightly. Thus the capital account added to the external stimulus in 1973 but cushioned the external restraint in 1974–75.

During 1976–77 rising export volumes and prices, together with continued capital inflow, permitted substantial gains in reserves to the non-oil-exporting developing countries. According to the data in table 2-4, these reserve gains have continued into 1978 and 1979, despite a widening current account deficit due to terms of trade losses in both years. In 1978, non-oil-exporting commodity prices fell 7.4 percent in dollar terms, reducing export earnings by perhaps $5 billion, while developing country import prices rose some 10 to 13 percent. The resulting $12 billion deterioration in the current account was more than matched by increased capital flows in the easy credit environment of 1978.

The 60 percent increase in the price of oil imposed by OPEC between December 1978 and July 1979 translates into an average price hike of about 35 percent, comparing 1979 with 1978.[21] This will raise the oil import bill of the non-oil-exporting developing countries about $10 billion, of which $7 billion is allowed for in table 2-4. Again, this worsening of the current account deficit appears to be readily financeable in the aggregate, allowing a further buildup of reserves of some $5 to $7 billion.

The continued viability of the strategy of financing current account deficits with aid and private capital inflows is dependent upon several factors. These include a proper mix of concessional aid and private capital, with the bulk of aid going to socially productive areas not attractive to private capital and to the poorest countries. A further set of conditions for viable capital transfer concerns the growth of the ability to service the debt, involving intelligent policies to encourage trade, agriculture, and the accumulation of capital, as well as adequate world economic growth.[22]

Domestic Economic Disturbances

The domestic monetary consequences of the reserve inflows shown above are indicated in table 2-5. The data show that the overall external boom in 1972–73 led to sharply higher domestic monetary expansion in all areas, although delayed until 1973 in Latin America.

On the other hand, the slackening of reserve growth in 1974 and 1975 did not lead to a comparable slowdown in monetary growth. Thus monetary authorities transmitted the expansionary stimulus by not sterilizing reserve growth, but then sterilized to offset the contractionary impact of

21. See OECD, *Economic Outlook,* vol. 25 (July 1979), p. 3.
22. On appropriate developing country policies, see Krueger, *Foreign Trade Regimes and Economic Development,* chaps. 11 and 12.

the slowdown in reserves. This behavior suggests either that sterilization is feasible but was not practiced during 1972–73, or that feasibility is asymmetric.

With a lag of about one year behind monetary growth, inflation also accelerated sharply in all areas, as real GNP growth was particularly rapid at the same time that traded goods' prices were rising sharply. Interestingly, the inflation rate slowed down sharply after 1973 in Asia, the only geographical region to achieve a slowdown in monetary growth after 1973. For example, the IMF *Annual Report* for 1976 noted that "Stabilization programs were adopted by several Asian countries even before the end of 1974, and the policies pursued have been successful both in reducing inflation and in fostering growth."[23] Thus it appears that domestic policies can play a crucial role in transmitting an external shock through the monetary mechanism. Furthermore, it is notable that the rise in traded goods' prices slowed down abruptly in 1975–76, while inflation continued unabated in all developing country areas except Asia. Thus, after the external source was removed, the internal process kept the inflation going in most developing countries on a self-sustaining basis.

Other internal sources of stabilization problems discussed earlier included government budget deficits, crop failures, subsidies to hold down prices, and excessive wage increases. These factors, more or less by definition, are likely to affect individual countries rather than broad groups at the same time. Thus the detailed statistical analysis later in this chapter should provide further evidence of their role in developing country stabilization problems. Nevertheless, there have been some efforts to study their impact in the 1970s in systematic fashion. For example, Bhalla has shown that budget deficits and wage inflation did not contribute abnormal stimuli to most developing countries during 1972. He has also examined food production and prices to determine whether widespread crop failures in 1972 contributed to domestic instability. These data show that twelve out of twenty-seven developing countries experienced a more than 3 percent decline in food production per capita in 1972, as world production per capita fell 2.8 percent.[24] Since the shortage was worldwide, it would have been particularly difficult to offset its domestic effects through imports, as developing country food import prices rose some 10

23. IMF, *Annual Report, 1976*, p. 23.
24. Bhalla, "The Transmission of Inflation." The countries were Argentina, Chile, Ecuador, El Salvador, Ghana, India, Indonesia, Mexico, Nigeria, Philippines, Sri Lanka, and Thailand.

Table 2-5. *Growth of Reserves, Money, and Prices*

Percentage change

Area	1962–72[a]	1972	1973	1974	1975	1976	1977	1978
Non-oil-exporting developing countries								
Reserves	12.2	37.0	23.5	8.0	0.7	38.1	21.5	19.5
Money supply	18.4	22.1	34.5	30.9	26.7	37.6	34.8	30.8
Consumer prices	13.0	14.0	22.8	28.2	28.6	28.3	29.1	24.7
Western Hemisphere								
Reserves	16.5	64.9	32.8	−2.4	−11.9	52.5	27.0	33.5
Money supply	27.9	29.8	49.5	42.3	38.7	57.2	46.7	42.8
Consumer prices	21.6	22.0	31.7	30.1	44.6	54.8	47.3	40.2
Middle East								
Reserves	10.5	31.8	33.4	7.9	14.1	12.3	23.7	21.9[b]
Money supply	10.7	18.4	21.0	24.2	25.1	25.7	30.5	28.4[b]
Consumer prices	4.8	5.8	12.0	22.6	21.4	17.9	20.4	22.7
Asia								
Reserves	11.3	24.2	13.2	18.8	8.2	43.0	18.8	15.2
Money supply	11.5	15.1	22.2	16.1	10.7	17.0	20.6	17.3
Consumer prices	6.3	7.2	16.7	29.0	9.6	−0.7	7.9	5.7
Africa								
Reserves	6.8	15.6	14.7	11.5	−2.2	10.5	17.0	2.6[b]
Money supply	10.0	12.4	17.9	25.1	21.8	23.6	27.7	21.6
Consumer prices	5.4	5.8	9.2	18.8	18.1	18.9	21.8	19.4

Source: *International Financial Statistics*, May 1978 and July 1979.
a. Compound annual rate of change.
b. Estimated.

Table 2-6. *Coefficient of Variation of Developing Country Export Volume and Unit Values*

Export item	Volume		Unit values	
	1969–69	*1970–76*	*1960–69*	*1970–76*
Primary products, except fuel	0.080	0.063	0.029	0.319
Manufactured goods	0.300	0.256	0.097	0.260

Source: Calculated from *UN Monthly Bulletin of Statistics*, Special Table G, June 1978 and December 1971.

percent in 1972, 39 percent in 1973, and 42 percent in 1974.[25] Therefore, one could reasonably argue that domestic crop failures in many countries contributed significant internal disturbances in 1972.

A recent study by Murray found that in fifteen out of twenty-one developing countries, most fluctuations in export earnings during the 1960s were caused by fluctuations in export volumes and in particular by fluctuations in the supply of exportables, presumably due to domestic causes.[26] But in the 1970s, price fluctuations have become far more important than quantity fluctuations. According to table 2-6, the variability of developing country export volumes of both nonfuel primary products and manufactured goods decreased significantly in the 1970s as compared with the 1960s. At the same time, the variability of export prices for both groups of products drastically increased. The implication is that world demand factors have played a considerably larger role in export fluctuations in the 1970s.

Finally, domestic food price subsidy programs have been shown to be significant factors both in government budgets and in causing heavy food imports in eight to ten selected developing countries during the 1970s, in a recent study by Davis.[27] As noted earlier in this chapter with respect to Argentina, it is also quite possible for other forms of domestic price

25. Based on unit value indexes for developing countries' food imports from *Networks of World Trade by Areas and Commodity Classes: 1955–1976*, Studies in International Trade, no. 7 (Geneva: GATT, 1978), table E.2.

26. See David Murray, "Export Earnings Instability: Price, Quantity, Supply, Demand," *Economic Development and Cultural Change*, vol. 27 (October 1978), pp. 61–73. Similar findings on the importance of quantities are reported by Constantine Glezakos, "Export Instability and Economic Growth: A Statistical Verification," *Economic Development and Cultural Change*, vol. 21 (July 1973), pp. 670–78.

27. Jeffrey M. Davis, "The Fiscal Role of Food Subsidy Programs," *IMF Staff Papers*, vol. 24 (March 1977), pp. 100–27. The countries include Bangladesh, Egypt, India, Indonesia, Korea, Mali, Morocco, Pakistan, Sri Lanka, and Tanzania.

subsidy to have destabilizing monetary effects, although documentation of such factors is more difficult.

In conclusion, the overall macroeconomic experience of the developing countries during the 1970s appears to have been dominated by external disturbances such as the inflationary boom of 1972–73, the oil price increases of 1974 and 1979, the recession of 1974–75, and the slowdown of 1977–79 in industrialized countries' growth. At the same time, numerous internal disturbances caused serious financial difficulties for individual countries. Furthermore, the differing domestic policy responses to external disturbances led to significant differences in the performance of individual developing countries.

External and Internal Factors in Stabilization Problems

Objectives and Methodology

The preceding discussion has reviewed the mechanisms by which stabilization problems arise and are transmitted in developing countries during the 1970s. Yet real understanding of the problems faced by these countries can come only from the study of individual cases, impossible here because of length considerations. The alternative approach taken is a statistical analysis of the differences between countries, which seeks to throw light on the factors making for success or failure in macroeconomic management in individual developing countries.

The methodology used is discriminant analysis, which chooses a set of linear functions of the discriminating variables, here taken to be various internal and external factors such as those discussed earlier, as well as country characteristics such as size, development, and openness. These functions are chosen statistically so as to explain as well as possible into which of a number of groups an individual country falls.[28] The classes used in this analysis are group 1, countries which defaulted on their in-

28. See Robert A. Eisenbeis and Robert B. Avery, *Discriminant Analysis and Classification Procedures* (Heath, 1972), and appendix A to this paper. Previous applications in this area include Charles R. Frank, Jr., and William R. Cline, "Measurement of Debt Servicing Capacity: An Application of Discriminant Analysis," *Journal of International Economics*, vol. 1 (1971), pp. 327–44, and Danny M. Leipziger, "Short-term Stabilization and Long-term Development," presented at the Washington, D.C., meetings of the Southern Economic Association, November 8–10, 1978.

ternational payments; group 2, countries which had an upper-tranche standby agreement with the IMF and are not members of group 1; group 3, countries which had a regular, compensatory, or oil facility drawing from the IMF and are not in another group; group 4, countries which borrowed in the syndicated Euro-loan market and are not in groups 1, 2, or 5; and group 5, countries which issued either international or foreign bonds and are not in groups 1 or 2.[29]

The choice of these groups means the discriminant functions try to distinguish the factors that make a country creditworthy in international markets. This is an imperfect but objective measure of success or failure in stabilization policy (not development!). The measure is imperfect because it ignores countries that do not seek access to international credit and because it neglects stabilization difficulties which do not spill over into international payments. On the other hand, it is a better measure than inflation or the rate of change of GNP, which may merely reflect the disturbances to which a country has been exposed rather than its success or failure in managing its affairs.

The discriminating variables used in the analysis, which are defined precisely in appendix B, include five *country characteristics*: size (1976 GNP in U.S. dollars), development (1976 GNP per capita), openness (ratio of imports to GNP), commodity concentration of trade (share of exports in largest two-digit SITC), and direction of trade (share of exports to largest trading partner). The analysis also includes six *external variables* not under the control of the domestic authorities: rate of change of import prices (in U.S. dollars), terms of trade (relative to 1975), change in reserves, rate of change of export volume, rate of change of world oil prices, and rate of change of world wheat prices. Finally, it includes nine *internal variables* more directly under the control or influence of the domestic authorities: change in import or exchange controls, ratio of debt service to exports, ratio of debt service to total debt (the inverse of debt maturity), rate of change of consumer prices, ratio of reserves to imports, rate of change of money stock, ratio of government deficit to GDP, real interest rate, and real exchange rate (ratio of export unit value to consumer prices).

Although several of the internal variables relate to external payments, they are primarily under the control of the domestic government. As

29. The manner in which overlaps are eliminated in the classes follows from the lexicographic ordering: [(Default, Standby)−, (Bond issue, Euro-loan)+, Drawing].

noted previously, a country has several options available in responding to a fluctuation in export volume or the terms of trade. Its own domestic response to these fluctuations will show up in the four variables related to import controls, debt service, and the ratio of reserves to imports. Furthermore, these four variables also can reflect the external effects of domestic policies that spill over into the balance of payments. The "real" exchange rate, which attempts to measure the price of traded goods (exports) relative to the price of nontraded goods (here proxied by consumer prices), reflects the exchange rate policy of the domestic government. The remaining four internal variables are rather more explicitly internal. Consumer prices include import prices as well as domestic prices, but since import prices are separately measured as an external variable, the remaining effect should reflect mostly internal policies.

The nineteen discriminating variables can be entered into the analysis in either of two ways: the direct method, which uses all of the variables regardless of their individual relative power of discrimination; and the stepwise method, which enters variables in order of their relative discriminatory power, and only if they contribute significantly to the overall discrimination process. The criterion for measuring the significance of contributions of individual variables in this analysis is Bartlett's V, a measure of the generalized distance between groups when projected into the subspace spanned by the linear discriminant functions.

The data required for classifying the countries into the five groups were collected for forty developing countries for each of the eight years from 1971 through 1978, for a total of 320 observations. The forty countries, which are listed in appendix B, were selected by a stratified random sampling process that weighted countries according to size, as measured by IMF quotas, and that insured regional coverage. Of the eighty-five non-oil-exporting IMF members in developing areas with quotas greater than or equal to SDR 10 million (as of April 30, 1979), the sampling method chose all of the twenty-one members with quotas greater than SDR 100 million and nineteen out of the sixty-four remaining countries, stratified by area. Thus five of the nineteen were in the Western Hemisphere, two were in the Middle East, three were in Asia, and nine were in Africa. The rationale for sampling in proportion to size is that variability in some of the data is likely to be proportional to size. Furthermore, the relevance of the analysis is increased by substantial coverage of large countries.

The effects of the discriminating variables on the countries' stabiliza-

Table 2-7. *Group Size and Missing Values*

Group	Number (1)	Total (2)	Missing values (3)	Excluding missing values (4)
Default	1	21	6	15
Standby	2	25	6	19
Drawing	3	74	30	44
Bank borrowing	4	22	1	21
Bond issue	5	56	13	43
Total active		198	56	142
Inactive	0	122	53	69
Total		320	109	211

tion performance are expected to occur with significant time-lags. Therefore, the data on the discriminating variables were collected for the period from 1969 to 1977. The averages of the two preceding years' data were then used to explain the country groupings for a given year. A simple one-year lag was also tried, with inferior results.

Table 2-7 tabulates the number of country/year observations that fall into each group, including a group 0 for countries that were completely inactive in international credit markets. Column 3 of the table indicates how many observations in each group had to be excluded from the analysis because of missing values for some of the discriminating variables. Column 4 gives the remaining number of observations.[30] Thus of the 320 observations for which data were sought, 122 were left unclassified because they did not fall into any group. Of the remaining 198 observations, 56 had to be excluded because data could not be obtained for all of the discriminating variables. Most of the missing values occurred for countries in groups 0 and 3, countries that were either inactive or in the middle group. These groups tended to be the smaller countries, with 1976 GNP averaging around $5 billion, compared with an overall average GNP of $18 billion.

Results

The results of the analysis can be examined in several aspects: the statistical significance of each of the four derived discriminant functions in

30. These numbers exclude the government deficit from the list of discriminating variables, since it was missing for 122 observations. The effects of including this variable will be discussed below.

separating the five groups; the percentage of observations correctly classified by the derived functions as belonging to one or another group; the coefficients of the individual discriminant functions and the factors contributing to each one; and the order of entry and relative contribution of each individual variable to explaining the overall differences between the groups. All but the last of these can be examined for both the stepwise and the direct methods of analysis, while the last is only available for the stepwise technique.

The coefficients of the four discriminant functions estimated by the direct method (that is, using all of the explanatory variables), together with the statistics on their overall statistical significance, are given in table 2-8. The statistics referring to the overall contribution of each function are given in the lower part of the table, indicating that the first three functions all contribute very significantly to discriminating between the five groups of countries. For example, the first function contributes 41 percent of the total separation achieved, with a canonical correlation between the function and the groupings of 0.70. The estimated value of Wilks' lambda has a chi-square value of 220.86, which with 76 degrees of freedom is virtually impossible to achieve by chance.[31]

The individual coefficients in table 2-8 indicate the relative importance of each variable in the functions. Function A, for example, is primarily dependent upon commodity concentration of trade, the real interest rate, and the level of development; export volume, the reserves/import ratio, and the terms of trade play lesser roles. Thus all three types of variables—external, internal, and country characteristics—are important in classifying countries among groups. The largest contributions come from two country characteristics, followed by two internal variables, with the two external variables being the least important.

Again in function B the real interest rate is very significant, but now in combination with export volume, debt maturity, openness, and commodity trade concentration. The real exchange rate, direction of trade, money growth, and inflation are also relatively important in the function.

Function C includes as its leading variables inflation, the real interest

31. The distribution theory on which these tests rely assumes that the groups have equal variance-covariance matrices. While this could not be tested directly, a test was made of the equality of variances of some relatively unstable variables. The value of chi-square for the variances of rates of increase of consumer prices was 168.23, which is significant at approximately the 10 percent level with 137 degrees of freedom. Therefore a quadratic discriminant function is likely to give better results. See Frank and Cline, "Measurement of Debt Servicing Capacity."

Table 2-8. *Estimated Discriminant Functions*

Variable and type[a]	Function			
	A	B	C	D
Country characteristics				
Size (4)	−0.02	−0.19	−0.77	−0.21
Development (1)	−0.37	−0.13	−0.25	−0.18
Openness (15)	0.12	−0.40	−0.01	−0.07
Concentration of trade (2)	0.61	−0.40	−0.20	−0.41
Direction of trade (11)	0.17	−0.27	0.05	0.09
External				
Import prices	0.18	−0.16	0.46	0.45
Terms of trade (8)	0.22	0.19	0.23	−0.23
Change in reserves (9)/(14)	−0.08	−0.13	0.11	0.26
Export volume (7)	−0.27	0.43	0.03	−0.10
Oil price (17)	−0.06	0.17	−0.04	−0.84
Wheat price	−0.09	0.16	−0.12	0.47
Internal				
Controls (13)	−0.08	0.16	0.27	0.06
Debt service	0.05	−0.06	0.30	−0.12
Debt maturity (3)	−0.07	−0.42	0.70	−0.10
Consumer prices (5)	0.04	−0.22	1.43	0.04
Reserves/imports (12)	0.24	0.14	−0.10	−0.13
Money growth (10)	0.02	0.24	−0.10	−0.62
Real interest rate (16)	0.39	−0.50	1.40	−0.63
Real exchange rate (6)	−0.19	0.32	−0.27	0.45
Summary statistics				
Eigen-value	0.94	0.80	0.45	0.09
Relative contribution	0.41	0.35	0.20	0.04
Canonical correlation	0.70	0.67	0.56	0.29
Wilks' lambda	0.18	0.35	0.63	0.91
Chi-square	220.86	135.50	59.62	11.51
Degrees of freedom	76	54	34	16
Significance level	0.000	0.000	0.004	0.777

a. Numbers in parentheses give the order of entry.

rate, size, and debt maturity, with import prices playing a subsidiary role. Function D, which does not contribute significantly to the analysis, has the rate of change of oil prices as its most important variable. Thus virtually all types of variables enter the analysis in some way or other. Some further understanding of the functions can be obtained by plotting the function values of the individual observations and the group means. This amounts to projecting the observations into the subspace spanned by the

Figure 2-1. *Plot of Groups versus Functions A (Horizontal) and B (Vertical)*

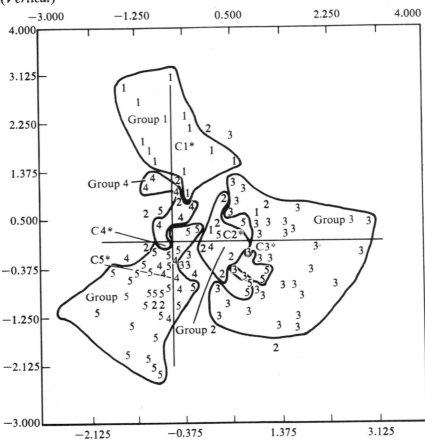

* Indicates a group centroid.

four functions (two at a time). Figure 2-1 shows that groups 1, 4, and 5 have similar (low) values of function A, while groups 2 and 3 have higher values. Just focusing on the leading element of function A, this suggests that groups 1, 4, and 5 tend to be more developed than group 2, which tends to be more developed than group 3. This certainly makes sense if it is argued that a country has to be able to borrow a lot before it can default.

In function B, groups 2, 3, and 4 have similar values, while group 1 has high values and group 5 low values (figure 2-1). This accords with treating function B as an indicator of domestic policy, as indicated by the

Table 2-9. *Percentage of Observations Correctly Classified*

Group	Within-sample	Out-of-sample	Total
1	73.3	50.0	66.7
2	47.4	0.0	36.0
3	68.2	56.7	63.5
4	61.9	100.0	63.6
5	65.1	38.5	58.9
Total	64.1	46.4	59.1

real interest rate, the real exchange rate, and debt maturity, in combination with export volume, openness, and trade concentration.

Function C, primarily measuring inflation and size, gives high values to groups 4, 2, and 3, in descending order, and low values to 1 and 5. Thus size appears to be positively correlated with the likelihood of borrowing, while inflation is negatively correlated with borrowing.

A third measure of the discriminant functions is their success in predicting into which category a given country will fall. This measure can be calculated both for the 142 observations used in the analysis (see table 2-7) and for the 56 that were excluded from the sample because of missing data for some variables. According to table 2-9, the analysis correctly classified 64 percent of the within-sample observations, ranging from 73 percent for group 1 to 47 percent for group 2. For the out-of-sample observations, the success ratio was 46 percent. Of course, some of the data were missing for these observations, diluting the power of discrimination. A random allocation of countries to groups would produce an average success ratio of 20 percent, so the results seem highly significant on this criterion.

The results in table 2-9 are based on the direct method of analysis including all of the variables. The stepwise method produced very similar results, with essentially the same statistical significance (for example, chi-square values of 213.78, 128.49, 53.6, and 8.8). Furthermore, the same variables dominated each of the individual discriminant functions, with some variation in the order of importance.

The stepwise technique allows the determination of the order of entry, shown in parentheses in table 2-8, which indicates the relative significance of the contributions of individual variables. Of the first five variables to enter, three were country characteristics (development, trade concentration, and size) and two were internal variables (inflation and debt maturity). Of the next five, two were internal (the real exchange

Table 2-10. *Contribution to Distance between Groups*

Country characteristics		Internal variables		External variables	
Size	26.2	Controls	8.8	Terms of trade	16.4
Development	45.5	Debt maturity	22.1	Reserves	9.0
Openness	8.8	Inflation	25.3	Exports	18.7
Trade concen-		Reserves/imports	12.7	Oil price	7.7
tration	48.6	Money	9.9	Total	51.8
Direction of trade	10.9	Real interest rate	9.8		(17%)
Total	140.0	Real exchange rate	16.3		
	(47%)	Total	104.9		
			(35%)		

rate and money growth), and three were external (export volume, terms of trade, and reserve change). Four variables were excluded from the analysis as not contributing significantly: import prices, the price of wheat, debt service, and the change in reserves, which was dropped from the analysis in step 14. In an effort to test whether consumer prices were preventing import prices from entering, a test was run in which consumer prices were not allowed to enter until after import prices, but import prices still did not contribute significantly. A further test, using a restricted sample of size 122 for which government deficit data were available, showed the deficit to be a marginally significant variable, the last one entered.

A final measure of the relative contribution of different variables to the analysis is their contribution to the generalized distance between the different groups of observations, when projected into the subspace spanned by the four discriminant functions. This measure is given in table 2-10 for each of the variables entering the stepwise analysis. The largest contribution, 47 percent of the total discrimination, comes from the country characteristics. The second largest, 35 percent, comes from the internal variables. The smallest fraction, 17 percent, comes from the external variables.[32]

Thus, although external factors have generated many of the disturbances to which developing countries have had to respond in the 1970s, it appears to have been largely country characteristics and the internal

32. An alternative calculation of the percentage of total distance contributed by each block of variables when entered last gives 41 percent for characteristics, 38 percent for internal variables, and 19 percent for external variables. If the reader prefers to reallocate certain variables from one category to another, the "contributions" in table 2-10 can be reallocated.

responses to those disturbances and other internally generated disturbances that have spelled success or failure for stabilization policy.

Policy Issues

Two major sets of policy issues are raised by the data and analysis in this chapter. First, to what extent has instability in the world economy caused instability in developing countries, and how can such global instability be reduced? Second, to what extent is instability in developing countries a domestic policy problem, caused by unwise policies that either transmit external disturbances or generate domestic disturbances? How can such policies be avoided?

To begin with the first issue, it seems clear from the data in the earlier section on global and domestic economic conditions and from the statistical analysis in the previous section that external disturbances have played an important role in the stabilization problems of the developing countries in the 1970s. The boom-and-bust cycle in the early 1970s followed by stagnation in the latter part of the decade led many developing countries to overexpand and then face painful readjustments. This is shown both by the aggregate data and by the significance of external variables and transmission variables in the discriminant analysis.

Mismanagement in the industrialized countries in the early 1970s indeed made life harder for developing countries. Of course, this was significantly reinforced by the oil price increase of 1974, which both directly raised developing country import prices and reduced their export volumes and worsened terms of trade by lengthening and deepening the 1974–75 recession. The appropriate policy response was forthcoming from the industrialized world and the international institutions in the form of increased compensatory financing, financing of oil deficits, larger aid flows, and other forms of lending to the developing countries. In fact, the heavy provision of foreign capital in 1973 and 1974 seems to have stimulated an excessive rise in developing country import volume in those years that could not be maintained in 1975–76.

Several policy conclusions emerge from this discussion. Obviously, the avoidance of excessive cyclical fluctuations in industrialized countries is of first importance, followed by the avoidance of excessive abrupt increases in the price of oil, like the increase in 1979.[33] When such fluc-

33. For some references on the first point, see footnote 1.

tuations do occur, it is absolutely necessary for international lending institutions and aid donors to provide financing for at least some of the export shortfall and/or increased cost of imports. Thus the recent liberalization of the IMF's Compensatory Finance Facility is to be welcomed,
along with the evidence cited earlier in this chapter that financing for the
1979 current account deficit of the non-oil-producing developing countries appears to be readily available.

Nevertheless, some guidelines for lending institutions in boom periods
could help avoid the tendency to extrapolate present good fortune into
the unknowable future. While the IMF cannot veto borrowing programs
of member countries not using its credit tranche facilities, perhaps it
should utilize the consultation process to bring its analytical expertise
to bear on such programs. Furthermore, it would be unfortunate if the
provision of liberal financing for externally generated disturbances led
to the adoption of domestic policies that transmit these disturbances to
the domestic economy. The provision of compensatory financing to a
country, for example, should continue to require cooperation with the
IMF ". . . to find, where required, appropriate solutions for its balance
of payments difficulties."[34]

On the second major set of issues, the degree of internal responsibility
for stabilization successes and failures, there is substantial evidence in
this chapter that internal policies matter a great deal. In particular, it
appears that the differential responses of different countries to the external disturbances of the 1970s, along with their differing sizes, levels
of development, diversification, and openness, have been the main factors determining success or failure in stabilization policy. Thus the developing countries themselves have it in their power to make many of
the crucial policy decisions concerning stabilization.

These domestic policies relate to the control of domestic inflation,
maintenance of adequate real rates of interest, maintenance of adequate
foreign exchange reserves, and maintenance of a realistic exchange rate
policy. The continuing success of a substantial number of developing
countries, especially in Asia, in controlling inflation (see table 2-5) has
enabled them to avoid stabilization difficulties while moving rapidly forward in development and the growth of foreign trade at the same time.

34. Text of Decision on Compensatory Financing, *IMF Survey,* August 20,
1979, p. 253.

These results have not been achieved without some stringency in monetary and fiscal policy.

The low-inflation countries have found it easier to maintain real rates of interest and realistic exchange rates, but other countries have found it possible to achieve these even with higher inflation via indexation and crawling or floating exchange rates.[35] Avoidance of distortions in the savings-investment process and in the allocation of resources to production of traded goods is of primary importance.

Finally, the response a country makes to external disturbances as well as its propensity to generate internal disturbances that spill over into the balance of payments can readily be observed in the ratio of reserves to imports. One encouraging aspect of the data in table 2-4 is the indication of a desire by developing countries to continue accumulating foreign exchange reserves at reasonable rates. However, it is clearly necessary to avoid excessive monetary stimulus from such reserve gains, and many countries have much to learn in this regard, according to table 2-5 and the evidence cited earlier on the lack of sterilization.

In conclusion, while the world of the 1970s has been a rough one for developed and developing countries alike, much experience has been gained in dealing with both external and internal disturbances in developing countries to enable better management of the disturbances of the 1980s.

Appendix A: Discriminant Analysis[36]

Given k groups of n observations on m variables, define the matrices of sums of squares and cross products among groups A and the pooled sums of squares and cross products within groups W as

$$A = [a_{ij}] = \sum_{g=1}^{k} N_g(\bar{x}_{gi} - \bar{x}_i)(\bar{x}_{gj} - \bar{x}_j),$$

and

$$W = [w_{ij}] = \sum_{g=1}^{k} \sum_{n=1}^{N_g} (x_{gin} - \bar{x}_{gi})(x_{gjn} - \bar{x}_{gj}).$$

---

35. See Jud, *Inflation and the Use of Indexing in Developing Countries.*
36. Based on Eisenbeis and Avery, *Discriminant Analysis and Classification Procedures.*

Figure 2-2. *Separation by Discriminant Function: The Two-Group Case*

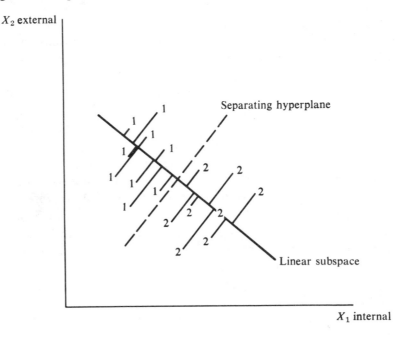

Problem: to choose $k - 1$ linear functions $v_g'x$ to divide the m-dimensional space into k regions in the best way. When the data are projected into the $k - 1$ dimensional subspace spanned by the linear functions, the groups will be separated in the best way. Solution: to maximize $|V'AV|/|V'WV|$, the ratio of among-group variance to within-group variance, by choice of V, solve the eigen-value problem $|A - \lambda W| = 0$. The groups will then be relatively "tight" and "well separated." See figure 2-2 for the two-group case.

The solution to the problem yields eigen-values λ_g associated with each eigen-vector v_g. The value of Wilks'

$$\Lambda = |W|/|A + W| = \prod_g (1/1 + \lambda_g),$$

which is analogous to the unexplained variance, should be reduced by the functions v_g to as low a level as possible. It has a chi-square distribution. We may also calculate the relative contribution of each function $\lambda_g/\Sigma\lambda_g$ and the canonical correlation $[\lambda_g/1 + \lambda_g]^{-1/2}$ of the "scores" $v_g'x$ with the groupings.

The stepwise approach adds variables which maximize the increments to

$$-\left(n - 1 - \frac{m + k}{2}\right) \ln \Lambda,$$

known as "Bartlett's V," which is approximately $1 - \Lambda$ adjusted for degrees of freedom, or the analogue of the explained variance. This is a measure of the generalized distance between groups, when projected into the subspace spanned by the discriminant functions.

Assuming the a priori probabilities of randomly chosen countries falling into different groups are equal, we predict the classification into which a country will fall as group g if $v_g'x \geq v_k'x$ for all $k \neq g$.

Appendix B: Data

A. *Classification Variables* (0 if absent, 1 if present).

1. Debt reschedulings, both multilateral and bilateral, listed in Albert C. Cizauskas, "International Debt Renegotiation: Lessons from the Past," *World Development,* vol. 7 (1979), pp. 199–210, footnote 17, and text.

2. Upper-tranche IMF standby agreements, from IMF, *Annual Reports,* various years, tables I.4, I.6, I.8, and text discussion; and *IMF Survey,* press releases.

3. Compensatory finance or regular drawing or oil facility drawing, from IMF, *Annual Report, 1977,* table I.9; various *Annual Reports,* table I.6; and *International Financial Statistics,* various issues.

4. Euro-dollar borrowing from banks, from Morgan Guaranty Trust Company, *World Financial Markets* (March 1978), p. 4; OECD, *Financial Market Trends,* vol. 8 (June 1979), p. 13; OECD, *Financial Statistics,* vol. 12, no. 1 (1978), table B.232.

5. International and foreign bond issues, from *World Financial Markets* (March 1978), p. 3; World Bank, *Annual Report* (1978), table 10, p. 133; OECD, *Financial Statistics,* vol. 12, no. 1 (1978), tables B.222.1 and C.22.1.

B. *Discriminating Variables* (from *International Financial Statistics,* country pages, specified line number, unless otherwise noted).

1. Annual rate of change of consumer price index, *IFS,* line 64.

2. Commodity trade concentration, share of exports in largest two-digit SITC in 1976, UN, *Yearbook of Trade Statistics* (1977).

3. Direction of trade, share of exports to largest trading partner in 1976, UN, *Yearbook of Trade Statistics,* or IMF, *Direction of Trade.*

4. Reserves/imports, yearly, *IFS,* line 1. . d ÷ line 77 abd.

5. Government deficit/GDP, yearly, *IFS,* line 80 ÷ line 99b, or IMF, *Government Finance Statistics Yearbook,* vol. 2 (1978), or World Bank, *World Tables* (1976).

6. Real interest rate, yearly, *IFS,* line 60 or national sources, minus item 1 above.

7. Real exchange rate, export unit value/consumer price index, yearly, *IFS,* line 74 ÷ line 64.

8. Annual rate of change of money supply, yearly, *IFS,* line 34.

9. Controls, ± 1 for significant strengthening or weakening of import and/or exchange controls, yearly, IMF, *Annual Report on Exchange Restrictions.*

10. Annual rate of change of import prices, yearly, *IFS,* line 75 ÷ line af converted to 1970 = 100, or *IFS,* World Tables Import price index for Other Less Developed Areas or Other Asia, as appropriate.

11. Terms of trade, yearly, *IFS,* line 74 ÷ line 75 or weighted component indexes or *IFS,* World Tables Export price index ÷ Import price index for Other Less Developed Areas or Other Asia, as appropriate.

12. Change in reserves, yearly, *IFS,* line 1. . d.

13. Annual rate of change of export volume, *IFS,* line 72.

14. Annual rate of change of price of petroleum, Saudi Arabia, yearly, *IFS,* Commodity Tables, line 76 aaz.

15. Annual rate of change of price of wheat, U.S. gulfports, yearly, *IFS,* Commodity Tables, line 76 d.z.

16. Openness, imports of goods and services/GDP in 1976, *IFS,* line 98c ÷ line 99b or line 77 abd plus line 77 add ÷ item 17 below.

17. Size, 1976 GNP in U.S. dollars, *World Bank Atlas* (1978).

18. Development, 1976 GNP per capita in U.S. dollars, *World Bank Atlas* (1978).

19. Debt service ratio, debt service/exports of goods and services, yearly, World Bank, *World Debt Tables,* vol. 1 (October 20, 1978), table II-12, and supplements.

20. Debt maturity, debt service/total debt, World Bank, *World Debt Tables,* vol. 1 (October 20, 1978), tables I-9.8 and I-10.1, and supplements.

C. *Countries*

Latin America	*Middle East*	*Asia*	*Africa*
Argentina	Egypt	Bangladesh	Benin
Barbados	Israel	China (Taiwan)	Chad
Brazil	Syrian	India	Ghana
Chile	Arab Rep.	Korea	Ivory Coast
Colombia	Yemen, P.D.	Malaysia	Kenya
Dominican	Rep.	Nepal	Mali
Republic		Pakistan	Mauritania
Guyana		Papua	Mauritius
Mexico		New Guinea	Morocco
Nicaragua		Philippines	Togo
Peru		Singapore	Upper Volta
Surinam		Sri Lanka	Zaire
		Thailand	Zambia

Comments by Sidney Dell[37]

This chapter shows that "external disturbances have played a very important role in the stabilization problems of the developing countries in the 1970s." What Black calls "mismanagement in the industrialized countries" created difficulties for developing countries, and these were "significantly reinforced by the oil price increase of 1974." He suggests, quite properly, that where cyclical fluctuations or increases in import prices occur, "it is absolutely necessary for international lending institutions and aid donors to provide financing for at least some of the export shortfall and/or increased cost of imports."

However, since this recommendation is consistent with past practice, and the main emphasis of the chapter is on anti-inflationary prescriptions with a strongly traditional flavor, the impression is left that there is little need for any basic rethinking of policy in this field. Yet the situation that Black describes is quite different from that customary in the past, when balance-of-payments difficulties in developing countries were often primarily a reflection of excess aggregate demand. In the 1970s, the difficulties have been and continue to be largely, though not exclusively, of external origin. Conventional formulas involving large doses of standard

37. The views expressed in these comments are those of the author and do not necessarily represent the views of the United Nations Secretariat.

deflationary medicine are not merely inappropriate in such circumstances; they also involve serious internal inconsistency for the international monetary system as a whole.

Developing countries must, of course, adjust to irreversible changes— this issue is not in dispute. But in determining the appropriate policy mix, including the amount of balance-of-payments support required and the period over which adjustment should be programmed, it is important to distinguish between those elements of a balance-of-payments deficit for which a developing country is itself responsible, and those elements that are due to factors beyond its control.

This is not a revolutionary idea. At one time, levels of activity had to be cut back even where external imbalance was due to a temporary decline in foreign demand for exports. The introduction by the IMF of the compensatory financing facility, and later of the oil facility, indicated recognition that it was improper to force standard adjustment policies on developing countries in circumstances for which they were not responsible.

But the full implications of the principle involved have yet to be recognized. Indeed, the current failure to renew the oil facility and the replacement of low conditionality support from that facility by supplementary financing on stringent terms are serious setbacks to the evolution of more appropriate methods of dealing with externally generated balance-of-payments difficulties.

The international community accepts the fact that there are large structural surpluses in the system and that stagnation combined with inflation in the industrial countries is not a short-term phenomenon. But the countries that have no choice but to try to cope with the counterpart deficits that are the inevitable consequence of these external pressures are frequently required to adjust within the relatively short periods characteristic of conventional stabilization programs. In a number of cases, the consequential degree of deflation has been of draconic proportions involving declines in real wages of 20 to 40 percent and even more within a short time frame, to say nothing of the complete disruption of development programs.

Of course, given the unavoidable and persistent character of the structural surpluses in the system, the only effect of the insistence on asymmetrical short-period adjustment in the developing countries is to shift the deficits backward and forward from one country to another, with a cumulative deflationary impact upon the world economy as a whole.

A further inconsistency lies in the perverse distribution of the burden of adjustment as between rich and poor countries. Black's view that financing for the current account deficit of the non-oil developing countries is "readily available" is at odds with the expectation of the IMF that for many developing countries "the financing of such large incremental payments for imports may pose problems";[38] and with the statement of the managing director at Belgrade that "I am deeply concerned about the external position of the low-income subgroup of developing countries." Black's view also ignores that in many countries, growth rates or even levels of production and income have been forced down below those previously attained, so as to suppress external deficits that could not be financed. Particularly hard hit in this sense have been countries at the bottom of the income scale that lack the access to private capital markets enjoyed by more advanced countries—a deficiency that the official financing institutions have not made good.

Thus a disproportionate share of the burden of adjustment has been shouldered by the countries least able to bear it. Although evidence on changes in income distribution is always difficult to obtain, especially in developing countries, there are also indications that a number of stabilization programs have impinged with particular severity on the poorest groups within the developing countries, notwithstanding professed international concern that these groups should receive special protection.

Finally, while the international community, as mentioned earlier, often requires prompt adjustment in countries faced with balance-of-payments deficits, it tolerates increasingly restrictive trade measures in the industrial countries that frustrate the efforts of the deficit countries to adjust. These restrictive measures are sometimes defended as a means of giving the industrial countries adequate time in which to adjust to imports from low-wage countries. In the case of textiles, the period of adjustment since the first international textile arrangement of 1962 has already lasted over seventeen years, with no end in sight. No such stretching out of the rate of adjustment is possible in cases of balance-of-payments difficulty calling for structural changes. Moreover, while great emphasis is placed on exchange rate realignment as a means of correcting external imbalance, by improving the export competitiveness of the countries concerned, the efficacy of the exchange rate weapon is continually eroded by the growing wave of protectionism that removes products of export interest to developing countries from the influence of the price mechanism and the

38. IMF, *Annual Report, 1979*, p. 2.

forces of competition—partly as a reaction to the exchange rate changes themselves.

It is inevitable that such inconsistencies in the present configuration of international monetary and trade policy generate great conflicts and tensions in the system. The weakest and poorest countries are least able to fend for themselves in the confusion that results. But the more advanced developing countries also face great difficulties because the process of sustaining growth under adverse world conditions by borrowing from capital markets cannot continue indefinitely.

Against this background, what is one to make of Black's ingenious excursion into discriminant analysis? The analysis seems vulnerable to the manifest interdependence of variables, and as in the case of other statistical measures of association, there is a question whether causal relationships are established thereby. If the purpose of the exercise was simply to establish the conclusion that "the developing countries themselves have it in their power to make many of the crucial policy decisions concerning stabilization," one would have thought that few would need the elaborate demonstration provided to concede the point. One is not sure, in the end, whether Black does not have a good deal more harness than horse, especially since he does not reach the more crucial issues of the day referred to earlier.

Whatever discriminant analysis may show in regard to the importance of domestic stabilization measures, the real issue lies elsewhere—namely, the appropriate degree of cooperation by the international community in the solution of current problems of disequilibrium. One may well ask why the facts that world market prices are rising and that industrial countries wish to slow down their economies in the search for price stability should be regarded as reasons for developing countries to have to adopt drastic programs of stabilization disruptive of their development goals.

The IMF's 1979 *Annual Report* estimates that the combined current account deficit of non-oil-exporting developing countries rose from $21 billion in 1977 to $43 billion in 1979. Of this $22 billion rise, some $16 billion is attributed by the IMF to deterioration in terms of trade, and about $6 billion reflects increased net payments of interest and other forms of investment income. Despite this testimony to the fact that the enormous increase in deficits of developing countries from 1977 to 1979 and the further enlargement of these deficits expected in 1980 are due to factors for which these countries are not responsible, many of them will be forced to undertake severe retrenchment, without the support of the kind of low conditionality finance that the oil facility provided in 1974–75. Is this the kind of international policy that one expects at the threshold of the Third Development Decade? Is it not incumbent on the international community to make an effort to insure that developing countries have at least as much time and elbow room in which to program their adjustment, and at least as much opportunity to avoid disruptive forms of adjustment, as are enjoyed by the countries whose decisions, whether to raise prices, to reduce levels of business activity, or to restrict imports, are at the root of current and prospective balance-of-payments difficulties of the Third World?[39]

Discussion

Ernest Stern (World Bank) welcomed the emphasis in Black's chapter, and in the conference overall, on stabilization measures that developing countries can take themselves. Moralizing about the share of blame for instability that is attributable to the international community is not fruitful; what is needed are pragmatic policy options for developing countries to deal with stabilization problems. These problems have become long term, not short term, because of higher energy prices, political attitudes toward capital flows, increased uncertainty, and other factors. Stern raised the issue of the willingness of some of the developing countries to take proper adjustment measures in the face of highly liquid international capital markets. He also noted the need to link stabilization measures to the longer-term economic development strategy.

Stanley Black agreed with Sidney Dell's point that low-income countries will have difficulty financing external adjustment, pointing to the importance of the income variable in his discriminant analysis.

39. For proposals for action along these lines, see the UNDP/UNCTAD report by Sidney Dell and Roger Lawrence, *The Balance of Payments Adjustment Process in Developing Countries* (London: Pergamon Press, 1980).

CHAPTER THREE

Interactions between Inflation and Trade Regime Objectives in Stabilization Programs

ANNE O. KRUEGER

EXAMINATION of the relationship between macroeconomic growth and the trade objectives of stabilization programs is an exceptionally difficult assignment. Three separate bodies of relevant literature—relating to trade regimes, to inflation and its causes and consequences, and to the determinants of economic growth—are pertinent to the analysis, and each has numerous points of contention. This in itself makes the assignment challenging. In addition, the kinds of problems that arise with inflation, trade and payments regimes, and development strategies in general are sufficiently different between countries so that no single model is appropriate for all of them.

To make the task manageable, a very elementary framework is used to analyze the relationship between the trade regime and monetary-macro aggregates. Within this framework, it is readily seen that in principle the interaction between different types of inflation and the trade regimes can be minimal. The costs of altering either the anticipated rate of inflation or the nature of the trade regime, and the effects of those states and changes on economic growth, are then briefly set forth. This chapter then examines the more prevalent case in which the authorities' efforts to contain inflation are reflected in a trade regime and real exchange rate different from that which would be chosen in the absence of the inflationary pressures, and traces the interaction between inflation and the trade regime. With that background, the next section presents a classification of the types of stabilization programs and analyzes the kinds of policy issues that arise in each category and their relationship to economic development. Finally, the main trade-offs that arise in deciding on the components of a stabilization program are examined.

The Price Level/Exchange Rate/Trade Regime Relationship

Depending on the question at hand, the appropriate model for analyzing any one of the three topics discussed here can be quite different. Determination of the price level is a macromonetary phenomenon, although in the short term cost-push and microeconomic phenomena (such as a good harvest) can enter into its determination. In an open economy with full convertibility and no quantitative restrictions upon international transactions, the exchange rate is likely to be a monetary phenomenon as well. If, however, quantitative restrictions apply to a large number of international transactions, the exchange rate will also be an important variable in affecting two significant relative prices: that between home goods and tradable goods, and that between the domestic prices of exportables and of import-competing goods. Finally, the trade regime itself consists of the policies and instruments used by a country to achieve two targets: first, the relationship between domestic prices of import-competing and exportable goods; second, the balance in transactions between residents and foreigners.

In principle, appropriate use of policy instruments can achieve total separation of the causes and consequences of the rate of price-level increase from any impact upon the trade regime. Such a circumstance is seldom found in the real world (although as will be argued, the sliding-peg regime can provide a fairly close approximation to it), but it is useful to establish the basic relationships. Within that context, analysis of alternative trade regimes, and their causes and consequences for economic growth, can be carried out.

Table 3-1 provides a schematic representation of the three markets and their relationship to trade regimes. The basic proposition underlying the analysis is that for any price level, an exchange rate corresponds that will leave the real variables in the system unaltered. This is nothing other than an application of the dichotomy to the international arena; if all demand and supply functions are homogeneous of degree zero in prices and money income, then it follows that for any rate of increase in the money supply, there is a corresponding (and equal) proportionate ap-

Table 3-1. *Characterization of Alternative Market Interactions*

Item	Flexible exchange rate	Payments deficit	Exchange control
Traded goods market	clears	deficit	clears
	$p_x^d = E p_x^*$	$p_x^d = E p_x^*$	$p_x^d = E p_x^*$
	$p_m^d = E(1 + t) p_m^*$	$p_m^d = E(1 + t) p_m^*$	$p_m^d > E(1 + t) p_m^*$
Money market	clears	surplus	clears
	$m^d = m^s$	$m^d < m^s$	$m^d = m^s$
Home goods	clears at	clears at	clears at
	$P_h/E = (P_h/E)_o$	$P_h/E > (P_h/E)_o$	$P_h/E \gtrless (P_h/E)_o$

preciation or depreciation of the currency that will leave all excess demand functions in the system unaltered by the change.[1]

The three markets involved are traded goods, home goods, and the money market.[2] Under a flexible exchange rate regime, all three markets clear with individuals free to carry out their desired transactions at prevailing prices. The traded goods market clears with the exchange rate (price of foreign exchange), E, equating the foreign prices of the home country's importable and exportable (p_m^d and p_x^d) with foreign prices of the same goods, denoted with an asterisk. The term $(1 + t)$ is included in the import price relation to indicate that flexible exchange rates are compatible with any tariff structure and level of desired protection for import-competing industries, a point developed later. Under flexible exchange rates, the money market naturally clears, as does the market for home goods. For later reference, the market clearing price for home goods is denoted under flexible exchange rates as $(p_h/E)_o$. This notation is useful in that the home goods market always clears. What differentiates different regimes is the relative price of home goods (and therefor their relative importance in domestic production): a higher market-

1. For economy of language, I am assuming throughout that the rest of the world is stationary and that there is no inflation or other change abroad. An alternative would be to phrase every statement in terms of maintaining a constant difference in the rates of price increase between the country under consideration and the rest of the world. In the context of economic growth, of course, real exchange rates may have to alter even in the absence of changes in the inflation rate.

2. In principle, there is also a bond market in the system. But in keeping with conventional macroeconomics, I follow the time-honored tradition of assuming that if the money market clears or if all three other markets taken together clear, then the bond market must clear. In practice, among countries with convertible currencies, it can and has been argued that the excess supply of money is more likely reflected in an excess demand for bonds than in the goods market. For present purposes, however, that set of questions is well away from our central concern.

clearing price for home goods corresponds to greater domestic production and, of course, consumption of those goods.[3]

Under a flexible-rate regime, any change in the anticipated rate of inflation is reflected in a shift in the excess demand function for foreign exchange. Abstracting from short-term phenomena (such as J-curve responses of exports and imports to the changed short-run price of tradable goods relative to home goods), the market for tradable goods will be unaffected in real terms. Thus, if inflation were perfectly anticipated, the time path of the exchange rate and the domestic price level would coincide in such a way that the relative price of tradable and home goods remained stable.

To be sure, inflation is never smooth and perfectly anticipated. Under fixed exchange rates, the real exchange rate is affected, as is explained below. For present purposes, however, the central point is that there is a way in which the payments regime can be fairly well insulated from the effects of inflation, permitting or insuring that the real exchange rate is not influenced by changes in the domestic price level.[4] For purposes of analysis, it is useful first to proceed to discuss the costs of inflation and the costs of alternative trade regimes on the assumption that inflation does not affect the real rate of exchange and that the real exchange rate does not affect the rate of inflation.

Growth under Alternative Trade Regimes

In the context of developing countries' economies, the key link between the trade regime and economic growth is the way in which the trade regime is employed in relation to the domestic growth pattern. Economic theory tells us that new resources should be allocated among tradable

3. At first sight, it seems paradoxical that a higher relative price of home goods is associated with greater production. The paradox is resolved if one considers the move from a "full equilibrium" under flexible exchange rates to a new "equilibrium" with the exchange rate held constant but with aggregate demand increased: an upward shift in the demand for home goods means the price of home goods must rise, *and* production of home goods increases. Production of traded goods falls while consumption rises, thereby generating a payments deficit in the new "equilibrium." Increased demand for home goods, in turn, usually arises because of excessive money creation or fiscal policy.

4. This is not to state that the real exchange rate should remain unaltered under all circumstances; the proposition is that the underlying determinants of the real exchange rate that will clear the market for traded goods are probably independent of the determinants of the rate of inflation and changes in the rate.

goods industries in such a way that at the margin resources devoted to saving a dollar of foreign exchange should be the same as the marginal resources devoted to earning a dollar of foreign exchange. However, there is also a need on the part of developing countries to provide infant industry support to many of these activities. Such support can be of several kinds, but prominent among the techniques used in many developing countries has been the trade regime, which has been employed to protect domestic producers against competition from imports. Such a policy, import substitution (IS), has generally resulted implicitly or explicitly in discouragement of exports. The alternative means of encouraging growth of tradable goods industries consists of providing incentives primarily for production, in which case it usually results that a large fraction of incremental output is exported. Very often, encouragement is given to exports directly.

For a variety of reasons, most countries seem to have industrialization and trade policies that result in a significant bias toward either export promotion (EP) or IS. The extent of bias is defined as the degree to which the ratio of the domestic prices of importables to exportables diverges from their international price ratio. Thus, using the terminology of table 3-1 and assuming the appropriate aggregation across commodity categories has been performed, bias, B, can be defined as

$$(1) \qquad B = \frac{p_m^d}{p_x^d} \bigg/ \frac{p_m^*}{p_x^*}.$$

The greater the divergence of B from unity in either direction, the more biased the regime; B's that are greater than unity represent a bias toward import substitution, while those less than unity represent biases toward export promotion.

Without detailing the reasons, IS regimes tend to become increasingly biased toward IS over time as export earnings fail to grow as rapidly as demand for imports, as the exchange rate tends to be set at unrealistic levels, as the incremental value of output per unit of investment decreases with small sizes of domestic markets, and as opportunities for further IS diminish rapidly. Also, IS regimes often tend increasingly toward quantitative restrictions upon imports and fairly detailed quantitative controls over domestic economic activity. All of these phenomena seem to result in a fairly unsatisfactory rate of economic growth for the countries undertaking the policies. A simplistic summary of experience with IS for most developing countries would be that after opportunities for "easy" IS

were exhausted, growth rates have tended to slow significantly, either sec-
ularly or in a stop-go pattern as foreign exchange availability has determined the rate at which the economy could grow. For present purposes,
one of the self-reinforcing phenomena with IS is that the implicit discouragement of export growth tends to increase the apparent "shortage"
of foreign exchange.

The built-in tendency for IS to decelerate as it continues may be the
most important long-run growth cost of IS regimes, but there are also
other costs that should be noted briefly. Chief among these is that IS
regimes tend to promote a fairly indiscriminate pattern of industrial development. High-cost, inefficient industries develop alongside lower-cost,
potentially efficient ones. Even where the domestic market for the product
is sufficiently large to permit efficient-size plants to be established, low-
cost firms have difficulty expanding at a rate much faster than the rate of
growth of domestic demand. Low-cost and high-cost firms therefore tend
to expand pari passu, in part because the disincentive to export is so great
that few firms can profitably do so, and in part because controls tend to set
up quasi-monopoly positions for individual firms that ensure maintenance
of market share: allocation of rights to import scarce intermediate goods
and raw materials very often rigidify individual firms' market shares. Not
all of these costs of an IS regime are inevitable, because alternative means
of fostering IS can have significantly different results. Nonetheless, the
evidence strongly suggests significant tendencies in this direction.

Export promotion policies can also be carried out in a variety of ways,
and some are superior to others. The reader should bear in mind that the
definition of bias indicates the extent to which an EP strategy is followed.
All countries have "export promotion" strategies, but in many cases those
strategies are really only a means of offsetting some of the disincentives
built into the system by IS policies, as IS industries receive stronger incentives still. In those cases, exports often consist of "excess capacity"
output of IS industries and do not necessarily represent industries with
long-term comparative advantages.

The reasons that countries which have genuinely biased their regimes
toward export promotion have tended to experience more satisfactory
growth rates can be summed up as the counterpart of the IS problems:
stop-go patterns do not seem to emerge due to foreign exchange bottlenecks; efficient low-cost firms can expand very rapidly well beyond the
limits of the domestic market; and domestic monopoly positions do not
spring up as firms are forced to compete for their customers abroad and

heed quality control and specifications. In addition, despite bias toward EP, the extent of the bias cannot get too great. Countries adopting IS with the domestic price of importables twice or more the international price are frequently noted; countries with EP with a bias of more than 25 or 30 percent toward exports are rare.

From this brief glimpse of the factors differentiating growth patterns under EP and IS,[5] it is evident that the choice of strategy adopted can significantly affect economic growth rates. But, in the presence of a fairly convertible exchange rate permitted to move with changes in the rate of inflation, it is not evident that the rate of inflation need be a factor in the choice of trade strategy; the two are, or can be, independent.

Inflation and Growth

There is presently in economics a revival of interest in the costs of inflation and little time need be spent on those costs here. As inflation accelerates, transactions costs rise and individuals seek stores of value to replace money in that function. These can be costly activities, as potentially productive resources (such as those producing gold and real estate) are diverted to providing a store of value, resulting in little increase in society's real product. In addition, to the extent that countries have geared their spending and taxing policies to stable prices, the costs of the distortions introduced by the tax system may be quite large. Finally, in cases where there is credit rationing and borrowers pay negative real rates of interest, as has occurred in many developing countries, significant resource misallocation can arise on that account.

These costs may be highly significant, and it is not intended to minimize their importance. There is little hard evidence, however, that the rate of inflation itself affects the rate of growth via these channels. Given the structure of production in most developing countries, it is likely that the biggest impact of inflation on growth in developing countries has arisen when the underlying premise of this section has been violated: the erosion of the real exchange rate with significant results for a country's trade and payments position and the nature of its trade regime. These costs must be analyzed to evaluate the impact of stabilization programs upon economic growth.

5. For a fuller discussion of these issues, see my book, *Foreign Trade Regimes and Economic Development: Liberalization Attempts and Consequences* (Ballinger for the National Bureau of Economic Research, 1978), especially chaps. 11 and 12.

Altering the Trade Regime

If bias toward IS were provided only by tariffs or export subsidies, alteration of the trade regime could be accomplished by altering the tariff or subsidy rates. However, as already stated, IS policies are often carried out through quantitative restrictions, and alteration of the bias of the regime entails shifting from reliance upon quantitative restrictions (QRs) to reliance upon prices and may indeed involve replacing the bias imparted by QRs with a similar bias imparted by tariffs.

One of the difficulties of altering trade regimes is that the extent of bias frequently is not known. Especially when QRs are important, it turns out that a move from QRs to tariffs alters the bias of the regime much more than intended by the authorities; they are simply unaware of the protective equivalent of the quotas.[6]

Regardless of the way in which bias toward IS is reduced,[7] resource reallocation will follow. Should the profitability of existing industries be reduced (as, for example, if there is an increase in the value of import licenses issued) without any offsetting stimulus to other industries, a reduction in the level of economic activity is the likely outcome. This is especially the case if expansion of the industries whose relative profitability has increased will require investments to expand capacity, while output can contract immediately in IS industries. Entrepreneurs without experience in exporting activities may be very reluctant to base large-scale investments on the expectation that they can profitably sell in international markets. On one hand, they may be inexperienced in those markets and be unaware of the opportunities facing them; on the other hand, they may be well aware of those opportunities but fear that the altered bias of the trade regime (with a more favorable real exchange rate) may not last, thereby rendering investment unprofitable.

6. There are at least two historical instances which are well documented and where the authorities were apparently surprised by the preexisting level of protection prevailing. See Michael Michaely, *Foreign Trade Regimes and Economic Development: Israel,* and Robert Baldwin, *Foreign Trade Regimes and Economic Development: Philippines* (both: Columbia University Press for the National Bureau of Economic Research, 1975).

7. The analysis is similar, although not entirely symmetric, for increasing bias toward IS. The reason for the difference is that entrepreneurs can be expected to be more familiar with the domestic market when IS strategies are adopted or intensified than they can be for moving toward EP. The reason for couching the discussion in terms of a move toward EP is that most stabilization efforts, discussed below, entail a reduction, or an attempted reduction, in the extent of bias toward IS.

These considerations pinpoint two aspects of any adjustment process that involves a shift in the bias of the regime. There is likely to be something of a disparity between the rate at which existing industry cuts back production and the rate at which potentially new industries increase output;[8] however, the role of expectations is crucial in determining how significant and long-lived the disparity is. If entrepreneurs are convinced that the change in incentives is permanent, the disparity may not last long. If, conversely, there are significant doubts about the ability of the authorities to maintain the new relative price structure, output of industries encouraged by the former bias of the regime may contract while there are few moves made to start increasing output along new lines. It is this latter case in which the growth costs of a shift in the trade regime can be potentially substantial.

It seems evident, therefore, that an attempt to alter the bias of a trade regime should be accompanied by some stimulus to activity in the newly profitable industries, and perhaps also some increase in the general level of aggregate demand to offset whatever decline will come about in the adversely affected industries. The severity of the downward pressure on the level of economic activity depends upon a number of factors, including the degree to which bias is being altered, the height of the protective barriers being reduced, the degree of uncertainty as to the permanence of the altered incentive structure, and the length of time the incentive structure has been in place. Even in the absence of inflationary pressures or other objectives, a policy shift with regard to trade strategies is likely, therefore, to entail some short-term costs in terms of the rate of economic growth. If the shift is successful, however, the short-term loss may be earning a relatively high rate of return in the form of improved resource allocation and more rapid growth in future periods. A major question, of course, is how the costs of such a shift may be minimized and, simultaneously, the extent to which policies can be introduced to offset part or all of the short-term losses. It seems best, however, to consider that question in the context of a total stabilization policy package.

8. If the existing bias of the regime has been relatively short-lived at the time of the policy shift, it is possible that excess capacity might exist in EP lines to pick up the slack from reduced IS activities. That outcome is less likely the longer IS policies have been in place. A more frequent pattern is that IS industries find that they can cover marginal costs in exporting out of existing capacity once incentives change. The commodity composition of exports in the year or two after shifting strategies, therefore, may bear little relation to the longer-run mix of exports.

Costs of Reducing the Inflation Rate

Little needs to be said here about the difficulties involved in reducing the rate of inflation in developing countries. There have been a few notable instances of successful, and fairly painless, sharp drops in the rate of inflation, but they are the exception rather than the rule. Israel in the mid-1950s, Turkey in 1958–59, and South Korea in the late 1950s and early 1960s were able successfully to bring about a reduction in their inflation rates of two-thirds or more. In those instances, there was little retardation in the rate of economic growth.[9]

A more prevalent pattern appears to be one in which "stabilization" programs are adopted, and some deceleration of inflation occurs. That deceleration, however, is accompanied by recession. In some instances, such as Brazil in the mid-1960s, the costs of stabilization in the form of below-capacity output were borne for several years, until the inflation rate had been significantly reduced. Even more frequently, however, recession and its effects have put such pressure on the political authorities that the stabilization attempt has been abandoned. The Chilean experience of the 1950s and 1960s seems to have been characterized by this sort of stabilization.[10] The cost of reduced inflation was recession, and resumption of economic growth occurred only after the stabilization effort was abandoned; with resumed growth, the rate of inflation (and the bias toward import substitution) once again increased.

For later reference, there is one aspect of attempts to reduce inflation that should be noted. There is one type of deflationary policy that can simultaneously help alter the bias of the regime and reduce the inflation rate: increasing the flow of imports. To the extent that financing can be found to achieve such an increase, purchasing power is absorbed while the implicit or explicit bias toward import substitution is substantially reduced. This feature is of special significance in considering stabilization policies and ways in which measures can be taken to improve the likelihood of their success and reduce their short-term costs.

---

9. All three have reverted to relatively high inflation rates in the mid-1970s and seem to be encountering much more difficulty at present in reducing their inflation rates than they had earlier experienced.

10. See Jere R. Behrman, *Foreign Trade Regimes and Economic Development: Chile* (Columbia University Press for the National Bureau of Economic Research, 1976), for a full account.

Interactions between Inflation and the Trade Regime

As already mentioned, determinants of the rate of inflation and of the bias of the trade regime are, in principle, largely separate. One of the policy measures that can be taken to reduce the distortion and growth costs of inflation is a sliding-peg exchange rate regime. To be sure, the optimal real exchange rate, which is itself a function of the desired bias in trade strategy and other variables, will not under all circumstances remain the same. As Carlos Diaz-Alejandro has noted, with the fluctuations that Colombia has faced in the price of coffee, there is probably no exchange rate that was not an equilibrium rate at one time or another.[11] Nonetheless, while alterations in the real exchange rate may prove desirable in response to altered prices for the country's exports on the world market or for other reasons (including a desire to shift the bias of the trade regime), there is little likelihood that rates of inflation will reflect only those changes.

Thus, if a country with a fixed exchange rate found that its price level was beginning to increase more rapidly than that of its trading partners, the best policy in the absence of willingness to allow freely fluctuating exchange rates would most likely be some form of indexation (sliding peg) of the exchange rate. Various formulas are possible; for example, the exchange rate can be set relative to a major trading partner in conformity with the differential between the country's and the trading partner's inflation rates, or a weighted average of the rates of inflation adjusted for exchange rate changes of several major trading partners can be deducted from the country's own rate of inflation. In different circumstances, the number of countries it is desirable to include in the calculus can differ, but in all cases adjustment must be made at fairly short time intervals. Under any of these formulas, changes in the rate of inflation will not have a significant impact upon the nature of the trade regime. Such an indexation works best when inflation rates are fairly stable or declining; there is some tendency toward balance-of-payments deficit when inflation generated by excess demand is accelerating over into the foreign exchange market. Nonetheless, contrasted with the maintenance

11. Carlos Diaz-Alejandro, *Foreign Trade Regimes and Economic Development: Colombia* (Columbia University Press for the National Bureau of Economic Research, 1976).

of a fixed nominal rate of exchange under inflation, a sliding-peg policy is vastly preferred.

The difficulty, and one which results in the important interaction between trade regimes and inflation, arises in countries that fail to adopt such a strategy. In those cases, inflation tends to increase the purchasing power of domestic currency when spent abroad relative to its value when spent at home. As a consequence, domestic nationals tend to increase their purchases abroad and reduce their sales abroad. In the absence of capital controls, they also try to exchange domestic assets denominated in domestic currency units for foreign assets denominated in foreign currency units.

In those instances, countries have three choices: to incur open balance-of-payments deficits; to alter the price paid and received for foreign exchange de facto or de jure; or to impose quantitative restrictions upon international transactions. In practice, the response is usually to adopt some price measures, such as surcharges upon imports and subsidies for minor exports, to impose some QRs, and to permit a deficit in the balance of payments to emerge, financed by running down foreign exchange reserves or borrowing from abroad. Indeed, one characteristic of many inflation-prone countries attempting to maintain a fixed exchange rate is the proliferation of fairly detailed, ad hoc measures designed to curb excess demand for foreign exchange side by side with the continued need to borrow from abroad to finance deficits that emerge despite measures taken. This welter of detailed and fairly specific measures itself has economic costs and can be one motive for a stabilization operation—"tidying up" the regime.

For purposes of analysis, however, it is convenient to set aside the use of price measures and mixed responses. If sufficient price measures were undertaken on an across-the-board basis to remedy the underlying tendency toward excess demand for foreign exchange, such measures would amount to a sliding-peg exchange rate policy. It is the absence of sufficient pricing measures that forces countries experiencing inflation at fixed exchange rates to adopt alternative measures.

The alternatives consist of incurring open balance-of-payments deficits, which are financed by running down reserves or borrowing from abroad, or of imposing quantitative restrictions. Each of these measures has costs and affects the nature of any subsequent stabilization program. For purposes of analysis, it is useful to analyze each type of response separately, although as already indicated the two are often found in combination.

Table 3-1 is again useful as a frame of reference. It will be recalled that the sliding-peg (if pegged at the appropriate level) or flexible exchange rate case was one where each market cleared and participants were free to carry out desired transactions at the prevailing prices. Incurring an open payments deficit is equivalent to permitting an excess supply of money in the home market to spill over into realized excess demand for goods and services from abroad (which is reflected in the payments deficit). By contrast, exchange control is a case in which individuals are not permitted to carry out their desired transactions; the domestic price of importables exceeds the foreign price-cum-tariff, and the money market consequently clears. The precise mix of these two policies in use is a critical factor in determining the effects of policies that are undertaken in a stabilization program.

Payments Deficit

The key characteristics of a response to excess demand by permitting a payments deficit are two: there is an excess supply of money; on the other hand, the relative price of home goods is "too high," as aggregate consumption is above sustainable levels, consumption of home goods increases, and the failure of the price of tradables to rise induces production to shift toward home goods.

The excess supply of money is in part a reflection of the fact that the fixed exchange rate acts as a suppressant to the inflation that would otherwise result from aggregate demand pressures. In the case of a sliding-peg exchange rate policy, the entire inflationary stimulus is passed through both the home goods and the traded goods sector: both prices increase nominally and there is no relative price change. In the case of a fixed exchange rate, home goods' prices rise (although not by as much as they would under a sliding peg because consumers are permitted to substitute traded goods for home goods in their consumption bundle while producers shift production away from traded and toward home goods), but traded goods' prices are stable. The payments deficit can be thought of as a reflection of that part of the inflationary pressure that was not reflected in price increases.

A straightforward way of viewing the problem of a country experiencing inflation and a payments deficit at a fixed exchange rate is to recognize that the inflation rate is held below that which would otherwise be realized as long as the exchange rate can be maintained, both because the price of tradable goods does not rise and because the increase in the price of home goods is less than it would otherwise be. Under those circumstances, devaluation is inflationary; it permits the inflationary impulse to be passed on to the domestic market. Devaluation would therefore accomplish little if a country could continue indefinitely to finance its payments deficits.[12]

The fact is, however, that countries cannot indefinitely run down reserves or borrow from abroad for purposes of financing their deficits. Just as an individual consumer can live well beyond his means by running up credit card charges, borrowing from a bank, and depreciating consumer durables, so too can a country live beyond its means. In both cases, the situation is not sustainable.

It is for this reason that analysis of the costs, in terms of growth prospects, of measures taken to eliminate an unsustainable deficit is extremely difficult. In a sense, the economy incurring a deficit and then reducing its expenditures relative to its income is on a nonoptimal path; its early level of expenditures and outlay is too high, at the cost of a later reduction in that level. For purposes of analysis, the best that can be done is to pose the question in the following way: given an economy that has

12. It is important to recognize that foreign lending and aid, motivated by prospects of a reasonable rate of return or undertaken for development purposes, can sustain a current account deficit and contribute, as long as the deficit lasts, to development objectives. In those cases, the current account deficit is offset by "autonomous" capital inflows. Deficits, as used in the text, refer to payments imbalances in which the desired transactions by individuals result in an excess demand for foreign exchange which must be met by the authorities by running down their reserves or seeking foreign financing which they would not seek simply for long-run developmental objectives. While the distinction is conceptually clear, there are often significant difficulties in practice of identifying particular types of transactions as being "autonomous" and others as being "accommodating." In practice, however, few worry about the "deficit" of Korea, as the financing is motivated by long-term commercial prospects, while it is straightforward to identify countries whose borrowing needs originate from their efforts to sustain an infeasible exchange rate. At the time of writing this chapter, Turkey represents a classic case of a country attempting to maintain an unrealistic exchange rate, borrowing for that purpose in excess of the amount she would otherwise borrow. It should be noted, however, that in an alternative economic context, Turkish net capital inflows might be much larger than they currently are. The reason, of course, is that commercial lending and investing has virtually ground to a halt as expectations of an exchange rate alteration lead potential creditors with commercial motivations to delay their activities.

incurred an unsustainable deficit, what is the lowest-cost way of altering its expenditure/income relationship to reattain a sustainable future expansion path? Consideration of this question is deferred until later in this chapter. At this point, the line of analysis sketched out here applies to any country's attempt to reduce the size of its payments deficit, actual or prospective. In many instances, stabilization programs have objectives pertaining both to reducing the size of the prospective deficit and to liberalizing the trade regime. Before analysis of those programs can be carried out, it is necessary to examine the differences between the goals and the problems implicit in the two alternatives.

Liberalizing the Trade Regime

As mentioned, inflation at a fixed exchange rate cannot long be sustained without incurring a payments deficit. That is unsustainable, and the alternative is alteration of the exchange rate or imposition of quantitative restrictions once access to further foreign credits becomes limited, as it eventually must. The key characteristic of using QRs to keep foreign exchange payments in line with receipts, as shown in table 3-1, is that the money market is permitted to clear while the domestic price of importables rises above the imported price (inclusive of landing costs, tariffs, and surcharges). Thus, whereas an open payments deficit is characterized by the inappropriate relative price of tradable to nontradable goods (for any chosen tariff structure), the quantitative restrictions equilibrium is characterized by a greater bias of the trade and payments regime toward import-competing activities domestically than would be chosen simply on the basis of the industrialization strategy. Whether home goods' relative prices are likely to be higher or lower than in the flexible exchange rate alternative is not clearcut; depending on the nature of the structure of production and the degree of substitution between exportables, importables, and home goods in both consumption and production, that relationship can go either way.

The difference between the price that prevails for an import in the home market if individuals were allowed to import all they wished at the prevailing price and the price that would prevail in the presence of quantitative restrictions upon imports is referred to as the *premium* on an import license. The fact that there are premiums on import licenses is usually sufficient evidence to indicate that quantitative restrictions are binding. Under those circumstances, the bias of the trade and payments regime toward IS is almost always greater than intended, and resource allocation costs can mount well above those associated with the tariff-generated protection.[13]

Thus, although either an open payments deficit or the tightening of quantitative restrictions can result from inflationary pressure at a fixed exchange rate, the symptoms and resource allocation effects of the two alternative responses are quite different. The realized rate of inflation for a given monetary stimulus will be greater under a QR response than under a deficit response; the degree of bias of the regime will be greater under the QR response than under the deficit response; and the home goods sector will likely expand more under the deficit response than under the QR response.[14] When stabilization programs are adopted, therefore, crucial considerations include the mix of the two policies chosen and how severely restrictive[15] the QRs have become or how sizable the deficits are.

When the response to potential deficits has been the imposition of quantitative restrictions, increasing the price of foreign exchange will operate rather differently than it will in the case of open deficit. Suppose, for example, that an open deficit has been incurred. Raising the price of foreign exchange while holding tariffs constant will, in the absence of quantitative restrictions, raise the price of tradable goods relative to the price of nontradables. For a small country with no monopoly power in trade, the relative price of exportables and import-competing goods will remain unaltered; the bias of the regime is unaffected, although production of both import-competing and exportable goods becomes more profitable relative to the profitability of producing home goods.[16] If, in-

---

13. There are exceptions, of course. Notable among them is the Korean case. The Koreans appear to have maintained quantitative restrictions upon import of luxury consumer goods which were not domestically produced. Interestingly, licenses to import those goods were awarded to exporters, thereby linking QRs (which were not intended as a balance-of-payments measure in the first place) to profitability of exporting.

14. This is because the higher price of import-competing goods under QRs are likely to pull some resources out of the home-goods sector.

15. A regime is said to be more restrictive the larger the aggregate value of premiums expressed as a percentage of the landed cost of the import bill.

16. This statement assumes that raising the price of foreign exchange is not accompanied by a sufficient increase in aggregate demand so that the domestic price level increases still further. Obviously, a devaluation of x percent, followed by an increase in the domestic price level of ax, with $a > 1$, will lead to a decline in the relative price of tradable goods and should intensify either the restrictiveness of the regime or the size of the deficit.

stead, QRs are in effect prior to the increase in the price of foreign exchange, part of the increase in price will go to absorbing the premiums on import licenses (thereby perhaps reducing the variance in effective exchange rates across commodity categories). If, as is usually the case, export subsidies are much smaller than premiums on import licenses, a far higher fraction of the increased price of foreign exchange will be reflected in the domestic price of exportables than it will be in the domestic price of import-competing goods. At the limit, in cases where the size of the devaluation is less than the size of the preexisting premium on import licenses, there is no reason to expect the domestic price of importables to rise following a devaluation.[17]

Several points should be noted. First, as a consequence of premium absorption, the increase in the price level following a devaluation in the context of preexisting QRs should be considerably smaller than the recorded price increase following a deficit-reducing devaluation. In a sense, this is the counterpart to the statement that a given inflationary stimulus will result in a larger rate of inflation under QRs than it will under an open deficit given a fixed exchange rate; the devaluation has more work to do correcting the relative prices of exportables and import-competing goods and less work to do in adjusting the price level. Second, in the absence of other policy moves, any devaluation is still likely to result in a reduction of the restrictiveness of whatever quantitative restrictions are in effect. That is, for given quantitative amounts of permitted imports, devaluation automatically liberalizes a given trade regime, unless other measures are taken to offset the increase in the price of foreign exchange.[18] Third, because devaluation absorbs premiums upon imports, it automatically alters the bias of the regime and thereby induces the resource reallocation mechanisms discussed earlier.

Finally, there is the question of the macroeconomic impact of a pure "liberalizing" devaluation. Unlike the open deficit case, where expenditures clearly have to be cut relative to income, the liberalizing devalua-

17. The empirical results from the Foreign Trade Regimes and Economic Development project tended to confirm the results. See chapter 8 of my *Liberalization Attempts* and the individual studies, especially Colombia and Chile, for analysis of this phenomenon.

18. If, for example, surcharges on imports and export subsidies are removed simultaneously with the devaluation, the changes in the effective exchange rates perceived by producers and consumers will be considerably smaller than the size of the devaluation. It is useful to refer to "net devaluation" as being the change in the price of foreign exchange once account is taken of the removal of export subsidies, import surcharges, and the like.

tion has no such imperative, except insofar as it was underlying the erosion of the real exchange rate which led to the necessity to impose QRs in the first place. In principle, therefore, if a QR regime were the result of past inflationary pressures which had subsided, leaving the exchange rate overvalued by a stationary amount, no deflationary stimulus or reduction in the level of aggregate demand would be necessary. Indeed, in the pure QR case, it can even be argued that the absorption of the premium by the exchange rate increase, combined with the benefits from resource allocation resulting from the change in the bias of the regime, might well result in a mild deflationary pressure on the economy.[19] Quantitatively, however, it is not evident that this deflationary pressure is likely to be significant.

Stabilization Programs and Long-Term Development

As the foregoing has indicated, there is no one action that can be described as a "stabilization program." The policies undertaken and their effects vary, depending on the underlying situation and the goals of the policy makers.

It has already been indicated that the task of reducing the rate of inflation is an exceptionally difficult one. Almost inevitably there is a short-term reduction in the rate of growth of output, and in many cases, recession. In these circumstances, deflationary policies are sometimes reversed so that few, if any, benefits are realized. Likewise, the resource reallocation that must accompany a successful effort to liberalize the trade regime and alter its bias away from import substitution cannot be achieved without inevitable adjustments of resources within the economy.

For these reasons, there are bound to be short-term adjustment costs of any stabilization program, whatever the nature of the policy package and regardless of the degree to which it is successful. There are, of course, ways to reduce those costs, but it is doubtful whether stabilization can be accomplished in the presence of unwillingness or political inability to withstand some short-term disallocations. The first and most important conclusion that can be drawn, therefore, is that it is senseless to incur the costs of adjustment only to reverse policies before they have had any chance to affect resource allocation and growth. Yet, the evi-

19. Egon Sohmen, in "The Effects of Devaluation on the Price Level," *Quarterly Journal of Economics,* May 1958, made this point.

dence is that a significant number of stabilization programs have foundered precisely because the authorities have been unwilling or unable politically to survive political pressure during the adjustment period.[20]

A second conclusion, which follows readily from the first, is that the reallocations will take longer and be more difficult, the greater are expectations that the realigned structure of relative prices and incentives will not continue. If it is expected that the devaluation and liberalization will be short-lived, businessmen and consumers are likely to stockpile foreign goods in anticipation of possible future reimposition of QRs. In doing so, they increase the current account deficit and therefore the foreign exchange outflow required to sustain the liberalization program through the adjustment period. In the context of a situation in which foreign exchange has earlier been in excess demand because of the trade regime, increases in imports and current account deficits may stimulate further speculation against the exchange rate, in turn tending to force the reimposition of controls. In addition, expectations of reversal discourage resource reallocation, thus blunting the increase in exports that might otherwise be experienced.

One objective of policy should be to ensure that a stabilization program, once undertaken, can be sustained long enough to provide an opportunity for its results to be felt. This in turn suggests that a desirable feature of any stabilization program is that it should be designed in such a way as to suggest to economic agents that it will succeed; expectations are likely to be self-fulfilling. This conclusion has numerous implications for policy, especially for the evaluation of the optimal lending strategy for donors in connection with stabilization programs.

For the longer term, the effects of stabilization on the rate of growth are a function of the objectives of the program (and especially the extent to which the bias of the regime is shifted away from undue emphasis upon import substitution) and the degree to which they are accom-

---

20. The difficulties are very real. Richard Cooper, in his "An Assessment of Currency Devaluation in Developing Countries," chap. 13 of Gustav Ranis, ed., *Government and Economic Development* (Yale University Press, 1971), documented these problems neatly. A sizable fraction of finance ministers at the time of devaluation lost their jobs within eighteen months. There is also no doubt that luck is an element. As Cooper showed, perhaps the best indicator of the likelihood of success is the quality of the harvest; a good harvest provides a buffer which makes the reallocation vastly easier. Of the twenty-two devaluations in the NBER project on Foreign Trade Regimes and Economic Development, in fifteen cases the inflation in the ensuing two years was larger proportionately than was the initial devaluation. See *Liberalization Attempts and Consequences*, pp. 82–83 and table 5-3.

plished. If stabilization policies are undertaken in the first place because existing policies are unsustainable, it is difficult to talk about the growth effects of a particular package except in the context of the alternative stabilization packages; continuation of the status quo ante is infeasible. It is for this reason that one can regard the biggest growth cost of stabilization programs as lying in their failure. When a program does not succeed, it is generally inevitable that another program, with the same sort of short-term costs, will have to be adopted in the future. To the extent that every failure of such a program intensifies expectations of failure of the next one, an unsuccessful stabilization program may itself have growth costs, not only in the current slowdown in economic activity which by definition has no payoff, but also in the heightened cost of achieving the same objectives at any future date, when memories of past failures result in skeptical expectations about the likelihood of success.

The Colombian experience of the late 1950s and early 1960s is perhaps an excellent example. After unsuccessful devaluation attempts in 1956, 1959, 1961, and 1966, the authorities successfully began altering the bias of the related policies in 1967. Carlos Diaz-Alejandro concluded that one of the major impacts on Colombian growth was that the consequent growth of foreign exchange earnings from increasing exports meant that the stop-go cycle of fiscal and monetary policy surrounding stabilization efforts finally stopped, which in turn permitted a more rapid rate of growth of the entire economy.[21]

It therefore seems appropriate to attempt to categorize stabilization programs in terms first of the primary objectives of the program, then of the preexisting situation, and finally the policy measures taken.

Objectives

Despite the fact that almost all stabilization programs by definition have some bearing on both inflation and balance-of-payments objectives, the relative importance of the two objectives can differ. In some instances, stabilization programs are geared primarily toward reducing excess aggregate demand, with balance-of-payments targets secondary.[22] In other instances, the infeasibility of continuing to incur indebtedness or of

21. Diaz-Alejandro, *Foreign Trade Regimes and Economic Development: Colombia,* pp. 237 ff.

22. Many Latin American programs, especially those of Chile and Argentina, seem to have been geared primarily toward inflation.

further tightening QRs makes the primary target an alteration in the trade regime.[23]

One fundamental lesson that seems to emerge from examination of the cases in which devaluation did not succeed in relaxing the foreign exchange constraint is that it does not make sense to tie the success of the measures aimed at the foreign trade sector to success in reducing the rate of inflation. It appears that it is significantly easier to alter the real exchange rate and to increase the rate-of-growth earnings than it is to reduce the rate of inflation permanently. This is perhaps the strongest argument that can be made on behalf of a sliding-peg policy; it permits the success of the trade component of a stabilization program independently of whether the rate of inflation drops or not. In light of the already-stated result that one of the significant costs of inflation lies in the distortions introduced by a fixed exchange rate, it is difficult to understand countries that attempt to alter their trade and payments regimes and inflation rates by adopting a new, fixed exchange rate. If the rate of inflation does drop, a sliding peg will not significantly alter the exchange rate, and both objectives of the program will be met; if, however, inflation is not successfully controlled, both objectives of the package are bound to fail if a new fixed exchange rate is set.

Because controlling inflation is inherently the more difficult objective in most circumstances and because those primarily concerned with bringing the rate of inflation down are likely to object to a sliding peg as being more inflationary than a new fixed exchange rate, it seems to be the case that stabilization programs motivated more by a desire to alter the trade and payments regime have a somewhat greater probability of partial or total success than do programs aimed primarily at the rate of inflation.

To be sure, neither change—alteration of the trade regime or changing the inflationary nature of the economy—is likely to be easy, for reasons already mentioned. Nonetheless, there are degrees of difficulty, and controlling inflation does seem much the more difficult of the two objectives.

Preexisting Conditions

A number of circumstances in the preexisting situation also have a bearing on the probable outcome of the stabilization package. Among the most important are "chance" elements, the set of macroeconomic

23. Turkey and India are examples of this type.

influences currently operating on the economy, the extent to which the trade regime has been characterized by QRs or by open deficit, and the magnitude of foreign short-term indebtedness.

Two chance factors should be noted. First, favorable harvests can significantly increase the probability that a stabilization program will prove successful. This is because good harvests tend to keep the domestic prices of foodstuffs relatively low, thereby exerting downward pressure on the overall price index, and also because bumper crops tend to increase quantities available for export, thus increasing foreign exchange earning. The latter results either in increased foreign exchange reserves, and thus conviction that the altered incentives will continue, or in an enhanced flow of imports, which in turn permits a relatively greater degree of bias toward exportables than would otherwise be possible. The other event that can positively affect the outcome of a stabilization program is favorable movements in the terms of trade. Such an outcome has the same sort of impact as the increased export earnings that can be attained with a good harvest, although the impact is less favorable on the inflation rate, and appropriate policies must be followed to prevent increased prices of key exports from resulting in large increases in domestic money supply and purchasing power. There have been instances of stabilization programs which, on the historical record, appear to have had a good chance of success that have foundered on unfavorable movements in the terms of trade. The Brazilian devaluation and stabilization effort of 1957 appears to have been one such case; the volume of exports increased almost 50 percent over the ensuing twenty-four months, but export earnings rose hardly at all.[24]

There are several macro influences. First, there is the nature of the monetary and fiscal policies in effect in the six to twelve months prior to the stabilization effort. When those have been highly expansionary, the difficulties entailed in successfully carrying out stabilization are likely to be much greater than when monetary and fiscal stimuli have been moderate. Indeed, it can even be contended that in the presence of highly expansionary monetary and fiscal policy over the preceding year, a country would be better off to postpone (if possible) altering the trade regime (especially if a sliding peg is not a realistic alternative) until monetary and fiscal magnitudes have been brought under control.

Second, there is the extent to which price controls have prevented

---

24. See Albert Fishlow, "Foreign Trade Regimes and Economic Development: Brazil," paper prepared for Bogota Seminar, April 1975.

excess demand pressures from being realized. When those factors have been of importance, it is usually necessary to remove those price ceilings at the time the stabilization package is inaugurated. As prices must rise from their formerly controlled levels, any cost-push responses within the economy will be triggered by those increases as well as the increase in the price of tradable goods, thereby making the task of reducing the rate of inflation more difficult. Nonetheless, when price controls have been operative prestabilizaton, their removal can be an essential part of the stabilization package. When those controls are over public sector products, they may have been a significant factor in contributing to the public sector deficit and thus to increases in the money supply. Such was the case in Turkey in the late 1950s, when public sector enterprises were required to maintain prices well below costs of production. Deficits, financed by central bank credits, were a chief source of inflationary pressure. Raising the prices of public sector enterprise outputs resulted in a once-and-for-all increase in the price level by 20 percent, but simultaneously eliminated the further extension of central bank credits. The consequence was that after several years of inflation recorded at 25 percent or more annually (despite the price controls which had suppressed it), prices actually fell in the two years following the increase in public sector enterprise prices.

Finally, there is the preexisting situation with respect to the trade regime and the balance of payments. For reasons outlined above, it makes a significant difference if the stabilization program is aimed primarily at reducing or correcting an existing or prospective open deficit, or whether instead it is intended to liberalize the trade and payments regime and to reduce or eliminate quantitative restrictions as a means for keeping foreign exchange receipts in line with payments. In addition, the degree to which debt-servicing difficulties are being experienced and imports have been curtailed prior to the stabilization program is also significant in influencing the nature of the package and the probable effect of any given set of policy changes.

In general, if imports have been sharply curtailed in the months or years prior to stabilization, the prospects are that an increased import flow can significantly affect real output, even in the short term.[25] If, however, imports are running at high levels, a stabilization program that curtails imports will probably be necessary. Import curtailment is in itself

25. This clearly happened in Turkey following the 1958 devaluation.

inflationary and may also impair domestic production levels if imports of intermediate and capital goods are used more or less in fixed proportions in domestic production.

The extent to which debt-servicing commitments exist prior to the stabilization package and the ways in which rescheduling is needed and handled within it are also important. The existence of debt-servicing obligations that cannot be met reflects the fact that the country has lived beyond its means in the past. The fact that stabilization packages are often postponed until debt-servicing obligations force governments into negotiations with consortia of creditors is also a reflection of governments' unwillingness to take the short-term costs of stabilization.

The difficulties that can arise as a result of bargaining over debt rescheduling can be important, both politically and psychologically, in affecting a stabilization program. Pressing debt-service obligations can induce governments to accept conditions from consortia of creditors as a prerequisite for debt rescheduling. In some instances, this may enable politicians to take measures they would not otherwise be able to take politically. In other cases, politicians may not accept the necessity for those measures, in which case they may carry them out only belatedly and begrudgingly. In that case, prospects for the longer-term success of the stabilization program are small; the objectives are really those of the creditors and not those of the debtor country.[26] When debt-service rescheduling becomes critical, however, donors as well as debtors are caught. Failure to impose some conditions upon borrowers at that time will force them to lend more later in the absence of policy measures and, if a government is unresponsive, creditors will eventually use the country's prospective default as a means of correcting the situation.

Policies

As already stated, there is no single set of policies that constitutes a "stabilization program." Programs can range from fairly minor adjustments of exchange rates and macroeconomic policies with only limited

26. For an analysis of the political implications of donor behavior with respect to one devaluation, see Jagdish Bhagwati and T. N. Srinivasan, *Foreign Trade Regimes and Economic Development: India* (Columbia University Press for the National Bureau of Economic Research, 1975), chap. 10. Diaz-Alejandro, *Foreign Trade Regimes and Economic Development: Colombia,* reports that, prior to undertaking its own liberalization program in 1967, the Colombian president even went on television to state that he would not abide by the wishes of Colombia's creditors!

Table 3-2. *Financial Programs as a Component of Stabilization Programs, Seventy-nine Countries, 1963–72*

Number of programs

	Credit policy to be implemented	
Main purpose	Deceleration	No deceleration
Correction of overly expansionary demand policies	26	. . .
Modification of exchange system and correction of overly expansionary demand policies	4	. . .
Modification of exchange system	7	13
Other (of which)	3	26
Antirecessionary program	(−)	(5)
Cope with temporary shortfall in exports	(−)	(11)
Total	40	39

Source: Reichmann and Stillson, "Experience with Programs of Balance of Payments Adjustment," p. 297.

objectives to attempts to correct high rates of inflation and severely restrictive QRs. In terms of their effects on economic growth, the successful stabilization programs are those that succeed in one or more of the following: (1) significantly alter the bias of the trade-and-payments regime away from import substitution; (2) move the economy away from reliance upon quantitative restrictions and toward pricing measures; or (3) permit a movement away from stop-go cycles of growth resulting from a foreign exchange "bottleneck."

Here, we discuss the policies that can constitute part of such a program. First, there are the already-mentioned monetary and fiscal policies. These often entail a reduction in the extension of credit within the economy, ceilings upon levels of government expenditures, and measures to increase tax collections. In addition, they may involve the removal of price ceilings and other measures that may have contributed to government deficits and increases in the money supply. Reichmann and Stillson[27] have tabulated the "financial programs" implemented as part of stabilization programs for the seventy-nine instances in which higher credit tranches were utilized during the 1963–72 period. These cases involve both developed and developing countries but are nonetheless instructive. Their classification of cases is reproduced in table 3-2 above. In their terminology, "no deceleration" refers to cases where credit expan-

27. Thomas Reichmann and Richard Stillson, "Experience with Programs of Balance of Payments Adjustment: Stand-by Arrangements in the Higher Credit Tranches, 1963–72," *IMF Staff Papers*, vol. 25 (June 1978), p. 297.

sion was to be permitted to continue at its present rate. As can be seen, the single largest group of countries resorting to higher credit tranches in IMF standbys were categorized as having "overly expansionary demand policies," and their rate of credit expansion was to be reduced as part of their stabilization programs. There were, however, thirteen cases in which the objective was to modify the exchange system, and deceleration of credit expansion was not called for. In some of these cases, the authorities had begun instituting restrictive credit policies prior to the standby agreement, so no further deceleration was warranted.

In some developing countries, notably Korea, a significant component of the altered growth structure of the economy originated from interest rate reforms undertaken in conjunction with the reform of the exchange system. In Korea, inflation had made the real interest rate significantly negative, and interest rate reforms raised the nominal rate of interest from 5 to 8 percent to 25 to 30 percent (with an inflation rate of about 20 percent). Although other factors also contributed, the Korean savings rate rose dramatically after the interest rate reforms, and this factor contributed to the large jump in the growth rate achieved subsequently.

With the exception of the interest rate reforms, however, most macroeconomic policies adopted as part of a stabilization program do not directly affect the three variables listed above as being significant for growth prospects. Rather, they constitute part of the background setting for alterations in the trade and payments regime; their chief significance is in determining whether the chosen nominal fixed exchange rate can remain realistic in real terms for a significant time.

The trade and exchange rate components of stabilization programs are even more varied than their macromonetary counterparts. The kinds of policies adopted can be loosely categorized under four main headings: exchange rate changes, liberalizing the import regime, altering the bias of the regime, and debt rescheduling.

Exchange rate changes have been discussed. As indicated, a part of the change in the nominal exchange rate is often absorbed by the removal of export subsidies, import surcharges, and other partial measures taken prior to devaluation; and it is "net," and not gross, devaluation that affects individuals' decisions. To be sure, there is probably some improvement in incentives resulting even from this tidying up, as the replacement of surcharges and subsidies with the exchange rate usually results in greater uniformity of incentives and effective exchange rates across transaction categories than exists prior to the change.

The preceding analysis also demonstrated that the impact of a net devaluation can be quite different depending on whether the preexisting situation was one of a QR-achieved balance in payments or of an open deficit. In the former case, alteration of the exchange rate automatically results in some liberalization of the regime and, insofar as export subsidies were not as large as import premiums, a reduction in the bias toward import substitution. In an open-deficit prior situation, devaluation is more likely to result in an equiproportionate rise in the domestic prices of tradables, and the chief relative price effect is the relative price of tradables in terms of home goods.

Liberalizing the import regime can come about not only through exchange rate changes when import premiums on licenses are absorbed, but also through alterations in the control mechanism itself.[28] Many stabilization programs have been accompanied by a revision of the licensing system, often with the introduction of a group of "priority" or "liberalized" imports for which licensing procedures are streamlined if not abandoned. Several techniques for achieving liberalization have been used. In some countries, a shift from a "positive" list (only items listed are permitted to be imported) to a "negative" list (all items not listed may be freely imported) has resulted in significant liberalization. In other countries, removal of "guarantee deposit" requirements, under which would-be importers deposit amounts equal to some multiple of their import license with the central bank pending receipt of the import, can represent a sizable liberalization. In Chile, for example, the authorities have imposed guarantee deposit requirements of 10,000 percent in periods of severe foreign exchange shortfalls prior to devaluation, and removal of those requirements has de facto permitted a resumption of imports.[29] Even moving from monthly to quarterly or semiannual import programs can result in liberalization of the regime, as can measures such as permitting the resale of import licenses and removing restrictions on currency areas in which licenses are utilized.

Alteration of the bias of the regime comes about through the exchange rate change itself (insofar as it is net), with absorption of premiums on

28. Liberalizing the regime cannot be carried very far without increasing the flow of imports. In the short run, that can usually be achieved only when financed by foreign credits, which are discussed below.

29. Removal or reduction of guarantee deposit requirements can have a significant effect on the money supply. For this reason, it sometimes makes sense to provide for their gradual removal, rather than to abandon them at the time of devaluation.

import licenses as the regime is liberalized and also through policies designed to encourage exports directly. Especially important can be assurances to exporters that the newly achieved real exchange rate for exports and other incentives for exports will continue. In some instances, this has been accomplished in part by the removal of domestic taxes on export production. In Brazil, for example, removal of state and federal taxes on exports made selling domestically and selling abroad at two-thirds the price approximately equally profitable.[30]

Finally, there is the matter of debt rescheduling and borrowing to finance an increased flow of imports. Debt rescheduling is often a prerequisite for any degree of liberalization of the regime and continued economic growth, because by the time of the stabilization program, the country's existing debt-service and repayment obligations are so large that the alternatives are default or an import bill so small that domestic economic activity will have to be severely curtailed. In addition to rescheduling, creditors and especially aid donors have often extended additional credits to the country at the time of stabilization to permit an immediate increase in the import flow before export earnings and other foreign exchange receipts respond to the altered incentives provided by devaluation and its accompanying measures.

Trade-Offs in Stabilization Programs

Enough has been said already to pinpoint the chief areas of trade-off in deciding upon the nature of a stabilization program. Essentially, there are three crucial and interrelated areas where significant trade-offs exist. The first is between the short term and the long term. The second is between gradual but continuing small changes and large changes. The third is between more foreign borrowing and greater deflationary pressure as part of the stabilization program.

Short-Term versus Long-Term Trade-Offs

If one were to pinpoint the most significant trade-off in stabilization programs, it is clearly the trade-off between short-term costs and longer-

30. See Jose Carvalho and Claudio Haddad, "Brazil," in Anne O. Krueger, Hal B. Lary, Terry Monson, and Narongchai Akrasanee, eds., *Trade and Employment in Developing Countries, 1: Individual Studies* (University of Chicago Press for the National Bureau of Economic Research, 1981).

term benefits. For reasons already spelled out, stabilization programs almost inevitably entail some short-term costs as a necessary price for achieving longer-term benefits. Especially when the changes that must be brought about involve both the rate of inflation and the bias of the trade regime, short-term adjustment is inevitable. Two or three additional percentage points per year of growth of GNP can be achieved by countries successfully altering their trade bias and payments regime. For those countries, the short-term costs, which are probably on the order of one or two percentage points of GNP for a year or eighteen months, are greatly exceeded by the discounted value of higher GNP at later dates.[31]

The difficulty, of course, is that politicians must inevitably face the short term before reaching the long term. The myopic nature of the political process is well understood. Thus one can well imagine situations in which alteration of the bias of the regime might well yield a social rate of return in excess of 15 percent on the short-term costs yet be rejected by the political process.

The fact that the politics of stabilization are difficult makes matters worse. Not only are politicians likely to use higher rates of discount than may be warranted, but the fact that they may be unwilling to withstand the pressures that arise during the transition period raises the possible costs of embarking on a stabilization program. Although the benefits to be achieved by a successful stabilization program that involve moving away from import substitution are not likely to be affected, the fact that politicians may decide to abort a stabilization program before its benefits begin to be realized raises potential costs. A donor, considering whether to push for a stabilization program and shift of trade orientation, must weigh the possibility that the program may be aborted (which will raise costs for the next attempt) as well as weigh the costs of a successful program against the potential benefits. In large part, such a judgment is of necessity political, but that makes the calculus no less necessary.

Gradualism versus Shock

The fact that there are likely to be short-term costs associated with any change makes the case for some degree of gradualism: it may dimin-

31. See *Liberalization Attempts*, chap. 11, for the statistical evidence on this point for a pooled time-series cross-section of devaluations in the NBER project countries. See also Bela Balassa, "Exports and Economic Growth: Some Further Evidence," *Journal of Development Economics*, vol. 5 (June 1978), pp. 181–89.

ish the costs of adjustment. However, the fact that there are likely to be built-in resistances to change (especially among successful import substitution establishments) and that entrepreneurs must perceive changes in incentives makes a powerful case for a fairly rapid shift in relative prices and in the trade and payments regime.

Here again, the trade-off is much like that between the short term and the long term. There is no doubt that a gradual shift in signals is the more desirable policy if such gradualism does not affect the chances of success of the policy package. If, however, gradualism provides more of an opportunity for failure (as it almost surely does) than a once-and-for-all reversal of signals, then the case for a sharp, once-and-for-all shift in policies is stronger.

As with the short-term/long-term trade-off, there are differences among countries in the likelihood that gradual alteration of the regime can be sustained. However, there is undoubtedly some critical minimum initial shift that is essential in order for businessmen and others to perceive that the regime is really altered, and it is probably a mistake to accept too gradual an approach. Indeed, there is not a great deal of evidence available as to the different costs of larger once-and-for-all changes and smaller ones spread out over a longer period of time. Nonetheless, in view of the political difficulties that are likely to arise if there is a long period during which adjustment is taking place with few visible signs of success, there is a presumption in favor of a once-and-for-all sharp adjustment.

Foreign Borrowing versus Recession

To achieve a given degree of liberalization of imports (and consequent alteration of bias of the regime), either the level of imports must be increased or income must be reduced in such a way that the demand for imports shifts downward. Thus, liberalization can be achieved either by increasing the size of the flow of imports or by domestic recession. If, as is usually the case,[32] an increased flow of imports can be financed during the initial stabilization period only by foreign credits, an immediate question arises: under what conditions is a country justified in borrowing

---

32. In some instances, expectations of an exchange rate alteration induce exporters to withhold their goods and importers to stock up. Reverse flows after devaluation can then finance increased imports. While that can happen, it is difficult to rely on it.

from abroad in the present (to finance increased domestic consumption) rather than accepting a reduction in the level of economic activity?

Again, an answer to the question is partly related to the probability of success of the stabilization program. If the country will, in any event, revert to exchange controls and a strong bias toward import substitution within a short period, it seems to make little sense to borrow currently and to mortgage the future for that purpose. However, to start out with the view that the program is likely to fail also is not acceptable.

Assuming that a program is started, therefore, it seems worthwhile to borrow from abroad to sustain the increased flow of imports. This can be seen in several ways. Suppose a country has a marginal propensity to import (with respect to income) of m. Then, for every dollar borrowed from abroad, domestic income can be greater than it otherwise could (for the same degree of liberalization) by $1/m$. Unless the marginal propensity to import is extremely high, this would suggest that borrowing from abroad may have a very high social marginal productivity in terms of the additional level of domestic income it will permit.

Another way to view the importance of foreign credits during the stabilization period is to recall that increased flows of imports simultaneously liberalize the regime faster than would otherwise be possible (except with recession) *and* are deflationary in that they absorb excess aggregate demand. Contrasted with the alternatives of cutting back on the level of economic activity or of less liberalization, financing larger import flows appears to be superior, as long as the stabilization program appears to have a good chance of success.

Implications for Donor Countries

The implications for aid-givers are several. First and most important, aid to support a sustained flow of imports at the time of a stabilization program may, if all goes well, have a very high marginal product *if* an objective of the stabilization program is to alter the bias of the trade and payments regime. Such aid can be used not only to finance an enlarged flow of imports, but also to reassure potential speculators that the new policies are permanent. Aid that simply increases reserves can be extremely productive.

Second, despite the fact that a country *should* devalue, considerations pertaining to the domestic political situation are not irrelevant to the decision to undertake a stabilization package, especially decisions about its timing. Particularly since the failure of a given stabilization policy makes the next attempt more difficult, there is something to be said for waiting, if possible, for domestic political sentiment to support the package. While increasing demands for new loans may force aid donors' and creditors' hands, postponement of pressure to stabilize may be warranted when feasible. In this connection, other fortuitous circumstances may affect the outcome of the stabilization effort; especially if signs are for a below-average crop or for deteriorating terms of trade, postponement of pressures on the debtor country may be wise.

Finally, a successful stabilization program will have its significant growth impact through the resource reallocation and restructuring of the economy that can result. Those achievements, in turn, can occur only insofar as countries are able successfully to compete in world markets. On the one hand, that requires that the countries altering their regimes provide appropriate incentives and support for their enterprises attempting to export. On the other hand, it also requires that donors be willing to permit entry of exports from developing countries into their markets. In terms of the prospects for increased growth through alteration of the bias of the trade regime, the most significant determinant in the long term will be the growth of world markets. For developed countries, the creditors', as a group, maintaining free access to their markets for the products of developing countries may be the single most important policy they can undertake to ensure the success of stabilization programs with positive effects on the rate of economic growth.

Comments by Hollis B. Chenery*

Anne Krueger takes as her starting point the useful National Bureau studies of *Foreign Trade Regimes and Economic Development*. These analyses give a solid empirical background for her evaluation of the political and economic context in which trade and stabilization policies are formulated. From this base, Krueger provides a number of useful insights into the costs of shifts in trade regimes, the lags involved, the effects of uncertainty, and the like.

---

* Further comments on this chapter, by Ronald McKinnon, are at the end of chapter 4.

In contrast to Krueger's highly empirical treatment of trade policy, the changes in the external environment that have led to the current inflationary situation are analyzed in a very general fashion. Stabilization is assumed to be an end in itself, and the degree of stabilization that is possible or desirable under current conditions is not seriously examined.

This limitation becomes more serious in the latter part of the chapter, in which the relations among stabilization, long-term development and foreign borrowing are examined with little reference to the different internal or external origins of the stabilization problem (excess demand, worsening terms of trade, etc.). Although some generalizations derived from the relatively stable and expanding world economy of the 1960s carry over to the unstable and depressed 1970s, others need to be seriously qualified.

The overriding destabilizing factor of this decade has been the enormous rise in the price of petroleum and the inability of most oil-importing countries to adjust their economies to this price in a reasonably short period. A complete adjustment will require a substantial restructuring of international trade and capital flows involving reciprocal actions by the surplus countries, so that the burden of adjustment does not fall too heavily on the weaker, deficit countries.

In this context an optimal strategy for stabilization and development would involve a more extensive reallocation of resources and probably a different combination of instruments than did the relatively smaller, independent adjustments of the 1960s on which Krueger's analysis is based. For some developing countries the magnitude of structural change required is comparable to that accompanying a minor war. Changes of this magnitude cannot be adequately treated in the short-term, relatively static context of this chapter.

The conventional separation between stabilization and development, or short-term and long-term policies, has become increasingly inappropriate to the international economic problems of this decade, in which the adjustment policies of individual countries must be assessed over periods of five to ten years and are heavily dependent on actions by other countries.

This observation applies equally to the design of the long-term development policies. The countries that have fared best in recent years—apart from the oil producers—have been those with flexible economies that could adjust their volume and composition of trade in response to large changes in world markets. For the foreseeable future we can anticipate a return to the disequilibrium conditions of the 1950s in which trade limita-

tions to growth and development will predominate and will require a combination of long- and short-term policies. In this setting it is misleading to
consider stabilization as a primary objective in itself rather than as a
means to a broader developmental goal.

Discussion

Constantine Michalopoulos (Agency for International Development)
noted the study focused on domestic sources of instability, whereas external shock makes adjustment more difficult. He also raised the question
of why developing countries do not seek remedies at an earlier stage, and
wondered whether there is some distortion in the international system
that, in addition to domestic politics, leads to this costly delay. *Joseph
Winder* (U.S. Treasury Department) asked about the study's implications
for program versus project lending. *Lance Taylor* emphasized the need to
consider distributional consequences of liberalization, such as the fact
that devaluation in the presence of import quotas eliminates rents formerly received by holders of quotas. The government may lose these
rents, as occurred in Egypt after eliminating dual exchange rates.

Daniel Schydlowsky disputed Krueger's view that macroeconomic stabilization can be separated from resource allocation issues. Citing excess
capacity in the services sector and in import substituting industries as the
result of past overinvestment, in the presence of excess demand for agricultural goods and imports, he argued that excess industrial capacity can
be used for export through promotional measures. Thus stabilization can
be combined with reallocation of resources.

Anne Krueger responded to Hollis Chenery's comment by allowing that
there might be some bias from generalizing on the basis of the specific
country experiences observed, but asked what the alternative was. Regarding worsening external conditions in the 1970s, she noted that we
have heard arguments for export pessimism for more than two decades
and the forecasts were too pessimistic. Failure of export earnings to grow
seriously injures growth prospects, as shown by experience in the 1970s.
Moreover, domestic policies are so distorted in many developing countries that it is still worth their while to carry out reforms even if the international economic environment has deteriorated and the best performance
potential is not as great as it would have been during more buoyant times.
Concerning program loans, Krueger emphasized the need to avoid the

appearance of imposing external performance requirements. Krueger was dubious about Schydlowsky's approach; she noted that trade reform causes changes in the industrial mix, and that policy makers should not try to identify which sectors to subsidize for export promotion. Indeed, export promotion is successful partly because incentives are fairly uniform and across-the-board. Moreover, evidence from Korea and elsewhere shows that capital utilization rises after stabilization programs.

CHAPTER FOUR

Southern Cone Stabilization Plans

CARLOS F. DIAZ-ALEJANDRO

THIS CHAPTER deals with stabilization plans with costs that raise the question of whether the cure is worse than the disease; or what may be named the Southern Cone case, after the experience of countries located in the southern part of South America. At the outset, however, it should be noted that not all stabilization plans are accompanied by sharp falls in output and massive income redistributions. And not all such benign stabilizations occur in Asia or Africa; within Latin America there are also examples of relatively small short-term costs of stabilization followed by rapid growth. Colombia in 1967 is one case, but there are more.[1]

The first part of the chapter outlines the initial conditions and the historical background to Southern Cone stabilization plans. The typical package of policy measures will also be discussed briefly. The second part describes a stylized scorecard of the consequences of the plans. The third part discusses some fresh complications introduced into stabilization plans by the high degree of international capital mobility observed in the late 1970s. Normative sections will close the chapter, covering both the national and international dimensions of the Southern Cone case.

The topic at hand is controversial. In its purely economic dimension it deals with an area—short-term macroeconomics—which during the late 1970s was unsettled. Debate in the industrialized countries echoes issues

I gratefully acknowledge comments from Edmar Bacha, Mario Brodersohn, Guillermo Calvo, William Cline, Albert Fishlow, Paul Krugman, Jorge Braga de Macedo, Juan Carlos de Pablo, Pedro Pou, Gustav Ranis, Carlos Rodriguez, and John Sheahan. They cannot be blamed for the opinions or possible errors in this paper.

1. See Thomas M. Reichmann and Richard T. Stillson, "Experience with Programs of Balance of Payments Adjustment: Stand-by Arrangements in the Higher Credit Tranches, 1963–72," *IMF Staff Papers*, vol. 25 (June 1978), pp. 293–309; and Anne O. Krueger, *Foreign Trade Regimes and Economic Development: Liberalization Attempts and Consequences*, vol. 10 (Ballinger for the National Bureau of Economic Research, 1978).

discussed in Latin America at least since the 1950s; just as in those old debates, it is often difficult to establish where scientific economics ends and political preference begins. Judgments about the speed of adjustment in different markets and evaluation of the social costs of alternative dynamic paths are still based mostly on hunches and sketchy evidence. The eclecticism of this chapter reflects the troubled state of macroeconomics.

It would be disingenuous to hide one's political preferences behind the technicalities of stabilization plans, at least when discussing the Southern Cone case; the awesome events of the 1970s in that part of Latin America rule that out. The reader is warned that what follows reflects a perplexed centrist political position, which to reject the horrors of the bureaucratic authoritarian state[2] finds it unnecessary to cover up the economic "chien-lit" of populism. The key underlying assumption will be that a mixed economy is a desirable and feasible model for most Latin American countries.

Many will find the combination of eclectic economics and centrist politics comfortable only for a fence-straddling academic critic. Perhaps. For what it is worth, the hope that the 1980s will see that messy and undramatic formula gaining ground in Latin America encourages the writing of this chapter.

Historical Background and Initial Conditions

The economic history of Southern Cone countries after World War II is littered with failed stabilization plans; in some cases the failures go further back. The basic failures are the inability to bring inflation down to U.S. (or in earlier days, U.K.) levels, and to eradicate tendencies toward disequilibrium in the balance of payments. A plausible hypothesis is that, ceteris paribus, the longer the history of failed stabilization plans, the smaller the chances of success (and/or the greater the costs of success) of any new plan. Besides reading daily newspapers, economic agents carry in their heads an economic history inducing them to discount any claim that "inflation will be down to zero within a year," regardless of how fiercely those claims are backed up. The expectations forming their behavior are based less on textbook models than on memories of previous failures within their own country. If, as appears to be the case, the private

2. This label, coined by Guillermo O'Donnell, seems more accurate than others, such as fascist, for referring to Southern Cone military regimes.

cost of erring on the low side is greater than that of too high an estimate of inflation, the stage is set for a viscous inertia in the inflation rate.[3] Inflation turns out to be more like Sisyphus' rock than Alexander's knot.

A typical Southern Cone stabilization plan will be preceded, say, during the one or two years before its announcement, by an acceleration of the chronic inflation. That acceleration will be accompanied by an increased variability in relative prices, a variability having little justification from the viewpoint of economic efficiency. Both the rate of inflation and relative prices become less predictable at this stage. Part of the erratic fluctuations in relative prices will arise from government attempts to control inflation by sporadically freezing some prices regarded as strategic, such as those for foreign exchange, necessities, public utilities, transport, and credit, followed by abrupt upward adjustments. Because those adjustments are only partial, most of those prices, including interest rates, will move far away from plausible equilibrium values.

Deficits in the balance of payments, vanishing foreign exchange reserves, and difficulties in servicing the foreign debt will be of more immediate concern than the acceleration of inflation and the growing variability and distortion of relative prices to governments that will be called populist in this stylized description of events.

Both internal and external factors contribute to this lamentable state of affairs. The early stages of populist governments are likely to have witnessed substantial expansion in government expenditures not financed by tax collections, either because the opposition blocks efforts to raise taxes or because the government regards fiscal and monetary management as less important than structural reforms. Fiscal deficits are more likely to be financed by borrowing from the central bank than from either the domestic or foreign private sectors. Increased public expenditure will be channeled more toward consumption than investment, although in human capital formation important advances may be registered. Across-the-board massive wage increases also accompany the early stages of populist governments. Because these measures will be felt first in output expansion, especially of wage goods, rather than an acceleration of inflation (which may even decline during the early stages of populism), the government will be confirmed in the wisdom of its heterodoxy. Pressure on the balance of payments in those early times can be handled by strengthening adminis-

3. See Joseph Ramos, "Inflación persistente, inflación reprimida e hiperstanflación. Lecciones de inflación y estabilizatión en Chile," *Desarrollo Económico,* vol. 18 (April–June 1978), pp. 3–49.

trative import-repressing mechanisms, drawing down reserves, and seeking foreign loans. Even sympathetic observers warning of future dangers due to excesses in fiscal, monetary, exchange rate, and income policies will be dismissed by the remark that "now the economy works differently." Under those euphoric circumstances concern for economic efficiency, export promotion and a minimum of concern for fiscal and monetary prudence will be regarded as prima facie evidence of "reactionary positions" not only by most populist politicians, but also by government economists giving top priority to achieving structural reforms, or seeking a rapid transition to a centrally planned economy, or simply believing that economic efficiency, export promotion, and prudent fiscal and monetary policies are of little consequence for the welfare of most people in the country.

External events may or may not add to the euphoria of the early stages of populism but frequently add to its closing troubles. The external shocks may come from a deterioration in the terms of trade, or from hostile foreign governments intending to "make the (populist) economy scream." Even when the external shocks (or an exogenous domestic one, such as a drought) are relatively minor, they can seriously destabilize an economy already weakened by the consequences of populist economic policies.

During the last stages of populism there will be general agreement that "things cannot go on like this" and that something must be done. Within the populist coalition, some will argue for a bold move toward centrally planned socialism, thus further encouraging capital flight and a slump in private investment. Moderate populist technocrats may be able to attempt their own stabilization plans, which will come too late. The opposition will move for the kill, culminating in a military coup.

The new government then launches its stabilization plan, usually in consultation with the International Monetary Fund (IMF). The plan will have several targets: a restoration of balance-of-payments equilibrium and the orderly servicing of the foreign debt; control and elimination of inflation; and the creation of a structure of relative prices conducive to an efficient allocation of resources. Plans undertaken most recently are more emphatic, and even radical, regarding the need for basic policy reforms, especially in the areas of foreign trade and domestic financial markets. Earlier plans, say those of the 1950s, focused mostly on short-term balance-of-payments and inflation targets, leaving the system of protection and "financial repression" largely unaffected.

The instruments are well known: strict limits on the expansion of overall banking credit; reduction in the share of that credit expansion claimed by the public sector; adjustment, often large and abrupt, in the prices which had lagged behind inflation, especially the price of foreign exchange and interest rates; the removal of distortions, such as import controls and excessive tariffs; and, somewhat inconsistently with the new dominant philosophy, a special kind of incomes policy consisting primarily of tough limits on wage increases. Once-and-for-all steps will accompany the stabilization package, such as the renegotiation of the foreign debt. Naturally, each plan will have sui generis targets and instruments, but for a given epoch their differences are less remarkable than their similarities.

The circumstances under which these policies are undertaken will not allow for much "fine tuning" of the instruments, nor a careful phasing of the different measures through time. The "something-has-to-be-done" syndrome, however, will give the new authorities some room to maneuver; for a considerable time, they can blame economic difficulties on the deposed populists, and a relieved bourgeoisie, with their property rights confirmed, will contemplate short-term economic hardships with equanimity. Entrepreneurs in particular will find the reestablishment of their authority within factories ample compensation for sluggish sales. Social groups openly opposing the new policies will be handled *manu militari*.

The coherence and steadiness of application of the stabilization plans should not be exaggerated. Authoritarian regimes are not free of hesitations, internal divisions, or personality clashes. Even when The Minister does not change, policies may be significantly modified, as in Argentina since 1976. Two different views of the exchange rate, for example, may claim the mantle of orthodoxy: one advocating a fair degree of flexibility, another wishing to use the exchange rate to guide the price level toward stability. The former or "old orthodoxy" regards the money supply as the main determinant of the domestic price level and orients the exchange rate toward balance-of-payments targets. The "new orthodoxy" will favor manipulation of domestic credit expansion as the key for achieving balance-of-payments targets, sharing with old structuralists the belief that the exchange rate can influence the price level, but not relative prices. While the old orthodoxy relied on models developed for large industrialized countries, the new orthodoxy views Southern Cone circumstances as not very different from those of Benelux and Central America. What follows will necessarily abstract from changes and countermarches in stabilization plans, but will return to the variety of views on exchange rate policies.

The Scorecard

The stabilization plans achieve their clearest and quickest success in the balance of payments. Within months, international reserves will be on the rise and foreign creditors becalmed. Developments in the capital account, having to do with financial flows, explain a good share of the short-term turnaround. Debt renegotiation, IMF credits, the end and reversal of capital flight, and the end of speculation against a previously overvalued exchange rate all contribute in the same direction. These considerations, which were already important in stabilization plans adopted during the 1950s, have become even more so under the circumstances of the late 1970s. Some special characteristics of stabilization plans undertaken in a world of high financial capital mobility will be discussed in the next section.

Help from the current account will be modest in the short term. However, a drop in the quantum of merchandise imports may contribute something to balance-of-payments equilibrium even in the very short term. A number of conflicting forces influence the import quantum: the levels of domestic output and capital formation; the new domestic relative price of importables (itself subject to contradictory influences from devaluation versus liberalization and tariff cuts); the cost and availability of foreign export credits; and the levels of domestic inventories of importables at the time of the launching of the plan. The net result of these influences will be in doubt and will provide a clue as to whether the stabilization plan is having severe short-term costs: a steep drop in the import quantum is likely to signal a severe slump in real output and investment.

An increase and diversification of exports have been major secondary targets of stabilization plans, with some variety in the instruments brought to bear for that purpose. An increase in the real exchange rate applicable to exports is a common feature; its greater stability has also been sought by a crawling-peg policy. In addition, some plans introduce or expand selective tax, credit, and other subsidies as part of the export promotion package, despite IMF disapproval. In the very short term, these measures are unlikely to be reflected in an increase in the export quantum. But their success in increasing nontraditional exports in the medium term, often aided by the excess capacity created by a fall in domestic demand, has been a more noteworthy feature and one of the most impressive successes of stabilization plans. Evidence indicates a clear victory for export optimists.

Inflation has proven to be more stubborn than the authors of stabilization plans had expected. Before the start of the plans, hyperinflation was often at hand; it is unclear whether, ex post, this provides a good explanation for the disappointing results obtained in this front, as it could be argued that hyperinflation provides conditions making its abrupt termination possible, as in the Central European cases of the 1920s. No Southern Cone stabilization plan has attempted a currency reform, and in the very short term the adjustment of lagging strategic prices has in fact frequently led to an acceleration of inflation. After the burst of "corrective inflation," authorities will take pride in the deceleration of price increases, even if the deceleration does not match official forecasts. Even the consolation of ever declining rates of inflation comes to an end after four years or so, before reaching, say, U.S. levels. Very seldom is the rate brought down below the 15 to 20 percent per annum range; it may remain above what the country had historically experienced in what the new authorities depict as the "bad old days." Ironically, at this late and frustrating stage, there may be moves to squeeze inflation further by delaying not only wage adjustments, but also the crawling peg and other key prices, such as public utility rates. Standard price indices may be revised, leaving out items experiencing the largest price increases. As under populism, these tactics will contribute to expectations contrary to those the authorities had hoped for.

Even in cases where excess demand was a plausible explanation for the high rates of inflation during the preplan period, its explanatory power declines as the months go by and excess capacity and foreign exchange reserves pile up. Remaining fiscal deficits and/or high rates of increase in the money supply provide weak explanations under conditions of declining output and of shrinking real credit and cash balances. Excessive trade union power can hardly be blamed when real wages collapse and union leaders are jailed, or worse. One is left with still imprecise references to lags and expectations, to increasing markups, to monopoly power in industry and commerce, or to imported inflation. This state of affairs is also found in industrialized countries; what makes the Southern Cone case unique in the bewildering quantitative dimensions of the stagflation problem.

The failure of import liberalization and tariff reductions to contain price increases in the very short term has been disappointing; far-from-competitive commercial firms or recalcitrant customs officials may block a result expected a priori and emphasized with hope in the 1960s literature. The upward thrust provided by exchange rate devaluation works faster than the downward pressures generated by tariff cuts and the elimination of import quotas. More generally, the Law of One Price, so important for models underpinning the new orthodoxy, appears to work better on the side of exportable goods than elsewhere; the line between importable and nontraded goods is blurry, especially in countries that have lived under rigorous protection for many years. An Argentina is not quickly turned into a Netherlands (nor into a Guatemala).

It can be argued that the inflation persisting after the start of the stabilization plan may be surprisingly stubborn, but at least it is accompanied by fewer distortions and less erratic relative price changes than the pre-stabilization plan. The payoff to a more rational structure of relative prices in terms of increased real output, however, will be slow in coming. Indeed, either stagnation or a decline in output has been more usual in the Southern Cone. Given the restructuring of incentives, one could have expected a decline in production of some sectors, such as those producing highly protected importables and some nontraded goods. But their decline is often not only speedier than the expansion of sectors now enjoying favorable incentives, but it also unnecessarily drags down the output of many nontraded goods.

Despite continuing price increases, one may diagnose this situation as rising from a reduction in aggregate demand going beyond what is required to make room for an expansion in the production of exportables and in the production of those importables and nontraded goods benefiting from the new constellation of relative prices. This overkill is one of the more puzzling economic features of Southern Cone stabilization plans and perhaps cannot be fully explained without reference to the new authorities' wish to "discipline" the labor force partly by creating a soft labor market. The high priority given to a quick restoration of balance-of-payments equilibrium and smooth foreign debt servicing also contributes to the overkill.

The cut in real aggregate demand arises partly from policies already mentioned, such as the reduction in domestic credit expansion for both the public and the private sectors, as well as from redistributive effects generated by the policy package, which have asymmetrical spending consequences. The most spectacular of these is a reduction in real wages of the (previously) best-organized segments of the urban working class. This reduction is quickly reflected in a fall in consumption of wage goods. Real wage rates in these economies influence aggregate demand as well as profit rates and international competitiveness; in the short term, the output-depressing effect of wage cuts outweighs their expansionary impact via the latter mechanisms.

The success achieved in the fight against inflation, modest though it may be, is to be credited to a large extent to the wage-repressing incomes policy, while the balance-of-payment success derives support from the sagging real aggregate demand.

The restructuring of relative prices generates many other short-run redistributive effects. A priori, there is no reason why they should influence overall income distribution in a systematic way: losers in highly protected industries—those which had access to artificially cheap credit or cheap imports—are likely to have been in high-income groups, while producers of exportable goods could include small farmers. Consumers of previously subsidized foodstuffs in the cities may have income levels higher than those of rural food producers. In the Southern Cone case, however, the net effect of the policy package appears to have a regressive effect on income distribution, although the general picture is murky. Open urban unemployment, for example, has been substantial in the post-1973 Chilean case and relatively minor in the post-1976 Argentine plan. Argentina, like Germany, seems to have exported its unemployment to neighboring countries. The decline in real wages in Argentina and Chile, which had started before the change in government, was so steep as to raise questions as to how households managed their budgets; in the Chilean case, the combination of falling real wages with increasing unemployment for a nontrivial length of time has been particularly striking. The workings of formal and informal labor markets under these peculiar conditions remain unclear, but it appears that structural changes have occurred and that wage dispersion has increased.

During the early stages of stabilization plans, asset markets will be especially volatile, as expected changes in relative prices and in the rules of the game are capitalized. Those who are well informed and have access to national or international institutional credit can make large sums in a short time. The long-term efficiency gains from such financial speculation, especially when it is based on privileged knowledge of future public policy, are moot. Sensational capital gains by a few will not improve willingness by the many to tighten their belts.

A cut in consumption is less painful when accompanied by an increase in investment. Perhaps the most disappointing feature of many of the Southern Cone stabilization plans is the weakness shown by capital formation, particularly when the public sector leads in reducing its investment, as in the Chilean case (in contrast with the more pragmatic Brazilian example). A skeptical private sector shows caution in undertaking long-term commitments, particularly when the newly liberated financial markets offer fairly liquid investment outlets with high yields. Excess capacity in many industries producing importables and nontraded goods provides little encouragement for capital formation, but even in those sectors where incentives are favorable and capacity limits output, entrepreneurs with long memories prefer to wait until the dust settles. Foreigners will not act very differently from domestic entrepreneurs: they will show more interest in buying paper than in installing machinery and equipment. The new open-door policies will reap only modest results, at least in the short and medium terms, in direct foreign investments; the new investments are more likely to go into natural resources and finance than into manufacturing. From the viewpoint of the balance of payments, however, the sluggishness in overall capital formation will be most clearly reflected in a decline in imports of machinery and equipment.

Even a perfectly rational constellation of prices and investment incentives cannot fully convince entrepreneurs that such an edifice will be in place tomorrow. When economic rationality is built upon an arbitrary political regime, which may depend on one general's heartbeat, entrepreneurs will not be easily persuaded that today's relative prices are good predictors of future ones. While the economic team builds policy on the assumption that households and firms behave rationally and process information intelligently, the political team assumes citizens cannot be trusted to choose their leaders nor to read an uncensored press.

Some Additional Complications of the Late 1970s

Stabilization plans differ in design and consequences not only from one country to another, but also for the same country at various times. For example, external circumstances changed between the 1955 and the 1976 Argentine stabilization plans in some crucial aspects. During the 1970s, inflationary impulses coming from abroad made domestic disinflationary efforts even more difficult. Indeed, it is frequently argued that inflation in the dollar prices of the basket of tradable goods relevant for Southern Cone countries has been far greater than the inflation registered in standard U.S. price indices. Volatility in external terms of trade has also risen during the 1970s; for some countries, especially oil importers such as Chile and Uruguay, there have been sharp deteriorations in terms of trade at crucial stages of their stabilization plans. The 1970s have also witnessed a large increase in international short-term capital mobility; this section will focus on how this fact has influenced Southern Cone stabilization plans.

As noted earlier, these plans have coupled more liberal trade and exchange rate policies with some liberalization of domestic financial markets. Complete liberalization of those markets has not been usually achieved,[4] but enough has been done to generate fresh dilemmas.

The major dilemma can be sketched as follows. Trade liberalization reforms have sought a higher and more stable real exchange rate, so as to expand and diversify exports and to reduce reliance on import controls and tariffs. The liberalization of local financial markets tends to increase real returns on domestic financial assets, even when the stabilization plan achieves only modest results fighting inflation. Restrictions on domestic credit expansion typically accompany the policy reforms, so that local interest rates can go substantially beyond those abroad plus the expected exchange rate depreciation. Domestic and foreign wealth owners will increase their net holdings of local financial assets, while local entrepreneurs will seek foreign loans. Some of these tendencies were already present in stabilization plans of the 1950s; since then, however, the interest elasticity of the international supply of financial funds has increased dramatically, and the local financial markets have become more fluid and sophisticated.

With an unrestricted link between the domestic and the international financial markets, large portfolio adjustments will occur, and a capital inflow will result. The real exchange rate will appreciate relative to what it would have been without such an inflow. The liberalization of the domestic financial market and of its links with those abroad will work at cross-purposes with export promotion. If at the same time the authorities are dismantling import-repressing mechanisms, the import-competing sec-

4. For a helpful review of the evidence until 1976, see Vincente Galbis, "Inflation and Interest Rate Policies in Latin America, 1967–76," *IMF Staff Papers,* vol. 26 (June 1979), pp. 334–66.

tor will be doubly damaged. Eventually the portfolio adjustment should be completed, and a larger net debt will have to be serviced so that the real exchange rate, to the delight of exporters, will have to depreciate relative to the days of the capital inflow. In a growing world, some gross inflows will persist, but pressures on the exchange rate will be similar to those outlined.

In practice the transition is proving to be far from smooth. Many imperfections remain; some segments of the local financial market are still controlled, leading to a high variance in interest rates. Most transactions are short term; efforts to build a local market for financial instruments with maturities of more than a few months have met with little success. High reserve requirements introduce a large wedge between active and passive interest rates when the central bank pays no interest on those reserves. Even when the passive rate eventually becomes equal to the foreign interest rate plus the expected depreciation of the exchange rate, those borrowers who have no international financial links must pay the often extravagant local active rates. Such differentiation among entrepreneurs, according to their borrowing facilities, will have consequences for both equity and efficiency.

Southern Cone authorities have been reluctant to allow the exchange rate to fluctuate freely; they either maintain a crawling peg whose formula is only vaguely known, or announce what the gradually depreciating exchange rate will be for several months in advance. In either case, capital inflows will be reflected in changes in official foreign exchange holdings, which will swell the money supply. An increasing share of the expansion in local money will come from changes in exchange reserves, at the expense of domestic credit expansion. The more fluid the link between domestic and international financial markets, the greater the loss of control over the money supply. While Southern Cone monetary authorities hesitate between the old and new orthodoxies, the management of domestic credit, exchange rates, and international financial flows can become erratic.

Argentine experience during 1978 and 1979 illustrates most clearly some of the troublesome short-term dynamic processes that can occur under the new circumstances.[5] Argentine authorities announced the exchange rate with respect to the U.S. dollar for several months ahead of time, hoping that such information would help to cluster inflationary ex-

5. This experience is being analyzed formally by Guillermo Calvo, Ana Maria Martirena-Mantel, and Carlos A. Rodriguez.

pectations around a lower path.[6] At the start of this policy, domestic interest rates, or at least a significant group of them, substantially exceed foreign dollar interest rates, after adjusting for expected devaluation of the peso relative to the dollar. Massive financial inflows occur, expanding central bank reserves and the money supply. This injection of liquidity will relieve at least some agents pressed by ceilings on domestic credit expansion. If future devaluation schedules are sensitive to accumulating foreign exchange holdings, so that there is a slowdown in the pace of peso devaluation, certain instability will be introduced, as that slowdown will further increase the attractiveness of domestic financial assets, thus leading to an even greater capital inflow. Exporters and previously protected producers of importables will find these short-term dynamics singularly perverse and will clamor for faster devaluation or subsidies. Authorities will point to bulging reserves as evidence that faster devaluation is unnecessary, a proposition that net borrowers from abroad, importers, and outflowing tourists will find very sound. Those in charge of battling inflation will also look kindly upon the revaluation trend, because under the new orthodoxy the exchange rate is expected to determine the price level, while money supply is regarded as endogenous (domestic credit expansion being the policy variable under the control of the authorities). Even if the pace of devaluation is not adjusted downward because of large reserves, producers of tradable goods will face a difficult period of transition, during which it is likely that the prices of nontraded goods will rise at a faster pace than prices for traded goods. In countries historically concerned with foreign exchange shortages, the Swiss-type embarrassment of riches brought about by capital inflows is a novel situation and a bitter surprise to exporters who expected that the new policies would encourage their activities.

Debates as to whether a given currency is overvalued or not have become more complex in the 1970s than they were in earlier years. Even if one takes a simple purchasing-power-parity (PPP) approach to what the exchange rate should be, one has to agree on the relevant index for "rest-of-the-world" price increases. One problem, already noted, is that world prices for the Southern Cone basket of tradables seem to have behaved differently from standard U.S. (or UN) indices. Then one has to consider fluctuations among key currencies to devise a suitably weighted effec-

6. In 1975, Chilean authorities used an unexpected revaluation to attempt breaking inflationary expectations, generating windfall losses to exporters and windfall gains to those with foreign debt.

tive exchange rate. Moving beyond a simple PPP approach, allowances would have to be made for the effect on equilibrium exchange rates of changes in external terms of trade as well as in domestic commercial policies that are considered permanent. Tendencies in long-term capital flows, as well as judgments about productivity growth in different sectors of the economy (for example, has there been a permanent change in Pampean rural productivity growth?), also have to be considered. Reasonable people can disagree on a number of these judgments, a disagreement encouraged by erratic world market conditions and compounded by faulty data. The urge to "let the market decide" is checked by doubts as to the desirability of a clean float in countries where, in spite of recent reforms, domestic financial markets remain limited.

It was noted earlier that in several Southern Cone countries local interest rates have remained substantially above those abroad plus exchange rate depreciation, even when large capital inflows have been registered. A number of hypotheses, which cannot be explored here, are compatible with this stylized fact. Note, however, that domestic interest rates can be negative, defined with respect to local inflation, yet incentives could remain for an inflow of short-term capital. Such a situation, which prevailed in Argentina sporadically during 1978–79, is quite plausible when prices of nontraded goods are rising faster than the pace of exchange depreciation and/or when the "world" nominal interest rate is lower than "world" inflation. Note further that under these circumstances the indexing of public debt instruments so as to make their interest rates positive with respect to local inflation will introduce downward stickiness to domestic interest rates. That indexing will also encourage speculative shifts among different financial assets depending on inflationary expectations. A generous indexing of public debt could then be said to be "crowding out" not only private capital formation, but also the production of tradable goods via the induced capital inflow and the resulting real appreciation of the exchange rate. Public expenditures financed by such borrowing are less likely to involve capital formation in some cases (such as Argentina) than in others (such as Brazil). The future servicing of such public debt could raise serious problems.

The important role played by indexed public borrowing in the liberalization of domestic capital markets coupled with the also extensive public sector borrowings in international capital markets raises the issue of the optimal mix of both types of borrowing, both from a narrow public finance viewpoint as well as from the viewpoint of strengthening and developing local capital market institutions. So far, domestic capital markets appear unable to compete with international capital markets in medium- and long-term maturities; it is often asserted that in Southern Cone (and other Latin American) countries, international capital markets are still used to intermediate between domestic residents except for short-term and marginal transactions.

Even authorities as committed to laissez faire as those in Chile have been unable to handle pressures arising from international short-term capital flows without recourse to ad hoc compulsory deposit requirements for foreign loans to the private sector, raising their effective interest costs. The more pragmatic Brazilian authorities have frequently used those measures as well as other forms of exchange controls, plus a crawling peg that keeps speculators guessing, all of which limit the short-term links between domestic and international capital markets.[7]

Are These Hardships Really Necessary?

To what counterfactual situation should one compare Southern Cone stabilization plans? Earlier sections have emphasized the difficult economic and political conditions under which they are undertaken; it will not do to criticize those plans in a spirit of self-confident ahistorical perfectionism. The present state of macroeconomic theory would make such pretension doubly rash. Furthermore, these stabilization plans include measures, particularly in the area of foreign trade, whose details and timing may be debated, but whose major thrust was long overdue in the Southern Cone. It would be tragic if those justifiably revolted by the political excesses of the bureaucratic authoritarian state were to make a one-to-one association between, say, export promotion policies and those regimes. At least when evaluating economic policies, a spirit of selectivity and restraint should guide the critique. The architects and apologists of Southern Cone stabilization plans would also benefit from this stance; their strident expressions of triumph and claims to scientific superiority, facilitated by the suppression of domestic criticism by brute force, are at best ridiculous. It is indeed a melancholy spectacle to see those trained

7. See *Business Latin America,* April 25, 1979, for a description of recent Brazilian measures designed to increase the cost of foreign borrowing (p. 129), and similar Chilean policies (p. 135).

in free debate and fierce contempt for economic irrationality becoming meek political minions of madmen in authority.[8]

Accepting that some sort of stabilization plan was necessary, one can discuss the importance given to different targets, the use made of various instruments, and the time frame adopted in the use of instruments and to achieve targets.

It was seen earlier that major costs of Southern Cone stabilization plans included a reduction in output and a lag in capital formation. Austerity in consumption has not necessarily led to more investment, but to under-utilization of the labor force and installed capacity. It is difficult to accept that this waste is necessary either as atonement for past excesses or for future efficiency. Too simple a diagnosis of inflation leads to an excessively sharp reduction in aggregate demand, credit use, and fiscal and incomes policies. A doctrinaire faith in private, as compared with public, invest-ment contributes to these costs. Here one can contrast the Brazilian and Colombian practice with that of Chile; Brazil and Colombia have main-tained fairly active public investment programs even during stabilization plans. The more those public investments contribute to expand capacity in bottleneck sectors, or the more they fit with the restructuring of the economy along more efficient lines, the better; but even public construc-tion, the old employment-generating standby, could be preferable to severe underutilization of labor and capacity.

Even while proclaiming faith in laissez faire, Southern Cone stabiliza-tion plans have adopted incomes policies, albeit of an unbalanced sort. Official action has tended to repress wages more directly than prices. Some argue that competition, particularly that from abroad, will be enough to restrain prices, but that state power is needed to countervail that of trade unions. Blaming Southern Cone trade union power seems ghoulish in the late 1970s; faith in the speedy competitive discipline seems overly opti-mistic. As noted earlier, countries which for many years have had fairly closed economies are likely to take some time before developing commer-cial channels that effectively enforce the law of one price between foreign and domestic markets. At least during the transition period there is room

8. After months of bizarre military posturing, war between the armed forces of Argentina and Chile was narrowly averted by papal mediation in December 1978. Public expenditures backing this display of irrationality must have been substantial. Economic officials on both sides are known to have been unhappy. Their public utterances, however, showed little evidence of that. Fixed or preannounced exchange rates may have been partly motivated by technocratic hopes of using the fear of reserve losses to curb military expenditures.

for price guidelines covering the largest industrial and commercial firms, guidelines that could be based on projected changes in exchange rates, tariffs, and foreign prices. Those guidelines could help cluster private expectations about future inflation better than exaggerated claims often heard at the start of harsh stabilization plans. Given the historical record, the goals of more rational, less volatile relative prices and of a more predictable overall inflation rate deserve greater weight than "whipping inflation now." In countries with a tradition of price stability, it makes sense to take extraordinary measures to suppress the beginning of inflationary pressures, yet for countries with long histories of chronic inflation, sporadic fits of monetary machismo will buy few positive tangible results.

Reliance on a preannounced and declining rate of exchange rate devaluation as *the* key instrument to lower inflation also appears as excessively risky. Stubborn inflation in the prices of nontraded goods can lead to overvaluation. The real prices of exportables could be both less favorable and more unstable than under a crawling-peg regime whose devaluation pace is not announced, as in the Colombian and Brazilian cases. The latter system has the virtue that while it signals that the government will maintain "reasonable" and steady real prices for exportables over the medium and long term, it keeps speculators guessing, thus helping to reduce short-term capital flows that may be destabilizing. Preannounced exchange rates reduce the uncertainty of financial speculators while increasing that of exporters, a peculiar trade-off. It could be argued that for the sake of maintaining the momentum of export expansion and diversification, the Colombian-type crawling peg adopts an accommodating stance toward inflation. Yet if the preannounced and slower devaluation pace fails to reduce inflation fairly quickly, expectations will grow that sharper devaluations lie ahead. The government will be faced with the 1950s dilemma of giving in to such expectations, rekindling after all the inflationary spiral and losing any remaining credibility, or adopting very contractionary policies to validate the overvalued exchange rate.

Stabilization plans have usually improved the fiscal machinery of the public sector: tax collection has been tightened up, and prices of public enterprises have been raised. Generally, however, even the most authoritarian regimes have been timid in using selective fiscal measures improving both efficiency and income distribution, such as land taxes, or in taxing windfall profits and luxury consumption. These measures could help to spread austerity more evenly without harming efficiency and growth.

The combination of steadier real aggregate demand, larger capacity-augmenting capital formation, and firmer and more balanced incomes policy may result in higher or lower overall rates of inflation than those actually registered. Improvements in the balance of payments and reserve accumulation, however, would clearly be less dramatic than those observed. Looking just at the results of Southern Cone stabilization plans, one could conclude that the balance-of-payments target has been the one authorities *really* care about. Such a stance makes more sense for the IMF and for foreign creditors eager to see punctual debt servicing than for domestic authorities. Maintaining higher levels of real demand and capital formation would lead to substantially higher imports than those observed, and it could marginally reduce the upsurge in nontraditional exports. An easier credit stance could mean lower real interest rates and a less frantic pace of financial capital inflows; direct foreign investment, however, could be more buoyant. On the whole, balance-of-payments and reserve targets will have to be more modest, and a different mix of private and public debt may be necessary.

Policies redressing the balance of incentives as between exports and import substitution were long overdue. During the 1960s, steps had been taken in this direction by some centrist Southern Cone governments, such as those of Presidents Frei and Illia, but not boldly enough. More recent efforts to open up the current account cover a variety of approaches, from the eclectic Brazilian and Colombian policies to the fiercely textbookish Chilean ones. The former have included, besides exchange rate policy, selective export incentives, such as tax and credit subsidies, and direct deals with large companies while never completely dismantling import controls or reducing tariffs to almost free-trade levels. It is unclear to what extent the very rapid elimination of import-repressing mechanisms in Chile and Argentina have contributed to short-run output and investment sluggishness independently of cuts in real aggregate demand; it could be that the latter have been much more powerful than the former. What is clear is that the Brazilian and Colombian policy packages have been compatible both with reasonable growth rates in output and investment *and* with significant expansions in nontraditional exports. In the Colombian case, import liberalization came after substantial progress had been registered in export promotion.

While foreign trade policies of semi-industrialized countries have been exhaustively studied and discussed for at least twenty years, fewer efforts have been invested in the study of the capital account of their balance of payments other than those related to obsolete discussions of foreign aid and inconclusive debates on costs and benefits of direct foreign investment. As noted earlier, the interaction of liberalization of domestic financial markets with a highly efficient and ubiquitous international capital market generates pressures which policy makers could safely ignore during the exchange-control-riddled world of the 1950s. While much additional work is necessary in this area, it appears that a liberalization of the current account should take precedence over liberalizing the capital account. This approach is similar to that of the Bretton Woods charter and is consistent with the postwar practice of a number of small open European economies, such as in Denmark and Finland, which have maintained restrictions on the freedom of domestic residents to choose their financial portfolios among all international assets and have also exercised market as well as nonmarket controls over financial inflows. In some cases the exchange rate applicable to capital transactions has differed from that used for current account operations. These policies may be discussed as to efficacy (can they be enforced?) as well as to their long-term effects on economic efficiency. But their presence even in sophisticated economies indicates the seriousness of the concern that capital flows can generate disruptive short-run macroeconomic disturbances. Given the magnitude of domestic disequilibriums during the implementation of Southern Cone stabilization plans and the weakness of the monetary tools available to the authorities, the real costs of the disturbances that could follow a premature lifting of controls over international financial flows could be substantial.

One may also wonder whether local financial markets will be able to grow beyond marginal short-term intermediation without some "infant market" protection. Even in the United States, there are troublesome inequities in the fact that smaller domestic banks and their customers have less access to the Euro-currency market than do the large international banks and their customers; the former are said to absorb a disproportionate share of the burden of restrictive policies.[9] In the Southern Cone this dichotomy will overlap with that involving domestic firms and transnational enterprises.

Both in Argentina and Chile, the rebirth of a variety of financial instruments offering handsome returns has probably contributed to a sluggish rate of real capital formation. Indeed, the coexistence of high real interest

9. Statement by Henry C. Wallich to the House Committee on Banking, Finance, and Urban Affairs, July 12, 1979, p. 9.

rates with mediocre output and investment performance, as in Chile, raises the question as to which projects or activities generate returns sustaining the interest charges. The liberalization of the domestic financial market appears to have shifted the burden of the "inflation tax" from savers toward marginal investors, with substantial deadweight losses in the process. A more expansive domestic credit, at the expense of capital inflows, could reduce those losses while maintaining the gains that domestic financial liberalization has brought to savers, especially small and medium savers.

The International Framework

The rest of the world provides credit to a country with a current account deficit. It may do so in a variety of ways: by buying its short- or long-term paper, which may originate in its public or private sector; by buying real assets; and by other means. Under normal circumstances, these arrangements can be made following standard market procedures; that is, foreign finance will be hired paying the going market rate. At Bretton Woods it was thought that such a mechanism should be supplemented by an internationally controlled public source of short-term finance, cheaper and more stable than alternative private sources. Under the assumption that these funds would have a nontrivial social opportunity cost, access to them could not be automatic, so that the IMF, acting as the agent for the rest of the world, would impose conditions to ration their use. Presumably the rest of the world would have two major concerns when dealing with a given country: how that country's policies affect world economic conditions and how to get the money back. In dealing with small countries one at a time, the latter consideration would be paramount. Longer-term interactions between the small country and the rest of the world would presumably be handled via other mechanisms and institutions, such as the World Bank.

These broad notions, which probably command widespread support, in practice can be implemented with different degrees of liberality. Not all countries are equally likely to be borrowers from the IMF, so differences will arise regarding "conditionality." This was already true in 1944 and was reflected in the contrasting British and U.S. approaches about access to the IMF. Since then, the creditors' view has been reinforced, so that developing countries as a whole regard the IMF as a niggardly source of credit. Semi-industrialized countries, confident of their ability to obtain private finance on their own, have bypassed the IMF; Brazil has been an example of this attitude. Other countries have attempted such a stance, but either because of bad luck or internal mismanagement have had to return to the IMF as a lender of last resort and dispenser of an internationally credible "Good Housekeeping seal"; Peru is the obvious example. Under the latter circumstances, harsh conditions will be likely, in turn reinforcing the IMF's Gothic image.

Regardless of who is to blame for this state of affairs, the consequence has been an underutilization of IMF credit, prima facie evidence that something is amiss in the international framework within which the balance-of-payments adjustment of semi-industrialized countries occurs. Within the Southern Cone context, there is tangible evidence of this point. The IMF's purpose includes not only supplying adequate credit flows while adjustment takes place, but also providing a prudent stock of international liquidity. Even semi-industrialized countries that adopted somewhat more flexible exchange rate policies have maintained a strong demand for international reserves. Indeed, world economic conditions during the 1970s, from the floating of key currencies to the increase in the probability of various shocks, may have increased that demand. During 1977 and 1978, for example, the ratio of international reserves to merchandise imports in Argentina and Brazil reached levels substantially above averages for the past twenty years.[10] Even if this ratio had remained at average levels, rising world prices would have induced an increase in the demand for reserves. The contributions of SDRs and IMF credit in the increase in Argentine and Brazilian reserves have been small; most of the increase in liquidity has been obtained by a more expensive and precarious fashion, that is, expanding the foreign debt, mainly to private banks.

IMF-generated increases in international liquidity may improve the environment for stabilization plans, but they will not drastically help to minimize their short-term costs. Traditionally the IMF viewed stabilization plans within a one-year horizon, which tended to increase the chances of severe cuts in output and capital formation. In recent years, this position has gradually changed, and stabilization plans have come to be viewed with a longer-term horizon. New credit facilities have been used to support stretched-out adjustment programs, which attempt to parcel out

10. According to data on international reserves and imports reported in *International Financial Statistics* published by the IMF, various issues.

blame for balance-of-payments disturbances between exogenous shocks (that is, those arising from worsening terms of trade or earthquakes) and those created by domestic policies. Analysis has expanded beyond the simplest versions of the monetary approach to the balance of payments, which assume away underutilization of capacity and sectoral imbalances.

These positive, although modest, changes come after many years of criticism of the IMF's encouragement of stabilization plans, whose only targets appeared to be the punctual servicing of the foreign debt and balance-of-payments equilibrium, at whatever cost. During the early years of the Alliance for Progress and then in the late 1960s, at the time of the Pearson Report, the advice was frequently heard that stabilization efforts should be placed within the framework of development plans, and that the IMF and the World Bank should cooperate to this end.[11] The changes that have occurred in the international economy during the 1970s, including the greater bargaining power of some developing countries, have also contributed to the modification of the IMF's advice.

The crawling peg and export subsidies were two of the most successful policy instruments used by South American countries during the 1960s and 1970s. The IMF's predilection for exchange rate adjustments that were massive and presumably "once and for all" and its hostility to any semblance of multiple exchange rates made the IMF (or its Western Hemisphere department) oppose or at least frown on the use of those policy instruments. In these areas it appears that many in the IMF's staff are reluctant to abandon their old views, although it is difficult to document this conjecture. Indeed, the exact IMF role and advice in stabilization plans have remained shrouded in mystery, because its officials are reluctant to disclose details and documentation, pleading the need to protect the confidential nature of their links with governments. Permission to scholars to consult documents older than, say, ten years would contribute to clarify the IMF role in stabilization plans.

Regardless of the explanation for the IMF's modifications in its stabilization advice and facilities, its views could be expected to have declining influence in the policy making of, for example, Argentina and Brazil, in contrast to Jamaica and Zaire. Only gross mismanagement could place the former type of economy at the mercy of more or less enlightened IMF advice on short-term policy. Rather, the larger Southern Cone countries could be expected to have a greater voice in discussions about the IMF's

11. See *Partners in Development,* Report of the Commission on International Development (Praeger, 1969), p. 220.

role in such systemic issues as international liquidity, exchange rate surveillance, and supervision of international capital markets. It remains to be seen how these influential developing countries, with strong voices at the IMF's board of directors, will view staff proposals for stabilization plans in countries such as Jamaica and Zaire.

Comments by Ronald McKinnon

I shall comment briefly on Anne Krueger's chapter before turning to Carlos Diaz-Alejandro.*

In collaboration with Jagdish Bhagwati and the NBER,[12] Anne Krueger has done as much as anybody to document the need for the liberalization of foreign trade in developing countries. The incredible resource misallocations from variable tariffs, quota restrictions, and exchange controls are accompanied in most developing countries by a severe and generalized bias against exporting.

What is not worked out in Krueger's paper is the nature of appropriate financial policies that best complement the liberalization of foreign trade. The model that Krueger presents has no formal capital market; the banking system provides money as a means of payment but does not intermediate between savers and investors. The structure of domestic interest rates, bank reserves, and private foreign capital flows and the way they are systematically linked to foreign exchange policy are omitted. Besides noting that a liberalized domestic financial system is necessary to facilitate the sweeping resource reallocations associated with the removal of restrictions on foreign trade, I shall consider just one specific difficulty with Krueger's analysis that has financial roots.

After a major liberalization of foreign trade and (possibly) a discrete devaluation, Krueger suggests that forward assurance should be given to exporters by indexing the "real" exchange rate against inflation. A few countries have adopted a downward crawling peg—Chile in the late 1960s, Brazil and Colombia in the 1970s—that successfully insulated exporters from a profit squeeze in the face on ongoing domestic inflation. Although official policy toward the foreign exchange rate in these coun-

---

* Editors' note: Additional discussion of Anne Krueger's study appears in the final part of chapter 3.

12. Jagdish Bhagwati and Anne Krueger, eds., *Foreign Trade Regimes and Economic Development,* 10 vols. (NBER, 1975–78).

tries is not easy to spell out exactly, the rate of downward crawling was accelerated when domestic inflation was high (and vice versa) such that exporting was somewhat protected despite incomplete trade liberalization.

Unfortunately, such variable downward crawling can severely destabilize the domestic monetary system if liberalization of QRs, exchange controls, and internal usury restrictions on interest rates is complete! In a fully liberalized economy, continual variations in the rate of downward crawling will destabilize the domestic demand for money and lead to surges of financial capital flowing in or out of the economy that further upset control over the monetary base.[13] Paradoxically, only if liberalization is incomplete—QRs remain on many imports with tight exchange controls on capital flows—can a government feasibly "index" the real exchange rate against domestic inflation by variable downward crawling as in the three cases mentioned above. But to understand points such as this as applied to, say, liberalizations in the Southern Cone at the present time, the role of financial processes and capital markets must be incorporated into formal models of trade liberalization.

In the recent "shared" economic history of Chile, Uruguay, and Argentina, Carlos Diaz-Alejandro has usefully identified five stages: (1) populist euphoria, (2) economic collapse, (3) military coup and retrenchment, (4) partial liberalization and ongoing inflation, and (5) full liberalization and ending inflation.

A succinct way of characterizing the populist euphoria is that the government promises the people a level of real wages plus social security benefits that may exceed by, say, 50 percent the maximum feasible production capacity of the economy. The government then tries to make good on its promises, and to a limited extent succeeds for a year or two by heavy external borrowing (or by the drawing down of exchange reserves) and by a willingness to run down the domestic capital stock. Then uncontrolled internal borrowing by the government eventually is monetized by the central bank, as are the cheap credits going to newly "liberated"[14] farms and factories. But a populist tenet is that prices should not rise, only wages; hence, domestic price controls spread rapidly, and the exchange rate is prevented from depreciating. In Chile, the crawling-peg experiment of the 1960s was discontinued. Then QRs spread to virtually every cate-

---

13. This point is developed in more detail in R. McKinnon, "Monetary Control and the Crawling Peg," in J. Williamson, ed., *The Crawling Peg: Past Performance and Future Prospects* (forthcoming).

14. The opposite of "liberalized."

gory of tradable goods in order to ration the increasingly limited supplies of foreign exchange.

Stage 2 is economic paralysis: exports decline, vital intermediate inputs for protected domestic industry are cut off, the regular flow of food supplies from country to city is halted, and urban services such as transport, electricity, and communications are interrupted. Ordinary people (as well as the bourgeoisie) become badly frightened by the economic chaos, and civil disorder erupts with paramilitary groups from both right and left engaging in terrorist activities. Unfortunately, the elected populist government is too technically incompetent either to appreciate the consequences of what it did or to have any clear idea of what to do next. A takeover by a more authoritarian regime has become inevitable; the only question is whether it will be from the right or the left. Afterward, there is a widespread sense of relief giving the new government an implicit popular—albeit unconstitutional—mandate.

As a footnote to stages 1 and 2, real wages rise in stage 1 and then fall in stage 2 *before* the military takes over. In the last months of the populist regime, the real value of people's money wage claims (as measured by official price indices) bears no relationship to what they can actually buy in price-controlled commissaries—whose supplies of consumer goods become progressively more limited as queues become very long.

In stage 3, Diaz emphasizes that the IMF and private foreign creditors may well support the new government by rolling over old debts and injecting new capital in return for promises to rationalize—and most particularly to restrict credit expansion by the domestic banking system. Although this pattern is quite common, it did not happen in Chile in the first crucial years, 1973–76, of the military junta. Quite the contrary, because Chile was a political pariah, no new official credits were extended and direct borrowing in private capital markets was effectively closed to the military government. Moreover, huge debt amortizations inherited from the populist period actually had to be paid rather than simply refinanced. Hence, the harsh Chilean retrenchment in the 1975 recession was done neither with the guidance of the IMF, nor with reliance on inflows of capital from official international lending agencies.

In stage 4, all three countries managed to reduce public sector deficits greatly, reduce subsidized credits to favored borrowers, and raise real yields to domestic savers holding time deposits in domestic banks. Only Chile, however, has had a complete liberalization of foreign trade, with export restrictions, QRs on imports, and protective tariffs totally removed.[15] Uruguay and Argentina both removed onerous taxes on certain classes of exports, with Uruguay doing some import liberalization and Argentina none (as of October 1979).

As Diaz points out, the response of foreign trade to liberalization, coupled with some exchange rate rationalization, has been very buoyant and probably exceeded expectations in Chile with the development of new export products. Exchange reserves have been rebuilt, and private foreign credits are flooding in so that now there is danger of a surfeit of foreign exchange rather than a shortage. In Chile and Uruguay, real growth in GNP has been about 7 to 8 percent in 1978 and 1979 and was about 4 percent per year in 1976 and 1977. (Argentina has too little liberalization to really make a judgment regarding its relationship to real growth.)

How can one evaluate export-based rates of growth of this order of magnitude? Countries like Brazil and Chile had even higher measured rates of growth in GNP in some of their highly protected import-substitution phases of the 1950s and early 1960s. Diaz is disturbed that these current rates of growth in the Southern Cone are not high and that measured unemployment has not come down much—although productive employment is growing at a healthy rate. He notes that domestic investors remain cautious in the face of very high real borrowing rates of interest thrown up by the newly liberalized domestic financial system. And I would agree that voluntary domestic saving and investment are not yet robust.

For a standard of comparison, consider the common classroom theory of immiserizing growth. In the presence of trade distortions, it is easy to show that high "growth" in measured GNP can lead to a loss of real consumer welfare in the economy. Import substitution so reduces the efficiency of foreign trade that welfare could decline in the economy as industrialization proceeds. At the very least, growth in real welfare under a high tariff policy leads to much lower increases in potential consumption than measured increases in GNP would suggest.

But in a general move toward free trade, one can turn the immiserizing-growth argument on its head! Conventional measured growth in "real" GNP may well understate the potential welfare gains to the economy. On the one hand, households now have an increasingly broad consumption basket from which to choose. On the other hand, the modest investment that has taken place is more likely to be socially efficient; the high cost of

15. A uniform 10 percent revenue tariff is all that remains as of June 1979.

domestic borrowing and international competition in the goods market rule out subsidized investments that are not socially profitable—unlike the period of import substitution. At undistorted world prices, measured growth in GNP of 4 to 8 percent would seem like a reasonably good performance.

While doing fine on the "real" side, the liberalizing economies have all had great trouble in getting inflation under control: stage 5. Chile has brought its inflation rate down from "several hundred" percent in the middle 1970s to about 35 percent in 1979. Uruguay and Argentina are doing less well. Nevertheless, the Chileans want to phase out the inflation tax altogether because there is now no fiscal need for it. At the same time, uncertain inflation destabilizes the financial system and prevents the lengthening of the term structure of borrowing and lending. In all three economies, the failure to assert full monetary control and to curb inflation is now associated with the foreign exchanges. Why should this be the case?

As Diaz notes, when inflationary expectations are highly developed, financial liberalization requires very high nominal, and high real, rates of interest to equilibriate the supply of and demand for funds in the domestic capital market. But the very success of trade reform in improving the state of the balance of payments creates a financial disequilibrium; the expected exchange rate depreciation is much less than the nominal rate of interest in pesos and less than the anticipated ongoing domestic inflation. Thus the real rate of interest that foreigners see from investing in the liberalized economy is too high. An uncontrolled capital inflow overwhelms the central bank and causes undue expansion in the domestic monetary base. The fact that world rates of interest on dollar securities have been negative in real terms for the last several years exacerbates this problem.

One partial solution is to have an active downward crawl in the exchange rate according to a calendar, as all three countries tried in 1979. The rate of crawl is not linked to past rates of price inflation, but rather initially reflects the difference between foreign and domestic rates of interest so as to repel foreign capital to some moderate extent. However, the rate of active crawling must decline systematically to bring domestic inflation down to the world level. The theory is that interest differentials would be similarly reduced as the rate of crawling declines.

I agree with Diaz that using the exchange rate as a method of controlling the domestic price level—even in an economy as liberalized as Chile—has yet to prove fully satisfactory. One runs considerable risk of getting back to an overvalued currency. Yet the authorities cannot simply index the exchange rate against domestic inflation once liberalization is complete (see my comments above on Anne Krueger). Hence, there is a serious—and as yet unresolved—financial dilemma in the Southern Cone countries. This dilemma is much more pronounced in Uruguay and Argentina because they removed all exchange controls on foreign capital movements *before* they fully liberalized foreign trade, and they continue to suffer very high domestic inflation in the face of a virtually fixed exchange rate.

One moral seems to be that complete removal of exchange controls on foreign capital movements should come last in the liberalization process, whereas domestic financial liberalization should accompany any move toward free trade. In this respect, Chile has come closest to getting the order right and remains the purest example of a comprehensive economic liberalization in the Third World.

Discussion

Sidney Dell remarked that although liberalization and consequent capital inflows in the Southern Cone might remove the need for financial support from the international financial institutions, this conclusion could not be generalized (for example, to countries such as Uganda). *Gustav Papanek* stated that the regional bias of the discussion led to inadequate attention to factors such as the use of imported foodgrains to stabilize prices of wage goods, an important element in Asian experience.

Carlos Diaz-Alejandro, citing the monetary expansion derived from capital inflows, argued for greater use of domestic credit expansion instead of accumulation of foreign reserves (which earn little interest) in meeting any given target of monetary expansion. He noted the puzzlingly sluggish behavior of nominal interest rates, determined by either foreign interest rates combined with the exchange rate crawl (in the open economy) or by domestic inflation plus the real interest rate. The two converge if the inflation rate for home goods (in excess of foreign inflation) equals the rate of devaluation. If the price of home goods rises faster than that of tradables, however, there will be capital inflow. If the government indexes bonds with respect to the domestic price level, the result can be an interest rate very different from that consistent with foreign interest arbitrage. Brazil and Colombia dealt with this problem by using a variable crawling peg, giving more certainty for relative prices but not enough certainty to set up a one-sided bet for financial speculators. In the active or preannounced crawl used by Argentina and Chile, excessive certainty is provided to speculators, causing a loss of control over the domestic money supply, while not enough certainty is given to producers of tradable goods. Diaz doubted the complete effectiveness of capital controls, but noted that some countries such as Finland and Norway seem to use them successfully. With respect to McKinnon's hypothesis concerning fictitious growth at artificially high industrial prices, Diaz argued that no plausible recalculation of growth rates for Brazil or Colombia would show growth to have been primarily fictitious; McKinnon's high growth rates for Chile use the trough of the cycle as base period. As for McKinnon's proposed stage 5 of full liberalization, Diaz felt that it risked both giving up on the anti-inflationary goal as well as creating political backlash that could bring back stage 1, populist euphoria.

CHAPTER FIVE

Employment, Income Distribution, and Programs to Remedy Balance-of-Payments Difficulties

MONTEK S. AHLUWALIA *and* FRANK J. LYSY

BALANCE-OF-PAYMENTS difficulties sometimes appear to be an endemic disease among developing nations. Current economic orthodoxy teaches that, in order to qualify for short-term international loans to tide over the present crisis, the developing country should first enact a package of "reforms" to remedy the situation in the medium term. The basic features common to most of these packages are that the government agrees to devalue the currency and to follow a program of fiscal and monetary restraint to deflate the economy. In practice, the IMF is usually the immediate party which must extend the international loans and, therefore, decide if the package of reforms will suffice.

Almost always, the governments (whether of developing or developed countries) forced to enact such programs complain to the IMF about these conditions, saying that they will increase unemployment, lower the real national income, harm the distribution of income, and may not even improve the balance of trade. Empirically, it seems they have often been correct on this[1] but the IMF has normally not been moved by such complaints. It should be immediately stated, however, that it is not clear

Much of the work reported on in this paper was undertaken at the Development Research Center, World Bank. Support of that institution is gratefully acknowledged. The views expressed in this paper are those of the authors and do not necessarily reflect those of the World Bank or the present institutional affiliations of the authors.

1. Richard N. Cooper, "An Assessment of Currency Devaluation in Developing Countries," in Gustav Ranis, ed., *Government and Economic Development* (Yale University Press, 1971), pp. 472–513.

that the IMF, given the tools at its command and its legal charter, has had much power to respond in any way other than it has. But what this calls for is a reexamination of the tools and the charter, so that such constraints can be eliminated.

Part of the problem lies in traditional economic theory, which concludes that the complaints of the developing countries' governments are unfounded. Traditional theory would say that the IMF package is the correct one to remedy balance-of-trade deficits, since the devaluation will lead to increased profitability, and therefore increased production, of export goods and import-competing goods. Production in these sectors will be spurred, and devaluation by itself is therefore *necessarily* expansionary. These expansionary effects would then be countered by the second half of the standard package: the contractionary fiscal and monetary policies. Finally, the traditional theory does agree that real incomes may occasionally fall in the short term as a consequence, but this is due only to the nation "living beyond its means" previously. The medicine may be bitter, they would agree, but the only alternative is massive, outright charity.

In recent years, certain economists have begun to argue that there are, indeed, problems with the traditional view. By analysing the problem in a more macro- or general-equilibrium frame than the essentially partial-equilibrium argument stated above, a good theoretical case has been made that devaluation can be contractionary, in and of itself, and that when accompanied by explicitly contractionary policies the result may be a deep recession. Profitability in general can fall; investment in new production facilities can collapse as a result; and while the balance of trade may improve in the short term as imports fall with the decline in incomes, the long-term prospects are bleak as production and investment stagnate. The new argument does not say that this will necessarily be the outcome, but that it is a possible one.

The theoretical analysis of these possibilities has been developed by Richard Cooper, Paul Krugman and Lance Taylor, Carlos Diaz-Alejandro, and others.[2] The distinction between short- and long-term conse-

2. Richard N. Cooper, "Devaluation and Aggregate Demand in Aid-Receiving Countries," in J. N. Bhagwati and others, eds., *Trade, Balance of Payments, and Growth* (Amsterdam: North-Holland, 1971); Paul Krugman and Lance Taylor, "Contractionary Effects of Devaluation," *Journal of International Economics,* vol. 8, pp. 445–56; and Carlos Diaz-Alejandro, "A Note on the Impact of Devaluation and the Redistributive Effect," *Journal of Political Economy,* vol. 71, pp. 577–80.

quences has been forcefully brought out in a nontechnical paper by Richard Eckaus.[3] What has been lacking in this work, however, is an analysis of how likely some of the possible outcomes might be. While it is useful to know, for example, that deflation is possible as a consequence of a devaluation, it is much more useful to know when deflation is likely and how severe it is likely to be.

This chapter will try to answer some of these questions. No new theoretical ground will be broken; rather, an attempt will be made to quantify some of the possible responses of a developing country's economy to programs of devaluation and stabilization designed to remedy balance-of-payments difficulties. To do this, two numerical models developed by the authors of Malaysia will be used.

Among our important results, we will find that deflation as the consequence of a devaluation is a genuine possibility in some economies. Devaluation will have important effects on real incomes and employment that should not be ignored. It will also be found that devaluation is basically a clumsy tool in effecting a balance-of-payments improvement, because of the higher import costs that accompany it. Policies designed to work directly on exports will be more efficient, if such are possible. With regard to distribution per se, as opposed to movements in the real incomes of certain classes, it will be found that distribution is fairly insensitive to the programs considered. Real incomes *do* fluctuate a great deal, but under the assumptions that we will generally make with regard to the pricing of exports, profits and wages will move up or down together, with only small changes in the relative incomes of the two groups. Finally, it will be found that for quite reasonable parameters, the short- and long-term consequences of policies to improve the balance of payments are often opposed. The balance of payments will improve in the short term when the economy is deflated, which may result either deliberately or unwittingly; however, this is often accompanied by decreased profitability of investment, which worsens the long-run position.

It should be stressed that these results are not really new, nor are they definite consequences. What is new is the analysis of what conditions or parameter values will lead to them. Hard and fast conclusions will not be presented; rather a framework will be developed of a fairly general nature, which can then be applied to particular situations of interest.

3. Richard S. Eckaus, "Is the IMF Guilty of Malpractice?" *Institutional Investor,* September 1977, pp. 13–15.

This chapter will first briefly summarize some of the received theory on ways to improve the balance of payments and the likely consequences of such actions. It will then look at these issues in a quantitative framework through numerical exercises with each of the two models.

A Summary of Received Theory

There are several basic results of received theory (as extended by Cooper, Diaz-Alejandro, Krugman and Taylor, and others)[4] that are useful to state clearly at the outside. The purpose of this is to establish the context in which the model results should be viewed.

First, it should be clear that a devaluation of, say, 10 percent, will leave real wages the same if, as a consequence, money wages respond by rising 10 percent. Employment levels and production would therefore not change; the competitive positions of exporting and import-competing industries would be exactly the same as before the devaluation, and all that would result is that wages, prices, and nominal magnitudes would be 10 percent higher. The devaluation would have been completely thwarted in its goal of improving the balance of payments.[5]

Furthermore, if it can be assumed that *real* levels of investment, government expenditure, and consumption are independent of the general price level,[6] then no real effects at all will result from the devaluation. There would be no reallocations across tradable and nontradable sectors, for example. These assumptions are, perhaps, reasonable for many developing countries, and are, in fact, the ones made in the models to be discussed below. It should be recognized, however, that they imply that real balance effects are unimportant, that monetary policy is either neutral or does not matter, and so on.

In recognition of this, it might be noted that if one assumes, as a good neoclassical economist would, that full employment is maintained in an economy through variation in money wages, then a devaluation will always be frustrated. The economy is assumed to start at full employment,

4. Cooper, "Devaluation and Aggregate Demand"; Krugman and Taylor, "Contractionary Effects of Devaluation"; and Diaz-Alejandro, "A Note on the Impact of Devaluation and the Redistributive Effect."

5. Michael Bruno, "Exchange Rates, Import Costs and Wage-Price Dynamics," *Journal of Political Economy,* vol. 86, pp. 379–403.

6. As would follow from any system of demand equations which are linearly homogeneous in prices and nominal incomes.

though perhaps with a balance-of-payments deficit, the currency is devalued relative to others, and the level of money wages will then rise in the exact proportion as the devaluation to bring the economy back to the original state of (full) employment. The balance-of-payments deficit (when expressed in a foreign currency) will remain exactly as before. The devaluation would be completely frustrated.

Such an analysis is not terribly interesting to pursue, partly because there is little more to be said, and partly because of the basic unreality of the assumptions. Economies, especially developing countries' economies, are not in a continuous state of full employment, and money wage rates do not respond quickly and smoothly in such a fashion as to match, always and necessarily, a devaluation. There are various theories on how money wage rates would respond to such a shock, but few would predict they would necessarily follow in step with the devaluation. Perhaps the most common theory is that, in the short term at least, the money wage rates would be constant. Another common theory would be that they respond in such a way as to keep constant the real value of the wages, defined in terms of some consumption bundle. This real consumption wage will differ from the real wage defined in terms of what labor produces (which we will call the real product wage) because even in a one-sector model imports will enter. And there is no reason to assume that the real product wage (that is, the wage in terms of steel or whatever labor produces) should be constant.

When one allows the possibility of less than full employment, a much more interesting set of results can be found. For example, it is easily shown that devaluation may or may not improve the balance of payments, depending on, among other things, the values of the price elasticities of demand for exports and imports. If, for example, the export price elasticity is less than one, total export revenues will fall as a result of the devaluation. The old and well-known Marshall-Lerner conditions have to be satisfied. Although empirical studies have often found that the Marshall-Lerner conditions are not satisfied for many developing countries' economies, such studies are usually ignored by those recommending devaluation. In our models, the values of certain of the key parameters will determine whether these conditions are met.

A more recent finding in the theoretical literature (although not to government officials) has been the conclusion that devaluation, by itself, can depress or can stimulate the economy, depending again on the values of a few key parameters. The best demonstrations of this are found in the papers cited previously of Cooper, Diaz-Alejandro, and Krugman and Taylor.[7]

Several factors lead to the result that devaluation may be contractionary. First, for many economies the factors that traditional theory uses to predict expansion may be weak. Traditional theory predicts that exports would be stimulated by the devaluation, as would import-competing industries. In many developing countries, however, exports are dominated by primary commodities whose supply is rigidly limited in the short run by sector-specific capital, such as the number of rubber trees. At the same time, imports have often been reduced by developing countries' governments to the minimal necessary imports of raw materials or capital goods for which there were no domestic industries that could come close to competing. If there were viable domestic sectors that had the possibility of competing with imports, developing countries' governments would normally have previously promoted such sectors through the use of prohibitive tariffs, quotas, or other such measures to the point where such imports would be negligible.[8]

With the stimulative forces weak, the depressant forces of a devaluation can easily dominate. There are several possible depressant factors; the two which are most often cited are the effects of higher import prices, and the possibility of a redistribution of income from low savers to high savers. The higher import prices that result from a devaluation act as a depressant just as a higher import tariff (or any other tax) would. Standard Keynesian reasons can be cited for this.

The redistributive effect results when it is assumed that exports will be sold at or close to their original prices, expressed in foreign terms, which translates into higher domestic prices after the devaluation. Profits would then rise, even after taking into account higher costs of imported inputs, since imports make up only a part of total costs. Real wages have fallen, however, due to the higher import costs and higher prices of export goods which may, perhaps, also be consumed domestically (as in the case of beef in Argentina). There has been a redistribution of real income from wages to profits. If one assumes, as is reasonable, that there is a greater

7. Cooper, "Devaluation and Aggregate Demand"; Krugman and Taylor, "Contractionary Effects of Devaluation"; and Diaz-Alejandro, "A Note on the Impact of Devaluation and the Redistributive Effect."

8. It should be clear that we are not taking a stand, one way or the other, on whether developing countries' governments *should* have pursued such policies, or whether they had any choice. We are just trying to lay out the essential facts as they now stand for most of the developing countries.

marginal propensity to consume out of wages than out of profits, then consumption demand will decline even if national income would have otherwise remained the same.

Crucial to the redistributive effect is the assumption made with regard to how exports are priced. Implicit in the redistributive argument is the assumption that the world prices of the export goods are fixed, while the supply is fairly limited. Windfalls, which accrue to domestic firms, are thus generated by the devaluation. If one had assumed neoclassical marginal cost pricing of the exports, then such windfalls would not be generated. Rather, we would have a neoclassical theory of distribution, where the relative shares would shift according to the shape of the supply functions. The only windfall that could be said to have been generated by the devaluation would be one that would arise if the export demand elasticity was less than infinity, and it would accrue to foreigns. The foreigners would then be receiving the same physical volume of exports (or more) at a lower price.

If the economy contracts as a result of the devaluation, several important consequences follow. First, it is likely that profits will fall, or at least not rise, by as much as the cost of producing new investment goods, if the redistributive effect is weak. As noted in the paragraph above, this depends on the export-pricing assumption. If profits fall relative to the cost of producing new investment goods, then by several theories of investment new investment will decline.[9] Employment and domestic production also fall, as the direct result of the contractionary effects of the devaluation as well as of the lower investment. With lower incomes, imports fall. There may therefore be an improvement in the balance of payments in the short term, but the cost is greater unemployment, stagnation, and slower growth in the long run. The long-term competitiveness of the economy is also hurt by the lower investment, which points to renewed balance-of-payments difficulties later.

A last point should be made about the wage-rate assumption. The models used below will assume that, in at least the short run, nominal wages are fixed with regard to changes in the exchange rate. The only reasonable competing assumptions that could be made would be that either the real product wage or the real consumption wage was fixed. It was previously noted that there is no basis for assuming a fixed real product wage (why should wages be fixed in terms of semiconductors?). Even

---

9. This statement is rough. Qualifications are necessary to make it rigorous. This theory is discussed later in this chapter.

if there were, such an assumption would lead to the conclusion that a devaluation will always be completely frustrated, given not unreasonable assumptions on how domestic demands respond to changes in the price level.

A stronger case can be made for a fixed real consumption wage. Such an assumption is in keeping with that of a long line of development economists (such as Sir Arthur Lewis). However, it can easily be seen that the effect of such an assumption would be the same as assuming a fixed real product wage when analyzing a devaluation. Suppose there is a 10 percent devaluation. This will raise the price of consumption goods, due to the imported component, and will therefore lead to a *rise* in the nominal wage. One can already see that assuming a fixed real consumption wage will be *less* favorable to the case for devaluation than assuming a fixed nominal wage.

The rise in the nominal wage will touch off a wage-price spiral (assuming marginal cost pricing) which will only end when the real consumption wage is back at its original level. This will occur when nominal wages have risen by 10 percent with the 10 percent devaluation, and, at this point also, the real product wage will be back at its original level. The devaluation will have been completely frustrated again.

Although it is interesting to find that such wage-price spirals will result from a devaluation under certain assumptions, there is little more that can be said about them. But, as this analysis shows, a devaluation will "succeed" only if wages do not catch up with prices, that is, only if employed labor sees a reduction in its real wage. Cooper noted this,[10] and also found that empirically such a reduction did occur in most of the cases of actual devaluation that he examined.

A One-Sector Model

Introduction and Presentation of the Basic Model

The macro analysis of devaluation is the most interesting for the issues we will be examining, and even when sectoral effects are considered the macro context often dominates. A simple, one-sector model serves best to present such issues.

10. Cooper, "An Assessment of Currency Devaluation in Developing Countries."

Before going into the actual equations of the model, it is useful to state some of the main features.[11] There is one good produced by the economy, which can be used interchangeably for consumption, investment, or exports. Labor, capital, and imported inputs are used to produce this good, and a two-level structure of production is assumed. Labor and capital combine at the lower level to produce value-added; imports then combine with value-added at the upper level to produce domestic output. A constant elasticity of substitution (CES) function is assumed to hold at the lower level, while fixed proportions are assumed at the upper level. That is, we assume here that all possibilities of import-competing industries substituting for imports, when imports become somewhat less price competitive after a devaluation, have been previously used up. All the effects of increased price competitiveness have been placed in the export demand function. Exports are assumed to face a world demand curve of constant price elasticity, and the value of this price elasticity will be one of the crucial parameters that will determine the character of the results.

As noted previously, the export pricing assumption is a crucial one in determining the distributive effects of a devaluation. In a macromodel where (1) the same good is used for exports as for other uses, (2) the neoclassical assumption is made that output will expand to the point where the price is equal to the marginal cost, and (3) exports face a less than infinitely elastic demand curve, the only reasonable assumption is that after a devaluation, the price of the export good (in foreign terms) will fall, and production and sales will expand until once again price equals marginal cost. At the new equilibrium, the price to foreigners (converted through the new exchange rate) is the same as to domestic users, and producers are indifferent about who buys their products.

As a result of this, we have a strictly neoclassical theory of distribution. Changes in the factor shares will depend on the shape of the product supply curve, which in our CES case depends only on the elasticity of substitution assumed.

Labor is assumed to be available at a fixed money wage. As stated previously, assuming labor is always fully employed is boring, even if one believes it. Capital, however, is limited in supply, and this leads to upward-sloping supply curves. In the CES case, the shape will be like those shown

11. The model is essentially the same as that developed in Frank J. Lysy, "Investment and Employment with Unlimited Labor: The Role of Aggregate Demand," *Journal of Development Economics*, 1980. The article contains a more complete description.

Figure 5-1. *Form of the CES Supply Function*

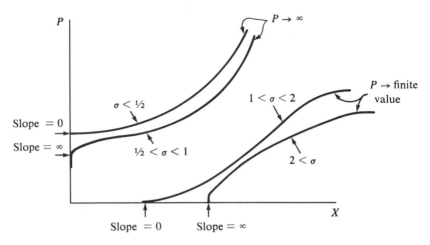

in figure 5-1.[12] As is seen, the form basically depends on the value of the elasticity of substitution, σ. The reason we bring this up here is that it is easy to see from figure 5-1 that when output expands the share of profits will rise if the elasticity of substitution is less than unity and will fall if the elasticity exceeds unity. This is our neoclassical theory of distribution.

Finally, to keep the model simple, we have abstracted from government. Government expenditure has been combined with investment, and taxes have usually been added to profit income. All domestic savings will come out of profit income.

The equations of the model are given in table 5-1. Equations 1a and 1b are the CES unit cost and production functions. Given the marginal cost conditions (that a factor will be hired until its price is equal to the value of its marginal product), one can derive equations 4 and 5. These can also be gotten directly from Shephard's Lemma. Given equations 4 and 5, it is easy to see that equations 1a and 1b are dual to each other. Thus, in any equations counting exercise to see if the system is determined, one must be dropped.

The domestic price of imports, P_M, will be the local currency/foreign currency exchange rate, r_F, times the world price of these goods (equation 2). The price of output, P_X, will then be as in equation 3, given the as-

---

12. For a derivation of this, see the appendix to chapter 3 of Frank J. Lysy, "A Keynesian Model of Malaysia" (Ph.D. dissertation, Stanford University, 1981).

Table 5-1. *The One-Sector Model*

Equation number	Equation
1a	$P_V = [\alpha_L^\sigma P_L^{1-\sigma} + \alpha_K^\sigma P_K^{1-\sigma}]^{1/(1-\sigma)}$
1b	$V = [\alpha_L L^{(\sigma-1)/\sigma} + \alpha_K K^{(\sigma-1)/\sigma}]^{\sigma/(\sigma-1)}$
2	$P_M = r_{F\pi} \pi_M$
3	$P_X = vP_V + mP_M$
4	$L/V = \left[\dfrac{\alpha_L P_V}{P_L}\right]^\sigma$
5	$K/V = \left[\dfrac{\alpha_K P_V}{P_K}\right]^\sigma$
6	$Y_L = P_L L$
7	$Y_K = P_K K$
8	$P_X C = c_L Y_L + c_K Y_K$
9	$X = C + I + E$
10	$E = A \cdot \left[\dfrac{r_F}{P_X}\right]^\varepsilon$
11	$I = \bar{I}$
12	$M = mX$
13	$V = vX$

sumption of fixed coefficients. If one scales so that all prices are initially one, then $v + m = 1.0$.

Incomes are determined in equations 6 and 7, and consumption in equation 8, where we have allowed the possibility of differing propensities to consume out of wage and profit income. The total demand for output is determined in equation 9, where export demand comes from equation 10 and investment demand from equation 11. The export demand function is a constant price elasticity function, where ε is that price elasticity, and A is a constant scaling parameter. Equations 12 and 13 determine the demand for value-added and imports, given the output level.

The model is a simple one, but not so simple that explicit expressions can be found for the price of output or its production level. The best that can be done is to solve for two expressions, which can be interpreted as aggregate supply and demand curves. It is easiest to work with value-added for this purpose.

By rearranging equation 5 to obtain an expression for P_K, inserting this into 1a, and solving for P_V, one obtains

$$(14) \qquad P_V = \alpha_L^{\sigma/(1-\sigma)}[1 - \alpha_K(V/K)^{(1-\sigma)/\sigma}]^{1/(\sigma-1)}P_L.$$

This is basically a supply function, with P_V a function of V and other variables which are all exogenous. The form of this function is that shown in figure 5-1. Not surprisingly, P_V is a function only of the *ratio* of V to K in this constant returns system, and is a linear function of P_L, the only variable factor in the production of value-added.

The demand for output can be gotten by starting basically with the material balance (equation 9) and substituting for each component of demand. The expression that will be obtained is:

(15)

$$V = v\left[\frac{c_L\alpha_L^\sigma P_L^{1-\sigma}P_V^\sigma V}{vP_V + mP_M} + \frac{c_K\alpha_K KP_V(V/K)^{1/\sigma}}{vP_V + mP_M} + I + A\left(\frac{r_F}{vP_V + mP_M}\right)^\epsilon\right],$$

where the first term in the brackets is consumption demand out of wage income (which will sometimes be referred to as C_L), the second term is consumption demand out of profit income (C_K), the third is investment demand, and the fourth is export demand.

The basic data used for the numerical simulations are presented in table 5-2, where it should be noted that government demand has been combined with investment demand. The numbers are for Malaysia in

Table 5-2. *Base Data, Malaysia, 1970*

All nominal amounts in millions of 1970 Malaysian dollars

a.	$V =$	12,491	V	$=$ 12,491	$V =$ 12,491		$v =$	0.7296145
	$C =$	7,328	Y_L	$=$ 6,046	$M =$ 4,629		$m =$	0.2703855
	$I =$	4,478	Y_K	$=$ 6,445	$X =$ 17,120			
	$E =$	5,314						
	$-M =$	$-4,629$						
b.	$K =$	32,096	$K/V = 2.5695$					
	$L =$	6,046						

c.   Total investment $= 4,478 =$ Total savings
                        $-685 =$ Balance-of-trade deficit
                       $5,163 =$ Domestic savings

d. $c_L = 1.0$
     $c_K = 0.1989139$

e.   Initial price scalings
     $P_L = \pi_M = P_M = r_F = 1.0$
     $P_V = P_X = 1.0$
     $P_K = Y_K/K = 0.2008038 =$ profit rate

f. $\alpha_L = 0.616474$ when $\sigma = 1.5$
     $\alpha_K = 0.376707$ when $\sigma = 1.5$

1970 and are derived from an aggregation of the numbers used in a multi-sectoral model developed by the authors.[13]

Algebraic Derivation of the Effect on Output of a Devaluation

The model as presented above can be solved algebraically to find the impact effect on output levels of a devaluation. One can basically work from equation 15 for the demand for value-added to find how V will change after a devaluation. The change in V will have second-round effects, of course, through a resulting change in P_V (equation 14), but we will not examine such general equilibrium relations here. It is not difficult to see (by Le Chatelier's Principle) that when, say, the impact effect is a rise in V, and the rise in V leads to a rise in P_V, the resulting rise in P_V will not be so strong as to lead to a reduction in V. That is, if the impact effect of a devaluation is such as to raise or lower output, then output will still move in the same direction after interactions with the price level are taken into account. The numerical simulations of a devaluation which will be reported on below will, of course, take full account of the general equilibrium effect.

The form of equation 15 is as follows:

$$(16) \qquad V = f(r_F, V).$$

When we take the partial derivative of equation 15 with respect to the exchange rate, we should take into account not only the direct effects of the exchange rate on production, but also the full indirect effects through consumption. Therefore, consumption will be a function of r_F and V:

$$(17) \qquad C = g(r_F, V).$$

Taking partial derivatives and solving for $\partial V / \partial r_F$ yields:

$$(18) \qquad \frac{\partial V}{\partial r_F} = \frac{\dfrac{\partial f}{\partial r_F} + \dfrac{\partial f}{\partial C}\dfrac{\partial g}{\partial r_F}}{1 - \dfrac{\partial f}{\partial C}\dfrac{\partial g}{\partial V}}.$$

This expression can be easily interpreted. The numerator shows the effect on V due directly to a devaluation ($\partial f / \partial r_F$) and indirectly through the effect on consumption. The denominator can best be interpreted as a

13. For details on their derivation, see Montek S. Ahluwalia and Frank J. Lysy, "A General Equilibrium Model of Malaysia," Development Research Center, World Bank, 1979.

multiplier, which arises due to the dependence of consumption on the level of production.

Inserting the required partials into equation 18, simplifying slightly, and using the initial price scalings of unity will yield:

(19)
$$\frac{\partial V}{\partial r_F} = \frac{v[\epsilon E - m(C + \epsilon E)]}{1 - \dfrac{C_L + C_K/\sigma}{X}}.$$

The interpretation of this equation is not difficult. Note that the first term in the numerator is just the traditional expansionary effect on exports, which will be stronger the greater the price elasticity of demand for exports. The second term, which enters with a negative sign, is the contractionary effect of higher import prices. This will affect the two components of output whose level can vary, consumption and exports (with exports being multiplied by their demand elasticity again), and will be more important the greater the import coefficient, m. The effect arises because both consumption and exports are inverse functions of P_X ($= vP_V + mP_M$, see equation 15) when all else is held constant, and P_X will rise due to the import component after a devaluation.

The denominator of equation 19 is best interpreted as a multiplier. The denominator is basically one minus the propensity to consume, though the "propensity to consume" of the expression is not quite the normal one. The elasticity of substitution enters, where normally (that is, in a simple Keynesian model where wages and profits are not distinguished) one would have expected just the marginal propensity to consume (equal to the average propensity for a linear consumption function with no intercept). The reason for this arises in how wages and profits differ in their response to changes in the level of output. Although it is mathematically possible for σ to be so low that the multiplier could become negative, it is unlikely. It is impossible if all profits are saved (that is, C_K is zero).

More likely, and hence more interesting, is the possibility that the numerator in equation 19 is negative, leading to a contraction after a devaluation. From the numerator of equation 19 (using our initial price scalings), the critical value for the export price elasticity of demand will be

(20)
$$\epsilon^* = \frac{mC}{E(1 - m)}.$$

If the export elasticity is, in fact, less than this, the devaluation will be contractionary. For our data for Malaysia (table 5-2), the critical value will be 0.511. This critical value will be higher the greater the level of consumption or the import coefficient (because the higher import costs are contractionary) and will be lower the greater the level of exports (because the devaluation will cause exports to expand).

The critical export elasticity is not really small at 0.5, and it is quite possible that in many situations the export elasticity would, in fact, be less than this. Note that here we are primarily concerned with the short-term elasticity. The possibility of an economic recession within the current year following a devaluation is of concern, and it is often unlikely that new export markets can be found in such a short time to make the elasticity very high. Econometric evidence suggests that a low export elasticity should be expected in such circumstances.

We have seen here that the net effect of a devaluation can be contractionary. The possibility arises due to the contractionary effects of higher import prices, which may not be fully offset if exports do not respond rapidly to their increased price advantage. For Malaysia, the critical export elasticity was found to be about 0.5. It should be noted, however, that this analysis has so far assumed no import substitution will occur as a result of the increased price competitiveness of domestic industry. To the extent that such is possible, the critical export elasticity would be lower.

Numerical Simulations of Policies Designed to Improve the Balance of Payments

Not many more interesting results can be easily obtained through working only with the equations of the model. But interesting games can be played by numerically simulating the model using the national accounts of a fairly typical developing country. Malaysia was chosen since it exhibits the main structural features of the developing countries' economies we are interested in. It is a small, semi-industrialized, trade-dependent economy that earns a major, though declining, share of its export revenues from a few primary commodities. Malaysia is atypical primarily in its luck with export prices in recent years.

The policies this section will examine are a devaluation, a shift in the world demand for exports, a reduction in investment (and government consumption) demand, and a redistribution of product from its use for investment (and government consumption) to the export use. Various combinations will also be examined, and the effects of alternative assumptions on the values of certain key parameters (mainly the export elasticity)

Table 5-3. Effects of a 10 Percent Devaluation

Expressed as a ratio to base

	r_F	σ	ϵ	P_V (1)	P_X (2)	V (3)	E (4)	D_F (5)	L (6)	Y_K (7)	C_L (8)	C_K (9)	θ_L (10)	θ_K (11)
A. Base	1.0	...	...	1.0	1.0	12,491	5,314	−685	6,046	6,445	6,046	1,282	0.4840	0.5160
B. Variations in ϵ														
1.	1.1	1.5	0.0	0.9798	1.0123	0.9719	1.0000	0.5711	0.9426	0.9613	0.9311	0.9497	0.9899	1.0095
2.	1.1	1.5	0.5	0.9994	1.0266	0.9991	1.0351	0.7426	0.9982	0.9988	0.9723	0.9729	0.9998	1.0002
3.	1.1	1.5	1.0	1.0135	1.0369	1.0191	1.0609	0.8707	1.0398	1.0264	1.0028	0.9899	1.0068	0.9936
4.	1.1	1.5	3.0	1.0446	1.0596	1.0647	1.1189	1.1661	1.1367	1.0892	1.0728	1.0279	1.0221	0.9793
5.	1.1	1.5	10.0	1.0755	1.0821	1.1119	1.1783	1.4782	1.2401	1.1543	1.1461	1.0667	1.0372	0.9651
C. Variations in σ														
1.	1.1	0.5	1.0	1.0207	1.0422	1.0096	1.0555	0.9353	1.0200	1.0404	0.9787	0.9983	0.9899	1.0095
2.	1.1	0.8	1.0	1.0179	1.0401	1.0133	1.0576	0.9099	1.0278	1.0349	0.9882	0.9950	0.9965	1.0033
3.	1.1	3.0	1.0	1.0088	1.0335	1.0254	1.0644	0.8286	1.0526	1.0173	1.0186	0.9843	1.0178	0.9833

Symbols used

r_F = foreign exchange rate (domestic currency/foreign currency)
σ = capital/labor elasticity of substitution
ϵ = price elasticity of demand for exports
P_V = price of value-added
P_X = price of exports
V = value-added level
E = export level

D_F = balance-of-trade deficit in foreign currency
L = labor employment (= wage bill)
Y_K = income to capital
C_L = real consumption level of labor
C_K = real consumption level of capital
θ_L = share of wages in national income
θ_K = share of profits in national income

will be included. The model was solved on a programmable hand calcula-tor by iteratively solving equations 14 and 15 for P_V and V until an equilibrium was found.

The effects of a 10 percent devaluation are shown in table 5-3, under alternative assumptions on the values of the export elasticity and of the capital/labor elasticity of substitution. The effects on most of the endog-enous variables are shown, and are expressed as a ratio to their base values. The first two columns show the effects on the two main prices: that of value-added and that of output. The price of imported goods in domestic terms, P_M, will always rise by 10 percent in a devaluation, and therefore P_X will always rise by more than P_V if P_V rises by less than 10 percent (as it does in all the experiments shown).

Columns 3 and 4 show the effects on value-added and exports. Total output, X, and imports, M, will always rise or fall in the same proportion as V and hence are not shown separately here. Column 5 shows the effect on the balance-of-trade deficit expressed in terms of foreign prices. This happened to be in surplus in 1970, but note that, for simplicity, we have assumed that all profits earned by foreign corporations were saved and not transferred abroad under the current account. This is all accounting, however, and a different system of accounting would not affect any of the results.

The last six columns show the effects of each experiment on the two classes, labor and capital. Column 6 gives the effect on employment (which will be the same as on total wage income, given the assumption of a fixed money wage rate); column 7 shows the effect on the level of nominal profits; columns 8 and 9 on the real consumption levels of labor and capital; and columns 10 and 11 on the shares in national income (value-added) of labor and capital. By definition, these two shares always sum to unity, so if one rises, the other must fall.

As was seen previously, a devaluation will be deflationary given the Malaysian data if the export elasticity is about one-half or less. Two such cases are shown in lines B1 and B2. When the export elasticity is close to the critical value of about 0.5, the increased demand from exports just offsets the reduced demand from real consumption. Therefore, real out-put levels stay the same, the price of value-added remains the same, and employment and profits remain the same. However, the higher cost of im-ports has pushed up the price of output, P_X, and this factor was respon-sible for the decline in real consumption despite the constancy of domes-tic production and employment. Furthermore, since the price of exports on world markets has fallen to 0.9333 ($= 1.0266$ of $P_x \div 1.10$ of r_F) and real exports rose by only 3.51 percent, total export revenue has fallen, in foreign currency terms. Import costs in foreign currency has remained the same, so the balance of trade worsens. The devaluation has made the balance of trade worse, and has at the same time reduced real income levels in the economy. It is tempting to ascribe the worsening of the balance of trade to the fact that Marshall-Lerner conditions have not been met, but it is not just this, as will be seen below when we examine the case of an export elasticity of 1.0.

Matters are even worse if the export elasticity is truly zero. A sharp contraction results, with real output falling about 2.8 percent and employment falling by an even greater percentage of about 5.7 percent.[14] Profits also contract, and since the price of output has risen, the real levels of consumption by labor fall 6.9 percent, and real consumption by capital falls 5.0 percent. The price of value-added falls in the contraction,[15] but *not* by so much that the price of output, P_x, would also fall. P_x is kept up by the 10 percent rise in the cost of imports. Export receipts fall in the devaluation, but export volume remains the same if the export price elasticity of demand is zero, so the balance of trade worsens, despite the fact that imports have fallen in proportion with output in the recession. Prospects of gain from a devaluation, both in terms of real income levels and in terms of the effect on the balance of payments, appear to be dismal when the export elasticity is low. And such appears to be the case for many developing countries. Stagflation results, with higher prices accompanied by lower output and employment.

The case of an export elasticity equal to unity is shown in line B3. The Marshall-Lerner condition is just met in such a case, but it is seen that the balance of trade still deteriorates in terms of foreign currency. The reason is that higher import prices reduce the competitiveness of exports, just as they raise the price of all domestic goods, so export volume does not rise by 10 percent after the 10 percent devaluation even though the elasticity is unity. Furthermore, imports rise by about 1.9 percent as the economy

---

14. Employment will always fall by a greater percentage than output in a contraction, and rise by a greater percentage in an expansion. The reason is that labor and capital combine to produce value-added in our neoclassical production function, and capital can be thought of as always being "fully employed." Furthermore, since the initial wage and profit shares are about equal, the percentage change in employment will always be about twice the percentage change in output.

15. It is not difficult to see that P_V will always move in the same direction as V in this model. See equation 14.

now expands with the export elasticity above the critical value of about one-half, contributing to the deterioration in the balance of trade.

It might be remarked that, due to our one-sector assumption, we have unfairly assumed that export goods exhibit the same import intensity as consumption goods and investment goods, and that this is a major cause of the balance-of-trade deterioration in this experiment. This is true, and we may be approaching the limits of what can be drawn from a macrosystem. However, as many developing countries' governments have found to their dismay, it is not completely safe to assume the competitiveness of exports will be unaffected when tariffs on imports are raised. Furthermore, even in an economy such as Malaysia's, where the export sector consists of goods such as rubber, palm oil, tin, and petroleum, imports still constitute a major input into exported goods. Using the data for Malaysia for the five-sector Keynesian model used below, imports (direct *and* indirect) constituted 20.4 percent of the total cost of inputs into the production of export goods. This compares to import shares of the total cost of 27.3 percent for consumption goods, 45.6 percent for investment goods, and 28.1 percent for all goods.

With an export elasticity of one, the system expands slightly, and this increases employment and profits. The cost of final goods, P_x, has risen by 3.7 percent, however, so real consumption by labor remains almost constant, while that of capital falls.

One result that has not been discussed so far is the likely effect of the devaluation on the long-run state of the economy. In particular, the question should be asked of the likely effect on fixed capital formation. Investment is taken as fixed in this macromodel, but we can still determine the likely pull on investment. For this, some theory of investment is needed.

The theories of investment propounded by Keynes in *The General Theory*, the theory used in the five-sector model below, and the theory based on James Tobin's "q-ratio"[16] can be interpreted as theories where the demand price for capital goods plays the crucial role. The demand price is determined by expected profitability and is compared to the supply price of newly produced investment goods at the current rate of production. When the demand price exceeds the supply price, the rate of production of investment goods will rise, and the rate of production will fall if the demand price falls short of the supply price.

16. James Tobin, "A General Equilibrium Approach to Monetary Theory," *Journal of Money, Credit and Banking*, vol. 1, 1969, pp. 15–29.

It is quite reasonable to assume that changes in *expected* profitability will move in the same direction as changes in *current* profitability, and hence that the demand price for capital will move in the same direction as current profits. Furthermore, if one makes the not unreasonable assumption that expected profits will move in the same proportion in every year of the lifetime of the capital asset as the proportion that current profits move, then the demand price will move in the same proportion. The supply price of investment goods is P_X in this macrosystem. Therefore, one can say that investment will rise if the ratio of profits (column 7) to P_X (column 2) rises, and will fall if this ratio (which is the same as Tobin's q) falls. Because this is a one-sector system, this ratio will change in the same way as real consumption out of capital income changes. Therefore, when the ratio shown in column 9 falls below 1.0, there will be a pull to reduce investment, and vice versa when the ratio in column 9 is above 1.0.

As shown in column 9 of table 5-3, there is a downward pull on investment in each of the cases when the export elasticity was 1.0 or less. This is not surprising when the economy was deflating in output and employment terms, but was also true when the export elasticity was 1.0 and the economy was inflating slightly (assuming investment would not yet be changed). The reason in the last case was the higher supply price of new investment goods, due to higher import costs. When the likely fluctuations in investment are taken into account, we can therefore predict that the contraction due to the devaluation when the export elasticity was low would have been exacerbated, while the slight expansion with the export elasticity of 1.0 would quite likely have been turned around by a decline in real investment.

The results found so far, with export elasticities of about 1.0 and below, have not been encouraging. Real incomes have fallen, real investment would have declined, the economy has contracted, output prices have been higher, and the balance of trade has worsened. This is not at all the traditional story. But things become better when a high export elasticity is assumed. Experiments with export elasticities of 3.0 and 10.0 are shown in lines B4 and B5.

With high export elasticities, exports expand to such an extent after the devaluation that the economy definitely inflates. Real production is higher, employment is much higher, profits grow, and real consumption is higher despite the higher prices. The balance of trade improves, although not to the extent one might have expected given the export growth. The reasons for this are the greater imports in the economic expansion and the lower prices the exports receive (which was the inducement for more sales to be made).

Another parameter for which there is a great deal of dispute as to the appropriate value is the capital/labor elasticity of substitution. This was varied in the experiments shown in panel C of table 5-3 (to which may be added the experiment of line B3). It turns out, for the experiments of interest to this study, that the results do not differ a great deal depending on whether this elasticity takes on very low or very high values. With an export elasticity of 1.0, the economy always expands slightly when real investment is held constant; employment rises; profits rise, but by less than prices; and the inducement is for investment to fall. When the elasticity of substitution is lower rather than higher, the economy is more rigid, so prices rise by more. But no essential result changes.

A possible exception to this arises with regard to the income distribution between capital and labor, which has not been mentioned. The well-known result of neoclassical distribution theory, described previously, is that an expansion in production will increase the share of profits if the elasticity of substitution is less than unity and will increase the share of labor if it exceeds unity. The opposite follows in a contraction. But since an expansion will raise both wages and profits (and a contraction will reduce both), the change in *shares* will generally be small relative to changes in other things, such as the absolute level of output or employment. The predicted changes in distribution are as predicted in table 5-3, and the main feature of interest is that they are uniformly small when one assumes neoclassical distribution theory.

Because the elasticity of substitution does not appear to matter too much, it will always be kept at the value of 1.5 in the experiments that follow. This will not affect any of the conclusions, except that one should keep in mind that when an economic expansion leads to a slight shift in distribution toward wages, the opposite would have occurred if we had assumed an elasticity of substitution of less than unity.

A different set of policies, designed to improve the balance of payments, works with components of aggregate demand rather than through an attempt to change relative prices (as a devaluation is supposed to operate). Two such policies examined here will be one that directly shifts, somehow, the world demand for the developing country's exports, and one that reduces the level of domestic expenditure on investment and/or gov-

Table 5-4. *Effects of Increased Export Demand or Reduced Investment Demand*[a]

Expressed as a ratio to base

r_F	σ	ϵ	P_V (1)	P_X (2)	V (3)	E (4)	D_F (5)	L (6)	Y_K (7)	C_L (8)	C_K (9)	θ_L (10)	θ_K (11)
A. Shift the export demand function 10 percent												
1.	1.0	1.5	0.0	1.0551	1.0402	1.0806	1.1000	1.5743	1.1712	1.1111	1.1259	1.0682	1.0273	0.9744
2.	1.0	1.5	1.0	1.0388	1.0283	1.0560	1.0698	1.3972	1.1180	1.0772	1.0872	1.0476	1.0192	0.9820
3.	1.0	1.5	3.0	1.0243	1.0178	1.0348	1.0434	1.2454	1.0728	1.0480	1.0541	1.0297	1.0122	0.9886
B. Reduce investment demand by the equivalent of 10 percent of base exports												
1.	1.0	1.5	0.0	0.9417	0.9575	0.9211	1.0000	1.2029	0.8417	0.8915	0.8791	0.9311	0.9705	1.0277
2.	1.0	1.5	1.0	0.9597	0.9706	0.9448	1.0303	1.3728	0.8883	0.9241	0.9152	0.9520	0.9798	1.0190
3.	1.0	1.5	3.0	0.9751	0.9818	0.9655	1.0566	1.5229	0.9297	0.9525	0.9469	0.9702	0.9876	1.0116

a. For symbols used, see table 5-3.

ernment consumption. Both will improve the balance of payments, but they will come associated with certain benefits and costs in other areas, such as employment and real incomes.

The increase in the world demand for the developing country's exports is implemented by shifting out the export demand curve by 10 percent. That is, at the original set of prices, 10 percent more exports can be sold than previously. Such shifts occur naturally over time, as world incomes grow, but it might be questioned whether such is possible in the short term. From the developing country's own actions, perhaps little can be done. It can send out more trade missions and generally promote sales of its goods more than before, and some such development of new markets must have been important to explain the rapid export growth of South Korea and Taiwan. But economists generally presume that such promotion is already going on to an optimal extent.

From the international viewpoint, the prospects are quite different. Imports from developing countries are often discriminated against by the OECD nations. This can come about indirectly, as through a reciprocal lowering of tariffs between developed countries in some new trade agreement, leaving developing countries the only ones paying the high tariffs. Or there can be direct quotas on textiles and other goods that often are among the first major manufactured exports from a developing country. Such discriminatory measures could be dropped for, say, a five-year period, for some developing county suffering from balance-of-payments difficulties and underutilization of capacity (such as Turkey), as part of the package accompanying an IMF loan.

Assuming that the export demand functions could be shifted, the results of such a shift are shown in panel A of table 5-4. Not surprisingly, such a policy would always be expansionary, with employment, profits, and real incomes growing by quite large amounts. With fixed capital supplies, such an expansion will be accompanied by higher rentals, and therefore higher prices. The higher prices will result in some cutback of the actual export growth from the 10 percent that would occur with no price increase, if the export price elasticity differs from zero. The higher the export elasticity, the more exports will be cut back for any given price increase, and the smaller the expansion in the system. Therefore, the increases in output, employment, real incomes, and prices will be smaller the greater the elasticity. In the limiting case of an infinite export elasticity, a shift in the export demand function will have no effect and is, in fact, quite meaningless.

But when the export elasticity is in a reasonable range, the expansion is significant and the results quite beneficial. For example, the case of an export elasticity of 1.0 is interesting, since in that case, if prices did not change, a 10 percent devaluation and a 10 percent shift in the export function would be equivalent in terms of the effect on the export volume. But while the balance of trade worsened by 13 percent in the devaluation, it improved by 40 percent when the exports were shifted. The reason, of course, is the effect on export prices of the devalued currency. Import volumes were, in fact, significantly lower in the devaluation case since the economy had not been spurred. Furthermore, real consumption by labor and capital grew by 8.7 percent and 4.8 percent when export demands are raised, while they were about constant in the devaluation case. Finally, since real profitability rose in the case where export demands were raised, investment would have been spurred, while in the devaluation case, the inducement was to reduce investment.

While developing countries' governments do not have much power over the position of the export demand curve they face, they do have significant control over the level of government consumption and development expenditure, and quite often over the level of private investment expenditure as well (at least when it is a *reduction* in investment which is called for rather than an expansion). In addition, a common element of the "standard" IMF stabilization package is a reduction in government expenditure. The experiments in panel B of table 5-4 look at the effects of a reduction in the level of investment (and government consumption) expenditure by an amount equal to 10 percent of the base-year export levels. This level was chosen to make it comparable to the experiments where export demand was shifted 10 percent, since an experiment that combined these two shifts would leave total output the same.[17]

The reduction in investment demand leads to a contraction in the economy, not surprisingly. Capital rentals fall, so prices fall and exports rise as a result when the export elasticity is not zero. The economy does not become as depressed, therefore, as it would have if exports had not responded. In the limiting case of an infinite export elasticity, exports would have grown to fill completely the "gap" left by the reduced investment and the economy would not have contracted. But such a rapid response is not a reasonable assumption.

The balance of trade always improves, primarily because of the reduced imports due to the depressed state of the economy. When the export

17. Such an experiment will be studied below.

elasticity is zero, the improvement is entirely due to the reduced imports, as export volume would not have grown, but the price at which it was offered to foreigners (as well as to domestic users) would have been reduced. With an export elasticity of unity, the increased volume is entirely offset by the reduced price, leaving revenues the same. Only with an export elasticity greater than 1.0 will exports begin to contribute in terms of foreign exchange.

When the export elasticity is equal to unity, the improvement in the foreign exchange position is 37.3 percent, which is close, by accident, to that achieved when the export demand function shifts 10 percent. But with the reduced investment, real incomes of labor and capital fall by 8.5 percent and 4.8 percent, while they grow by 8.7 percent and 4.8 percent when export demand increases. Employment falls by 11.2 percent rather than growing by 11.8 percent. The results are close to mirror images of each other, which had to be the case for some export elasticity, given the one-sector nature of the system. Finally, real profitability falls when investment (and government) demand is reduced, and this is an inducement to pull down investment even further.

The effects of various combined policies are shown in table 5-5. Normally these are fairly easily interpreted, and the results are usually close to the multiplicative effect of the experiments forming the basis for the combined experiment. The three combinations examined were (1) shift export demands by 10 percent and reduce investment demands by the equivalent; (2) shift export demands 10 percent and devalue 10 percent; and (3) shift export demands 10 percent, reduce investment demands by the equivalent, and devalue 10 percent.

When export demands are shifted 10 percent and investment demands are reduced by an equal amount, total production, employment, incomes, and prices in the system remain unaltered. One has just shifted output from one use to another, and as the system does not inflate or deflate, the values of the export elasticity and the elasticity of substitution do not matter. Exports are 10 percent higher and are sold at constant prices, imports remain the same, and the balance of trade improves. The only real harm is long term, if it is investment in useful forms rather than wasteful expenditure (such as for military jets) that has been reduced. The real question, however, is whether such a switch in the pattern of production is possible in a short period of time. There is no problem in this, by definition, in a one-sector model; however, things may be different in the real world.

Table 5-5. *Effects of Combined Policies*[a]

Expressed as a ratio to base

r_F	σ	ϵ	P_V (1)	P_X (2)	V (3)	E (4)	D_F (5)	L (6)	Y_K (7)	C_L (8)	C_K (9)	θ_L (10)	θ_K (11)
A. Shift export demand function 10 percent and reduce investment demand by the equivalent of 10 percent of base exports													
1. 1.0	any	any	1.0	1.0	1.0	1.1000	1.7758	1.0	1.0	1.0	1.0	1.0	1.0
B. Shift export demand function 10 percent and devalue 10 percent													
1. 1.1	1.5	0.0	1.0346	1.0523	1.0498	1.1000	1.0688	1.1047	1.0687	1.0499	1.0156	1.0171	0.9839
2. 1.1	1.5	1.0	1.0532	1.0658	1.0776	1.1353	1.2511	1.1647	1.1070	1.0928	1.0386	1.0262	0.9754
3. 1.1	1.5	3.0	1.0702	1.0782	1.1037	1.1680	1.4234	1.1811	1.1429	1.1332	1.0600	1.0345	0.9676
C. Shift export demand function 10 percent, reduce investment by the equivalent, and devalue 10 percent													
1. 1.1	1.5	0.0	0.9798	1.0123	0.9719	1.1000	1.2850	0.9426	0.9613	0.9311	0.9497	0.9899	1.0095
2. 1.1	1.5	1.0	1.0158	1.0385	1.0224	1.1651	1.6242	1.0467	1.0309	1.0078	0.9927	1.0079	0.9926
3. 1.1	1.5	3.0	1.0473	1.0615	1.0687	1.2240	1.9410	1.1454	1.0947	1.0790	1.0313	1.0233	0.9781

a. For symbols used, see table 5-3.

When the export demand function is shifted 10 percent and the currency devalued 10 percent, the system always expands, as the expansionary effects of the export shift outweigh the contractionary effects of the devaluation when the export elasticity is low; both are expansionary when the elasticity is high. When a reduction in investment is added in (panel C), the results can be contractionary or expansionary, depending on the export elasticity, and the movements in real incomes largely follow.

To conclude, it appears that in terms of an improvement to the balance of trade, a simple shift in export demands is best when the export elasticity is low, while a combination of export shift, investment reduction, and devaluation seems to work best when the export elasticity is high. But this result arises at least partly because we have assumed that there is no problem in shifting production from one use to another. In addition, the assumptions of the one-sector system tend to break down as the assumed export elasticity takes on higher values, as the implicit assumption being made is that export production can respond as quickly as the production of any other good to take advantage of the increased price competitiveness. For these reasons, it is best to turn next to a model that distinguishes export goods from other goods to see how our tentative conclusions hold up.

A Five-Sector Model

As previously noted, the assumptions of the one-sector system tend to break down for a number of issues, particularly when the export price elasticity is high. For this reason, a five-sector model that distinguishes goods according to the type of intended use will be used to examine the effects of policies designed to improve the balance of trade. The goods distinguished are consumption goods (C-goods); export goods (E-goods); and investment goods for the production of consumption goods (IC-goods), export goods (IE-goods), and more investment goods (II-goods).

Export goods production which is constrained by limited resources, either natural or man-made, can be handled in this system, so we will switch our assumptions from one where exports were as freely available as other goods to one where they are rather severely constrained. That is, the output of Malaysian rubber will be assumed to be fairly rigidly constrained by the number of rubber trees, in the short term.

An endogenous investment theory can also be handled adequately now that investment goods are distinguished. It may not be immediately obvious why this was impossible in the one-sector model. We outlined above what the pull on investment would be in each of the experiments examined, but we kept real investment constant. The problem is that, in a one-sector system, the model would be unstable if investment was allowed to fluctuate according to changes in current profitability and if it is assumed interest rates are constant. It would be unstable in the sense that a shock to some endogenous variable, which should leave the system unaffected after a solution is found again, would in fact lead to a different solution or even no solution at all. The reason can be seen by taking as an example a shock which was expansionary. Profits would therefore rise, and this would lead to higher investment. The increased production of investment goods would require more output from the one sector of the model, and this would increase profits even further, which would raise investment demand again, and so on ad infinitum. Under a wide variety of conditions the series would diverge, but even if it converged, the new equilibrium would differ from the old. The problem is that investment would feed on itself in such a system.

This problem does not arise when the sector producing I-goods differs from the one using the I-goods as part of its capital stock. In this case there is no direct feedback whereby higher demand raises profits which, in turn, raise demand again.

A more complete description of the model can be had by referring to figure 5-2.[18] The supply and demand curves for each of the three types of sectors are shown there. The first diagram (A), that of the export-goods sector, shows that we have assumed an infinite price elasticity of demand for E-goods at a fixed world price, with a supply curve that is very steep at the point where it intersects the demand curve. Since the E-goods sector is totally independent of the operation of the economy, one can solve for its price, output level, employment, and profits first.

The rest of the economy is interdependent, and a solution is found iteratively. It is easiest to start with a guess at profit levels for the C-goods and I-goods sectors (profits on E-goods are already known). One then solves for the production levels of I-goods; given the income levels determined there, one can solve for the production levels of C-goods. The re-

18. For a complete discussion of the model and the data set underlying it, see Lysy, "A Keynesian Model of Malaysia," chaps. 3–4.

Figure 5-2. *Supply-Demand Curves in the Five-Sector Model*

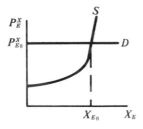

A. Export-goods sector

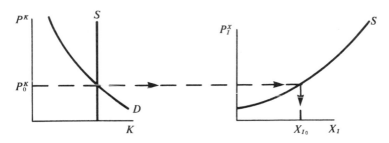

B. Investment-goods sectors

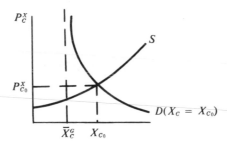

C. Consumption-goods sector

sulting profit levels are compared to those guessed, and if they differ significantly the iterations continue.

The theory of investment is based on that in Keynes' *General Theory*, in which the demand price for capital plays the crucial role. This price is determined in a market for stocks, since the stock of capital is a stock and not a flow as some economists often implicitly assume. The price that wealth-owners are willing to pay for capital, either new or old, is determined by the profits they expect to earn in holding it, and the assumption is that current profitability is an important determinant of this expectation. We assume that the stream of expected profits will equal current profits in the current period and then decline or increase exponentially to a level of "normal profitability."

Given the stream of expected profits, the demand price for the K-goods will be the present discounted value of that stream, using the money rate of interest (since money is the alternative asset investors can hold) as the discount rate. The money rate of interest is set exogenously, either by the developing country's government or by the conditions in the rest of the world. Given the fixed supply of capital in the short term, one then has the price at which capital can be bought or sold. This is depicted in the first half of panel B in figure 5-2.

Producers of new capital goods, that is, of I-goods, can sell their product at this price without any appreciable effect on it in the short term through a change in supply. This forms their demand price. Their supply price is determined according to an upward-sloping supply curve, which varies with the rate of production of I-goods. The rate of production will therefore vary until the supply price equals the demand price. The rate of investment is thus determined, as well as employment, labor incomes, profits, and so on in the I-goods sectors.

There are three I-goods sectors, but each operates on the principles just outlined. There are three different types of capital goods, and thus three markets for stocks of different types of capital. Capital going to the E-goods sectors will be valued according to the profits in the E-goods sector, and similarly for capital going to the C-goods sector. Capital used to produce more capital (either the IE-goods or the IC-goods) will be valued according to the maximum of the two profit rates in the IC-and IE-goods sectors. Finally, capital is not used to produce capital which, in turn, helps produce C-goods and E-goods, but the supply curve in the II-sector is still upward sloping due to a limited supply of "managerial expertise."

The rate of production of C-goods depends primarily on the incomes generated in producing E-goods, I-goods, and the C-goods themselves. The demand on goods for government consumption is also assumed to go to this sector. The supply/demand situation is shown in panel C in figure 5-2. The supply curve is upward sloping, due to fixed capital, and the demand curve is well defined and downward sloping for a *fixed* rate of production of C-goods. Since, in fact, this rate of production is part of the problem to be solved, the implicit aggregate consumption curve need not be so well behaved, and may slope upward. Another iterative procedure is required, but this poses no problem in practice.

Imports are assumed to enter as an input into the production of each of the five goods and are allowed to substitute with purely domestically produced output (that is, value-added) in each use. A CES formulation was used, with elasticities of substitution of 0.6 for C-goods, 0.3 for E-goods, and 0.2 for I-goods. We have therefore departed from the fixed coefficients assumption of the macromodel used earlier so that a devaluation, for example, will lead to some import substitution as a result of the increased price competitiveness of domestic product.

This brief outline of the model should suffice for the results we will examine next. For a more complete description, the reader is referred to Lysy.[19] Three experiments will be examined. The first two will be of a 5 percent devaluation, one of which has a "normal" investment response and one of which has made expectations of profitability completely rigid. The third will have the world price of exports raised 5 percent. The results are presented in tables 5-6, 5-7, and 5-8.

The devaluation with the normal investment response will be discussed first. It is easiest to start with the E-goods sector. The devaluation, in effect, raises the horizontal demand curve for E-goods by 5 percent, although, at the same time it also raises the supply curve as the price of imported inputs has also risen. However, as imports form only a part of total costs, the supply curve will not rise by the same proportion as the demand curve, so total profits rise. As is seen in table 5-6, profit in the E-goods sector rises by 11.4 percent, and this raises the demand price for capital, P_K, by 7.4 percent.[20]

The price of the output of the IE-sector as a result will also rise by 7.4 percent. And although part of its costs (the import cost) has risen by 5 percent, its profits will still be higher, by 20.4 percent in this case. This in turn raises the price investors would have to pay for new or old capital in that sector by 15.8 percent. And with the increased profitability of IE-goods (due to the greater profitability of E-goods), the rate of production

19. Ibid.
20. It rises by less than current profits because they are expected to decline exponentially through time to a normal rate. The exponential rate used was 0.5. A higher value for this rate would have led to a smaller increase. See below.

Table 5-6. *Devalue Malaysia's Foreign Exchange Rate 5 Percent, with Base Data*

Expressed as ratio to base

Item	C-goods	E-goods	IC-goods	IE-goods	II-goods	All goods
A. Prices						
1. Domestic good (P^D)	1.0177	1.0500	1.0399	1.0967	1.2865	⋮
2. Output (P^X)	1.0282	1.0500	1.0447	1.0739	1.1584	⋮
3. Capital (P^K)	1.0447	1.0739	1.0672	1.1584	1.4186	⋮
4. Imports (P^M)	1.0500	1.0500	1.0500	1.0500	1.0500	⋮
B. Levels						
1. Profits (Y^K)	1.0456	1.1135	1.0734	1.2036	1.5779	1.0863
2. Employment (L)	1.0364	1.0217	1.0434	1.1176	1.3147	1.0377
3. Imports (M)	1.0029	1.0118	1.0172	1.0666	1.1772	1.0183
4. Domestic output (D)	1.0219	1.0118	1.0192	1.0574	1.1303	1.0216
5. Total output (X)	1.0156	1.0118	1.0183	1.0618	1.1543	1.0201

Table 5-7. *Devalue Malaysia's Foreign Exchange Rate 5 Percent, with Expected Profitability Kept Constant*
Expressed as a ratio to base

Item	C-goods	E-goods	IC-goods	IE-goods	II-goods	All goods
A. Prices						
1. Domestic good (P^D)	1.0006	1.0500	0.9552	0.9528	0.9428	...
2. Output (P^X)	1.0166	1.0500	1.0000	1.0000	1.0000	...
3. Capital (P^K)	1.0000	1.0000	1.0000	1.0000	1.0000	...
4. Imports (P^M)	1.0500	1.0500	1.0500	1.0500	1.0500	...
B. Levels						
1. Profits (Y^K)	1.0014	1.1135	0.9193	0.9048	0.8936	1.0223
2. Employment (L)	1.0011	1.0217	0.9508	0.9418	0.9348	1.0034
3. Imports (M)	0.9721	1.0118	0.9589	0.9508	0.9478	0.9762
4. Domestic output (D)	1.0007	1.0118	0.9773	0.9695	0.9684	1.0009[a]
5. Total output (X)	0.9912	1.0118	0.9683	0.9602	0.9571	0.9927

a. Real GDP in constant 1971 prices = 0.9996.

Table 5-8. *Raise World Price of Exports 5 Percent*
Expressed as a ratio to base

Item	C-goods	E-goods	IC-goods	IE-goods	II-goods	All goods
A. Prices						
1. Domestic good (P^D)	1.0411	1.0654	1.1801	1.1735	1.5734	...
2. Output (P^X)	1.0275	1.0500	1.0939	1.0881	1.2594	...
3. Capital (P^K)	1.0939	1.0881	1.2511	1.2594	1.8208	...
4. Imports (P^M)	1.0000	1.0000	1.0000	1.0000	1.0000	...
B. Levels						
1. Profits (Y^K)	1.1075	1.1486	1.3420	1.3729	2.2179	1.1746
2. Employment (L)	1.0851	1.0281	1.1930	1.2094	1.6127	1.0801
3. Imports (M)	1.0764	1.0346	1.1165	1.1345	1.3453	1.0877
4. Domestic output (D)	1.0507	1.0152	1.0802	1.0987	1.2287	1.0462
5. Total output (X)	1.0590	1.0196	1.0967	1.1155	1.2847	1.0590

of IE-goods rises by 6.2 percent in real terms. This is much greater than the increase in the rate of production of E-goods, which was only 1.2 percent, since although the output of rubber is rather rigidly limited in the short term, the planting of new rubber seedlings is not.

With profits substantially higher, and output (and therefore employment) somewhat higher, the demand for C-goods will have grown. The demand curve for C-goods will have shifted out. The supply curve has also shifted up from the higher import costs, but not by enough to offset it. There will be an increased rate of production of C-goods, which will raise the demand for C-goods even more due to the higher incomes. This raises profits on C-goods and therefore raises the demand for IC-goods. This in turn has a feedback effect on C-goods.

In the final equilibrium, employment has grown by 3.8 percent, real output by 2.0 percent, domestic output (value-added) by 2.2 percent, and imports by 1.8 percent. Imports grow at a slightly slower rate than domestic output due to import substitution arising from the increased competitiveness of domestic industry. But note how minor this is. And it is interesting to note that since imports have grown by substantially more than exports (in real terms or, equivalently, in terms of foreign prices), the balance of trade will have become worse. This is a short-term result, of course, but the short term can be important. In the long term, as the increased investment in the E-goods sector bears fruition, the production of E-goods will be able to expand.

The lags can be long, however, and IMF lending policy is currently not of the nature to support such balance-of-payments deficits. In this devaluation experiment, it turned out that 78 percent of the increased imports were for the production of investment goods. Without long-term financing to purchase these imports, the investment may become impossible, and the devaluation would have been completely frustrated.[21]

The devaluation we have examined was expansionary, and an interesting question to ask is, under what circumstances would one expect a contraction? The contractionary forces operating were due to the higher import costs. Is it possible that they could dominate the expansionary forces? In certain sectors, we will find that such would be possible, but not in others, so the answer will depend on the structure of the economy.

First, in the E-goods sector, since the price of the product will rise by a full 5 percent in a 5 percent devaluation, and since only one input (im-

21. For a similar argument and for some examples of the IMF actually pursuing such policies, see Richard S. Eckaus, "Is the IMF Guilty of Malpractice?"

ports) will have a 5 percent price increase, the sum of profits plus the wage bill will have to rise. With output rigidly limited by available capital, employment will not increase much, so the wage bill will be about constant and profits will rise. If profits are largely saved, the demand for C-goods will not be affected greatly. But with greater profitability, the demand price for capital will have risen, so one must next look at the IE-goods sector.

At least three factors will lead to a small response of IE-goods output. The first arises when expectations are such that the current high profitability of E-sector capital is not expected to last, so the demand price for the capital good will not rise by much. The second is that the output of the IE-sector may itself be fairly limited by a rigid capital constraint in the short term (the rubber seedlings may have to come from London's Kew Gardens nurseries). The third is that if the IE-sector is heavily dependent on imported inputs, and if the demand price for its product has not grown by much, profits in the sector could fall and output could contract. If any of these factors apply, employment will not grow by much and may actually decline. Profit incomes will grow only if the second applies. Again, if profits are largely saved, the demand for C-goods will not grow by much.

It is therefore quite possible that the demand for C-goods may not rise by very much, if at all, as a consequence of what has happened in the E- and IE-sectors. Yet the supply curve has risen due to higher costs of imported inputs. Therefore profits in the C-sector could fall and output and employment contract. This will have feedback effects through the decline in employment in the C-goods sector, as well as through the consequent contraction of the IC-sector. It is quite possible, therefore, that the devaluation could be contractionary, overall.

A case of this is provided by the experiment shown in table 5-7. The base structure of the economy was maintained, but the assumption on profit expectations was changed. It was assumed that investors acted as if current changes in profitability were completely transient, so that they would not change their demand price for capital as current profitability changed.

As can be seen from table 5-7, the E-goods sector is completely unchanged from the previous devaluation experiment, except that the demand price for its capital is still at the base solution value rather than increasing by 7.4 percent, although profits still rose by 11.4 percent. The price at which the IE-sector output can be sold is therefore unchanged.

But its costs have risen (due to the higher import costs), so it contracts. This is true for all the I-goods sectors. The price of their output is unchanged, but their import costs have risen, so their profits fall and they contract.

The demand for C-goods declines very slightly, in the end. There is a balance between the higher demands from the extra employees in the E-goods sector (which, though proportionally a small change, is still significant due to the size of the sector), and the lower demands from those formerly producing I-goods. However, although the total output of C-goods is unchanged, there is a small increase in the domestic component of C-goods due to import substitution resulting from the price advantage gotten by the devaluation. Therefore employment and profits in the C-goods sector rise very slightly, by 0.1 percent.

The net effect on the economy is so small that by some measures it would be called expansionary and by some contractionary. Employment grows slightly, but total output declines, and real GDP in base-year prices is essentially constant. Income distribution moves against wages, however, as the much higher profits in E-goods production outweigh the declines in the I-goods sectors.

The last experiment we will look at with this model will be one where the world price of the export goods has been raised by 5 percent. We will not go into detail on how this might be done except to note that this again is a factor over which the developing country's government has little control but over which the international community may have considerable control. That is, the major OECD nations may agree, as part of an IMF package to assist a developing country's economy in balance-of-payments difficulties, to guarantee a remunerative purchase price for certain of that developing country's commodity exports.

The results are shown in table 5-8. We can be quite brief in their analysis, since they follow the effects of the 5 percent devaluation of table 5-6, except that import costs have not been raised. The expansionary forces are therefore not partially (or fully) counteracted by the depressive force of higher import costs. The effects on employment, profits, investment, and output are strong.

The only problem in this scenario is, perhaps surprisingly, the balance of payments. Even though export prices are 5 percent higher, export volume grows only 2.0 percent, so total receipts grow 7.1 percent. Imports, however, grow 8.8 percent in the expansion, where the substitutability between domestic and imported goods now works against the economy, as domestic prices have risen. Furthermore, with profits high, repatriated profits also increase. But the balance of payments does not worsen by appreciably more than in the devaluation, and, once again, it is probably a short-term phenomenon, as investment in E-goods capital has grown by a large amount. But without long-term financing to support this investment and the resulting deficit, all would be lost.

Conclusions

The primary conclusion from this chapter is that the prospects for a developing country's economy facing balance-of-payments difficulties are much brighter from the international standpoint than from the national one. Devaluation is an inefficient tool due to the resulting higher costs of imports and terms of trade losses on exports, and contractionary monetary and fiscal policies succeed only to the extent that they reduce real incomes. Quite often the result is stagnant investment, with long-term troubles added to the short-term ones.

From an international standpoint, things improve as OECD nations do have the wherewithal to purchase the exports of a developing country in difficulty either in increased quantities or at higher prices. To put this more concretely, if the OECD nations truly are concerned about Turkey's ability to repay its deutsche mark loans, then it should agree to take more of Turkey's exports. Given the gross underutilization of capacity in Turkish industry, there should be no problem in supplying such exports, if minimal loans are provided for the necessary imports.

This can be written in as part of the IMF package accompanying a loan to Turkey. And it is in keeping with the original Bretton Woods agreements stating that the burden of adjustment in cases of balance-of-payments problems should not fall solely on the debtor nation. The granting of generalized trade preferences to developing countries is not a new one, of course. Authors as diverse as Harry Johnson, Raul Prebisch, and Gunnar Myrdal have supported it.[22] What does seem to be new is the specific targeting of such preferences to developing countries requiring IMF assistance, such as Turkey. Among the specific policies that could be followed by the OECD nations would be a raising of quotas on textile

22. Harry G. Johnson, "Trade Preferences and Developing Countries," *Lloyds Bank Review*, no. 84, pp. 1–18; Raul Prebisch, *Toward a New Trade Policy for Development*, E/CONF.46/3 (New York: United Nations, 1964); and Gunnar Myrdal, *The Challenge of World Poverty* (Pantheon, 1970).

imports from Turkey, a lowering of tariffs, and so on. The agreement would be guaranteed to last for some fixed period of time, such as five or ten years. The main problem to be watched would be that the practical effects of such policies may simply shift Turkey's exports for those of some other developing country, which can ill afford to lose the OECD markets.

For other, less-industrialized developing countries which depend on exports of primary commodities, the appropriate policy would be a price guarantee for several of its commodity exports. Again, the policy should be written into the IMF accord and guaranteed to last for some minimum period, such as five or ten years.

The model simulations have shown that such policies would raise rather than lower real incomes, stimulate rather than depress employment, and stimulate rather than depress real investment.

It has also been found that policies to remedy the balance of payments that should be judged as successful can still increase the balance-of-payments deficit in the short term. The reason is that investment in the export industries may have been spurred, leading to greater import requirements. Such a situation requires long-term financing of this foreign exchange requirement, and the IMF currently does not do this. The World Bank can, so perhaps greater coordination is needed between these two institutions. Some coordination already occurs in such situations on an informal basis, and perhaps it should be made formal.

We have also seen that it is possible, for certain parameter values, for a devaluation to be deflationary. We do not wish to argue that this result is necessarily likely, just that the orthodox view that such is impossible is wrong. What will happen in a particular country at a particular time depends on many things. Our goal will have been achieved if economists approach this with an open mind.

A deflation will result from a devaluation if the export supply elasticity is low, and there is a low investment response to higher profits. The deflationary forces come from the higher import costs. The export demand elasticity could be anything for this result. If there is a high export supply elasticity, devaluation can be deflationary if the export demand elasticity is low. Therefore, we can be certain of a stimulus from a devaluation only in the cases where the export supply response is significant in the short term, *and* the export demand elasticity is high.

Finally, even in those cases where a devaluation *by itself* would not be deflationary, the effect of the entire orthodox "package of reforms" could be. The reason is that the accompanying contractionary fiscal and monetary policies may not be operating against a strong expansion due to the devaluation. What was left out of the calculations were the depressant forces which accompany the devaluation, forces which have already partially counteracted the expansionary forces. When the packages are deflationary, all our goals are often hurt. Real incomes, employment, and output are all reduced, and the balance of payments may even have become worse.

Discussion*

Sherman Robinson (World Bank) noted that the models resemble others recently developed by Taylor, Lysy, Krugman, Ahluwalia, Cardosa, and Bacha, all in the tradition of the Latin American structuralist school (as expanded to include honorary members such as Portugal, Egypt, and Malaysia).

While Ahluwalia and Lysy claim to adapt Keynesian ideas to developing countries, Robinson considered their models easier to understand when viewed through classical or neoclassical glasses. The models contain no money, no liquidity preference, virtually no expectations, and no uncertainty; other features are in the Walrasian general equilibrium tradition. Their special structuralist features drive the models and largely determine their empirical results. They specify a fixed nominal wage and nominal exchange rate. Real investment is fixed (even in the multisector model, it does not depend directly on savings). Imports are tied to domestic production. There are downward-sloping export-demand functions in the one-sector model (but infinitely elastic functions in the multisector model). Finally, labor and capital have different propensities to save.

Robinson identified two important adjustment mechanisms in the models by which a change in the exchange rate affects the economy: domestic price level or trade balance. If the elasticity of demand for exports is low, then the balance of trade is quite insensitive to changes in the exchange rate. In this case, the major adjustment mechanism is Kaldorian, with the domestic price level changing until the real wage and the functional distribution are set so as to equate desired savings and the inde-

---

* Both formal discussants for the session on income distribution, Arnold Harberger and Albert Fishlow, commented on both of the papers for the session (Ahluwalia-Lysy and Foxley). Accordingly, the two formal comments appear at the end of chapter 6 by Alejandro Foxley. This discussion therefore includes only comments on the Ahluwalia-Lysy study. The first is an extended comment by Sherman Robinson.

pendently determined investment. If the elasticity of demand for exports is infinite (the "small country" assumption), domestic prices and real wages cannot adjust independently of the exchange rate, and adjustment falls largely on exports and the balance of trade, which must then change to validate the savings-investment gap.

Robinson pointed out that the models' exchange rate mechanism is rather special. Expenditure switching between tradables and nontradables is precluded in the one-sector model and minor in the multisector model. Given the fixed nominal wage, changes in the exchange rate work through changes in domestic prices, the real wage, the distribution of income, and/or a sort of vent-for-surplus export theory. Whether these features fairly represent the views of "structuralists" is an open question, but they are nonetheless interesting.

Danny Leipziger (U.S. State Department) rejected as politically impractical the Ahluwalia-Lysy policy recommendation that industrial countries should take preferential trade-liberalizing measures for countries (such as Turkey or Zaire) that are in external account difficulties. *Arnold Nachmanoff* (U.S. Treasury Department) questioned the study's conclusion, advocating more external financing and more gradual adjustment, because delay makes the final adjustment and recessionary consequences more severe, and extra foreign financing will not necessarily be used to make needed structural changes.

Joanne Salop (International Monetary Fund) disagreed with the study's conclusion that there are major alternatives to traditional stabilization measures, because the only real alternative cited by the authors is more external aid, not an active policy option comparable to domestic stabilization. Moreover, she maintained that in the normal case where devaluation is needed—cases of overvalued currencies—supply elasticities for exports tend to be high, contrary to the study's main assumptions. Expressing surprise at the paper's lack of focus on income distribution, Salop outlined current work in this subject at the IMF. That analysis examines the distributional consequences of moving from an overvalued exchange rate and other distortions (as outlined by Krueger) to sustainable policies, through considering price changes for nontradables and tradables (for example, a required decline in the price ratio of the former to the latter) and determining whether the real wage must fall.

Frank Lysy responded that his policy recommendations referred to freer trade, not aid. He disputed that one could say clearly whether a country had incorrect relative prices or excess absorption, and he maintained that devaluation typically will worsen the terms of trade.

CHAPTER SIX

Stabilization Policies
and Their Effects on Employment
and Income Distribution:
A Latin American Perspective

ALEJANDRO FOXLEY

THIS CHAPTER deals with economic stabilization policies and their impact on employment and income distribution from a Latin American perspective. In the following pages I will discuss at a conceptual level some of the general issues that arise from the varied attempts at stabilization in Latin America.

What is the relationship among stabilization policies, employment, and the distribution of income? Obviously there is no unique answer to that question, except perhaps that stabilization efforts usually imply reductions in real income and some increase in unemployment. In the short term, the kind of stabilization policies chosen determine who bears the burden of the decrease in income and employment. In the long term, the distributive effects depend on the changes in asset ownership that the stabilization policies might bring about and on the nature of the structural changes accompanying stabilization.

A Latin American perspective on the problem must begin by referring to the two main currents that have influenced the thinking about inflation for the last three decades: structuralism and monetarism. The interest is not purely academic. In fact, as will be shown further on in the paper, both schools of thought have deeply influenced the design and application

The author is grateful for comments by J. Arellano, R. Cortazar, V. Corbo, R. Ffrench-Davis, P. Meller, O. Muñoz, and N. Flaño; valuable research assistance was provided by J. Marshall; and J. Notaro was kind enough to let me have access to his data for Uruguay. Responsibility, as usual, remains with the author.

of stabilization policies in Latin America. By contrasting theoretical conceptions and historical experience, we can learn something about the effects of policies conceived under radically different assumptions.

The subject is of interest not only to Latin Americans. The so-called new inflation in developed countries and the subsequent discussion as to why the traditional monetary-fiscal approach has failed to bring it down within a reasonable period of time resulted in increasing attention to structural factors behind the inflationary forces in developed countries today. The parallel with debates in Latin America in the late 1950s and 1960s is striking, as Hirschman and Diamand have recently pointed out.[1]

The basic policy question, in a paper dealing with the employment and income effects of economic stabilization, is the following: which policy approach not only succeeds in moderating inflation, but does so without recourse to massive unemployment and regressive income distribution effects? I will take up this question in the final section, after first examining the results of the policies and some hypotheses that might explain the results.

The rest of this chapter is organized in five sections. The first provides a historical background of ideas prevailing during the 1950s and 1960s in Latin America about stabilization policies. The next section describes the main features of the "new" stabilization policies of the 1970s, and in the third I give the results of these new policies in terms of employment and income distribution. The fourth section analyzes some of the macro-adjustment processes that help to explain the nature of the employment and distributive results. In the final section, I discuss some policy conclusions drawn from the preceding analysis.

Historical Perspective

Structuralism is usually associated with gradualist stabilization policies. The structural approach asserts that the roots of inflation are im-

---

1. See F. Modigliani, "The Monetarist Controversy or Should We Forsake Stabilization Policies?" *American Economic Review* (March 1977); A. Hirschman, "The Social and Political Matrix of Inflation: Elaborations on the Latin American Experience," Brookings Project on the Politics and Sociology of Global Inflation (October 1978); M. Diamand, "Towards a Change in the Economic Paradigm Through the Experience of Developing Countries," *Journal of Development Economics,* vol. 5 (March 1978).

bedded in the economic structure. This is characterized in developing countries by resource immobility, market segmentation, and disequilibriums between sectoral demands and supplies. As growth proceeds, the economy is prone to develop extended bottlenecks since the changes in demand associated with higher income levels are not followed by an adequate supply response.

A characterization of the main bottlenecks would include the supply of food products; the availability of foreign exchange; the rigidity in the tax and expenditure structure of the government; the inability to raise enough internal saving; and the supply of various intermediate inputs, whose relative scarcity varies depending on the country's resource base and, in some cases, on the level of development achieved.[2] I refer to inputs such as fuels, fertilizers, transport facilities, and credit availability.

A stabilization policy that does not recognize the existence of such bottlenecks, according to the structural view, is doomed to failure. It may reduce one disequilibrium (the rate of inflation), but at the expense of creating other disequilibriums: excess capacity, unemployment, and concentration of income and wealth. The main thrust of a structuralist stabilization policy would then lie in doing away with the bottlenecks that are forcing the economy to go through inflationary cycles. Almost by definition, this would be basically a long-term policy, since structural disequilibriums can be eliminated only by a reallocation of investment. Thus, bringing inflation under control is necessarily a gradual process.

The structuralist view of stabilization is not only gradual and rather long-run in its flavor, but it is also part of a reformist or, in some historical cases, even revolutionary process of change. According to this view, deep institutional reforms are needed if bottlenecks are to disappear: land reform, tax changes, and state intervention in various areas of economic activity. All these changes would negatively affect the income of those who control the scarce resources where bottlenecks originate: the owners of land and those who control key raw materials or exports. Resources extracted from these sectors would be channeled to the state. They would provide the basis for sustaining productivity increases and income redis-

2. See C. H. Kirkpatrick and F. I. Nixson, "The Origins of Inflation in Less Developed Countries: A Selective Review," in M. Parkin and G. Zis, eds., *Inflation in Open Economics* (Manchester University Press, 1976); O. Sunkel, "La inflación chilena: un enfoque heterodoxo," *El Trimestre Económico* (October 1958); A. Pinto, *La inflación, raíces estructurales,* Serie de Lecturas, *El Trimestre Económico,* no. 3 (México, 1973).

tribution in the lagging poorer segments of the economy. Structural reforms would produce a progressive income redistribution in the long term.

The monetarist view is generally thought, as a contrast, to be short term and favoring a rapid control of inflation. In a somewhat ambiguous but revealing statement, a monetarist has asserted that "the monetarist is a structuralist in a hurry."[3]

Inflation is negative for efficient growth according to this view. It also produces negative income distribution effects, mainly through the presumably regressive "inflation tax."[4] Thus, the monetarist approach to stabilization is consistent with a strong preference for zero inflation. The shorter the period in which this goal is achieved, the better. In this sense, a "shock treatment" approach to stabilization might be more desirable than a gradual adjustment to equilibrium.

The monetarist approach is usually focused on the use of very few policy instruments: control of money supply, reduction of the government deficit, exchange rate devaluation, freeing of prices, and doing away with subsidies. These instruments are assumed to produce neutral distributive effects as a consequence of the application of a uniform "rule" for all economic agents: the working of a free price system. These were roughly, and in a very summary form indeed, the views on stabilization prevalent in the 1950s and 1960s in Latin America. These ideas were tested in various countries and political circumstances.

The late 1950s saw the application of numerous monetarist programs, including Chile (1956–58), Argentina (1959–62), Bolivia (1956), Peru (1959), and Uruguay (1959–62). The results of these experiences have been compared and described by many authors.[5] The policies applied followed rather closely the orthodox package: monetary and credit contraction, reduction in public expenditures, decrease in real wages, exchange rate devaluation, increases in utility rates, and elimination of subsidies and price controls. The short-term results of the policies were judged to

3. The expression is attributed to Roberto Campos.
4. See D. Laidler and J. Parkin, "Inflation: A Survey," *Economic Journal* (December 1975).
5. For comparative reviews of the policies, see "Papel de las políticas de estabilización," *Economía de América Latina* (México: Centro de Investigación y Docencia Económica [CIDE], September 1978); O. Sunkel, "El fracaso de las políticas de estabilización en el contexto del proceso de desarrollo latinoamericano," *El Trimestre Económico* (October 1963); and R. Thorp, "Inflation and the Financing of Economic Development," in K. Griffiin, ed., *Financing Development in Latin America* (Macmillan, 1971).

be, on the whole, unsuccessful. While typically the inflation rates decreased for a short period, production at the same time fell, unemployment went up rapidly, and the income share of wage earners deteriorated.

The structuralists' turn in applying their policies came in the 1960s and early 1970s. A good example is the stabilization program during the Frei administration in Chile.[6] The idea was to stabilize the economy gradually and at the same time undertake those long-term reforms needed to overcome the basic bottlenecks in the agricultural, external, and fiscal sectors. At the same time, income redistribution, an explicit policy objective, was to be achieved by (1) land reform, (2) the reorientation of public developmental programs toward small producers, (3) increasing expenditures in housing, health, and education, and (4) generous wage policies.

After six years, the results showed an inflation rate stabilizing around 30 percent a year, moderate growth, and significant gains in labor participation in national income.[7]

The relatively high rate of inflation at the end of the reformist structuralist experiment was only an external sign of a problem inherent in this type of stabilization package: it must, to be successful, advance consistently on three fronts: price stability, structural reforms, and income redistribution. The balance is precarious and may easily be disrupted by dissatisfied pressure groups (organized labor, in the case that we are examining). If, for example, wage increases get out of line, they are bound to be reflected in a higher rate of inflation than was originally programmed.

Besides the monetarist and structural experience, one finds another type of stabilization policy in the populist regimes in Latin America. These programs typically apply extended price controls, while at the same time expanding wages, government expenditures, and money supply. The Peron administrations in Argentina (1946–52 and 1973–76) and the Radical Party government (1963–66) are adequate illustrations of populist policies.[8] As can be easily predicted, detailed price controls

6. R. Ffrench-Davis, *Políticas Económicas en Chile 1952–1970* (Santiago: Ediciones Nueva Universidad, 1973).

7. The share of salaried income, according to national accounts estimates, increased from 44.8 percent in 1964 to 52.3 percent in 1970. See ODEPLAN, *Cuentas Nacionales.*

8. See A. Canitrot, "La experiencia populista de redistribución de ingresos," *Desarrollo Económico,* vol. 15, no. 59 (Buenos Aires, October 1975).

and large increases in expenditures make for an inconsistent policy package. After a short initial success in redistributing income toward wage earners and in moderating the rate of inflation, the imbalances generated by the policy result in accelerating inflation and a regression in the initial distributive gains.

The "New" Stabilization Policies of the 1970s

The previous pages have described the evolution of ideas about stabilization policies and their relationship to experiences in the 1950s and 1960s in Latin America.

The 1970s have witnessed a return to prestructuralist policies with some important new features, as will be shown later on. The failure of populist experiences brought about not only a full reversal in economic policies but also the breakdown of the democratic political system in many countries. A growing body of literature tries to establish the link between the two.[9]

Here I will stress only that one factor was "the low propensity of policy makers to defer to normal economic constraints" when implementing stabilization policies during the populist experiences.[10] This was one of the factors that lead to high inflation, extended bottlenecks in production, scarcity of basic goods, and losses in real income for almost all groups in society. The result was that wrong economic policies reinforced the political instability of the regimes and contributed to replacement of the regimes with authoritarian military governments.

As a reaction to the previous experience, these governments chose to apply strictly orthodox policies, heavily influenced by the modern monetarist approach. At the same time, they reversed the previous trend toward increased economic and political participation by excluding workers and workers' organizations from decision-making mechanisms in both the political and economic spheres.

9. D. Collier, ed., *The New Authoritarianism* (Princeton University Press, forthcoming); G. O'Donnell, "Reflexiones sobre las tendencias de cambio en los regímenes burocrático-autoritarios," *Documento de Trabajo,* no. 1 (Buenos Aires: Centro de Estudios de Estado y Sociedad [CEDES], 1976).

10. The quotation is from A. Hirschman, "The Turn to Authoritarianism in Latin America and the Search for Its Economic Determinants," in Collier, ed., *The New Authoritarianism.*

It would seem on the surface that as far as stabilization policies are concerned, the process had come full circle, back to the approach to stabilization of the late 1950s. Although many of the policies being applied today in several Latin American countries bear strong resemblance to those of the 1950s, there are at least two new components that must be considered.

One is a political component: orthodox policies are being applied today by authoritarian military governments. The relative independence of these governments from popular pressure seems to solve what the monetarists saw as the reasons for the previous failures: the premature reversal of the policies, caused by the adverse reaction of the social groups most affected, mainly the workers; and the "partial" application of the package.

Obviously, an authoritarian government should have no problem in disciplining the workers and in controlling the political and social environment so that a sustained application of a consistent stabilization policy is made possible. Thus, authoritarianism is presented almost as a requisite for the success of the orthodox economic policies.

The second new element in the orthodox policies of the 1970s is their strong long-term component. Monetarism is usually associated with short-term adjustment policies and their degree of success is judged accordingly. In their present version in Latin America, the orthodox policies put a heavy emphasis on changing the more fundamental ways of working of the economy. In a curious parallel to structuralist thinking, inflation is increasingly viewed as the result of an economic system that does not work.

Solving the problem of inflation requires a radical transformation in the economy. This involves such "structural" changes as reducing the size of the public sector, reorienting the surplus to the private capitalist sector, creating private capital markets, opening up the economy to free trade, and redefining the participation of private enterprise vis à vis labor organizations in decision-making mechanisms. Thus the original problem, inflation, is escalated to a generalized malfunctioning of the economy.

In this sense, it could be argued that the new stabilization policies in Latin America are a form of structuralism using orthodox instruments. Obviously the direction, content, social support, and alliances behind it are entirely different. For example, while the structuralism of the 1960s was integrating the poorer masses of workers and peasants into the benefits of the system, the main aim of the new structuralism of the 1970s is to integrate the domestic economy into the world economy. If achieving this goal requires excluding those very same social groups from political and economic participation, then it must be undertaken.

Summing up, the two new elements in the recent stabilization policies in Latin America seem to be (1) the political framework within which they are applied (authoritarianism), and (2) the heavy emphasis on long-term transformation of the economy as a condition for price stability. Both factors, together with the nature of the specific short-term policies applied, will influence the pattern of employment and income distribution that will emerge from the period of economic stabilization.

The Policies and Their Employment and Distributive Effects

When discussing recent orthodox stabilization policies, I refer to the experiences in Chile (1973–78), Argentina (1976–78), Uruguay (1974–78), and, to a limited extent, the original experiment by Brazil (1964–67).[11] These policies had some features in common and several differences, particularly with respect to the intensity with which some instruments are applied. Since this is not a comparative study of the various national cases, I will just give enough elements to typify the policies and describe their effects on employment and income distribution.

The stabilization policies, relying on the assumption that inflation is "always and everywhere a monetary phenomenon," centered on control of the money supply and the factors affecting it, mainly the fiscal deficit. Government expenditures were reduced, the rates for public utilities increased, subsidies eliminated, and real wages drastically curtailed. At the same time most prices were freed. Import controls were gradually eliminated, and the exchange rate was devalued to reduce the balance-of-payments deficit.

So far the policies look very much like those of the late 1950s. The new elements were more structural. The goals were to reduce the size and importance of the public sector by reducing public employment, by turn-

11. The Brazilian case is perhaps the most heterodox, as has been shown in A. Foxley, "Stabilization Policies and Stagflation: The Cases of Brazil and Chile," *World Development,* forthcoming.

ing public enterprises over to the private sector, and by redistributing real and financial resources toward the private capitalist sector.[12]

The economy was also supposed to operate under free market rules to the maximum extent possible. Opening up the economy to the world markets was one way to achieve this. Tariff reductions were planned and implemented with different intensity, but they were very much at the core of the programs.[13] Previous rigid regulations for the flow of foreign capital were substantially eased, if not eliminated altogether.

Simultaneous with the stabilization programs, private capital markets were developed. Public resources were transferred to these financial markets; and public enterprises, under a policy of self-financing, were required to borrow from these new financial institutions. After a few months the interest rate was free to fluctuate according to market conditions.

A more detailed description of the policies, from which it is easy to infer both common elements and differences, can be found elsewhere.[14] We will summarize here some of the aggregate results that bear more di-

12. These goals, shared by all the governments concerned, were not applied systematically, except in Chile. Argentina, for example, succeeded in reducing the salaries of public employees by 53 percent, but employment in the public sector remained fairly constant. In Chile, public sector employment went down by 25 percent between 1973 and 1978. On the other hand, out of 464 firms in the public sector by 1974, all but 31 had been turned over to the private sector by the end of 1978, and the privatization process continued in 1979, including many activities in the areas of health, housing, and education that were traditionally undertaken by the government. For references on Argentina see, A. Ferrer, "El retorno del liberalismo: reflexiones sobre la política económica vigente en la Argentina," *Desarrollo Económico,* no. 72, vol. 18 (January 1979); A. Canitrot and R. Frenkel, "Estabilización y largo plazo: la experiencia Argentina 1976–1979" (Buenos Aires: CEDES, June 1979); and for the Chilean case, A. Foxley, "Stabilization Policies."

13. Tariff reduction targets vary widely. Argentina, starting from an average nominal rate of 55 percent for 1976, will gradually decrease it to 15 percent by 1984. Uruguay did not reduce tariffs at all until the fifth year of application of the policies. The program is gradual and has set a target average tariff of 35 percent for 1985. Chile reduced tariffs very rapidly, from 94 percent average in 1973 to a uniform rate of 10 percent in 1979. See M. Rimez, "Las experiencias de apertura externa y desprotección industrial en el Cono Sur," *Economía de América Latina* (México: CIDE, March 1979).

14. A. Foxley, "Stabilization Policies"; D. Hachette, "Aspectos macroeconómicos de la economía chilena: 1973–1976," *Documento de Trabajo,* no. 55 (Instituto de Economía, Universidad Católica de Chile, 1977); A. Canitrot and R. Frankel, "Establización y largo plazo"; A. Ferrer, "El retorno de liberalismo"; L. González and J. Notaro, "La política de estabilización uruguaya 1974–1978" (Montevideo: Centro de Investigaciones Económicas [CINVE], June 1978).

Table 6-1. *Variation in GDP and Consumer Prices*

Percent

	Argentina			Brazil			Chile			Uruguay	
Year	(1) GDP	(2) Consumer prices	Year	(3) GDP	(4) Consumer prices	Year	(5) GDP	(6) Consumer prices	Year	(7) GDP	(8) Consumer prices
1974	6.5	40.1	1962	5.2	51.3	1973	−1.1	605.9	1973	0.8	77.5
1975	−1.3	334.9	1963	1.5	81.3	1974	4.2	369.2	1974	3.1	107.3
1976	−2.9	347.5	1964	2.9	91.9	1975	−16.6	343.3	1975	4.4	66.8
1977	4.7	160.4	1965	2.7	34.5	1976	5.0	197.9	1976	2.6	39.9
1978	−4.1	169.9	1966	3.8	38.8	1977	8.6	84.2	1977	3.4	57.3
			1967	4.8	24.3	1978	6.0	37.2	1978	2.2	46.0

Sources: (1) Banco Central, *Memoria Anual*; (2) Comisión Económica para América Latina (CEPAL), *Estudio Económico de América Latina*; (3) *Coyuntura Económica* (November 1972 and July 1977); (4) Antonio C. Lemgruber, "Inflation in Brazil," in Lawrence B. Krause and Walter S. Salant, eds., *Worldwide Inflation: Theory and Recent Experience* (Brookings Institution, 1977); (5) ODEPLAN, *Cuentas Nacionales*; (6) R. Cortázon and J. Marshall, "Indice de Precios al Consumidor 1970–1978," *Colección de Estudios CIEPLAN*, no. 4 (1980); and (7) and (8) Banco Central, *Indicadores Económica-Financieros*.

Table 6-2. *Unemployment Rate*

Percent

Year	(1) Buenos Aires	(2) Montevideo	(3) Santiago
1972	6.6	7.7	3.8
1973	5.4	8.9	4.6
1974	3.4	8.1	9.6
1975	3.7	...	16.3
1976	4.5	12.8	16.7
1977	3.0	11.8	13.2
1978	...	10.1	14.0

Sources: (1) Programa Regional de Empleo para América Latina y el Caribe (PREALC), *Archivo de Datos Ocupacionales sobre América Latina y el Caribe* (1979); (2) Dirección de Estadísticas, *Encuesta de Hogares;* (3) Departamento de Economía, Universidad de Chile, *Ocupación y Desocupación.*

rectly on the employment and equity effects. Figures for GDP, rates of inflation, wages and salaries, and the distribution of income or consumption for households are given in tables 6-1, 6-2, 6-3, and 6-4.

1. The inflation rate was resistent despite stabilization efforts: in three of the four cases considered, it took between four and five years to bring the inflation rate to around 40 percent a year; in Argentina, after three and one-half years inflation is still around 150 percent.[15]

2. High inflation coexisted with recession during an equivalently long period (notice that in two of the four cases—Argentina and Chile—GDP per capita actually fell in real terms).

3. Unemployment went up sharply in at least two of the four cases, the extreme case being Chile where the rate of unemployment was, at one point, between three and four times higher than the historical rate.

4. Wages fell from 20 to 40 percent in real terms in all four cases.

5. The family income distribution, when available, showed a deterioration in the income share of the poorer classes and a significant gain for the higher quintile.

In the Chilean case, an example of the more thorough and radical application of the monetarist package, the initial rate of inflation was 360 percent; it stayed in the three-digit level for three years and came down to 30 percent in the fifth year of application of the policy. GDP per capita fell in absolute terms, reaching in 1978 the 1970 level. Open un-

15. Grouping all cases together is not totally fair, given the differences in the initial conditions (inflation in Brazil and Uruguay was about 90 percent; in Argentina and Chile, more than 300 percent).

Table 6-3. *Real Wage Index*

ARGENTINA (1973 = 100)

Year	(1) Average wages, public sector	(2) Average wages, industry	(3) Average salaries, industry	(4) Basic wages, industry	(5) Basic wages, agriculture
1973	100.0	100.0	100.0	100.0	100.0
1974	110.0	114.0	116.0	103.8	114.7
1975	85.0	105.0	109.0	101.7	106.4
1976	58.0⎫	72.0	78.0	58.5	58.9
1977	42.0⎭		89.0	52.9	53.6

BRAZIL (1961 = 100)

Year	(6) Median wages, industry (Rio)	(7) Wages, rural sector (S.P.)	(8) Minimum wages (Rio)
1961	100.0	100.0	100.0
1962	93.2	99.4	83.5
1963	89.6	92.2	77.4
1964	...	102.1	77.4
1965	85.4	116.7	71.3
1966	83.1	108.2	66.1
1967	86.5	117.6	63.5

CHILE (1970 = 100)   URUGUAY (1970 = 100)

Year	(9) Average wages	(10) Average salaries	Year	(11) Average wages, industry	(12) Average wages, agriculture
1973	87.2	74.2	1973	84.0	81.2
1974	66.5	63.7	1974	83.5	87.8
1975	61.1	64.6	1975	75.7	86.0
1976	65.0	64.7	1976	68.5	90.2
1977	71.1	71.8	1977	58.8	70.4

Sources: (1), (2), and (3) Canitrot and Frenkel, "Establización y largo plazo"; (5), (11), and (12) PREALC, *Asalariados de bajos ingresos y salarios mínimos en América Latina* (1979); (7) Bacha, "Economic Growth, Rural and Urban Wages"; (6) and (8) Bacha and Taylor, "Brazilian Income Distribution"; (9) and (10) Instituto Nacional de Estadísticas, "Household Expenditures Survey."

employment in Santiago was over 20 percent of the labor force in early 1976 and stayed at around 14 percent during the next three years.[16] If a make-work employment program, with those employed in it earning half the minimum wage, is added to the unemployed, the figure would go up to 17 percent. Unemployment in other urban areas has proven to be even

16. See A. Foxley, "Stabilization Policies." The initial rate of inflation corresponds to the twelve-month average rate prevailing as of September 1973, calculated correcting for black market prices, by the Departamento de Economía, Universidad de Chile.

Table 6-4. *Income Distribution in Brazil and Uruguay (Montevideo) and Consumption Distribution in Chile (Santiago) by Household*

Percent

BRAZIL

Quintile	(1) 1960	(2) 1970
I	3.49	3.16
II	8.07	6.85
III	13.81	10.81
IV	20.26	16.94
V	54.35	62.24

CHILE (Santiago)

Quintile	(3) 1969	(4) 1978
I	7.6	5.2
II	11.8	9.3
III	15.6	13.6
IV	20.5	20.9
V	44.5	51.0

URUGUAY (Montevideo)

Quintile	(5) 1973	(6) 1976
I	6.53	5.52
II	11.34	10.21
III	15.94	15.06
IV	22.65	22.49
V	43.54	46.72

Sources: (1) and (2) Bacha and Taylor, "Brazilian Income Distribution"; (3) and (4) Instituto Nacional de Estadísticas, *Encuesta de Presupuestos Familiares;* (5) and (6) Bensión and Canmant, *Política económica y distribución del ingreso en Uruguay 1970–76* (Montevideo, 1979).

higher.[17] The unemployed are heavily concentrated in the two lower quintiles.[18]

Real wages in Chile went down by as much as 40 percent in 1975 and recuperated slowly afterward. As a result of the extremely high unemployment and the reduction in wages, income distribution deteriorated

17. Typical regional unemployment rates for 1978 in Chile are the following: central region, 22 percent; central-north, 13.3 percent; central-south, 18.99 percent; southern region, 15.2 percent. See Departamento de Economía, Universidad de Chile, *Ocupación y desocupación* (March 1979).

18. See Instituto Nacional de Estadísticas, Chile, "Household Expenditures Survey, Summary of Results," *El Mercurio,* February 25, 1979; and Departamento de Economía, Universidad de Chile, "Encuesta especial a desocupados del Gran Santiago, December 1978," *Documento de Extensión,* no. 12 (June 1979).

sharply. The share of wages and salaries in national income went down from 44.3 percent in 1970 to 34.7 percent in 1976, the latest year for which figures are available.[19] The distribution of household consumption by quintiles shows a sharp deterioration for the lower 20 percent of the families. The upper 20 percent, on the other hand, increased its share of consumption from 44.5 percent to 51.0 percent, as can be seen in table 6-4.

In Argentina, the rate of inflation, 335 percent in 1975, actually increased to 347 percent during the first year of the stabilization program and has stabilized at around 160 percent a year since then. GDP decreased by 2.5 percent, and total consumption fell by 14.4 percent in real terms between 1975 and 1978.[20] Unemployment has stayed at around 4 percent for Buenos Aires.[21] Real wages in the industrial sector fell by 32 percent between 1975 and 1977, while basic real wages dropped even more, nearly 47 percent as can be seen in table 6-3.

The Uruguayan stabilization policy resulted in a reduction of the inflation rate from 97 percent to 45 percent between 1974 and 1978. The distributive signs are consistent with the cases previously examined: private consumption decreased at a rate of 1.4 percent a year; real wages continuously fell since 1973. In 1978 they were 28 percent below the initial level and 40 percent below the more "normal" 1968–72 period.[22] Unemployment went up from an average of around 8 percent for the previous five-year period to 13 percent in 1976, and decreased slightly afterward.

19. The figures do not include social security contributions by employers. If they are included, the share goes down from 52.3 percent to 41.1 percent respectively. See ODEPLAN, *Cuentas Nacionales.*

20. See Banco Central de la República Argentina, *Memoria Anual 1977 y Anticipo Memoria Anual 1978;* CEPAL, *Estudio Económico de América Latina 1977;* International Monetary Fund, *International Financial Statistics.*

21. This seems to be due to a reduction in the supply of labor caused by several factors. The flow of international migration of labor from neighboring countries has been reversed due to government policy and reduced real wages. The participation of women in the labor force has also decreased due to lower wages. Other factors are a shift from salaried to self-employed positions, given that the very low wages often compare unfavorably with the income of the self-employed; and a decrease in internal migration from rural to urban areas for the same reason (extremely low wages in the cities). From the demand side, public sector employment has remained high during the whole recession, thus alleviating what could have been a worse situation for the labor force. See E. Kritz, "Escasez de mano de obra como dilema estructural," *Suplemento Económico Clarín* (July 22, 1979).

22. Figures from L. González and J. Notaro, "La política de estabilización uruguaya 1974–1978."

The previous results are consistent with the household income distribution figures for Montevideo (table 6-4). The income share for the lowest quintile fell from 6.5 percent to 5.5 percent from 1973 to 1976. The upper 20 percent of the families, on the other hand, increased its share from 43.5 percent to 46.7 percent. Further declines in real wages while unemployment stayed up make it likely that the picture has further deteriorated since 1976.

The results of stabilization in Brazil in the 1960s are sufficiently well known (see table 6-1 to 6-4). The stabilization policy implied a reduction in the growth rate by half during the 1964–67 period, and existing evidence seems also to show a deterioration in real wages and the distribution of income.[23] Data for income distribution in the rural sector are not available. However, rural wages show a tendency to decline in Argentina and to remain approximately constant in Brazil and Uruguay.[24]

Some of the previous results were the consequence of a deliberate policy, the best example being the fall in real wages. Wage repression was a basic element of the orthodox policy package. Other results, like the prolonged period of stagflation and high unemployment were not expected at all,[25] yet they are very important in explaining the process of income concentration that accompanied these experiences.

Adjustment Processes for Economic Stabilization

To understand the distributive and employment effects of the stabilization policies I have been examining, it is useful to look more carefully at some of the adjustment mechanisms chosen by policy makers to bring the economy back to price stability. The description of the processes will re-

23. A. Fishlow, "Some Reflections on Post-1964 Brazilian Economic Policy," in A. Stepan, ed., *Authoritarian Brazil* (Yale University Press, 1973); E. Bacha and L. Taylor, "Brazilian Income Distribution in the 1960s: 'Facts,' Model Results and the Controversy," *Journal of Development Studies*, vol. 14, no. 3 (April 1978).

24. See table 6-3. For Brazil, see A. Fishlow, "Some Reflections," and E. Bacha, "Economic Growth, Rural and Urban Wages: The Case of Brazil" (Rio de Janeiro: Pontífica Universidad Católica, March 1979). Evidence for Chile is scarce. Although legal minimum wages increased, effective wages paid apparently fell with respect to 1970, according to information in S. Galleguillos, "Remuneraciones agrícolas: teoría y evidencia" (Escuela de Economía, Universidad de Chile, forthcoming).

25. The following quotation from P. Baraona, who was to become Minister of Economics in the Pinochet government, is illustrative. In October 1973 he declared that, "Before a year, we will have a zero rate of inflation." See *El Mercurio*, October 17, 1973.

flect stylized facts rather than any particular country experience. It will also concentrate selectively on just a few of these mechanisms of adjustment; the criterion for selecting these and not others is that they seem particularly relevant for explaining the stagflation and income concentration that accompanied these experiences.

I will examine the following adjustment mechanisms: (1) asymmetrical treatment of goods prices and wages, (2) financial sector adjustments, (3) effects of external supply shocks and devaluation, and (4) the fiscal adjustment and its impact on employment and income distribution.

General Disequilibrium and Price Adjustment: Asymmetric Treatment of Goods Prices and Wages

Let us assume that the economy is initially in a state of disequilibrium, characterized by repressed inflation. A generalized system of price controls does not allow the market to provide the signals that restore equilibrium. As a result, goods are scarce, and black markets develop. Suddenly prices are set free. At the same time, nominal wages are fixed so that real wages will fall. However, if prices are set too high and wages too low, there will be a tendency for an excess supply of goods to develop, possibly causing a reduction in output levels and an increase in unemployment, with a probable regressive effect on the ditribution of income. These arguments will be examined in more detail later.

When prices are suddenly freed after a period of repressed inflation, producers must make decisions concerning output and prices. Information about the future is highly imperfect at this time. The market provides no uniform guide to follow. The expected rate of price increase differs markedly among the various economic agents, and so do their expectations about the set of relative prices that they will face.

The variance of expected inflation tends to be higher with higher inherited disequilibrium. Under these conditions—extreme uncertainty and large price increases expected—firms will attempt to protect themselves from the risks of huge losses attached to an underestimation of future inflation. They will do this by raising prices initially at a higher rate than they expect the rate of inflation to be.[26] Thus, given the lack of adequate

26. R. Frenkel has developed a mathematical model that shows this result as a rational outcome for firms facing high inflation and uncertainty. See R. Frenkel, "¿Qué expectativas: la inflación Argentina 1975–1978?" (Buenos Aires: CEDES, May 1979).

Table 6-5. *Prices, Money Supply, and Exchange Rate Increases,*
Argentina

Ratio to level in December 1970

Date	(1) Prices	(2) Money (M_2)	(3) Exchange rate
June 1976	49.4	39.1	35.2
December 1976	89.4	74.6	69.3
December 1977	232.8	241.7	153.2
December 1978	628.0	656.7	261.3

Sources: (1) CEPAL, *Estudio Económico;* (2) IMF, *International Financial Statistics;* and (3) CEPAL, Estudio Económico; and Canitrot and Frenkel, "Establización y largo plazo."

Table 6-6. *Prices, Money Supply, and Exchange Rate Increases, Chile*
Ratio to level in December 1969

Date	(1) Prices	(2) Money (M_2)	(3) Exchange rate
October-December 1973	39	29.5	30.6
December 1974	227	118.0	163.2
December 1975	1,085	507.1	831.7
December 1976	2,883	1,912.5	1,716.7
December 1977	4,688	5,015.0	2,781.3

Sources: (1) Instituto Nacional de Estadísticas, see Foxley, "Inflación con recesión"; (2) and (3) Banco Central.

market signals and high variance of expectations, there is an inherent tendency for prices to overshoot what might have been a reasonable expected rate of inflation.[27]

This is not just an abstract speculation; it is what figures show for at least two of the cases that we have been studying, as can be seen in tables 6-5 and 6-6. In Argentina, after three months of free prices (June 1976) the general price level had increased forty-nine times with respect to a base of December 1970. Money supply had increased only thirty-nine times and the exchange rate thirty-five times during the same period. The picture for the Chilean economy looks very similar. While prices rose thirty-nine times between December 1969 and the last three months of

27. J. Ramos was the first to describe this phenomenon in the case of Chile. His paper on hyperstagflation has certainly been influential in my thinking about the importance of the initial price overshoot. See J. Ramos, "Inflación persistente, inflación reprimida e hiperestanflación," *Cuadernos de Economía,* no. 43 (Santiago).

1973 (when prices were decontrolled), money supply and the exchange rate had grown only thirty times, and wages, twenty-four times. This trend persisted for a sustained period thereafter.

Why would this initial overshoot in prices generate more than a once-and-for-all effect that should be rapidly corrected by market forces? Part of the explanation lies in expectation formation. In fact, the fast pace of price increases that follows decontrol sets a benchmark that influences inflationary expectations. After the initial upsurge in the prices of goods, other prices, such as the nominal interest rate, the exchange rate, and utilities rates, tend to be readjusted in proportion to the initial price increase. This affects the costs of imported raw materials, domestic inputs, and working capital. If firms set prices as a markup over variable costs, a second round of price increases will follow. This way the initial disequilibrium is passed on through the indexation it induces in the prices of those variables most determinant of firms' variable costs.

On the other hand, at the same time as the price overshoot, nominal wages are fixed, and the rate of expansion of money supply is falling as part of the demand-centered stabilization effort. A significant drop in effective demand follows. The overshoot in prices makes real wages and real cash balances fall well below what had originally been programmed.[28]

There is then an income-constrained adjustment process. Producers and consumers alike cannot realize their "notional" demands. Their market signals correspond to a level of effective demand below the potential level. Resources are underutilized. An excess supply of goods develops and is transmitted to the labor market as a reduced demand for labor. This generates excess labor supply, which in turn reduces effective demand again. Income falls. Unemployment goes up.[29]

The drop in demand should eventually help to curb the rate of price increase. But the speed with which this happens depends on several factors; my hypothesis is that the price adjustment process will tend to be slow partly because (1) firms are continuously facing changed initial conditions that represent disequilibrium in other markets, and (2) after the initial price overshoot and consequent departure further away from equilibrium, firms would not behave as atomistic competitors but rather

28. See J. Ramos, "El costo social: hechos e interpretaciones," *Estudios de Economía* (Universidad de Chile, second semester 1975).

29. This kind of dynamic adjustment is fully described in A. Leijonhufvud, *On Keynesian Economics and the Economics of Keynes* (London: Oxford University Press, 1968); and also in H. Muellbaner and R. Portes, "Macroeconomic Models with Quantity Rationing," *Economic Journal* (December 1978).

as an oligopoly. The reasons for this kind of behavior of the firm under disequilibrium have been extensively developed by several authors.[30]

The argument runs as follows: with imperfect information and no market auctioneer, departures from equilibrium imply that firms are necessarily price setters. Since information is imperfect, their profits will depend on other firms' and consumers' reaction to their own pricing and output decisions. They face a demand curve whose slope is not known.

In such an environment producers will be very cautious about price changes. They will set up simple markup rules so that cost increases are passed on to prices in a predictable way. On the other hand, if demand changes, they will adjust prices slowly. If demand falls, they will not reduce prices for fear of not gaining a larger share of the market. They will be cautious until they can get enough information to minimize the risk of profit losses due to wrong price decisions.

Most of the effect we have described is transitory and will last as long as the disequilibrium persists. But one factor would permanently affect the speed of price adjustment: the existence of oligopolistic structures as such. And large segments of the modern manufacturing sector appear to be oligopolistic in semi-industrialized economies, such as the ones we have been discussing. The prevalence of oligopoly will only reinforce the tendency for low price adjustment in the economy vis à vis changes in demand.

These considerations on market structure add up to the following: when, as a result of the drastic relative price changes brought about by the stabilization policy, disequilibrium prevails and demand falls sharply, it is quite likely that the economy will adjust mainly by reducing output and employment levels first, and only then and gradually, by reducing the rate of increase in prices.[31] The lower-income levels and higher unemploy-

30. K. Arrow, "Towards a Theory of Price Adjustment," in M. Abramowitz, ed., *The Allocation of Economic Resources* (Stanford University Press, 1959); and A. Leijonhufvud, *On Keynesian Economics,* chap. 11.

31. The behavior of this type of economy, under disequilibrium, would probably be closer to the fixed-price models of Barro and Grossman, Patinkin, Leijonhufvud, and Malinvaud, than that predicted by the competitive model with auction markets a la Walras. Employment would be more sensitive to expected demand than to wage levels. A decrease in real wages would have a contractionary effect in demand, and through the Keynesian multiplier, in output and employment. Real income effects would be important during the adjustment process, giving rise to marked income distribution changes. See R. Barro and H. Grossman, "A General Disequilibrium Model of Income and Employment," *American Economic Review* (March 1971); A. Leijonhufvud, *On Keynesian Economics;* E. Malinvaud, *The Theory of Unemployment Reconsidered* (New York: Halsted Press, 1977); H. Muellbaner and R. Portes, "Macroeconomic Models."

ment that result from this type of adjustment affects income distribution, probably reinforcing the regressive impact due to the sharp reduction in real wages.

Financial Markets, Stagflation, and the Redistribution of Assets

A second process of interest is the development of private financial markets simultaneous with a policy of monetary restraint. Suppose that, while monetary contraction is underway and recession is setting in, private financial intermediaries are created, and the previously controlled interest rate is allowed to fluctuate freely according to supply and demand conditions. This happened in Chile during 1974, when private *financieras* were allowed to operate under a system of free interest rates. At the same time the rate charged by banks was under control of the monetary authorities. Typically the former would be about 50 percent higher than the latter.[32] In April 1975, bank rates were set free. They jumped by more than 100 percent in nominal terms during the first semester of 1975 (see figure 6-1).

Similar behavior occurred in Argentina. A *Reforma Financiera* was implemented in May 1977, when banks were allowed to operate in the short-term financial market with free interest rates.[33] At the same time, the demand for funds by public enterprises was channeled to this market. The effect was that nominal monthly rates rose from 6 percent in May to 13 percent by the end of the year. (See figure 6-2, which gives equivalent rates for 90 days.)

The effect of such a sharp rise in interest rates is equivalent to a supply shock. The cost of financial capital for firms rises, and this will eventually affect prices. Cavallo has provided empirical evidence that this effect might be important in the context of semiindustrialized countries.[34]

An explanation of why the cost of borrowing may be an important factor in the pricing behavior of firms and the macroeconomic implications of borrowing cost are developed by Cavallo and more recently by Bruno.[35] Conventional macrotheory has emphasized wages as the main cost-push factor behind price determination by firms in the short term. The under-

32. Average nominal monthly rates for the first three months in 1975 charged by *financieras* was 14.3 percent as compared to 9.6 percent charged by banks.

33. See A. Canitrot and R. Frenkel, "Establización y largo plazo."

34. D. Cavallo, "Stagflationary Effects of Monetarist Stabilization Policies in Economies with Persistent Inflation" (Ph.D. dissertation, Harvard University, 1977).

35. M. Bruno, "Stabilization and Stagflation in a Semi-Industrialized Economy" (Hebrew University of Jerusalem, December 1977).

Figure 6-1. *Chile, Selected Indicators (Quarterly Variations and Index)*

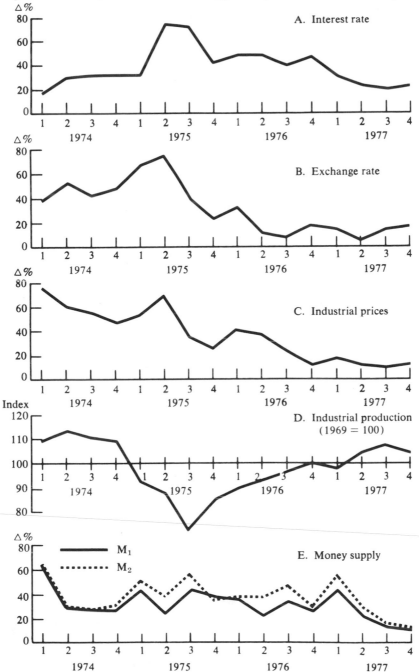

Sources: Panel A, Banco Central, *Boletín Mensual*, no. 601; panels B and E, Banco Central; panel C, Instituto Nacional de Estadísticas, "Household Expenditures Survey"; panel D, Sociedad de Fomento Fabril.

Figure 6-2. *Argentina, Selected Indicators (Quarterly Variations and Index)*

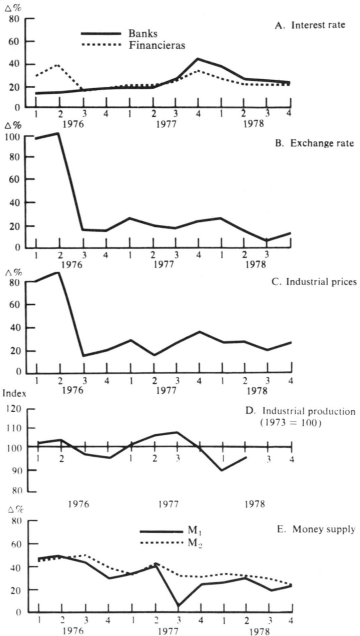

Sources: Panels A and B, Canitrot and Frenkel, "Establización y largo plazo"; panels C and D, Frenkel, "¿Qué expectativas: la inflación Argentina 1975–1978?"; panel E, IMF, *International Financial Statistics*.

lying assumption is that capital is constant and that raw materials prices do not change significantly throughout the cycle.

The assumption seems to be justified with respect to physical capital, but not necessarily with respect to working capital, which is not a fixed cost. Working capital is in fact a function of the funds required to finance labor and physical inputs and of the interest rate.

If for some reason the demand for funds increases or the supply is rationed and interest rates rise sharply, there will be a cost-push effect on firms. A higher cost of borrowing shifts aggregate supply upward. How important this effect will be depends on the relative importance of the rise in interest rates. Ordinarily, in economies with developed, homogeneous capital markets, these changes are not large, even in the face of a restrictive monetary policy.[36] The same cannot be said for semi-industrialized economies with segmented financial markets. Here a restrictive monetary policy may have a very sharp effect on the cost of borrowing. This policy may force firms out of the official low-interest-rate market into the high-cost financial market.[37] In fact, the higher the cost of alternative credit supply and the more segmented the financial market, the more significant the cost effect.

What kind of financial market segmentation were these economies facing? During the first phase, the market was segmented between an official, regulated market (the banking system) and a higher-cost, free market (the *financieras*). Both were essentially domestic markets. Then the interest rates were set free, and they rapidly reached a much higher level than the official rate. This made external borrowing more attractive. The cost of borrowing abroad, for those banks and firms that had access to foreign capital markets, was substantially lower than the costs of domestic borrowing.[38] Since there were regulations concerning the maximum volume of foreign borrowing allowed, the external financial market acted as a rationed, cheap credit market as compared with the domestic one. Thus, in some ways the external market became a substitute for the original domestic official credit market, where interest rates were also substantially lower than the domestic free market.

36. J. Tobin, "The Wage-Price Mechanism," in O. Eckstein, ed., *The Econometrics of Price Determination* (Washington, D.C.: Federal Reserve Board, 1977).

37. For example, borrowing from banks at the official rate during 1974 in Chile may not have been possible for many firms due to the contractionary monetary policy. They were, then, forced to borrow, at a cost higher by 50 percent, from the *financieras*.

38. In Chile, for a sustained period of time, the external cost of borrowing was between one-fourth and one-half the internal cost.

At the same time, since demand was falling due to the restrictive monetary policy, firms were piling up inventories. The higher cost of credit forced them to reduce stocks. They did this by cutting production. The effect of the higher financial cost was not only to increase prices, but also to reduce output, a typical stagflationary effect.[39] The trends shown by the variables in figures 6-1 and 6-2 seem to be consistent with this hypothesis.

The effect will be temporary and may, thus, be considered unimportant.[40] But given that it tends to happen simultaneously with other macro-adjustments, such as devaluation and monetary contraction, it tends to reinforce the stagflationary effects produced by some of these other mechanisms. On the other hand, given that the economy is facing a very high rate of inflation for a sustained period, inflationary expectations perform an important amplifying role vis à vis any changes in such critical indicators as the exchange rate, wages, and the interest rate. Thus there are powerful reasons for not underestimating the impact of financial costs on the rate of inflation and on the level of economic activity and employment, at least while financial market segmentation is a significant structural characteristic of the economy.

A side effect of this policy concerns important processes of asset redistribution that are facilitated by a macroeconomic environment such as the one we have been describing in this section. The prevalence of high real interest rates—in Chile they have been over 40 percent a year for about three years—implies huge distortions that affect resource allocation.[41] Resources do not flow into new real investment unless rates of return similar to those prevailing in the financial markets can be obtained. Such high rates of return can only be achieved through a gross undervaluation of assets. The price of productive assets will drastically go down.

On the other hand, recession and higher financial costs that firms are simultaneously facing make them vulnerable financially. But not all firms are equally affected; large firms can rapidly develop access to foreign

39. Notice that the stagflationary effects occur simultaneously with a general policy of monetary contraction. And, at least during the period that the financial supply shock is absorbed, what would be observed is not reductions in output and rates of inflation, but lower output with higher inflation, a "perverse" result according to conventional theory.

40. The rise in domestic interest rates could be very temporary if, simultaneous with setting it free, external capital were allowed to move in with no restrictions.

41. Notice that the interest rates given in figures 6-1 and 6-2 are nominal quarterly rates. They are consistent with the yearly real rates given above.

borrowing. Since the external rates are equivalent to one-half or one-third of rates prevailing in the domestic markets, foreign borrowing gives large firms a significant advantage.

Thus, liquidity concentrates in larger firms. As a consequence, it is easy for them to buy undervalued assets of medium-sized firms that are in trouble because of low sales and increased borrowing at the very high rates prevailing in the domestic market. The mechanism we have described is not merely an abstract exercise. At least in the Chilean case, it has proved to be a very powerful mechanism to concentrate assets in a few large conglomerates.[42] The process is accelerated if it coincides with the denationalization of public enterprises, a common objective of the "new" orthodox stabilization policies in Latin America. Undervalued public enterprises are transferred at low prices and bought by those very few who have access to liquid funds under favorable conditions.[43]

Summing up, the persistence of financial market segmentation, together with general recessionary conditions in the economy, has two kinds of effects: (1) it sets in motion a powerful process of asset concentration, and (2) it generates stagflation. Both effects have a negative impact on the distribution of income.

External Shocks and Devaluation

Chronic balance-of-payments disequilibrium has been a structural feature of most Latin American economies for decades. These imbalances have been aggravated by the external supply shocks—autonomous price increases of imported raw materials—that have become a part of the scene in the 1970s. These external disequilibriums are the reason for the drastic and recurrent devaluations that have gone together with monetary control, wage repression, and the other policies that form part of the orthodox package in the cases analyzed in this chapter.

Consider the cases of Chile and Argentina as illustrations. A look at

42. In 1978 five conglomerates controlled an estimated 53 percent of the assets of the 250 largest firms, and nine controlled 82 percent of the assets of the banking system. Among 100 firms sampled, real assets held by five conglomerates rose 97 percent from 1969 to 1978, while those of other firms rose only 14 percent. F. Dahse, *Mapa de la Extrema Riquez* (Ed. Aconcagua, 1979).

43. Again, an example from Chile will be illustrative. Of 121 public firms that were sold to the private sector between 1975 and 1977 for $290 million, the assets of only 21 were valued at $301 million in 1977, according to their balance sheets. See A. Foxley, "Stabilization Policies."

figures 6-1 and 6-2 indicates the various instances in which a devaluation of the peso was taking place. In Chile, starting in November 1974 and during the first semester of 1975, the peso was devalued at a faster rate than during the first ten months in 1974.[44] This process was accompanied by an upsurge in prices.[45] Similar but even more discontinuous devaluations took place in Argentina in the first and last quarters of 1976, and again in the fourth quarter of 1977. These devaluations were also accompanied by price increases, as suggested in figure 6-2.

What are the effects of devaluations on semi-industrialized economies such as those examined? Conventional theory predicts that devaluation, by improving the relative price of traded vis à vis nontraded goods, shifts resources toward export- or import-substituting activities, thus helping reduce the balance-of-payments deficit. At the same time, an excess demand for the relatively cheaper nontraded goods develops. This results in either an increase in price of domestic goods if the economy is in full employment or in an expansion of nontraded goods production. Introducing money and capital flows in the analysis does not change the basic conclusions, although the transmission mechanism might be a little more complicated.[46]

This approach does not stress some important effects that might accompany the change in relative prices resulting from exogenous changes in import prices or from devaluation. One is a probable strong and immediate impact on inflationary expectations, particularly when the economy is suffering from very high inflation rates.[47] Another less conventional

44. In 1974, average devaluation during the first nine months was 43 percent per quarter; in the last quarter, 58.5 percent; and in the first and second quarters of 1975, 71.9 percent and 64.3 percent.

45. While average rate of price increases for the period October–December 1974 was 41 percent; between January and March 1975, the rate of inflation went up to 60 percent; and in the second quarter, the inflation rate increased to 73.7 percent.

46. Essentially a real cash balances effect reduces income, thus depressing imports until a surplus in current account is developed. This very short-run effect is accompanied by a flow of foreign capital, given that the original trade deficit creates an excess demand for money. Interest rates rise and capital flows in, helping cover the deficit and expanding money supply. See R. Dornbusch, "Real and Monetary Aspects of the Effects of Exchange Rate Changes," in R. Z. Aliber, ed., *National Monetary Policies and the International Financial System* (University of Chicago Press, 1974). See also L. Calmfors, *Prices, Wages and Employment in the Open Economy* (University of Stockholm, Institute for International Economic Studies, 1978).

47. L. Sjaastad and H. Cortés find evidence of this in Chile. See their paper, "El enfoque monetario de la balanza de pagos y las tasas de interés real en Chile," *Estudios de Economía,* no. 11 (Universidad de Chile, 1978).

impact of devaluation might be a contractionary effect on effective demand and income of a more permanent nature than predicted by conventional theory.

Suppose nominal wages are constant or only partially indexed to the rate of inflation. When the price of traded goods increases as a result of devaluation, a cost increase for firms follows because the price of imported inputs raises. Some of the cost pressure is transferred to domestic prices through a markup mechanism. Now the prices of traded and nontraded goods are rising. But nominal wages do not keep up with the price increase caused by devaluation.

Real wages and the wage share fall. Income distribution shifts toward profit earners, exporters particularly; and toward the government via increased export and import tax revenues. It suffices that the saving propensities of the latter two be higher than those of wage earners for the net effect on aggregate demand to be contractionary. Savings would be in excess of required levels, and the economy would adjust by reducing income. The impact of devaluation would be recessionary.[48]

The same type of result is obtained if it is assumed that devaluation acts over a large and chronic balance-of-payments deficit. In this case, even if the trade balance improves in terms of foreign currency after devaluation, it may actually result in a larger deficit in domestic currency.[49] If money supply is endogenous and directly dependent on the trade balance in domestic currency, nominal money balances will fall as a result of devaluation. Since at the same time prices are rising, real balances fall even more, and the final effect is recessionary.

These results depend on some key assumptions. One assumption, explicit in both the Taylor and Bruno approaches, is that the price elasticities involved (demand for imports, supply of exports) are small. In other words, they share a pessimism about the capacity of the economy to respond quickly to devaluation through higher exports and lower imports.

In effect, Krugman and Taylor's argument is that income distribution effects will reduce aggregate demand (absorption) and that this reduction will dominate any improvement that might be achieved in the trade balance. This is the only way that the net effect is recessionary.

48. This approach has been developed in an interesting paper by P. Krugman and L. Taylor, "Contractionary Effects of Devaluation," *Journal of International Economics*, no. 8 (1978); see also L. Taylor, *Macro Models for Developing Countries* (McGraw-Hill, 1979).

49. A model along these lines has been proposed by M. Bruno, "Stabilization and Stagflation."

But recent experience in countries such as Uruguay, Brazil, and Chile seems to suggest that export pessimism is not warranted, given the success of these countries in expanding nontraditional exports, when the exchange rate bias against exports is eliminated. This conclusion is in agreement with empirical studies for a large number of countries.[50]

If this is so, the impact of devaluation could go either way. Devaluation would be recessionary only if, in spite of significant improvements in the trade balance, the depressive effect on internal demand were very strong and dominant. This seems to be the case in Argentina, where the basic traded exportables are food products that represent a large share of domestic consumption. Devaluation has a very large and direct impact through higher prices of traded consumption goods and lower real wages on real domestic consumption. This impact generates an almost immediate recessionary tendency. This relationship is suggested in figure 6-1 and has also been demonstrated at the theoretical and empirical level in several studies.[51]

Another important premise in the previous analysis is that international capital flows are controlled by the government. If this were not the case, the recessionary tendency would be checked because any reduction in real monetary balances caused by the price increases that follow devaluation would be compensated by a higher flow of external capital. This flow of capital would expand money supply;[52] a recession would not necessarily be a consequence of devaluing the domestic currency.

On the other hand, when these conditions are not met, as is often the case in most semi-industrialized economies, particularly a condition of free capital movements, the likelihood of recession following devaluation increases. And a direct impact on prices, through both higher costs and inflationary expectations, is almost a certainty.[53] Neither effect helps

---

50. See J. Bhagwati and R. Martin, "Trade and Investment Strategies, Jobs and Poverty" (Massachusetts Institute of Technology, August 1979).

51. The pioneering work was done by C. Diaz-Alejandro, *Exchange Rate Devaluation in a Semi-Industrialized Country: The Experience of Argentina* (MIT Press, 1965).

52. See L. Sjaastad and H. Cortés, "El enfoque monetario." See also A. Harberger, "Una visión moderna del fenómeno inflacionario," *Cuadernos de Economía* (Universidad Católica de Chile, December 1977).

53. The impact on prices is a certainty unless the effect of devaluation is compensated by tariff reductions. But in that case, an important expected result of the policy, that of checking import expansion by increasing its relative price, is cancelled.

improve income distribution, particularly when nominal wages are fixed or only partially indexed.

Fiscal Adjustment and Distributive Effects

The public sector deficit has been an important source of monetary expansion in Latin America for a long time. During stabilization attempts, particularly those focused on the reduction of money supply, policy makers have given a high priority to balancing the fiscal accounts. Figures for Brazil, Uruguay, and Chile, given in table 6-7, show a uniform pattern of reduction in the public deficit during the years corresponding to the orthodox stabilization programs.

There are many ways to reduce the fiscal deficit, including increasing taxation or cutting government expenditures. Among the latter, there is a choice between reducing current expenditures or public investment.

Table 6-7. *Fiscal Deficit as a Percentage of Gross Domestic Product*

ARGENTINA

Year	(1) Public sector deficit
1972	2.7
1973	5.5
1974	6.2
1975	11.9
1976	8.2
1977	4.2
1978	3.4

BRAZIL

Year	(2) Federal government deficit
1963	4.2
1964	3.2
1965	1.6
1966	1.1
1967	1.7
1968	1.2
1969	0.6
1970	0.4

CHILE

Year	(3) Fiscal deficit
1970	2.9
1971	9.3
1972	10.5
1973	8.8
1974	8.9
1975	2.9
1976	2.0
1977	1.5

URUGUAY

Year	(4) Central government deficit
1970	1.8
1971	5.7
1972	2.6
1973	1.4
1974	4.3
1975	4.3
1976	2.6
1977	1.3

Sources: (1) IMF, *International Financial Statistics*; for 1976–78 the price deflactor was estimated; (2) Lemgruber, "Inflation in Brazil"; (3) Ministerio de Hacienda and ODEPLAN; (4) Banco Central.

The choice of instruments will be probably influenced not only by short-term considerations, but also by the role assigned to the state in the long-term development strategy. Brazil chose to expand the public sector, while Chile favored its drastic reduction.

These two long-term models have very different implications for fiscal policies. Brazil reduced the fiscal deficit by increasing taxes and reducing current government expenditures[54] and, at the same time, expanding public investment. For example, in 1965 in the middle of a recession, when industrial production was falling by 4.7 percent, investment by the central government increased by 8 percent and that by public enterprise by 70 percent. This countercyclical policy no doubt helped in terms of lowering unemployment during the recession.[55]

Fiscal adjustment in the Chilean case came mainly through a reduction in public expenditures. Government expenditures decreased from 29.1 percent of GDP in 1974 to 22 percent in 1977. During the same years, the share of public investment in GDP fell from 11.8 percent to 6.3 percent. In 1975, during a critical period of the stabilization program, public investment fell by 48 percent in real terms. A large part of this decrease was in investment in public works and housing, a highly labor-intensive activity, that contracted by 50 percent in real terms in just one year. This particular fiscal policy contributed to the 20 percent unemployment rate in Chile in early 1976.

The distributive consequences of the fiscal adjustment differ widely according to the instruments chosen. When the adjustment implies a drastic reduction in public expenditures, activities that have a progressive effect on income distribution—the so-called social sectors, such as health, education, housing, and social security—are bound to be affected. In the Chilean case, public expenditure in these sectors decreased from ninety dollars per person in 1970 to seventy dollars in 1976.[56] On the other hand, reducing public investment in infrastructure causes high unemployment, mostly among unskilled or semiskilled laborers.[57]

The other side of fiscal adjustment is taxation, and most countries will

---

54. Tax revenues increased from 7.8 percent of Gross National Product (GNP) in 1963 to 11.1 percent in 1966.

55. See J. R. Wells, "Growth and Fluctuations in the Brazilian Manufacturing Sector During the 1960s and Early 1970s" (Ph.D. dissertation, Cambridge University, 1977).

56. A. Foxley and J. Arellano, "El Estado y las desigualdades sociales," *Revista Mensaje,* no. 261 (August 1977).

57. The unemployment rate for construction workers in Chile was 31 percent during 1975 and 34 percent in 1976.

try to increase tax revenues as a way of reducing the public deficit. But there are alternatives here also. Referring to the previous example, look at the way tax revenues were increased in Chile after 1974. The main source was a value-added tax with a uniform rate of 20 percent. At the same time, several taxes were eliminated: the net wealth tax, the capital gains tax, and the tax on interest payments. Through these changes, the share of direct taxes fell from 33.4 percent of the total tax revenue in 1974 to 26.6 percent in 1977, while indirect taxes increased from 66.6 percent to 73.4 percent.

The example of Chile is useful to stress the cumulative effects that a certain adjustment for the fiscal accounts may have in terms of employment and income distribution. Most distributive signs seem to be negative in this particular case, but it need not be so generally. Given a target reduction in the fiscal deficit, there are several different ways to achieve the objective. The equity and employment implications of each one are also very different, as this discussion has suggested.

Why wouldn't policy makers always choose the package that has the least negative distributive impact? I have suggested that the answer lies in the nature of the long-term development model and the role assigned within it to the various economic agents. If, for example, the model postulates a reduced public sector and an increased role for private capital, then it is likely that this will be reflected in the fiscal policy as in other areas. This policy orientation may imply negative distributive effects. The extent that the conflict is solved in favor of a larger control over resources by private capital at the expense of equity only confirms the preeminence of that objective over others.

The explanation of why this option was taken in several of the recent economic stabilization programs in Latin America is related to the nature of the political changes that have occurred and the preferential access to power that authoritarian regimes seem to give to private capitalists at the expense of most other groups in society.

Conclusions

In this chapter I have analyzed the distributive consequences of stabilization policies from a Latin American perspective. Beginning with a review of the early attempts in the 1950s, attention was focused on the "new" stabilization policies of the 1970s. Some of the mechanisms that produce negative distributive and employment effects were studied. In selecting these, I considered those adjustment mechanisms that may produce unexpected or unconventional impacts in the level of employment and on the distribution of income. This choice does not mean that I underestimate the importance of such adjustment mechanisms as the control of money supply. This variable plays a key role, particularly in periods of high inflation as are observed in Latin America.

Relative prices policy, wage policy, devaluations, the development of financial markets, and fiscal sector adjustment were emphasized because these instruments, if not properly used, may reinforce each other in producing negative employment and distributive effects, particularly in a framework of monetary contraction. These negative effects, if taken in isolation, may be only short term and thus not too important. But when considered together, as part of a policy package, their impact may be magnified, particularly when they influence inflationary expectations in addition to increasing costs and depressing aggregate demand.

The need to identify properly the interdependencies between these various adjustment mechanisms is one obvious lesson from the previous analysis. What follows from a policy point of view is that stabilization policies should be applied simultaneously in various fronts if the negative equity effects of a one-sided monetarist policy are to be minimized. Under conditions of generalized market disequilibriums and less than perfectly flexible prices, it is essential to act on inflationary expectations and guide some critical prices back to equilibrium. Relying only on money supply to achieve this goal would be inefficient, slow, and painful from the equity point of view.

On the other hand, throughout this paper I stressed the importance of supply factors. This emphasis is very much in the structuralist tradition. The kind of perverse distributive and employment effects observed in Latin America often occurred in the presence of structural features associated with semi-industrialized economies: financial market segmentation, chronic disequilibrium in the balance of payments, and supply bottlenecks that make the economy vulnerable to frequent exogenous supply shocks.

Of course some of these phenomena have also been important in the recent inflationary upsurge in the developed world.[58] The application of

58. M. Diamand, "Towards a Change in the Economic Paradigm"; F. Modigliani, "The Monetarist Controversy"; A. Okun and G. Perry, "Innovative Policies to Slow Inflation, Editors' Summary," *Brookings Papers on Economic Activity, 2:1978.*

conventional contractionary monetary and fiscal policies to reduce the level of demand, in the developed countries' framework, has produced poor results and stagflation. Both had already been observed in the Latin American economies in the late 1950s (see the first section of this paper).[59]

The question then is, what policies are best suited to deal with inflationary pressures that have a strong causal factor on the supply side? The Latin American structuralist reply of the 1950s and 1960s would be to eliminate supply bottlenecks. Since this may require a very significant reallocation of investment resources, the approach to stabilization must necessarily be gradual and rather long term.

Bottlenecks, either in sources of energy, other intermediate inputs, food products, or foreign exchange, will not disappear in the short period of time for which stabilization programs are usually designed. This was mentioned in the first section of this paper as one of the basic weaknesses of the structuralist approach of the 1960s in Latin America.

What should be done in the 1970s, when the structural component of inflation has, if anything, increased? The challenge is to strike the right balance between demand management policies and supply disinflationary shocks.[60] One extreme to be avoided is the exclusive concentration in long-term reallocation of resources (to exports, agriculture, energy, etc.) accompanied by extended (and inefficient) price controls, while at the same time expenditures grow at a fast pace. The other extreme is the naive view that by controlling money supply and the fiscal deficit, everything else will come into place in a reasonably short period of time and without large costs in terms of equity or unemployment. Avoiding these extremes is essential, not only from the point of view of efficiency, but also to reduce to a minimum the regressive effect of the policies on wage earners and the poor.

---

59. The following quotation, describing the state of the U.S. economy in 1973–74 is eloquent as a parallel: "In that interval, prices accelerated much more than did wages. The relative moderation of wages helped to limit the severity of inflation, but it also contributed a squeeze on the real purchasing power of American families. The Federal Reserve kept firm control on the growth of money in the face of soaring prices and interest rates, and the federal budget was brought close to balance. As a result of the squeeze on real incomes and the restraint of monetary and fiscal policies, the economy fell into the most severe recession since the 1930s. . . . The persistence of rapid inflation in a slack economy was a new experiment: it was the first time in U.S. history that a severe recession had failed to stop inflation." See A. Okun and G. Perry, "Innovative Policies."

60. The expression is from A. Okun and G. Perry, "Innovative Policies."

What types of supply disinflationary shocks can be applied, in such a way as to minimize the adverse social effects of the policies? The most common suggestion in the past has been to reduce the cost of labor. This can be done, as in the Latin American orthodox policies, by outright reductions in real wages or by elimination of the minimum wage, or both. It is not irrelevant to stress that this policy has been viable for more than very short periods of time only in the presence of authoritarian governments that eliminated labor legislation, outlawed labor organizations, and were extremely repressive toward labor in general.[61] The reason is obvious: the negative income distribution effect may be dramatic, as has been shown previously in this chapter. Other possibilities, such as reducing indirect taxes while increasing direct taxation and reducing social security contributions, must be examined carefully for their distributive impact.

A different, but related, point has to do with the question of gradual vis à vis abrupt adjustment during stabilization programs. The subject is very broad. Here I will stress only two aspects. One, already mentioned, is that to the extent that there are structural problems behind inflation, gradualism seems unavoidable. A second aspect, a lesson learned from the previous discussions in this chapter, is that abrupt, partial, and asymmetric adjustments in an economy in a state of disequilibrium are bound to produce even more disequilibriums, even if successful in reducing imbalances in one particular market. Once this has happened, various kinds of effects will follow: subsequent adjustment will be slow and difficult—more stagflation, for a longer period—and very significant processes of redistribution of income and assets will take place. The direction of these effects will depend on the nature of the disequilibriums, on the instruments chosen to eliminate them, and on the social and political groups behind the policies.

The groups behind the policies in the recent orthodox stabilization schemes in Latin America have been the private capitalist sector allied with the military. They have provided a political framework that has been quite efficient in transferring resources precisely in favor of private capitalists. This process has required diminishing the role of the state

61. When these policies were applied in a democratic environment in Latin America in the 1950s, they often had to be abandoned in a short period of time due to worker resistance to the large income losses implied by the policy of wage reduction.

and disciplining the workers. As a result, income distribution has deteriorated.

Thus, because the short-term stabilization policies have been accompanied by a drastic reorientation in the way the economy functions, income distribution changes are not only a short-term transitory phenomenon in the authoritarian orthodox experiences. The previous conclusion is familiar to political economists: the distribution of income and property rests, finally, in the structure of power in society. If this is authoritarian and nonparticipatory and excludes important social groups from the political process, the outcome of the distributive process will almost necessarily be regressive.

When the problem of policy alternatives for better income distribution is posed, it is inescapable to associate the technical recommendations to the political framework within which they will be applied. More egalitarian policies in the past were usually associated with either populist or reformist governments in Latin America. The former were successful in producing short-lived gains in the income of the poor, but given their disregard of fundamental economic constraints, they generated the conditions for increased economic instability and, eventually, a full reversal of the policies. In a technical sense, reformist regimes were more successful in producing a coherent set of policies, but their attempts to advance simultaneously in stabilizing the economy, redistributing income, and undertaking structural reform encountered numerous difficulties. The policies were opposed by the groups affected by reforms, and political support in favor of them was often weak and unstable.

At this point one has to choose. If one considers an open, democratic society to be a superior and more desirable political environment than that of an authoritarian regime, the challenge to design policies adequate for that environment has to be met. Policies that require a good deal of political repression to have a reasonable chance of success are certainly not a satisfactory solution.

Although there are no easy answers, there are some lessons to be learned from the past. Short-term policy consistency is important. A gradual approach to stabilization does not mean that money does not matter. Structural change is necessary if production bottlenecks are to be eliminated, but is not a panacea that cures all ills. And, developing political consensus is perhaps the most basic prerequisite to make a more efficient, egalitarian policy work within an open, democratic society.

Comments by Arnold C. Harberger*

In commenting on the chapter by Ahluwalia and Lysy, I start from their concluding section. The main conclusion is that the solution to the balance-of-payments difficulties of developing countries lies in the developed countries' committing themselves to import more from the developing countries in question by reducing trade barriers, raising import quotas, or by extending price guarantees to specific exports of specific countries.

The first thought that crossed my mind on reading this recommendation is that it is supremely easy for any country to put itself in balance-of-payments difficulties. Sidney Alexander taught us many years ago how this could be done by fiscal policy (the expenditures approach to balance-of-payments deficits); now Harry Johnson and others have taught us how it can be done by monetary policy (the monetary approach to the balance of payments). Needless to say, if there is an international arrangement that fills in balance-of-payments gaps by issuing quantity and/or price guarantees on exports, there will be a genuine temptation for countries to act in such a way as to create their own balance-of-payments problems.

Ahluwalia and Lysy do not explore how they would deal with this possibility, but there is an important clue in the third section of the paper. The authors say, "we assume here that all possibilities of import-competing industries to substitute for imports . . . have been previously used up." This clue serves to help us interpret the models in the paper. The results are meaningful when applied to a foreign-exchange-constrained economy, and a country becomes foreign-exchange constrained when the shadow price (or social opportunity cost of foreign exchange) is greatly in excess of the market exchange rate.

The only way that I know to get a country into this situation is by policy measures. Drastic import substitution against anything nonessential will drive the system to the point where only essentials are imported and, in the process, will drive the exchange rate to a position so overvalued that only items of supreme comparative advantage for the country can be exported. Many countries have got themselves into this sort of situation in the past, and some are still there in the present. But I thought

---

* Editors' note: These comments and those by Albert Fishlow refer to both this chapter and chapter 5 by Montek Ahluwalia and Frank Lysy.

that the main lessons of recent years were that countries could and should rectify that sort of situation.

The great lesson of effective protection theory, for example, is that only by having a uniform tariff can we even *know* how much protection we are giving to our domestic products. Yet a uniform and moderate tariff—which is where effective protection analysis points—leads to an economy for which the Ahluwalia-Lysy model just does not apply.

As far as I can see, if a developing country is pursuing reasonable trade and capital market policies, there will be no way to assure or guarantee that all its imports are essential. No line of argument moving from an assumed deficit to a conclusion calling for foreign aid to cope with the deficit can survive as a general rule for developing countries. Where such a line of argument has plausibility, it is because the developing countries in question have not heeded the policy lessons of recent decades and have opted for an extreme form of import substitution.

Alejandro Foxley's paper surprised me in its revival of the structuralist-monetarist debate, which I thought had been substantially resolved at a famous Rio de Janeiro conference more than fifteen years ago. Arthur Lewis, in a brilliant summary of the proceedings of that conference, concluded that if chronic and large fiscal deficits were defined as a structural phenomenon, then we were all structuralists; and that if they were defined as a monetary phenomenon, then we were all monetarists.[62] For other definitions of structuralism, there is no evidence. Neither before the Rio conference, during it, or after it, has any systematic evidence been assembled indicating a tendency for inflation to be greater in countries with balance-of-payments deficits, or in countries with slow-growing agricultural sectors, or in countries (or at times) when food prices are relatively high. I do not think it is helpful to allude to inflation being caused by bottlenecks until evidence to that effect has been presented.

As far as I can see, structuralism is not a theory in the sense that monetary theory is. By and large, monetary analyses of inflation work with the demand function for money (or for real cash balances). Evidence supporting the existence of such a function abounds, drawn from many countries and for many time periods. Efforts to understand monetary events, including the phenomenon of inflation, while ignoring the relevance of the demand for real balances are, in my view, doomed to

---

62. See W. Arthur Lewis, "Summary of the Conference," in Werner Baer and Isaac Kerstenetsky, eds., *Inflation and Growth in Latin America* (Homewood: Richard D. Irwin, 1964).

Table 6-8. *Percentage Increase in Money Supply*
During year ending December 31

Country	1973	1974	1975	1976	1977	1978
Argentina	103	70	406	296	126	143
Brazil	49	34	39	39	37	41
Chile	317	272	257	194	108	67
Uruguay	80	64	64	66	38	80

failure. It seems to me that Foxley would have served the science better in trying to delineate what the current state of our scientific knowledge is, rather than by trying to revive an old and ill-defined controversy that has little scientific content. At the very least, if structuralism is to be thought of as a serious scientific theory or approach, its scientific content (e.g., some counterpart of the demand function for real cash balances) should have been set forth.

The space remaining allows me to comment on only a very few of the substantive points made in Foxley's paper. First, let me say that, however one might characterize government economic policy in Chile during the Frei administration (1964–70), it certainly did not have an anti-monetarist cast. Indeed, its policy was more firmly based on good monetary theory than that of the great majority of other administrations, both in Chile and in the rest of Latin America. The same cannot be said of its successor government (Allende, 1970–73), which blatantly ignored the lessons of simple monetary theory.

Second, it is completely wrong to give the impression that monetary restraint has been a leading feature of recent economic policy in the Southern Cone countries. This can be seen directly from table 6-8, which gives the percentage rates of increase in the money supply in Argentina, Brazil, Chile, and Uruguay over the period since December 1972. There is no evidence whatever of a "monetary crunch" here; gradualism is the order of the day.

Third, although fiscal deficits have been sharply reduced in Argentina, Chile, and Uruguay, they have been brought to levels that bespeak a reasonable flexibility of budget policy—not a doctrinaire balanced-budget approach. After the budgetary contraction, Argentina's deficit was still 3.4 percent of GDP, Chile's was 1.5 percent, and Uruguay's 1.3 percent (see table 6-7, data for 1977).

Finally, Foxley exaggerates both the coherence of policy in the Southern Cone countries and its dependence on authoritarian government. The tax reforms of 1974 and 1975 in Chile came before any serious effort was made to disinflate the economy. The main components of this package were (1) a value-added tax copied from Europe and (2) an income tax reform drawn from the Report of the Royal Commission on Taxation in Canada. Liberalization was partial in all cases—Chile liberalized trade while maintaining capital market controls; Argentina and Uruguay liberalized capital movements while doing little or nothing about trade restrictions. Wage restraint played different roles in different places. While wage controls were a significant feature (I am told) on the Argentine scene, no such controls were imposed at any time by the military government in Chile.

My own view is that in actual fact the various components of policy in the Southern Cone countries came about in quite independent ways. They were not parts of a single package, imposed all at once. Moreover, the validity of one piece did not depend in any great degree on the presence of the others. Chile could have imposed a value-added tax with or without the reform of the income tax system, with or without tariff reduction, with or without a gradual move to a fixed exchange rate.

I not only believe that the separate components of policy came about via essentially independent processes; even more I feel that we are capable, professionally, of analyzing them separately and on their merits. In particular, I am disturbed by Foxley's apparent desire to condemn the policies pursued in the Southern Cone countries through "guilt by association" with authoritarian governments. In my opinion, no single component of policy in the Southern Cone countries is without its precedents in a democratic setting. Economic policies should be judged on their merits.

Comments by Albert Fishlow

The consequences of stabilization policy for income distribution derive from three principal sources: the generalized reduction in real income that is encouraged to curb aggregate demand and imports; the changes in relative goods and factor prices that are promoted to induce an altered production profile in the economy; and the reduced size of the public sector that is the concomitant of fiscal restraint.

Ahluwalia and Lysy touch upon all of these effects in their Keynesian model simulations but focus on the possibilities of a perverse response to devaluation. Instead of offsetting restrictive and monetary policies by re-directing resources to exports and import substitutes, devaluation may—through increased savings from windfall export gains, through real balance effects, and through reduced consumption from higher import prices—provoke declines in aggregate demand. The authors consider only the last of these mechanisms and estimate the critical parameter values for export demand that determine the balance of forces.

Their contribution makes clear that, even in a world of neoclassical goods and factor price equations, the absence of money in the determination of the price level, and immediate and direct return to equilibrium, there are possibilities for a perverse response to devaluation. They are much greater, of course, when expectations are taken into account and the initial price adjustment necessitated by devaluation ramifies throughout the economy; when uncertainties afflict foreign capital inflow; when domestic firms encumbered by foreign debt find their liabilities much enhanced; when access to new credit is limited; when, in short, the readjustment of the exchange rate in a more realistic setting makes the immediate negative repercussions on expenditure carry further than intended and fall on production decisions more severely than the stimulus to exports and import substitutes.

As the authors recognize, the distribution implications in their models are limited by their same assumptions. Returns to factors depend on elasticities of substitution and levels of output; there is no asymmetrical effect on labor or capital, nor, even in their more complicated model, are there changes in the relative returns to different skill classes. This misses the reality of cyclical response in stabilizing economies—in part, perhaps, because the authors base their simulations on an economy that has managed to avert successive stabilization crises. In tracking historical Malaysian experience and developing abstract models appropriate to it, Ahluwalia and Lysy have implicitly started from initial conditions that do not require the therapy applied and have thereby diluted the applicability of their experiments.

Foxley paints with a broader brush. The historical experience of Latin America is a richer one of stabilization policies. From the 1950s until the most recent cases of Argentina, Chile, Mexico, and Peru in the 1970s, the IMF has been an active participant in that experience, not always by the desire of the countries involved, and almost always controversially. At this writing, the next situation looming on the horizon is that of Brazil, the largest developing country debtor, where the internal debate about appropriate stabilization strategy is at the heart of economic policy.

Foxley's position essentially consists of two major propositions: (1) market imperfections and supply bottlenecks cause a demand-oriented approach to stabilization to be inefficient, if not ineffective, with the burden falling disproportionately on sectors having limited, and sometimes negative, political weight; (2) the priorities of stabilization policy are diverted to the balance of trade and short-term economic indicators to the exclusion and detriment of long-term growth, let alone distribution implications. He seeks to document the validity of his case by reference to the varied measures imposed and the results achieved in the four Southern Cone countries of Argentina, Brazil, Chile, and Uruguay.

It is important to note the convergence in one respect between earlier monetarist and structuralist approaches to stabilization policy. Foxley's descriptions of the far-reaching interventions undertaken in labor, financial, and product markets as part of recent stabilization policies make clear that radical and structural reform has been integrated into more orthodox approaches. Demand management is inadequate. It is also relevant that policies in Argentina and Chile now incorporate features of global monetarism rather than old-fashioned orthodoxy. Domestic inflation is regarded as determined by the world rate plus the pre-fixed rate of devaluation; the money supply is an endogenous result of capital flows equilibrating domestic and international interest rates. Long-run equilibrium conditions have not had a full counterpart in actual observations. The weight given to international constraints carries over to product markets: free trade is the instrument of preference to ensure productive efficiency.

The fundamental issue dividing structuralists and monetarists is not whether stabilization policies are necessary, but which ones are appropriate. Accelerating inflation, public sector deficits, shortages of foreign exchange, and stagnant exports eventually take their toll on economic development. There is no division on the question of whether one ought to get prices right, but there is on deciding what they ought to be. The more orthodox view is that it is necessary and sufficient to give fuller rein to market determination dominated by private interests and transactions. Structuralists emphasize the continuing need for social priorities and public guidance.

The distributive implications of orthodox stabilization policies are almost inevitably adverse. Since wages lag behind prices in adjustment, even a continuing constant wage share in income is likely to imply a real loss compared to previous experience. In fact, constancy is difficult to ensure. Since private production and savings are priorities, returns to capital are typically permitted to rise and encouraged by policy; since prices must be restrained, wage costs must be limited: bargaining is no longer free. Beyond the economics there is also a political motivation: stabilization policy finds few supporters in the urban or rural masses.

From the orthodox perspective such a redistribution is justified as part of the transition to a new equilibrium, unfortunate, perhaps, but inevitable. Critics tend to chronicle its existence but not to confront the issue of whether real wages have become so high as to prejudice incentives to invest and to impede the creation of new job opportunities. The question is too important to be resolved by assumption. Social priorities and private returns do not coincide, but there is no reason for the prestabilization disequilibrium to define a viable set of relative factor prices, any more than an appropriate exchange rate.

Another central unknown, at least in the Latin American context, is the means of influencing inflationary expectations. Declines in output are an expensive social means for reversing views about price increases, the more so since the burden does not afflict income classes equally. Devaluation and fiscal restraint inevitably produce an initial upward readjustment of relative prices that can easily generalize to broad inflationary pressures. Can and should price controls be used to get prices right rather than have the market nullify, at least for some time, the transition toward a more adequate productive structure?

Despite the increasing sway held by orthodoxy, its claims are not unblemished, theoretically or empirically, as these papers demonstrate. Sometimes we seem to make a virtue of the very costs of restrictive stabilization policies, as if the willingness to accept them (and to repress others less inclined to do so) were proof of their appropriateness. A large part of the appeal of orthodoxy is the failure of alternative strategies, perverse in their insistence that the costs are minimal and that multiple policy objectives can be pursued with impunity. A more persuasive option remains to be fully defined. Otherwise long-term aspirations for more equitable and just societies may continue to suffer at the hands of apparent short-term imperatives.

Discussion

Margaret E. Crahan (Woodstock Theological Center, Georgetown University) commended Foxley's study for documenting the degree of social injury in stabilization cases such as that of Argentina and Chile.

She cited the need to determine what responsibility for the results could be attributed to foreign governments and international institutions, and whether the economic options really necessitated such deleterious effects. She concluded by urging that the validity of economic policies be tied not only to economic criteria, but also to the degree to which they promote the fulfillment of basic needs and encourage popular participation in political and economic decision making.

Danny Leipziger (U.S. State Department) stated that devaluation unaccompanied by structural change is unlikely to succeed, and that conditionality imposed by the IMF and other financial sources should take account of the gradual change required for structural problems. Greater linkage between IMF and World Bank lending would help. He maintained that stabilization programs typically needed to reduce the real wage but not employment. Because alternative resource allocations have alternative employment implications, employment targets should be part of adjustment programs, and trade-offs between transfers and employment generating expenditures should be considered in any cutbacks of government spending.

Gustav Papanek (Boston University) noted that contrary to the findings of the Ahluwalia-Lysy and Foxley studies, stabilization in Bangladesh and Indonesia had been progressive in terms of income distribution and expansionary in terms of real GDP. Real wages rose dramatically. Both cases were shock treatments (in Indonesia inflation fell from approximately 1,000 percent to 8 percent in three years). Supply expansion was the key to price and external account stabilization. It was possible to expand exports with no decline in world price (the normal case for a single country, contrary to the Ahluwalia-Lysy assumption). Increased foreign aid, especially for food, made foreign exchange available for imported wage goods and inputs to raise exports and output; and increased export revenue further eased the foreign exchange constraint on production.

Alejandro Foxley agreed with Harberger that there had not been a monetary crunch in Chile. Public enterprise deficits had kept the government from reducing monetary growth as much as it desired, and the private capital market had created money substitutes.

CHAPTER SEVEN

The Role of Private Banks
in Stabilization Programs

IRVING S. FRIEDMAN

THE FOCAL POINT of this paper is the behavior of commercial banks in lending to developing countries, particularly countries engaged in programs designed to relieve balance-of-payments pressures and reduce inflation. I have drawn heavily on my commercial bank experience during the last six years in dealing with Zaire, Turkey, Peru, Jamaica, Nicaragua, Gabon, Sudan, and Zambia. Case studies of the first four (appended) illustrate the interaction between the International Monetary Fund (IMF) and private commercial banks.

Growth of Private Bank Lending to Developing Countries

The private banks are playing an increasingly important role in financing development. In this part, I describe the recent evolution of this role and how the banks view their role.

Evolution of Lending to Developing Countries

At year-end 1978, total disbursed external term debt outstanding in about 100 developing countries (including the major capital-importing, oil-producing developing countries) amounted to about $340 billion. This was almost five times the amount in 1970.[1] Of the $340 billion outstanding at year-end 1978, about three-quarters consisted of public sector, or publicly guaranteed debt; one-quarter was outstanding with private sector

1. Term debt, as defined here, is debt with original maturities exceeding one year. Short-term debt, that is, debt with maturities of one year or less, is not considered here.

Table 7-1. *Estimate of Disbursed External Term Debt Outstanding in Developing Countries, 1970–80*[a]

Billions of U.S. dollars unless otherwise specified

Type of debt	1970	1971	1972	1973	1974	1975	1976	1977	1978	1979	1980
Public or publicly guaranteed term debt[b]	54.3	63.9	74.1	90.2	110.2	132.9	163.6	201.1	250.0	290.0	330.0
From official sources	36.6	42.9	48.6	56.7	66.7	77.0	89.2	104.2	126.0	150.0	170.0
From private sources	17.7	21.0	25.5	33.5	43.5	55.9	74.4	96.9	124.0	140.0	160.0
From private financial institutions	5.6	7.8	10.9	17.2	24.9	36.4	51.5	69.5	88.0	106.0	124.0
As a percentage of total	10.3	12.2	14.7	19.1	22.6	27.4	31.5	34.6	35.0	36.6	37.6
Nonguaranteed term debt (from private sources)	14.0	16.1	20.5	26.3	32.6	40.1	54.4	71.0	90.0	110.0	130.0
Total external disbursed term debt	68.3	80.0	94.6	116.5	142.8	173.0	218.0	272.1	340.0	400.0	460.0

Source: *World Bank Annual Report 1979*, and estimates by the author. Figures for 1978 are preliminary; for 1979, estimated; and for 1980, projected.
a. Approximately 100 developing countries, including capital deficit oil exporters.
b. External debt exceeding one year in original maturity.

borrowers and was not guaranteed by a public entity in the borrowing country (table 7-1). About $126 billion, or 37 percent, of these borrowed funds came from official creditors; and $214 billion, or more than 60 percent, came from private creditors, mostly banks. Commercial banks accounted for about $160 billion, nearly 50 percent, of the outstanding term debt. Of the public sector term debt of $250 billion outstanding at year-end 1978, about half came from official sources.

At year-end 1970, private financial institutions held about $5.6 billion of the public sector's (or publicly guaranteed) external term debt outstanding, accounting for 10 percent of the total. At year-end 1978, private financial institutions accounted for $88 billion, or approximately 35 percent of the total. Private nonfinancial institutions provided about another 15 percent.[2]

After World War II and until the beginning of the 1970s, official creditors, both governments of developed countries and multilateral organizations, were the most important sources of debt capital to the developing world. In 1972, disbursements of funds from private sources to the Third World's public sector exceeded disbursements of official funds. By 1976, disbursements from private financial institutions alone exceeded disbursements from official sources. In 1978, private financial institutions disbursed an estimated $40 billion to the public sector of the developing world, compared with disbursements of about $25 billion from official creditor sources.[3] Between 1974 and 1976, disbursements from private financial institutions to public sector borrowers in developing countries almost doubled. By 1978, there was another doubling in disbursements from private financial institutions.

The rapid nominal growth of Third World debt and the growing share of debt to private lenders—debt which generally involves shorter maturities and harder terms than official credits—have been cause for concern among observers of international monetary and financial developments. Is the concern warranted for lender or borrower? This depends on the use to which the debt is put.

If the nominal increase in outstanding external debt from 1970 to 1978 is deflated for price changes, the increase comes to about 75 percent,

2. See Irving S. Friedman, *The Emerging Role of Private Banks in the Developing World* (Citicorp, 1977), for a discussion of the growing role of private banks as lenders to developing countries.
3. World Bank, *Debtor Reporting System* (Washington, D.C.: World Bank), and *World Bank Annual Report 1979*.

Table 7-2. *Debt Service Ratios*

Debt service payments on external public debt as a percent of exports of goods and services

Country	1971	1972	1973	1974	1975	1976	1977	1978
Zaire	4.9	8.1	8.3	11.2	15.3	n.a.	n.a.	n.a.
Zambia	9.8	12.9	30.1	7.1	10.1	10.1	18.6	27.1
Sudan	13.4	13.8	11.9	14.2	21.7	14.1	7.6	9.4
Gabon	7.1	7.1	14.1	4.1	5.5	6.1	9.5	20.5
Peru	15.6	15.6	29.1	23.0	25.3	25.9	30.3	31.0
Jamaica	3.4	4.6	5.8	5.9	7.0	11.5	14.9	20.6
Nicaragua	13.7	9.8	19.3	10.7	11.6	12.4	13.8	17.0
Turkey	18.1	17.7	11.1	11.2	13.0	10.9	14.1	14.5
Average	10.8	11.2	16.2	10.9	13.7	n.a.	n.a.	n.a.
Average without Zaire	11.6	11.6	17.3	10.9	13.5	13.0	15.5	20.0
Average of 47 developing countries	11.0	11.3	11.1	9.1	11.1	10.8	11.9	16.3

Sources: IMF, *International Financial Statistics*, December 1979; and World Bank, *World Debt Tables* (and Supplements), 1978 and 1979.
n.a. Not available.

rather than almost fivefold, or an annual average increase in volume of term debt of about 7 percent.[4] By comparison, the volume of world trade over the same period increased by 60 percent, or at an annual average of about 6 percent.[5]

Tables 7-2 and 7-3 provide debt service ratios for selected developing countries. Other quantitative indicators are used by banks to assess creditworthiness. None of these indicators is wholly satisfactory in determining whether a private bank should curtail lending to a developing country. In assessing risk, private banks must pay attention to these indicators, especially a country's total debt and the debt profile.

However, in answering the question of whether countries have borrowed excessively, banks must look beyond these indicators to a country's economic management and its political and social framework. These

4. Deflated by the World Bank's international price deflator which is that of c.i.f. manufactured goods exports (Standard International Trade Classification 5-8) from Organization for Economic Cooperation and Development (OECD) countries, adjusted for exchange rate fluctuations.

5. Measured as world exports (excluding the trade of the centrally planned economies) and deflated by the index of world export prices.

Table 7-3. *Modified Debt Service Ratios*

Debt service payments on external public debt as a percent of exports of goods and services including net unrequited transfers

Country	1971	1972	1973	1974	1975	1976	1977	1978
Zaire	4.3	8.0	8.1	11.2	14.6	n.a.	n.a.	n.a.
Zambia	12.4	15.4	33.6	7.8	11.8	11.2	20.3	30.0
Sudan	13.5	13.5	11.8	13.5	20.0	13.8	7.4	9.2
Gabon	7.2	6.8	14.1	4.1	5.5	6.1	8.8	21.2
Peru	15.0	15.1	28.2	22.4	24.6	25.1	29.5	30.3
Jamaica	3.3	4.4	5.5	5.8	6.9	11.4	14.6	20.1
Nicaragua	13.4	9.6	16.6	10.3	11.2	12.3	13.6	16.8
Turkey	11.1	10.9	6.6	6.6	7.6	7.8	9.9	10.7
Average	10.0	10.5	15.6	10.2	12.8	n.a.	n.a.	n.a.
Average without Zaire	10.8	10.8	16.6	10.1	12.5	12.5	14.9	19.8
Average of 47 developing countries	9.7	10.1	10.3	8.2	9.9	9.8	10.7	13.9

Sources: IMF, *International Financial Statistics,* December 1979; and World Bank, *World Debt Tables* (and Supplements), 1978 and 1979.
n.a. Not available.

issues, as well as quantitative criteria, determine whether the would-be borrower will continue to enjoy the confidence of the external lending community.

A sample of forty-seven of the largest debtors among the developing countries shows that, on average, the ratio of disbursed external term debt of the public sector (or publicly guaranteed) to GDP has been fairly stable over the period 1971–78, averaging 20 percent of GDP. Variations among individual countries are very large, with disbursed external public debt ranging from about 60 percent of GDP (Zaire) to less than 10 percent (Thailand). Similarly, the ratio of disbursed external term debt of the public sector to export earnings has, on average, remained fairly stable. Again, variations among countries are substantial. In some countries external term debt is a multiple of annual export earnings (Bangladesh, India); in others, external term debt amounts to less than half of annual export earnings (Yugoslavia). The average ratio of this debt to export earnings has been about 111 percent.

The public debt service ratio (the ratio of interest and amortization payments on external public sector debt to export earnings) averaged 16 percent in 1978 in forty-seven countries. In Mexico it reached 58 percent, in Chile 34 percent, and Brazil 27 percent, whereas in Kenya and Thailand this ratio was as low as 8 percent and 4 percent, respectively. The higher percentages usually reflect the strong credit standing of the country concerned. The ratio of export earnings to import costs has remained generally stable over the past decade. Export earnings, on average, have covered more than 80 percent of the cost of imports. This was the case in 1972 as well as in 1978. In 1975, following the increased cost of oil imports and the effects of the recession in the industrial countries, export earnings dropped to 75 percent of import costs. Again, there are substantial differences in the export performance of individual countries.

The importance of private commercial bank lending to sustaining development programs in developing countries can be summarized by citing statistics. During 1978, private commercial banks in the Group of Ten countries (plus Switzerland, Austria, Denmark, and Ireland) reported an increase in term claims on developing countries of about $30 billion.[6] By comparison, in 1978 the World Bank Group approved $8.7 billion of credits.[7] The net flow of official development assistance (ODA) from industrial to developing countries during 1978 was $18.3 billion.[8]

Role and Criteria of Commercial Banks in the External Financing of Developing Countries

Personal conclusions and suggestions on the role of commercial banks and the criteria they use in external financing of developing countries are listed below:

1. International lending by commercial banks will continue to expand, although the relative importance of individual banks in this incremental lending will change. Non-U.S. banks are likely to increase in relative importance, but U.S. banks should remain the largest single group for the foreseeable future.

2. Per capita income is not of decisive importance in country creditworthiness, although higher-income countries are likely to be the largest borrowers because of their absorptive capacities. Nevertheless, many low-

---

6. Bank for International Settlements, *Maturity Distribution of International Bank Lending, End-December 1978* (Basel, July 1979).

7. *World Bank Annual Report 1978.*

8. Press release, OECD, "Resources for Developing Countries 1978 and Recent Trends," June 25, 1979.

income countries use commercial banks as an important source of development finance.

3. Balance-of-payments ratios become significant elements in country risk assessment mainly when confidence in a country is waning.

4. As they gain experience, borrowing countries become increasingly aware of the lending criteria of commercial banks. This evolution will increase the importance for commercial banks of improved information about country conditions. The multilateral institutions, for example, the IMF and the development banks, could be helpful; but unless there are changes in the willingness of their members to provide information to banks, such help necessarily will be limited.

5. Quality of economic management is likely to weigh heavily in the judgment by banks of a country's creditworthiness. What constitutes good economic management will vary from country to country and from time to time; absolute criteria or tests will not be feasible.

6. The acceptance by borrowers and multilateral institutions of the fact that private banks will remain the largest single category of development finance will result in adaptations of domestic policies of borrowers and of lending practices of multilateral institutions.

7. The regulatory authorities of creditor nations should continue their efforts to improve their understanding of conditions in borrowing countries, of the risks involved in lending, and of how to fulfill their regulatory functions without impeding acceptable international lending and borrowing. Further domestic and international consideration should be given to the differences in national regulatory behavior and to the implications for the international competitiveness of the banks involved.

8. Developing countries can rely on commercial banks as a source of external finance only so long as their governments maintain policies that keep them creditworthy for international borrowing. Private bank "conditionality" is unavoidable. Private banks must always, implicitly or explicitly, be applying country lending criteria in deciding when to reduce, maintain, or increase levels of exposure in countries to which they lend. Widespread dollar liquidity does not mean that banks make loans they regard as risky. It does mean, however, that many more banks are willing to meet competition by lending to creditworthy borrowers and on financial terms that borrowers find relatively favorable, for example, longer grace period and maturities.

9. While the demands of developing countries are likely to increase

for foreign currency project financing from both official multilateral development agencies and private commercial banks, the financial terms and conditions from the commercial banks are likely to reflect the general market conditions for credit rather than the nature of the investment for which financing is sought.

10. Countries that have balance-of-payments problems and that are nevertheless on balance creditworthy should expect to have great importance attached to their productive use of loans, the credit standing of the borrowing entity, and the past record of debt servicing.

11. Private banks are likely to insist that borrowers give debt servicing obligations to them the highest payment priority. Banks cannot give debt relief for political reasons. Public agencies, however, may wish to be treated similarly to banks and to public creditors in other countries, even though they have an option to act more leniently. This is, in effect, a political decision that should be kept separate from private bank decisions. Various "clubs," like the Paris Club, have been formed on an ad hoc basis to deal with public creditors in a particular country. At times questions have arisen on the comparative treatment of publicly and privately extended debt. Common or even similar actions on debt may not be feasible.

12. In many developing countries, the priority list of debt service to private lenders is—

a. Amounts due to foreign commercial banks,

b. Contractual payments to external suppliers who are also lenders,

c. Payments under buyers/suppliers' credits, and

d. Remittances for miscellaneous purposes, including imports.

13. Borrowing countries must have up-to-date operating judgments on their foreign currency indebtedness, on the debt profile they can manage, and on how private markets regard their creditworthiness. External sources of credit are likely to remain attractive to domestic borrowers because of higher domestic interest rates, even after discounting for exchange rate devaluation. The lack of domestic equity markets, combined with limited long-term funding in local currency, further enhances the attractiveness of external sources of funds. Countries may wish from time to time to place limits on foreign currency indebtedness, magnitudes, and terms. Various measures are available to the monetary authorities to dampen or restrain demand for external credit. Borrowing countries should monitor continuously the interactions between their external borrowing and domestic conditions.

Relationships between Private Banks
and the International Monetary Fund

Relationships between private commercial banks and the IMF are informal and varied. Each bank, indeed each banker, would describe the relationships differently. There are no formal arrangements for either transmitting information or exchanging views. In this part, I examine the relationships between the banks and the IMF in countries with reasonably stable economic conditions and in countries with extraordinary conditions requiring stabilization efforts.

Ordinary Cases: No Stabilization Programs Negotiated or Being Implemented

Despite the informality, relationships between the banks and the IMF are often mutually beneficial. Formal arrangements would be difficult because of the intergovernmental nature of the IMF and the private character of commercial banks. The IMF must respect the confidentiality of its information and of its discussions with member countries, and the IMF staff must avoid doing injury to its members by violating this confidentiality.

For their part, commercial banks are guided by their private needs and obligations. They cannot divulge to IMF staff members confidential information that might be detrimental to the banks' borrowers, depositors, or shareholders. Moreover, banks are separate entities with greatly differing interests, objectives, and decision-making mechanisms and responsibilities.

Countries that come to the IMF to negotiate a standby or extended arrangement in the higher credit tranches are often in financial trouble; in commercial bank parlance, the IMF deals often with "workout" or "near workout" cases. In such cases, emphasis is on policies to ameliorate or eliminate the immediate difficulties. Such countries may need the IMF's presence either to reinforce persons within the government and central bank who wish to pursue policies to overcome existing difficulties or who need the technical assistance the IMF can provide. These countries usually also need access to IMF financial resources. External finance, both public and private, is more likely to be forthcoming if a country in difficulty pursues stabilization policies endorsed by the IMF. Under these conditions, when external financing in addition to IMF resources is required, relations between the commercial banks, the country in difficulty, and the IMF become more urgent and more involved than under ordinary circumstances. These cases will be discussed later.

Commercial banks feel more comfortable lending to countries that do not require major changes in economic policy or management. Thus, the typical case is that of private banks lending to a country that is not seen to be in need of new stabilization policies. Problems may exist, such as a decline in commodity prices, a rise in the cost of imports, or the introduction of external protectionist measures affecting export earnings. These are warning signals and may imply that the country must adjust. Banks usually rely on their own capability to judge whether or how a country will adjust.

Countries not in immediate difficulty have little incentive to come to the IMF for technical or financial assistance. For a country with balance-of-payments difficulties, the use of unconditional IMF drawing rights may be attractive because it does not imply that the country is being mismanaged, an implication which is hard to avoid when stabilization programs involve conditional drawings on IMF resources in the higher credit tranches.

The question arises whether countries that need major adjustments in policies and would otherwise adopt stabilization programs, presumably with the assistance and endorsement of the IMF, are able to avoid this action by borrowing from private commercial banks. This evasion of adjustment may occur when non-IMF sources of financing are truly unconditional, that is, the country obtains the resources without substantive changes in policy or management despite the need for change. But this lack of attention to policy is not true of borrowings from private banks; banks do not lend significant sums without serious consideration of the country risk. It is true that at times banks may be willing to have a small exposure within a country with little or no attention to country risk. For instance, loans guaranteed by government institutions in creditor countries may be undertaken with little attention to country risk in the borrowing country. However, these situations are exceptional. The bulk of international lending does not involve creditor government guarantees. Most international lending is to countries in which the lending institutions already have significant exposure. Marketing considerations, particularly profitability, may well create incentives or internal pressures within a bank to lower standards of country evaluation. Similar pressures operate to lower standards of individual credit evaluations. Less obvious but ever present, however, are internal control mechanisms to prevent dangerous lowering of credit or country evaluation standards. High-risk interest rate premiums are not deemed acceptable reasons for lending to countries with a high-risk environment.

Whenever they see reason to do so, banks voice their concern to borrowers about the borrowing country's past performance and its outlook for the future. The expressed concerns of private banks do not go unheeded. The governments of borrowing countries are aware that if existing difficulties are allowed to proceed to points of crisis, the governments will lose their access to external sources of finance. This conditionality is informal but constant. Lending by private banks thus encourages the pursuit of policies that avoid the creation of conditions which simultaneously require drastic changes in policies and cause a cessation of commercial bank lending to the country in difficulty.

In countries not engaged in a stabilization program but seen by banks as being on the brink of a crisis, informal exchanges with both the IMF staff and the government are likely to take place. However, for reasons stated earlier, even in thees cases banks must be guided by their own knowledge and by the actions of the IMF, rather than by information received from the IMF.

Role of Private Banks in Fund Stabilization Programs

I will assume that readers of this essay are reasonably familiar with the content of IMF stabilization programs.[9] In difficult stabilization cases,

9. In addition to other essays in this volume, recommended recent readings are H. Johannes Witteveen, "Financing the LDCs: The Role of Public and Private Institutions," *IMF Survey* (May 22, 1978), pp. 145–50; J. J. Polak, "The Relationship Between Economic Growth and Balance of Payments Adjustments in Present World Economic Conditions," *IMF Survey* (July 17, 1978), pp. 210–13; T. M. Reichmann and R. T. Stillson, "Experience with Programs of Balance of Payments Adjustment: Stand-by Arrangements in the Higher Credit Tranches, 1963– 72," *IMF Staff Papers,* vol. 25 (June 1978); T. M. Reichmann "The Fund's Conditional Assistance and the Problems of Adjustment, 1973–75," *Finance and Development* (December 1978), pp. 38–41; S. Mookerjee, "New Guidelines for Use of Fund Resources Follow Review of Practice of Conditionality" (including text of Decision of March 2, 1979, on Access to Resources from Fund and Use of Stand-By Arrangements), *IMF Survey* (March 19, 1979), pp. 82–83; T. A. Connors, "The Apparent Effects of Recent IMF Stabilization Programs," International Financial Discussion Paper 135 (Federal Reserve Board, April 1979); and various official histories of the IMF.

international confidence in a country must be restored. In such cases, the standby and extended arrangements with the IMF acquire an importance far beyond the actual magnitude of financial assistance made available to countries by the IMF. Sources other than the IMF in the international credit and capital markets can contribute much larger amounts of balance-of-payments support to developing countries. The IMF's presence is valued by the banks because it increases confidence in the quality of the program and enhances the likelihood of implementation.

As of June 30, 1979, fifteen member countries had standby arrangements, and eight other members had arrangements under the Extended Fund Facility. Of these, five were not in the higher credit tranches. The members with arrangements included some countries in serious balance-of-payments difficulties when the programs were agreed, but also a number that undertook these arrangements primarily as preventive medicine.

The criteria of private banks in judging a stabilization program are likely to be similar to those of the IMF. Their advice will deal with fiscal, monetary, and exchange rate policy, as normally does the IMF's, but their advice goes beyond this in some respects. For example, banks are also likely to emphasize that the country should—

1. End undue government interference in the market mechanism, particularly actions that interfere importantly with the efficient allocation and use of resources;

2. Encourage domestic savings and encourage more sophisticated and nondiscriminatory money and capital markets to distribute savings;

3. Eliminate or reduce regulations and laws that discriminate against foreigners;

4. Recognize the principle that full and prompt servicing of external debt to private lenders must have top priority in foreign exchange usage;

5. Create conditions that will enable the country, if it chooses, to borrow externally from private and public sources and to attract equity investment;

6. Improve statistical services to improve the evaluation of conditions in the country;

7. Encourage decisive management of a country's balance of payments as well as its domestic economy to reduce the uncertainty of doing banking business with and within the country;

8. Encourage more efficient management of productive enterprises, private and public; and

9. Maintain or strengthen the productive capacity and efficiency of enterprises.

Banks obviously are uneasy when their criteria of stabilization needs in any country differ from IMF's criteria. The approach of commercial banks reflects the factors of risk, profitability, liquidity, and solvency that are the natural concerns of a commercial bank. Coincidence between the views of the IMF and of commercial banks will occur much more frequently than not, but it is neither automatic nor inevitable. More important, much of which private banks might favor in any particular case may simply not fall within the scope of stabilization programs endorsed by the IMF, for example, restrictions on foreign enterprises or nationalization; or the IMF may assume unrealistically the willingness of banks to refinance outstanding debt or extend new monies. The banks walk the tightrope of following the IMF's lead and of trying to strengthen the IMF's role in stabilization programs, while retaining the freedom to act in accord with their own special corporate needs and constraints.

Actions of Private Banks during Stabilization Program Period

Stabilization programs under standby or extended arrangements that involved commercial banks to an important extent account for only a small fraction of bank business. Some stabilization cases in which the private banks have been involved significantly are set forth in the appended case studies.

Each case is different, but certain key aspects can be generalized based on actual experience. Banks begin by having both short-term and long-term exposure. The conventional dividing line is one year. Short-term exposure can be decreased by amortization payments that are not offset by new loans to the same or other entities. The mix of bank maturities varies greatly from country to country. On average, half the maturities are short and half are long, but this cannot be taken as a rule of thumb for a particular country. During a standby arrangement period in which commercial banks feel significant risk and their actions are part of the program, banks are usually involved in the following actions:

1. Banks assess a country's situation from their viewpoint and review their exposure in each country to position themselves to defend against losses.

2. If the risks in maintaining or increasing exposure are regarded as

great, banks can take steps to maintain or reduce existing exposure or otherwise to make exposure less vulnerable, for instance, by substituting new borrowers deemed stronger and by reducing the average maturity of portfolio.

3. A country can ask banks to maintain their levels of exposure or reduce their exposure in a particular way, for example, by maintaining their short-term exposure and reducing their term exposure as maturities fall due and are paid. Demonstrated willingness to have a stabilization program endorsed by the IMF is likely to weigh heavily in obtaining a favorable response from the banks.

4. A country can ask creditor banks to consider restructuring outstanding debt and/or additional lending as part of a stabilization program. A country can begin to explore with banks the timing of new credits it hopes to obtain if it adopts and implements a stabilization program endorsed by the IMF.

5. If approached by a country for refinancing or new money, banks request IMF assurance that the country has indicated its willingness to prepare a stabilization program for which it will seek IMF endorsement; at the same time, the banks can express their own views on what needs to be done.

6. Any commitments obtained from banks on rescheduling, restructuring, or new money can be subject to adoption or implementation of stabilization measures.

7. Banks principally involved may arrange for some coordinating mechanism to work with other banks concerned, at least during the formation and implementation of the stabilization program or, in other words, until more normal conditions and relationships are restored. Lead banks, perhaps in an informal coordinating committee, can help arrange for visits by officials of the country to explain their problems and programs to other bankers. IMF representatives and others from multilateral institutions might also be present.

8. The IMF can try to provide the *masse de manoeuvre* needed for stabilization. This can be accomplished by giving appropriate waivers on limits of IMF resources or by front-ending the access of IMF resources and by obtaining support from other multilateral institutions. This would be particularly appropriate when the commercial banks feel that a considerable period of time is needed for implementing a program. Private banks should not be expected to perform this support or aid function prematurely. In exceptional cases, a quick contribution from banks to a pro-

gram agreed with the IMF could be in the form of restructuring country debt profiles in such a manner as to be particularly helpful in the early period of implementation.

9. If external funds are needed to assure the feasibility of the implementation of the stabilization program, and such funds cannot come primarily from multilateral institutions or official sources, the commercial banks may become the most important, single source of external finance. In such cases, it may take considerable time before banks have the necessary confidence in the new situation and outlook. In making their decisions, banks presumably would have the benefit of discussions with officials of the country and of the IMF and other multilateral institutions involved. As implementation progresses satisfactorily, banks can increase their exposure with new loans. This can be done by phasing drawings on agreed banks' credits. If use of IMF resources is also phased, the banks could phase in a parallel schedule. The pattern of phasing might well be inverse: the IMF starting high and coming down, the banks starting low and coming up.

10. Commercial banks try to avoid restructuring of outstanding debt. Since countries involved in stabilization programs are likely to have reduced external creditworthiness, restructuring of past debt may be difficult to avoid. Here, restructuring means situations in which the outstanding bank creditors renegotiate the repayment terms applying to existing debt. The creditor banks are not changed. In any event, the terms and conditions of restructuring the debt will be greatly influenced by the country's willingness to negotiate a standby or extended arrangement in the upper credit tranches. In such cases, in contrast with new or additional credits, the agreed restructuring would probably come into effect at the beginning or very early stages of implementation of the stabilization program rather than be delayed to assure that the program is reasonably well implemented.

11. If the IMF will not certify the good efforts of a country in difficulties, banks can be expected to take defensive measures. Countries in difficulties are aware when this happens. The influence of banks on stabilization programs stems primarily from the fact that new lending by the banks will not be resumed in substantial amounts until the country's economic management performance meets the country creditworthiness criteria of the lending banks.

12. When reestablishing creditworthiness with private banks and/or restructuring past debt are of crucial importance for the success of the

country's stabilization program and are so perceived by the country and the IMF, bankers may be invited to participate informally in deliberations with country officials and officials from the IMF, the World Bank, and other multilateral institutions. This process is facilitated when the private banks most concerned have formed some kind of coordinating group, without prejudice to any individual bank having its own informal bilateral discussions with the country's officials or the IMF. In such cases, bankers' participation is entirely advisory and informal as their advice has no contractual or legal implications. The formal conditions are set forth in loan contracts.

Twenty or thirty banks in various countries account for the bulk of international lending, but hundreds of banks around the world have a stake in most stabilization programs. This was dramatically illustrated by experiences in Zaire, Peru, and Turkey when questions arose on external indebtedness and possible responses of private banks to requests for debt relief and more credit to help implement stabilization programs and achieve more normal conditions. In many countries in difficulty, there is not precise knowledge of outstanding external debt to commercial banks.

Banks repeatedly have informally urged countries to turn to the IMF when the countries' external financial standing was coming into question or had been seriously impaired or was in danger of becoming so. In some cases, countries were reluctant to have standby arrangements in the higher credit tranches; in a few cases, countries did not wish to do anything which was not routine in their relations with the IMF. In all cases, to the best of my knowledge, no decision to avoid an IMF standby was taken because the countries were advised that they could borrow from banks and thus avoid such agreements. In very few cases, bank lending went to countries that the IMF staff may rather have seen turn first to the IMF. This is not likely to happen when banks know that this is the case and, by implication, that the IMF regards further debt accumulation by the borrowing country as dangerous for the lenders.

Conclusions and Suggestions for Private Bank Participation in Stabilization Programs

1. Stabilization programs cannot be regarded as successful even if rates of inflation are moderated unless the programs eliminate the fundamental causes of inflation. Similarly, I do not regard stabilization programs as

successful if they reduce a country's current account balance-of-payments deficit, but over a significant period of time lower its rate of fixed capital formation, thus impairing the country's long-term growth prospects.

Stabilization efforts have typically resulted in reduced rates of inflation and improved balance-of-payments and reserve positions for one, two, three, and sometimes even four years, only to be followed by a resurgence of inflation, often at rates exceeding those which led to the stabilization programs and often with balance-of-payments difficulties of a more serious and intractable character.

There were great debates in the 1950s as to whether the gradualist approach to ending inflation was superior or inferior to the nongradualist approach. It was agreed that ending inflation had to be a gradual process, but the gradualism became transformed into acceptance of continuing inflation. I believe this happened because we changed the objective of stabilization from ending inflation to moderating it.

I still believe that ending inflation has to be a gradual process. Indeed, in most countries it requires structural changes in consumption, savings, and investment and therefore changes in habits, practices, and institutions that may take years to accomplish. However, there is a great difference between recognizing that policy packages have to be maintained and adapted over many years before the goal of ending inflation can be achieved and designing policy packages that from the outset are not intended to end the inflation.

My view on stabilization is closely related to my views on development. The defeat of development creates unfavorable conditions for external financing. If we are to judge stabilization programs adequately, we must judge them by developmental criteria as well as by short-term stabilization criteria. As long as inflation persists, there will be a hostile environment for policies designed to overcome poverty, illiteracy, maldistribution of income, and ill health. Acceptance of continuing inflation is tantamount to acceptance of the ultimate defeat of the objectives of economic and social development. Needless to say, in coming at stabilization problems from this point of view, I evaluate country conditions differently from those who place less emphasis on the importance of ending inflation.

2. Private banks essentially play a developmental role. Their function is to strengthen the productive capacity and productivity of the countries in which the borrowing entities are found. In a well-managed development process, the private banks find themselves performing an important role—the degree of importance varies from country to country and from time to

time—in strengthening the ability of the developing country to achieve higher and more satisfactory levels of output and services. This is true at all stages of economic and social development, although the relative importance is likely to increase as countries broaden their modernized sectors. The advances can be in the public or private sector, but they all require financing and they all involve the activities of private banks, whether domestic or foreign.

Private banks dare not follow the lead of institutions that define good economic management as consisting of the pursuit of short-term or, at most, medium-term policies. The private banks must have confidence that the longer-range developmental objectives of the country are being pursued efficiently. The private banks do not live only in the short term. The banks hope to keep even their short-term customers and clients for many years. Investing in establishing branches, providing capital, maintaining contacts, and developing personnel are longer-term decisions. Private banks have a continuing, long-term profit-making position in the country, and it is the longer-term future of the country that is most meaningful to them.

Defending against adverse developments in the short term is relatively easy. The difficulties arise in defending against adversities that are not clearly perceived because they are long term in nature. This constraint, however, does not make the longer term less important; it just makes it more vulnerable and more difficult.

Banks need the capability to examine and evaluate long-term trends in the countries to which they are lending, however qualified the findings might be. They must learn to apply developmental criteria as they now have learned to apply short-term and medium-term criteria. In so doing they will find themselves, paradoxically, on more familiar ground. Banks know how to assess production, foreign trade, technology transfer, and other important variables. After all, the banks finance the real world. They operate within a monetary environment, but their technical knowledge must relate to such real world activities and sectors as aircraft, mining, energy, transportation, manufacturing, agriculture, and trade. Thus, the private banks are experienced in looking at problems in the context of the long run. They deal with long-established corporations—public and private—that will exist for a long time. They evaluate management from the longer-term point of view, as well as from the short- and the medium-term view. No private bank would think of lending to an entity whose management was considered to be efficient only in the short term.

I would strongly urge banks to pay more attention to the longer term and to the application of developmental criteria in their lending decisions. If developing countries are concerned about whether they are borrowing too much, or at excessively high costs, or in other ways unwisely, they should test their borrowing by applying developmental criteria. This test would eliminate much unwise borrowing and misuse of resources. The difficult cases we have had have not been cases where monies were borrowed for developmental purposes. Countries have gotten into difficulties when they placed nondevelopmental objectives ahead of developmental objectives and borrowed externally to sustain these nondevelopmental objectives. The practice of the World Bank in relating program lending to development performance, including phasing of funds borrowed, should greatly help private banks judge their own lending activities in countries. An expansion in international lending by private banks could be mutually beneficial to the banks and their customers if they both pay much more attention than they have in the past to the developmental aspects of their activities.

3. The main impact of private banks on stabilization programs is likely to be to encourage countries experiencing increasingly adverse conditions to improve these conditions before the countries lose their external creditworthiness. Private banks will continue to be concerned deeply about stabilization programs designed to overcome severe balance-of-payments difficulties. They are likely to emphasize increasingly that the IMF is the appropriate source of advice and resources to facilitate balance-of-payments adjustment called for in the stabilization program. The IMF will need to consult more often and earlier with banks in cases where bank actions will be necessary. The IMF is likely to be looked to by the banks to monitor the progress of stabilization policies, with the banks giving great weight to the views of the IMF, but exercising independent judgments on lending during the stabilization period.

4. The IMF should continue to explore ways and means of providing a larger proportion, if not all, of the balance-of-payments support needed for stabilization programs.

5. Relationships between the commercial banks and countries with IMF stabilization programs have undergone an evolution over many years, from ad hoc responses by all concerned to the present situation in which the ground rules of relationships are reasonably well known and understood. No formal understandings or guidelines directed this evolution, and relationships varied as the country conditions and the position

of commercial banks as creditors varied. At the same time, certain common features have begun to emerge: the need for direct relationships between the commercial banks and the governments and central banks of the countries; the role of the IMF as the adviser to the country, the negotiator of the stabilization program, and the judge of the adequacy of the program and its implementation; the use of the IMF as a channel to inform banks concerned of the progress in the stabilization efforts and the use of informal coordinating mechanisms by the leading banks, where necessary; and the banks' insistence on agreements with the IMF before providing either restructuring or refinancing of existing debt or new money. As these informal arrangements and modes of operation have taken root, new stabilization situations have been met with greater ease, efficiency, patience, and confidence in the ability to solve the immediate problems. Informality and flexibility, including the acceptance of the inevitability of misunderstandings, ill feelings, and false starts as part of the entire process, have enabled realistic and healthy relationships to thrive among the parties concerned.

6. In dealing with countries with stabilization programs, banks usually have many concerns other than the balance of payments, such as the impact of stabilization measures on money market conditions, lending opportunities, earnings, and wage and rent costs. Banks, however, accept these changes as a part of doing business within and with the borrowing countries.

7. Private banks must operate on the principle that outstanding loans are serviced fully and promptly. This is a clear aspect of all loan contracts. Elaborate provisions are made within banks regarding loans that are either in default or in serious prospect of coming into default. Income streams are immediately affected by such developments. Private banks reschedule or refinance outstanding debt in exceptional circumstances where the only feasible alternative is outright default. Banks can absorb defaults and do so repeatedly. However, borrowers that have to reschedule or refinance debt out of weakness are perceived as weak borrowers; the very act of such rescheduling or refinancing erodes their international position with private lenders.

Conclusions

I have summarized my conclusions and suggestions in various sections. A point that cannot be emphasized too much is that the world of development finance has been fundamentally altered as a result of the current role of commercial banks.

At present, issues for most developing countries do not center on availability of finance or the ability to service debt, but how to ensure productive use of borrowed funds within a framework of economic management that keeps the confidence of external lenders.

Issues for lending institutions and creditor countries will not center on magnitudes of total lending by banks to developing countries, but rather on the portfolio diversification of the individual lender and the existence of satisfactory processes to evaluate country risk and, when needed, to defend the lender in crisis situations. Issues like balance sheet consolidation, possible reserve requirements against deposits held offshore, appropriateness of existing capital/asset ratios, and distinctions in risk among various usages of loans will get increasing attention. On balance, it will be found, I believe, that international lending to developing countries strengthens a bank's portfolio as long as diversification is part of the management process. More borrowing countries mean more choices and options to the lender, not less. Temptations to lend to doubtful borrowers can be met by lending to clearly creditworthy entities in countries where experience has already indicated that they are acceptable risks. The developing countries have only begun to be known to the international financial world. Therefore, lending to them will continue to be done with caution. Banks will gain increasing confidence in such lending as the developing countries maintain their good record of debt servicing. Confidence, however, is a plant of slow growth.

Catastrophes can be conjured; at most, they spell disaster for the borrower, not the lender. And, if they happen, it will not be due to high levels of external borrowing, but to the mismanagement of the country and the waste of its resources, internal and external, in unproductive activities. This does not happen instantaneously. A bank is not likely to be taken by surprise if it is doing a professional job in monitoring countries in which it has a significant stake.

As experience is gained, the role of commercial banks in stabilization programs will be seen in proper perspective, that is, as arising only in cases of exceptional difficulties. The more important relationships of the banks with the IMF and other multilateral agencies will be the more normal, day-to-day relations affecting all developing countries. There is much room for improvement in these relationships—to the mutual benefit of lender and borrower. The manner of dealing with the difficult cases, however, can greatly influence the willingness of private banks to lend to developing countries and the willingness of developing countries to pursue policies that will enable them to regard such banks as continuing major sources of development finance.

The theme of this paper has led me to concentrate on commercial banks and conditions in borrowing countries. However, much of what will happen in lending to developing countries will be influenced by the world economic and monetary environment, including the size of the IMF, the magnitude of official development assistance, changes in the international monetary system, and international efforts to deal with global inflation, energy, growth, protectionism, and so forth.

Appendix: Case Studies

Zaire

Zaire was the first major developing country "workout" case faced by the private banks in the 1970s, and from this experience significant ground rules for future relations between private banks and developing countries evolved. By mid-1975 Zaire's ambitious development plan, which the banks were helping to finance, had been undercut by plummeting copper prices and economic mismanagement. This in turn had exhausted Zaire's foreign reserves and led to debt service interruption of $80 million in principal and interest due on the country's $2 billion in foreign debt.

Zaire moved in late 1975 to reestablish its credit in three stages: (1) it brought in the IMF to assist in establishing an economic stabilization program, signing first-tranche standby agreement of 42 million Special Drawing Rights with the IMF in February 1976; (2) in June 1976, it negotiated a ten-year partial rescheduling of the $1 billion it owed its government creditors (known collectively as the Paris Club); (3) in November of 1976, it signed a memo of understanding with the private banks (the London Club) covering $375 million in consortium debt due to private banks. The memo was not a legally binding document but rather a gentleman's agreement. It stipulated that the private banks would not declare a default and that one of Zaire's major international creditors would undertake to raise up to $250 million in new credits to help get the economy back on its feet. Usage of this line depended on Zaire bringing current the $80 million in principal and interest arrears; negotiating a new and stricter IMF standby agreement in the higher tranches, and thereafter maintaining eligibility to draw under the standby by meeting IMF-stipulated economic targets; and suffering no further damage (material adverse change) to its credit rating.

The Zaire-private banks negotiations took the form of face-to-face meetings in London, Paris, and New York. The Governor of the Banque du Zaire (the central bank) represented the Republic, and 13 agent banks represented nineteen international loan syndicates involving more than 100 private banks.

Throughout the negotiations, the IMF played an important role behind the scenes. In addition to providing informal counsel and updated country data, the IMF worked to mesh the private bank-Zaire understanding into the new higher-tranche IMF standby. In contrast, the relationships between the private banks and certain of Zaire's government creditors were at times strained, with such governments fearing that the private banks would somehow induce Zaire to pay them off while leaving the governments holding the bulk of Zaire's debt. Indeed, in the Paris Club rescheduling agreement of June 1976, Zaire had to agree to obtain "comparable" terms from the private banks—a caveat that impeded private bank efforts to raise new incremental credits for Zaire afterward.

Over the 1976–77 winter, Zaire pursued its London Club obligations by paying $40 million in past due interest and negotiating an SDR 45 million higher-tranche standby with the IMF. However, in spring 1977, Zaire's southern province of Shaba was embroiled in an invasion and rebellion, forcing the banks to postpone the syndication. Although the agent banks had nearly completed the $250 million credit syndicate by August, Zaire fell behind in its IMF stabilization program and lost its eligibility to draw under the Fund standby, thereby violating a key condition of the London Club memo of understanding. Moreover, Zaire's government creditors, the Paris Club, forced Zaire to turn down the private bank syndicate on the grounds that the revolving LC facility was not comparable to the government's ten-year rescheduling scheme as mandated by the Paris Club agreement.

In the fall of 1977, the agent banks designed a new five-year term loan facility acceptable to the Paris Club and by February 1978 had raised $220 million from a syndicate of U.S., British, Canadian, French, Belgian, German, Italian, and Japanese banks.

In late summer 1978, the government brought in foreign advisers for the Banque du Zaire and the Ministry of Finance. Also, Zaire continued to keep the banks current on interest and in spring 1979 started up new negotiations for yet another IMF standby, which the Fund formally approved in the amount of SDR 118 million in August 1979. At this writing, it is understood that Zaire will reopen negotiations with the private banks to refinance its $375 million in debt (now around $380 million in arrears).

In summary, the private banks may have lost the battle to get a wealthy but problem-plagued Zaire to pay off its arrears without rescheduling. However, it can be argued that the banks won the war over how developing country debt would be handled in the future. Zaire was widely considered a test case. Its handling has set several critical precedents. Most important, the Zaire case forestalled two strong unfavorable trends in international finance that might have drastically curtailed private bank lending to the developing countries. First, by responding to Zaire's problems positively—that is, by refraining from declaring default and by trying to raise new incremental money—the banks helped forestall a strong movement among the developing countries to declare unilateral moratoriums on their private bank debts. No one talks seriously of moratoriums today. Second, the banks forestalled a bias developing among developing country creditors, specifically government creditors, to grant quick and easy reschedulings without the tough conditionality of reform needed to assure revitalization of a country's economy. The Paris Club today often sets as tough workout conditions as do the private banks when dealing with developing countries. Had either moratoriums or unconditioned reschedulings become the rule of the day, private banks would have had to back away from developing country markets.

The following ground rules have emerged for cases in which a developing country falls into arrears on its private bank debt. The country agrees (1) to acknowledge unconditionally the debts (no talk of moratoriums) and to confirm its willingness to give highest priority to the earliest possible repayment of those debts; (2) to keep the banks current on interest; and (3) to acknowledge full responsibility for devising and carrying out monitorable reform programs—often with the aid of the IMF. For their part, the private banks agree (1) to stand still (maintain outstanding loans at current levels and refrain from declaring default); (2) to be patient (acknowledging that in designing an economic reform program, securing the political mandate to carry it out, and executing it decisively, a developing country faces an immense task); and (3) to support a viable reform/recovery program, once it is in place, not only by restructuring creatively old debt but also by raising new incremental credit.

These ground rules are not in writing, but they have today become a kind of general practice guiding both private bank lending to developing countries and the workouts that followed Zaire. This pattern is reflected in the following summaries.

Turkey

Turkey's debt is the largest among financially troubled developing countries: $10 billion, of which roughly half is short term, mostly due to banks and in arrears. In addition, debt negotiations have been hampered by successive Turkish governments' failure to obtain strong mandates for reform and inability to sustain a stabilization program.

Turkey's balance-of-payments troubles began in the early 1970s, in part due to a government decision to focus its development program on domestic production to the neglect of exports. Three windfalls postponed the crisis: the 1973–74 world commodity boom, which temporarily boosted agricultural exports; growing remittances from Turkish workers in Europe; and, finally, the introduction of the short-term Convertible Turkish Lira Deposit (CTLD)[10] scheme, which quickly attracted some $2 billion in foreign exchange, 90 percent coming from 250 foreign banks.

In 1976, the Turkish current account deficit surpassed $2 billion. Toward the end of the year a major international bank, concerned about the deteriorating balance-of-payments situation and mounting short-term external debt, offered to raise a Eurodollar standby credit. This facility, to be called upon only in case of need, was to support the authorities' efforts to restructure liabilities under the CTLD. As the authorities did not at the time perceive any inherent problems in the CTLD maturity structure, the bank's proposal was rejected.

In early 1977, Turkey faced the first serious problem resulting from the critical payments imbalance. The country's international reserves reached the point of near exhaustion; and after some emergency measures, reserves recovered to some extent but fell again when import controls were relaxed in summer 1977 during a national election campaign. At the same time the country's creditworthiness was seriously eroded. That fall, as the

---

10. Under the Convertible Turkish Lira Deposit scheme, financial institutions, corporations, and individuals are permitted to deposit the lira countervalue of foreign currencies with commercial banks established in Turkey. Such deposits enjoy exchange convertibility guarantee and protection from exchange risk. Further, interest earned on these deposits tends to exceed that paid on deposits of similar amounts and maturities placed in the Eurodollar market.

current account deficit approached $3 billion and arrears $2.5 billion, the government started negotiations with the IMF for a standby agreement but ended in disagreement over what stabilization terms to accept. Elections in spring 1978 gave a new government at best an uncertain mandate to negotiate a program with the IMF. An agreement for a two-year standby of SDR 374 million was signed in April 1978, with drawings conditioned on meeting IMF targets. In July, Turkey negotiated the rescheduling of much of its government debt. However, by September the Turkish government, under political pressure to relax reform at home, had fallen short of several program targets. By November 1978, it became evident that the stabilization effort and the IMF agreement were not succeeding. By July 1979, the authorities and the IMF had agreed on a financial program; and, in consequence, Turkey became eligible for a new two-year SDR 250 million standby.

Throughout, the private banks worked closely with the Turkish government on debt restructuring, encouraged by the fact that the Turks never went into arrears on their Eurodollar loans and kept the banks current on interest due in respect to CTLD and other debts. On the basis of the original standby agreement reached with the IMF, eight international banks with major exposure to Turkey (three U.S., two German, two Swiss, and one British) formed an ad hoc steering committee. The objective of the ad hoc committee was to put together a financial package, including restructuring maturities under the CTLD, rescheduling existing commercial bank debt, and providing new money. Negotiations were long and arduous because the financial package was contingent on Turkey's compliance with the IMF's stabilization program.

Following the conclusion of the new IMF standby facility and by late August, agreement was reached to restructure maturities amounting to $2.1 billion under the CTLD, to reschedule commercial bank debt of $429.3 million, and to provide $407 million in new money in the form of a letter-of-credit facility.

Turkey's utilization of the facilities made available by the banks was made conditional on Turkey's compliance with the program agreed upon with the IMF and the drawdown under the standby arrangement.

Peru

The Peruvian government requested and successfully negotiated two balance-of-payments facilities from the private banks during 1976–78.

The first one, for $250 million, involved nineteen U.S. banks and was fully disbursed by February 1977. The background to this first balance-of-payments facility was unusual in that the Peruvians made it clear from the outset that they did not want to go to the IMF, although they were counseled to do so by the bankers involved. Instead, the government formally requested its principal bankers to review the stabilization program that was to be implemented beginning in mid-1976 as a basis for making a decision on the requested facility.

After reviewing this program on July 20, 1976, six U.S. banks expressed their willingness to constitute a steering committee and to proceed on a best efforts basis to raise $200 to $250 million of the requested financing within the United States subject to, among others, the following stipulations:

1. Peru had to raise outside of the United States an additional $100 million from Canadian, European, and Japanese banks;

2. Participation by other U.S. banks having substantial exposure in Peru was mandatory. (Because it was widely believed by the steering committee banks that the proceeds of the loan would be used to repay current maturities of term debt falling due during the balance of 1976 and 1977, the steering committee banks wanted to ensure widest participation in the balance-of-payments facility, thereby assuring that the risks were shared by as many of the lending banks as possible. The insistence on participation by the European and Japanese banks resulted in parallel negotiations between the Peruvian government and the U.S. banks on the one hand, and the Peruvian government and the foreign banks, on the other. The resulting inefficiences in communication and coordination with respect to this first loan were later to influence the composition of the steering committee formed two years later for the second balance-of-payments loan.)

3. Monthly information on the progress of the 1976–77 stabilization program was to be provided by the Peruvian government to the banks both during and following disbursement. (Early in the negotiations and in the context of this third stipulation, the U.S. steering committee made the following key decisions: to set up a special subcommittee to monitor progress made under the stabilization program, and not to list in the eventual loan agreement any specific numerical targets that Peru had to meet to qualify for the final loan disbursements in February 1977. Instead, 75 percent of the lenders (by dollar participation) had to agree that Peru was making satisfactory progress under the stabilization program.)

During 1977, the program ran into difficulties, and by midyear it was obvious that the Peruvian program had failed. Reportedly, opposition to the program within the Peruvian cabinet had become increasingly vocal, with a faction committed to expansionary policy. A number of key, moderate government officials resigned. At the same time, foreign exchange availability was constrained adversely; in the first place, due to a fall-off in export proceeds from Peru's main commodities; and in the second, by some contraction in the level of short-term, trade-related credits extended by both banks and suppliers. The Peruvians in their 1976 stabilization program had assumed throughout that they would be able to maintain the same level of short-term, trade-related credits while they were using the proceeds from the balance-of-payments facility for general purposes, including the repayment of current obligations of long-term debt.

After the failure of the 1976 program, the private bankers involved in the existing arrangement again counseled and urged strongly that the Peruvians go to the IMF to work out a new program that could be successfully implemented; that in the absence of effective stabilization measures they must not assume that current levels (1977) of trade-related exposure could be maintained; and that any delays in defining a new coherent, well-integrated policy package, preferably in conjunction with the IMF, could create a most difficult, if not impossible, balance-of-payments situation.

By August 1977, the Peruvians had met in New York with their principal U.S. bankers; had assured the bankers that they were in fact going to work out a program with the IMF; and, based on this intention, requested their bankers to maintain short-term lines and outstandings at then present levels until the IMF program could be negotiated and implemented. While they were successful in getting most banks to go along, some smaller lenders did not.

The agreement with the IMF was reached in late 1977, but by December of that year some targets under the standby had not been met. The Peruvians, however, initiated a new dialogue with the IMF to work out new targets.

By February 1978, the U.S. banks' steering committee had evolved into a six-bank international steering committee representing U.S., Canadian, Japanese, and European banks. To ensure the IMF/Peruvian dialogue would continue under the best possible conditions, this international steering committee recommended to the banks that a cohesive and unified approach be taken in respect to the maintenance of trade-related credits. On the recommendation of the international steering committee, the banks also agreed to roll forward until January 3, 1978, approximately $180 million of current maturities of term debt owed to private banks and falling due in the second semester of 1978. These credits were to be refinanced if a satisfactory program with the IMF could be worked out. Aside from these decisions, the Peruvians requested the banks to provide a new facility that would essentially refinance a substantial portion of current maturities of central government and/or public sector entities owed to private bankers falling due in 1979 and 1980. The international steering committee felt and communicated to the banks that their actions should be linked to an IMF extended term facility, which the Peruvians had indicated they wished to have.

A new extended term facility with the IMF for SDR 184 million was negotiated in September of 1978. The IMF also approved a 120 million SDR financing facility to compensate Peru for the decline in prices of its main export commodities.

The banks were additionally encouraged by the fact that Peru had by this time already restructured its debt with the Eastern bloc countries, having obtained relief for bilateral payments due over the following three years (that is, 90 percent relief for the following two years of payments; 65 percent for the third year), rescheduled over eleven years with a three-year grace period.

Prior to triggering their own refinancing package, the private banks required as a formal precondition the successful rescheduling of 1979 and 1980 maturing obligations on external debts owed to governments and official agencies. This was done in a Paris Club meeting in early November 1978. Finally in December 1978, 285 private banks worldwide signed a refinancing agreement that rescheduled 50 percent of the 1978 roll-forward credits (deferring payment on the balance to year-end 1979); rescheduled 90 percent of 1979 current maturities on term debt to be paid in nine semiannual installments commencing in February 1982; and subject to negotiation in the last quarter of 1979, made a provision which would allow 90 percent of all 1980 current maturities on term debt to be repaid in seven semiannual installments commencing in February 1983.

Jamaica

The private banks played a role in the deliberations with the Jamaican government that was similar in some respects to the role they played in the Peruvian case. For example, during March and April 1977, bankers were counseling and urging the Jamaican government to negotiate a standby program with the IMF as a mechanism for getting access to additional private bank credits. Negotiations between the government and the IMF had broken down late in 1976, presumably due to the unwillingness of the Jamaican government to devalue its currency to the extent deemed appropriate by the IMF to meet the necessary conditions for the establishment of a standby. Rumors abounding in the financial marketplace in the spring of 1977 that Jamaica was about to default on its external debt because of the poor performance of commodity exports and tourism, alarming decline in international reserves, and the impasse with the IMF were communicated to the key Jamaican government officials by private bankers. Jamaica quickly took the initiative, began a new dialogue with the IMF, devalued its currency, and initiated new discussions related to a standby.

Once negotiations with the IMF began, the Jamaican government approached a few leading private banks and requested a facility to provide the funds to meet a substantial part of Jamaica's medium-term public sector obligations falling due to private banks in fiscal year 1979, that is, from April 1978 to March 1979. At the same time, government officials made it known to these private banks that eventually it would become necessary to address the issue of the refinancing of current maturities of the public sector owed to private banks and falling due in fiscal years 1980 and 1981.

As in the case of Peru, a steering committee of Jamaica's principal banks was formed to facilitate negotiations related to the first loan.

The steering committee agreed to consider the first facility and to recommend approval to other potential participating banks, provided that the facility was linked to performance under the IMF's standby.

By mid-1977, the government had negotiated a two-year standby with the IMF for SDR 74 million. By December, however, the Jamaicans had failed to meet specified targets, and negotiations between the private banks and the government on the first loan were at a standstill. The Jamaican government then reopened negotiations with the IMF for a loan through the Extended Term Facility for SDR 200 million. The loan was approved in mid-June 1978.

Complications similar to those of the Peru case arose in the first loan concerning the composition of the steering committee. Initially, the committee included representatives from Canadian and U.S. banks, but none from Japanese or European banks. This resulted in inefficiencies in communications, and the first refinancing was not completed until December 1978.

The negotiation and closing during April 1979 of the second balance-of-payments facility, covering public sector debt owed to private banks and falling due in fiscal years 1980 and 1981, was considerably abetted by the fact that the steering committee had become international in nature by the inclusion of European and Japanese banks.

The Peruvian example was followed in all its essential elements in both loans, that is, 12½ percent of outstandings due to the private banks was to be repaid, with 87½ percent rescheduled over seven years with two years' grace, subject to successful implementation of the stabilization program and compliance with targets therein.

The role played by the private banks in the Jamaican stabilization program was in other respects dissimilar to the role played in Peru. For one, private banks had proportionately less short-term, trade-related claims on the Jamaican public sector. Therefore, the Jamaican arrangements did not provide for short-term debt. In addition, Jamaican overall external debt structure did not require a Paris Club rescheduling of public sector outstandings due to governments and/or official agencies as current maturities of such obligations were more manageable than was true for Peru, and the level of assistance received from donor nations was and continues to be proportionately greater.

The Jamaican case is different in another respect. The original extended term facility of SDR 200 million provided by the IMF in mid-1978 was augmented in mid-1979 by IMF approval of additional drawing rights for Jamaica under the new supplementary facility. Total assistance is now SDR 330 million over the three-year period of the program rather than SDR 200 million—relatively the most assistance ever rendered by the IMF to a member country.

In the Jamaican case, as in the Peruvian case, the loan discussions began as consideration of requests for general balance-of-payments support and ended by being restructuring of some maturities together with some immediate payments of outstandings falling due. In both cases, as noted above, the actions were tied to performance and agreements with the IMF.

Comments by H. Robert Heller

"The Role of Private Banks in Stabilization Programs" offers a well-balanced, comprehensive, and in-depth treatment of this increasingly important topic. As Friedman emphasizes, the role of private banks in lending to developing countries has increased sharply in the last decade and consequently has attracted an increasing amount of attention. The main characteristic of this newly developed relationship—and this point cannot be overemphasized—has been its smooth, largely trouble-free development. This fact is all the more astounding because the global environment during this period was not characterized by tranquility and stability. Excessive global inflation and unprecedented changes in world trade flows dominated the world economy in the 1970s.

The paper not only gives a perceptive analysis of the growing role of commercial banks in lending to the developing countries, but also offers a comprehensive assessment of the relationships between commercial banks and the IMF. The latter connection especially is all too often shrouded in mystery; therefore, it is most helpful that a person as uniquely qualified for this task as Friedman has addressed this delicate topic.

I would like to follow the outline of the chapter and comment first on the role of private bank lending to developing countries and, in particular, the role of country risk analysis in that process. Second, I will deal with the relationship between the private banks and the IMF.

The most important message pertains to the necessity to use the proceeds from commercial bank loans for productive purposes. As such, private loans can play a central and supportive role in the development process by aiding in the construction of new capital projects and financing of the ensuing trade. Loans will have to be repaid with interest; therefore, it is of the utmost importance that they generate sufficient cash flow in terms of foreign currency to enable the borrowers to fulfill their obligations. This does not imply an exclusive use of the loan proceeds for investment projects, although in the ultimate analysis, repayments can be effected only from the earnings generated by productive investment. Under appropriate circumstances, foreign borrowing may also enhance the stabilization efforts of a country. For instance, by temporarily financing a limited balance-of-payments deficit with external funds, a country may avoid the economic disruptions and the loss in productivity that would be involved if it had to resort to restrictive economic policy measures. But it cannot be overemphasized that such circumstances are the exception rather than the rule, and Friedman correctly calls for a greater role for the IMF in financing such stabilization policies.

Where I differ somewhat with Friedman is in the role of quantitative techniques to assess a country's creditworthiness, but our differences are probably a matter of degree and emphasis rather than fundamental approach. Friedman argues that "in evaluating country risk, banks should not be guided by a uniform set of variables." In contrast, I would argue that—at least as a first step—uniform quantitative criteria are essential to ensure that countries that have very different characteristics are treated on an equal basis. Global consistency and, in particular, global portfolio balance can be achieved only if an effort is made to render diverse economies comparable as far as risk is concerned. Quantitative techniques can be most helpful in providing a baseline for such an assessment. Of course, no single formula can take into account all relevant parameters. It is, therefore, frequently necessary to adjust the numerical indicators to incorporate appropriate judgmental factors. Two basic reasons for judgmental adjustment are particularly important: (1) not all relevant variables can be incorporated in a formula lest it become too unwieldy and cumbersome; (2) some variables are difficult or impossible to quantify, especially those of a political or socioeconomic character, and are perhaps better handled in a judgmental manner.

I would also reverse the sequence of confidence and balance-of-payments ratios in creditworthiness evaluations. While Friedman states that "when confidence in a country is waning, the balance-of-payments ratios become significant elements in country risk assessment." It may be more appropriate to view a deterioration of the balance-of-payments situation as a necessary precondition or as the leading element in debt service problems. But not all countries whose objective indicators deteriorate actually get into difficulties. It is here that confidence plays such an important role. If the country is able to maintain the confidence of the world financial community, even high debt burdens can be carried and financed. It is in this context that appropriate stabilization measures are often of great significance, and this brings us to the second topic covered by Friedman—the relationship between the private banks and the IMF.

Friedman emphasizes the informal character of the relationships between commercial banks and the IMF, in which each side retains its independence and respects the confidentiality of its relations with the various countries. Although these two principles should always be maintained, it may be possible to develop greater cooperation in the information area. For instance, there is little reason why the largely factual IMF reports on recent economic developments in member countries should not be shared with banks because the reports contain little or no confidential information. Such a sharing of information would be particularly helpful to the smaller commercial banks, as they do not have the resources to monitor a large number of relatively small countries. The quality of bank lending decisions would consequently be improved. The countries would benefit because the information would reduce the uncertainty faced by the banks, which in turn would probably be more willing to lend to these countries. In contrast, IMF country consultation reports and staff appraisals of the economic situation should rightfully remain confidential. Facts should be shared, but judgments should be arrived at independently.

Friedman offers a comprehensive set of stabilization measures that might enhance a country's credit standing with the commercial banking community and emphasizes the important role of the IMF in the implementation of such programs. The important distinction between the banks and the IMF is that while countries are likely to rely on commercial bank financing on a continuing basis, their use for IMF resources is likely to be temporary. While commercial banks are likely to have a long-term perspective emphasizing projects that have payoffs in terms of economic growth and development, the use of the IMF's resources is appropriately focused on short- and medium-term stabilization measures. Greater use of the IMF's resources in the context of stabilization programs would be a most helpful complement to commercial bank lending, as Friedman points out. Of course, the IMF should maintain its ongoing relationship with member countries through regular consultation procedures. A good fire department offers assistance to the community through continuing preventive counseling and emergency services. Similarly, the IMF should provide constant advice and surveillance and should also supply needed liquidity in emergency situations. But just as the fire department should not be called upon to provide regular transportation services, the IMF should not be lending to countries on a continuing basis to finance development needs, nor should the commercial banks attempt to assume the role of the IMF as far as surveillance and adjustment advice are concerned. The existence of both commercial transportation and the fire department are important for the well-being of a community, just as both private banks and the IMF are essential for the prosperity of the community of nations.

Discussion

Robert Pelikan (U.S. Treasury Department) agreed with Friedman that it is difficult to formalize creditworthiness comparisons quantitatively.

He raised the issue that the banks may have been lending too much in the wrong places, lending even when there were clear signs that it was unadvisable to do so (in countries such as Peru, Turkey, and the Dominican Republic). He suggested the need for more cooperation between the IMF and the private banks to reduce this problem.

Marilyn Seiber (U.S. Commerce Department) felt the Friedman study downplayed the prospective deterioration in ratios of debt service to exports. Arguing that banks may be only fair-weather friends to developing countries, she maintained that banks should share in the responsibility for poor loans. She stated that international financial markets are excessively liquid and highly competitive, possibly leading to inadequate lending standards.

Robert Slighton (Chase Manhattan Bank) identified two potential problems: too little or too much lending. He noted that although the traditional critique was of the former problem, financial markets have improved greatly in the past twenty years. Slighton held that, in general, bank lending had contributed to an orderly adjustment process. He pointed out the difficulty for banks in knowing whether funds would be wisely used; and, with regard to catastrophic risk, he said banks have little idea of the true costs to them of a debt rescheduling.

Henry Wallich (Federal Reserve Board of Governors), commenting on whether the banks are lending too much, observed that any market growing at 20 to 25 percent annually raises that question. He saw recent risk spreads as too low to cover the additional equity the bank needs to make more loans, and he noted that some American banks have drawn back from risky loans with low spreads while increasingly active foreign banks have taken their place. He cited as a possible problem the fact that foreign bank regulators do not evaluate the consolidated balance sheets of their banks' foreign and domestic loans as American regulators do. While accepting the role of judgment, Wallich argued for greater attention to standard ratios. Loans for ten years and more must stand the test of major changes in the world economy and in the government, and when one sees leading borrowers exceeding debt service ratios of 50 percent on grounds of special confidence in country management, there is cause for concern. He noted the possibility of catastrophic risk in foreign lending that is absent in domestic lending because of the national central bank.

Wallich felt that under current conditions countries should adjust sooner and rely less on foreign bank financing than during the period following the first OPEC price rise. For their part, banks should restrain themselves. Wallich would welcome more bank conditionality, but feels that when a bank has put its foot down it has been too late and too severe. The availability of bank financing has slowed the move to the IMF. Instead, banks should smooth a country's path to the IMF, which should be a friend with an ongoing relationship to the developing country rather than a lender of last resort. Notwithstanding these reservations, Wallich agreed that what the banks had accomplished had been amazing.

Lawrence Krause (Brookings Institution) stated that banks should not be making public policy decisions, but should lend on a commercial basis. He asked why spreads do not reflect risks, and he suggested that the IMF might provide country credit risk ratings.

Joel Bergsman (World Bank) noted that the Bretton Woods system envisioned the IMF as the principal source of international finance for stabilization, and he asked how well the Bretton Woods institutions could perform at present when they have so little money compared with the private bank flows.

Irving Friedman acknowledged the need for quantitative indicators as advocated by Heller, but said banks must go beyond them and use considerable judgment. He accepted Pelikan's point on problem cases, saying there have been fewer since 1975 and citing the special circumstances of the Convertible Lira Account in Turkey. He stated that the system cannot have the IMF telling banks not to lend to specific countries. Friedman agreed with Wallich on the problem of capital adequacy for banks. He cited market penetration goals by foreign banks as a reason for low spreads, which in turn inhibit the ability of banks to build up capital from earnings. He considered it difficult for any outside entity to define risk, and he noted that regardless of past experience, debt rescheduling now does have significant costs for banks.

CHAPTER EIGHT

Case Study of Economic Stabilization: Mexico

SIDNEY WEINTRAUB

IN 1976, Mexico faced its worst economic crisis in forty years. At the time, there was speculation about the continued viability of the Mexican political system.[1] The overt economic manifestations of the crisis were massive capital flight, a substantial devaluation of the Mexican peso on August 31, 1976 (after some shifting, the peso found its level at between 22 and 23 to the dollar, a devaluation of 84 percent with respect to the 12.5 rate that had prevailed since 1954), the provision by the United States of interim credits from the Exchange Stabilization Fund and the Federal Reserve of up to $900 million,[2] and the entry into a stabilization program between Mexico and the International Monetary Fund (IMF).

This program, under the extended IMF facility, imposed conditions on Mexico's external borrowing, its international reserve buildup, the deficit of its nonfinancial public sector, changes in the net domestic assets of the Bank of Mexico, payments restrictions for current transactions, and the use of import restrictions for balance-of-payments purposes.

Now, several years later and after three successive stabilization agreements with the IMF (covering calendar years 1977, 1978, and 1979), the acute crisis has passed. President José López Portillo has since commented that his administration's initial plan was to devote two years to overcome the crisis, two years to consolidate the economy, and then the

1. See Soledad Loaeza, "La Política del Rumor: México, Noviembre–Diciembre de 1976," in Lorenzo Meyer and others, *La Crisis en el Sistema Político Mexicano, 1928–1977* (El Colegio de México, 1977), pp. 119–50.

2. U.S. Department of the Treasury, *Exchange Stabilization Fund Annual Report for Year Ended June 30, 1976 and Three-month Period Ended September 30, 1976,* p. 7.

final two years to economic growth.[3] Except for controlling the rise in consumer prices, the plan is reasonably on target.

The crisis was many years in the making. It might have taken longer to manifest itself or come in a different form if not for the efforts by President Luis Echeverría to deal with inequities in the distribution of income and basic services in Mexican society. These underlying problems remain, and it is not clear how López Portillo intends to deal with them.[4]

This paper will focus on the buildup to the crisis during the six-year term of President Echeverría and the subsequent stabilization measures under President López Portillo. The Echeverría period was a classic example of mismanagement under which a difficult situation was made intolerable without accomplishing the administration's main objectives of improving equality and creating jobs. However, to understand the motivations behind Echeverría's actions, it will be necessary to trace briefly the earlier Mexican development strategy of *desarollo estabilizador* (stabilizing development). The sacrifices imposed by the post-Echeverría stabilization measures obviously were intended as a necessary short-term step to make sustained economic development possible. One result of Mexico's experience since 1970 is that the development strategy that Echeverría inherited is discredited among Mexican intellectuals. Despite the initial success of Mexico's stabilization effort, the more formidable and fundamental problems are still to be addressed.

The Buildup to the Crisis

For two decades prior to 1970, Mexico was considered one of the success stories of economic growth. Table 8-1 provides data on which this perception was based. Despite Mexico's high population growth rate, gross domestic product (GDP) per capita grew at a compound annual rate of about 3 percent. An industrial structure was established. The country enjoyed political stability.

3. *Second State of the Nation Report* by José López Portillo, President of Mexico, September 1, 1978.

4. For example, the *Plan Nacional de Desarrollo Industrial, 1979–1982,* published in 1979 by the Secretaria de Patrimonio y Fomento Industrial, deals only peripherally with employment and distribution issues.

Table 8-1. *Growth of Mexican Gross Domestic Product and Its Components, 1950–78*

Compound annual percentage rates of growth in constant prices (1960 = 100)

Component	1950–65	1965–70	1970–75	1976	1977[a]	1978[a]
Gross domestic product	6.4	6.9	5.6	1.7	3.2	6.6
GDP per capita	3.1	3.3	2.0	−1.9	−0.5	3.5
Agriculture, livestock, forestry, and fisheries	4.6	2.3	2.0	−2.8	2.7	3.1
Mining	1.9	3.3	3.6	2.0	0.9	−2.0
Petroleum and petrochemicals	9.3	9.6	7.5	10.6	15.9	15.5
Manufacturing	7.1	8.6	5.9	2.7	3.6	8.5
Construction	7.2	9.7	8.3	−1.9	−2.0	12.5
Electricity	12.7	14.1	8.6	7.4	7.7	10.0
Trade	6.6	7.0	5.2	−1.0	2.0	n.a.
Transport and communications	5.4	7.8	9.9	5.0	5.2	n.a.
Government	6.6	7.6	10.5	8.2	1.8	n.a.
Other services[b]	5.4	5.4	3.7	2.2	2.3	n.a.

Sources: Nacional Financiera, *Statistics on the Mexican Economy, 1977*, pp. 32–37, for 1950 sectoral data; Banco de México, *Producto Interno Bruto y Gasto, Cuaderno 1960–1977* (August 1978), pp. 28, 29, and 46, and Banco de México, *Informe Anual 1978*, for 1978 percentages.

n.a. Not available.

a. Preliminary figures.

b. Contains adjustment for banking services.

Problems Inherited by President Echeverría

The beginnings of problems can be seen well before the 1970s. Table 8-1 shows the sharp slowdown in agricultural growth (to a rate less than population growth) in the late 1960s. The outwardly satisfactory rates of growth in manufacturing during the 1950s and 1960s were stimulated by protection against external competition, by tariffs and import licensing, and through fiscal and other financial stimuli both for production and exports.[5] In effect, other sectors (particularly argiculture and mining, which also grew slowly) subsidized the manufacturing sector.[6] Bergsman, in a 1974 article, estimated the cost of protection in Mexico (stemming mostly

5. Gerardo Bueno, "The Structure of Protection in Mexico," in Bela Balassa, ed., *The Structure of Protection in Developing Countries* (Johns Hopkins Press, 1971), pp. 69–202.

6. Ruth Rama and Robert Bruce Wallace, "La Política Proteccionista Mexicana, Un Analysis Para 1960–1970," *Demografía y Economía*, vol. 11, no. 2 (1977), pp. 167–214.

from the tolerance of inefficiency and monopoly returns) at 2.5 percent of gross national product.[7] Many authors have noted that Mexico's industrial policy of capital intensive import substitution was increasingly forcing Mexico's industry to look inward.[8]

The most serious problem inherited by Echeverría was the inability of this development model, with its focus on protected industry, to produce enough jobs to meet the supply. According to Altimir, while the demand for labor kept up with or exceeded the supply offered in the 1950s, it did not in the 1960s, leading to significant overt unemployment.[9] By the 1970s, unemployment and underemployment combined affected about 40 percent of the economically active population.[10]

Mexico's inability to adequately utilize its labor force also was reflected in the high degree of inequality in income distribution when Echeverría became President[11] (see table 8-2). Income distribution data are subject to substantial error, and the figures in table 8-2 are best evaluated as a tendency rather than as an accurate portrayal at any point in time. Moreover, the data for different years are not directly comparable. However, the direction of income distribution in Mexico over the past thirty years is fairly consistent; there has been a reduction in the proportion of total income received by families with the highest incomes (the highest 5 percent and the highest 10 percent) and the lowest incomes (the lowest 10, 20, and even 40 percent), and an increase in the share of families 30 percent above the median.[12] In his final presidential message, Echeverría re-

7. Joel Bergsman, "Commercial Policy, Allocative Efficiency and 'X-Efficiency,'" *Quarterly Journal of Economics,* vol. 88 (August 1974), pp. 409–33.

8. One example is Gustav Ranis, "¿Se esta tomando amargo el milagro Mexicano?" *Demografía y Economía,* vol. 8, no. 1 (1974), pp. 22–33.

9. Oscar Altimir, "La Medición de la Población Economicamente Activa de México, 1950–1970," *Demografía y Economía,* vol. 8, no. 1 (1974), pp. 50–83.

10. Saúl Trejo Reyes, "La Política Laboral," in Gerardo M. Bueno, coordinador, *Opciones de Política Económica en México Despues de la Devaluación* (México, D.F.: Editorial Tecnos, 1977), p. 150.

11. This characterization of "high" inequality comes from Hollis Chenery and others, *Redistribution With Growth* (Oxford University Press for the World Bank, 1974), p. 8; Adalberto R. Garcia, "La Distribución del Ingreso en México," *Demografía y Economía,* vol. 8, no. 2 (1974), p. 118, notes that Mexico's Gini coefficient in 1968 (0.53) was higher than that of all major Latin American countries other than Brazil and Peru.

12. Orel Javier Salinas Arizpe, "Análisis del Efecto del Desarrollo Económico sobre la Distribución del Ingreso Familiar en México" (thesis, Universidad Autónoma de Nuevo Leon, 1974). David Felix, "Income Inequality in Mexico," *Current History,* vol. 72 (March 1977), p. 112, shows the growth in the shares of the 40th to the 80th percentiles.

Table 8-2. *Estimated Distribution of Family Income in Mexico, 1950, 1968, 1975, and 1977*[a]

Households	Total income received (percent)			
	1950	*1968*	*1975*[b]	*1977*
Lowest 20 percent	6.1	3.6	1.9	3.3
Lowest 40 percent	14.3	11.2	8.1	10.9
Highest 20 percent	59.8	56.5	60.4	55.1
Highest 5 percent	40.2	29.0	30.7	25.5

Sources: For 1950, Ifigenia M. de Navarrete, "La distribución del ingreso en México; tendencias y perspectivas," in David Ibarra et al., *El Perfil de México en 1980,* vol. 1 (México, D.F.: Siglo Venitiuno Editores, S.A., 1970), p. 37. For 1968, Banco de México, *La Distribución del Ingreso en México* (México, D.F.: Fondo de Cultura Económica, 1974), p. 8. For 1975, calculated from Centro Nacional de Información y Estadísticas del Trabajo (CENIET), *Encuesta de Ingresos y Gastos Familiares, 1975* (México, D.F.: CENIET, 1977), and World Bank estimates. For 1977, from Enrique Hernandez Laos and Jorge Cordova Chavez, "Estructura de la distribución del ingreso en México," *Comercio Exterior*, vol. 29, no. 5 (May 1979), p. 507. Their 1977 data come from Salvador Kalifa, "La distribución del ingreso en México: una reconsideración al problema distributivo" (Ph.D. dissertation, 1977).

a. There are problems of comparability of the data in the table, and hence the percentages should be viewed as approximate and not directly comparable.

b. Preliminary. The figures may overstate the decline in the share of the lowest 20 and 40 percent of households; for that reason, the 1977 data are shown.

peatedly referred to the efforts of his administration to improve Mexico's inequitable income distribution.[13] As table 8-2 shows, he apparently failed.

Two other themes stand out in Echeverría's recapitulation of the objectives of his administration. They are the importance he attached to (1) the growth of the public sector to correct deficiencies in the provision of services (such as education, housing, nutrition, and health) to the lower income groups and to compensate for shortfalls in private sector investment, and (2) the effort to maintain the value of the Mexican peso with respect to the dollar. He accomplished the first; public sector expenditures did increase in his administration, but the manner in which they were financed was the main cause of Mexico's destabilization. He did not succeed in maintaining the peso-dollar parity.

These six areas, however, provide a reasonable recapitulation of problems that antedated Echeverría and a basis for judging the effectiveness of his administration:

1. A slowdown in the growth of agricultural production;
2. The subsidization of industry at the expense of other sectors;
3. Inadequate job creation and excessive population growth;

13. Citations regarding Echeverría's "Sexto Informe Presidencial," of September 1, 1976, come from *Comercio Exterior,* vol. 26 (September 1976), pp. 1097–114.

4. Substantial economic and social inequalities;

5. Inadequate public revenues to rectify these inequalities by means of more complete public educational, health, and other services; and

6. A policy that deemed defense of an overvalued exchange rate as a vital national interest.

The seeds of disequilibrium existed in 1970; the history of the 1971–76 sexenio is that they were nourished into a full-scale panic.

Public Sector Expansion

The critical destabilizing decision of the Echeverría administration was to expand the public sector as the main vehicle for stimulating economic growth and rectifying social inequalities, but then doing so on an inadequate tax and revenue-generating base. Early in the administration, Echeverría made an effort to increase taxes but failed. Public sector expansion was sharp. The overall public sector deficit, which had averaged 2.5 percent of gross domestic product annually between 1965 and 1970, averaged 5.7 percent of GDP in the 1971–76 period; the deficit was 9.5 percent of GDP in 1976. Current expenditures of the public sector increased from an annual average of less than 6.5 percent of GDP in the previous sexenio to more than 17 percent of GDP in the final two years of the Echeverría period. Public sector investment expenditures increased from an annual average of less than 6 percent of GDP in the first year of the Echeverría term to more than 12 percent in the last year. Since private sector gross fixed investment remained fairly constant at 12 to 13 percent of GDP between 1971 and 1976, this meant that total gross fixed investment (public plus private) increased to an annual average of 21.3 percent of GDP, compared with 18.2 percent from 1965 to 1970. By contrast, public sector savings as a percent of GDP declined from an annual average of 3.3 percent in the previous sexenio to 2.6 percent in the Echeverría sexenio.[14]

Looking only at the federal government's budget (that is, not at the entire public sector), Auguiano Roch calculated that the balance of current receipts over current expenditures covered 76 percent of capital ex-

14. Data cited come from various sources: publications of the Secretaria de Programación y Presupuesto; the World Bank; Nacional Financiera, *Statistics on the Mexican Economy;* and Edmund V. K. FitzGerald, "Patterns of Public Sector Income and Expenditure in Mexico," Technical Papers Series 17 (Austin: University of Texas, Institute of Latin American Studies, 1978).

penditures in 1971, but only 24 percent in 1975.[15] The ratio of current expenditures to current revenue, which had averaged 84 percent in the 1965–70 period, averaged 90 percent between 1971 and 1976.[16] Since current revenue tends to be between 97 percent and more than 99 percent of total budgetary revenue of the federal government, this savings decline inevitably resulted in increased federal government deficits to finance investment, which was itself growing.[17]

The largest increases in current federal government expenditures in the Echeverría period were for transfers, most of which went to public enterprises. The most important of these under budgetary control are the oil company (Pemex), the electricity companies, and the railways. This is not the place to analyze the more than 800 parastatal enterprises in Mexico, but rather to note the substantial subsidy element involved in the operations of many of them and the consequent burden on public sector expenditures.[18] FitzGerald has calculated that transfers to these enterprises increased from 2.3 percent of GDP in the period 1960–68 to 3.4 percent in 1973–76 (or if decentralized activities in health, education, and other services are included, the increase was from 4.6 to 6.4 percent of GDP for the same periods).[19] The largest subsidies are to reduce energy prices (oil, fuel, and electricity), operate the railroads, and lower food prices. FitzGerald's calculations are that subsidies from the central government to public sector enterprises and to the private sector in the form of reduced prices came to an average of 5.3 percent of GDP in the 1973–76 period, compared with 3.5 percent of GDP from 1969 to 1976.[20]

Public sector revenues increased, but not commensurately with expenditures. The increase, in relation to GDP, was from 11.3 percent as an annual average in the previous sexenio to 17 percent in the 1971–76 period. There was no substantial tax reform under the Echeverría administration. As a consequence of the spending-saving disparity, the annual

15. Eugenio Auguiano Roch, "La Política del Gasto Publico," in Gerardo Bueno, coordinador, *Opciones de Política Económica en México* (México, D.F.: Editorial Tecnos, 1977), p. 114.

16. Calculated from Banco de México, *Indicadores Económicos,* various issues.

17. Luis Bravo Aguilera, "La Política Impositiva," in Bueno, *Opciones de Política Económica,* p. 168.

18. René Villareal and Norma Rocío R. de Villareal, "La Empresa Publica," in ibid., shows the growth in the number of parastatal enterprises in Mexico from 84 in 1971 to 845 in 1976 (p. 86).

19. FitzGerald, "Patterns of Public Sector Income," pp. 8–9.

20. Ibid., p. 13.

Table 8-3. *Financing Granted by the Banking System, 1965–72 and 1970–76*

Annual average percentages based on amounts outstanding on December 31 of each year

Years	To businesses and individuals[a]	To the federal government
1965–70	75	25
1971–76	63	36

Sources: Nacional Financiera, *Statistics on the Mexican Economy, 1977;* Banco de México, *Informe Anual,* various issues.
  a. Includes pubic sector enterprises.

borrowing requirement rose from about 3 percent of GDP in the previous period to 8 percent in the final years of the Echeverría period. Of this, more than two-thirds came from internal sources and less than one-third from external sources.[21]

Much has been written about the nature of the Mexican banking system and the use of legal reserve requirements of financial intermediaries set by the Bank of Mexico, not only as an instrument of monetary policy, but also as a technique to absorb government paper and thus provide compulsory loans to the government. The legal reserve requirements are also a way of allocating credit between the public and private sectors. Funds available to the government in the mid-1970s through these reserve requirements represented about one-third of the liabilities of the financial system.[22]

This technique of financing the public deficit had its costs. As the level of deposits appropriated by the government increased, monetary policy as a macroeconomic instrument became increasingly ineffective. In addition, as can be seen in tables 8-3 and 8-4, the share of credit from the banking system to the private sector fell during the Echeverría period, forcing rationing, which probably favored borrowers seeking large loans.

The atmosphere in which these budgetary and related credit developments were occurring was one of increasing hostility between the administration and the private sector. The animosity was substantively based

21. Ibid., p. 16.
22. Gilberto Escobedo, "The Response of the Mexican Economy to Policy Actions," *Federal Reserve Bank of St. Louis Review,* vol. 55 (June 1973), p. 21. Leopoldo Solís states that the weighted average of legal reserves was more than 40 percent during the *desarrollo estabilizador* period. See "Equilibrio Interno y Externo en la Economía Mexicana durante la Decada de los Sesentas," paper presented at seminar sponsored by the Instituto Torcuato Di Tella and the Organization of American States, Buenos Aires, September 1978.

Table 8-4. *Allocation of Total Credit, Selected Years, 1970–76*
End-of-year stocks as percentage of GDP

Year	Total credit	To public sector	To private sector
1970	44	22	22
1971	47	24	23
1973	47	25	22
1975	46	27	19
1976	42	27	15

Source: World Bank, *Mexico Manufacturing Sector: Situation Prospects and Policies* (March 1979), p. 75, based on data from Bank of Mexico.

because fiscal policy was inflationary (the annual average increase in the wholesale price index in Mexico City was 14.5 percent from 1971 to 1976 compared with 2.9 percent from 1965 to 1970),[23] and credit policy was accommodating the growing public sector demands. The conflict also was ideological in that the president regularly castigated the private sector for its lack of patriotism.

The decline in private sector confidence was reflected in capital flight estimated at $4 billion in the eighteen months preceding the devaluation.[24] From December 1975 to December 1976, the increase in peso liabilities of the banking system was only 10 percent (less than half the percentage increase of the previous twelve months), whereas liabilities denominated in foreign currencies increased by 72 percent (more than double the percentage increase of the previous twelve months).[25] Reserve requirements on dollar deposits were 100 percent, compared with about 40 percent for peso deposits. The disintermediation is apparent from data starting in 1972, but the process accelerated in 1976. The "dollarization" in 1976 took a quantum leap and reflected the crisis mentality that existed.

The costs of the president's budgetary decisions and of the emphasis on increasing the public sector generally are apparent enough. These decisions resulted in increasing deficits, in some crowding out of the private sector from bank credit (which the private sector may not have wanted under the circumstances), in rising inflation, in growing internal and external debt, and eventually in massive capital flight, reflecting the lack of confidence in government policy. As will be discussed in the next section, the balance of payments inevitably deteriorated.

23. Collected from data in *Indicadores Económicos*, various issues.
24. Supplement, "The Future for Mexico," *Euromoney* (April 1978), p. 2.
25. Banco de México, *Informe Anual 1976*, p. 40.

Were there countervailing benefits to the president's policies? Perhaps the best way to assess this is to ask whether priority objectives were accomplished. It already has been noted that inequality in income distribution apparently increased during the Echeverría sexenio (as it had during the *desarrollo estabilizador* period of the previous two decades). In this regard, therefore, the Echeverría policy of shared development *(desarrollo compartido)* was no more successful than the policies of his predecessors. The declining trend of agricultural production was not reversed. However, at least one significant project was begun, PIDER (Investment Program for Rural Development, started in 1973), which was designed to foster integrated rural development; this project may have important consequences in time. The import substitution technique of development, with its inherent subsidization of industry at the expense of other sectors, was not altered under Echeverría (although some change now seems to be taking place). Job creation was no more adequate under Echeverría than it was during the 1960s and, indeed, the problem probably worsened because of the lower rates of economic growth combined with demographic trends of the previous two decades. One accomplishment of the Echeverría sexenio, perhaps the one that will have the greatest long-term consequences, was the institution of a population program.[26] The data are inadequate to assess whether more was accomplished in 1971–76 in improving literacy and education, housing, nutrition, and health services than in prior sexenios. Except at the eleventh hour, there was no attempt to change significantly the land tenure pattern.

Echeverría's exchange rate policy during most of his administration was patently costly in seeking to maintain the peso-dollar rate when the peso had become clearly overvalued. However, Echeverría did render a service to his successor by taking the onus and consenting to the inevitable devaluation at the very end of his term.

The Balance of Payments

Because of the predominance of the United States in Mexican trade in goods and services (in recent years, the United States has accounted for about 60 percent of Mexico's trade in goods and 70 percent of Mexico's

---

26. Victor L. Urquidi, "Empleo y Explosión Demográfica," *Demografía y Economía,* vol. 8, no. 2 (1974), pp. 141–53, discusses employment and population trends in Mexico.

Table 8-5. *Wholesale Price Indexes, United States and Mexico City,*
1954–70 and 1954–76

1954 = 100

Year	United States[a]	Mexico City
1970	126.0	174.1
1976	208.9	355.6

Sources: For the United States, *Economic Report of the President, January 1978*, p. 319. For Mexico City, Nacional Financiera, *Statistics on the Mexican Economy, 1977*, pp. 218–19.

a. Data converted from 1967 = 100 base to 1954 = 100.

tourist receipts),[27] the critical exchange rate relationship for Mexico is between the peso and the dollar. Keeping it fixed was a Mexican fetish that Echeverría inherited and maintained. Yet, even at the time Echeverría became president in 1970, there was evidence that the peso was overvalued. Table 8-5 gives data on the relative increases in wholesale prices in the United States and Mexico from 1954 (when the Mexican peso was pegged at 12.50 to the dollar and held until September 1976) to 1970 and 1976. (The wholesale price index for Mexico is that for Mexico City, since a national wholesale price index is not available. Using the index for Mexico City may introduce some bias, but it is not likely to be significant and its direction is uncertain.) The degree of overvaluation was relatively modest in 1970 compared with the next six years. (If 1970 were set at 100 for each country, the wholesale price index comparison in 1977 would be 176 for the United States and 288 for Mexico.)

Mexico was able to maintain the peso-dollar parity set in 1954 as long as it did through earnings on invisibles (such as tourism, border transactions, and remittances from Mexicans working in the United States), large capital inflows, and protection of domestic industries against the competition consequences of overvaluation. However, this protection had its costs. One cost of protection, that of subsidizing industry at the expense of other sectors, already has been mentioned. The overvalued exchange rate also encouraged the importation of capital goods by reducing their peso cost, thus distorting relative factor prices. This distortion was often exacerbated by freeing capital goods imports from duties. Mexican industrial growth inevitably was forced to turn inward since exports were discouraged by the combination of a noncompetitive sheltered industry and an overvalued exchange rate. (There is also evidence of substantial smug-

27. Calvin P. Blair, "Mexico, Some Recent Developments," *Texas Business Review*, vol. 51 (May 1977), pp. 98–103.

Table 8-6. *Elements of Mexico's Balance of Payments, 1965–77*
Millions of dollars

Year	Merchandise balance[a,b]	Balance on current account[a]	Errors and omissions[c]	Long-term capital	Short-term capital[d]
1965	−431	−398	218	111	n.a.
1966	−420	−391	−193	213	n.a.
1967	−618	−635	69	346	n.a.
1968	−710	−757	545	379	n.a.
1969	−633	−609	−270	693	n.a.
1970	−923	−1,123	425	504	n.a.
1971	−647	−836	34	766	164
1972	−728	−916	650	828	−383
1973	−837	−1,415	−411	1,819	165
1974	−2,348	−2,875	−845	3,046	748
1975	−2,817	−4,040	−1,229	4,667	763
1976	−1,761	−3,408	−3,039	4,994	551
1977	−442	−1,779	−257	4,527	−1,840

Sources: International Monetary Fund, *International Financial Statistics* (*IFS*), August 1976, p. 65, until 1970; Nacional Financiera. *Statistics on the Mexican Economy,* for long-term capital 1965–70, pp. 380–81; *IFS*, January 1979, for all data 1971–77, p. 273.

n.a. Not available.

a. The IMF data differ from those used by the Bank of Mexico in several respects. The merchandise trade account in the IMF data includes nonmonetary gold and silver trade, whereas the Bank of Mexico's publication *Indicadores Económicos* shows this item separately. The IMF merchandise trade data are on an f.o.b. basis both for imports and exports since 1971, whereas the *Indicadores* shows imports c.i.f. The IMF data show reinvested profits as an outflow in the current account and an inflow in the capital account, whereas the *Indicadores* apparently abstracts from this issue in both accounts. The result is that since 1971 the trade deficit given is larger in the Bank of Mexico data, and the balance on current account is larger in the IMF data.

b. The trade data are exports f.o.b. and imports c.i.f. until 1970 and f.o.b. for both imports and exports from 1971 on.

c. The IMF errors and omissions figures since 1970 are substantially larger than those given by the Bank of Mexico in *Indicadores Económicos* or the *Nacional Financiera* publication listed in the source. The difference is explained by the effort of the Bank of Mexico to sort out some private sector short-term capital movements as a separate item whereas the IMF includes these in errors and omissions.

d. Not reported separately by the Bank of Mexico for years 1965 through 1970.

gled imports into Mexico to escape Mexican tariff and licensing requirements.)[28]

Table 8-6 shows key elements in Mexico's balance of payments since 1965. The deficit in merchandise trade grew during the latter 1960s, but the explosive growth of the deficit began in 1974. This certainly was associated with Mexico's accumulating inflation, which led to the growing overvaluation of the peso. Money supply increases (M_1, cash plus demand deposits) also were larger in the 1970–76 sexenio than in the previous six-year period (19 percent annually compared with 11 percent),[29]

28. An article in the *Washington Post,* February 13, 1979, using Mexican sources, gave an estimate of $1 billion a year for these contraband imports.

29. Figures constructed from *Indicadores Económicos,* various issues.

and some of this demand must have spilled over into imports. The recession in the United States and elsewhere dampened demand for Mexican exports, although this slowdown did not become manifest until 1975. Mexico's total merchandise exports grew by 37 percent in 1974, but this growth was dwarfed by the almost 60 percent increase in imports. Exports did not grow at all in 1975. The evidence, however, is that the growing merchandise trade deficit starting in 1972 is explained more by the increased growth of imports than by the recession-induced slowdown in export growth.

Table 8-6 also shows the growing deficit on current account. Put in terms of its relationship to gross domestic product, the annual deficit averaged 2.4 percent in the 1965–70 period and 3.7 percent in the 1971–76 period. In the final two years of the Echeverría administration (1975 and 1976), the current account deficits were 5.1 and 4.3 percent of GDP.[30] This deficit had to be financed, and table 8-6 shows the growing level of capital imports into Mexico during this period. One final point worth highlighting from table 8-6 is the dramatic growth of errors and omissions, which presumably reflects capital flight.

Concluding Comments on Destabilizing Period

A survey article on Mexico in *The Economist* contained the following harsh judgment on the Echeverría period:

Enter in 1970 President Luis Echeverría, a man whose political instinct far outran his political abilities, whose economic ambitions outran his economics, and whose populism outran his popularity. Exit in 1976, three months after having devalued the peso following 22 years of financial stability, and thereby giving rise to fears for the stability of the whole Mexican system.[31]

As one looks back, destabilization was costly, and the causes were mostly made in Mexico. As can be seen from table 8-1, growth was modest in the Echeverría sexenio. The recession in the United States in 1974 and 1975, often adduced as a partial explanation for Mexico's problems in those years, does not explain the inability to control fiscal deficits and

30. The numerator was calculated from IMF data, and the denominator from the publication of the Banco de México, *Producto Interno Bruto y Gasto* (1978), using IMF exchange rate data to convert pesos into dollars. Using the Bank of Mexico's definition of the current account deficit, the figure would be 4.9 percent of GDP in 1975.

31. David Gordon, "Mexico: A Survey," *The Economist*, April 22, 1978, p. 18.

inflation or to moderate the rise in imports. However, it does partly explain the year-to-year decline in exports of goods, services, and transfers from 10 to 8 percent of domestic product in 1975. Neither the inflation nor the burgeoning balance-of-payments deficit can be attributed to the increased cost of oil imports. (Mexico was a modest net importer of energy in 1974 to the extent of about $250 million, but became a net exporter in 1975.)

Javier Marquez summarized some dichotomies of the Mexican economic scene during the Echeverría period. These included the desire to use fiscal policy to reform the social scene, but then doing this on an inadequate tax base; the desire to raise exports, but seeking to do this while maintaining a fixed exchange rate in the face of accelerating inflation; the desire to strengthen public sector enterprises while freezing their prices; and the striving for greater industrial efficiency under a policy of protectionism.[32] Mexico was forced to address these dilemmas when it embarked on its stabilization program in 1977.

The Stabilization Period

Judging the stabilization program on the basis of its limited objectives, it must be deemed to have been mostly, but by no means fully, successful. The broad objectives of the program were to

1. Restore conditions conducive to higher rates of sustained growth;
2. Reduce inflation; and
3. Lower the current account deficit in the balance of payments to some level deemed acceptable in terms of external financing.

Table 8-7 summarizes the results in these three areas. GDP growth remained modest in 1977, the first year of the program, but then recovered in 1978. Industrial production grew by an estimated 10 percent in 1978, compared with an average of 7 percent over the preceding 10 years. However, agricultural production does not seem to have recovered in 1978 to the 1975 level.[33] Inflation (measured by the consumer price index) remained high, and in this respect the stabilization program failed. The increase in Mexico City wholesale prices moderated in 1978. The current

32. Javier Marquez, "La Economía Mexicana en 1977 y su Futuro," article based on a seminar given in Madrid, October 25, 1977.

33. Banco Nacional de México, *Review of the Economic Situation of Mexico*, December 1978, pp. 446 and 469.

Table 8-7. *Mexican Economic Growth, Inflation, and Balance-of-
Payments Indicators, 1975–78*

Annual growth rate except as indicated

Indicator	1975	1976	1977	1978ᵃ
Gross domestic product[b]				
Total	4.1	1.7	3.2	6.6
Per capita	0.4	−1.9	−0.5	3.5
Inflation				
Mexico City wholesale				
prices[e]	10.5	22.2	41.2	15.8
National consumer prices[d]	15.2	15.8	28.9	17.5
Current account deficit as				
percent of GDP[e]	5.1	4.3	2.4	2.7

Source: GDP data, Banco de México, *Producto Interno Bruto y Gasto* (1978), p. 31, up to 1978; Banco de México, *Informe Anual 1978*, p. 22, for 1978. Prices, Banco de México, *Indicadores Económicos* (December 1978), pp. 48 and 52, and *Informe Anual 1978*, for 1978 data. Current account/GDP percentage calculated from *Producto Interno Bruto*, p. 31, and IMF, *International Financial Statistics*, May 1979.
  a. Preliminary figures.
  b. Constant prices, 1960 = 100.
  c. Base 1954 = 100.
  d. Base 1978 = 100.
  e. For year indicated.

account deficit as a percentage of GDP has been reduced substantially. (Because of growing oil exports, this objective has a different urgency from that which existed in 1976 when the stabilization program was initiated. This will be discussed later.) Real wages declined in 1977 and 1978, an outcome that cannot be repeated indefinitely, and it is therefore likely that real wages, which were a deflationary factor in the first two years of the stabilization effort, will be an inflationary or, at best, a neutral factor in the years ahead.

IMF Agreement

The agreement reached between the IMF and Mexico was under the IMF's extended facility, involving a three-year program for 1977–79, with annual renewals at the end of the first and second years. This program was combined with a Mexican purchase under the IMF's compensatory financing facility and a Mexican purchase in its first credit tranche. Total potential Mexican use of IMF resources under the agreement amounted to SDR 837.125 million (the equivalent at the time of $965 million).[34] As already noted, this agreement with the IMF, announced in October 1976, was preceded in September by a bridge financing with the

34. *IMF Survey* (November 1, 1976), pp. 332–33.

United States of up to $600 million in addition to the $300 million already in the swap arrangement between the Bank of Mexico and the Federal Reserve.

When the agreement with the IMF was announced, there also was a specification of measures the Mexican government already had taken (the so-called preconditions). These included the imposition of some export taxes to prevent windfall profits from the peso devaluation and to augment government revenue; the suspension of many export incentives (or tax rebates under the Mexican system of CEDIs, which had averaged 15 percent ad valorem before devaluation), and some dismantling of import license requirements. Subsidies (price controls) for essential consumer goods and raw materials were allowed to continue.

This was only the second time any country had made use of the extended facility.[35] This facility, established in September 1974, was designed to mitigate the impact on a country of stabilization measures by extending the time for implementation. Under the facility, Mexican repurchases (repayments) would take place quarterly, over four years, with the first repurchase beginning four years after the purchase (drawing).

Elements of the agreement have been discussed publicly. One aspect which attracted much attention was the limitation of $3 billion during 1977 on public borrowing from abroad, including debts with maturities of less than one year, over the level of the disbursed public debt as of the end of 1976. As of the of end of 1976, Mexico's disbursed public debt with original maturity of more than one year was about $16 billion, and if short-term debt is added, close to $20 billion.[36] This combination had been growing at a rate of about $4 billion a year over the previous three years, and the $3 billion ceiling therefore represented a cutback. In addition, the debt structure placed a severe burden on Mexico for interest payments and for debt refinancing over the following five-year period.[37] Mexico complied with this condition of the agreement for 1977. It had been expected that the 1978 external borrowing limit would be less than in 1977, but the figure was kept at $3 billion to accommodate additional borrowing requirements of Pemex. The same $3 billion ceiling was set for 1979 for the same reason. Maintaining a constant level of borrowing

35. IMF, *Annual Report 1977*, p. 53.
36. World Bank, *World Debt Tables*, vol. 2, EC-167/78 (October 20, 1978), p. 117; and *Euromoney* (April 1978).
37. The interest payments/GDP ratio was more than 2 percent in 1977.

meant a reduction in relation to the GDP. According to the finance minister, the debt profile also has been improved.[38]

Mexico's external public debt, including short-term debt, was $26.3 billion at the end of 1978 (about 35 percent of GDP).[39] Debt ratios are extremely high, but Mexico is an atypical case because of potential oil export revenue. The concern about borrowing during the destabilizing period was not just on the amount and its profile, but also whether the funds were being used for investment or to finance current fiscal expenditures. This concern has been allayed, particularly with respect to the borrowing to expand Pemex operations.

Other quantitative targets in the agreement with the IMF were to progressively reduce the global deficit of the public sector and to raise its rate of savings; to increase international reserves using increases in currency issue as a benchmark; and to limit the increase in net domestic assets of the Bank of Mexico. These are typical conditions imposed by the IMF under stabilization agreements. From the public evidence available, all the targets were met in 1977 and 1978.

The gross international reserves of the Bank of Mexico declined by about $300 million in 1976 (to $1.3 billion) and then recovered in 1977 and 1978 (to about $2 billion).[40] The public sector deficit, which was 9.5 percent of GDP in 1976, dropped to 6.6 percent in 1977 and rose to 7.5 percent in 1978. Public sector savings, which traditionally have been low in Mexico, fell drastically during the Echeverría period (to about 0.3 percent of GDP in 1976), but have since recovered (to about 4.5 percent of GDP in 1978).[41]

Some brief comment may be useful regarding the nonquantitative conditions under the agreement with the IMF, namely, not to intensify nontariff import restrictions for balance-of-payments purposes or to use payments restrictions for current transactions. These conditions are concerned primarily with the longer-term development of Mexico.

Mexico does not have payments restrictions. Such restrictions probably would not be effective if introduced because of the ease of evasion, given the great human and economic interaction with the United States, particularly along the border.

38. "The Future for Mexico," *Euromoney*, pp. 14–15.
39. Banco de México, *Informe Anual 1978*, p. 78.
40. IMF, *International Financial Statistics* (May 1979).
41. Banco Nacional de México, *Examen de la Situación Económica de México* (January 1979), p. 11.

As noted, prior to the entry into force of the agreement with the IMF, Mexico eliminated import licensing requirements for some tariff items and reduced some tariffs. Since then, thousands of additional tariff items have been freed from the licensing requirements, and tariffs were adjusted to provide the desired level of protection. Export tax rebates were eliminated at the time of the devaluation but were reintroduced in 1977. It remains to be seen how far this process of trade liberalization will go.[42]

It was noted earlier that Mexico's potential for oil and natural gas exports has radically altered the original calculations made at the end of 1976 under the stabilization plan about the seriousness of Mexico's balance-of-payments current account deficit and of the burden on Mexico of servicing its external indebtedness. Indeed, Mexico could have surpluses in its current account in the near future rather than the deficits the stabilization plan was intended to correct. For example, the recently proposed industrialization plan noted that because of the revenue from projected oil exports, Mexico would have a current account surplus in its balance of payments in the 1980s (on the order of 0.8 to 1.8 percent of GDP) in the absence of a special effort to augment industrial growth.

It is indeterminate what such an outcome (a current account surplus) would do to Mexico's exchange rate without also specifying the outcome of other variables (such as the level of inflation in Mexico relative to that in the United States or the state of lender and investor confidence in Mexico). However, a current account surplus could reinforce the tendency—so costly during the Echeverría period—to prevent depreciation of the peso relative to the dollar, even if the peso is overvalued. Reinforcement of this tendency could weaken Mexico's already weak competitive position in external markets for manufactured goods. The industrial development plan seems to recognize this possibility and posits as a basic condition that the current account deficit should not exceed 2 percent of GDP in any year. The plan obtains this outcome by assuming import growth of 15 percent a year in real terms during the 1980s. Mexico is apt to face a complicated balancing problem in the 1980s; Mexico must conduct its external economic policy to avoid either damaging its industrial

42. The fragility of Mexico's commitment to trade liberalization can be seen from the intense debate in the Mexican press after Mexico indicated in early 1979 that it might accede to the General Agreement on Tariffs and Trade. The debate focused on Mexico's continued ability to protect its agriculture and industry. See, for example, the statement opposing accession of the Colegio Nacional de Economistas published in the newspaper *Uno Mas Uno,* May 25, 1979, p. 12.

sector by too heavy reliance on earnings from oil exports, or wasting its earnings by seeking too rapid an increase in imports in order to sustain GDP growth of at least 10 percent a year starting in 1982.[43]

The precise targets of the stabilization plan to limit both the balance-of-payments deficit and the increase in new external indebtedness were essentially out of date soon after their promulgation in 1976. The non-quantitative targets relating to import liberalization, which were a proxy for encouraging export competitiveness, were more significant even if less precise mathematically.

Costs and Benefits of Stabilization

Among the major criticisms of IMF stabilization programs have been that the conditions imposed (1) require too rapid an adjustment, (2) are too uniformly applied to countries without sufficient regard to domestic political circumstances, and (3) impose too great a burden on the poorest groups in the society.[44] How should the Mexican experience be judged based on these criticisms?

The first two criticisms are not particularly germane to the Mexican case. The rapidity of the stabilization effort was tempered by the three-year time frame of the agreement with the IMF. While some rapid policy shifts were required, particularly in slowing the expenditure growth of the public sector, the gradualism of the total program permitted Mexico to soften the hardships on the society generally. In this sense, the program did not ignore the political context of Mexico. In addition, the program was altered once it was clear that Mexico's balance-of-payments position had changed.

However, the burden of adjustment did fall heavily on wage earners. Real wages declined in 1977 and apparently again in 1978. President

---

43. Cited figures are from the *Plan Nacional de Desarrollo Industrial, 1979–1982*, pp. 24, 45, 48, and 121.

44. See paragraph 12 of the communique of the Group of 24 (finance ministers of developing countries), *IMF Survey* (October 2, 1978), p. 305; Danny M. Leipziger, "Short-Term Stabilization and Long-Term Development," draft of paper prepared for the Southern Economics Association, November 8–10, 1978; and Robert Frenkel and Guillermo O'Donnell, "The 'Stabilization Programs' of the International Monetary Fund and their Internal Impacts During Bureaucratic-Authoritarian Periods," paper presented at a conference on U.S. Foreign Policy and the Latin American and Caribbean Regimes, Woodrow Wilson International Center for Scholars, Washington, D.C., March 1978.

López Portillo made particular reference to the sacrifices of the wage earners in his second report on the state of the nation.

This is not the place for an analysis of Mexico's labor structure. Trejo Reyes has noted that the real living standard of workers covered by labor legislation appears to have improved from 1960 to 1976; during that time, nominal daily minimum wages increased from 9.89 to 78.81 pesos. According to Trejo, salaries increased in 1960–72 at an annual rate of 9.5 percent, which was considerably higher than the rate of increase in prices. In 1972–77, nominal salaries increased 21.9 percent a year, an annual increase of about 3.3 percent in real salaries. The nominal minimum salary doubled between 1974 and 1977, but did so "in response to price increases and converted itself into one additional element in the inflationary spiral."[45] In September 1976, before the stabilization effort began, there was a general emergency wage adjustment of 23 percent to maintain purchasing power following the devaluation. Thereafter wage policy became part of the adjustment. On January 1, 1977, minimum wages were increased by only 10 percent. The September 1977 pay increases for government employees was kept to 10 percent. For 1978, the government wage guideline for contractual settlements was set at 12 percent. Minimum wage increases, differentiated by urban and rural areas and by level of wages, averaged 14.5 percent nationally in 1978 (and 18.6 percent in 1979).[46] Actual wage and salary increases did not greatly exceed these norms in 1978.[47]

Much more than wage and salary earners, the disadvantaged groups in Mexico are the unemployed and underemployed. Although real wages declined during the first two years of the stabilization program, they had increased during the previous years of growing inflation. Those who presumably suffered most from the inflation were those who had no regular wages or incomes. The stabilization program may have hurt this group, but they probably were hurt much more from the inflationary developments and the economic stagnation prior to the stabilization program.

45. Trejo Reyes, "La Política Laboral," p. 151.

46. The minimum wages for the coming year can be found in an annual publication, *Salario Minimos,* issued by the Comision Nacional de los Salarios Minimos.

47. According to the U.S. Department of Labor, Bureau of International Labor Affairs, "Profile of Labor Conditions—Mexico," 1979, about 30–50 percent of employers of urban workers and as many as 80 percent of employers in rural areas fail to pay the minimum wage. On the other hand, wages in unionized industries tend to run higher than legal minimum rates, and in the first half of 1978, exceeded the government guidelines (p. 6).

The most telling piece of evidence on this score is that cited earlier on the deterioration of the share of total income of the lowest income group during the Echeverría period. It is also the underemployed and unemployed (particularly in rural areas) that benefit least from educational and health services provided by the state, so that a reduction in the growth of fiscal expenditures probably affected them less than it did other groups.

Mexico entered into its stabilization program following a period of growing inflation and economic stagnation. Per capita GDP growth remained negative in 1977, the first year of the program, but even that negative indicator was an improvement from the 1976 outcome (as can be seen from table 8-1, per capita GDP fell by 1.9 percent in 1976 and by 0.5 percent in 1977). By 1978, the worst of whatever hardships the stabilization program might bring were over.

Conclusions

By the close of 1976, Mexico needed some program to reverse the inflationary and balance-of-payments trends of the previous five years, particularly since the destabilizing policies being followed were not accomplishing their primary growth and distributional objectives. Therefore, judging the stabilization program in 1977 and 1978, the relevant issues are whether the measures adopted were well conceived, whether they accomplished their objectives with a minimum of hardship and of distributional inequality, and whether the program lays a foundation for future Mexican growth.

In terms of most of its immediate objectives, the stabilization program clearly was successful. GDP growth per capita, which was low in 1975 and negative in 1976, remained negative in 1977, but recovered in 1978 and seems to be recovering even more in 1979. The deficit in the current account of the balance of payments declined sharply as a percentage of GDP following the devaluation. The principal failure in 1977 was the continued increase in prices. These moved downward in 1978, but remain excessive. All observers attest to a sense of confidence in the economy since 1978, reversing the pessimism which prevailed in 1976.

It is hard to evaluate the degree of hardship imposed by the program on the poor majority in Mexico since a standard of comparison (to make before and after judgments) does not exist. The unemployment (and underemployment) problem was severe before the stabilization program, as was income inequality. For those who had jobs, a pattern of wage and salary increases chasing price increases had become endemic. The stabilization measures permitted continuation of subsidies of vital consumer goods in order to mitigate the hardships on those least able to cope with the retrenchment measures. It is hard to say whether the burdens demanded under the program were greater than those being extracted during the latter phases of the destabilization period. The burdens were greater in 1977 and 1978 for wage earners; they probably were not greater for the unemployed and underemployed, about 40 percent of the economically active population.

Mexico was fortunate in the timing of its program. The program coincided with the discovery of large oil and gas reserves and the beginnings of increased earnings from petroleum exports. Imports of goods and services grew as a percentage of GDP (from 13.5 percent in 1976 to 14 percent in 1977), but exports increased at an even greater rate (9.2 to 11.1 percent). The timing of the program also coincided with periods of high growth in the United States, facilitating Mexico's export growth. The balance-of-payments constraint under the program did not impose a great hardship. For the foreseeable future, the balance of payments will not be a constraint to Mexican growth.

Significant imponderables for the future include the following: How extensively will Mexico liberalize its import structure to promote competitiveness of its industry? Will Mexico follow an exchange rate policy that encourages exports and makes unnecessary quantitative import restrictions (or excessively high tariffs) of the type employed since 1947? In both cases, the initial steps were encouraging, and they flowed directly from the stabilization program. The most important imponderable of all is how Mexico will seek to create sufficient jobs for its economically active population. The successful stabilization program permits this question to be addressed under reasonably favorable circumstances, but no more than that.

Comments by Saúl Trejo Reyes

Sidney Weintraub's chapter touches on some very important structural characteristics of the Mexican economy that are not normally discussed in relation to stabilization policy. In particular, his discussion of the agricultural sector, protection and efficiency of the industrial sector, insufficient government revenues, the external competitiveness of the Mexican economy, and the level and structure of public sector subsidies to private activity, as well as unemployment and inequality, contributes to a fuller understanding of the context in which stabilization policy must work in Mexico. The chapter should also help us appreciate the difficulty of evaluating the effectiveness of such policies according to the criteria commonly used for such purpose, that is, short-term criteria.

Weintraub attempts to evaluate recent Mexican macroeconomic policy, particularly during the 1970–76 administration, in terms of the objectives of growth, price stability, and balance-of-payments equilibrium. He also points out what he considers the failure of government policies during the period under discussion to make much of a dent on the problems of unemployment and inequality. It is important in this respect to make some qualifications. The first is that in order to evaluate government's attempts to make development less unequal, one must understand that the tendencies toward inequality, balance-of-payments disequilibrium, and a slowing down of agricultural growth, among others, are in many ways a logical result of the policies followed in the postwar industrialization period. One should therefore not start in 1970, but much earlier. At the same time, the political elements which gave rise to, or even forced, some key decisions during the period under discussion can be ignored only at serious risk. Finally, much more empirical work is needed on the short-term dynamics of the Mexican economy to prove fully the assertion that government investment displaces private investment activity. This is important in discussing the question of whether government is "too big" or not.

With regard to the long-term tendencies of the Mexican economy, one must emphasize the general level of efficiency of all activities. It is not only industry that is inefficient; commerce, services, and agriculture—both modern and traditional—are also highly inefficient when measured in terms of their primary resource use per unit of output. Government subsidies have tended to concentrate on certain regions and on modern sector activities in general so that these are, at market prices, more profitable. Thus, the problem of efficiency must be viewed in terms of the need for different technological, educational, and other policies and of the international system of which the Mexican economy is a part. In this view, foreign trade liberalization can play only a minimal part in the achievement of higher levels of efficiency in the various sectors of the Mexican economy.

Growth, by its nature, often implies a substantial redistribution of income which normally tends to heighten social and political conflict among competing groups. This has most certainly been the case in Mexico, where the state early in postrevolutionary development fostered the growth of an indigenous business class that naturally, as it became stronger, has attempted to gain for itself a larger share of wealth and income and a more direct part in policy-making activities. On the other hand, organized labor has perhaps been government's best organized and strongest ally. The conflicts inherent in the growth strategy, which left a majority of the population outside the benefits of growth, have become more open during the last few years, but they were present long before 1970.

These long-term conflicts have made short-term economic policy rather difficult. Each recent administration, on assuming office, has faced a progressively larger fiscal deficit as well as growing social and balance-of-payments problems. At the same time, each has faced great resistance on the part of the middle and upper classes to any substantive fiscal reform.

The first year of an administration is normally a recession year, given the fact that government investment expenditures are at their lowest level in a six-year cycle. Although Weintraub sees public and private investment as competing with each other for available savings, the observed first year recessions, as well as empirical work,[48] seem to support the hypothesis that public investment does not compete with private investment, but rather with private consumption. Public investment really appears to have been the motor behind private investment activity. In 1971 and 1972, public investment did not crowd out even private consumption, much less private investment, which was at particularly low levels. It was only the recovery of public investment in 1972 that made possible a return to the traditionally higher rates of growth. Of course, high inflation rates began in 1973.

Weintraub's chapter shows a keen appreciation of some of the motivations behind the past administration's policies. However, he attributes the economic events of the period after 1972 to pure and simple mismanagement, and therefore does less than full justice to an unresolved question of fundamental importance for Latin American countries: how to maintain short-term stability while at the same time advancing toward dis-

48. See Edmund V. K. FitzGerald, "Patterns of Saving and Investment in Mexico: 1939–1976," Working Paper 30 (University of Cambridge, Centre of Latin American Studies, 1979).

tributional and social justice goals. As Weintraub rightly points out toward the end, it is not yet clear how this can be done in Mexico. Social justice and economic equality remain primary objectives of Mexican governments and are the basis for their legitimacy, so equity goals are of great importance.

It should also be pointed out that the long border and close financial ties with the United States set strong restrictions on monetary policy. Such policy, however, has not been managed very flexibly in the 1970s. The resulting capital movements have been large and, of course, in 1973–76 they were amplified by expectations about changes in the parity of the peso. Expectations of this type tend to be self-fulfilling, and it is true that in this case it would have been advisable to devalue sooner. However, devaluation could not be expected to be the whole answer, given the structural nature of inefficiency in the Mexican economy, as has been pointed out. The relative success of economic policy in recent years should perhaps be attributed to oil more than to any other single element, although government's efforts to restore business confidence have certainly played a key role.

Serious problems remain. Given the internal pressures to maintain a high rate of growth and at the same time increase the level of spending on social infrastructure to at least avoid creating a larger backlog than already exists, government investment spending must increase continuously. This would require a large increase in government saving, except that increases in prices by government corporations, given the oligopolistic nature of the Mexican economy, might be highly inflationary, so that market structure policies become important. Oil revenues will help, but there will still be the problem of generating enough domestic savings to utilize oil income most productively.

Discussion*

Abraham Katz (U.S. Commerce Department) emphasized Mexico's problem of industrial inefficiency, citing strong resistance to efforts to reduce protection and shift industry from import substitution to exports. He noted business group opposition to policies of the Echeverría regime as one source of destabilization, saying that it was too early to tell whether

* The general discussion on both the Mexico and Peru studies appears at the end of chapter 9.

the new administration's pro-business tone would bring forth business group cooperation. He emphasized the advantages to the current regime provided by oil revenues.

Sidney Weintraub (Brookings Institution) said he agreed with Trejo that Echeverría inherited many problems of long standing that constrained his freedom of action. However, Echeverría's policies often worsened the very problems he set out to ameliorate. When he left office, not only was the public sector deficit greater than before, but inequality in income distribution had increased, unemployment was up, inflation was higher, the balance of payments was in crisis, and no national consensus had been created.

Weintraub agreed with several commentators that there is little profit in looking back and that the crucial issues for Mexico are those that lie ahead. The generally successful stabilization program carried out by López Portillo did not by itself correct the most serious problems both he and Echeverría inherited—those of stagnant agricultural production, rising unemployment and underemployment, and rigidities in the government's ability to increase its share of the GDP. The balance-of-payments problem was corrected by the fortunate discovery of vast quantities of oil. The López Portillo stabilization program is significant in that its success permits the more deep-seated problems to be addressed from a position of economic strength rather than an atmosphere of turmoil.

CHAPTER NINE

Economic Stabilization in Peru, 1975–78

WILLIAM R. CLINE

FROM 1975 through 1978, Peru experienced a severe imbalance in its external accounts that led to a succession of attempts at economic stabilization, street riots, near default on debt, severe economic recession, and accelerating inflation. The purpose of this study is to examine the Peruvian experience to evaluate the appropriateness of the stabilization strategy adopted and to derive broader lessons about stabilization policies in developing countries.

Table 9-1 shows several basic economic indicators for the Peruvian economy from 1967 to 1978. It is clear from the table that the crux of the problem was an external sector out of control beginning in 1974 and 1975. The cumulative current account deficits drove Peru into heavy external indebtedness and reduced net reserves to nearly intolerable levels by 1978. By late 1978, the external crisis was somewhat under control: the current account deficit had been cut dramatically, and Peru successfully carried out a debt rescheduling. The successive, and at first abortive, stabilization episodes beginning in 1975 and continuing beyond 1978 appeared finally to have achieved success in the external sector. At the same time, however, real GDP per capita fell by approximately 8 percent from 1976 to 1978. Moreover, domestic inflation, not initially a major stabilization problem, had reached 57.8 percent in 1978 (year over year), taking the place of external balance as the primary stabilization problem.

Without question, Peru experienced one of the most wrenchingly painful stabilization processes of all the developing countries in this period. The central analytical questions are these: Could Peru have achieved economic stabilization at a lower cost in terms of sacrifice of real growth?

For generous cooperation and invaluable insights, I am indebted to Roberto Abusada, Claudio Herzka, Linda Koenig, Manuel Moreyra, Alonso Polar, Raúl Salazar, Richard Webb, and Felipe Ortíz de Zevallos. None of these individuals bears any responsibility for the views expressed in this study.

Table 9-1. *Peru: Selected Economic Indicators, 1967–78*

Year	Real growth rate of GDP (percent)	Increase in consumer price index (percent)	Imports[a] (millions of dollars)	Exports[a] (millions of dollars)	Current account balance (millions of dollars)	Net external reserves (millions of dollars, year-end)
1967	3.5	9.8	810	742	−311	n.a.
1968	0.0	19.0	673	850	−59	n.a.
1969	4.2	6.3	659	881	−29	n.a.
1970	7.3	4.9	599	1,072	158	423.2
1971	5.1	6.9	730	890	−73	347.0
1972	6.0	7.1	812	945	−71	397.4
1973	6.2	9.5	1,097	1,113	−303	410.6
1974	6.9	16.9	1,909	1,506	−773	692.5
1975	3.5	23.6	2,389	1,291	−1,591	115.8
1976	3.1	33.5	2,099	1,360	−1,252	−751.7
1977	−1.0	38.1	2,164	1,726	−976	−1,100.9
1978	−1.8	57.8	1,600	1,941	−192	−1,025.0

Sources: IMF, *International Financial Statistics* (June 1979 and May 1978); Banco Central de Peru, *Proyección Financiera a Diciembre 1979: Compendio Estadístico* (Lima: Banco Central de Peru, May 4, 1979), table 3; and Banco Central de Peru, *Reseña Económica, Cuarto Trimestre de 1978* (Lima: Banco Central de Peru), pp. 11, 15.
n.a. Not available.
a. F.o.b.

Would superior alternative strategies have been feasible within the same constraints on externally available resources? Is Peru now past the crisis stage, or are slow growth, high inflation, and severe pressure in external accounts likely to persist? A first step toward analysis of these issues is to review briefly how the economy got into its crisis and what stabilization measures were taken.

Origins of the Economic Crisis

A growing monographic literature on the Peruvian experience provides a substantial basis for diagnosis of Peru's stabilization experience.[1] The

1. Daniel M. Schydlowsky and Juan J. Wicht, "The Anatomy of an Economic Failure: Peru 1968–78," Discussion Paper Series 32 (Boston University, Center for Latin American Development Studies, February 1979); John Sheahan, "Peru: International Economic Policies and Structural Change, 1968–1978," Latin American Program Working Paper 21 (Smithsonian Institution, Woodrow Wilson Center, 1978); Barbara Stallings, "Peru and the U.S. Banks: Privatization of Financial Relations" (University of Wisconsin, July 1978); Rosemary Thorp, "The Peruvian Experiment in Historical Perspective," Working Paper 31 (Smithsonian Institution, Woodrow Wilson Center, Latin American Program, 1978); and Rosemary Thorp, "Inflation, Stabilization, and Attempted Redemocratization in Peru, 1975–79" (Oxford University, 1979).

military regime of General Velasco that took power in October 1968 entered on the heels of an episode of foreign exchange crisis and corrective tax increases and devaluation with an International Monetary Fund (IMF) stabilization package that had largely laid the foundation for subsequent years of growth without external imbalance.[2]

The reformist military regime carried out a land reform that was sweeping even though land was distributed to only 25 percent of the rural population. The regime restructured the industrial sector by creating the "industrial communities" providing for worker participation in profits and management. The regime continued the Peruvian development strategy of import substitution, imposing nearly total prohibitions on imports of products enumerated under the "industrial register" protecting domestic industry.

From 1969 until 1974 the Peruvian model seemed to work relatively well. Growth rates averaged about 6 percent annually, inflation was low by Latin American standards, and the government clearly achieved some redistributive results (although primarily from the very top to the upper-middle income groups, bypassing the low-income groups[3]).

By 1975, however, the model began to disintegrate. The emerging features of economic failure included several elements:

1. Exports had been allowed to stagnate. The quantum of exports fell by 28 percent from 1968 to 1974 (table 9-5, below), strangling the supply of foreign exchange vital to the strategy of import substituting industrialization. The lack of new foreign mining projects (given political uncertainty) and the bias against exports inherent in the import substitution model (with an overvalued exchange rate and high protection) were contributing factors.

2. Economic management was chaotic in state enterprises, and in the "reformed private sector," fear of socialist rhetoric as well as disincentives to profits under profit-sharing provisions limited investments for expansion.

3. Private investment declined markedly, only partially offset by rising public investment.

2. Precipitating the coup was the Belaunde government's attempt to lay an even firmer foundation by resolving the outstanding nationalization dispute with the International Petroleum Corporation and thereby become eligible for U.S. economic assistance. See Pedro Pablo Kuczynski, *Peruvian Democracy under Economic Stress: An Account of the Belaunde Administration, 1963–1968* (Princeton University Press, 1977).

3. Richard C. Webb, *Government Policy and the Distribution of Income in Peru, 1963–1973* (Harvard University Press, 1977), p. 101.

Table 9-2. *Selected Data on the Peruvian Economy, 1955–76*
Percentage of GNP

Item	1955–58	1959–63	1964–68	1969–73	1974–76
Investment					
Total	22.3	18.6	15.4	12.7	15.3
Private	17.5	15.3	10.8	7.9	6.5
Public	4.8	3.3	4.6	4.8	8.8
Exports minus imports[a]	−5.2	−1.1	−1.4	1.6	−7.1
Government deficit					
Central government	n.a.	n.a.	n.a.	3[b]	7[c]
Total pubic sector	n.a.	n.a.	n.a.	n.a.	10[c]
Real exchange rate[d]	n.a.	139	99	100	104

Sources: Thorp, "Inflation, Stabilization, and Redemocratization," p. 3; *International Financial Statistics* (May 1978 and June 1979); Sheahan, "Peru: International Economic Policies," p. 15; table 9-5, below.
  n.a. Not available.
  a. Goods and nonfactor services (national accounts concept).
  b. 1970–74.
  c. 1975–77.
  d. Index, 1970 = 100.

4. Ambitious government investment programs were not matched by tax increases, and the government budget deficit (including state enterprises) rose to 10 percent of GNP by 1975.[4]

5. The regime resorted to external financing as a substitute both for domestic revenue and for faltering exports, and Peru ran up a massive foreign debt that stood at $3 billion at the end of 1975 (about 2.3 times exports) and $4.7 billion at the end of 1977 (about 2.7 times exports).[5]

To add to the dislocations caused by all of these features of questionable economic policy, Peru suffered severe exogenous economic shocks: fishmeal exports fell because of the disappearance of anchovies in 1973; world copper prices fell sharply in 1975; and the tantalizing prospects of massive oil discoveries proved illusory (as examined below).

Detailed analyses of the origins of Peru's economic crisis have appeared in the literature cited above. However, table 9-2 presents in summary form data that help explain the emerging crisis. The table shows the long-term decline in Peru's investment rate, from 22 percent of GNP in the late 1950s to 15 percent in the mid-1970s. Declining investment per-

4. Sheahan, "Peru: International Economic Policies," p. 16.
5. World Bank, *World Debt Tables,* supplement (February 12, 1979). These figures are for disbursed public and publicly guaranteed debt with maturities over one year. According to Thorp, if short-term and private sector debt are included, the figure for 1978 reaches $9 billion. (Thorp, "Inflation, Stabilization, and Attempted Redemocratization," p. 18.)

formance contributed to the declining growth rate that began in 1975. Moreover, in the period of the military regime (after 1968) there was a sharp drop in private investment and a rise in public investment. To the extent that public investment was less efficient than private, this shift would have led to a slowdown in growth as well.

Table 9-2 also shows exports minus imports of goods and nonfactor services as a percentage of GNP. This figure represents a comparison between domestic production of goods and services and domestic use. Through the 1960s the balance was close to zero, but by 1974–76, domestic use exceeded domestic production by 7 percent of GNP.[6]

Table 9-2 also shows the sharp increase in government deficits. The central government deficit more than doubled as a percentage of GNP from 1969–73 to 1974–76, and total public sector deficits reached 10 percent of GNP. These figures strongly suggest the presence of excess demand in the economy caused by ambitious government spending unmatched by revenues.

Finally, table 9-2 reports the index of the real exchange rate, corrected for foreign and domestic inflation. The index fell sharply from the early 1960s to a relatively constant level for 1964–76, meaning that the incentive to import was higher (and the incentive to export lower) throughout the late 1960s and early 1970s than in the early 1960s.

In sum, the table suggests (1) lagging investment performance, (2) expansion of public investment at the expense of private investment, (3) surging excess demand as shown by external and budget deficits, and (4) lagging exchange rate incentives as causes of the emerging crisis.

Special Factors

Problems of economic management were not the only source of Peru's economic crisis in the mid-1970s. In addition, bad luck and questionable political priorities added up to a series of major special factors influencing the external account. The bad luck included disappearance of the anchovies, decline in the price of copper, and failure of glowing hopes about oil finds to materialize. The political issue was military spending.

6. The 5 percent figure for 1955–58 also represented a sizable deficit, but it occurred when investment was high, indicating that capital inflows were going to finance investment. The low investment figure for 1974–76 suggests that external inflows went more to finance consumption, public and private.

Table 9-3. *Imports of Arms, 1968–77*

Year	Imports (millions of dollars)
1968	30
1969	30
1970	20
1971	50
1972	70
1973	80
1974	80
1975	100
1976	200
1977	430 (464)[a]
1978	299[a]

Sources: U.S. Arms Control and Disarmament Agency, *World Military Expenditures and Arms Transfers, 1968–1977* (Washington, D.C.: ACDA, 1979), and Banco Central de Peru, *Reseña Económica*, p. 15.
a. "Other" imports, generally understood to be military imports.

The encouraging discoveries of oil in 1973 and 1974 led even cautious analysts to project large oil export revenues. Thus in 1975 the World Bank projected oil exports of $396 million in 1977 and $565 million in 1978, rising to $2.4 billion by 1985. Official projections of the Peruvian government were twice as high for the period 1978–85.[7] In reality, oil exports reached only $75 million in 1977 and $180 million in 1978 because discoveries fell far below expectations.[8] These sanguine forecasts of oil prospects in 1974 and 1975 undoubtedly contributed to the willingness of private banks to lend to Peru (and to the judgment by Peruvian policy makers that high borrowing temporarily was safe). Correspondingly, when the oil bonanza failed to arrive, Peru's external accounts came under severe pressure.

Nature dealt Peru a blow even earlier when the disappearance of anchovies from coastal waters in 1973 reduced fishmeal exports by 78 percent in volume, although because of higher prices, the reduction in value was only about one-half. Using the 1970–72 average value of fishmeal exports ($268 million) as a reference basis, if this value of exports could have been maintained in real purchasing power terms (adjusting for inflation in dollar import prices), fishmeal exports would have averaged $492 million annually for 1974–77 instead of their actual average of $171

7. According to the World Bank country report for Peru issued March 1975.
8. Banco Central de Peru, *Reseña Económica, Cuarto Trimestre de 1978* (Lima: Banco Central de Peru), p. 11.

million. In that event, overall exports would have been higher by approximately 22 percent.[9]

The decline in world copper prices was another exogenous shock, although the costs appear to have been relatively small. Copper prices in the London market fell by 40 percent from 1974 to 1975. However, they had risen by 92 percent from 1972 to 1974, so that the 1974 price had to be considered a short-term windfall.[10] Moreover, Peru's own volume of copper exports declined from an index of 144 in 1972 to 107 in 1974 (too early for slack world demand to be an explanation), so that much of the subsequent decline in copper earnings was attributable to Peru's lower export volume rather than to lower prices. An approximate estimate of the size of the windfall loss attributable to lower copper prices would be only a $34 million annual average for 1975–77.[11]

The rise in the world price of oil in 1974 represented another exogenous shock to Peru, still a petroleum importer in the period 1974–77. From 1973 to 1974, Peru's net imports of petroleum products rose from $39.4 million to $97.4 million.[12] Stated at a 1976 purchasing power level, this loss amounted to $66 million annually.

Another source of "exogenous" strain on the foreign sector was military spending for imports. Table 9-3 shows the levels of military imports for the period 1968–77. In 1974–75, Peru made massive arms purchases amounting to more than $2 billion. As shipments began to arrive in volume by 1976 and 1977, arms imports became a major burden on the foreign sector, accounting for approximately 10 percent of total imports in 1976 and 20 percent in 1977. Comparing a base period of 1970–72 to the period 1974–77, and taking into account higher general import prices, the rise in the annual average of military imports between the two periods amounted to $116 million (in 1976 dollars). Unlike oil discoveries, anchovies, and world copper prices, military imports were subject to gov-

---

9. Calculated from IMF, *International Financial Statistics,* selected issues.

10. IMF, *International Financial Statistics* (May 1978), p. 53.

11. Using a 1970–72 base for copper exports by value, maintenance of their import purchasing power would have implied exports of $384 million years, 1975–77. Because volume fell by 27.5 percent from 1970–72 to 1975–77, this reference figure must be reduced by that proportion. Thus with 1970–72 "real" prices, copper exports in 1975–77 would have averaged $278 million, only $34 million more than the actual figure. Calculated from IMF, *International Financial Statistics* (May 1978 and June 1979).

12. United Nations, *Yearbook of International Trade Statistics: 1977,* vol. 1 (New York: UN, 1978), p. 755.

Table 9-4. *Impact of Exogenous Shocks and Military Imports on Peru's Trade Balance, 1974–77*

Influence	Impact on trade balance[a] (millions of dollars, annual average)
Disappearance of anchovies, 1973	−321
Decline in copper prices, 1975–77 versus 1970–72	−34[b]
Rise in oil price, 1974–77 versus 1973	−66
Subtotal, economic shocks	−421
Military imports, 1974–77 versus 1970–72	−116
Total	−537
Memorandum items	
Exports	1,471
Current account balance	−1,148
Effects as percentage of current account deficit	
Economic (percent)	36.7
Economic and military (percent)	46.8

Source: Calculated from *International Financial Statistics* (June 1979 and May 1978). See text.
a. Expressed in dollars with 1976 import purchasing power.
b. Refers to 1975–77 average.

ernment control, and it appears indisputable that the government decision to spend heavily on arms imports represented a major source of Peru's external economic problems. The government did eventually recognize the need to cut back; in 1978, its military imports fell from $464 million to $299 million (table 9-3).

Table 9-4 summarizes the impact of the "special factors" of fishmeal, copper prices, oil prices, and military imports on Peru's external economic position. The four factors together represent a cost of over half a billion dollars annually in the period 1974–77, representing more than one-third of actual export earnings and nearly one-half of the average current account deficit. The decline in fishmeal exports was the most important factor (representing 60 percent of the total loss from these special factors), and military imports were next in importance at 22 percent of the loss.

In sum, bad luck and a costly military appetite accounted for a large part of Peru's external economic crisis. If the failure to find oil in quantities expected is included, the influence of economic "chance" was even more dramatic.

It does not necessarily follow, however, that because bad luck was a major factor, Peru should have received more help from the international community. Only the copper price decline represented the kind of temporary bad luck that is typically eligible for international assistance (at market rate terms), and yet copper prices appear to have played only a small role in the overall crisis. Fishmeal decline, higher oil prices, and absence of oil discoveries were essentially permanent phenomena, and higher loans to cover a "temporary" burden were not appropriate (although some degree of gradual adjustment through external financing rather than immediate adjustment was appropriate in the face of fishmeal decline and higher oil prices). Military imports represented a burden that was at Peru's own discretion.

The Stabilization Programs

The emerging economic crisis marked by outsized trade deficits in 1974 and early 1975 (spurred by the policy-induced and exogenous factors discussed above and import surges related to government investment projects) and by accelerating inflation, served as a catalyst for the coup by General Francisco Morales Bermudez in August 1975. The coup marked an economic turning point of the regime. The Bermudez government largely nullified the reformist "industrial community" law, although the regime did not reverse land reform. Despite somewhat more orthodox economic policies, the balance-of-payments crisis continued.

Private Banks' Package, 1976

In March 1976 the Bermudez government sought a large balance-of-payments loan from major U.S. banks, without a prior IMF standby agreement. The government felt that agreeing to IMF conditions would be unacceptable politically, although in its discussions with the banks, the government proposed a program very much like that which might have secured IMF support. Partly out of fear of a more leftist coup if Bermudez lost power, the banks eventually agreed, but only after the regime demonstrated willingness to take unpopular stabilization measures. In June 1976 the government devalued the sol by 31 percent and raised excise taxes and prices for electricity and transportation; the immediate result was rioting in Lima.[13]

The program called for an initial $200 million in loans with a second

13. David O. Beim, "Rescuing the LDCs," *Foreign Affairs,* vol. 55 (July 1977), p. 725.

$200 million to follow after several months, contingent on government adherence to the policy package. Signed only by the end of 1976, the package soon demonstrated the frailty of such direct intervention by banks; for reasons of data availability, technical capacity, and political sensitivity, it proved impossible for the banks to enforce their lending conditions, and adverse publicity for the intervention (plus its ineffectiveness) caused the leading bankers involved to resolve that they would not become entangled in similar packages in the future but would rely on the IMF as the monitoring authority.[14] Nevertheless, for the first six months (June to December 1976), Peru fulfilled its commitments, and in early 1977, the banks released the second tranche of the loan package. By the first quarter of 1977, however, Peru had departed widely from the program, as the military government's spending demands far exceeded the bounds prescribed by the Central Bank of Peru.

IMF Packages, 1977–78

The IMF mission of March 1977 set forth stringent conditions for a standby loan to Peru: a target inflation rate of 15 percent, a budget deficit of 20 billion soles, higher gasoline prices, tax reform, 30 percent devaluation, elimination of import quotas, and wage increases limited to 15 percent.[15] The central bank proposed a milder program (25 percent inflation, 40 billion soles budget deficit), but negotiations failed because even these targets were highly unlikely to be met given pressures for more spending in the rest of the government. (In fact, the 1977 budget deficit reached over 89 billion soles.)[16] Faced with the impasse, Finance Minister Luis Barua resigned. His replacement, Walter Piazza, successfully negotiated a draft agreement with the IMF, but the cabinet rejected the agreement (in part for unrelated political reasons), and Piazza resigned. Nevertheless, the government implemented the price rises called for by the draft agreement, provoking the first general strike in Peru since 1919.[17]

Declining reserves forced the government back into negotiations with the IMF, and in November 1977, Peru entered into a formal standby

14. Nancy Belliveau, "What the Peruvian Experiment Means," *Institutional Investor* (October 1976).

15. Stallings, "Peru and the U.S. Banks," pp. 48–49.

16. Sheahan, "Peru: International Economic Policies," p. 16.

17. Stallings, "Peru and the U.S. Banks," p. 50.

agreement with the IMF. By February 1978, however, the IMF found Peru in serious violation of the agreement, causing a suspension of IMF credits and leading the foreign banks to halt plans for $260 million in rollover loans.[18]

The turning point came in May 1978. With net reserves (gross reserves minus short-term obligations) at approximately −$1.2 billion, and with debt service of approximately $1 billion falling due in 1978, the economy was near external bankruptcy. The government brought in a new economic team, Manuel Moreyra of the Central Bank and Silva Ruete of Economy and Finance, who insisted on severe measures as a condition of acceptance. The government devalued the sol from 130 to 150 per dollar, changed the exchange rate to a crawling peg, raised prices of fuel by 60 percent and milk and bread by 40 percent, eliminated most subsidies, took new tax measures, raised interest rates, and restrained government spending. Altogether the measures were designed to reduce the budget deficit by 31 billion soles in the second half of 1978.[19] Political response was sharp: there were riots in major cities that caused several deaths, and a general strike, leading to imposition of martial law. The financial results were the successful postponement until 1979 of $185 million due to foreign commercial banks in the rest of the year,[20] the negotiation of a new agreement with the IMF in July (signed on September 15, 1978) and a successful rescheduling of external debts late in 1978.[21]

The hardening of policy in mid-1978 appears to have reflected the absence of any alternative rather than a change in political orientation. As a gauge of how severe the external crisis was, for several months in mid-1978, private imports were virtually suspended. The government stopped granting import licenses for intermediate goods and even prohibited the payment of letters of credit, thereby drying up the normal funds financing imports. Under these conditions of quasi-bankruptcy, Peru had little alternative to the adoption of stringent measures. To an important extent, the firm measures of 1978 appear to have represented a final success of economic advisers in convincing military authorities that there was no alternative. In this light, the earlier, abortive stabiliza-

18. *Peru Económico,* vol. 2 (January 1979), p. 2.
19. *Peru Económico,* vol. 1 (August 1978), p. 5.
20. *Peru Económico,* vol. 2 (January 1979), p. 3.
21. More than $2 billion in external debt was rescheduled, including $800 million in commercial bank lending for which repayment was spread out over seven years. *New York Times,* December 30, 1978.

tion programs (in 1976 and 1977) were part of a learning process within the political-economic context.

From mid-1978 to mid-1979, the Peruvian government strictly followed the conditions of the IMF standby agreement, staying well within the allowed ceilings for total credit (net domestic assets of the Central Reserve Bank) and on net bank credit to the public sector, adhering to limits on the contracting of external debt, and meeting nonquantitative performance criteria in areas such as improving tax collections. In the same period, the external sector began to improve because of sharply lowered imports (caused by restrictions, the downturn in GDP, and lower military imports) and higher export earnings (resulting from higher prices and from the coming on line of some petroleum exports).

Softening the Terms?

Although IMF standby conditions are not in the public domain, there is some evidence that the IMF accepted softer terms in the July 1978 negotiations than it had required in the November 1977 package. With the benefit of hindsight, most Peruvian analysts now appear to regard the 1977 package as having been impossible to achieve, and indeed the program's terms had already been violated within the first two months (although budgetary dissembling disguised the fact).[22] By the time of the 1978 agreement, the IMF had sent a more senior negotiator widely regarded in Peru as more flexible, and the agreement included notable elements of greater flexibility, including the fact that credit limits were to be applied only to the Central Bank, rather than to the entire banking system.[23] Apparently, the riots, the deaths, and the likelihood that the Moreyra-Silva team represented the last chance for an agreement con-

22. See, for example, *Peru Económico*, vol. 2 (January 1979), p. 2.

23. *Peru Económico*, vol. 1 (August 1978). Also see Nicholas Asheshov, "Peru Hits the Comeback Trail," *Institutional Investor* (July 1979), pp. 71–84. Unfortunately, a more rigorous analysis of the degree of severity of the successive standby agreements would require their complete details, which are confidential. In broad terms the IMF and the government appear to have been choosing between gradual adjustment, with higher fiscal deficits, inflation, and devaluation, and more rapid adjustment with smaller magnitudes for these three variables. Until 1978 the government appears to have been unable to make a consistent choice of one course or the other and deliver on all of its elements. Thus, the 1978 package may have meant the adoption of a consistent gradualist approach, accepting the devaluation consequences, whereas the failed 1977 package called for more rapid adjustment but its elements, especially fiscal deficit targets, were not met.

tributed to a learning process on the part of the IMF as well as the generals.

Role of the Banks

Private foreign banks played a critical role in the Peruvian crisis. Essentially, they switched from a position of providing large capital inflows from 1974 through 1976 to one of expecting large repayments (causing capital outflows) by 1978. The foreign banks' confidence in Peru dropped dramatically by 1977, causing the reversal.

Thus in 1974, 1975, and 1976, Peru's external debt (over one year's maturity) to private foreign financial institutions rose by $455 million, $380 million, $705 million, respectively (to a total outstanding of $2.35 billion), representing an average net inflow of about $500 million annually. By contrast, in 1977, this debt rose by a paltry net inflow of approximately $30 million, and in 1978, if there had been no debt rescheduling, the banks would have withdrawn hundreds of millions of dollars on repayments due while making negligible new long-term loans.[24]

The sharp turnabout in foreign bank lending was therefore a major element in Peru's economic crisis in 1977–78. Three factors appeared to cause this reversal. First, the bright prospects for oil exports in 1974–75 seemed to justify massive lending, although it was clear even then that Peru's official export projections were too high (for example, from the World Bank's more cautious, albeit still overly optimistic, projections). Second, in the period 1974–75, worldwide bank lending to developing countries was high as banks awash in OPEC funds to recycle (and facing slack demand in industrial countries) pushed loans aggressively.[25] In this atmosphere, it was easy for the banks to lend too much, too fast to Peru. Third, the failure of oil exports and the general economic crisis turned Peru from a good bet to a bad one by 1977, and the banks sought to get out as avidly as they had earlier moved to enter.

The large inflows from private banks in 1974–76 helped finance the unsound economic policies of the regime in this period, high military imports and high government budget deficits in particular. The banks even financed questionable investments (such as certain irrigation schemes)

24. World Bank, *World Debt Tables* (February 12, 1979).
25. See, for example, Richard S. Weinert, "Why the Banks Did It," *Foreign Policy*, vol. 30 (Spring 1978), pp. 143–48.

that had been rejected by the World Bank. In retrospect, Peru probably would have fared better if foreign bank financing had been more limited in the period 1974–76, forcing the government to deal with the emerging crisis before it reached such severe dimensions. Lower lending earlier, the adoption of sustainable policies, and then continued bank lending in 1977–78 (instead of a complete drying up and reversal to capital outflow) would have been better for Peru and for the banks. Indeed, the experience of Peru may have served to make the banks more cautious about similar future situations in other countries.

Evaluation of the Stabilization Experience

Given the conditions of the Peruvian economy in 1974–76, including the elements of exogenous shocks, the shift from euphoria to despair in private bank sentiment, and the errors of economic policy management, what would have been the appropriate response? Was the IMF stabilization package the correct approach? Many critics have charged that Peru represents the prototype case in which the IMF enters with a heavy hand and imposes stabilization measures that cause both political upheaval and economic dislocation in the form of a loss of real GNP and special hardships for the poor.[26] Nor is the critique limited to pundits; "structuralist" economic analysts old and new have argued that standard stabilization packages are inappropriate for developing countries.

The Structuralist Critique

The Latin American structuralist school of the 1950s argued that structural bottlenecks caused inflation and that far from reducing money growth and government spending, governments facing inflation should invest more to break supply bottlenecks. More recently, analysts have modernized the structuralist critique. Using mark-up pricing models driven by import prices and a modified IS/LM approach, Taylor has concluded that the standard stabilization package is disastrous in the typical case of the developing economy because (1) devaluation has little impact

26. See, for example, Ron Chernow, "The IMF: Roughest Bank in Town," *Saturday Review* (February 3, 1979), pp. 17–20.

on trade and mainly aggravates inflation and (2) domestic credit restriction causes a loss of real output, essentially because operating credit for firms acts like a real input in the production function and cutting this credit cuts output.[27] Similarly, Schydlowsky has argued that the standard stabilization package (devaluation, reduced government spending, and reduced credit expansion) is ineffective because (1) imports and exports are unresponsive to the exchange rate and (2) real output will fall as higher prices induced by devaluation reduce purchasing power and demand, and as the credit squeeze cuts firms' output. Schydlowsky recommends measures that increase exports by means other than general devaluation (subsidies, dual exchange rates) and increases instead of decreases of credit to the private sector; aided by the excess capacity (idle shifts) he considers typical, the economy will respond by raising output rather than by reducing absorption.[28]

In the specific case of Peru, Thorp, Stallings, and Schydlowsky and Wicht all criticize the stabilization measures as excessively costly in terms of lost output, and they fault devaluation and credit restriction in particular on structuralist grounds.[29] Sheahan focuses on the policy flaws of excess demand and inadequate attention to the external sector that led to the crisis in the first place, considering the corrective stabilization measures (and their costs) as relatively inevitable.[30]

Whatever the merits of the structuralist case, it seems clear that the case cannot be made independently of the origins of the crisis. In an economy with high investment and savings, high fiscal revenues, and a realistic exchange rate, it is possible that the appropriate response to an exogenous shock causing inflation and/or trade deficit will not be the standard stabilization package (especially if trade response is inelastic). When conditions have been patently overexpansive and trade distortions have been extreme, however, it is difficult to accept that devaluation and

27. Lance Taylor, "Short-Term Policy in Open Semi-Industrialized Economies," *Journal of Development Economics,* vol. 1 (September 1974), pp. 85–104; and Lance Taylor, "IS/LM in the Tropics: Mechanics of the New Structuralist Macro Critique" (Massachusetts Institute of Technology, 1979).

28. Daniel M. Schydlowsky, "Containing the Costs of Stabilization in Semi-Industrialized LDC's: A Marshallian Approach" (Boston University, January 1979).

29. Schydlowsky and Wicht, "Anatomy of an Economic Failure"; Thorp, "Peruvian Experiment" and "Inflation, Stabilization, and Attempted Redemocratization"; and Stallings, "Peru and the U.S. Banks."

30. Sheahan, "Peru: International Economic Policies."

fiscal and monetary restraint must be avoided for structuralist reasons. Yet this latter set of conditions characterized Peru in 1974–77. Moreover, the structuralist critics are singularly vague on the correct policy response, having ruled out the standard stabilization package; to the extent that they have a response in mind, it typically involves the assumption that somehow considerably more external resources can be obtained to facilitate a smoother adjustment.[31]

Structural Rigidities: Empirical Tests

It is possible to test some of the "structuralist" hypotheses by examining the statistical relationship between exchange rates, demand levels, and imports and exports. In particular, the structuralist critics argue that imports and exports are not responsive to the exchange rate, and some critics even argue that imports are unresponsive to the level of aggregate income and demand.[32]

Table 9-5 shows evidence on the exchange rate and trade performance. The table shows generally stagnant imports beginning in 1968, with the exception of a surge in 1974 and 1975. The "industrial register" mechanism virtually prohibited imports of goods produced domestically beginning in 1970. Exports also are stagnant and are especially low beginning in 1973, although they rebound partially by 1977 and 1978. The collapse of fishmeal exports in 1973 and after (discussed above) is an important influence.

The nominal exchange rate shows a pattern of being held at a fixed level over long periods (1959–66, 1968–74) despite rapid domestic inflation. As a result, the real exchange rate compensated for both domestic and foreign inflation (table 9-5, column 4) falls sharply from 1959–63 to low periods in 1965–67 and 1971–72, with a real increase coming only by 1976–77. With the secular decline in "real" soles per "real" unit of foreign exchange, the incentive grew over time to import (although import protection stifled the incentive), and the incentive to exports de-

31. For example, Schydlowsky and Wicht, "Anatomy of an Economic Failure," pt. 3.

32. For example, Thorp argues that because imports are concentrated in inputs into a few sectors, general demand restriction will do little to reduce imports; that the intermediate and capital goods dominating imports are not responsive to price; and that exports are determined by supply constraints, not competitiveness. Thorp, "Inflation, Stabilization, and Attempted Redemocratization," pp. 25–27.

Table 9-5. *Trade Performance and Exchange Rates, 1959–78*

Year	Real imports excluding military (millions of dollars, 1970 prices) (1)	Quantum index of exports (1970 = 100) (2)	Exchange rates (soles/$) (3)	Index of real exchange rate adjusted for home and foreign inflation (1970 = 100) (4)	Index of nominal dollar export prices (1970 = 100) (5)
1959	323	49	27.9	163.3	52
1960	378	65	27.4	148.1	58
1961	472	77	26.8	135.9	58
1962	541	84	26.8	127.9	60
1963	585	80	26.8	120.3	63
1964	577	89	26.8	109.7	71
1965	744	85	26.8	96.4	71
1966	870	87	26.8	91.3	83
1967	878	90	30.7	95.3	79
1968	697	101	38.7	103.5	85
1969	668	92	38.7	101.2	90
1970	679	100	38.7	100.0	100
1971	643	92	38.7	97.7	90
1972	643	96	38.7	97.7	90
1973	734	72	38.7	104.1	167
1974	1,068	73	38.7	105.7	215
1975	1,190	68	40.8	98.3	192
1976	978	65	57.5	107.6	194
1977	791	73	83.8	122.5	219
1978	n.a.	84	156.3	n.a.	210

Source: Calculated from *International Financial Statistics*, selected issues, and tables 9-1 and 9-2 above. The 1978 figure, column 2, was calculated from U.N. CEPAL, *Notas sobre la Economía y el Desarrollo de America Latina*, no. 286/287 (January 1979), p. 6. Column 4 for 1959–69 was calculated as $[E/P_p]/[P_u]$, where E = exchange rate, P_p = consumer price index, Peru, P_u = wholesale price index, United States; for 1970–78, calculated as $[E/P_p]/[\Sigma_i \phi_i P_i (R^{it}/R^{io})]$, where ϕ_i and P_i are trade turnover shares and wholesale price indexes of country i, respectively, and R^{it} and R^{io} are exchange rates of country i in current year and 1970, respectively (for Germany, Japan, United Kingdom, France, Netherlands).
n.a. Not available.

clined. The disincentive to exports was partially counteracted, however, by high export prices beginning in 1973 (table 9-5, column 5).

To test the "structuralist" hypotheses that imports are unresponsive to the exchange rate and to aggregate demand, the following equation was estimated:

$$M = -35.4 - 1.762E + 0.589R_{(t-1)} + 2.376Y - 352.0D,$$
$$\quad (0.1) \quad (0.9) \quad\quad (1.98) \quad\quad (4.3) \quad\quad (3.1)$$
$$\bar{R}^2 = 0.76$$

where t-statistics are in parentheses, M = real imports (nonmilitary),

E = index of inflation-compensated exchange rate, $R_{(t-1)}$ = reserves in prior year, Y = real GDP at 1975 prices, and D = dummy variable (zero before 1970; one for 1970 and after). This regression shows a statistically significant influence of income on imports, rejecting the proposition that aggregate demand does not affect imports. The results show a strong negative influence of the regime of import prohibitions beginning in 1970 (dummy variable D) and a behavioral relationship whereby reserves in the prior year significantly affect imports (representing a willingness to relax import restrictions when reserves are higher).

In these absolute forms, the equation fails to find a significant influence of exchange rates. However, when specified in terms of annual percentage changes, the exchange rate variable becomes significant:

$$\dot{M} = -11.0 - 1.049\dot{E} + 3.01\,\dot{Y}_{t-1}.$$
$$(1.3) \quad (2.13) \qquad (2.04)$$
$$\bar{R}^2 = 0.41$$

In this formulation, the variables are as defined above except that the overdot refers to annual percentage change. Although the $\bar{R}^2$ (fraction of variation explained) is lower, the degree of explanation is relatively good for specification in annual percentage changes. The results of this model indicate that a 1 percent rise in aggregate demand (as represented by gross domestic product) causes a 3 percent rise in imports, and a 1 percent rise in the real exchange rate causes a 1 percent decline in imports. Both parameters are statistically significant.[33] Thus real imports do respond demonstrably to both aggregate demand and the real exchange rate, and the empirical evidence contradicts the critique against using devaluation and demand restraint for adjustment on the grounds that these measures will not affect imports.

Similarly, it is possible to test the hypothesis that exports do not respond to the exchange rate. For data from 1959 through 1978, the following model was estimated:

$$X = -28.4 + 0.863\,Y_{am} + 0.354PXE^* - 60.1DX,$$
$$(1.3) \quad (6.0) \qquad (2.3) \qquad (5.6)$$
$$\bar{R}^2 = 0.71$$

33. In the percentage-change regression form, dummy variables for 1970 and after (simple or interactive with exchange rate and income) are not statistically significant.

where X = quantum index of exports; Y_{am} = real GDP in agriculture and mining;[34] $PXE^* = [P_x][E^*]$, where P_x = index of nominal dollar prices of exports and E^* = exchange rate deflated by the consumer price index for Peru; and DX is a dummy variable with a value of one beginning in 1973 and zero before.

This model uses the IMF quantum index of exports, which reflects traditional mining and agricultural exports. Real exports are explained by output supply (Y_{am}) and a dummy variable used to capture the loss of fishmeal exports beginning in 1973. The variable PXE^* represents combined influences of the dollar price of exports on world markets, and the translation of those prices into incentive for the exporter as represented by the exchange rate deflated by the domestic consumer price index.

The main result of the export model is that real exports do respond significantly to the exchange rate incentive. Evaluated at the means, the elasticity of exports with respect to the real exchange rate–export price variable is 0.45. Thus a 1 percent rise in the real exchange rate calls forth about 0.5 percent rise in exports. Moreover, the actual response is probably even greater. For traditional exports the short-term responses (probably agriculture, fishing, and small to medium mining firms) captured in the equation do not include the longer-term responses of major mining expansions that require a gestation period of years. Furthermore, Sheahan has shown that nontraditional exports (although still only about 10 percent of export value) respond briskly to the real exchange rate.[35] In sum, another critique of the stabilization approach—that exports will not respond to devaluation—is contradicted by the statistical evidence.

In fact, Peru's trade balance did show substantial improvement in 1977–78 when stabilization measures including devaluation and demand restriction were being applied. Imports fell dramatically from a peak of $2.4 billion in 1975 to only $1.7 billion in 1978, and exports rose from $1.3 billion to $1.9 billion over the same period (table 9-1). Thus both on the basis of observed results for 1976–78 and in light of the statistical estimates for the last two decades, the evidence indicates that imports re-

34. Estimated by linear interpolation of these sectors' share in GDP between 1950 and 1977. United Nations, Comisión Económica para América Latina (CEPAL), *El Desarrollo Económico y Social y las Relaciones Económicas de América Latina,* vol. 1, E/CEPAL/1061 (January 23, 1979), p. 23.

35. "Peru: International Economic Policies," p. 11.

spond to the real exchange rate and aggregate demand, and exports respond to the real exchange rate.[36]

Excess Demand: A Misdiagnosis?

Schydlowsky and Wicht argue, even more specifically than the generalized structuralist critics, that the Peruvian government and the IMF misdiagnosed the economic crisis as one of excess demand.[37] The policies of devaluation, import controls, and tighter money caused recession, inflation, and an increased government deficit, according to these authors.[38]

It is of course possible in principle for recession to cause a government deficit, so that a growing deficit does not necessarily mean excess demand (instead, the "full-employment" budget might show a surplus). This argument appears to have been irrelevant in the Peruvian case, however. Table 9-6 shows the revenues, expenditures, and deficits of the central government from 1972 through 1977, in nominal and constant price values. It is clear from the table that the mushrooming deficit of 1975–77 was not caused by recession-induced declines in revenue. On the contrary, real revenues rose by 10 percent for the 1975–77 average over the 1972–74 average. Real expenditures rose by 27 percent from the 1972–74 average to the 1975–77 average. These data are clearly consistent with the hypothesis that rising government spending caused rising real deficits and rising excess demand. The data are inconsistent with the hypothesis that the government deficits were primarily the result of recession-induced reductions in revenues.

36. Model predictions were for 10.4 percent and 16.7 percent reductions in real nonmilitary imports in 1976 and 1977, respectively, versus actual reductions of 17.8 percent and 19.1 percent, respectively. (Note that the model implies an 11 percent reduction if there is no change in exchange rates and economic growth is zero.) The large drop in imports in 1978 reflected the severe import restrictions imposed, in addition to further devaluation; 1978 is not included in the estimating period. For exports, the model predicted an increase of 15 percent in the quantum of exports from 1975 to 1978, whereas the actual rise was 24 percent. Larger than predicted increase was probably due in part to the coming on line of exports from the Cuajone copper mine, which began sizable exports in 1977, and higher oil export earnings.

37. Schydlowsky and Wicht contend that, on the contrary, ". . . there was no generalized excess demand. Indeed, not much of a dent had been made in the chronic underutilization of capacity in industry." Schydlowsky and Wicht, "Anatomy of an Economic Failure," pt.2 , p. 17.

38. Ibid., pt. 2, p. 18.

Table 9-6. *Central Government Revenues and Expenditures, 1972–77*
Billions of soles

Year	Current prices			Constant 1975 prices[a]		
	Revenues	Expendi- tures	Deficit (−)	Revenues	Expendi- tures	Deficit (−)
1972	45.6	56.5	−10.8	73.3	90.8	−17.4
1973	53.4	67.4	−14.0	74.8	94.4	−19.6
1974	68.6	82.7	−14.1	82.4	99.4	−16.9
1975	87.9	118.5	−30.6	87.9	118.5	−30.6
1976	111.4	159.8	−48.4	82.9	119.0	−36.0
1977	154.1	233.2	−79.1	82.8	125.4	−42.5

Source: *International Financial Statistics*, July 1979, p. 306.
a. Deflating by the implicit GDP deflator.

Nor do the data on industrial production support the Schydlowsky-Wicht critique. From an index of 100 in 1973, industrial production rose to 108.7 in 1974, 113.8 in 1975, and 118.9 in 1976 and fell to 113.3 in 1977.[39] Therefore, there was no clear evidence of rising excess capacity in 1975–76, disputing the hypothesis that measures restricting aggregate demand had a serious impact in increasing excess capacity. By 1977–78 the recessionary impact was felt, but the point here is that industrial production data contradict the notion that the initial policy response to the external crisis (1975–76) provoked serious excess capacity.[40]

Income Distributional Effects

Another popular image of the stabilization program in Peru is that it adversely affected the poor in absolute terms and concentrated the distribution of income in relative terms. The evidence usually cited is that real wages declined substantially and that the government phased out subsidies for mass consumption goods.

39. United Nations, *Estudio Económico de América Latina: 1977*, vol. 2, E/CEPAL/1050 (New York: UN), p. 780.
40. It is another question whether there exists "chronic" excess capacity on the basis of hypothetical three-shift capacity. The longer-term structural distortions and rational economic calculations that lead to the presence of less than three-shift operation should not be confused with the shorter-term issues of macroeconomic stabilization, it would seem. Otherwise, there will be an expansionary bias, caused by the belief that there always exists excess capacity even when, operationally, none exists.

Table 9-7. *Real Wages in Lima, 1970–78*

December 1973 = 100

Year	Blue collar	White collar
1970	87.5	81.6
1971	93.3	89.2
1972	100.5	96.6
1973	102.3	105.9
1974[a]	94.6	100.1
1975[b]	86.9	82.5
1976[c]	81.6	93.4
1977[c]	67.4	75.8
1978[c]	58.1	67.6

Sources: Calculated from *Informe Estadístico* (January–June 1979), pp. 64, 65; and Ministerio de Trabajo, *Anuario Estadístico del Sector Trabajo 1977* (Peru: Ministerio de Trabajo, 1977), table 36.
a. June.
b. August.
c. Average of March, June, and September.

Table 9-7 shows the trend of real wages for blue collar and white collar workers in Lima, 1970–78. Taking the period 1970–73 as a base and 1976–78 as the terminal period of stabilization, real wages fell by 28 percent for blue collar workers and by 36 percent for white collar workers. White collar workers are primarily in the upper portion of the national income distribution. According to 1961 figures used by Webb, three-fourths of white collar workers are in the upper quartile of Peru's income distribution and 39 percent are in the top decile. Even blue collar workers stand relatively high in the income distribution: one-quarter of the blue collar workers are in the top quartile of the distribution and 59 percent are in the top 50 percent of income recipients. The rural Sierra workers constitute the bulk of the poor, with about half in the lowest quartile of the distribution.[41]

During the stabilization period there was clearly a decline of real earnings for urban workers in the organized sectors. However, because these workers were in the upper-middle section of the national income distribution, this decline probably tended to equalize the distribution of income nationally (at a minimum, the distribution of labor income). Even within the urban sector, wages of the higher-income group—the white collar workers—deteriorated the most (in part the result of government measures that decreed absolute instead of percentage wage increases).

There are no data on the real incomes of workers in the urban "in-

41. Calculated from Webb, *Government Policy,* p. 10.

formal" sector (such as sidewalk peddlers), but because this sector derives its income from the formal sector, the economic recession probably caused real incomes in this sector to decline as well. Indeed, severe declines below "poverty levels" probably occurred in this group. There is indirect evidence that the incidence of serious poverty increased in the urban areas. Official statistics report that the consumer price index for the lowest of three urban income groups rose from 100 in 1973 to 695 in June 1979, whereas the index for the upper-income group rose only to 587 (primarily because of the lower weight of food and beverages, for which prices increased the most over the period).[42] As other evidence, a sample survey of 1,500 households in Lima (June 1978) found that low-income households (42.2 percent of households) spent 67.4 percent of their income on food, compared with only 58 percent on the basis of the 1971–72 consumer price index weights for low-income households.[43]

With respect to the distribution of income between labor and capital, national accounts data show the following labor shares of national product at factor cost from 1973 through 1977 (percentages): 45.3, 41.9, 42.8, 43.5, and 41.5, respectively.[44] Thus while labor share fell, it did so as early as 1974, well before the stabilization programs. There is no clear erosion of labor share during the stabilization period. Because profits are generally more sensitive to the business cycle than wages, the labor share might have been expected to rise during the stabilization period. The fact that labor share did not rise probably reflects the severe real wage decline (urban) as well as the fact that some firms earned extraordinary profits because of export subsidization schemes during this period.

It is by no means certain that the reduction of government subsidies on consumption goods caused a concentration in the distribution of income. Subsidies for food imports and gasoline were major sources of government deficits in 1973 and 1974. The largest loss by a public enterprise was from the Empresa Publica de Servicios Agropecuarios (EPSA). This agency, which provided foodstuffs at controlled prices, had large losses in 1973 and 1974 because of high prices of imported wheat. Similarly, Petroperu experienced large losses in 1973–74 because of the increase in world oil prices. Peru had maintained the price of gasoline unchanged at

42. *Informe Estadístico* (January–June 1979), pp. 58–59.
43. Telegram, "Current Malnutrition in Peru—A Quantitative Study on the Situation in Lima" (U.S. Embassy, Lima, March 30, 1979).
44. Institución Nacional de Planificación, *Cuentas Nacionales del Peru 1950–1978* (Lima, 1979), p. 88.

9 soles per gallon from 1968 through 1974 (when this rate amounted to only twenty-three cents). From 1975 through 1978 the food distribution agency (EPSA) at first raised prices by about one-third for wheat, rice, and potatoes and by more than 50 percent for corn and vegetable oils and subsequently made periodic increases to keep up with inflation. The price of gasoline rose to 15 soles per gallon in 1975 (still only thirty-five cents), but by mid-1976 the government raised the price to 50 soles (seventy-seven cents) and readjusted the price periodically thereafter, keeping it generally in a range of approximately sixty to ninety cents.[45]

Was it regressive to phase out gasoline subsidies? According to family budget survey data for Lima, spending on public transportation plus vehicle operation rose from 4.4 percent of family expenditure for the lowest quartile of families to 5.3 percent for the highest.[46] Even allowing for capital costs of owned vehicles for richer families, the income distributional incidence of higher gasoline prices would appear to be essentially neutral within Lima. Considering that gasoline consumed is probably a smaller fraction of family budgets in rural areas, for Peru as a whole, gasoline subsidies were probably regressive in nature. Therefore, phasing out these subsidies probably improved the income distribution rather than concentrated it.

As for food subsidies and price controls on food, a major effect of the system was to keep prices artificially low to farmers. Foodstuffs are produced primarily on a small-farm basis (especially potatoes, wheat, and corn). Higher food prices therefore meant, in general, a redistribution of income away from urban residents to farmers, almost certainly a progressive redistribution. (Because there is very little rural labor in a landless, salaried labor force, higher food prices would not be a disadvantage for much of the rural work force.)[47]

In summary, the phasing out of government subsidies for food and petroleum, and increases in their prices, probably represented either a pro-

45. U.S. Embassy, *Annual Petroleum Report—Peru* (Peru: U.S. Embassy, 1977 and 1978)

46. Philip Musgrove, *Consumer Behavior in Latin America: Income and Spending of Families in Ten Andean Cities* (Brookings Institution, 1978), p. 332.

47. Because wheat consumed in the urban areas is almost wholly imported, higher wheat prices might have represented a regressive measure (because low-income farmers would not benefit directly, while low-income urban families would lose directly). Over time, however, the potential to shift land into wheat meant this change could also benefit small farmers.

gressive or, at worst, neutral redistribution of income. The measures shifted the terms of trade favorably for the rural areas.[48]

Taxation was the principal area in which the stabilization programs appeared to fail to be as equitable as possible. A relatively standard criticism of the stabilization policies is that they failed to rely more heavily on increased collections of direct taxes from upper-income groups.[49]

Overall Evaluation

The real failure of stabilization policy in Peru was that it was not implemented earlier and more vigorously. The need for stabilization was evident by 1975. Yet the government kept pursuing excess demand policies through 1977, running budget deficits of 10 percent of GNP in 1975, 10 percent in 1976, and 9 percent in 1977,[50] and increasing the heavy outlays for imported arms (table 9-3) through 1977. Thus, while special factors helped cause the crisis (fishmeal decline, copper price decline, higher oil price, failure to make major oil discoveries), the bulk of the problem was, in fact, caused by bad economic policies in terms of excess demand and distortions to foreign trade incentives. Through 1975 the problem was that the majority of economic advisers (including many from international agencies) counted the petroleum chickens before they hatched. In 1976 the technocrats launched a program that would have worked, but the military government shattered the program with an excessive budget in 1977. Until May 1978 the bad policies appear to have reflected the ultimate control by military leaders who, unlike their Brazilian counterparts, were unwilling (1) to base the major economic decisions primarily on the advice of the technocrats and (2) to withstand the popular outcry that some of the necessary measures implied. Moreover, the foreign banks underwrote the persistence of bad economic policies in 1974–75 and, though only under duress, in 1976–77.

It may be that the structuralist and neostructuralist critiques have merit and that devaluation, reduction in budget deficits, and credit re-

---

48. However, the national accounts failed to show any corresponding rise in agriculture's share in GDP, which fell from approximately 13 percent in 1972–74 to 12 percent in 1975–78. *Cuentas Nacionales*, p. 62.

49. The World Bank country study issued in mid-1979 made this critique, according to press reports. *Peru Económico* (April 1979), p. 7.

50. Sheahan, "Peru: International Economic Policies," p. 16.

straint can be bad stabilization policies and can cause loss of real output rather than smooth correction of external and internal imbalances in some cases. Peru was not one of those cases. Excess demand policies, external borrowing, and the delay in corrective policies made the situation so bad that by 1977–78 there was virtually no alternative to the extreme measures taken. Furthermore, results did begin to appear following the 1977–78 measures; devaluation and the slowing of aggregate demand reduced the trade deficit (as the statistical tests above, rejecting the structuralist view, indicate).

Ideally, Peruvian stabilization would have gone as follows. In 1975 the government would have raised taxes sharply, reducing excess demand caused by government deficits and, as a dividend, opening the way for a more equitable sharing of stabilization burdens among income classes. The government would have sharply cut back military imports (and military spending generally), devalued the sol more dramatically (in 1975 the real exchange rate actually appreciated; table 9-5), and avoided taking in the massive private foreign bank loans that flowed in 1975 and 1976. In short, the government would have taken its 1978 measures in 1975, although probably to a considerably milder degree. Had this scenario occurred, it is highly likely that the external imbalance would have been corrected in 1976 and 1977, that Peru would not have approached bankruptcy, and that the total sacrifice in growth would have been much smaller.

Future Prospects

By mid-1979, the medium-term prospects for the Peruvian economy had improved considerably. Real GDP in the first half of 1979 was 3.4 percent higher than the year before (though some suspected the accuracy of the data), and the trade balance for the first six months showed a surplus of $688 million.[51] Export earnings were soaring because of higher prices and volume for oil exports (forecast at $682 million for 1979)[52] and higher prices for copper. Ironically, the turnaround in the external account was so sharp and external reserves were increasing so rapidly that policy makers had come to consider monetary expansion resulting

51. *Informe Estadístico* (January–June 1979).
52. Central bank estimates.

from reserve growth to be an important source of inflationary pressure.[53] In the face of windfall export earnings, policy makers were even considering reverting to payment of at least some of the external debt originally due in 1980—that is, foregoing the 1980 debt reschedulings negotiated in 1978. Another strong positive factor was the government's intention to move to a more open import regime, greatly reducing the number of prohibited items, unifying the tariff rate for each item (by eliminating surcharges and exemptions), and reducing the average tariff level.[54] If aggressively implemented, import liberalization could boost the Peruvian economy greatly by reducing inflationary pressure and by increasing the efficiency in allocation of resources.

The less-favorable aspects for the near-term future were the problem of inflation, the lack of private investment, and the depressed state of urban incomes. For the year ending June 1979, the consumer price index rose 61.8 percent.[55] The problem of money supply expansion based on increased foreign reserves was one factor.[56] Even more important in the view of many analysts was the continuing state of inflationary expectations, combined with oligopolistic market structure. (As an indicator of inflationary expectations, the velocity of money rose by 20.3 percent in 1976, 14.3 percent in 1977, and 7.4 percent in 1978.)[57] Furthermore, some policy makers considered the rates of devaluation during 1978 to have been excessive (in the light of subsequent windfall gains on oil and copper exports), thereby leading to greater inflationary pressure than was necessary in the event.

For its part, private investment remained stagnant. Two reasons appear most important. First, with elections and return to civilian rule scheduled for May 1980, entrepreneurs were not willing to undertake major investment commitments until the new political environment became clear. Second, the very program of demand restriction that had made the turnaround on external account feasible had, by repressing ur-

---

53. Thus, whereas international reserves had fallen by $870 million in 1976 and $350 million in 1977, they rose by $76 million in 1978 and were forecast to rise by nearly $300 million in 1979. Banco Central de Peru, *Proyección Financiera,* fig. 9.

54. "Política Arancelaria y Desarrollo Industrial," speech by the Minister of Industry, Commerce, Tourism and Integration, Lima, August 8, 1979.

55. *Informe Estadístico* (January–June 1979), p. 57.

56. The narrowness of the government bond market appears to make sterilization infeasible. Policy makers appear to be unwilling to make the bonds more attractive by indexing them, on grounds of general opposition to indexing.

57. Banco Central de Peru, *Proyección Financiera,* fig. 1.

ban salaries and wages, depressed the only significant domestic market for industrial products. Although industrial firms were compensating in part by exporting, they were generally unprepared to make new investments in the face of slack demand domestically.

Overall, the future prospects for Peru appear bright on purely economic grounds, although growth and stability could be frustrated by political developments or by a serious reversal of the windfall gains on mineral exports. An important factor will be whether oil exports grow or decline over future years; this will depend on new discoveries. Inflation could remain a serious problem over the near term, although the strong balance of payments may help decelerate the rate of inflation as it permits an opening of the import regime and, perhaps, a slowing down of devaluation. Peru still appears to lack a cohesive strategy for longer-term growth, however, and an essential task of the new government elected in 1980 will be to design such a strategy.

Lessons from the Peruvian Case

One lesson from the Peruvian case seems to be that the international financial system lacks effective coordination between the IMF and the banks. The private banks probably loaned more money to Peru, and kept lending it longer, than they would have if they had been following a strategy coordinated by the IMF (perhaps jointly with the World Bank); under such a strategy, Peru might have taken effective measures earlier. It is unclear whether this lesson implies any formal institutional reform, however. After the learning process with increased lending to developing countries in 1974–76, it is now less likely that private banks will indulge in heavy lending to an economy with highly dubious economic policies; indeed, the banks' bias now may be toward conservatism, as they find themselves already "loaned up" to many developing countries. (On the other hand, the new flood of petro dollars to be recycled because of higher oil prices may make the banks less cautious, especially smaller regional banks that missed the first act in 1974–75.)

The problem of "bringing the IMF in earlier" remains, however. Some analysts have argued that the IMF's own funds have become so small that countries now bypass the IMF until it is too late to achieve a smooth adjustment and these analysts conclude that larger IMF resources are necessary.[58] This argument really reflects the recent lack of IMF–private bank coordination, however, because it implies that in recent years, developing countries have been able to go directly to the private banks without IMF participation.[59] Again, this seeming problem may be resolving itself by the apparent tendency of the banks to revert to a more cautious posture and heavier reliance on IMF judgment.

A second lesson from the Peruvian experience may be that there is a need for an international refinancing facility for converting private loans with short maturities into longer-term loans (but still at market interest rates). While Peru's tax, spending, subsidy, and exchange rate measures of 1978 were appropriate, the extreme situation forced other measures that were clearly disruptive—in particular, the prohibition of imports of even intermediate goods. The immediate cause of the extreme measures was the reversal of bank flows, adding prospective capital outflow to the already large need to reduce the trade balance deficit. The presence of an international mechanism to prevent the outflows by converting the bank loans to longer maturities would have made the 1978 adjustment much less traumatic.[60] To some extent, the debt rescheduling which was eventually arranged accomplished the same purpose, but only after months of potentially avoidable agony for the economy from cessation of imports.

A third lesson from the Peruvian case is a negative one. Peru does not prove valid the structuralist critique that typical stabilization programs (devaluation cum reductions in government deficits and in credit growth) are bound to fail and to cause unnecessary loss of real output for the economy. The statistical tests here reject the structuralist propositions that trade is unresponsive to the exchange rate and (according to some of the critics) to aggregate demand. The degree of excess demand in the economy was so extreme that Peru makes a poor case to argue for a structuralist alternative. Moreover, an examination of possible income

58. Sidney Dell, "The Balance of Payments Adjustment Process in Developing Countries: Report to the Group of Twenty-Four," UNDP/UNCTAD Project INT/75/015 (UNDP/UNCTAD, 1979).

59. According to one IMF study, there was a sharp drop in the percentage of developing country deficit cases financed by IMF standby loans in 1974–76 (10 percent) as compared with 1967–69 (43 percent), as cited by Danny M. Leipziger, "Short-Term Stabilization and Long-Term Development" (Department of State, 1978), p. 30.

60. There will of course be critiques of "bailing out the banks" for any such proposals, but the terms can be such that the banks have to pay some price for the opportunity to get out.

distribution consequences of stabilization in Peru does not confirm the popular impression that stabilization had inequitable results. More generally, the loss of output in 1977 and 1978 appears to have been the result of the fact that policies of excess demand and inappropriate exchange rate were carried on for so long that the shock of corrective adjustment became much larger than it would have been if adjustment had been undertaken earlier.

A final implication of the Peruvian case is that it can be costly and time consuming for political authorities to learn about economic reality and, the case may be argued, for the IMF to learn about political reality. It may be too much to expect for other countries, or even Peru, to take the economic lesson to heart. As for the IMF, it has already shown recent signs of greater effort toward political accommodation;[61] however, it cannot bend too far in that direction without losing its credibility with the private banking sector and thereby losing its chief value to most developing countries—that of unlocking the larger flows of private capital.

Comments by Daniel M. Schydlowsky

For Cline, Peru in 1976–78 followed the right stabilization policy: massive devaluation, tight money, and a cut in government expenditure (especially subsidies). "The real failure of stabilization policy in Peru was that it was not implemented earlier and more vigorously." Those who argue that there was a less costly and less disruptive alternative are neo-structuralists and are wrong: statistical analysis demonstrates this.

Were Cline right, it would be most distressing, for a reduction in per capita GNP of 8 percent resulting from bad economic policy is no laughing matter. Fortunately, Cline's defense of the standard deflationary package for Peru does not stand up to close examination.

Was There an Alternative?

Cline says there was no alternative: Peru suffered from excess demand, and hence demand needed to be cut. The evidence he offers is at best circumstantial: both the fiscal sector and the balance of payments

61. "New Guidelines Issued on Fund Conditionality," *IMF Survey* (March 19, 1979), pp. 82–83.

were in deficit. The facts say otherwise. In the industrial sector, substantial increases in output were possible in 1976 even within the shifts and days worked. Moreover, an increase in shifts was possible within the days worked, and an increase in number of days worked during the year was also possible. Data on these points are available in the industrial survey of the Ministry of Industry for 1976 as well as in the study on the export potential of manufactured products conducted by ESAN, a private graduate school of business, in mid-1977.[62] That this situation should be so is not too surprising since between 1971 and 1977 Peru imported approximately $1.3 billion worth of machinery for its industrial sector, thereby duplicating its real installed productive capacity, while industrial output grew only about 4 percent per year.[63] Moreover, that the number of shifts worked by enterprises in Peru depends on the policy environment and therefore can be affected by policy change has been established by Millan[64] and Abusada.[65] Thus it is not appropriate to dismiss the potential output from multiple shifting and additional days worked as merely "theoretical."

Furthermore, not only the industrial sector could expand output. In the service sector, considerable room for expansion existed, for this sector, is labor intensive and thus has a very elastic supply curve. Since industry contributes 26 percent of GNP and easily expandable services contribute 43 percent, it turns out that *more than two-thirds of the economy* had ample supply capacity at the time of the alleged excess demand!

Given the available productive capacity in industry and services, the alternative certainly existed to convert the potential output of these sectors into realized output. Detailed estimates of the magnitudes involved have been provided by this author elsewhere; suffice it to say that the potential economic output would have been adequate to cover the 1975 balance of payments and fiscal deficits.[66] However, it is more likely that

---

62. Escuela Superior de Administración de Negocios, "Estudio del Potencial Exportador de Productos Manufacturados de Consumo del Peru" (Lima: ESAN, March 1978).

63. Roberto Abusada-Salah, "Reformas Estructurales y Crisis Económica en el Sector Industrial Peruano" (November 1978).

64. Patricio Millan, "The Intensive Use of Capital in Industrial Plants: Multiple Shifts as an Economic Option" (Ph.D. dissertation, Harvard University, 1975).

65. Roberto Abusada-Salah, "A Statistical Shift-Choice Model of Capital Utilization," Center for Latin American Development Studies Discussion Paper 15 (Boston, November 1975).

66. Daniel M. Schydlowsky and Juan J. Wicht, *Anatomía de un Fracaso Económico, Peru 1968–1978* (Universidad del Pacífico, 1979), pp. 97–104.

supply expansion by itself could not have been implemented and taken effect with enough speed to avoid the need for some demand management policy as well. All the same, even a gradual expansion of supply would have allowed a more balanced approach toward an economic equilibrium rather than the inflation-propelled deflation toward balance-of-payments equilibrium which left all the domestic disequilibriums and distortions untouched.

Balance of Payments and Fiscal Deficits without Excess Demand?

If large potential output existed in industry and services, there could not have been generalized excess demand in the economy. But how can these facts be squared with balance of payments and fiscal deficits? The answer lies in a mismatch between the structure of demand for goods and the structure of installed capacity to produce such goods. At 1975 income levels, the demand for agricultural goods could not be satisfied by that sector's installed capacity; hence import demand ensued. Moreover, while demand for industrial products and services fell well short of capacity output, these sectors required imported inputs. Even at their modest output levels, these import requirements could not be met by the foreign exchange available from the export of primary sectors working at full capacity, after paying for the required food imports. Had enough of the "surplus" capital stock in industry and services instead been in the mining sector, no balance-of-payments problem would have existed. Thus the deficit was fundamentally caused by a maldistribution of the capital stock.

Given maldistribution of the capital stock and the resulting shortage of foreign exchange, output in industry and services was well below productive capacity. As a result, the tax base was reduced, which in turn signified a revenue shortfall compared to the full utilization level. Hence although the government might well have been in a full utilization surplus, it found itself in a realized deficit. Such a situation is not, however, inconsistent with the separate finding that a part of government expenditure was misguided, undesirable, or even wasteful. However, the macro- and microeconomic aspects of government expenditure are best kept distinct.

It is appropriate then to characterize the 1975 situation as one of excess demand for foreign exchange but not of generalized excess demand, and as one of realized fiscal deficit but possible full utilization surplus.

Recapping the Causes of the Crisis

The Peruvian crisis is fundamentally the result of the application of an internally inconsistent development policy. Import substituting industrialization was pursued with extreme vigor. As a result, sectors demanding foreign exchange in the form of inputs and capital goods grew much more rapidly than sectors supplying such foreign exchange. Once the respective growth trends crossed, a balance-of-payments crisis was inevitable. However, the situation was aggravated by several reform policies that systematically increased the foreign exchange intensity of demand and reduced the growth of those sectors supplying foreign exchange. Bad luck and military expenditures played a minor but not unimportant part.[67]

Cline's Statistical Tests

Cline tests the elasticity of demand for imports and supply of exports to changes in the exchange rates, and he examines the impact of Peru's stabilization policy on the government deficit. The following discussion will review these tests.

EXCHANGE RATE ELASTICITY OF IMPORTS. Cline reports that when the percentage change of imports is regressed on the percentage change in the real exchange rate and on the percentage change in income, both independent variables are statistically significant with values of -1 and 3, respectively. "Thus real imports do respond demonstrably to both aggregate demand and the real exchange rate, and the empirical evidence contradicts the critique against using devaluation and demand restraint for adjustment on grounds that these measures will not affect imports."

---

67. Cline's table 9-4 is very misleading in this regard for it assumes that the trade account balance was independent of the economic "shocks" that he analyzes. For example, fishmeal revenues being higher by the $321 million Cline calculates were lost would more than likely have had a repercussion on domestic income in accordance with the respective foreign trade multiplier. Naturally, this increased revenue would have signified an increase in import levels, which means that the $321 million would not have been available to cover the preexisting deficit that Cline is analyzing. Moreover, with the higher exports receipts, foreign exchange authorities would have had increased revenues against which to issue licenses to import and would probably have increased such licensing by the same $321 million. Hence increased fishmeal revenues would not have affected the current account balance at all! When account is had of the functional relationships between the macrovariables of the economy, the exogenous shocks perhaps account for a third as much of the deficit as Cline calculates in this table.

Let it be said at the outset that Wicht and I argue vigorously that imports are crucially affected by income levels[68] but not by the exchange rate. Thus, speaking for myself at least, I have no quarrel with the income elasticity that Cline obtains. However, Cline's time series regression is not pertinent to the question posed. The exchange rate elasticity of imports in Peru *in 1976* cannot be estimated from data stretching back to 1959 because the increasingly stringent import licensing imposed from 1969 onward fundamentally changed the effective determinant of imports. Where until 1969, prices (exchange rate plus tariff) determined the quantity imported, after 1969, scarcity premia rapidly built up and the quantitative restrictions directly regulated the amounts imported—over a wide range, price was irrelevant.[69] I have rerun Cline's regression on his own data separately for the periods 1960–68 and 1969–77.[70] The first of these periods gives a significant exchange rate elasticity of −1.2. For the second period, which corresponds to the regime of the Peruvian military government and spans the years of the crisis, the estimated exchange rate elasticity is +0.46 with a *t*-ratio of 0.42, which makes it not statistically different from zero, in addition to having the wrong sign.

EXPORTS. Cline states, "The main result of the export model is that real exports do respond significantly to the exchange rate incentive. Evaluated at the means, the elasticity of exports with regard to the real exchange rate export price variable is 0.45." However, this regression is on absolute levels, a specification that Cline correctly abandoned in favor of percentage changes for the import regressions. Moreover, the same objection to the use of time series can be made here as in the previous case. Rerunning Cline's own regression in percentage changes renders the elasticity coefficient for the real exchange rate—export price variable insignificant (*t*-value of 1.1) and also gives it a wrong sign. Restricting the data to 1969–74 causes no noticeable further change.[71] It thus appears that the statistical results do not show an exchange rate export price elasticity for exports in 1976.

Conventional wisdom is therefore not buttressed, nor are the critics refuted by the empirical data from either the import or the export side.

68. Schydlowsky and Wicht, *Anatomía de un Fracaso Económico*, chap. 2, sec. H.
69. The situation was no more than the usual textbook case of binding quotas.
70. This is a simple way of doing covariance analysis.
71. Note that complete data for running this regression through 1976 are not available; Cline had to interpolate GNP shares. Moreover, 1960–68 produces an insignificant coefficient (*t* = 1.8) but with the right sign.

FISCAL EFFECTS OF STABILIZATION. Cline argues that deficits of 1976 and later were caused by "rising government spending causing rising real deficits and rising excess demand" and shows real revenues in 1976–77 at 1974 levels and 1977 real expenditure at 25 percent above the 1974 level (table 9-6).

A look beneath the surface of these data reveals a rather different story. On the revenue side during 1976 and 1977, tax rates were substantially raised, and new taxes were created to offset reduction in tax revenue caused by the stabilization policy.[72] Thus it would appear that Cline mistook ex post for ex ante revenue elasticity. For instance, the revenue from the new 15 percent tax on traditional exports alone amounted to 4.2 percent of total current revenue in 1976 and 9.9 percent in 1977.[73] Substract these amounts from Cline's table 9-6, and 1976 and 1977 revenues are 3.6 percent and 9.4 percent short of 1974 receipts, respectively. A more proper comparison is with 1975, however, the last year before the induced depression began. Now 1976 shows a loss of current revenue of 9.7 percent, and 1977 shows a loss of 15.2 percent. Sad to say, stabilization-induced depression contributed to the loss of taxation and to the magnitude of the government deficit.[74]

Government expenditure was also affected by the stabilization policy. One major item was interest and repayment on the foreign debt. The exchange rate differential (compared with 1975) on this item alone amounted to 2.6 percent of total expenditure in 1976 and 7.4 percent in 1977. Evidently, other purchases of imported material also rose proportionately to the exchange rate.[75] Thus again it is clear that stabilization policies increased expenditures and hence the deficit.

Summing both sides, just the two effects discussed quantitatively above account for 19.3 percent of the government deficit of 1976 and 44.2 percent of the deficit of 1977. When these amounts are substracted from the realized figures, the deficits for 1976 and 1977 in real terms turn out to

72. Banco Central de Reserva del Peru, *Memoria* (1977), p. 31.

73. Another important new revenue source was a tax increase on gasoline that caused revenues to increase from 1975 to 1976 by 353 percent and then from this higher base by another 176 percent in 1977. Thus in 1977, revenue from gasoline taxes alone were 7.0 percent of current revenue, compared to 2 percent in 1975.

74. Such a finding is, of course, consistent with the decline in the index of retail sales which began in 1976. Banco Continental, *La Situación Económica del Peru, IV Trimestre* (Lima, 1978), p. 2.

75. Note that the devaluation leads the GDP deflator, thus causing an index number problem when real government expenditures are to be calculated as in Cline's table 9-6.

be 5 percent and 21 percent *below* that of 1975. Hence, contrary to Cline's contention, the stabilization policy was directly responsible for the increase in the deficits of 1976 and 1977.

The Lessons from Peru

Cline states "In an economy with high investment and savings, high fiscal revenues, and a realistic exchange rate, it is possible that the appropriate response to an exogenous shock causing inflation and/or trade deficit will not be the standard stabilization package (especially if trade response is inelastic). When conditions have been patently overexpansive and trade distortions have been extreme, however, it is difficult to accept that devaluation and fiscal and monetary restraint must be avoided for structuralist reasons."

This viewpoint gets the match of patient and medicine precisely wrong. Countries with few distortions, where effective exchange rates are fairly uniform and where price signals have been allowed to operate, may not require more than broad economywide stabilization measures, for they are unlikely to have encapsulated localized problems, and moreover, they have the flexibility of response necessary to adjust well to undifferentiated macromeasures. On the other hand, economies with many distortions, where markets have been segmented and have not been allowed to operate fully and foreign exchange scarcity has become a major problem, across-the-board measures are likely to do more harm than good, and specific antidistorting measures are needed to counteract the preexisting rigidities and to restore the flexibility that the economy has lost.

In analyzing such an economy, and Peru in 1975–78 is a good example, great care must be taken in looking beneath the aggregates, for one runs great risk that by paying attention only to the macro forest one does not notice the type of tree it contains. It is unfortunate that Cline should have fallen into precisely this pitfall.

Discussion*

John Holsen (World Bank) said the most important point is that both the Mexican and Peruvian stabilization problems were homemade. He

* The following discussion refers to both the Mexico and Peru studies, chapter 8 and this chapter.

agreed with Weintraub on the central role of increased public spending without adequate financing, and he found Cline's study overly generous to Peru in attributing so much of the problem to special external factors. Both countries were typical cases of excess demand and poor public finance, as well as excessive wage increases, leading to balance-of-payments problems. More than excess demand was involved, however; there was also need for restructuring, as in the neglected area of agriculture. Stabilization programs in both countries caused faster inflation in the short term because of "corrective inflation" resulting from long delayed adjustments of some officially fixed prices. Holsen agreed with Cline on the relatively destabilizing role of private banks but was skeptical about formal coordination between the IMF and the banks. He urged development of better rules of the game and disputed Friedman's position that commercial banks should be treated as preferred creditors for repayment.

Jack Sweeney (U.S. Treasury Department) expressed general agreement with both studies. He emphasized the lesson from both cases that early action is essential in order to minimize adjustment costs.

Richard Weinert (Leslie, Weinert & Co., Inc.) agreed with Cline on the role of the banks in Peru. The banks considered Mexico a good risk up to 1976 and were shocked when the crisis came; thereafter the banks shunned Mexico for six months, a position just as unrealistic as their previous inability to anticipate crises in light of structural problems. The banks resumed lending after the IMF's seal of approval, showing that critics of the IMF's limited resources ignore its catalytic and supervisory role. Weinert doubted the effectiveness of stabilization, noting that if oil is deducted, the 1978 trade deficit exceeded that in 1976. *Sidney Dell* said he would go beyond Schydlowsky in saying that excess demand was not Peru's problem in 1974–75. The evidence then justified increased investment, and the World Bank thought projected borrowing and investment were reasonable. *Jorge del Canto* (formerly of the IMF) commended both studies for balanced assessments of the role of the International Monetary Fund.

William Cline responded to Schydlowsky that the study does not say the problem was simply one of excess demand but cites structural problems. Cline cited Schydlowsky's own reference to labor legislation as one example for skepticism about the practicality of a change to multiple-shift operation as a technique of stabilization. On the issue of whether there was excess demand in 1975–76, Cline cited widespread consensus with the study's position among economists at the World Bank, the IMF, the Peruvian central bank, and many Peruvian academic and economic journalists. Responding to Dell, Cline noted that there was already a sharp criticism of overexpansion from the central bank in 1975 and that the massive budgetary expansion in 1975 went far beyond levels foreseen by the World Bank in 1974. Cline noted that Schydlowsky's data on increased tax rates do not disprove the criticism that deficits were not caused by recession. Built-in tax revenue typically lags behind GNP (the World Bank estimates an elasticity of 0.7), so that taxes are always in need of increases just to keep pace with GNP. The real test of Schydlowsky's argument concerning recession-induced deficit is the ratio of revenue to GNP. If Schydlowsky is right, that GNP decline would have caused declining revenue and rising deficit but that tax increases sustained revenue, then the ratio of revenue to GNP should have risen. Instead, this ratio fell (by about 2 percent for 1976 and 1977). Regarding the tests for import response, Cline suggested Schydlowsky's separate results for 1969–76 failed to find a significant relationship to the exchange rate because there were too few observations for a statistical test. He pointed out that dummy variable tests in the percentage-change model showed no significant change in the period 1969–76 from before, contrary to Schydlowsky's position. In any event, general scientific procedure supports the simplest model with statistical significance and consistency with theory, and failure to find statistical significance in an alternative specification does not invalidate results that are statistically significant in an equally or more appropriate specification. Cline noted that Schydlowsky's comment on net foreign exchange availability after taking into account an import spending policy response would apply to Schydlowsky's proposed export expansion strategy as well as to the "special factors" examined in the study.

CHAPTER TEN

Stabilization and Development of the Tanzanian Economy in the 1970s

JAMES H. WEAVER *and* ARNE ANDERSON

THIS PAPER contains an analysis of stabilization policies in mainland Tanzania during the 1970s. We did not include Zanzibar in our analysis because the two economies were managed quite independently during the period under discussion.

We feel obliged to make our bias explicit. We are quite sympathetic with the Tanzanian effort to build a socialist society. That said, we have tried to present the data objectively and the critics' views effectively.

The objective of this paper is to examine Tanzania's economic crises of the 1970s and the government's response to those crises. Any such examination will depend on an understanding of the unique nature of Tanzania. To that end, the chapter begins with a brief survey of Tanzania's institutions and goals. The chapter then describes the extent of the crisis. Next, the government stabilization policy is examined on its own merits; what the government tried to do and wanted to happen is compared with what it did and what did happen. The next section presents critiques of Tanzania's policy. The final section contains our conclusions.

Background[1]

The physical resource base for Tanzanian development is quite limited. Although the country has a land area of 365,000 square miles, only 60

We express our gratitude for the assistance we received from the people concerned with Tanzanian economy at the U.S. Agency for International Development, the World Bank, the International Monetary Fund, and the Tanzanian Embassy.

1. This section is based on Richard Blue and James Weaver, "A Critical Assessment of the Tanzanian Model of Development," Occasional Paper 1 (U.S. Agency for International Development, Development Studies Program, 1977).

percent is arable, and much of that is not habitable because of the widespread occurrence of the tsetse fly. Shortage of rainfall for agriculture is a chronic problem, as is soil erosion in parts of the country. The Tanzania-Zambia Railroad has opened untapped areas for mineral and agricultural development. There is considerable potential for hydroelectric power, and the potential for fishing in the enormous lakes is largely undeveloped.

Tanzania had a population of approximately fifteen million in 1975 and a growth rate of 2.6 percent. Approximately 90 percent of the population lives in rural areas and engages in agriculture. Life expectancy is about forty-five years. The infant mortality rate is approximately 150 per 1,000 live births.

Estimates of adult literacy range from 15 percent to 60 percent, the only consensus being that the government has made great strides in establishing both universal primary education and adult literacy classes. There is also a widespread opinion that the Tanzanian education program has been costly and that its cost will increase dramatically.

Per capita income in Tanzania is approximately $180 per year and has grown, in real terms, 2.6 percent per annum since 1960. Tanzania is one of the world's poorest countries as measured by per capita income.

Tanzania is a one-party state. Tanganyikan-African National Union (TANU) led the struggle for independence and has shaped the political life of the country since independence.[2] Considerable competition exists for leadership positions within the party and before the electorate. Within clearly defined constraints, Tanzanians are active politically.

Tanzanian Goals

The transition to independence in 1961 was peaceful. The Tanzanians inherited a colonial educational system, a colonial health system, a colonial tax system, and so forth, that were designed to perpetuate colonialism. President Nyerere argued in a speech in Mozambique that Tanzanians thought ". . . the task was to let the people with black faces do the work previously done by people with white faces. The independence struggle had not demanded a fundamental change in thinking. It had not been a revolutionary experience." The fundamental change in thinking to which Nyerere referred has been gradually taking place over the years since independence.

2. In February 1978, Tanganyikan-African National Union (TANU) was merged with the Afro-Shirazi party of Zanzibar, which is gradually merging with Tanzania. The new party is named Chama Cha Mapinduzi, or the Revolutionary party.

The Tanzanian leadership is attempting to build a society that will overcome or bypass some of the major problems of modern and modernizing societies, whether socialist or capitalist. Tanzania represents a remarkable experiment in the reordering of human values and relationships. In choosing a socialist approach, Tanzania hopes to achieve both growth and equity. It is unwilling to accept as historically necessary a development pattern that sacrifices equitable distribution to economic growth.

Nyerere and TANU have departed from the notion that socialism is a more efficient means of producing a high material standard of living associated with an industrialized society. Rather, they advance a model of an economic order based on an agrarian society, with limitations on the accumulation of material wealth, but capable of providing an adequate level of material existence for all citizens. They hope to avoid and prevent the emergence of social classes and invidious distinctions between elites and masses. Their vision of the new society has little room for either the capitalist elite or the elite based on state bureaucratic power. Instead, the ideology foresees a social-political order based on moral and group material incentives, leading to a condition of equality, freedom, and essential material well-being for all people.

There are two major strategies for achieving the goals described above. First, private ownership of industry is to be abolished and replaced with state ownership. Second, private ownership and control of agricultural production is to be replaced by collective ownership and production of agricultural products within the framework of the Ujamaa village.

The Mwongozo guidelines decree that the mode of leadership in the society must change from the individualistic to the collective in politics, government administration, and industrial and agricultural management. This change means workers' councils, sharing of managerial responsibility between the bureaucratic and the elected political leadership, and the active participation of small farmers in the planning and execution of agricultural and rural development.

Tanzania's long-term goals are thus laid out and will probably remain the same for the foreseeable future. These goals can be broadly summarized as socialism and self-reliance. Tanzanian socialism means achieving equity and participation.

The first goal, equity, has ramifications for the ownership of property, for the distribution of income from labor, and for the distribution of public services. The goal is to achieve equity in all these areas without regard for place of residence, urban or rural; rich or poor; whether in large or small enterprise or public or private enterprise. In addition, the Tanzanians want to achieve equity between generations so that no generation is sacrificed so that another may have a better life.

The second goal, participation, implies both traditional political democracy, the choice of who governs and the capacity to influence political decisions, and participation in the decision-making process at the workplace. It means worker self-management in the factories, firms, and farms; it means new egalitarian relationships between managers and workers; and it means new interpersonal relationships based on courtesy, not deference.

The government adopted specific targets for improving human welfare in the fifteen-year, long-term development plan for 1964–79.[3] These goals included increasing per capita income by 90 percent over the fifteen years (not achieved), achieving manpower self-sufficiency by 1980 (largely achieved), and increasing life expectancy to fifty years (not achieved). The two most important institutional changes initiated were the creation of Ujamaa villages and the decentralization of government.

In Tanzania, people and resources are both scarce. It makes sense that the resources could be spread more widely if the people were spread less widely, and this is the logic behind the government's push to move the rural population into villages. Originally, the villages were intended to create a "socialist man" via increased communal farming, but this idea has been postponed. Between 1974 and 1976, more than half the population was moved into villages. Now, the villages are best thought of as administrative units.

With nationalization of economic activity and the rapid growth of a central state bureaucracy, a real danger of creating a new and privileged bureaucratic class emerged. The response to this problem was a radical decentralization of government administration. This process started in 1972 and is still evolving.

The Crisis

The gross domestic product (GDP) of Tanzania increased by 5 percent per year during the first five-year plan (1964–69). Population increased 2.7 percent per year; thus per capita income increased 2.3 percent

3. United Republic of Tanzania, *Third Five-Year Plan for Economic and Social Development 1976–1981* (Dar es Salaam: Government of Tanzania, 1976), pp. 2–5.

per year. During the second five-year plan (1969–74), the gross domestic produce increased 4.8 percent per year. During the period 1974–78, the gross domestic product increased 6.1 percent per year.[4]

As can be seen from table 10-1, agriculture is the dominant sector of the economy, accounting for 40 percent of GDP in 1978. Total agricultural output increased approximately 50 percent between 1966 and 1978 in real terms, or 3.6 percent per annum, keeping ahead of the population increase in this same period.

When we look at the percentage increase in material product in the monetized sector in table 10-1, we see great year-to-year variations. Growth was above 5 percent every year between 1967 and 1972. The performance has been less impressive since 1972, showing a drop in 1974 and no increase in 1978. Only 1976 and 1977 were up to pre-1972 levels of performance.

The respectable growth of gross domestic product disguised several problems. Agricultural production was keeping ahead of population growth but was highly unstable. Productivity in the industrial sector was declining. Much of the increase in GDP came from expansion of services, particularly of public administration. The rate of domestic saving and investment was high, but the resulting growth in output was disappointing. Finally, an increasing share of the development budget was being financed externally. Approximately 60 percent of the development budget was coming from external sources in 1977–79.

The country had an excess of imports every year since 1967. The imbalance was particularly large from 1970 on. The value of exports fell slightly in 1975 and dramatically in 1978, and increased very little in 1971–74. The only years of sizable export growth were 1976 and 1977, and this growth was in value, not in volume.

Imports

Imports increased steadily throughout the period 1965–73. There was a very large increase in the value of imports in 1974. There was a decline in volume in 1975–77. A quantum jump occurred in 1978.

When imports are analyzed by Standard International Trade Classification (SITC) divisions, it is seen that the big increase in 1974–75 was

4. Computed from table 10-1. The gross domestic product is heavily dependent on volatile agriculture and agricultural export earnings. Changing the base year and terminal year leads to great changes in growth rates.

Table 10-1. *GDP by Industrial Origin, 1970–78*

Millions of T Sh, constant (1966) prices

Industry	1970	1971	1972	1973	1974	1975	1976	1977	1978
Agriculture	3,205	3,166	3,425	3,458	3,315	3,596	3,988	4,316	4,515
Monetary	1,589	1,522	1,620	1,625	1,516	1,567	1,722	1,831	1,774
Subsistence	1,616	1,644	1,805	1,833	1,799	2,029	2,266	2,485	2,741
Mining and quarrying	97	152	119	91	88	73	77	63	46
Manufacturing	716	784	850	888	900	903	961	1,017	1,062
Electricity and water	92	96	106	114	127	139	142	148	163
Construction	327	380	402	418	413	392	360	350	294
Wholesale and retail trade	984	972	990	1,039	1,068	1,074	1,092	1,195	1,327
Transportation and communications	729	814	869	905	958	997	1,034	1,088	1,160
Finance and real estate	763	800	831	867	929	941	961	1,003	1,040
Public administration and other[a]	767	837	947	1,020	1,222	1,438	1,550	1,648	1,822
Total GDP (at factor cost)	7,680	8,001	8,539	8,800	9,020	9,553	10,165	10,828	11,429
Addendum:									
Subsistence	2,179	2,223	2,401	2,445	2,430	2,677	2,934	3,172	3,449
Monetary sector	5,501	5,778	6,138	6,355	6,590	6,876	7,231	7,656	7,980
Monetary material product (constant prices)	3,550	3,748	3,966	4,041	4,002	4,071	4,296	4,497	4,499
Percentage change per year	6.8	5.6	5.8	1.9	−1.0	1.7	5.5	4.7	0.0

Source: Computed by the IMF from United Republic of Tanzania, *The Economic Survey* (Dar es Salaam: Government Printer), various years.
a. Net of imputed bank service charges.

in food. These imports increased from 274 million Tanzanian shillings (T Sh) (T Sh 8 = approximately U.S. $1) in 1973 to T Sh 1,066 million in 1974, stayed at T Sh 1,011 million in 1975, and then dropped backed to around T Sh 500 million in 1976, 1977, and 1978. Other categories showing large increases in 1974 and continuing at high levels were fuel, chemicals and fertilizer, manufactured goods, machinery, and transport equipment.

The authors of the recent study by the United Nations Development Program (UNDP)[5] found that in 1973–74, approximately 43 percent of the increase in imports could be accounted for by increased food imports. Of this, 37 percent could be attributed to increased quantity, and 6 percent to higher prices. Twelve percent of the import increase could be traced to higher fuel imports despite control over quantities imported. Approximately 10 percent of the increase could be accounted for by higher prices for fertilizer. Approximately 15 percent of the increased imports could be attributed to machinery and transport equipment— about evenly divided between higher prices and increased quantities. Sixteen percent of the increase was accounted for by increased imports of manufactured goods, but no attempt was made to break this down between increased price versus increased quantity.

Exports

Most of Tanzania's exports are of primary products (see table 10-2). It appears that the drop in the value of exports in 1975 was due to drops in cotton, sisal, and cashew nuts. The drop in 1978 came in all commodities except tobacco, due mainly to a sharp decline in unit prices. Until 1978, the prices of Tanzanian exports had increased significantly. In 1975 the major products exported (except tea) received prices significantly higher than in 1967–69.

However, even though export prices were generally above the 1967–69 base year in the 1970s, they were subject to extraordinarily erratic movements (see table 10-3). The export price of cotton in 1975 was 19 percent lower than in 1974, and sisal was 40 percent lower. The export prices of cashews, tea, and tobacco were higher in 1975. Even greater

5. Reginald Green, Delfin Rwegasira, and Brian van Arkadie, *The Balance of Payments Adjustment Process in Developing Countries—The Case of the United Republic of Tanzania,* Project INT/75/015 (UNDP/UNCTAD, December 1978), pp. 21–24. (Hereafter *UNDP Study.*)

Table 10-2. Indices of Value, Volume, and Prices of Six Major Agricultural Exports, 1970–78

Product	1970	1971	1972	1973	1974	1975	1976	1977	1978
				Value: 1967–69 average = 100					
Cotton	96.4	95.6	131.1	129.9	184.5	115.9	239.2	211.5	163.5
Coffee	123.3	89.7	119.8	195.6	148.2	190.9	506.7	739.1	511.9
Sisal	103.3	77.3	83.7	128.1	267.2	174.3	138.5	131.6	125.8
Cashew nuts (raw)	110.3	115.1	143.8	135.2	187.9	169.7	125.6	180.2	154.4
Tea	92.7	108.2	340.0	119.2	152.3	178.8	298.0	397.4	370.9
Tobacco (unmanufactured)	124.0	118.5	135.0	154.3	242.4	228.7	517.9	567.5	611.6
				Volume: 1967–69 average = 100					
Cotton	88.1	99.2	76.5	70.4	46.5	23.3	33.7	24.5	28.8
Coffee	93.9	75.5	115.3	125.8	86.0	113.2	121.6	98.5	106.9
Sisal	115.2	85.4	81.2	59.9	49.3	54.1	42.4	36.6	41.9
Cashew nuts (raw)	99.8	123.7	145.6	141.8	146.9	125.0	85.1	96.6	56.7
Tea	101.5	177.8	200.0	222.2	222.2	222.2	266.7	266.7	333.3
Tobacco (unmanufactured)	133.3	111.1	133.3	133.3	200.0	133.3	244.4	266.7	244.4
				Unit prices: 1967–69 average = 100					
Cotton	97.3	106.7	124.5	132.5	229.9	186.1	265.4	320.5	217.8
Coffee	131.8	121.3	132.5	155.5	173.1	168.1	419.2	755.5	482.7
Sisal	89.8	90.8	103.2	213.2	541.3	325.6	309.7	378.9	300.8
Cashew nuts (raw)	110.9	93.0	99.2	95.8	128.5	135.5	147.3	187.2	271.4
Tea	90.4	97.5	86.9	84.9	106.4	116.4	166.5	221.8	167.5
Tobacco (unmanufactured)	94.0	114.3	110.4	114.5	125.4	164.9	213.3	224.7	252.8

Source: Same as table 10-1.

Table 10-3. *Yearly Percentage Changes in Unit Export Prices, 1971–78*

Product	1971	1972	1973	1974	1975	1976	1977	1978
Cotton	10	17	6	74	−19	43	21	−32
Coffee	−8	9	17	11	−3	149	80	−36
Sisal	1	14	107	154	−40	−5	22	−21
Cashew nuts	−16	7	−3	34	5	9	27	45
Tea	−3	−1	−2	25	9	43	33	−24
Tobacco	22	−3	4	10	32	29	5	13

Source: Computed from table 10-2.

volatility was shown in 1978. Cotton prices were 34 percent lower than in 1977, coffee was 41 percent lower, sisal was 17 percent lower, and tea was 25 percent lower. Only tobacco and cashews received higher prices in 1978 than in 1977. Thus even though export prices were higher throughout the 1970s than they had been at the end of the 1960s, they were subject to such extremely rapid and wide swings that they introduced great instability into the balance of payments and uncertainty into planning development expenditures.

Tea and tobacco are the only exports that have consistently increased in volume. Coffee exports have fluctuated widely along a generally upward trend. The volume of exports of cotton, sisal, and raw cashews has clearly fallen. However, domestic processing of raw cashews accounts for some of the decreased volume of exports for that product.

The volume of exports of primary products could drop for a number of reasons: (1) these products could be processed domestically and ex-

Table 10-4. *Total Production of Five Major Export Crops, 1964–78*

Year	Cotton (bales)	Coffee (tons)	Sisal (tons)	Tea (tons)	Tobacco (tons)
1964	293,246	33,837	233,540	4,812	2,124
1969	382,516	46,140	209,303	8,777	11,664
1970	421,332	49,669	202,180	8,492	11,066
1971	360,116	45,834	181,104	10,457	11,949
1972	428,033	51,738	156,846	12,706	14,181
1973	378,220	54,578	155,407	12,658	13,025
1974	394,000	44,671	132,000	12,974	18,150
1975	326,264	62,416	124,000	13,732	14,193
1976	448,845	55,359	113,698	14,074	19,126
1977	358,637	48,682	105,018	16,665	18,353
1978	285,706	43,000	91,873	17,331	17,087

Source: Same as table 10-1.

Table 10-5. *Balance-of-Payments Estimates*

Millions of T Sh

Item	1970	1971	1972	1973	1974	1975	1976	1977	1978
Goods									
Exports (including reexports)	1,626	1,680	2,086	2,302	2,719	2,434	3,828	4,264	3,553
Imports	2,284	2,779	2,925	3,410	5,137	5,424	5,180	5,980	8,650
Net	−658	−1,099	−839	−1,108	−2,417	−2,990	−1,360	−1,716	−5,097
Net services	226	209	256	130	152	451	436	602	504
Net transfers	92	41	−30	35	323	689	464	961	1,072
Balance on current account	−341	−849	−613	−942	−1,942	−1,850	−461	152	−3,521
Net capital	512	1,090	868	909	1,309	1,637	563	790	935
"Special funds" (net)	...	...	...	...	...	...	...	213	163
Errors and omissions	−286	−275	134	248	28	345	159	383	661
Overall balance	−114	−34	390	215	−606	−68	261	1,233	−1,762

Source: Same as table 10-1.

ported in a processed state, (2) they could be consumed domestically rather than exported, or (3) total production of these products could have dropped. Data are unavailable to test the first hypothesis. But table 10-4 contains the data on total production of five major export crops. This table reveals that cotton production exceeded 400,000 bales in 1970, 1972, and 1976 but has generally been lower, dropping to less than 300,000 bales in 1978. The drop in export volume of cotton was due to a drop in cotton production. The same decline in total production was also found for sisal. Coffee production fluctuated. Only tea and tobacco production experienced an upward trend. We did not find data for total production of cashew nuts, but most reports indicate a downward trend for production of this crop.

Balance of Payments

The trade account was in deficit every year from 1967 to 1978 (see table 10-5). Services were positive every year of this same period. Net transfers were also positive in every year from 1967 to 1978 except in 1972 and were very large (approximately T Sh 1 billion) in 1977 and 1978. Thus the effect of services and transfers was to reduce the deficit on current account significantly. Still, the deficit on current acount was almost T Sh 1 billion in 1971 and 1973, almost T Sh 2 billion in 1974 and 1975, and more than T Sh 3.5 billion in 1978.

Why did Tanzania experience a balance-of-payments crisis? Or rather, why has Tanzania experienced three balance-of-payments crises in the 1970s?

The way the question is posed of whether Tanzania faced one crisis (1974–75) or three crises is significant in the analysis. One view—forcefully presented in the UNDP study—holds that the Tanzanian economy functioned effectively in the 1970s and was beset by a series of major and minor shocks (drought, higher petroleum prices, and world stagflation) that disrupted this otherwise successful course. A second analysis, equally well articulated in two papers by Michael Lofchie,[6] concludes that the Tanzanian economy was badly mismanaged during the 1970s and avoided bankruptcy only by virtue of the generosity of the capitalist world, so

6. Michael Lofchie, "Agrarian Socialism in the Third World: The Tanzanian Case," *Comparative Politics,* vol. 8 (April 1976), and "Agrarian Crisis and Economic Liberalization in Tanzania," *Journal of Modern African Studies,* vol. 16 (1978).

much maligned by Tanzanian spokespersons, and by favorable world market prices of coffee exports. Each of these analyses will be discussed in detail later in the chapter.

The Government's Response

How did the Tanzanian government respond to the various crises? This section will focus on the response to the crisis of 1974–75, although brief mention will be made of the minicrisis of 1970–71 and the latest crisis in 1978–79.

The response to the 1970–71 minicrisis in the balance of payments involved steps that laid the foundation for the policies taken to deal with the much more severe crisis in 1974–75:[7] a foreign exchange budgeting procedure was devised involving import licensing and exchange controls to be implemented by the Bank of Tanzania; the government secured the services of a Swiss firm to monitor prices for key exports and imports; a credit budgeting system was initiated involving all domestic lending by commercial banks and the central bank; the government began regulating the uses made of surpluses earned by all public enterprises; and the government strengthened the role of the Price Commission in setting prices and established a new trading structure to handle domestic and international trade.

These policy measures were successful in reducing the deficit, which fell from T Sh 1,099 million in 1971 to T Sh 839 million in 1972. The overall balance showed a surplus in 1972 and 1973, thus allowing the government to increase net official reserves to a record T Sh 1,022 million by the end of 1973. It appeared that the crisis was indeed past. By 1974, however, it had become clear that the 1970–71 crisis had merely been a dress rehearsal for the drama that was to unfold in the middle of the decade.

The 1974–75 crisis marked the return to what some have called a sense of pragmatism in Tanzania. Public pronouncements have been marked by criticism of worker discipline, encouragement of privately owned small-scale enterprises, and abandonment of the communal farm-

---

7. Green and others, *UNDP Study,* pp. 10–11. The authors of the UNDP study of the Tanzanian balance-of-payments crisis included a former adviser to the government and a member of the staff of the central bank. They have provided an extremely comprehensive description of the government's stabilization policy.

ing aspect of Ujamaa, and so forth.[8] However, the general approach taken was heavily influenced by the goals of socialism and self-reliance. Specifically, the government attempted to shield the weaker groups in society from the costs of stabilization while continuing the development program.

The authors of the UNDP study[9] have laid out the goals, the policy instruments, and the expected costs of the stabilization policy.

Goals

1. To increase output and expand export earnings by increasing the value-added content of traditional exports (cashews, sisal, cloth, and leather) and to expand production of nontraditional exports.

2. To prevent greater inequality of income distribution.

3. To limit price increases to those made necessary by higher import costs and to limit expansion of credit to those increases necessary to accommodate adjustments in import costs, wages, and farm prices.

4. To maintain surpluses of private and public enterprises, to keep the recurrent budget in surplus, and to avoid permanent subsidy of consumer goods.

5. To expand basic services to peasants, including extension services and agricultural inputs, and to maintain real levels per capita of other services.

6. To give priority to directly productive investment likely to be remunerative in a short period.

7. To avoid the loss of development momentum.

8. To bridge the 1974–75 balance-of-payments gap with import cuts, reserves, and emergency funding (soft loans, IMF, World Bank, or commercial borrowing); to reduce imports in 1975–76 through output recovery and longer-term assistance; and to promote recovery in 1976–77 through structural changes in production and from long-term external finances.

Instruments

The stabilization policy package contained ten instruments designed to achieve these objectives.

8. For example, note the following quotation from Julius Nyerere's speech, "The Arusha Declaration: Ten Years After" (Dar es Salaam: Government of Tanzania, February 5, 1977). ". . . profit is necessary whether an enterprise is privately owned or not. . . . It is essential we should tighten up on industrial discipline."

9. Green and others, *UNDP Study*, pp. 29–33.

1. Major increases in agricultural producer prices (for food crops).

2. A 40 percent increase in the minimum wage, with other wage increases tapering down to 3 percent posttax for top civil servants and managers (to be discussed later).

3. Sharp retail price increases of basic foods.

4. Authority to the Price Commission to adjust prices for the main products to cover cost increases and to allow the parastatals (state-owned production and trading corporations) to maintain a surplus.

5. Restriction of credit increases to those necessary to accommodate requirements resulting from the new structure of prices.

6. Allocation of foreign exchange to high-priority imports, including minimal necessary supplies of basic foods, widely used consumer goods, fuel, fertilizer, pesticides, and spares; imports necessary for a continued investment program; and enough intermediate goods to prevent major cuts in production.

7. Maintenance of public service levels and expansion of adult education, primary education, agricultural extension, and rural health.

8. Moderate curtailment of public investment, particularly of infrastructure projects with long gestation periods.

9. Massive mobilization of external finance to cover the deficit until a return to normal conditions (envisaged for 1977–78).

10. Tax increases necessary to maintain a moderate government surplus.

Thus the objectives of the government's policies on the demand side of the economy were to attack the balance-of-payments problem through import controls, to restrict nonessential consumption to free resources for development, and to import food supplies for the poorest segments of society.

Costs

The government anticipated that some of the following costs would result from the stabilization program: some distortions in production, worsening of income distribution as richer peasants took advantage of higher producer prices, increased inflation, reduced saving, deterioration of rural water supply system and roads due to lack of maintenance, reduction in public investment, and postponement of the third five-year plan from 1974–79 to 1976–81. The government also feared that the increased dependence on external funding might force it to adopt a standard deflationist strategy as the price of funding.

Policy Implementation

On the demand side, the government utilized import controls as its prime instrument. In mid-1974 the government increased import controls on consumer goods (excluding food) and industrial raw materials. As the crisis worsened, import licensing was tightened even more significantly. The authorities also complemented the import restrictions with such control mechanisms as suspending remittances to foreign relatives, reducing travel allowances, and banning Sunday driving.

Although pricing measures were of secondary importance in reducing demand, several such measures were instituted: gasoline and electricity prices were allowed to rise to reflect increased costs, and food prices were increased. Indirect taxes were increased on textiles, beer, and cigarettes.

A one-year wage freeze was imposed after the increase in 1974. Aside from a minor adjustment in 1975, there were no other legislated wage increases in the period under examination. Public sector employment was reduced.

An extra note on Tanzania's wage policy is warranted here. The 40 percent increase in the minimum wage (with lesser increases in the higher brackets) in 1974 has been strongly criticized. Three explanations have been offered for the government's action: (1) the raise was needed to offset past price increases, (2) the raise was needed to offset future price increases, and (3) the raise occurred prior to the government's recognition of the severity of the crisis. Whatever the rationale, there is a general recognition that the raise had a negative impact on the government stabilization policy.[10] The wage freeze (post-1974) has been evaded to some extent by promoting workers into better jobs.

The credit system was used to facilitate the shift to the altered price and wage structure. The government argued that the expansion of the money supply was an effect of the increase in import prices and higher producer prices for food. The total money supply (M_1) had increased from T Sh 1,800 million to T Sh 3,000 million from December 1970 to June 1974—a 67 percent increase in three and a half years. But between June and December 1974, total supply increased T Sh 700 million, and almost another T Sh 1,000 million by December 1978. Thus the money supply increased almost threefold between December 1970 and December 1976.

10. The position that the wage increase can be understood as *a part* of the government stabilization policy broadly defined (that is, integrated with the government's commitment to equity) is best put forth by Green and others, *UNDP Study*.

Table 10-6. *Domestic Price Indices*
1969 = 100

Year	National consumer price index (18 towns)	Dar es Salaam minimum-wage earners retail price index	Dar es Salaam middle-grade civil servants cost-of-living index	GDP deflator
1965	...	89	89	96
1966	...	93	92	97
1967	...	95	96	97
1968	...	99	100	98
1969	100	100	100	100
1970	104	104	102	104
1971	108	107	103	108
1972	117	119	106	116
1973	129	129	122	128
1974	154	169	152	150
1975	194	249	204	171
1976	...	307	226	...
1977	...	358	252	...
1978	...	419	303	...

Source: Same as table 10-1.

The government was not successful in slowing the growth of government expenditures and deficit financing. Both higher import prices and higher producer prices for food increased government spending dramatically. Tax increases were insufficient to offset the increased expenditure. The government borrowed heavily from the banking system—more than T Sh 1,000 million in 1975–76.

Price increases had been moderate through 1971. The rate of inflation increased in 1972 and 1973. However, 1974 was the beginning of an unprecedented increase in prices. The retail price index for a minimum-wage earner in Dar es Salaam increased forty points in 1974, eighty points in 1975, fifty-eight points in 1976, fifty-one points in 1977, and sixty-one points in 1978. This index indicated that retail prices paid by a minimum-wage earner had increased more than 200 percent between 1969 and 1978. Other price indices moved up more slowly (see table 10-6.)

SUPPLY INSTRUMENTS. On the supply side, two major policy instruments were utilized: increasing producer prices and redirecting government investment. The use of producer prices to spur agricultural output marked a shift in government policy. Prior to the crisis, Tanzanian authorities had feared that increasing producer prices would cause increasing inequality of intrarural income distribution because the producers for the monetary economy were generally the better-off peasants. But in 1975, such worries were waived in the face of the crisis, and prices were drastically increased (maize 127 percent, wheat 75 percent, and paddy 35 percent).

The government restructured its development budget in 1974–75 and 1975–76 by redirecting expenditure to directly productive sectors (agriculture, industry, and mining). The development budget shifted from 23 percent (pre-1974) directly productive expenditure to 48 percent in 1975–76. Even more impressive is the fact that four-fifths of the new projects planned were in the directly productive sectors. The government attempted to use the crisis to provide an impetus to its import substitution campaign. Emphasis was placed on the engineering industry as well as the shoe, textile, bicycle, and cement industries.

EXTERNAL SECTOR. Tanzania devalued its shilling by 11 percent in October 1975 and sought to mobilize external finance. The hope was that the external finance would bridge the short-term balance-of-payments gap and that such external assistance would be available on terms that would not compromise long-term goals.

The international response to the balance-of-payments crisis was impressive. In 1974, Tanzania received commitments of more than $300 million in external financing—approximately $20 per capita. Most commitments were on soft terms, with the result that Tanzania owed only $1 billion at the end of 1977, and debt service required only 7 percent of export earnings in that year.

The IMF made T Sh 423 million available in 1974, T Sh 210 million in 1975, T Sh 203 million in 1976, and T Sh 46 million in 1977. The IMF worked out a first credit tranche agreement with the government of Tanzania during the 1974–75 crisis. Disbursements were made from the first credit tranche, the oil facility, and the compensatory export finance fund —all relatively unconditional sources of funds. No disbursement of the second credit tranche was made. Some observers argue that this was because the Tanzanian government refused to deflate the economy at the expense of the poor. Others say it was because the Tanzanian government was unable to reduce government spending and the growth of the money supply in accordance with the IMF's requirements.

Despite the IMF's unwillingness to disburse, the World Bank made two program loans to help the government survive the crisis. The first program loan was for $30 million in 1974, and the second was an International Development Association credit of $15 million in 1977. The conditions for those loans were essentially the stabilization program the government carried out.

IDEOLOGICAL CAMPAIGN. The government was active on the ideological front, placing heavy reliance on a massive campaign to mobilize people to grow maize. The president, in his New Year's Day address to the nation in 1975, threw out the challenge, "Grow more food or starve. The reserves are gone and the external assistance is not coming."

Easing of the Crisis

From late 1975 through 1977, Tanzania's economic fortunes improved. Food production rebounded strongly, as did the value of exports. The balance-of-payments gap was reduced to manageable levels. In short, virtually all of Tanzania's immediate macroeconomic goals were realized.

The 1975–77 period marked the return of normal (or better than average) weather. Concurrently, the world market witnessed sharp increases in tea and coffee prices. Earnings from coffee exports grew from T Sh 483 million in 1975 to T Sh 1,282 million in 1976, about 60 percent of the increase in export earnings. Increases in GDP in both 1976 and 1977 (which were near the targeted 6 percent) were led by agricultural growth that was well above its long-term trend. Imports were cut from T Sh 5,694 million in 1975 to T Sh 5,421 million in 1976 primarily as a result of a 60 percent drop in food grain imports. The balance-of-payments deficit was reduced substantially. In 1977 the balance of payments showed a surplus of T Sh 1,233 million, which allowed net reserves to increase to T Sh 250 million.

As a result of the import controls, the quantity of nonfood imports is estimated to have fallen approximately 12 percent to 13 percent from 1973 to 1976.[11] The best indication that the controls were biting **deeply** was the widespread reports of shortages of essential parts and raw materials. Such shortages undoubtedly had real costs in forgone production. The shortages of consumer goods also had costs in increased smuggling, corruption, and black market activity.

Agricultural output responded to the increased producer prices, and producer prices remain in the government's arsenal of policy instruments.[12] Most reports mention the "life or death" campaign as a positive

11. Green and others, *UNDP Study,* p. 48.
12. "These measures include . . . raising and announcing producer prices early in each crop season," speech by Ndugu E. I. M. Mtei, Minister for Finance and Planning (Dar es Salaam: Government of Tanzania, June 15, 1978).

factor. Undoubtedly, the wage restraint and the other resource-freeing measures (taxes, driving ban, etc.) enabled Tanzania to maintain a higher rate of real investment than otherwise would have been possible. A notable failure has been Tanzanians' attempt to limit recurrent government expenditure.

The level of external finance was sufficient to fulfill the role of bridging the immediate gap. However, there were significant problems in the timing of the assistance. Until the middle of 1975, the total was inadequate. Tanzania's hope of securing this external aid without an unacceptable debt service ratio and on terms compatible with its own national goals was fulfilled. Only a small portion was in hard loans, and Tanzania successfully avoided a general deflationary program.[13]

The credit policies had mixed results. Too much credit was created in 1975 and 1976 and too little in 1977, causing unnecessary loss of output.

There were real costs of the stabilization policy. The breakdown in public services (most notably public transportation and rural water supply) was a direct consequence of postponed maintenance. The worst hit service was the rural water supply; as many as 30 percent of the facilities were inoperative in 1977.

There has been no attempt to measure the effects of the stabilization policy on income distribution in Tanzania. Some argue that the rural-urban gap that had been widening was strongly offset, if not reversed. The increase in producer prices, relief food, and the educational and water campaigns heavily favored the rural population. Wage restraint, reduced employment, increased food prices and taxes, and consumption restrictions considerably reduced the urban sector's real income.[14]

However, there is a strong suspicion that increased producer prices may have significantly worsened the intrarural distribution since much of the marketed output is produced by the better-off farmers. It should be noted that this effect would be offset somewhat by the services received by the rural poor, especially education and clean water.

Tanzania's stabilization policy was adhered to tenaciously. The strategy's effects and costs were significant. However, without better weather and terms of trade, the turnabout would not have occurred.

An examination of the 1978 balance-of-payments data reveals that the

13. Green and others, *UNDP Study,* p. 47.

14. Green and others, *UNDP Study,* p. 41. The authors estimate a 10 percent to 15 percent drop in real wages for the minimum-wage earner, a 20 percent drop for other low-wage earners, and a 33 percent drop for the high-wage class between 1973 and 1978.

economy faced yet another severe crisis in that year. Preliminary estimates from 1979 indicate that the balance-of-payments deficit was even
greater than in 1978. The breakup of the East African community hurt
exports. The war with Uganda was costly and import intensive, as Tanzania imports weapons, ammunition, and fuel. So, the decade ended as it
started—with severe balance-of-payments problems.

Critiques

Some argue that expenditure reduction policies are inappropriate in
the developing countries in that most balance-of-payments deficits in developing countries during the 1970s were not caused by excessive domestic demand but by higher import prices, low export prices, a drop in export volume, or all three. Expenditure reduction reduces incomes and
employment that are already too low in developing countries. The cost of
adjustment is slowed growth of GNP, reduction of development momentum, and very high costs for the poor and unemployed. Sidney Dell
argues that balance-of-payments adjustments in many developing countries are best handled through long-term structural alterations and that
the deficits should be externally financed until those structural alterations
can take place.[15]

Some observers argue that stabilization policies in a socialist economy
must be fundamentally different from those that would be appropriate in
a capitalist developing country. The goals of socialist economies are different, the basic economic institutions are different, and therefore, it is
argued, stabilization policies must also be different.

Socialist Stabilization Theory

Thomas Fues has synthesized the classical theory of stabilization policies in centrally planned economies.[16] According to the theory, planned
economies rarely have to deal with external imbalances. The government
controls all external financial movements and all international trade.
Thus the government can always achieve equilibrium in the foreign trade

15. Sidney Dell and Roger Lawrence, *The Balance of Payments Adjustment
Process in Developing Countries* (London: Pergamon Press, 1980).

16. Thomas Fues, "Stabilization Policies in Centrally Planned Economies"
(Massachusetts Institute of Technology, Department of Economics, 1979).

balance and the balance of payments by contracting imports in line with foreign exchange availability or by stimulating exports. In practice, socialist developing countries have relied on many of the same stabilization policies advocated by traditional capitalist theory (monetary and fiscal policies of expenditure reduction or switching), although these are combined with direct controls.

Tanzanian Monetary and Exchange Rate Policy

The government largely rejected the two principal monetary policy instruments—devaluing the currency and raising the interest rate. There was a slight devaluation of approximately 11 percent in 1975 and a second devaluation of approximately 10 percent in 1979.

The government agreed with the standard critiques of devaluation in developing countries, that is, that there was an inelastic demand for imports. There were no domestically produced substitutes available for imports. Devaluation would not reduce import demand but would lead to the same volume of imports but at higher prices, leading to inflation in the economy. The government argued that export supply was also inelastic, at least in the short term. There was no excess capacity in the export sector that could be brought into production as a result of higher prices. Industrial goods being consumed domestically could not be exported because there were no markets for them.

The rejection of interest rate policy was based on the argument that higher interest rates were ineffective in mobilizing private savings. The government argued that the reason savings were low in the crisis years was that incomes were low. The government argues that the main barrier to higher private savings rates in normal years is lack of access to credit institutions, and there is an effort to bring credit institutions to all parts of the country.

Also, the source of saving in a socialist economy is different from that in a capitalist economy, where most savings come from owners of capital —from rent, interest, and profits. In a socialist economy, the capital is socially owned, so savings come primarily from government. The interest rate has little effect on the level of government savings. There may also be less incentive for private savings in a socialist economy because of social programs to provide for the aged, sick, and others.

The government was unable to control the money supply as it had intended. In part, this may have been due to a gap between the theory and practice of socialist economy in developed and in developing countries. In a developed socialist economy, money supply and credit play passive roles. The decisions on production and distribution are made in real terms, and the money supply is used merely to facilitate real economic activity. Little attention is paid to monetary policy in socialist planning.

In socialist developing countries, however, the government is often not able to control overall economic activity in the same way that developed socialist economies can. In Tanzania, almost all agricultural production —the mainstay of the economy—is in private hands. Private enterprise plays a considerable role in the rest of the economy as well.

Fiscal Policy

An attempt was made to reduce the budget deficit through tax increases on cigarettes, beer, and textiles. Beer and cigarettes were taxed because they were not necessities, the tax would not fall so heavily on the poor, and demand was somewhat inelastic, so considerable revenue could be raised.

The government also attempted to reduce spending. This attempt turned out to be extremely difficult, and in fact, the government has admitted its inability to bring recurrent spending under control.[17]

No reliance was placed on tariffs as an instrument to control imports. The government preferred direct import controls and foreign exchange budgeting. Higher tariffs would have allowed well-off people to import luxury goods even at higher prices. Banning such imports was a direct, more effective, and more equitable means in the government's view.

Direct Controls

The government placed primary reliance on direct controls to deal with the balance-of-payments crisis. These direct controls included banning imports of luxury goods, banning Sunday driving, controlling wages and reducing employment to restrain consumption, altering prices to restrain consumption and encourage production, controlling and allocating foreign exchange according to government priorities, rationing credit according to government priorities, and directly distributing drought relief.

Some actions were successful. Producer price increases did stimulate a great increase in production of food crops. Two problems arose as a

17. Mtei, speech of June 15, 1978.

result of raising producer prices. The higher prices increased income inequality in the rural sector. The higher prices were not matched by increased availability of consumer goods in the rural areas, so producers acquired excess liquidity. Thus the incentive to produce more was somewhat reduced. Higher prices for gasoline, electricity, food, textiles, and other products did restrain the growth of consumption. Foreign exchange and credit rationing did allocate scarce resources to the sectors favored by government. The success of the wage policy is in dispute. Some think wage policy was misguided and the minimum wage increase of 1974 fueled inflation. Others think the wage policy accomplished its purpose in protecting the poor from bearing an undue share of the costs of stabilization. Massive starvation—such as occurred in Ethiopia and the Sahel during this period—was avoided.

Ideological Campaign

Working for nonmaterial incentives is not a part of traditional capitalist theory, although virtually all governments make use of ideological campaigns. Socialist theory makes more allowance for the role of ideology and nonmaterial incentives in motivating human behavior. Many observers believe the "grow maize or starve" campaign was successful in stimulating maize production.

Leftist Critique

Several critiques of the Tanzanian stabilization program have emerged. One critique holds that the government had clear long-range objectives, that is, socialism and self-reliance, and that both these objectives were sacrificed during the 1970s, with the result that Tanzania is now more integrated in and dependent upon the international capitalist system than ever before. The most obvious examples of the retreat from socialism are abandoning communal farming; raising producer prices in agriculture; securing loans from the World Bank and other creditors that will have to be repaid with exports of primary products—a continuation of the old colonial relationship; reducing worker management and participation in the industrial sector and imposing piece rates and "worker discipline"; encouraging capitalist enterprise in retail trade and butchering; inviting the International Finance Corporation to return to Tanzania; and inviting agribusiness to develop large plots of land. All of these steps were pursued in response to the balance-of-payments crisis and demonstrate the inability of Tanzania to pursue a half-capitalist, half-socialist strategy.

Some leftist critics move beyond this limited critique to question the class nature of the Tanzanian state. They posit that the "bureaucratic bourgeoisie" is the ruling sector of the petty bourgeoisie. They argue that the so-called "socialist" actions of the Tanzanian government are the results of the bureaucratic sector carving out an economic base for itself. However, a truly socialist (internally classless and externally independent of imperialist relations) society will not be achieved by the present state because ". . . the 'bureaucratic bourgeoisie' is incapable of restructuring the internal society and thereby disengaging from the world capitalist system, their objective class interests in the long run converge (with the international bourgeoisie)."[18] What is needed is a worker-peasant alliance, with the most advanced (Marxist) elements of the working class in the lead, to create a socialist revolution.

Centrist Critique

A fully developed analysis of the causes of and responses to the crisis is contained in the UNDP study. The authors of this study concede that the minicrisis of 1970–71 "had been largely the result of policy developments."[19] But they go on to argue that "the crisis of late 1973 was largely a result of events outside the influence of domestic policies."[20] These events were a severe drought in 1973–74 (that reduced food grain production by about 30 percent) and an increase in import prices for food, fuel, fertilizer, and other products.

The drought severely reduced maize production (the basic food crop) and led to massive food imports at the time of worldwide food shortages and thus high prices in 1973–75. The drought also caused a drop in production of export crops, particularly cotton. This drop in production meant that Tanzania was unable to benefit from the higher prices for exports in 1974.

In response to the drought, Tanzania increased producer prices for food crops in 1974–76 to encourage food production. This change in relative prices between food and export crops led farmers to switch from

18. Issa G. Shivji, *Class Struggle in Tanzania* (Monthly Review Press, 1976), p. 85.
19. Green and others, *UNDP Study*, p. 14.
20. Ibid.

producing export crops (particularly cotton) to producing food. This drop in export production then prevented Tanzania from capitalizing on the booming export prices in 1976–77.

The authors of the UNDP study argue that there was one balance-of-payments crisis and that it was caused by external events. They hardly mention the disruptive impact of villagization, decentralization, elimination of the cooperative unions, and other occurrences. Any problems encountered by Tanzania were those inherent in being a developing country buffeted by drought and stagflation in the international capitalist system. Tanzania should have had more ready access to external finance so that it could have dealt with the crisis more flexibly without having to reduce development momentum.

Some World Bank staff members argue that Tanzania had the traditional stabilization objectives—to reduce imports and increase exports. The policy of reducing imports was successful in the short term primarily as a result of massive efforts to achieve food self-sufficiency. There was, however, no effort to increase exports, and in fact export volume fell as resources were shifted from export crops to food crops in response to changes in relative prices and input costs. This drop in export volume was masked by high prices for coffee and tea in 1976–77 but became apparent in 1978–79. Thus the effort to solve one problem—food imports—exacerbated another problem—sluggish exports—with the result that Tanzania faced another balance-of-payments crisis in 1978–79.

The World Bank staff members argue that the government carried out virtually every recommendation the World Bank made in accordance with the two program loans in 1975 and 1977. In the Tanzanian case, the World Bank was more active than the IMF in providing emergency finance and in recommending policy measures to deal with the crisis.

There were only two areas in which the government refused to follow World Bank recommendations. The government refused to slow down the villagization effort or to slow spending on social services—especially education. The government has moved to reinstate school fees, however, in an effort to reduce recurrent expenditure for education.

The World Bank argues that the crisis was brought on by drought and higher import prices. Villagization played some role, but it is hard to quantify the impact.

The World Bank staff assessed the possibilities for increasing nontraditional exports—processing sisal and other agricultural goods and producing instant coffee, textiles, and leather goods—and concluded that there were very limited possibilities for nontraditional exports. At the present time, 80 percent of Tanzania's exports are of agricultural goods, and this is likely to remain true in the near term. Expansion of traditional exports was seen as crucial for dealing with the balance-of-payments crisis.

However, the government has not encouraged production of traditional export crops because that policy reflected colonialism and dependency. When the balance-of-payments crisis hit in 1974–75, the government was forced to borrow heavily from foreign governments and aid agencies. Is this not dependency? Would Tanzania be better off if it had encouraged export crops in the first place?

The World Bank policy package for Tanzania included the following recommendations.

1. The first focus was on redistribution of resources to directly productive projects. The World Bank was concerned with the high percentage of the development budget going to social services and to infrastructure—particularly the railroad from Dar es Salaam to Zambia. (Even though this railroad was undertaken for political reasons—to free Zambia from reliance on Rhodesia and South Africa—it is now finished and earning foreign exchange.) The government responded well to this recommendation and expanded industrial investment. It will take time to see the results. The World Bank is still concerned about the efficiency of these operations, however, and argues that it is now time for consolidation and improvement of existing activities rather than for new industrial undertakings. The government also increased investment in agriculture. But the problems in agriculture do not relate to money. The record on investment in agriculture is very good. The problem is organizational, and the solution will take time.

2. The second focus was on raising agricultural producer prices. The government had subsidized urban consumption through low prices for food. The World Bank staff traced through the implications of this policy on food production. The World Bank and the UNDP provided technical assistance to the pricing commission in the Ministry of Agriculture. The World Bank was satisfied with Tanzanian performance on prices. The record was impressive. The response to increased prices for maize and cassava was dramatic, and a surplus of both crops developed. There were inadequate storage facilities, but the government was reluctant to lower producer prices or to export the surplus.

3. The third World Bank recommendation concerned demand. The World Bank argued against the minimum-wage increase of 1974 even though the staff recognized that urban workers were getting squeezed. The result of the minimum-wage increase was as the World Bank predicted—a rapid increase in prices. Later, the government accepted the World Bank's argument, and there has been virtually no increase in the minimum wage in the past five years. The World Bank wanted to tie wage increases to increased worker productivity to increase incentives. But incentives was a dirty word in Tanzania five years ago. Now the Treasury is linking wage increases to productivity increases. Piece rates and cash bonuses are being adopted.

4. A fourth recommendation concerned other attempts to reduce private consumption. These policies included reducing imported nonfood consumer goods; passing higher import costs on to final consumers; raising user charges for water; increasing taxes on textiles, beer, and cigarettes; and banning Sunday driving.

When the coffee price boom hit and export earnings soared, the World Bank argued that the government should liberalize imports—especially of spare parts and raw materials so as to allow fuller utilization of industrial capacity. The government did so and thus exacerbated the balance-of-payments problem. The World Bank staff feels that the increased imports will ultimately lead to increased production.

The World Bank staff argues that there is still a long-term export problem that calls for a new set of policies.

1. There is a need for organizational adjustments to improve delivery of inputs to the agricultural sector. The government should allow the private sector to deliver certain services, particularly truck transportation. The decision in 1976 to abolish agricultural cooperatives and replace them with parastatals led to a significant reduction in efficiency and a consequent reduction in production of some export crops, particularly coffee. The efficiency of the extension service has also declined. Necessary credit is not always available.

2. There is evidence that the private sector is being reinvigorated. The role of the private sector has been clarified. Nyerere gave the signal in "The Arusha Declaration: Ten Years After."[21] The World Bank is preparing a tourism project in Tanzania. Private industry is being encour-

21. Nyerere, "The Arusha Declaration."

aged. Some government firms have been denationalized. The International Finance Corporation (a World Bank subsidiary that makes equity investments in private firms) is now back in Tanzania.

So, all in all, the World Bank staff was satisfied with Tanzania's stabilization strategy. The main problem was lack of attention to exports. This area requires longer-term policy changes, some of which are already underway.

Rightist Critique

A third critique has emerged that blames the economic crises of the 1970s on the economic policies of the government. Michael Lofchie analyzed the limited meteorological data available and concluded that the country did suffer a serious shortage of rainfall in the late summer months of 1973. He thinks it plausible that this drought could have reduced the maize crop by about 20 percent, equal to the share usually marketed. However, Lofchie does not accept the argument that the severe drought continued in 1974. He presents data to support his argument that in 1974, rainfall was well within normally adequate amounts.[22]

Lofchie holds that the 1974–75 crisis was one of a series of crises facing Tanzania in the 1970s that were brought on primarily by bad policy and exacerbated by the drought and higher import prices. According to this argument, the periods of 1970–71, 1974–75, and 1978–79 must be seen as the norm. The aberrant years were 1972–73 and 1976–77, when there were no balance-of-payments crises. The cause of this decade-long crisis was a series of bad policies—primarily the attempts to establish communual agriculture in the Ujamaa villages and the failure to encourage production of traditional export crops.

Lofchie correlates the drop in agricultural production with the effort to move people into Ujamaa villages. He shows the relationship between the establishment of villages and the necessity to import maize. Since maize is the basic food crop in Tanzania, imports of maize are seen as a good proxy for subsistence food crop production. He argues that imports rose in 1971–72, when there was no drought, because of peasant resistance to villagization, communal farming, low producer prices, and other misguided policies. The same pattern held in 1973–74, until the government abandoned communal farming and raised producer prices. The

22. Lofchie, "Agrarian Socialism," pp. 462–63.

balance-of-payments crises of 1970–71, 1974–75, and 1978–79 must also be seen as resulting from the poor performance of the export sector.

Tanzania has had an ambitious development program. To accomplish the social goals, the gross domestic product must increase 5 to 6 percent per year. This growth requires sizable imports. Throughout the period 1965–75, imports were a minimum of 25 percent of gross domestic product. In 1971–75, imports were 30 percent to 35 percent of GDP.

Most of these imports were destined for the development effort. From 1967 to 1975, 40 to 45 percent of imports were intermediate goods, and 20 to 30 percent were capital goods. Except for the drought years, consumer goods constituted 30 percent or less of imports in the 1970s.

Thus the pace of development clearly depends on increasing imports. To pay for these imports, Tanzania must export or rely on the generosity of foreign aid donors. But there has been no emphasis on increasing production of export crops. The development plans have focused on import substitution and industrialization. Even the massive agricultural effort in 1975–76 focused on increasing production of food crops. Traditional exports have suffered. The threat of villagization and communal farming stifled investment and production in export crops. Cashew trees were abandoned in the move to villages. Producer prices, input subsidies, and input availability all favored food crops over export crops. The government was hostile to the better-off farmers who grew export crops and refused to assist them. Critics of the Tanzanian government conclude that even in 1979, the government had not learned the importance of exports. The stabilization effort was a failure in that it neglected to deal with these fundamental causes of the crisis.

Lofchie argues that most of the agricultural surplus (especially in export crops) had been generated by the larger, progressive, and prosperous farmers. The government mistakenly identified income inequality in the rural sector with exploitation. Thus efforts to reduce the land holdings and the incomes of these wealthier farmers have been misdirected. Such efforts have reduced total agricultural production (especially of export crops) and have drastically reduced the marketable surplus. Tanzanian peasants have practiced communal ownership of land but not communal farming or communal distribution, according to Lofchie. Nyerere's efforts to establish such communal farming are based on a misreading of the past and have antagonized those with medium and small farms as well as the richer farmers. Until such misdirected efforts are dropped, there is little hope for agricultural production to increase significantly. Thus another balance-of-payments crisis in 1978–79 followed on the heels of the one in 1974–75.

Lofchie argues that allowing progressive farmers to expand their operations is the most efficient way to transform traditional agriculture and could be consistent with a socialist economy. Several Eastern European socialist countries (Poland, Hungary, Czechoslovakia, and Yugoslavia) have virtually abandoned collective agriculture. Income redistribution can take place through taxes on the rich farmers to subsidize agricultural inputs and social services that benefit small farmers.

Inefficiency of governmental administration contributed significantly to the decline in agricultural production in 1974–75. The villagization effort was organized poorly, disrupted production, moved people away from productive tree crops, located villages where there was inadequate water and on soil that was quickly depleted by intensive cultivation, led to deforestation as people cut the wood for firewood, and led to soil erosion and drought as intensive cultivation and deforestation combined to disrupt the water cycle and the previous pattern of shifting cultivation, fallow periods, and so forth.

In addition to problems arising from villagization, there were disruptions in the transportation of agricultural inputs and products as a result of socialization of the transport sector. Farmers wasted fertilizer that was distributed on a subsidized basis. The extension service was ineffective.

Retail trade shops were nationalized and were inefficiently run. Few consumer goods were available for peasants to purchase—so there was little incentive to increase production because there was nothing to buy with the increased income. The threat of socialization of retail trade still hangs like a dark cloud over the retailers and keeps them from saving and investing in their businesses. They carry minimum inventories because they fear nationalization. They send their profits out of the country as fast as possible, thereby contributing to the balance-of-payments deficit.

TOURISM. Tourism could be a great source of foreign exchange earnings, but socialists have argued that rich tourists would undermine socialist values and spread the ideology of consumerism. Thus the vast game parks, Mt. Kilimanjaro, and the Ngorongoro Crater—the greatest tourist attractions in Africa—remain undeveloped. The expensive airport at Kilimanjaro, and the game park hotels operate at far less than capacity. The tourism policy is seen as another socialist idiocy.

INDUSTRY. Perhaps the most searing criticism of Tanzanian socialism centers on the industrial sector. Almost all observers of Tanzanian industry agree that most government-owned firms are inefficient in terms of worker productivity. Wages have not been related to production. Management rewards have not been linked to firm profitability. Much time is lost due to party activities, parades, and so forth.

Interest rates are kept low, which discourages saving. Interest rates are not used to allocate capital to efficient and profitable firms. Instead, capital is allocated on the basis of planners' preferences, and low interest rates are charged to all firms. Raising interest rates and allocating capital to the firms that can use the capital most profitably could be consistent with a socialist economy, as is illustrated in Yugoslavia.

BASIC INDUSTRY STRATEGY. The orthodox argue that the greatest idiocy of all is the basic industry strategy announced in the third five-year plan (1976–81).[23] The goal of this strategy is to achieve industrial self-reliance by 1995. Other considerations are to establish industries that can manufacture exportable products, use local resources, produce substitutes for imports, increase employment, and be established on a small scale.

The allocation of industrial capital for the third five-year plan is as follows:[24] steel industry 7.6 percent; chemical industry 8.6 percent; food and drink industry 19.1 percent; paper and timber industry 19.1 percent; non-steel and building construction industry 15.6 percent; cotton, hides, skins, and sisal industries 27.6 percent; and other industries and industrial services 2.5 percent.

The alternative industrialization strategy considered was the "efficiency strategy." This strategy would have (1) minimized the opportunity cost of factors of production and maximized value added measured at world (border) prices and (2) produced greater value added and greater employment than the basic industry strategy. However, the basic industry strategy was selected because of the great emphasis placed on industrial self-reliance. It must be pointed out that there was a large core of industries common to both strategies.[25]

Never was the cost of socialist ideology (the red man's burden) more apparent than in the choice of the basic industry strategy. In the face of a worldwide surplus of steel, with no hope of being able to produce steel as cheaply as it could be imported, and with a long record of inefficiency

23. United Republic of Tanzania, *Third Five-Year Plan*.
24. Ibid., pp. 86–87.
25. Michael Roemer, Gene M. Tidrick, and David Williams, "The Range of Strategic Choice in Tanzanian Industry," *Ekistics*, no. 259 (June 1979).

and underutilized capacity in government-run industries, the government of Tanzania is going to build a steel industry and aim for industrial self-reliance. Rightists ask, "when a decision like that was made in 1976, what hope can there be for advocates of economic rationality in Tanzania?"

APPROPRIATE SHORT-TERM RESPONSE. Advocates of economic orthodoxy argue that the immediate response to the balance-of-payments crisis should have been a sizable devaluation of the currency—perhaps as much as 50 percent.[26] Ideally, a flexible exchange rate would have been adopted, exchange controls would have been dropped, tariffs would be reduced over time, and markets would be allowed to allocate foreign exchange and determine what goods were imported.

Tanzania had no business trying to control every aspect of foreign trade and every unit of foreign currency. Market mechanisms can do that more efficiently and with a great saving of managerial and organizational talent—perhaps the scarcest resource in Tanzania.

If the government had devalued the currency and allowed flexible exchange rates, firms and parastatals could have bought the foreign exchange for necessary imports of spare parts and raw materials and avoided the delay and underutilization of capacity that resulted from the exchange control system. Market allocation of foreign exchange would also have avoided the black markets and rampant corruption that developed in the wake of the foreign exchange crisis and governmental efforts at allocation. This corruption has seriously undermined morale among the citizens.

APPROPRIATE LONG-TERM RESPONSE. Orthodox critics would argue that the stabilization program should have moved toward broad structural changes in the economy if it was to be successful. These changes would have included encouraging production of traditional export crops; encouraging entrepreneurial farmers to expand their operations; letting agricultural prices be set at world market levels; letting interest rates be set by demand and supply; using markets to channel savings to their most profitable use; denationalizing truck transportation and retail trade; setting wages to reflect worker productivity and management salaries to reflect firm profitability; letting the market set prices for the products of government-owned firms; letting inefficient government enterprises go bankrupt and/or be sold to private investors; setting user fees for high-cost public services such as water and education; giving regions, districts, and villages the capacity to raise tax revenues to pay for some of their own

26. The black market rate was approximately T Sh 12 = $1 in 1974–75, whereas the official rate was approximately T Sh 8 = $1.

services and thus limit the expansion of recurrent expenditures at the national level; reducing the expansion of the money supply and the monetizing of the government deficit; keeping the minimum wage from rising, thus reducing labor's share of national income and thereby increasing the surplus available for investment; inviting foreign capital to find and develop the country's minerals; encouraging tourism; and abandoning the basic industry strategy of building steel mills, etc., and instead invest in those efficient industries in which Tanzania has a comparative or potential comparative advantage.

Conclusions

There is a kernel of truth in each critique presented in the previous section. We agree that the shift to "pragmatism" represents a measured retreat from the heady march into socialism. The most striking example was the abandonment of communal farming. We agree that the government had a clear stabilization program and carried it out with considerable success. The short-term results were impressive. We agree also with the authors of the UNDP report that Tanzania was fortunate because it was able to borrow substantial sums on a concessional basis.

We agree that there was something of a zero-sum game in the performance of the Tanzanian economy. As food crop production went up, export crop production went down—leading to a new balance-of-payments crisis. The stabilization strategy was deficient in that it put almost sole emphasis on reducing imports and almost no emphasis on increasing exports.

There is some validity to the rightist argument that the Tanzanian economy has been mismanaged. A socialist economy requires extensive planning and organizational talent from skilled manpower, which in Tanzania is a scarce resource.

One alternative for dealing with scarce skilled labor power and managerial ability would be to make more use of private enterprise and markets within an overall socialist framework. The Tanzanian government is moving very slowly in this direction.

However, there is great reluctance to rely on private enterprise and markets. This reluctance stems from the analysis of the political economy of private enterprise and markets rather than from an economic analysis. Some Tanzanians argue that reliance on capitalist agriculture and market socialism would probably lead to increased economic and therefore to greater political power for rich farmers, retail traders, and bureaucratic elites. Eventually, these groups would abandon the socialist goals of equality and participation. So a rather small part of economic policy, such as stabilization policy, must be seen from the larger political economy perspective.

As an alternative to private enterprise and markets as a way of dealing with the scarcity of skilled manpower and managerial capacity, the government is trying to create more skilled managers and technicians. Much of the expenditure on education can be defended on the grounds that it is designed to break the bottleneck of scarce human capital.

Our study raises several issues that deserve further analysis.

1. What are the economic prospects for the developing countries following a non-Marxist socialist development path? John Gurley argues that the Marxist socialist developing countries have experienced a more rapid rate of economic growth than comparable capitalist developing countries and also have a better record of meeting basic needs for food, clothing, medical care, and so forth.[27] So there is apparently nothing inherently inefficient in the socialist model of development. And yet many of the non-Marxist socialist developing countries have faced extraordinary economic difficulties, particularly balance-of-payments crises (Jamaica, Allende's Chile, Guyana, Sri Lanka). Most of these countries are so small that they cannot follow a self-reliant development model like China. They do not have Cuba's client relationship with the Soviet Union, so they must rely on trade with the capitalist countries for necessary imports of capital goods. This reliance has presented great difficulties.

2. The cumulative effect of the Lofchie analysis is that the balance-of-payments problem is not within the realm of "should have done this, shouldn't have done that" but rather that the whole institutional framework is unsound. Lofchie argues that capitalist agriculture is a far more efficient means of transforming traditional agriculture than is communal farming. He argues that taxes can be imposed on prosperous farmers to reduce income inequality while utilizing the incentives private enterprise provides. This is a powerful argument. Can an effective alternative to capitalist agriculture be developed in Tanzania?

3. The growth of per capita GNP in Tanzania has been quite respect-

27. John Gurley, "Economic Development: A Marxist View," in Charles K. Wilber and Kenneth P. Jameson, eds., *Directions in Development* (Notre Dame University Press, 1979).

able for a low-income country (2.6 percent per year from 1960 to 1977).[28] Tanzania has out-performed all but six of the thirty-seven low-income countries analyzed in the 1979 *World Development Report,* including neighboring Kenya.[29] Yet many observers argue that the Tanzanian model of development is a failure. Is the perception based on reality? What are the appropriate criteria to use in measuring success?

4. Can the socialist countries come up with an alternative to the IMF? Or can the IMF be reformed to allow for pluralist development models?

5. Is there hope for commodity price stabilization schemes, common funds, and so forth to overcome the great instability of export earnings that makes development planning difficult? The Tanzanian experience is an excellent example of the need for such reforms.

6. Critiquing the Tanzanian government's stabilization policies in the 1970s is like evaluating the rowing techniques of a person cast adrift in a rowboat in the Atlantic Ocean. The international economy was so chaotic in the 1970s that even the richest country in the world—the United States —was unable to successfully manage its economy. To expect very poor countries to cope with these problems within the present international economic order is unrealistic and naive. Will another set of crises like the Great Depression and World War II be necessary before we restructure the international system? This is *the* question for the 1980s.

Comments by G. K. Helleiner

Without minimizing the unique features and difficulties of longer-term Tanzanian development efforts, I believe that we can take the 1974–75 experience in Tanzania as a case study. The Tanzanian case is peculiarly interesting for comparative study of economic stabilization policies in developing countries for the following reasons:

1. Tanzania is very poor, a least-developed country, with little prospect of significant borrowing from foreign private banks.

2. For a number of reasons—poverty, ideology, resource base—foreign direct investment has not recently been a major source of finance.

3. Tanzania's macroeconomic management, until the major shocks of 1974–75, has been "sound," cautious, and orthodox with resulting very

28. World Bank, *World Development Report 1979* (Washington, D.C.: World Bank, 1979), p. 126.
29. Ibid.

modest rates of inflation, reasonable rates of monetary expansion, adequate foreign exchange reserves, and a low debt-servicing ratio; management quality was considered to be fairly high.

4. The Tanzanian government is unusually committed to improving the equity of income distribution while continuing to pursue economic growth and development.

5. Tanzania experienced a severe short-term balance-of-payments shock in 1974–75 because of a combination of exogenous circumstances —food, oil, and other price increases and successive droughts—following which Tanzania was able to return, more or less, to its previous "track."

Tanzania's situation can therefore show what can generally be done to "stabilize" a poor country faced with large short-term shocks outside its own control by a reasonably efficient and honestly managed government whose concern over distributional equity (now much more fashionable than when Tanzania first announced it) is beyond dispute.

I do not believe that it is helpful, for the purpose of analyzing stabilization policies, to characterize Tanzanian government primarily in terms of its "socialist" or "unorthodox" policies. The pragmatic Tanzanian mix of policies on reserve use, foreign assistance, domestic pricing, government revenues and expenditures, and import controls constituted a fairly "normal" policy response to balance-of-payments pressures. Despite Tanzania's socialism, the effects were also "normal."

What *may* be of special interest, however, is the impact of Tanzanian stabilization policies on income distribution, which was a major concern of the government. Tanzania's experience may shed light on the "conventional wisdom" in this area of growing general interest.

In the case of the 1974–75 shock, beginning with the 58 percent increase in import value in 1974 and a consequent quadrupling of the current account deficit, the size and timing of the adjustment required in the Tanzanian economy depended, first, upon the extent and nature of assistance from abroad. As has been seen, Tanzania could expect little financing either from foreign private banks or from direct investors who might be impressed by any major new attempt to "restore confidence." Foreign financing had to come from official sources. The full story of such official financing has, unfortunately, not been told. Beyond those drawings that were virtually automatic (including some under the oil facility), Tanzania received no further assistance from the International Monetary Fund (IMF). Weaver and Anderson suggest that conditionality was responsible for Tanzania's failure to obtain more from the IMF, but they cannot tell us exactly what the relevant conditions or the crucial points of disagreement were. The authors imply that these conditions had to do with income distribution, the exchange rate, and the required speed of adjustment based on assessments of the likelihood and timing of recovery. If Tanzania *did* successfully adjust with its distributional objectives intact and *did* shortly thereafter successfully recover, and if IMF conditions *were* those described by the authors, then we would seem to have a case of IMF miscalculation and overrigidity as well as "success" of the country's own adjustment policy.

There is another fascinating strand to the foreign financing in Tanzania's case. At the same time that, for one reason or another, the IMF was refusing further credit to Tanzania, the World Bank (actually the International Development Association) decided to extend a program loan of almost the same size as the remaining Tanzanian upper credit tranche drawing rights in the IMF. (Obviously, this was a longer-term, softer loan than the IMF could have offered.) It seems that the World Bank view of Tanzanian stabilization policies was one that, in the language of the later (1979) IMF directive, took into account "the domestic political and social objectives of its members" and, to quote the present IMF managing director at Manila, allowed for "varying speeds of adjustment." Weaver and Anderson suggest that Tanzania took the World Bank's advice—especially on the redirection of government expenditure toward directly productive activities, and the raising of agricultural producer prices—and that Tanzania thus merely settled for World Bank, rather than IMF, conditions. The fact that the World Bank apparently disagreed with Tanzanian wage policy suggests, however, that Tanzanian stabilization policy was to some extent independently formulated, and that conditionality *was* reduced, rather than just altered in content, through the World Bank's lending. In any case, it is clear that the size of the required Tanzanian adjustment to the 1974–75 shock was thereby substantially reduced. It does not seem likely that the increased *bilateral* aid, which apparently occurred at this time as well, was in any way a "response" to the balance-of-payments crisis.

It is tempting to infer that the World Bank, newly concerned with income distribution, was at this time especially sympathetic to Tanzania's objectives. Consciously or not, the World Bank may have provided us with a test case (one which the IMF of the time may still have been unwilling to provide) of whether, with IMF-style support, short-term stabilization policies *can* have more equitable effects. In any case, in hindsight, the World Bank appears wiser than the IMF in its stabilization policies toward Tanzania.

In light of major cutbacks and redirection in government expenditures, the increase in taxes, the wage freeze, and the imposition of stringent import controls in 1974–75, it seems a little wishful to say that "Tanzania successfully avoided a general deflationary program." It is important to try to assess the overall distributional consequences of the Tanzanian adjustment program. The consensus is that in the seven or eight years after the Arusha Declaration, the government of Tanzania had already considerably narrowed intraurban after-tax incomes and had at least prevented intrarural or urban-rural differentials from widening at the previous pace. These results were achieved through determined political leadership, but also through political pressures from urban workers and cash crop farmers. This political pressure from below continued to influence the formation of government policy. How equitably was the burden of Tanzanian adjustment shared?

Weaver and Anderson's statement of Tanzanian objectives is correct in this regard, but their analysis of what actually transpired is less than totally convincing. The Weaver-Anderson (qualified) argument that the poorest were successfully shielded from the cost of stabilization policies rests upon the inference that the rural-urban gap narrowed (presumably *after* the 40 percent increase in the urban minimum wage in 1974). That inference is itself based on "the increase in producer prices, relief food, and the educational and water campaigns," all of which "favored the rural population," and the fact that "Wage restraint, reduced employment, increased food prices and taxes, and consumption restrictions considerably reduced the urban sector's real income." I would render a more Scotch verdict on the distribution of the overall burden of the decrease in Tanzanian real income of these years for the following reasons.

RURAL SECTOR

1. The government's announced increase in grower prices for food may not have raised farm incomes (or intrarural differentiation) or lowered urban incomes as much as it seems, since a high proportion of sales of these products was on black markets beforehand. However, privately traded goods were deflected to official marketing channels and storage facilities, so that some private traders' incomes were lowered. Although the production response was not as great as that in officially marketed surplus, it was probably significantly positive.

2. The impact of the food imports associated with the drought requires

careful analysis. It cannot be assumed that the sole, or even the principal, beneficiaries were the poorest rural dwellers, as Weaver and Anderson seem to believe. Typically, the depressing effects on urban food prices are important elements in relief food imports.

3. While there may have been an attempt to redirect education and water expenditures toward rural areas, the effect of this redirection would take some time to register. Moreover, government nonproductive expenditures were being severely cut back, so that the total change was probably small. The authors also note a subsequent breakdown in rural water supply systems due to inadequate maintenance during the stabilization period.

URBAN SECTOR. As for the urban economy, demonstration that real incomes fell obviously does not constitute proof that either relative or absolute urban-rural differentials decreased as well, at a time when overall incomes were falling. There are also some questions about changes in the intraurban distribution of income. While it is true that the 1974 wage increase was proportionately higher for minimum-wage earners than for medium- and higher-level wage earners, one must also take account of (1) wage changes in the informal, or unorganized, sector, on which there are no firm data; (2) the effect of relative price changes, that is, differential rates of price increase, upon different income groups, on which there are some figures; and (3) the level of urban employment, which fell.

Wages in the unorganized sector probably changed very little when the 40 percent minimum-wage increase took effect, although one cannot be sure of this. Since workers in this sector (including the newly unemployed) are generally at the bottom in the urban income distribution and, at least in Dar es Salaam, they, like the minimum-wage earners, experienced more rapid price increases for the items consumed in these years than did medium-level income earners (see table 10-7). Controls and increased duties on luxury imports undoubtedly, however, hit the highest-income earners harder than middle-income earners.

My guess is therefore that *the highest and the lowest* portions of the urban income distribution spectrum bore more than their share of the adjustment burden. The highest-income earners continued to bear the relatively high burdens (compared to, say, their Kenyan counterparts) that Tanzanian leadership and ideology demanded. But the organized and middle-level portions of the urban work force may have protected themselves more successfully at the expense of other, less-fortunate, urban and rural dwellers. My "surmises," however, are unfortunately no more

Table 10-7. *Annual Percentage Increase in Dar es Salaam Prices*

Year	Retail price index, wage earners (T Sh 2,000 to T Sh 4,000 a year) (percent)	Cost-of-living index, middle-grade civil servants (T Sh 8,000 to T Sh 20,000 a year) (percent)
1973–74	32	25
1974–75	49	34
1975–76	21	11
1976–77	17	12
1973–77	178	108

Source: Calculated from Bank of Tanzania, *Economic and Operations Report* (September 1978), vol. 10, p. 45.

conclusive than those of Weaver and Anderson. We need more data and more careful study to be certain. That Tanzania (with World Bank help) outguessed the IMF in 1974–75 is a foregone conclusion, whatever else we eventually conclude about the distribution of domestic adjustment costs.

Discussion

James Adams (World Bank) called the 1974–75 stabilization program a good one that the World Bank supported; by 1976, higher coffee prices helped as well. By mid-1978, crisis had returned because of declining price and volume for coffee exports, and war in Uganda aggravated the situation. Adams emphasized the importance of raising prices of food crops, commending the government for the adoption of a more realistic pricing policy, but noting that Tanzania still had not solved the crucial problem of raising the overall agricultural growth rate above population growth rate.

Stephen O'Brien (World Bank) made it clear that there had been no dispute between the World Bank and the IMF leading to lending by one but not the other. In 1974 both responded rapidly to the Tanzanian crisis, the IMF with a credit of 50 million Special Drawing Rights. In 1975 Tanzania and the IMF reached agreement on lending through a higher IMF tranche with conditionality, but Tanzania did not draw on these resources because the country did not meet the targets it had accepted, leading to some strain between Tanzania and the IMF. O'Brien noted more recent problems with deficits because of heavy government spending commitments.

CHAPTER ELEVEN

Stabilization Policies in Pakistan: The 1970–77 Experience

STEPHEN E. GUISINGER

BEFORE 1970, stabilization was not a major concern of economic planners in Pakistan. The fundamental economic problem of Pakistan was at that time, and will remain for the foreseeable future, the achievement of an acceptable rate of sustained economic growth. Price inflation was exceptionally moderate by world standards. The problems of both unemployment and disequilibriums in the balance of payments were of a structural rather than a cyclical character. From time to time, war or adverse weather unsettled the economic system, but these shocks were only temporary and were dealt with by ad hoc measures.

In 1970, conditions changed. The first five years of the decade were marked by political and economic turmoil arising both from within the country and from without. Inflation, which had averaged less than 3 percent per annum in the previous decade, jumped to an annual rate of 30 percent in 1973–74. The gross national product (GDP) gyrated wildly, rising from an average of 1 percent per annum in 1970–71 and 1971–72 to around 7 percent in 1972–73 before falling back in 1973–74 and 1974–75. The balance-of-trade deficit fell to as low as 3.1 percent of GDP in 1972–73 before rising to 11.6 percent two years later. In 1975–76 and 1976–77 the rate of inflation tapered off, although fluctuations in national output persisted.

This study attempts to sort out the government role in destabilizing the economy, especially the price level, and then in contributing to stabilization. So diverse were the forces of destabilization during the 1970–77 period that it is analytically impossible to clearly distinguish the role of

The author is grateful for suggestions and assistance from Ashraf Janjua, Dr. A. H. Niazi, and Jawaid Asfar. None, of course, should be held responsible for the final product.

government from other factors influencing the economy. Nevertheless, the government's strategies of monetary and fiscal policy to combat inflation and recession can be described, even though their effectiveness cannot be determined with a high degree of accuracy. However, before these policies are discussed, a brief sketch of Pakistan's development before 1970 is needed to put the government's actions in proper perspective.

Pakistan's Development, 1950–70

Pakistan was widely regarded as an economic wasteland when it was carved out of the subcontinent in 1947. During the first decade of its existence, the country did little to belie the skeptics. Agriculture stagnated in the face of meager incentives for farmers to improve productivity through the use of water and fertilizer. Manufacturing grew at astonishingly high rates but from a very small base. However, when the contribution of manufacturing is measured in world market prices instead of domestic prices inflated by tariffs and quota restrictions, real manufacturing growth was almost nonexistent. Inflation was modest during the decade of the 1950s, with the price level edging upward at a 2 percent per annum rate. The largest surge of inflation came on the heels of the 1955 devaluation, and on at least two occasions during the decade, the price level fell, an event that unfortunately was never to be repeated.

A major shift in Pakistan's economic policies that brought a marked improvement in economic performance occurred around the beginning of the 1960s. The internal terms of trade were shifted in favor of agriculture, and farmers responded by making extensive investments in tubewells to supply irrigation water and by purchasing fertilizers and pesticides. Toward the middle of the decade, the "green revolution" took hold, and agricultural productivity climbed still further. The average annual rate of growth of agriculture during the 1960s was 4 percent, far greater than anyone anticipated for such a poverty-stricken country with few natural resources.

Manufacturing continued to grow but at rates below those achieved in the previous decade. Industrial profits began to sag as easy opportunities for import substitution disappeared. Manufacturing for export became more attractive, compared to production for the domestic market, with the introduction of an export subsidy scheme known as bonus vouchers.

These vouchers represented entitlements to foreign exchange, which were freely transferable and commanded a considerable premium on the open market because of the scarcity of imports maintained by the exchange control system.

The rate of inflation averaged 3.3 percent during the decade of the 1960s. The major source of inflation during this decade apparently was not the rapid acceleration in the growth rate but rather disruptions caused by the 1965 war with India and two successive years of poor harvests.

Although marred by the military confrontation with India, the decade of the 1960s, in retrospect, was the golden age of Pakistan's development. In 1970 it appeared that the stage was set for a continuation of rapid growth with relatively stable prices experienced during the previous decade.

The Stabilization Problem

The decade of the 1970s proved to be one of slow growth under un-stabilized conditions. The major symptom of destabilization during the 1970–77 period was accelerating inflation. Prices began to climb in 1971–72, first reflected in the wholesale price index, as seen in table 11-1. Prices continued to rise until 1973–74, when they peaked at an approximately 30 percent per annum rate. Inflation eased the following year and then dropped sharply in 1975–76, leveling off at around 10 percent in 1976–77.

Caution must be exercised in interpreting these rates of inflation because for some products only official prices, not open market prices, were reported; for still other products, prices were officially fixed, but supplies were unavailable at those prices. For a number of years, there have been dual markets for wheat and sugar: a public market in which goods are rationed at fixed prices, and a private market in which prices are set by supply and demand. Whenever stocks in the ration shops are inadequate to meet consumer demand, open market prices escalate and the shift of consumers into the open market is not captured by the consumer price index. The products where the government attempted serious price control constitute less than one-quarter of the budget of the typical urban consumer. But the incidence of inflation is quite different between urban and rural areas, since ration shops do not exist outside urban areas.

Table 11-1. *Inflation, National Income, and the Balance of Trade, 1970–77*

Item	1970–71	1971–72	1972–73	1973–74	1974–75	1975–76	1976–77
Prices	*Annual percentage increase*						
Wholesale price index	4	10	20	28	26	11	11
Consumer price index	6	5	10	30	27	12	9
GDP deflator	4	6	14	27	20	15	10
Gross domestic product	1.3	0.6	8.6	1.9	7.6	1.7	1.7
Constant market prices of 1969–70	0.1	1.0	7.0	6.8	1.9	3.8	0.8
Balance of trade	*Millions of U.S. dollars*						
Exports of goods and services	n.a.	723	920	1,238	1,289	1,461	1,437
Imports of goods and services	n.a.	1,259	1,195	1,938	2,686	2,706	3,079
Balance	n.a.	−536	−275	−700	−1,397	−1,245	−1,642

Source: Prices, *Monthly Statistical Bulletin*, Government of Pakistan. National income, *Economic Survey, 1978–79* (Islamabad: Government of Pakistan, 1979). Balance of trade, State Bank of Pakistan. A fiscal year for Pakistan runs from July 1 to June 30. Since indices for a fiscal year represent an average over the July–June period, changes over a previous year reflect increases over approximately the January–December period.
n.a. Not available.

National output fluctuated sharply during the 1970–77 period. The rates of growth of gross domestic product in 1970–71 and 1971–72 were very low—around 1 percent in each year—and far below the average rate of growth achieved during the previous decade. In 1972–73, output soared, expanding by more than 7 percent. What happened the following years is subject to considerable statistical controversy: estimates of growth in GDP at market prices vary from a low of 1.9 percent to a high of 6.8 percent, and one estimate of GDP at factor prices put the increase at 7.7 percent. The data for the following year are equally confusing; some estimates show a sharp rebound in national output, while others show a continuing decline. What is clear is that the average expansion during the two years—1973–74 and 1974–75—is below the 1972–73 expansion but well above the slow growth of 1970–71 and 1971–72. Moderate growth continued in 1975–76, but the rate slipped somewhat in 1976–77. In all years except 1972–73, actual output expansion fell short of planned expansion, and perhaps most crucially, in five of the seven years, actual increases in gross national product were at or below population growth.

As for the balance of trade, the gap between imports and exports widened sharply in 1973–74, as shown in table 11-2. The constant price data in the same table indicate that the increase in the foreign deficit was due almost entirely to the deterioration in the terms of trade. In 1969–70 prices the postdevaluation deficits in the years after the price increase were actually lower than the deficits registered during 1970–71 and 1971–72. The rising deficits were financed by substantial increases in foreign assistance in 1973–74 and 1974–75, first from the Pakistan consortium and then from nonconsortium countries (mainly, the OPEC countries) whose aid increased eightfold in 1974–75 compared with the 1970–73 average. Together, consortium and nonconsortium aid disbursements increased sixfold between 1972–73 and 1974–75—from $146 million to $878 million.

Sources of Destabilization

The decade of the 1970s was tumultuous for all developing countries, but Pakistan may have a fair claim for having absorbed a greater variety and a greater intensity of shocks than other developing countries. Many of the destabilizing forces were outside Pakistan's control, and efforts at stabilization of prices, output, and the balance of trade were vexed by

Table 11-2. *Components of National Expenditure*

Billions of rupees

Component	1969–70	1970–71	1971–72	1972–73	1973–74	1974–75	1975–76	1976–77
					Current prices			
1. Consumption (C)	38.6	40.7	42.4	52.2	72.3	93.8	104.7	118.0
2. Investment (I)	7.5	7.9	7.7	11.6	18.2	22.9	27.1	…
3. Public consumption (G)	4.8	5.2	6.5	7.7	8.5	12.0	13.9	15.6
4. External balance (X − M)	−3.3	−3.5	−2.7	−2.1	−6.2	−12.9	−11.4	−15.1
5. GDP	47.7	50.4	53.8	66.5	86.2	111.1	130.0	145.6
6. Consumption deflator	100.0	105.7	110.7	121.5	157.7	199.0	223.0	242.3
7. Investment deflator	100.0	108.0	137.7	231.4	285.0	330.6	337.9	389.6
8. Public consumption deflator	100.0	106.1	111.3	123.9	159.3	201.7	227.2	250.0
9. Current surplus	…	0.5	0.2	−0.4	−0.5	−3.1	−2.5	−0.4
10. Expansionary financing	…	0.5	1.3	1.5	0.5	2.0	3.9	5.6
					Constant 1969–70 prices			
11. Consumption (C)	38.6	38.5	38.3	43.0	45.8	47.2	46.9	48.7
12. Investment (I)	7.5	7.3	5.7	4.1	4.3	5.9	6.8	7.1
13. Public consumption (G)	4.8	5.0	5.8	6.2	5.4	5.9	6.4	6.2
14. Home goods $X_h = C + I + G$	50.9	50.8	49.8	53.3	55.5	59.0	59.8	62.0
15. External balance	−3.3	−2.5	−1.1	−0.6	−1.7	−1.1	−0.9	−2.1
16. Exports	n.a.	n.a.	3.1	3.5	2.7	3.0	3.5	2.8
17. Imports	n.a.	n.a.	4.2	4.1	4.4	4.1	4.4	4.9
18. GDP at market prices	47.7	48.3	48.6	52.8	53.8	57.9	58.9	60.0
19. Current surplus	n.a.	0.5	0.2	−0.3	−0.3	1.5	0.9	−0.2
20. Expansionary financing	n.a.	0.5	1.2	1.2	0.3	1.0	1.4	2.2
21. Expansionary financing as percent of GDP (100 × row 20 ÷ row 18)	…	1.0	2.5	2.3	0.6	1.9	2.4	3.7
22. Growth of GDP at market prices (percent)	…	1.3	0.6	8.6	1.9	7.6	1.7	1.7

Source: Planning and Development Division, Ministry of Finance.
n.a. Not available.

the persistence of these external factors. The major "nonpolicy" factors responsible for inflation, output fluctuations, and the widening trade deficit were weather, separation of East Pakistan, and world economic conditions. The major policy-related cause of inflation was widely assumed to be devaluation.

Droughts and Floods

With most of its product in agriculture and agriculturally related industries, the economy of Pakistan is extremely sensitive to changes in weather. Drought conditions prevailed in 1970–71 and 1971–72; deliveries of water through the irrigation system fell sharply from their 1969–70 levels. Agricultural output fell 3 percent in 1970–71, but in spite of a drought, managed to regain the 1969–70 level of output in 1971–72. The importance of natural factors in determining national output can be seen by recalculating GDP for 1970–71 on the assumption that agriculture maintained its trend growth. With normal agricultural growth, the GDP increase would have been 3.5 percent instead of 0.1 percent.

Drought conditions were followed by floods in 1973. More than 10 percent of cultivated areas were inundated in August 1973, and the total losses from the floods have been estimated at more than 5 percent of GDP. Drought struck again in 1974–75, when the water supply in the irrigation system fell to its lowest level in twenty-five years. Agricultural output fell by 2 percent; had it grown by 5 percent instead, the rate of growth of GDP would have doubled.

The vicissitudes of nature, of course, plague all poor countries with a large rural sector. However, the fluctuations of the early 1970s seem exceptionally severe, and declines in output appear closely linked to floods and droughts.

The Separation of East Pakistan

East Pakistan formally separated from (West) Pakistan in December 1971, and the events leading up to the separation, including the war with India, placed great strains on the economy. During 1970 and 1971, labor disturbances arising from the political chaos disrupted manufacturing. Civil unrest put a damper on both trade and communications. Public resources were diverted into defense. Following the separation of East

Pakistan, Pakistan had to find new markets for goods previously exported to the eastern wing.

In many ways, 1972 was an ideal year for recovery from civil war and separation. The terms of trade improved sharply in both 1972–73 and 1973–74, and export volume increased by more than 10 percent. Moreover, aid donors were more sympathetic to Pakistan during this crisis than at the time of the 1965 war with India, when aid commitments were cut back. Aid commitments increased markedly in 1973–74 after a hiatus in 1972–73. Still, on balance, the growth of Pakistan was reduced to some degree by the secession of East Pakistan.

World Economic Fluctuations

During the first two years of the 1970s, moderate worldwide expansion aided Pakistan's exports, but the prices of imports rose faster than the prices of exports, worsening the terms of trade. In 1972–73 and 1973–74, a buoyant world market for cotton provided a sharp reversal in the terms of trade. However, the following year the effects of the oil price increase began to be felt, and the terms of trade plummeted by 40 percent. In 1975–76 and 1976–77 the terms of trade recovered somewhat, but at the end of the period they stood at only 80 percent of their value in 1969–70.

Devaluation

Devaluation of the rupee in 1972 has been assailed as perhaps the most severely destabilizing of the economic policies introduced by the Bhutto government, which assumed power in December 1971. In May 1972 the government announced a new official rate of exchange of eleven rupees (Rs) to the U.S. dollar, a 130 percent increase over the previous rate of Rs 4.76. The devaluation was accompanied by a major reform of the trade control system: import licensing was all but eliminated, the bonus voucher scheme was scrapped, tariffs on imports were lowered, and export duties on certain goods were introduced. Because of these reforms, the average increase in domestic prices of tradable goods was less than the 130 percent change in the official exchange rate.

Import licensing had been for many years the linchpin of Pakistan's policies to deal with disequilibriums in the balance of payments. Restrictive licensing, that is, where the supply of licenses for foreign exchange fell far short of demand, was introduced following the Korean War, when raw material prices tumbled. Rather than devalue the currency in 1953, Pakistan simply clamped down on the flow of imports. A 1955 devaluation reduced the demand for imports, but licensing remained the principal determinant of the domestic prices of tradable goods. Licensing as a short-term device had the obvious advantages of speed and certainty. But as a long-term instrument, licensing proved to be very inefficient, because the protection afforded domestic industry by the licensing system followed no rational scheme. Moreover, licensing was inequitable and provided a breeding ground for corruption. The elimination of privileged access to licenses, which generated large windfall gains to the holders, was at the top of the list of priorities for the Bhutto government.

The timing of the devaluation was unfortunate, because in 1972 prices of Pakistan's exports were rising rapidly. The initial fears of Pakistan's inability to sell on world markets those goods previously exported to East Pakistan proved to be overstated. On balance, devaluation combined with export taxes produced a 20 percent increase in the domestic price of exportables. The unit value of exports, expressed in dollars, rose slowly in 1972–73 but surged by more than 60 percent in 1973–74. On the import side, devaluation produced a 20 percent increase in prices, as tariffs were lowered and licensing was eliminated. However, this price increase came on top of an annual average increase in world prices of 15 percent between 1972 and 1974.

In February 1973, Pakistan chose to let its rupee appreciate against the dollar when the dollar was devalued. The decline in the rupee price of the dollar, from Rs 11 to Rs 9.9, eased pressures on import prices somewhat. Still, devaluation exacerbated the inflationary effects of the general rise in world prices. One layer of Pakistan's price inflation during this period was due to the general rise in world prices, but another layer was due to the direct, price-raising effect of devaluation, although as will be demonstrated later, the size of that layer has been exaggerated.

It is also possible that the devaluation could have abetted inflation through its expansionary impact on aggregate spending. Under normal conditions, devaluations are expansionary and, for economies at full employment, inflationary. However, Richard Cooper[1] and Lance Taylor[2]

---

1. Richard N. Cooper, *Currency Devaluation in Developing Countries,* Essays in International Finance 86 (Princeton University, International Finance Section, 1971).

2. Lance Taylor, *Macro-Models for Developing Countries* (McGraw-Hill, 1979).

have argued that the reverse may be true in developing countries. If imports are inelastic, the increase in the import bill (valued in the local currency) may exceed the increased demand for exports, producing a new contraction in aggregate demand. This effect is all the more strong when countries operate with a large trade deficit, a typical condition in most developing countries.

Taylor's model of the short-term impact of devaluation[3] can be adapted to the case of Pakistan to explore in a more systematic way the consequences of the 1972 devaluation. The model consists of thirteen equations and can be solved to express home goods (X_H), that is, all locally consumed goods including imports, as a function of the defined variables.

$$X_H = \left(\frac{1}{Q}\right)\left\{\left(\frac{X_E}{P_H}\right)[(\gamma_W - \gamma_Z)a_{LE}w + \gamma_Z P_E] + \left(\frac{1}{P_H}\right)\right.$$
$$\left. \times [\gamma_Z e(\text{REM}) - (\gamma_W T_W + \gamma_Z T_Z)] + I + G\right\},$$

where

$$Q = 1 - \gamma_W a_{LH} \frac{w}{P_H} - \gamma_Z \frac{z}{(1 + z)(1 + v_H)};$$

$1/Q$ = multiplier
X_E = real exports
P_H = price of home goods
γ_W = propensity to consume out of wage
γ_Z = propensity to consume out of profits
a_{LE} = labor input in export goods
w = wage rate
P_E = domestic price of exports
e = exchange rate
REM = value of remittance
T_W = value of taxes collected from wages earned
T_Z = value of taxes collected from owners of capital
I = value of investment
G = value of government consumption
Z = profit markup over prime costs, that is, labor and imported inputs
v_H = rate of indirect tax.

For 1971–72, gross domestic product and its components are as fol-

3. Ibid.

lows (all figures are in billions of rupees):

Consumption	(C)	42.4
Investment	(I)	7.7
Government	(G)	6.5
Home-goods output	(X_H)	56.6
Imports	(M)	6.7
Exports	(X_E)	4.0
Indirect taxes	(T)	4.5

Gross domestic product at factor cost:

$$C + I + G + X - M - T = 49.4$$

Remittances in 1971–72 were less than 0.1 billion and are ignored in subsequent analyses.

The other variables in equations 1 and 2 take on the following values for Pakistan:

Labor input to home goods	(a_{LH})	0.4813
Labor input to export goods	(a_{LE})	0.6
Import input to home goods	(a_{OH})	0.1184
Profit markup on home goods	(Z)	0.535
Propensity of workers to consume from disposable income	(γ)	0.98
Indirect tax rate on home goods	(v_H)	0.0864

The multiplier can be found by substituting these values for the appropriate variables in equation 2. In the predevaluation case the multiplier takes the value of 3.25. Thus an increase of Rs 1 billion in government spending or investment will raise demand for home goods by Rs 3.25 billion. A similar increase in exports, however, will produce only a Rs 2.8 billion response in home-goods demand.

Remittances, insignificant in the predevaluation period, have the lowest multiplier—2.24.

Table 11-3 presents the results of various simulations performed with these data. Column 1 is the basic solution. The figures in column 2 are derived on the basis of an assumed 20 percent effective devaluation with no change in the wage rate w or real exports X_E. The output of home goods declines by 3.4 percent, while gross domestic product declines by 1.2 percent. Domestic prices rise by only 4 percent because of the relatively small share of imports in home-goods production. Even if all im-

Table 11-3. *Simulation for Pakistan*

Item	(1) $e = 1$ $w = 1$ $X_E = 4.0$	(2) $e = 1.2$ $w = 1.0$ $X_E = 4.0$	(3) Change (percent)	(4) $e = 1.2$ $w = 1.2$ $X_E = 4.0$	(5) Change (percent)	(6) $e = 1.2$ $w = 1.2$ $X_E = 4.8$	(7) Change (percent)
GDP							
Nominal factor cost	49.4	49.6	0	59.4	20	61.3	24
Predevaluation factor cost	49.4	47.8	−1.2	49.5	0	51.0	3.2
Price of home goods	1.0	1.0395	4	1.20	20	1.20	20
Output	56.6	54.7	−3.4	56.7	0	58.9	4.0
Nominal fiscal deficit	1.4	...	...	...	...	...	...
Trade balance							
International prices	−2.7	−2.5	...	−2.7	...	−3.2	...
Domestic prices	−2.7	−3.0	...	−3.2	...	−3.8	...
Indirect taxes	4.5	4.3	...	4.5	...	5.6	...
Multiplier	3.25	3.07	...	3.25	...	3.25	...

ports are assumed to be used as inputs into home-goods production, the input coefficient for imports is 0.12, while the labor input coefficient is four times as large (0.4813). In the short term, with no response from exports, devaluation is definitely contractionary.

The second simulation assumes a 20 percent increase in wages as well as a 20 percent increase in the prices of tradable goods. Domestic prices also rise by 20 percent, and hence real wages remain constant, as compared with the previous case, where they declined by 4 percent. In the second case, the contractionary effects of the devaluation are just offset by the increase in nominal wages, leaving the real output of home goods and the real gross domestic product unchanged. Nominal GDP rises, of course, by the amount of devaluation, namely, 20 percent.

The final simulation assumes a response from exports of 20 percent, implying an elasticity of 1 to changes in the effective exchange rate. Home-goods demand rises by 4 percent, but GDP by a lesser amount because of the higher leakage through increased imports.

The conditions immediately following devaluation in 1972 are more in line with the second case than the first. The level of real wages not only did not fall but, according to some sources,[4] actually increased. The combined effect of the government's wage and exchange rate policy on overall demand was neutral in the short term. With time, of course, exports responded to the increased incentives and the multiplier effect began to filter through the economy.

In sum, devaluation was certainly a cause of inflation in Pakistan, but terms of trade effects and wage increases seem to be equally, if not more, important contributors to the rise in price levels. Wage increases appeared to neutralize the short-term contractionary effects of devaluation, but as exports began to respond to devaluation, the need for compensatory additions to aggregate demand clearly diminished.

Fiscal Policy

To what extent was the government's fiscal policy a cause of inflation or a cure? The role of government in the economy expanded rapidly during the 1970–77 period, and conventional wisdom holds that this involvement was expansionary and a primary source of inflation. The govern-

4. Stephen Guisinger, "Trade Policies and Employment: The Case of Pakistan," in Anne Krueger, *Trade Policies and Employment in Developing Countries* (National Bureau of Economic Research, 1980).

Table 11-4. *Consolidated Public Revenues and Expenditures*

Millions of rupees

Item	1970–71	1971–72	1972–73	1973–74	1974–75	1975–76	1976–77
Revenues	7,139	8,080	9,665	13,757	16,488	19,826	22,418
Current expenditure	6,606	7,837	10,078	14,272	19,633	22,333	22,846
Surplus	533	243	–413	–515	–3,145	–2,507	–428
Capital expenditure	3,065	3,449	5,086	7,024	11,308	14,456	16,482
Expansionary finance	505	1,305	1,507	499	2,038	3,901	5,611
Public consumption deflator	106.1	111.3	123.9	159.3	201.7	227	250.0
Investment deflator	108.1	137.1	231.4	285.0	330.6	337.9	389.6
				Constant 1969–70 prices			
Current revenues	6,729	7,260	7,801	8,636	8,175	8,734	8,967
Current expenditures	6,111	7,041	8,134	8,959	9,734	9,838	9,138
Capital expenditures	2,835	2,505	2,198	2,465	3,420	4,278	4,230

Source: *Economic Survey, 1978–79.*

ment was cognizant of the inflationary consequence of its expenditures, and the annual plans repeatedly referred to the need to trim expenditures, raise revenues, and reduce reliance on expansionary finance.

The evidence on the government's alleged expansionary role is certainly mixed, particularly with regard to magnitude. In current prices the government's share of economic activity rose from 17.1 to 23.6 percent over the 1970–77 period. However, in constant 1969–70 prices the increase was only to 18.6 percent. A major problem in gauging the government's fiscal role is lack of consistent data on public spending. Budget data suggest increasing government expenditures on consumption and capital formation and increasing revenues, in both current and constant prices, over the 1970–77 period (see table 11-4). However, national income accounts show a more or less constant level of public consumption outlays, in constant prices of 1969–70, after 1972–73, while public investment increased by around 50 percent. Budget and national income data differ because transfer payments, such as subsidies, are included in the former but not the latter.

Budget data on public revenues and expenditures suggest that the current account surplus/deficit declined in real terms, necessitating a rapid increase in government borrowing. Revenues rose in real terms in every year except 1974–75, when export duties were reduced to encourage exports faced with declining world demand. Revenues managed to keep pace with GDP growth, but the increase in government receipts was provided more by new taxes than by the elasticity of existing taxes. Pakistan's tax structure has traditionally been inelastic, in part because of its heavy reliance on indirect taxes. Import substitution has steadily eroded the base for import duties, and the rise of the largely untaxed service sector in the economy has placed a drag on indirect tax receipts.

Current expenditures increased by 50 percent, in real terms, over the period. Expenditures on defense are purposely obscured for reasons of security, but even the publicly reported data show a sharp increase, from 6 to 7 percent of GNP. This in part was due, of course, to the 1972 war with India and the outlays on internal security both before and after separation. Public expenditures on the social sectors mushroomed after 1972 as Bhutto sought to fulfill his campaign pledge to give more attention to the long-neglected social sectors. In 1973–74, provincial expenditures on education, health, and civil works increased by 80 percent, absorbing 40 percent of the total new revenues available to both federal and provincial governments.

Table 11-5. *Expenditures on National Product*
Billions of rupees; constant prices of 1969-70

Item	1970-71	1971-72	1972-73	1973-74	1974-75	1975-76	1976-77
Private consumption (C)	38.5	38.3	42.9	45.8	46.9	46.9	48.5
Government consumption (G)	4.9	5.8	6.2	5.3	5.9	6.4	6.3
Investment (I)	6.5	4.9	3.3	3.7	4.9	6.7	6.8
Public (I_g)	3.3	2.4	1.7	2.4	3.3	4.8	4.8
Private (I_p)	3.2	2.5	1.6	1.3	1.6	1.9	2.0
Changes in stocks	0.8	0.8	0.8	0.6	1.0	0	0.4
Exports (X_E)	3.7	3.1	3.3	2.7	3.0	3.5	2.8
Imports (M)	6.3	4.3	3.8	4.4	4.1	4.4	4.9
Net factor income	−0.1	0.1	0.2	0.2	0.2	0.4	0.7
GNP	48.2	48.7	52.9	54.0	57.9	59.4	61.6
Indirect taxes	4.7	4.6	5.3	6.0	5.8	6.0	6.3
Subsidies (R)	0.2	0.2	0.4	1.9	1.9	1.3	0.8
GDP at factor cost	44.0	44.3	48.0	49.9	54.0	54.7	56.1
$I_p + X$	6.9	5.6	4.9	4.0	4.6	5.4	4.8
$G + I_g + R$	8.4	8.4	8.3	9.6	11.1	12.5	11.9
$G + I + R + X$	15.3	14.0	13.2	13.6	15.7	17.9	16.7
$(G + I + R + X)^a$	15.3	15.7	16.2	16.7	17.2	17.7	18.2

Source: Current data from *Economic Survey, 1978-79*, deflated by price indices from Planning Division data.
a. Levels required to achieve 3 percent growth in income.

The most rapidly mushrooming expenditure item was subsidies. Real wage growth of the 1970s was made possible in part by subsidies that held in check prices of essential consumer goods, especially wheat. In 1970–71, government outlays on subsidies amounted to Rs 200 million, or roughly 2.3 percent of total government expenditures. By 1976–77, outlays on subsidies had grown to Rs 1,900 million, equal to 5.5 percent of total government expenditures. The major source of this increase was the subsidy to wheat. Wheat is procured from farmers at a set price and rationed to urban consumers at a slightly lower "issue" price. The difference between local procurement and ration demand is made up from imported wheat. The world price of wheat began rising in 1972–73 and peaked in 1974–75 at a price more than four times the 1971–72 price. The domestic open market price echoed world price movements, and the demand for ration wheat at the lower, fixed price soared. Issue prices were raised, but only moderately and with a considerable lag. Open market prices climbed by 160 percent over the period, but the issue price rose by only 80 percent. Procurement price changes lagged behind as well, so that farmers began shifting to other cash crops like sugar and rice, the prices of which increased relative to the price of wheat. In 1974–75, the subsidy to wheat alone came to almost 2 percent of GDP.

Subsidies to other products have been neither as substantial nor as recurring as the subsidy to wheat. After the oil crisis of 1973, subsidies to petroleum products—gasoline, fertilizers, pesticides—and sometimes directly to petroleum users, such as Pakistan International Airways, were increased to soften the impact of the surge in import prices on domestic prices. Many of the subsidies were phased out or greatly reduced by the end of the period.

Capital expenditures, like current expenditures, grew in real terms by roughly 50 percent during the period. But in the first two years, capital outlays declined. After 1972–73, public investment steadily increased with the launching of a number of major projects, such as the Karachi steel mill.

A slightly different picture is obtained from the national income accounts summarized in table 11-5. Current public expenditure rose between 1970–71 and 1972–73 but was fairly flat over the next four years. Public investment dropped sharply over the first two years of the period, then climbed steadily thereafter. Total government outlays grew by 40 percent between 1970–71 and 1976–77.

From either source of data, it is evident that government spending increased, and it is also evident that this increase was financed in large part by government borrowing. Under normal circumstances, government expenditures not backed by government revenues would be inflationary. But at the same time that public expenditures were increasing, private aggregate spending (excluding autonomous consumption) was on the decline. Private investment, in real terms, declined steadily after 1965. Although it recovered slightly after 1973–74, private investment in 1976–77 was only two-thirds of the level achieved in 1970–71. Exports, in real terms, showed no distinct trend during the period. Together, exports and private investment declined by Rs 2.1 billion, or 30 percent, between 1970–71 and 1976–77. The increase in government outlays of Rs 3.5 billion offset the decline in private spending. More important, the growth of government outlays fell far short of the required growth to maintain a constant per capita income. With population growth at 3 percent, an increase of 3 percent in GDP is necessary just to keep per capita income constant. The last row of table 11-5 shows the required levels of autonomous expenditures to achieve 3 percent growth in income. Only in 1975–76 did actual levels of autonomous expenditure equal or surpass required levels.

It seems fair to conclude that government spending per se was not a major contributor to inflation, although the mode of financing—from credit creation rather than increased taxes—may have added to inflation. But an increase in public spending to fill the gap in aggregate demand left by declines in exports and the weakening of private investment appear consistent with the desire to maintain a steady growth in GDP. The decline in private investment could be traced to the crowding out of private sector borrowers by the government, and this government action could then be viewed as "predatory" rather than compensatory. Indeed, some evidence for this explanation is adduced in the review of monetary policy below. But a sufficient explanation of the decline is the collapse of investor confidence following the 1965 war with India and especially after the 1972 nationalizations.

The one remaining mystery is the rapid rise in private consumption in the face of such a sluggish growth in autonomous spending. Private consumption rose by more than 25 percent against a 9 percent increase in autonomous spending over the period. A shift in the consumption function is the most likely explanation, since the rate of direct taxation showed no distinct trend. Since wages—nominal and real—were increased and profits shrank during the period, a shift in the consumption function prompted by redistribution of income is a possibility. Of course, some of this expansion in consumption was made possible by foreign borrowing to finance increased imports of consumer goods and imported inputs. Consumption liberalization and redistribution did not, however, produce a decline in savings, as the gross national product increased even faster than combined public and private consumption.

Monetary Policy

The objectives of monetary policy in Pakistan are standard ones for the developing countries: a steady, noninflationary expansion of the money supply and continued monetization of the economy. Pakistan fits the mold of the "underintermediated" financial system sketched out by McKinnon[5] and Bruno[6]. The public holds money but few other financial instruments. Credit is rationed by the state bank with low rates of interest on both advances and deposits. The money supply is governed by fiscal and balance-of-payments deficits and is therefore largely outside the control of the agency with nominal responsibility for the money supply, namely, the State Bank of Pakistan. Monetary restraint takes the form of restrictions on the flow of credit to the private sector. This restriction may lead to sharp increases in the curb rate of interest, pushing up costs of manufacturing and inventorying goods and thereby adding fuel to inflation rather than providing the intended damper.

One measure suggesting the degree to which the state bank lacks control over the money supply is the divergence between planned and actual expansions of the money supply. Each year, targets for the overall expansion of the money supply, as well as the sectoral allocations, are established by the National Credit Consultative Council (NCCC). The target rate of growth of the money supply is determined by adding together (1) the projected real rate of growth of GNP; (2) an allowance for the monetization of the nonmonetized sector (usually 1 percent to 2 percent per annum); (3) an allowance for the increased preference of individuals for holding cash balances (generally 1 percent per annum); and (4) more recently, an allowance for imported inflation. The planned money

5. Ronald I. McKinnon, *Money and Capital in Economic Development* (Brookings Institution, 1973).

6. Michael Bruno, "Stabilization and Stagnation in a Semi-Industrial Economy," in Rudiger Dornbusch and Jacob A. Frenkel, eds., *International Economic Policy: Theory and Evidence* (Johns Hopkins University Press, 1979).

Table 11-6. *Planned and Actual Increases in Money and Credit, 1971–76*
Values are in Rs crores

Year	Planned				Actual			
	Increase in monetary assets	Increase in total credit	Public	Private	Increase in monetary assets	Increase in total credit	Public	Private
1971–72	150[a]	n.a.	60	n.a.	282	302	177	125
1972–73	120	165	15	150 (156)	615	397	237	160
1973–74	160	251	65	186 (235)	354	421	150	271
1974–75	360	510	130	386 (445)	596	671	281	390
1975–76	375	525	100	425 (443)	894	820	504	316

Source: Data are from *Economic Surveys* of relevant year. For each fiscal year the planned amounts and the previous year's actuals are taken from the annual plan for that year. Numbers in parentheses represent planned targets drawn from the NCCC credit plans.
n.a. Not available.
a. Estimated.

stock growth can be combined with a projected balance-of-payments position to yield the permissible expansion of credit. The overall target for credit expansion is then partitioned between public and private sectors, and individual targets are set for various borrower categories, such as economic sector (agriculture, manufacturing), size of enterprise, and type of use (working capital, fixed capital).

The credit plans are not made public in their entirety, but certain targets are cited in official documents from time to time. The credit plans prepared by the Planning Division provide estimates that are often used as the starting point for the deliberations of the NCCC. Table 11-6 compares the planned increases in money and credit in the annual plans (credit plans data, when available, are in parentheses) with the increases actually observed.

It is evident that the targets were overachieved in every year for which data are available and that the prime culprit was the public sector. Only in 1973–74 did the actual expansion of credit in the private sector exceed the credit plan total to any significant degree. In every year, credit extended to the public sector exceeded the planned level, sometimes by a factor of five.

It is interesting to note that the NCCC consistently planned for a balance-of-payments deficit, permitting a greater expansion of credit than the stock of money. However, in every year during the period, the actual balance-of-payments deficit proved to be smaller than the planned deficit. In two fiscal years, 1973 and 1976, a balance-of-payments surplus was registered, largely because of increased foreign aid inflows.

Measurement of the supply of money during this period is complicated by the conditions that surrounded the separation of East Pakistan. At the time of the crisis, accounts were blocked and certain denominations of currency were demonetized to prevent Bengalis from removing their capital from West Pakistan. Estimates of the stock of money in (West) Pakistan after separation vary widely, according to how these demonetizations were treated. Preseparation estimates of West Pakistan's money supply suffer from the same problems that confront all estimates of regional money supply within a common currency area. Divergences in money stock estimates are evident in table 11-7, which provides data on the money stock from two sources: the State Bank of Pakistan (source I) and the International Monetary Fund (IMF) (source II).

The two sources show broad agreement on the average annual growth in the broader definition of money (M_2), but the state bank data suggest

Table 11-7. *Estimates of the Stock of Money and Its Velocity*

Billions of rupees

Year	GNP deflator	Change	GNP at current prices	Change	M_1	Change	M_2	Change	$\overline{M}_2$[a]	Change	V_1	Change
										Source I		
June 1970	100.0	...	47.8	...	13.1	...	21.2	...	21.2	...	3.65	...
June 1971	104.3	4.3	50.3	5.3	14.9	13.7	23.0	8.2	22.1	4.2	3.38	−7.5
June 1972	110.8	6.2	53.9	7.2	14.8	−0.7	24.5	6.7	22.1	0	3.64	7.7
June 1973	126.8	14.4	67.1	24.4	18.9	27.7	30.5	24.5	24.1	9.0	3.55	−2.5
June 1974	160.8	26.8	87.0	29.6	22.2	17.5	34.0	11.4	21.1	−12.5	3.91	10.1
June 1975	193.1	20.1	112.4	29.3	23.8	7.2	37.0	8.8	19.2	−9.0	4.72	20.7
June 1976	222.8	15.4	132.5	17.9	29.2	22.7	45.9	24.2	20.6	7.3	4.54	−3.9
June 1977	247.7	11.2	151.0	14.0	36.9	26.4	56.5	23.2	22.8	10.7	4.09	−10.0
Annual average growth, 1970–77	...	13.8	...	17.9	...	21.2	...	15.0	...	1.0	...	1.6

Source I: *Economic Survey, 1978–79.* Source II: *International Financial Statistics,* May 1978.
a. The overbar signifies real balance.

a faster rate of growth in M_1 than the IMF data. Most important, the two sources show very little agreement on year-to-year changes, and in some cases the disagreements are quite sharp. During fiscal year 1974, for example, the IMF data indicate a decline in M_2, while the state bank data show an increase of 11.4 percent. However, for the following year the IMF data suggest a much higher rate of growth of M_2, and the average growth for the two years is about the same. It is still somewhat perplexing to find that even in fiscal years 1976 and 1977, well after the separation of East Pakistan, the two sources differ quite significantly on the growth of the money supply.

Velocity, measured on either the narrow or broad concept of money, edged gradually upward during the 1970–77 period. Velocity followed the expected pattern during inflationary cycles: as the rate of inflation accelerated, velocity rose swiftly as demand for cash balances sagged; but when the rate of inflation showed signs of easing, velocity dropped as individuals sought to adjust their cash balances to the higher price levels.

Real cash balances, $\overline{M}_2$ in table 11-7, grew very slightly during the 1970–77 period—by between 1 and 2 percent. This rate of growth is far below the growth of real balances that would have been implied by the planned or actual growth rates of GNP. The annual rates of planned growth during this period averaged 7 percent. If allowance is made for the increased monetization of the economy and the increased preference for holding cash that the NCCC includes in their calculations of "safe" expansions of the money supply, the projected rate of growth of real balances should have been around 9 percent. The projected rates of growth

						Source II					
V_2	Change	M_1	Change	M_2	Change	$\bar{M}_2$	Change	V_1	Change	V_2	Change
2.25	...	14.0	−8−	20.8	...	20.8	...	3.41	...	2.30	...
2.19	−2.7	16.5	17.8	23.6	13.8	22.6	8.7	3.05	−10.6	2.13	−7.4
2.20	0	19.9	20.0	27.7	17.5	25.0	10.6	2.73	−10.5	1.95	−8.5
2.20	0	22.2	11.6	31.6	13.8	24.9	−0.3	3.02	10.6	2.12	8.7
2.56	16.4	22.5	1.4	31.2	−1.3	19.4	−22.0	3.87	28.1	2.79	31.6
3.04	18.7	25.6	13.8	37.8	21.2	19.6	1.0	4.39	13.4	2.97	6.5
2.88	−5.3	34.0	32.8	50.0	32.2	22.4	14.3	3.90	−11.2	2.65	−10.8
2.67	−7.3	39.9	17.4	58.5	17.0	23.6	5.4	3.78	−3.1	2.58	2.2
...	2.5	...	16.1	...	15.9	...	1.8	...	3.1	...	1.7

were not realized; the actual expansion of GNP in constant prices amounted to 3.5 percent. But the real money supply did not expand at 5.5 percent either. The "real" velocity of money obviously increased as individuals economized on cash balances to avoid the inflationary tax. On balance, it does not appear that the money supply was expanded at excessively high rates. Monetary expansion may have validated the inflation but was not itself a cause.

Traditional instruments of monetary policy have played almost no role, or at best a very passive role, in regulating the stock of money. Changes in reserve requirements have not been utilized. The discount rate was raised on four occasions between 1971 and 1977, rising from 5 percent at the beginning of that period to 10 percent at the end. However, the change was more symbolic than substantive. Little recourse to the discount window is made by commercial banks. Moreover, interest rates on advances and deposits are set by the state bank, and typically, changes in the discount rate have lagged rather than led changes in lending rates. Open market operations are inconsequential in their impact on the volume of credit and its cost. Government bonds bear such a low rate of interest that banks are required to hold a fixed share of their portfolios in government debt.

After the direct controls over the amount of credit available to the private sector, the next most potent source of public intervention in the financial system is the mechanism of selective credit controls. The scope and diversity of these controls are so broad that any summary judgment about their impact on the supply of credit and its allocation among sectors is extremely difficult. Selective credit controls generally take the form of changes in the margin requirements, that is, the share of the value of collateraled items that must be supplied by the borrower. In some cases, margin requirements are effectively 100 percent, tantamount to a ban on advances. The objective of the selective credit controls is ostensibly to curtail speculative hoarding of raw materials and final goods. But the government's practice of changing margin requirements on very short notice and frequently reversing policies adopted a few months prior suggests that the government was unsure of the effect of margin requirement changes on hoarding and the price level. If increased margin requirements pushed wholesalers into the curb market to finance inventories, the net result of the government's anti-inflationary selective control policies might very well have been more inflation, as wholesalers will pass through to consumers the increased costs of curb market financing.

Stabilization Policies: An Evaluation

The most difficult part in assessing the government's role in causing inflation and balance-of-payments disequilibriums and then in adopting appropriate policies to reduce inflation and payments deficits is the choice of a standard for comparison. By an absolute standard, there is little doubt that the government was a significant contributor to inflation and that its stabilization policies were ineffective to the extent that they did not eliminate inflation and restore balance-of-payments equilibrium. The devaluation in 1972 directly raised prices of exportable and importable goods, on average, by 20 percent. Had the government maintained a balanced budget and limited credit expansion to the planned real growth of the economy, the rates of inflation undoubtedly would have been much lower.

Internal inflation swiftly eroded the competitive effects of the 1972 devaluation. The failure of the government to maintain the real effective exchange rate for imports and exports at the levels attained immediately following the 1972 devaluation is responsible, in large measure, for the widening trade deficit. On the absolute standard, therefore, the performance of the government in the areas of monetary, fiscal, and exchange rate policies certainly fell short of the mark.

However, by a relative standard, government policies can be seen in a slightly more favorable light. First, in relation to overall economic objectives, some price instability and some worsening of the balance of payments appear almost inevitable prices to pay for the maintenance of aggregate demand in line with the planned growth of the economy. As noted earlier, the fundamental problem for Pakistan's planners is economic stagnation. Government spending financed by credit expansion was a necessary antidote to the shortfalls in export earnings and private investment in manufacturing, without which the rate of real growth would have slipped far below the rate of population expansion. Instability and growth are obviously interrelated: rapid inflation and short-term swings in output and employment may weaken the prospects for sustained growth. Rapid growth, on the other hand, may make stabilization of prices and employment easier to achieve.

Also, in relation to the pattern of inflation in other parts of the world, Pakistan's performance gets high marks. Much higher rates of inflation were registered in Latin America during the 1970s. In many countries, rates of inflation showed no tendency to decline throughout the 1973–77 period, whereas in Pakistan the rates peaked in 1974–75 and declined steadily thereafter.

Comments by Gustav F. Papanek

The reasons for price stability in Pakistan over twenty years are as interesting as reasons for inflation in the 1970s, on which Stephen Guisinger concentrates. Even the 1970s can be analyzed more effectively by contrast with the earlier period and with the experience of other countries in the region.

Stability

Stability in prices characterized the period following independence, although there were considerable annual fluctuations. Over an eighteen-year period (1952–53 to 1969–70), price changes of 5 percent or more took place in eight years and in five of these years, prices changed by 9 percent or more. But the average rate of inflation was far lower than in the 1970s and low by world standards.

The reasons for price stability probably varied over time.

1. Guisinger emphasizes the rate of growth rather than cyclical insta-

Table 11-8. *Growth, Inflation, and Real Wages*

Percentage change[a]

Country	Time period	GNP/GDP growth	Average agricultural product	Prices	Wages
Pakistan	1950s	3.3	3.1	1.2	(4)
	1960s	6.4	3.4	3.3	10
	1970s	3.0	−2.8	15.5	6
	(1973–77)	(2.1)[b]	(−1.8)	(21.7)	(−20)
Bangladesh	1950s	2.1	−1.0	2.5	0
	1960s	4.2	0.5	5.3	11
	1970s	−3.9	−7.4	38.6	−29
	(1974–76)			(−36.9)	(59)
Indonesia	1958–67	2.0	n.a.	190.3	−53
	1967–75	8.0	n.a.	ʻ5.6	47
	(1967–70)	(7.0)		(from 898 to 11%)	(50)
India	1950s	3.6	0.7	5.0	(−26)
	1960s	3.4	0.5	7.0	0
	1970s	3.0	−2.6	(5.4)	(2)

Source: G. F. Papanek, "Methodological and Statistical Appendix to Real Wages, Growth, Inflation, Income Distribution and Politics in Pakistan, India, Bangladesh, Indonesia," Discussion Paper 30 (Department of Economics and Center for Asian Development Studies, Boston University, 1979).

n.a. Not available.

a. All figures, except for real wages, are annual rates of change. Real wages compare averages for several years.

b. GDP between 1974 and 1977 increased by 2.1 percent according to official figures, but the rate almost certainly was less.

bility as Pakistan's principal economic difficulty. The rapid rate of growth in the 1960s was a major factor in moderating price increases. Pakistan then included its present area and what is now Bangladesh. The GDP growth rate for the two regions averaged about 5.5 percent, or 2.5 percent per capita. This is not very high by world standards but is very satisfactory by South Asian, including Pakistani, performance over the past thirty years. Aid inflows also increased in the 1960s, raising available resources even more. As a result, most politically important groups experienced a visible improvement in incomes (see wage changes in table 11-8). The government could therefore maintain monetary and fiscal policies that were conservative in relation to the increase in goods and services available, without being subject to strong pressures from disaffected groups for increases in nominal incomes that would have to be financed by monetary expansion.

2. In the 1950s, growth was slow, although not as slow as in much of the 1970s, but demands from potentially disaffected groups may have been muted by the recent experience of independence and partition. Several million people benefited from taking over assets left by departing Hindus, and several million were recent refugees, generally pleased to have escaped with their lives.

3. The economy was subject to severe shocks that sometimes resulted in sharp yet temporary price increases. A reduction in per capita agricultural output was followed by rising prices in 1959–60 and 1966–67, but with better weather and greater output in subsequent years, price rises moderated or were reversed. As a result, there were not two years in a row with a high rate of inflation. On the other hand, there were five years when price changes were zero or negative. Inflationary expectations, therefore, were not becoming built in.

Another shock was the devaluation of 1955. With adequate supplies of foreign exchange to import food, the devaluation produced no price rise. In fact, prices declined by 1.6 percent.

4. The civil servants and military, who dominated decision making for most of the twenty years, were inclined to conservative fiscal and monetary policies. They had a pre-Keynesian abhorrence of deficits. An attitude of "a gentleman does not incur debts he cannot meet" was carried over from family to national budgeting. The country's few economists, arguing that increases in output, imports, and monetization permitted increases in the debt, had to contend with this conviction.

5. Industrial wages in countries like Pakistan had little impact on the price level. Price level was dominated by the price of food grains, determined in turn by supply, the price of imports, and government procurement and subsidy policy. Industry contributed substantially less than 10 percent of GDP during most of this period. Wages were only one-third of value added in industry, so changes in industrial wages affected only 2 percent to 3 percent of GDP. Therefore even if minimum wages had been raised rapidly, it would not have affected inflation significantly.

6. In the labor surplus economies of Asia, changes in real wages throughout the economy—including agricultural and construction labor —seem to be related to the average product in the traditional sectors, where work and income sharing exist, notably in agriculture (see table 11-9). The average product determines the reservation wages. Real wages therefore rose when output per capita was increasing anyway, so wages

Table 11-9. *Factors Related to Changes in Wages*

| Country | Constant | Prices | | Average agricultural production | | R^2 |
		Current	Lagged	Current	Lagged	
Pakistan						
1. Textiles	5.69	0.52	...	...	...	...
	(1.6)	(1.7)				0.20
2. Textiles	−9.90	...	...	...	2.61	0.78
	(−5.7)				(8.3)	
3. Manufacturing	−9.56	...	...	...	2.55	0.70
	(−2.6)				(3.8)	
4. Urban casual	−21.9	...	...	...	2.07	0.86
					(9.6)	
Bangladesh						
5. Rural	0.02	0.35	0.3	0.14	0.06	0.86
	(1.2)	(2.9)	(2.4)	(1.1)	(0.4)	
6. Construction	0.01	0.45	0.39	0.34	0.46	0.79
	(0.6)	(3.3)	(3.0)	(1.4)	(1.9)	
7. Manufacturing	0.07	0.6	−0.6	0.62	0.73	0.87
	(3.1)	(0.1)	(−1.2)	(3.6)	(4.4)	
Indonesia						
8. Plantations	0.3	0.72	0.28	...	0.11	0.99
	(0.7)	(27.2)	(9.1)		(1.7)	
India						
9. Rural-Bihar	−0.03	−2.98	4.20	−3.13	3.21	0.50
	(−0.3)	(−1.8)	(2.6)	(−1.9)	(2.0)	
10. Manufacturing	0.03	0.39	0.02	−0.06	0.74	0.67
	(3.7)	(2.3)	(0.1)	(−0.3)	(3.0)	

Source: Papanek, "Methodological and Statistical Appendix." Regressions 2 through 4 have real wages as dependent variable. All others use nominal wages. Regression 8 uses "state of economy" dummy variable instead of average agricultural product. Regressions 2 through 4 and 9 use moving averages of three years for the average agricultural product. Figures in parentheses are *t*-statistics.

provided no inflationary stimulus. Moreover, wages responded with a two-year lag, if at all, to price changes.

Therefore wages (1) counteracted inflationary tendencies, falling in real terms when prices accelerated, rising when inflation slowed; and (2) rose and fell together with the GDP/GNP. A rapid growth of national income occurred generally when agricultural output (and that of other traditional sectors) was rising more rapidly than population. With rising per capita product, wages also rose, keeping income disparities from rising during periods of rapid growth. So growth was favorable for the absolute income of the poor and not unfavorable for income distribution.

Inflation

Inflation in the 1970s was influenced by the same factors as stability in the 1960s. Following Guisinger's analysis, one can conclude these points:

1. The per capita supply of goods and services from domestic production stagnated or declined. This decline was due in part to exogenous shocks, mostly bad weather, but equally due to disruption of production, and of input and output distribution due to nationalization so rapid that the administrative machinery could not cope with it; massive capital flight; investment concentrated in capital intensive, long-gestation period, low-productivity projects; and further distortion of relative prices.

As a result, the real income of at least some major groups had to drop. Quite naturally it proved more difficult to resist demands for excessive increases in nominal income when the society or government had to allocate declines in real income, than when it could allocate increases.

2. Reducing real incomes of some groups was especially difficult for a populist government that had aroused the hopes and expectations of previously disadvantaged groups, who were its political constituency. In an attempt to increase the income of organized workers despite stagnant output, the government rapidly raised minimum wages of an industrial sector far larger than was done a decade earlier. In the early 1970s, many businessmen and industrialists also increased wages not subject to minimum wage legislation because they were frightened.

In addition to raising nominal wages, the government subsidized the prices of urban wage goods. As a result of both factors, urban real wages rose temporarily. In addition, the government increased expenditures on the military, on open and hidden subsidies for public enterprises, and on patronage to some groups. Rising expenditures, despite stagnation in real per capita income, fueled inflation.

3. All but one year in the 1970s showed inflation rates of 5 percent or more, and two successive years had rates of 30 percent. As a result, inflationary expectations were built in, and every organized group pressed for increases in price.

4. In Bangladesh, the deterioration in the economy in the 1970s was even sharper, with an annual negative growth rate of nearly 4 percent.

Indonesia in an earlier period had experienced stagnation or decline in per capita income for a decade or more. In both instances, inflation was even more rapid than in Pakistan.

5. With average agricultural product declining, the reservation wage fell, and with it wage rates fell throughout these economies. Rapid and accelerating inflation, with nominal wages lagging, worsened the situation. Real wages declined as a result, reversing the initial spurt even in Pakistan.

Stabilization

Stabilization programs were successful in Indonesia (1967–70) and Bangladesh (1974–76) and provide useful lessons.

1. The programs reduced price distortions; emphasized economic rationality; and in general, increased output, exports, savings, and the inflow of foreign resources. The programs were expansionary, rather than contractionary, in the following ways: (1) a great increase in x-efficiency, the efficiency with which the economy was managed, was especially important and rapid with respect to agriculture as a result of more effective use of fertilizer and rehabilitation of irrigation (in this respect, these countries differed from what would be possible in Latin America); (2) double shifting instead of less than one shift in industry helped reduce the need for imports; (3) a substantial increase in imports of wage goods was financed by aid; (4) some increase in exports came about in response to higher local currency prices, since exports were supply, not demand, constrained; and (5) greater savings, less capital flight, and less capital inflow resulted from increased output, security, and price incentives.

The increased output stabilized prices; stable and more rational prices produced further savings and increases in output.

2. The stabilization effort was successful in the short term, with prices in Bangladesh actually decreasing over two years and price increases in Indonesia dropping from a rate near 1,000 percent to about 10 percent.

3. Since stabilization was expansionary, it benefited wage earners in two ways: (1) with average product in the traditional sectors rising, the reservation wage rose, and real wages increased throughout the economy; and (2) with inflation slowing sharply and nominal wages lagging behind prices, real wages rose in the short term for that reason as well.

Conclusions

1. As in the Guisinger paper, the emphasis in this essay is on supply. Changes in the supply of goods and services, as related to expectations of politically powerful groups, apparently were the principal determinants of price stability or instability. Monetary, fiscal, and trade policies, especially trade policies, affected supply, but so did nationalization, the effectiveness of government and of public enterprise, confidence and capital flight, and availability of foreign resources (especially wage goods). When supply was inadequate, macropolicies were designed to give important political groups the illusion of progress and rising incomes. Inflation was the result, but the principal culprit was not mismanaged short-term macropolicies, but mismanaged production policies.

2. Price stability, when accompanied by stagnant output (India, Pakistan in the 1950s), was consistent with stagnant real wages and therefore unchanged income distribution. But stabilization, as the result of more rapid growth in output, was accompanied by rising real wages throughout the economy, since wages are apparently a function of average product. Moreover, with wages in general lagging prices rather than anticipating them, stability could directly improve the income of wage earners. Thus stabilization benefited the poor when both stabilization and increased wages were the result of increased output, not reduced demand.

CHAPTER TWELVE

A Macroeconometric Model
of Inflation and Growth
in South Korea

ROGER D. NORTON *and* SEUNG YOON RHEE

IN THIS CHAPTER, a relatively small annual macroeconometric model of the South Korean economy is formulated, estimated, and applied to some hypothetical policy choices over the past decade and a half. The principal endogenous variables of the model are output, price level, wage rate, imports, fixed investment, inventory investment, savings, consumption, and employment. The model projects variables in both current and constant prices. Behavioral relationships are postulated for the real variables and the price level, and current price identities are used to derive values of some other variables.

In all, the model contains seventeen stochastic equations and twenty-four identities. Its structure is recursive for each time period, and hence the estimation is carried out via ordinary least squares or the Cochrane-Orcutt iterative procedure. The sample period for estimation is taken to be 1963–77, with earlier years used for lagged values as required. Most of the behavioral equations are expressed in terms of variables in percentage change (growth rate) form. This procedure tends to reduce, although not eliminate, problems of autocorrelation and multicollinearity, which often characterize time series of macrovariables in a rapidly growing economy.

The main policy instruments in the model are the exchange rate, the nominal money supply, and the farmers' selling price for agricultural pro-

The research reported here was sponsored in part by the Korea Development Institute and the World Bank. Helpful suggestions on an earlier draft were made by Micha Gisser, Arnold Harberger, Mahn Je Kim, Lawrence Krause, and Larry Westphal. Neither they nor the sponsoring institutions, however, bear any responsibility for the opinions expressed or for remaining errors.

Table 12-1. *List of Variables in the Model*

All real variables in 1970 constant prices

Variable	Definition
Purely exogenous variables[a]	
A	Real gross agricultural output
PIM	National accounts deflator for imports
IMUV	Import unit value index (index of dollar prices of imports)
NFID	Net factor income from abroad, in dollars
STD	Statistical discrepancy in the national accounts
WDUM	Wage rate dummy = 1.0 in each of 1974–77 and zero in prior years
PAB	Index of farmers' buying prices for inputs
POP	Total population
Policy exogenous variables[a]	
PAS	Index of farmers' selling prices
MM1	Monthly average nominal money supply
E	Goods and services exports, in constant domestic currency (won)[b]
ER	Exchange rate
IER	Import effective exchange rate[c]
EER	Export effective exchange rate[c]
EGD	Goods exports in current dollars
ESD	Services exports in current dollars
Endogenous variables	
YA	Agricultural value added
PYA	Agricultural value-added deflator
YN	Nonagricultural value added
PYN	Nonagricultural value-added deflator
IV	Inventory accumulation
Y	GDP
PY	GDP deflator
CG	Government consumption
PCG	Government consumption deflator
WC	Manufacturing wage index (nominal)
IF	Gross fixed capital formation
K	Capital stock
PIF	Fixed investment deflator
RDEPR	Depreciation allowances
PIV	Price deflator for inventories
IM	Total imports in domestic currency
IMPO	Commodity imports in current dollars
IMCD	Total imports in current dollars
IMS	Service imports in current dollars
ECD	Total exports in current dollars
BPCE	Balance of payments in current dollars
BPWC	Balance of payments in current won

Table 12-1 *(continued)*

Variable	Definition
SD	Domestic savings
S	Total savings
NMA	Manufacturing employment (in thousands of persons)
YLC	Total labor income in current prices
WS	Wage share in national income
UPOP	Urban population
RPOP	Rural population

a. Some of these variables are made endogenous in the "oil shock" policy experiments.

b. Clearly, there is interdependence among the exogenous valuations of *E*, *EGD*, *ESD*, and *ER* (or *EER*). In some versions of the model, *E* is made endogenous via use of a logistic share equation, as explained later in the text; when that is done, some of the other trade-related variables are made endogenous as well.

c. The export effective exchange rate (*EER*) is computed as the ratio of the national accounts won valuation of goods and services exports (in current prices) to the balance-of-payments (BOP) dollar valuation of goods and services exports. The *EER* differs from the official exchange rate because (1) the national accounts (NA) figure includes exports of deep-sea fishing products, whereas the BOP figure does not; (2) the BOP figure includes factor income from abroad, whereas the NA figure does not; (3) the BOP figure includes exports of freight and insurance services to foreign companies, whereas the NA figure does not; and (4) the *EER* concept implicitly is averaged over daily values for each year. Similarly, the *IER* differs from the *ER* because of the treatment of imports of freight and insurance by domestic companies and the daily averaging.

ducts. In alternative versions of the model the export level may be made purely exogenous, as a function of world exports, or a policy exogenous variable that may be varied in different solutions. The main purely exogenous variables are level of gross agricultural output, net factor income from abroad, population, and some export and import price variables. Table 12-1 lists all variables in the model.

The basic concepts underlying the model specification can be outlined as follows.

1. Output is determined by expectations[1] and by the availability of domestic credit. In the short term, the stock of fixed capital is not a binding constraint, but of course, investment accelerates when facilities are intensively used. The relevant expectations include prices and effective demand levels, and for the latter the government's annual export target is the key variable.

2. Output growth then determines investment, and investment needs determine savings. Many Korean economists have consistently stressed that savings do not constrain Korean growth but that savings will respond to investment needs.[2] Therefore to express this concept in the system, the

1. Lance Taylor, *Macro Models for Developing Countries* (McGraw-Hill, 1979).

2. Mahn Je Kim and Yung Chul Park, "A Study on Savings Behavior, 1953–1972," in Chuk Kyo Kim, ed., *Planning Models and Macroeconomic Policy Issues* (Seoul: Korea Development Institute, 1977).

model has no savings function (no consumption function). Consumption is determined by the national accounts identity.

3. Prices are determined mainly by the relative levels of nominal money supply and the real demand for money, plus movements in the key primary price—the price of imports.[3]

4. Nonagricultural employment is determined by nonagricultural output growth and real wage growth; there also is a wage equation for the labor share in national income and an equation for urban population growth.

In essence it is a demand-led model in a double (or triple) sense: demand expectations help determine output; (2) output determines the increment in capital stock; and (3) the capital increment, plus foreign savings behavior, determines domestic savings.

This model differs from some other macromodels by having a non-neoclassical output supply function and by not having a consumption function. The widespread view in Korea that savings is responsive to investment opportunities and trade policy tends to be supported by simple tests that show the Keynesian consumption function, in first-difference form, to be relatively unstable.

Arnold Harberger pointed out to the authors that this residual specification of consumption also appears to accord with Korean reality in another respect: whether by policy design or not, inflation has been a mechanism whereby consumption was squeezed to allow for more real capital formation. The national accounts deflator for private consumption grew more rapidly than both the deflators for gross domestic product (GDP) and fixed capital formation during 1963–77.

In the past six years, South Korea has suffered a much higher rate of inflation than in the previous ten years. Inflation has become a major social issue, with urban groups feeling that they are suffering disproportionately from its consequences. The government has been concerned not only with social inequities generated by inflation but also with inflation's effects on Korea's export competitiveness. The debate over appropriate

3. R. C. Vogel, "The Dynamics of Inflation in Latin America, 1950–1969," *American Economic Review*, vol. 64 (March 1974), pp. 102–14; David Laidler, "Inflation—Alternative Explanations and Policies: Tests on Data Drawn from Six Countries," in K. Brunner and A. H. Meltzer, eds., *Institutions, Policies, and Economic Performance*, Carnegie-Rochester Conference Series on Public Policy, vol. 4 (Amsterdam: North-Holland, 1976), pp. 251–306; and R. J. Ball and T. Burns, "The Inflationary Mechanism in the U.K. Economy," *American Economic Review*, vol. 66 (September 1976), pp. 467–84.

policies for curtailing inflation has intensified in the last year or two, and a variety of prescriptions have been offered. The government itself has shifted tactics from time to time. Until recently, price controls had been attempted, with a little success. In 1977 and early 1978, import liberalization moves were advocated and to some extent implemented, but subsequently they lost some of their appeal as the trade gap widened sharply, in a reversal of trends. Attempting to limit the rate of increase of grain prices has been an element of strategy from 1976 onward. Since the beginning of 1979, strong controls over the the rate of expansion of the money supply have been favored, although other approaches have not been disregarded.[4] Very recently, it has been considered necessary to diminish the growth rate of exports and gross national product (GNP), partly because of the lack of success of other measures and also because of the apparent conviction of the public that the sustained export drive is finally having deleterious side effects. Also, very recently, after five years of strong real wage increases, wage control measures have been discussed.

Given these concerns, we have attempted to address the model to some issues of inflation and growth, while making no pretense of a comprehensive examination of all strategies. Specifically, in a historical context, we have addressed the model to the role of exports in generating growth and, possibly, inflation; to the role of the money supply for growth and inflation; and to the effects of the 1974–75 "oil shock" on domestic economic performance. We also discuss other evidence on the role of wage increases, agricultural price increases, and import liberalization in determining overall inflation rates.

The remainder of this chapter presents the equations of the model's basic version, with some discussion; discusses sample period performance of the model; presents some historical experiments; and offers a policy summary and other concluding observations.

The Equations of the Model

As noted above, the system as a whole is triangular in structure, so that, for any time period, the solution of an equation depends upon information only from the equations above it in the structure. The equations are given here in their triangular sequence, with symbols as defined in table

4. Economic Planning Board, Republic of Korea, *The New Stabilization Program* (Seoul: Economic Planning Board, June 1979).

12-1. Some notational conventions are as follows: (1) the prefix *D* refers to the percentage-change form of the variable; (2) the prefix *T* refers to the first-difference form of the variable; (3) the suffix *C* means current price (nominal) valuation of the variable; and (4) subscripts denote annual time periods.

The model begins with equations for value added and prices in agriculture and nonagriculture; continues through other price and macroeconomic expenditure variables; and concludes with equations for wages, unemployment, wage share of national income, and urban population. Because there is no statistical private consumption function, private consumption is determined by the national accounts identity. Private consumption is a residual variable, below the other expenditure variables in the recursive order of the system. Hence the system's performance in tracking private consumption is a good indication of the amount of accumulated error in the entire set of expenditure variable equations.

Many of the other identities in the model are trivial relationships required to convert from current to constant prices, and vice versa.[5] The agricultural equations that initiate the system are little more than statistical regularities, based on near identities. Important behavioral relationships commence with the third equation, for nonagricultural income.

In the reporting of the equations, the numbers in parentheses are *t*-ratios, OLSQ means ordinary least squares, CORC is Cochrane-Orcutt iterative procedure, SM connotes the standard error of estimate of the equation divided by the mean value of the dependent variable, D.W. stands for the Durbin-Watson statistic, and the years refer to the regression sample, if the years are not 1963–77. In several instances, alternative equations are numbered a, b, and so forth.

Agricultural Income in Current Prices

(1) $DYAC_t = -0.02562 + 1.14706\ DA_t + 1.17413\ DPAS_t.$
            $(-0.9096)\quad (5.8862)\qquad\quad (8.7938)$

OLSQ; $R^2 = 0.9258$; D.W. $= 2.5845$; SM $= 0.1908$

COMMENTS. Equation 1 says that the percentage change in current price agricultural value added is closely related to the sum of the percen-

---

5. The identities required to convert from percentage-change form to level form of a variable are omitted.

tage change in agricultural output and the percentage change in the index of farmers' selling prices. This equation is a near identity, since the coefficients of the explanatory variables are close to unity in value and the intercept terms do not differ significantly from zero. Two factors prevent the equation from being specified as an identity: (1) omission of variations in agricultural input prices and input-output ratios and (2) statistical differences in coverage in the sample surveys for determining gross output, value added, and prices.

The change in gross agricultural output is exogenous for this model, but it could be made endogenous via inclusion of a production function. The agricultural price variable is regarded as a policy instrument, for it is strongly influenced by two annual policy decisions: the support price levels for grains and the amount of imports of agricultural products. However, it should be recognized that government control over the agricultural price index is limited and becomes weaker over time as nongrain products occupy an increasing share of total agricultural output.

Agricultural Value-Added Deflator

(2)
$$PYA_t = -0.00359 + 0.98953 \, PAS_t.$$
$$(-0.2791) \quad (131.458)$$

OLSQ; $R^2 = 0.9992$; D.W. $= 1.9137$; SM $= 0.0210$

Real Agricultural Value Added

(3)
$$YA_t = YAC_t/PYA_t.$$

Real Nonagricultural Value Added

(4) $\quad DYN_t = -0.04208(1 - \rho) + 0.29237(DMM1_{t-1} - \rho DMM1_{t-2})$
$$(-1.9293) \qquad\qquad (7.6488)$$

$$+ \, 0.23492(DE_t - \rho DE_{t-1})$$
$$(10.2065)$$

$$+ \, 0.06058(DPYN_{t-1} - \rho DPYN_{t-2}) + \rho DYN_{t-1};$$
$$(1.0780)$$

CORC; $R^2 = 0.8909$; D.W. $= 2.3933$; SM $= 0.1246$; $\rho = -0.56060$
$$(-2.6219)$$

(4a) $DYN_t = -0.02624 + 0.16541(DMM1_t + DMM1_{t-1})$
             (-1.1139) (5.8330)

             $+ 0.13959 \; DE_t + 0.07338 \; DPYN_{t-1}.$
             (4.8209) (1.1909)

OLSQ; $R^2 = 0.8596$; D.W. $= 2.7196$; SM $= 0.1414$

COMMENTS. Equation 4 is most readily interpreted as it is written in equation 4a, without the factors ρ and $(1 - \rho)$ and without the lagged terms involving ρ. These variables entered the equation in the course of the Cochrane-Orcutt iterations in order to remove some of the autocorrelation among the residuals. The variable $DPYN_{t-1}$ is taken to represent expectations for the rate of nonagricultural price change in year t. Following Taylor,[6] the relevant set of price expectation variables should include the interest rate and the wage rate, both with negative coefficients in the equation for DYN_t. Official interest rates have been controlled at non-market levels for most of the sample period, and no reliable survey of unofficial money market rates is available; hence that variable had to be dropped. Wage rates were included in some estimations, but their coefficient always proved to be statistically insignificant. The lagged price variable alone, then, becomes a proxy for expected profits, and its coefficient has the correct sign.

Export targets for each year have been announced in advance by the government and, through various incentive measures, were met almost exactly in all but one or two years. Hence the export variable (in rate of change form) may be regarded either as an expectational variable used in firms' production planning or as an autonomous expenditure variable.

The money supply is assumed to affect production through the availability of domestic credit to finance working capital expenditures.[7] The lag reflects the lead time required to plan raw materials purchases. The M2 concept of money supply worked as well as M1 in equation 4 and also in equation 5 below.

It has been suggested that because of the omission of physical capi-

6. Taylor, *Macro Models*.
7. For discussions of the role of money in the aggregate production function, see David Levhari and Don Patinkin, "The Role of Money in a Simple Growth Model," *American Economic Review*, vol. 58 (September 1968), pp. 713–53. Recently, Barro used *unanticipated* changes in the money supply to explain output (and price) changes. R. J. Barro, "Unanticipated Money, Output, and the Price Level in the United States," *Journal of Political Economy*, vol. 86 (August 1978), pp. 38–54.

tal stock, equation 4 may fit the data better in years of underutilization of capacity. However, while rigorous tests have not been performed on this point, casual inspection of the patterns of residuals in equation 4 shows that the equation fits as well in high-growth years as in low-growth years.

Nonagricultural Value-Added Deflator

(5) $DPYN_t = 0.05700 - 0.64306 \, DYN_t$
$\quad\quad\quad (1.1919) \; (-3.4749)$

$\quad\quad\quad\quad + 0.33281(DPYN_{t-1} + DPYN_{t-2}) + 0.21729 \, DPIM_t$
$\quad\quad\quad\quad (4.1515) \quad\quad\quad\quad\quad\quad\quad\quad\quad (5.4443)$

$\quad\quad\quad\quad + 0.14528 \, DMM1_{t-1};$
$\quad\quad\quad\quad (2.3466)$

$\quad\quad$ OLSQ; $R^2 = 0.8918$; D.W. $= 2.2534$; SM $= 0.1502$

(5a) $DPYN_t = 0.07022 - 0.94616 \, DYN_t$
$\quad\quad\quad (1.4969) \; (-3.6323)$

$\quad\quad\quad\quad + 0.32208(DPYN_{t-1} + DPYN_{t-2}) + 0.20389 \, DPIM_t$
$\quad\quad\quad\quad (3.9520) \quad\quad\quad\quad\quad\quad\quad\quad\quad (5.0559)$

$\quad\quad\quad\quad + 0.12492(DMM1_t + DMM1_{t-1}).$
$\quad\quad\quad\quad (2.1402)$

$\quad\quad$ OLSQ; $R^2 = 0.8849$; D.W. $= 1.6718$; SM $= 0.1450$

COMMENTS. The form of the above price equations is derived from a simple hypothesis based on portfolio balance and demand for real cash balances, plus a representation of the effects of international inflation.[8] The portfolio balance approach suggests that real demand for money may be determined partly by real output growth (DYN_t), which determines the increased transactions demand for money, and also by the expected return on money relative to other assets. For the latter, we have used a lagged inflation variable that is intended to represent inflationary expectations. Price increases then are a function of the difference between the rates of change of the nominal money supply and the real demand for money. In implementing this hypothesis empirically, it was found that the

8. A. C. Harberger, "The Dynamics of Inflation in Chile," in *Measurement in Economics: Studies in Mathematical Economics and Econometrics in Honor of Yehuda Grunfeld* (Stanford University Press, 1963); Laidler, "Inflation—Alternative Explanations and Policies."

coefficient of the *current* money supply growth variable ($DMM1_t$) was statistically insignificant.[9] A large number of alternative equations were estimated, and that variable's coefficient became significant only when combined with the lagged money supply change (as in equation 5a). The elasticity of inflation with respect to the nominal money supply is about 13 to 14 percent in alternative equations.

The real output variable DYN_t may also influence prices through greater supply on the goods markets: consumption growth tends to be rather smooth owing to permanent income effects, so short-term fluctuations in output represent fluctuations in net excess supply. In alternative equations the elasticity of prices with respect to this variable remained consistently around -0.6. This elasticity is higher in absolute value in equation 5a because the fifth right-hand term includes two variables and hence is larger numerically.

Expectations turn out to be quite important in determining price movements, with a rather stable elasticity of about 33 percent. Import prices also have been important, owing to the relatively inelastic demand for imported grains and petroleum products. The elasticity of domestic inflation with respect to imported prices turns out to be 21 percent to 22 percent.

In estimating alternative equations, it was found that output fluctuations and cost factors alone can explain 73 percent of the variation in the rate of inflation.

When substituted for the money variable, the government's net domestic borrowing is equally significant for two reasons: (1) it is the clearest measure of government deficit and (2) it represents an important component of high-powered money; thus it operates on the price level through both fiscal and monetary channels.

To derive a more complete money-inflation relationship, the effects of money supply on output and output on prices must be taken into account. Substituting equation 4 into equation 5 suggests that the total effect of money supply expansion on the price level has been nil over the sample period. This finding implies that within a limited range of variation around the actual historical money supply growth rates, changes in those growth rates would not have altered the rate of inflation. Apparently, most of the money supply growth over 1963–77 serviced genuine transactions de-

9. Vogel, "Dynamics of Inflation in Latin America." Vogel finds a similar result for a few countries in his Latin American sample. Aghevli and Rodriguez's price equation contains the same form of the output and money supply variables that ours does. B. B. Aghevli and C. A. Rodriguez, "Trade, Prices, and Output in Japan: A Simple Monetary Model," *IMF Staff Papers*, vol. 26 (March 1979), pp. 38–54.

mands; that is not surprising, given the low rate of monetization of the 1963 Korean economy, by international standards, and the rapid rate of real industrial output growth over 1963–77. This lack of monetary influence on prices is confirmed in the system simulation results reported subsequently, but we hasten to add that it is not necessarily correct to assume that the lack of influence will continue in the post sample period. Another caveat is that the expectational *mechanism* is assumed stable, that is, the double lag price increase term remains valid as the determinant of inflationary expectations. Either an abrupt or a prolonged shift in monetary policy could affect the psychology of inflation and hence change the structure of equation 5 as regards expectations.[10] These issues are discussed again in the concluding section.

Nonagricultural Value Added in Current Prices

(6) $$YNC_t = YN_t \cdot PYN_t.$$

GDP in Constant and Current Prices

(7) $$Y_t = YA_t + YN_t.$$

(8) $$YC_t = YAC_t + YNC_t.$$

(9) $$PY_t = YC_t/Y_t.$$

Government Consumption Expenditures and Their Price Index

(10) $$CG_t = 107.368 + 0.09103 \ YN_t.$$
$$(20.0759)(39.9658)$$

OLSQ; $R^2 = 0.9919$; D.W. $= 1.6568$; SM $= 0.0325$

(11) $$PCG_t = 0.10098 + 1.20803 \ WC_t.$$
$$(3.5795) \quad (58.4205)$$

OLSQ; $R^2 = 0.9962$; D.W. $= 1.7094$; SM $= 0.0522$

(12) $$CGC_t = CG_t \cdot PCG_t.$$

10. Equation 5 was reestimated via two-stage least squares (2SLS), using fitted values of DYN from equation 4. The results were very similar to those reported. With the 2SLS estimate, when equation 4 was substituted into equation 5, the total effect of money on prices increased slightly from the OLSQ case but still remained very low.

COMMENTS. The wage rate is used as the explanatory variable for the government consumption price index because wage costs are much greater than materials costs in the government budget. The wage variable WC_t is the manufacturing wage rate, but clearly, service sector wages closely follow the pattern of the manufacturing sector. Attempting to relate the government consumption deflator to the GDP deflator or other national accounts deflators yields a much poorer fit.

Gross Fixed Capital Formation

(13) $IF_t = -229.546 + 0.83467\ YN_{t-1} - 0.23038\ K_{t-1};$
          $\quad\quad (-1.5251)\ (2.0400) \quad\quad\quad (-1.0628)$

   OLSQ; $R^2 = 0.9699$; D.W. $= 1.3033$; SM $= 0.1156$

(13a) $IF_t = 142.863(1 - \rho) + 0.24332(YN_{t-1} - \rho YN_{t-2})$
          $\quad\quad (1.1353) \quad\quad\quad\quad (3.9393)$

          $+ 0.89950(TMM1_t - \rho TMM1_{t-1}) + \rho IF_{t-1};$
          $\quad (3.3388)$

   CORC; $R^2 = 0.9871$; D.W. $= 1.6361$; SM $= 0.0756$, $\rho = 0.76003$
   $\quad\quad\quad\quad\quad\quad\quad\quad\quad\quad\quad\quad\quad\quad\quad\quad\quad\quad (4.5294)$

(13b) $IF_t = 225.328(1 - \rho) + 0.36070(YN_{t-1} - \rho YN_{t-2})$
         $\quad\quad (1.3838) \quad\quad\quad\quad (2.9436)$

          $- 0.088624(K_{t-1} - \rho K_{t-2}) + 0.99637(TMM1_{t-1}$
          $\quad (-1.3065) \quad\quad\quad\quad\quad\quad (3.7586)$

          $- \rho TMM1_{t-2}) + \rho IF_{t-1};$

   CORC; $R^2 = 0.9888$; D.W. $= 1.8162$; SM $= 0.0738$, $\rho = 0.82742$
   $\quad\quad\quad\quad\quad\quad\quad\quad\quad\quad\quad\quad\quad\quad\quad\quad\quad\quad (5.7063)$

(13c) $IF_t = -47.9309(1 - \rho) + 0.40573(YN_{t-1} - \rho YN_{t-2})$
        $\quad\quad (-0.5856) \quad\quad\quad\quad (12.3721)$

          $- 17.6665 \left[\left(\dfrac{100 \cdot IV}{Y}\right)_{t-1} - \rho\left(\dfrac{100 \cdot IV}{Y}\right)_{t-2} \right] + \rho IF_{t-1}.$
          $\quad (-2.2064)$

   CORC; $R^2 = 0.9832$; D.W. $= 1.7413$; SM $= 0.0863$, $\rho = 0.61593$
   $\quad\quad\quad\quad\quad\quad\quad\quad\quad\quad\quad\quad\quad\quad\quad\quad\quad\quad (3.0280)$

COMMENTS. Equation 13 is of the standard accelerator form. An improved explanation of historical behavior can be obtained by including the lagged increment in the money supply, or inventories, in the right-hand-side arguments. Both variables are statistically significant, and inclusion of either of them reduces the forecasting error (standard error of estimate) by about one-third.

Price Deflator for Fixed Investment

$$(14) \quad DPIF_t = 0.04545(1 - \rho) + 0.44028(DPIM_t - \rho DPIM_{t-1})$$
$$\qquad\qquad (-2.9448) \qquad\qquad (11.0436)$$

$$0.13283(DIF_t - \rho DIF_{t-1}) + \rho DPIF_{t-1}.$$
$$(2.4452)$$

CORC; $R^2 = 0.8848$; D.W. $= 2.3317$; SM $= 0.2333$; 1962–77, $\rho = -0.46470$
$$(-2.0326)$$

COMMENTS. Given the large component of imported capital goods in total investment, the cost of investment goods was hypothesized to depend in part on the price index for imports. Also, supply and demand conditions on the capital goods market, as represented by the growth rate of fixed investment, contribute to explaining movements in the investment goods price index.

Depreciation and Capital Stock Accumulation

$$(15) \quad RDEPR_t = -163.683(1 - \rho) + 0.12856(Y - \rho Y_{t-1}) + \rho RDEPR_{t-1}.$$
$$\qquad\qquad (-4.1557) \qquad\qquad (13.3462)$$

CORC; $R^2 = 0.9905$; D.W. $= 1.5715$; SM $= 0.0690$; 1962–77; $\rho = 0.77317$
$$(4.7217)$$

COMMENTS. Real GDP and the level of capital stock worked about equally well as the explanatory variable for the level of (real) capital consumption allowances.

$$(16) \qquad\qquad K_t = K_{t-1} - RDEPR_t + IF_t.$$

Inventory Investment and Its Price Index

$$(17) \qquad IV_t = -31.6107 - 0.27651\, TE_t + 0.25855\, TY_t$$
$$\qquad\qquad (-1.8877)(-3.9449) \qquad\qquad (2.8602)$$

$$153.061\, DPY_t + 2.02127 \left[\frac{TIMPO}{IMUV} \right]_t$$
$$(2.2171) \qquad\qquad (2.4185)$$

OLSQ; $R^2 = 0.8393$; D.W. $= 1.3489$; SM $= 0.3965$

COMMENTS. The first difference in GDP (TY_t) stands for increases in the supply of goods and hence for inventory accumulation. The most dynamic element on the demand side, the first difference in exports (TE_t), represents inventory decumulation. Even though these two variables are positively correlated, as revealed by equation 4, they turn out to have the expected opposite signs in explaining inventory behavior.

The other two variables with positive effects on inventory accumulation are the expected future price increases, as represented by the current rate of inflation in the GDP deflator (DPY_t), and the real (dollar) increment in commodity imports.

$$(18) \qquad PIV_t = 0.25337(1 - \rho) + 0.01527(PAS_t - \rho PAS_{t-1})$$
$$\qquad\qquad\quad (2.7610) \qquad\qquad (28.3686)$$

$$-0.01019(IV_t - \rho IV_{t-1}) + \rho PIV_{t-1}.$$
$$(-5.8938)$$

OLSQ; $R^2 = 0.9635$; D.W. $= 2.1880$; SM $= 0.1618$; $\rho = -0.77392$
$$(-4.7331)$$

COMMENTS. Agricultural goods figure importantly in inventory accumulation, and hence the index of farmers' selling prices (PAS_t) is very important in explaining the price of inventories. Also, the (excess) supply of inventories has a negative influence on the price.

Total Imports in Domestic Currency

$$(19) \qquad DIM_t = 0.03671 + 0.73290 \, DIF_t + 0.76226 \, DYN_t$$
$$\qquad\qquad\quad (0.3863) \quad (4.5552) \qquad\qquad (1.1345)$$

$$- 0.23055 \, DIMUV_t - 0.49057 \, DIER_t.$$
$$(-1.8390) \qquad\qquad (-2.7505)$$

OLSQ; $R^2 = 0.9125$; D.W. $= 2.3618$; SM $= 0.3508$

COMMENTS. The close relation between investment demand and imported capital goods is revealed by the investment growth rate variable (DIF_t) in this equation, and the demand for other classes of goods is represented by the growth of real nonagricultural GDP (DYN_t). Imports contribute partly to the building up of stocks in some years, and so it is not surprising that lagged stock accumulation negatively affects current imports. The change in the won price of imported goods is decomposed in this equation into two components: inflation in the dollar price of imported goods (*DIMUV*) and change in the effective import exchange rate (*DIER*).

$$(20) \qquad IMC_t = IM_t \cdot PIM_t.$$

Imports in Dollars

(21) $\quad DIMPO_t = 0.11375 + 0.83413 \ DIF_t + 0.82465 \ DIMUV_t$
$\qquad\qquad (2.4654) \quad (5.4416) \qquad\qquad (6.4694)$

$\qquad\qquad - 0.59227 \ DIER_t;$
$\qquad\qquad (-3.8101)$

OLSQ; $R^2 = 0.9308$; D.W. $= 1.6999$; SM $= 0.2783$

(21a) $\quad DIMPO_t = 0.00784 + 0.65958 \ DIF_t - 0.03320 \left[\dfrac{100 \cdot IV}{Y} \right]_{t-1}$
$\qquad\qquad (0.0789) \quad (3.1072) \qquad (-1.4685)$

$\qquad\qquad 0.82817 \ DIMUV_t + 1.27008 \ DYN_t - 0.26934 DER_t.$
$\qquad\qquad (6.3131) \qquad\qquad (2.0656) \qquad\quad (-1.8381)$

OLSQ; $R^2 = 0.9398$; D.W. $= 1.4873$; SM $= 0.2870$

COMMENTS. The $IMPO_t$ denotes *commodity* imports in current dollars. The explanatory variables DER_t and $DIER_t$ represent the percentage change in the official exchange rate and the effective import exchange rate,[11] respectively; the variables have similar coefficients and degrees of significance in alternative equations.

The variable $DIMUV_t$ is the percentage change in the "import unit value index," an index of inflation in the dollar value of imports. The elasticity of real dollar imports with respect to this index of their price is $-(1 - \beta)$, where β is the coefficient of $DIMUV_t$ in the estimated equation. The value of $(1 - \beta)$ is stable at about 0.17. Owing to their typically discrete character, the exchange rate movements, to some degree, are anticipated, and hence importers' reactions are spread over more than one year. Hence we would expect import demand in the short term to be more inelastic with respect to dollar cost increases than to exchange rate move-

11. See definitional footnotes to table 12-1.

ments. The equation with the most significant coefficient for DER_t (equation 21a) tends to confirm this phenomenon: the elasticity with respect to the dollar price index is -0.17 and with respect to the exchange rate is -0.27. The same phenomenon is observed in equation 19.

In the equations below, total dollar imports are derived by converting total won imports, and then service imports are obtained by the difference with respect to dollar commodity imports. An alternative procedure is to eliminate equation 19 and to replace it with an equation for service imports in dollars. That procedure was tested and gave a poorer forecasting performance than the one used.

In another test, equation 21 was replaced by five equations for Standard International Trade Classification groups of commodity imports (food, minerals and fuels, and others). Some, but not all, of the commodity group equations turned out very well, and the best sample period forecasts of aggregate commodity imports were obtained using equation 21.

Figure 12-3 below shows the sample performance of equation 21.

Service Imports

(22) $$IMCD_t = IMC_t/IER_t.$$

(23) $$IMS_t = IMCD_t - IMPO_t.$$

Balance of Payments

(24) $$ECD_t = EGD_t + ESD_t.$$

(25) $$BPD_t = ECD_t - IMCD_t + NFID_t.$$

(26) $$EC_t = ECD_t \cdot EER_t.$$

(27) $$BPWC_t = EC_t - IMC_t + NFID_t \cdot ER_t.$$

COMMENTS. As a practical matter, exports are forecast by Korean policy-making bodies first in terms of current dollar commodity (EGD_t) and service (ESD_t) exports. These findings are then converted into current won imports by use of the export effective exchange rate (EER_t). Conversion of these variables into constant dollar and constant won exports requires use of the export unit value index ($EXUV_t$) and the national accounts export deflator (PE_t).

Private Consumption

(28) $CP_t = Y_t - E_t - IF_t - IV_t - CG_t + IM_t + STD_t.$

(29) $CPC_t = YC_t - EC_t - IFC_t - IVC_t - CGC_t + IMC_t + STDC_i.$

(30) $PCP_t = CPC_t / CP_t.$

COMMENTS. The variables STD_t and $STDC_t$ are the (exogenous) national accounts statistical discrepancy, in constant and current prices. These variables are used in the sample period simulations but not in forecasting beyond the sample period.

Savings

(31) $SD_t = Y_t - CP_t - CG_t.$

(32) $SDC_t = YC_t - CPC_t - CGC_t.$

(33) $S_t = SD_t + IM_t - E_t.$

(34) $SC_t = SDC_t + IMC_t - EC_t.$

Manufacturing Wage Index

(35) $DWC_t = -0.01383(1 - \rho) + 0.77422(DYN_{t-1} - \rho DYN_{t-2})$
$\qquad\quad (-0.2600) \qquad\qquad (2.8635)$

$\qquad\quad + 0.71774(DPYN_{t-1} - \rho DPYN_{t-2})$
$\qquad\qquad (4.7469)$

$\qquad\quad + 0.08347(WDUM_{t-1} - \rho WDUM_{t-2}) + \rho DWC_{t-1}.$
$\qquad\qquad (5.1134)$

$\qquad$ CORC; $R^2 = 0.8784$; D.W. $= 2.3479$; SM $= 0.1474$; $\rho = -0.54124$
$\qquad\qquad\qquad\qquad\qquad\qquad\qquad\qquad\qquad (-2.4084)$

COMMENTS. Short-term acceleration in output growth, represented by DYN_{t-1}, causes additional pressure on the labor market, and labor supply to urban areas reacts more slowly; hence the short-term effect is higher wages.

Lagged price changes are reflected in higher wage demands in the current year's wage negotiations.

The wage dummy variable registers the structural change that occurred about 1974, when massive migration of Korean labor to the Middle East began. During 1970–73, wages grew by about 12 percent per year, but during 1974–78 they grew by about 32 percent per year. In real terms, wages kept pace with productivity increases until 1974–78, when real wages grew more rapidly than productivity.

Manufacturing Employment

$$(36) \qquad TNMA_t = -6.6205 + 0.7514\,TYN_t$$
$$(-0.1850) \quad (5.4045)$$

$$- 517.493(DWC_{t-1} - DPYN_{t-1}).$$
$$(-2.9712)$$

OLSQ; $R^2 = 0.7088$; D.W. $= 1.8001$; SM $= 0.4832$

COMMENTS. The first explanatory variable is the increment in real manufacturing output (value added), and the second is the change in the wage rate relative to the general nonagricultural price index, lagged one year. As expected, output growth has a positive effect on employment, and relative wage increases have negative effects.

Wage Income and the Wage Share

$$(37) \quad TYLC = -50.1363 + 1744.86\,TWC_t + 0.27683\,TNMA_t.$$
$$(-2.0952) \qquad (24.4055) \qquad (1.9652)$$

OLSQ; $R^2 = 0.9860$; D.W. $= 2.9558$; SM $= 0.1576$

$$(38) \qquad WS_t = WS_{t-1}(1 + DYLC_t)/(1 + DYC_t).$$

COMMENTS. If the dependent variable were manufacturing wage income, then equation 37 would be an identity; as it is, we are assuming a regular statistical relationship between manufacturing wage rates and employment on the one hand and labor income for all sectors on the other.

Equation 38 is a first-order approximation to the labor share in national income, assuming that national income and GDP grow at approximately the same rate in the short term.

Urban and Rural Population

(39) $TUPOP_t = 2279.48 - 1510.21\left(\dfrac{YA}{YN}\right)_{t-1} - 756.056\left(\dfrac{PAS}{PAB}\right)_{t-1}.$

$\qquad\qquad\quad (5.2721)\ (-6.3609) \qquad\qquad (-2.0856)$

$\qquad\qquad$ OLSQ; $R^2 = 0.7713$; D.W. $= 2.0398$; SM $= 0.1868$

(40) $\qquad\qquad UPOP_t = UPOP_{t-1} + TUPOP_t.$

(41) $\qquad\qquad RPOP_t = POP_t - UPOP_t.$

COMMENTS. Equation 39 effectively is a simple annual migration function which says that the increment in urban population is a negative function of (1) lagged relative real output in agriculture and (2) lagged agricultural terms of trade.

Thus our description of the basic version of the model is completed. Some extensions are discussed later in this chapter. Clearly, several kinds of extensions are possible; the principal ones might involve (1) endogenizing some of the presently exogenous variables and (2) along with making the money supply endogenous, formulating equations for a financial subsector to incorporate more specific detail on monetary and fiscal policies.

Sample Period Performance of the Model

The system's historical validity can be assessed statistically by reference to (1) individual equations' regression statistics, (2) the system's "static simulation" performance, and (3) the system's dynamic simulation performance. A static simulation refers to an annual sequence of solutions of the model in which, for each year *t*, previous year's values of all variables are set at their actual levels. In a dynamic simulation, values for 1962 and prior years are taken as given, but sample period values of the endogenous variables are left at their endogenous levels when fed into later years.

In the static simulation, cumulative system error is transmitted down the recursive sequence for any given year, but it is not accumulated over time. In the dynamic case, error accumulates over time as well as across

Table 12-2. *Static Simulation Error Analysis*

	Level variable (percent)		Growth rate variable (percent)	
Variable	MAE/Mean[a]	Theil index[b]	MAE/Mean[a]	Theil index[b]
YNC	1.31	0.82	4.90	3.07
YN	0.85	0.49	8.40	4.77
PYN	1.86	1.14	12.46	7.48
YC	1.54	0.94	5.81	3.53
Y	0.51	0.29	6.08	3.75
PY	1.64	1.02	10.89	6.46
CPC	1.76	0.88	13.11	8.06
CP	1.69	1.00	23.24	13.29
PCP	2.20	1.39	21.95	10.93
CGC	3.61	1.59	24.73	14.01
CG	2.48	1.46	38.70	21.25
PCG	2.42	1.14	21.67	12.64
IFC	3.94	1.95	37.21	26.50
IF	5.10	2.82	54.16	32.59
PIF	1.85	1.06	18.48	10.11
IVC	25.61	12.51	n.a.	n.a.
IV	31.52	14.45	n.a.	n.a.
PIV	15.44	7.51	n.a.	n.a.
IMC	4.04	1.98	30.90	19.58
IM	5.09	2.53	45.48	23.25
WC	2.76	1.56	14.70	7.81
NMA	3.51	1.99	36.62	19.95
YLC	2.94	1.51	18.92	11.57
UPOP	0.72	0.47	12.79	8.10

n.a. Not applicable.
a. The ratio of the mean absolute error to the variable's actual mean value (see equation 42).
b. The Theil index is defined by equation 43.

equations. As remarked earlier, one main criterion of system performance is the amount of error in simulating private consumption, both in current and constant prices, since that variable is determined residually by the national accounts identity and other price and expenditure variables.

Regarding the individual equations' goodness of fit, the pertinent regression statistics are reported along with the equations in the previous section. The statistic SM, the ratio of the equation's standard error of estimate to the dependent variable's sample mean, is perhaps the most relevant for forecasting considerations. Loosely speaking, SM represents the average percentage forecasting error during the sample period. It is comparable to the system simulation error statistic called "mean absolute error divided by sample mean of actual values," which is reported in tables 12-2 and 12-3.

Table 12-3. *Dynamic Simulation Error Analysis*

	Level variable (percent)		Growth rate variable (percent)	
Variable	MAE/Mean[a]	Theil index[b]	MAE/Mean[a]	Theil index[b]
YNC	4.09	2.06	5.08	3.08
YN	0.84	0.49	12.25	7.28
PYN	3.76	1.98	12.89	7.29
YC	3.18	1.62	6.11	3.44
Y	0.80	0.45	13.44	7.64
PY	2.73	1.47	13.11	7.59
CPC	2.05	1.09	10.64	6.77
CP	3.49	2.20	30.11	18.43
PCP	3.44	1.87	18.50	9.82
CGC	4.21	2.16	24.41	15.86
CG	2.38	1.41	39.33	23.31
PCG	2.96	1.63	23.81	13.88
IFC	4.60	1.86	45.10	33.68
IF	5.98	3.14	66.35	42.12
PIF	1.51	0.83	21.00	11.98
IVC	34.81	19.94	n.a.	n.a.
IV	33.01	15.29	n.a.	n.a.
PIV	23.70	10.25	n.a.	n.a.
IMC	10.75	5.57	35.07	23.63
IM	10.09	5.23	51.87	28.75
WC	2.47	1.43	21.02	11.57
NMA	4.01	2.64	42.39	23.45
YLC	2.68	1.61	18.48	14.56
UPOP	0.92	0.50	13.73	8.50

n.a. Not applicable.
a. The ratio of the mean absolute error to the variable's actual mean value (see equation 42).
b. The Theil index is defined by equation 43.

Figures 12-1 to 12-3 below show the actual and estimated values from the individual equations for three key variables: the rate of inflation in the nonagricultural GDP deflator, the growth rate of real nonagricultural GDP, and the rate of change of commodity imports. In each case the hypotheses embodied in the equation appear to explain historical reality fairly well, taking each equation alone. However, the SM value for the import equation is quite a bit higher than for the other two equations, and so it has the greatest potential for disrupting system performance.

Tables 12-2 and 12-3 summarize the errors in both the static and dynamic simulations, and figures 12-4 through 12-10 report the annual simulation results for seven major variables. Dynamic simulation results for the other variables are given in the appendix tables.

Figure 12-1. *Annual Growth Rate of Nonagricultural GDP (DYN),*
1963–77

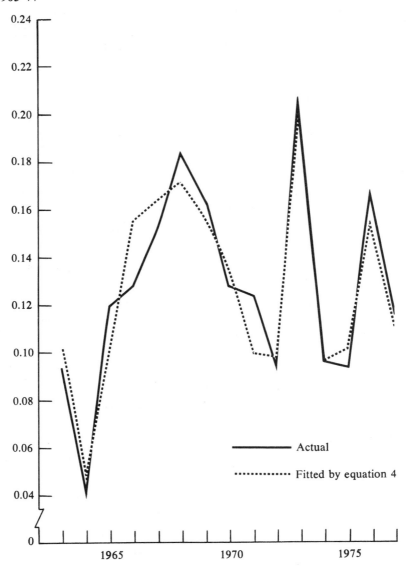

Figure 12-2. *Annual Inflation in the Nonagricultural GDP Price Index (DPYN), 1963–77*

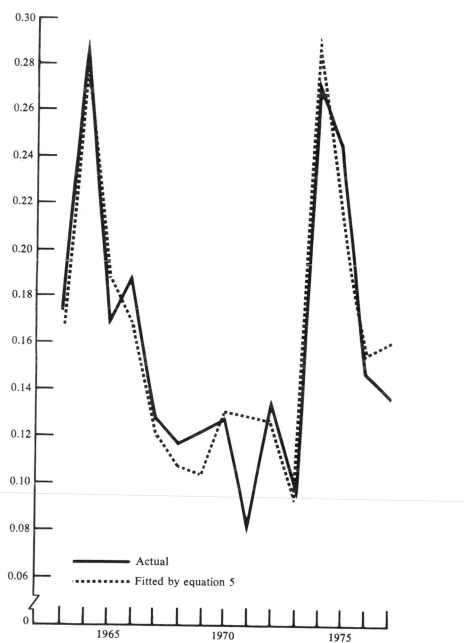

Figure 12-3. *Annual Percentage Rate of Change in Commodity Imports (in dollars, DIMPO), 1963–77*

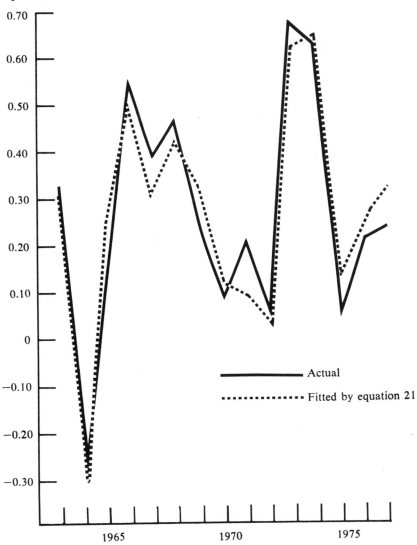

Figure 12-4. *DYNC: Actual Path and Static and Dynamic Simulations, 1963–77*

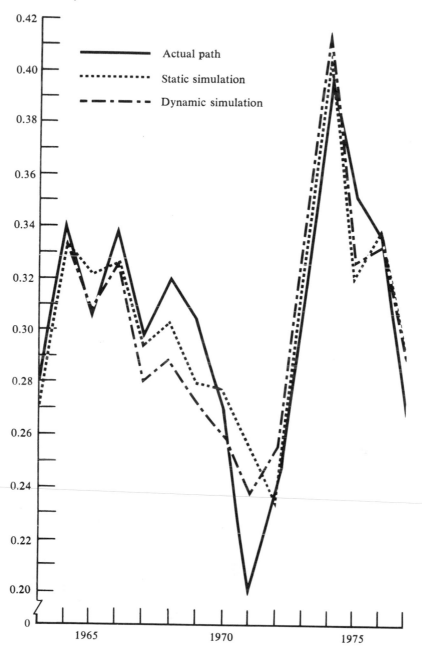

Figure 12-5. *DYN: Actual Path and Static and Dynamic Simulations, 1963–77*

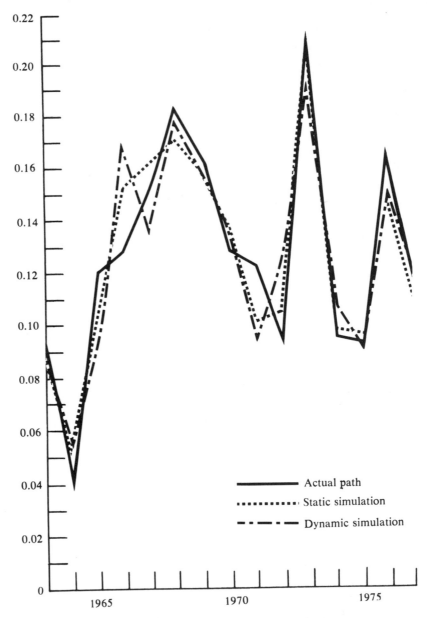

Figure 12-6. *DPYN: Actual Path and Static and Dynamic Simulations, 1963–77*

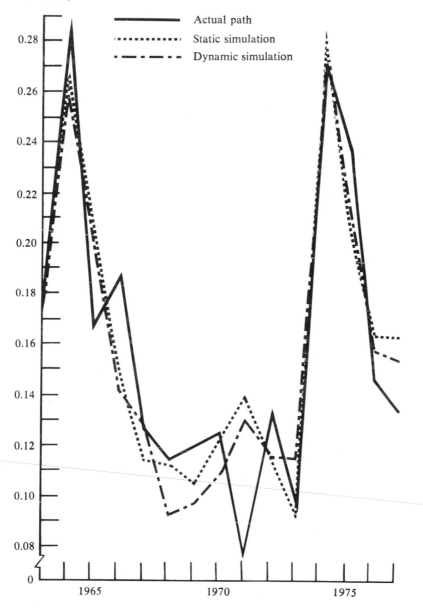

Figure 12-7. *DCPC: Actual Path and Static and Dynamic
Simulations, 1963–77*

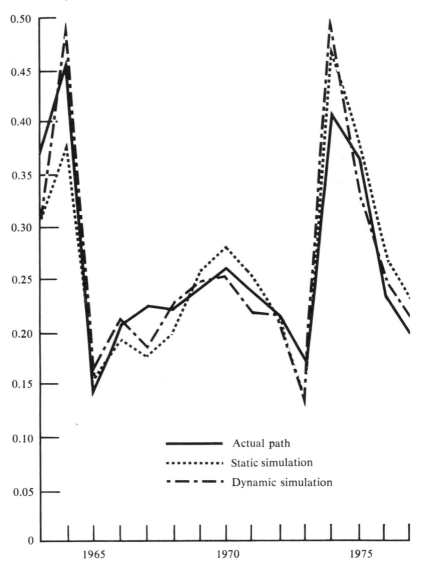

Figure 12-8. *DCP: Actual Path and Static and Dynamic Simulations, 1963–77*

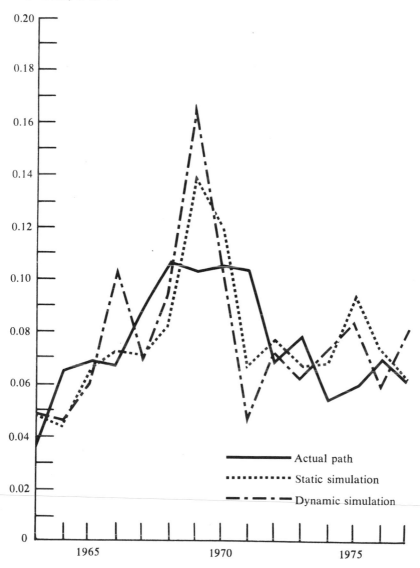

A review of tables 12-2 and 12-3 shows that the system tracks history fairly well and, as expected, the errors are larger in the dynamic simulations in most cases. However, there are a few exceptions in which the static simulation fares more poorly. The chief price and output variables, PYN and YN, are simulated with a level of accuracy equal to or better than that suggested by the single-equation regression statistics. The crucial residual, private consumption, also does well in current price terms but only moderately well in constant prices. Fixed investment also is predicted more accurately in current than in constant prices. A curiosity occurs in the case of GDP, where, owing to changing sign patterns of errors over time, the model predicts the *level* better in constant prices and the *growth rate* better in current prices. Imports and inventories are, not surprisingly, the worst-behaved national accounts variables. As a consequence of the import behavior, the model is not a very good predictor of the magnitude balance-of-payments situation, although the model does reflect the turning points fairly well (see appendix tables).

In tables 12-2 and 12-3, the first column for each type of variable reports the ratio of the mean absolute error (MAE) to the variable's actual mean value, where

$$(42) \qquad \text{MAE} = \sum_{t=63}^{77} \left| X_i^{\text{actual}} - X_i^{\text{simulated}} \right| \Big/ 15.$$

The Theil index in tables 12-2 and 12-3 is defined as follows:

$$(43) \quad \left(\sqrt{\sum_t (X_i^a - X_i^s)^2 / N} \right) \Big/ \left(\sqrt{\sum_t (X_i^a)^2 / N} + \sqrt{\sum_t (X_i^s)^2 / N} \right),$$

where $N = 15$.

As illustrated by figure 12-9, the model's simulation of *level* variables looks fairly good in all cases. However, because this model was designed for eventual use in forecasting, we emphasize that the performance of the percentage change variables is the concept by which the model should be judged.

Historical Experiments with the Model

The complete dynamic version of the model has been applied to three issues for the sample period: evaluating the impact of the 1974 oil shock on the Korean economy, evaluating the role of the "export push policy," and computing the effects of different monetary policies.

Figure 12-9. *CP: Actual Path and Dynamic Simulation, 1963–77*

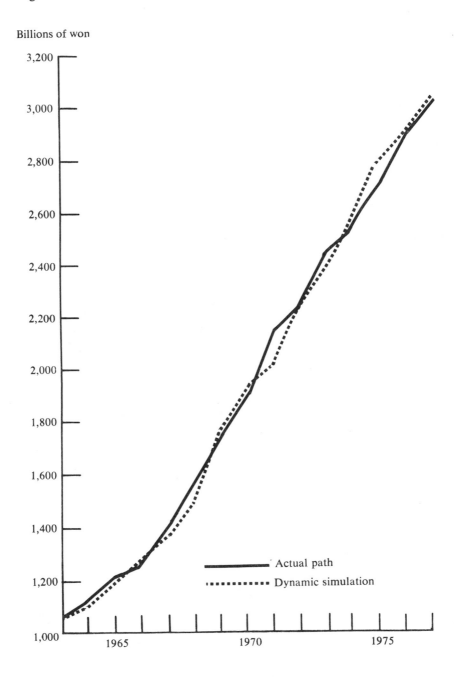

Billions of won

Figure 12-10. *DPCP: Actual Path and Static and Dynamic Simulations, 1963–77*

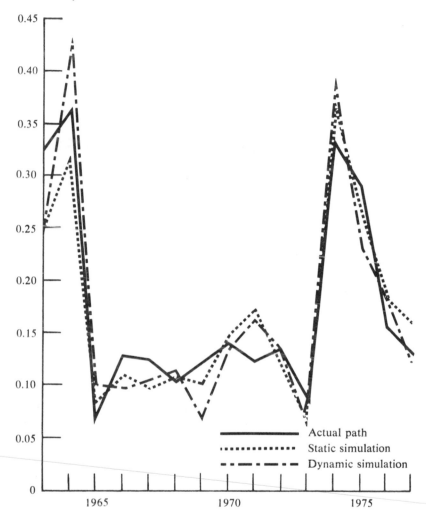

Actual path

Static simulation

Dynamic simulation

Table 12-4. *Exogenous Values for the Oil Shock Experiments*

Year	DIMUV		DEXUV		DWE: world export growth rate		
	Actual	Cases I and II	Actual	Cases I and II	Actual	Case I[a]	Case II[b]
1972	0.017	0.017	0.012	0.012	0.186	...	...
1973	0.335	0.020	0.266	0.020	0.393	...	...
1974	0.555	0.040	0.266	0.040	0.474	0.143	0.182
1975	0.029	0.040	−0.073	0.040	0.031	0.143	0.182
1976	−0.020	0.040	0.117	0.040	0.139	0.143	0.182
1977	0.022	0.040	0.095	0.040	0.129	0.143	0.182

a. In case I the 1974–77 *DWE* is set at the actual compound annual value for 1964–73.
b. In case II the 1974 *DWE* is set at the actual compound annual value for 1974–77.

Oil Shock Experiments

To simulate what might have happened in South Korea if the world price of oil had not increased dramatically in late 1973, it is necessary to posit alternative time paths of import and export price variables and of the volume of world exports. Clearly, this is sheer guesswork, but nonetheless, it is interesting to see approximately what might have occurred in the Korean economy under some set of international trade conditions that were much more favorable. We do not attempt to construct measures of the welfare loss resulting from the oil shock, but rather we use the model to simulate the consequences of a different set of historical circumstances. Obviously, the numerical results should not be taken literally, but their magnitudes are probably reliable.

In addition to hypothesizing different values for some exogenous variables, six previously exogenous variables, related to export levels and the international terms of trade, were made endogenous for this experiment. Table 12-4 gives the new assumptions, and equations 44 through 49 are the new behavioral relationships.

The new equations are as follows.

Exchange rate

$$(44) \quad ER_t = 215.55(1 - \rho) + 115.71(PYN_{t-1} - \rho PYN_{t-2}) + \rho ER_{t-1}.$$
$$(5.4333) \qquad\qquad (4.4839)$$

$$\text{CORC; } R^2 = 0.9317; \text{ D.W.} = 1.9687; \text{ SM} = 0.0859; \rho = 0.66119$$
$$(3.4134)$$

Effective import exchange rate

(45) $IER_t = 58.2124 + 0.73020\ ER_t + 27.1801\ PYN_{t-1}.$
          (2.0911)   (4.7122)   (1.0867)

OLSQ; $R^2 = 0.9558$; D.W. $= 2.2550$; SM $= 0.0656$

Effective export exchange rate

(46) $EER_t = 144.825(1 - \rho) + 0.28782(ER_t - \rho ER_{t-1})$
          (2.1880)   (1.1195)

          $+\ 79.8389(PYN_{t-1} - \rho PYN_{t-2}) + \rho EER_{t-1}.$
          (2.0922)

CORC; $R^2 = 0.9502$; D.W. $= 1.7989$; SM $= 0.0827$; $\rho = 0.65878$
                                                                 (3.3913)

National accounts import deflator

(47) $DPIM_t = -0.00054 + 0.98496\ DIMUV_t + 0.99603\ DIER_t.$
          (-0.04568) (16.6508)   (16.5135)

OLSQ; $R^2 = 0.9755$; D.W. $= 2.6868$; SM $= 0.2203$

National accounts export deflator

(48) $PE_t = -1.10526 + 0.02259\ EXUV_t + 0.00235\ EER_t.$
          (-10.2218) (7.4927)   (3.6998)

OLSQ; $R^2 = 0.9805$; D.W. $= 0.9312$; SM $= 0.0823$

Korean share of world export volume

(49) $KS_t = \dfrac{\alpha}{1 + \beta \exp(-\gamma t)}.$

Nonlinear estimation; $R^2 = 0.9833$; D.W. $= 2.0440$; SM $= 0.1171$; 1961–77

where $\alpha = 0.02327$ (2.1911)
      $\beta = 58.4406$ (3.4460)
      $\gamma = -0.21842$ (-7.1576)

$KS_t = ECD_t/WE_t$; $WE_t =$ world exports in current dollars
$t =$ annual time index.

The addition of these six equations (44 through 49) weakens the overall predictive power of the model slightly, but is preferable to attempting to make interdependent assumptions on these dependent variables without benefit of the statistical relationships.

Table 12-5 contains the results of the oil shock experiments. Absence of the oil price rise would have reduced 1974–77 inflation by six or seven percentage points per year. This outcome suggests that the oil shock was the major reason why Korean inflation rates from 1974 onward have been persistently above the rates of the previous ten years.

Import demand in the model is somewhat price responsive, and as a consequence, real import growth rates are seven or eight percentage points higher in the absence of the oil shock. And because of lower dollar inflation for Korea's export goods, real won exports grow more rapidly in the absence of the oil shock, even allowing the same or lower growth rates of current price world exports. Among other things, these effects add up to a slower rate of devaluation of the won: the model calculates that the 1977 exchange rate would have been 432 to 437 won per dollar, instead of 484 won per dollar.

The oil shock impact on the GDP growth rate is to reduce it by 0.8 to 1.6 percentage points per year, depending on the assumed path of world exports in the absence of the oil shock.[12] The absence of the oil shock also improves real wages slightly; thus the net effect on manufacturing employment is ambiguous, depending on whether the output effect or the factor substitution effect dominates.

Interestingly, the more favorable external trade position stimulates exports, investment, and savings sufficiently that real private consumption growth rates are slightly lower in the absence of the oil shock. In other words, Korea would have continued on the path of rapidly building up capital for future generations at the expense of present consumption. However, the absence of the oil shock would have led to a more equitable income distribution in Korea, as measured crudely by the wage share in national income.

Export Push Experiment

For the export push experiment, we return to the original version of the model, without the six new equations, and simply posit that the real won

12. For perspective, it should be noted that the Korean government made an explicit decision to sustain output growth after the oil shock by financing exporters' accumulation of finished inventories. As a result, by 1976, Korean exporters were in a position to capitalize on improved world market conditions.

Table 12-5. Oil Shock Experiments

1974–77 growth rates

Variable	Actual (DWE = 18.24%)	Case I (DWE = 14.32%)	Case II (DWE = 18.24%)	Variable	Actual (DWE = 18.24%)	Case I (DWE = 14.32%)	Case II (DWE = 18.24%)
Y	10.59	11.38	12.16	IF	15.86	16.31	17.01
YC	32.80	26.85	26.77	IFC	35.06	28.18	28.89
PY	20.16	13.88	13.01	PIF	16.97	10.20	10.16
YA	6.22	6.11	6.11	IV[a]	66.89	52.68	36.56
YAC	30.34	30.41	30.41	IVC[a]	212.39	200.92	130.12
PYA	22.67	22.87	22.87	PIV	31.06	32.87	34.79
YN	11.76	12.78	13.75	E	20.71	28.26	32.54
YNC	33.62	25.62	25.50	EC	40.43	32.23	36.38
PYN	18.67	11.37	10.32	PE	17.44	2.98	2.79
CP	6.13	6.07	4.80	IM	15.87	22.81	24.20
CPC	30.23	25.47	23.78	IMC	37.67	31.69	32.80
PCP	22.74	18.35	18.18	PIM	21.18	7.22	6.91
CG	9.85	11.10	11.85	BPD[a]	−1,307.20	−1,043.40	−517.16
CGC	42.20	38.52	39.37	BPW[a]	86.10	101.08	241.48
PCG	29.34	24.56	24.48	BPWC[a]	−476.33	−541.75	−326.46
S	16.41	16.65	16.78	WS	3.83	4.21	4.41
SC	33.56	26.24	25.38	UPOP	6.00	6.01	6.03
DS	21.95	24.36	28.79	IMUV	14.66	4.00	4.00
DSC	36.82	25.45	29.38	EXUV	10.13	4.00	4.00
WC	32.22	25.92	25.84	ER	5.26	2.40	2.08
YLC	37.70	31.06	31.18	IER	5.30	3.35	3.04
NMA	12.24	11.81	12.91	EER	5.28	2.57	2.25

Note: The oil shock experiments are described in the text. Six stochastic equations have been added in order to endogenize variables E, ER, IER, EER, DPIM, and PE. Two new exogenous variables have been added: IMUV and EXUV, which are the dollar import and export price indices, respectively.

Cases I and II are distinguished by assuming that in the absence of the oil shock, the 1974–77 world export growth rate would be (case I) equal to the 1964–73 growth rate (14.32 percent) and (case II) equal to the actual 1974–77 growth rate (18.24 percent) but smoothed over those four years.

a. Average *level* instead of growth rate.

Table 12-6. *Export Push Policy Experiment*
1968–77 growth rates

Variable	Actual (DE = 28.98%)	Case III (DE = 23.93%)	Variable	Actual (DE = 28.98%)	Case III (DE = 23.93%)
Y	11.24	10.33	WS	1.19	1.57
YC	28.60	29.41	UPOP	6.59	6.35
PY	15.68	17.36	IF	16.31	14.93
YA	4.74	5.27	IFC	31.20	29.87
YAC	24.84	25.50	PIF	13.03	13.15
PYA	19.16	19.21	IV[a]	55.24	64.40
YN	13.68	12.37	IVC[a]	120.83	165.97
YNC	30.12	30.98	PIV	30.84	27.02
PYN	14.57	16.65	IM	20.42	19.02
CP	8.13	8.97	IMC	37.19	35.66
CPC	25.64	28.57			
PCP	16.28	18.05	BPD[a]	−952.28	−1,784.67
CG	8.47	7.64	BPW[a]	−94.84	−264.52
CGC	31.38	31.64	BPWC[a]	−334.15	−746.83
PCG	20.98	22.30	S	16.57	15.25
WC	22.34	23.17	SC	32.73	31.77
YLC	30.14	30.98	DS	24.70	19.21
NMA	10.81	9.70	DSC	42.25	35.83

Note: In case III, each year's real won export growth rate was set at five percentage points lower than the actual.

a. Average 1968–77 *level* instead of growth rate.

export growth rate was five percentage points lower than the actual rate in each year during 1968–77. This experimental procedure has the disadvantage of overlooking the fact that other variables might have been lowered by this change; for example, the money supply growth rate might not have been as high. However, this experiment does have the advantage of enabling us to see the impact of one variable alone.

Table 12-6 reports the results of case III, the export push experiment. The lower export growth reduces annual GDP growth by 0.9 percentage point, and manufacturing employment by a slightly greater amount. This reduction would have meant 122,000 fewer jobs in manufacturing by 1977 had the slower export growth policy commenced in 1968. Import growth rates would have been only slightly lower, and so Korea's balance-of-payments position would have been markedly worse.

Contrary to some opinions on the causes of Korean inflation, lower export growth, ceteris paribus, would have meant higher inflation. The lower growth would have reduced the transactions demand for money, and hence the same nominal money stock would have been more inflationary. (On the other hand, as the next experiment indicates, it is not clear that reducing the money supply growth rate correspondingly would have helped control inflation.)

The welfare of the present generation, if measured by real private consumption, would have been greater with less emphasis on exports. Proportionately less of total consumption expenditure would have been made by the government. Real wages would have been somewhat lower by 1977, but the wage share in national income would have been greater.

The picture that emerges regarding exports is that the actual policies were successful in improving the country's balance-of-payments position and in promoting growth, employment, and capital stock for the benefit of future generations. Also, the policy was not inflationary, and it may even have helped somewhat with respect to prices. However, there was a sacrifice of overall private consumption in the medium term, and another cost of the policy was a worsened factoral income distribution. The export-cum-industrialization policy also contributed to greater urbanization (and presumably to the attendant congestion).

To test the robustness of these conclusions, the export push experiment was repeated with both the export growth rate and the money supply growth rate reduced by five percentage points per year. The results were similar to those reported in table 12-6, except that real GDP growth was yet lower, by a small amount, and inflation was a little worse.

Monetary Policy Experiments

Over the 1968–77 period, the nominal money supply ($M1$) grew at a compound annual rate of 33.08 percent. In case IV, with the original version of the model, each year's growth rate of $M1$ is reduced by five percentage points, and in case V a smooth annual growth rate of 30 percent is assumed. This experiment suffers the same methodological defect of the export experiment by assuming that other exogenous variables are unchanged and that structural relationships are unaffected. However, this experiment has the same advantage of permitting us to analyze the role of one variable in isolation, and by dealing with relatively small departures from reality, the assumption of unchanged structural relationships is more tenable. We would not extrapolate these results to large departures from historical experience, and the same proviso applies to the export push experiment.

As table 12-7 shows, and as would be expected from the nature of equation 4, the five percentage point drop in money supply growth would have meant a one percentage point drop in the real GDP growth rate. Investment expenditures would have declined proportionately more than other kinds of expenditures, and imports would have been significantly lower. Hence if the export growth rate could have been sustained at historical levels with lower money growth, the balance-of-payments position would have been more favorable.

On the other hand, inflation would have been slightly worse, real private consumption would have been lower (mostly because of higher prices), and manufacturing employment would have been less. The inflation result follows from the structure of equations 4 and 5: lower money growth means lower output growth, which in turn makes a given money supply more inflationary. The magnitudes of the effects are such that in net terms a reduction of money supply growth alone does not reduce inflation.

Of course this result appears counterintuitive but suggests that the observed expansion in Korean money supply has been very much in accord with increased transactions demands. Korea's rate of monetization in the 1960s was low by international standards, and the rapid industrialization required an increase in the ratio of money to GDP. The model results suggest that Korean monetary authorities responded rather sensitively to the economy's growing need for liquidity. It should be recalled that the form of inflation equation 5 is quite similar to that used successfully by both Harberger and Vogel[13] to explain Latin America inflation. The net money-price level result arises not so much from this equation as from the admission of money in the output supply function.

With these considerations, the money-inflation result appears plausible but cannot necessarily be extrapolated to larger changes in the money growth rate over the sample period or to future possibilities. A rather drastic and sustained change in the monetary policy, for example, could affect the shape of the expectation function and, by that route, have the expected kind of effect on inflation. In the model, expectations change over time, but the process by which expectations are formed is assumed to be stable.

One tentative policy conclusion therefore is that *if* monetary policy is

13. Harberger, "Dynamics of Inflation in Chile"; Vogel, "Dynamics of Inflation in Latin America."

Table 12-7. Monetary Policy Experiments

1968–77 growth rates

Variable	Actual (DMM1 = 33.08%)	Case IV (DMM1 = 28.07%)	Case V (DMM1 = 30.00%)	Variable	Actual (DMM1 = 33.08%)	Case IV (DMM1 = 28.07%)	Case V (DMM1 = 30.00%)
Y	11.24	10.17	10.62	WS	1.19	1.66	1.63
YC	28.60	28.26	28.62	UPOP	6.59	6.34	6.35
PY	15.68	16.49	16.37	IF	16.31	13.31	13.71
YA	4.74	5.27	5.27	IFC	31.20	27.81	28.57
YAC	24.84	25.50	25.50	PIF	13.03	12.93	12.99
PYA	19.16	19.21	19.21	IV^a	55.24	39.48	44.55
YN	13.68	12.17	12.76	IVC^a	120.83	85.96	111.86
YNC	30.12	29.45	29.93	PIV	30.84	28.11	25.82
PYN	14.57	15.50	15.37	IM	20.42	17.67	18.42
CP	8.13	6.45	7.36	IMC	37.19	34.16	35.28
CPC	25.64	24.98	25.58	BPD^a	−952.28	−284.52	−546.85
PCP	16.28	17.49	17.15	BPW^a	−94.84	8.87	−29.11
CG	8.47	7.49	7.92	$BPWC^a$	−334.15	−87.12	−203.76
CGC	31.38	30.52	31.29	S	16.15	13.16	13.78
PCG	20.98	21.44	21.65	SC	24.70	24.49	23.82
WC	22.34	22.28	22.50	DS	32.73	29.03	29.97
YLC	30.14	29.92	30.25	DSC	42.25	42.86	41.81
NMA	10.81	9.41	10.04				

Note: *DMM1* is the growth rate of the monthly average *M1* money supply; its actual compound annual 1968–77 value was 33.08 percent. Case IV was constructed by reducing each year's *DMM1* by five percentage points. Case V was constructed by imposing a constant annual *DMM1* value of 30 percent.

a. Average 1968–77 *level* instead of growth rate.

to be effective in combating inflation, the reduction in money supply growth cannot be temporary or marginal with respect to trends; it must be sharp and sustained. (The model, of course, does not guarantee that this condition is sufficient for inflation control.)

Another question about these results is the true degree of endogeneity of the money supply. Exploratory regression results indicate that over 90 percent of the variation of the annual *increment* in *MM1* can be explained by the following four variables: the increment in real nonagricultural GDP, the reserve ratio, the government deficit, and the increment of foreign exchange reserves (in domestic currency).

One equation for the first difference in the money supply is as follows:

$$(50) \qquad TMM1_t = 26.7184 + 0.42255\ TYN_{t-1}$$
$$(0.7433) \quad (5.0628)$$

$$- 201.938\ RR + 0.25938\ GMAFM_t,$$
$$(-1.5027) \qquad (7.6317)$$

$$\text{OLSQ; } R^2 = 0.9518; \text{ D.W.} = 1.7962; \text{ SM} = 0.2958$$

where the new variables are RR = reserve ratio and $GMAFM$ = sum of deficit on government and government agencies, and foreign sector money creation.

Similar results are obtained when government domestic borrowing is substituted for the total government deficit. These results suggest that the Korean money supply is partially controllable by policy action, but clearly a more definitive treatment of these issues would require an expansion of the monetary-fiscal side of the model.[14]

Concluding Remarks

A few concluding comments are offered on two topics: policy implications and needs for improvement in model specification. The policy experiments have been described in the preceding section, so here we wish

14. It has been suggested that the Korean government's extension of export credit has contributed to both export expansion and money supply expansion—and thereby to both growth and inflation. While this is an interesting suggestion, simple first-difference regressions of exports on, alternatively, (1) export credit and (2) total preferential loans result in extremely poor fits. In the model of this paper, we basically assume that export incentive policies have not fluctuated much in degree of intensity over the sample period, and therefore we abstract from them.

to review a few conclusions that seem the most reliable and also add some new observations.

There seems to be little doubt that the oil shock contributed significantly to the increased rates of Korean inflation from 1974 onward. By the model estimate, about one-third of the inflation in the past five years has been due to the oil shock. It seems clear that Korea's well-known export promotion policy has brought significant long-term benefits and equally clear that there have been medium-term costs, chiefly in personal consumption levels and the income distribution. Within the framework of this study, we do not find any evidence that rapid growth per se has contributed to inflation.

Although purposive policy no doubt has played a major role in the Korean export boom, it should be noted that the path of export expansion does respect some kinds of market restrictions, for example, declining rates of export market penetration as predicted by the logistic function description of adaptive behavior. The experience of new exporters tends to follow the three phases of a logistic curve: slow expansion during the period of familiarization with the market, accelerated expansion once the marketing techniques have been mastered, and slower growth again as a saturation point is reached and/or competitors begin to react. It may be only slightly fanciful to suggest that in the aggregate, Korean exporters behave as a single large socioeconomic institution. Since they face similar challenges, learn from each other's experiences, and share resources (including a skilled labor force and preferential bank loans), Korean exporters tend to be regarded as a single sector or entity by the government in the policy-making process.

Logistic functions for the export shares of Japan and Taiwan also were estimated with comparable goodness of fit. Comparing the three countries' functions, the long-term stable share of the world market (parameter α) appears to be highest for Japan (7.8 percent), lowest for Taiwan (1.1 percent), and in between for South Korea (2.3 percent). In 1961, Korea had the lowest exports of the three, but Korea's period of rapid export acceleration appears to have been longer lasting than Taiwan's.

Another point regarding trade policy is that imports may have been less subject to control by Korean government policy than is sometimes supposed. Equations 19 and 21 are based entirely on market variables and capture fairly well the uneven pattern of import growth over time.

As regards the role of money in inflation and growth, three cautious conclusions may be ventured from this study: (1) money significantly influenced real GDP growth, (2) transactions demand absorbed most of the 1963–77 growth in the money supply, and (3) small year-to-year variations in the money supply growth are not likely to influence inflation rates.

For the inflation equation alone, expectations (positively) and real output growth (negatively) are important determining factors. These findings are consistent with those of Harberger and Vogel.[15] The imported goods price index also is a consistently significant explanatory factor. Wages do not emerge as a statistically significant factor when all other variables are included, but when a "cost side" equation is estimated with only *DPIM* and *DYN* and the change in the wage rate as independent variables, the change in the wage rate is significant statistically and the equation explains 73 percent of the variation in nonagricultural inflation. Similar remarks may be made with respect to agricultural price movements and an "import liberalization index" (*IM/Y*): when only a few variables are included, they are marginally significant, but in the best-fitting equation they lose significance.

These considerations suggest that there are no easy answers to the Korean inflation problem. Clearly, the government must attempt to alter inflationary expectations, and some marginal help can be expected from a number of specific measures such as wage control, agricultural price control, and import liberalization. These measures all involve trade-offs of the interests of different socioeconomic groups such as workers, farmers, and entrepreneurs, respectively. Because of the sustained inflation of recent years, in Korea one hears increasing fears of loss of export dynamism through loss of competitiveness. If such fears are correct, devaluation would be appropriate, but via the import price variable (*DPIM*) devaluation would exacerbate inflation, which again would adversely affect export competitiveness. The net result depends on the coefficients, for instance, in equation 5 above but also on the price elasticity of demand for Korean exports, which thus far is unknown.

We feel that the present model contains some useful approaches for the equations for output, prices, imports, fixed investment, and inventories. However, the last three in particular leave room for empirical improvement. The most productive extensions of this version probably would not be in the direction of disaggregation of production sectors but rather in the incorporation of a more detailed fiscal-monetary block and perhaps in more careful investigation of the determinants of the structure of price expectations.

15. Harberger, "Dynamics of Inflation in Chile"; Vogel, "Dynamics of Inflation in Latin America."

Appendix: Dynamic Simulation Results for Additional Variables[16]

Table 12-8. *Dynamic Simulation Results: YC, GDP in Current Prices*

	Level form of variable[a]			Percentage-change form of variable[b]		
Year	Actual	Model	Error	Actual	Model	Error
1963	485.21	486.64	−1.43	0.4035	0.4077	−0.0041
1964	694.95	679.84	15.11	0.4323	0.3970	0.0353
1965	797.67	790.92	6.75	0.1478	0.1634	−0.0156
1966	1,019.07	1,003.35	15.72	0.2776	0.2686	0.0090
1967	1,248.00	1,212.29	35.71	0.2246	0.2083	0.0164
1968	1,574.86	1,522.34	52.52	0.2619	0.2558	0.0062
1969	2,056.49	1,956.83	99.66	0.3058	0.2854	0.0204
1970	2,577.36	2,409.81	167.55	0.2533	0.2315	0.0218
1971	3,153.81	3,010.45	143.36	0.2237	0.2492	−0.0256
1972	3,875.32	3,763.86	111.46	0.2288	0.2503	−0.0215
1973	4,938.63	4,801.24	137.39	0.2744	0.2756	−0.0012
1974	6,812.70	6,684.55	128.15	0.3795	0.3923	−0.0128
1975	9,239.18	8,805.96	433.22	0.3562	0.3174	0.0388
1976	12,278.83	11,824.30	454.53	0.3290	0.3428	−0.0138
1977	15,316.03	15,019.20	296.82	0.2474	0.2702	−0.0228
Mean	4,404.54	4,264.77	139.77	0.2897	0.2877	0.0020

a. Standard deviation ÷ mean = 0.0452; Theil index = 0.0162; percent mean squared error = 0.0339; and mean absolute error = 139.96.
b. Standard deviation ÷ mean = 0.0706; Theil index = 0.0344; percent mean squared error = 0.0739; and mean absolute error = 0.0177.

16. Because of space limitation, not all simulation results could be published, but complete sets of results may be obtained from the authors on request.

Table 12-9. *Dynamic Simulation Results: PY, GDP Deflator*

Year	Level form of variable[a]			Percentage-change form of variable[b]		
	Actual	Model	Error	Actual	Model	Error
1963	0.3675	0.3695	−0.0020	0.2898	0.2968	−0.0070
1964	0.4845	0.4674	0.0171	0.3184	0.2650	0.0535
1965	0.5245	0.5271	−0.0025	0.0826	0.1277	−0.0451
1966	0.5981	0.5829	0.0152	0.1403	0.1059	0.0344
1967	0.6828	0.6684	0.0144	0.1416	0.1468	−0.0052
1968	0.7641	0.7480	0.0161	0.1191	0.1191	0.0000
1969	0.8664	0.8308	0.0356	0.1339	0.1107	0.0233
1970	1.0000	0.9369	0.0631	0.1542	0.1277	0.0265
1971	1.1149	1.0884	0.0265	0.1149	0.1617	−0.0468
1972	1.2766	1.2347	0.0419	0.1450	0.1344	0.0106
1973	1.3974	1.3679	0.0295	0.0947	0.1079	−0.0132
1974	1.7723	1.7324	0.0399	0.2683	0.2665	0.0018
1975	2.2087	2.1115	0.0972	0.2463	0.2188	0.0274
1976	2.5531	2.4845	0.0686	0.1559	0.1767	−0.0207
1977	2.9005	2.8648	0.0356	0.1361	0.1531	−0.0170
Mean	1.2341	1.2010	0.0331	0.1694	0.1679	0.0015

a. Standard deviation ÷ mean = 0.0341; Theil index = 0.0147; percent mean squared error = 0.03051; and mean absolute error = 0.0337.

b. Standard deviation ÷ mean = 0.1624; Theil index = 0.0759; percent mean squared error = 0 2138; and mean absolute error = 0.0222.

Table 12-10. *Dynamic Simulation Results: CGC, Government Consumption in Current Prices*

	Level form of variable[a]			Percentage-change form of variable[b]		
Year	Actual	Model	Error	Actual	Model	Error
1963	54.74	62.40	−7.66	0.1032	0.2576	−0.1545
1964	61.95	72.03	−10.08	0.1317	0.1543	−0.0226
1965	76.02	88.12	−12.10	0.2271	0.2234	0.0038
1966	104.82	110.09	−5.27	0.3788	0.2493	0.1296
1967	132.17	137.66	−5.49	0.2609	0.2505	0.0104
1968	175.28	172.87	2.41	0.3262	0.2558	0.0704
1969	222.69	217.26	5.43	0.2705	0.2568	0.0137
1970	281.81	270.32	11.49	0.2650	0.2442	0.0213
1971	355.96	328.93	27.03	0.2630	0.2168	0.0463
1972	438.24	406.08	32.16	0.2312	0.2345	−0.0034
1973	479.35	526.75	−47.40	0.0938	0.2972	−0.2034
1974	741.90	717.12	24.78	0.5477	0.3614	0.1863
1975	1,020.23	1,022.59	−2.36	0.3752	0.4260	−0.0508
1976	1,487.55	1,462.74	24.81	0.4581	0.4304	0.0276
1977	1,944.23	2,044.77	−100.54	0.3070	0.3979	−0.0909
Mean	505.13	509.32	−4.19	0.2827	0.2837	−0.0011

a. Standard deviation ÷ mean = 0.0644; Theil index = 0.0216; percent mean squared error = 0.0829; and mean absolute error = 21.27.
b. Standard deviation ÷ mean = 0.3377; Theil index = 0.1586; percent mean squared error = 0.7024; and mean absolute error = 0.0690.

Table 12-11. *Dynamic Simulation Results: PCP, Private Consumption Price Deflator*

Year	Level form of variable[a]			Percentage-change form of variable[b]		
	Actual	Model	Error	Actual	Model	Error
1963	0.3821	0.3595	0.0226	0.3236	0.2453	0.0783
1964	0.5215	0.5116	0.0099	0.3649	0.4231	−0.0582
1965	0.5568	0.5614	−0.0046	0.0676	0.0973	−0.0297
1966	0.6279	0.6189	0.0090	0.1276	0.1024	0.0253
1967	0.7058	0.6855	0.0204	0.1242	0.1076	0.0165
1968	0.7793	0.7675	0.0118	0.1041	0.1196	−0.0155
1969	0.8757	0.8223	0.0534	0.1237	0.0714	0.0523
1970	1.0000	0.9289	0.0711	0.1419	0.1296	0.0123
1971	1.1236	1.0811	0.0426	0.1236	0.1638	−0.0402
1972	1.2778	1.2261	0.0518	0.1372	0.1341	0.0031
1973	1.3899	1.3191	0.0708	0.0877	0.0759	0.0118
1974	1.8557	1.8493	0.0064	0.3351	0.4019	−0.0668
1975	2.3937	2.2936	0.1001	0.2899	0.2403	0.0496
1976	2.7682	2.6919	0.0763	0.1564	0.1736	−0.0172
1977	3.1231	3.0084	0.1146	0.1282	0.1176	0.0106
Mean	1.2921	1.2483	0.0437	0.1757	0.1736	0.0021

a. Standard deviation ÷ mean = 0.0436; Theil index = 0.0187; percent mean squared error = 0.0396; and mean absolute error = 0.0444.

b. Standard deviation ÷ mean = 0.2254; Theil index = 0.0982; percent mean squared error = 0.2242; and mean absolute error = 0.0325.

Table 12-12. *Dynamic Simulation Results: PIF, Gross Fixed Investment Deflator*

Year	Level form of variable[a]			Percentage-change form of variable[b]		
	Actual	Model	Error	Actual	Model	Error
1963	0.4055	0.4021	0.0034	0.1124	0.1031	0.0094
1964	0.5250	0.5528	−0.0278	0.2947	0.3748	−0.0801
1965	0.6099	0.6425	−0.0326	0.1616	0.1622	−0.0006
1966	0.7092	0.6928	0.0164	0.1628	0.0783	0.0844
1967	0.7611	0.7467	0.0144	0.0733	0.0779	−0.0046
1968	0.8261	0.8040	0.0221	0.0854	0.0767	0.0088
1969	0.8650	0.8759	−0.0109	0.0471	0.0895	−0.0424
1970	1.0000	0.9590	0.0410	0.1561	0.0949	0.0612
1971	1.0721	1.0656	0.0065	0.0721	0.1111	−0.0390
1972	1.1837	1.1897	−0.0060	0.1041	0.1164	−0.0123
1973	1.3727	1.4223	−0.0496	0.1597	0.1956	−0.0359
1974	1.8688	1.8930	−0.0242	0.3614	0.3309	0.0304
1975	2.2084	2.1920	0.0164	0.1817	0.1579	0.0238
1976	2.3112	2.3113	−0.0002	0.0465	0.0544	−0.0079
1977	2.5173	2.5147	0.0026	0.0892	0.0880	0.0012
Mean	1.2157	1.2176	−0.0019	0.1405	0.1408	−0.0002

a. Standard deviation ÷ mean = 0.0190; Theil index = 0.0083; percent mean squared error = 0.0268; and mean absolute error = 0.0183.
b. Standard deviation ÷ mean = 0.2834; Theil index = 0.1198; percent mean squared error = 0.3406; and mean absolute error = 0.0295.

Table 12-13. *Dynamic Simulation Results: IVC, Inventory Investment in Current Prices*

	Level form of variable[a]			Percentage-change form of variable[b]		
Year	Actual	Model	Error	Actual	Model	Error
1963	22.22	37.09	−14.87	−8.0540	−12.7761	4.7221
1964	20.80	9.95	10.85	−0.0639	−0.7319	0.6680
1965	2.81	−1.60	4.41	−0.8649	−1.1610	0.2961
1966	15.79	18.62	−2.83	4.6192	−12.6312	17.2504
1967	8.01	18.38	−10.37	−0.4927	−0.0130	−0.4797
1968	16.21	32.51	−16.30	1.0237	0.7684	0.2553
1969	67.76	62.80	4.96	3.1801	0.9320	2.2482
1970	54.46	51.11	3.35	−0.1963	−0.1861	−0.0102
1971	75.63	62.53	13.10	0.3887	0.2234	0.1653
1972	25.25	56.96	−31.71	−0.6661	−0.0892	−0.5770
1973	119.46	107.51	11.95	3.7310	0.8875	2.8436
1974	347.11	277.00	70.11	1.9057	1.5765	0.3291
1975	146.54	193.54	−47.00	−0.5778	−0.3013	−0.2765
1976	209.73	183.11	26.62	0.4312	−0.0539	0.4851
1977	146.18	322.64	−176.46	−0.3030	0.7620	−1.0650
Mean	85.20	95.48	−10.28	0.2707	−1.5196	1.7908

a. Standard deviation ÷ mean = 0.6142; Theil index = 0.1994; percent mean squared error = 0.7809; and mean absolute error = 29.66.

b. Standard deviation ÷ mean = 17.4753; Theil index = 0.6320; percent mean squared error = 3.0612; and mean absolute error = 2.1114.

Table 12-14. *Dynamic Simulation Results: SC, Total Savings in Current Prices*

	Level form of variable[a]			Percentage-change form of variable[b]		
Year	Actual	Model	Error	Actual	Model	Error
1963	82.85	86.06	−3.21	0.9077	0.9815	−0.0738
1964	101.07	122.93	−21.86	0.2199	0.4285	−0.2086
1965	112.03	152.62	−40.59	0.1084	0.2415	−0.1331
1966	210.08	215.36	−5.28	0.8752	0.4111	0.4641
1967	264.67	285.18	−20.51	0.2599	0.3242	−0.0644
1968	402.65	362.50	40.15	0.5213	0.2711	0.2502
1969	594.20	496.57	97.63	0.4757	0.3699	0.1059
1970	672.51	581.74	90.77	0.1318	0.1715	−0.0397
1971	812.27	756.14	56.13	0.2078	0.2998	−0.0920
1972	792.34	889.94	−97.60	−0.0245	0.1770	−0.2015
1973	1,282.49	1,366.86	−84.38	0.6186	0.5359	0.0827
1974	2,212.98	2,195.53	17.45	0.7255	0.6062	0.1193
1975	2,658.88	2,687.31	−28.43	0.2015	0.2240	−0.0225
1976	3,028.90	2,933.22	95.68	0.1392	0.0915	0.0477
1977	3,865.48	3,999.54	−134.06	0.2762	0.3635	−0.0873
Mean	1,139.56	1,142.10	−2.54	0.3763	0.3665	0.0098

a. Standard deviation ÷ mean = 0.0600; Theil index = 0.0208; percent mean squared error = 0.1337; and mean absolute error = 55.58.
b. Standard deviation ÷ mean = 0.4563; Theil index = 0.1921; percent mean squared error = 2.1761; and mean absolute error = 0.1329.

Table 12-15. *Dynamic Simulation Results: BPCW, Balance of Payments in Current Won*

	Level form of variable[a]			Percentage-change form of variable[b]		
Year	Actual	Model	Error	Actual	Model	Error
1963	−55.69	−42.33	−13.36	0.3540	0.0292	0.3248
1964	−54.38	−78.89	24.51	−0.0235	0.8638	−0.8873
1965	−59.18	−101.54	42.36	0.0883	0.2871	−0.1988
1966	−101.01	−116.38	15.37	0.7068	0.1461	0.5607
1967	−134.81	−145.82	11.01	0.3346	0.2530	0.0816
1968	−207.51	−177.86	−29.65	0.5393	0.2197	0.3195
1969	−254.05	−236.23	−17.82	0.2243	0.3281	−0.1039
1970	−261.21	−307.07	45.86	0.0282	0.2999	−0.2717
1971	−351.74	−375.11	23.27	0.3466	0.2216	0.1250
1972	−199.71	−351.83	152.12	−0.4322	−0.0621	−0.3702
1973	−161.92	−315.57	153.65	−0.1892	−0.1031	−0.0862
1974	−845.16	−1,118.10	272.94	4.2196	2.5432	1.6765
1975	−864.14	−1,573.27	709.13	0.0225	0.4071	−0.3846
1976	−185.08	−824.76	639.68	−0.7858	−0.4758	−0.3101
1977	−10.96	−821.68	810.72	−0.9408	−0.0037	−0.9370
Mean	−249.77	−439.10	189.33	0.2995	0.3303	−0.0308

a. Standard deviation ÷ mean = −1.3468; Theil index = 0.3464; percent mean squared error = 19.1237; and mean absolute error = 197.44.

b. Standard deviation ÷ mean = 2.0278; Theil index = 0.3180; percent mean squared error = 11.0109; and mean absolute error = 0.4425.

Comments by Larry E. Westphal

Korean economic experience demonstrates that inflation is not inimical to sustained rapid economic growth so long as the balance of payments is properly managed. Past research into Korea's economic development provides a clear understanding of the sources of its successful balance-of-payments performance, but not of the causes of its persistent inflation. Unfortunately, the Norton-Rhee paper neither reflects what has been learned about the former nor contributes much to clarifying the latter, as a review of the salient features of Korean experience will indicate.[17]

17. The author thanks Yung W. Rhee for numerous discussions that have materially added to the author's understanding of Korean economic management. The author's views and interpretations expressed in this comment should not be attributed to the World Bank, to its affiliated organizations, or to any individual acting on behalf of these organizations.

Leaving aside the current recession, the Korean economy has experienced rapid growth without serious balance-of-payments problems since the mid-1960s. Prior to the mid-1960s, for the first decade following the Korean War, its growth performance was highly erratic due, in large measure, to factors that were also associated with recurrent balance-of-payments crises. The pronounced change in performance was the result of policy reforms in a number of areas which were implemented during the first half of the 1960s and led to a fundamental restructuring of economic activity.[18] Critically important were the exchange rate and related policy reforms which removed the antiexport bias of incentives and thereby fostered Korea's extraordinary export achievement.[19] Thus the principal element underlying Korea's exemplary record in managing both its growth and its balance of payments is the efficient resource allocation engendered by the policies stemming from its industrialization cum trade strategy.

The Korean economy has nonetheless experienced rather high rates of inflation, close to the average for all less developed economies except for the period following the rise in oil prices (see table 12-16). Korean inflation has thus consistently outstripped the rise in world prices, by a substantial margin.[20] A succession of anti-inflationary stabilization programs undertaken after 1964 did succeed in significantly moderating the variability of inflation, but it did not reduce the average rate by much.

It is tempting in Korea's case to infer that the excess of inflation over

18. David C. Cole and Princeton N. Lyman, *Korean Development: The Interplay of Politics and Economics* (Harvard University Press, 1971), and Gilbert T. Brown, *Korean Pricing Policies and Economic Development in the 1960s* (Johns Hopkins University Press, 1973), provide excellent discussions of these reforms. For a more recent assessment, see Edward S. Mason and others, *Studies in the Modernization of the Republic of Korea: The Economic and Social Modernization of the Republic of Korea* (Harvard University Press for the Council on East Asian Studies, forthcoming).

19. For a comprehensive description and evaluation of these reforms, see Anne O. Krueger, *Studies in the Modernization of the Republic of Korea, 1945–75: The Developmental Role of the Foreign Sector and Aid* (Harvard University Press for the Council on East Asian Studies, 1979). Larry E. Westphal, "The Republic of Korea's Experience with Export-Led Industrial Development," *World Development*, vol. 6 (1978), pp. 347–80, provides a shorter, summary discussion.

20. For example, according to IMF figures (*International Financial Statistics*, May 1978, pp. 50–51), the average annual rate of increase in import prices for all less developed countries was less than 1 percent between 1965 and 1971; Korean wholesale prices rose at an average annual rate of more than 8 percent during this period.

Table 12-16. *Average Annual Rates of Change, 1956–77*
Percent

Indicator	1956–64	1965–73	1974–77
Consumer price inflation			
Less developed economies, average	12.2	13.1	29.9
Korea	13.1	11.0	18.9
Taiwan	7.7	4.0	15.4
Growth of domestic product			
Korea	4.7	9.3	9.4
Taiwan	7.1	10.2	6.0

Sources: Consumer price inflation: IMF, *International Financial Statistics*, May 1978, pp. 42–43. Growth of gross domestic product: for Korea, Bank of Korea, *National Income in Korea: 1978*, pp. 205 ff.; for Taiwan, Directorate-General of Budget, Accounting, and Statistics, Republic of China, *Statistical Yearbook of the Republic of China: 1979*, pp. 420–21.

the rise in world prices is simply the unavoidable consequence of the imbalances that necessarily accompany very rapid growth. But this inference is contradicted by the experience of Taiwan, which embarked on a similar industrialization cum trade strategy in the early 1960s. Taiwan's economy both grew somewhat more rapidly and experienced far less inflation than did Korea's over the period from 1965 to 1973 (see table 12-16).

Inflation in excess of world rates should be, and has been, a matter of concern to Korean policy makers for several reasons. Perhaps most important, it increases the difficulty of managing the balance of payments. Indeed, a stable balance of payments with high growth becomes impossible when the exchange rate is controlled by a government that seeks to avoid devaluation, if only because export growth declines as export incentives are progressively eroded by inflation. Indeed, the Korean economy is currently suffering a severe recession caused largely by the maintenance for too long of a constant nominal exchange rate. Because of declining export incentives, the volume of Korea's exports fell in 1979 while the export volumes of its principal competitors increased, in several cases by as much as 15 percent or more.

Inflation is of further concern because it may reflect imbalances in the real structure of the economy which can, if left unresolved, directly impair continued rapid growth. Indeed, Korean inflation appears to have been caused by the simultaneous operation of a number of real imbalances, some transitory and others endemic. The most serious, long-lasting sectoral imbalance has concerned agriculture. Together with government control over agricultural imports, it has led a continuous relative rise in agricultural prices. During the 1970s, there is evidence as well of a lag in housing construction and in the provision of related infrastructure. These imbalances have led to sustained upward pressure on nominal wages which undoubtedly contributed to cost-push inflation in the rest of the economy. Closer to the present, imbalance in the labor market—particularly for highly qualified technical and managerial manpower, as well as for construction workers—has produced unsustainable short-term growth in real wages, which is one of the causes of the recent deterioration in Korea's export competitiveness.

Macroeconomic imbalance has had an even more clearly important role in Korean inflation. Given the government's direct control of the banking system and its use of credit as a major incentive policy instrument, excess aggregate demand arising out of government, investment, and export activities has been immediately translated into monetary expansion. Bank credit has financed a major share of the sometimes sizable government deficit and has been used to promote priority investments in the private sector. Exporters have for a long time been guaranteed immediate access to credit on preferential terms and within generous limits based on export contracts. Macroeconomic imbalance has thus been sustained by the responsiveness of monetary expansion to the growth of private and public investment as well as exports, with the consequence being a form of "forced savings."

Rising foreign exchange reserves have also produced considerable monetary expansion, especially in earlier periods. The wide differential between Korea's relatively high nominal interest rate and interest rates in the international capital market has been partly responsible for reserve accumulation, as it has provided a powerful stimulus for overseas borrowing to finance domestic expenditures.

Practically none of the salient features of the Korean economy discussed above find expression in the Norton-Rhee model. It is thus of extremely limited value for historical analysis as well as for current policy discussion. On the surface, the model does appear to embody the "forced savings" phenomenon, in that consumption is determined residually. However, as a moment's reflection will confirm, inflation plays no part in the model's depiction of "forced savings." Moreover, contrary to what would be expected given the close link between export activity and monetary expansion, acceleration of export growth leads in the model to lower inflation.[21] Even more implausible, and far more dangerously misleading, is the model's implication that lower export growth would have resulted in higher consumption growth over the twelve-year period from 1968 to 1977. Among other things, this result completely neglects the fundamentally important role that export expansion has clearly had in Korea of promoting efficient resource allocation, not simply through investment but also via increased resource utilization.[22] In short, "forced savings" through inflation is a far more complicated phenomenon than is captured in the model, for it has not meant that exports simply displace consumption but rather that part of the multiplier effect of export expansion is absorbed in higher prices. The Norton-Rhee model not only fails to capture the multiplier effect of increased exports, it also omits the feedback of the accelerator effect of output expansion through increased capacity to future increases in output.[23]

The model fares no better in relation to short-term policy issues. Its neglect of the underlying determinants of inflation precludes its use to assess policy changes or to evaluate possible trade-offs in the design of anti-inflationary measures. The model is equally inadequate for analyzing the effects of inflation, particularly on the balance of payments. Most debilitating in this respect is the failure to recognize the dependence of exports on incentives and relative prices.[24] The import equations are also defective, since they include only the exchange rate and foreign prices,

21. This result follows from the specification of just two equations: in the model the rate of change of the nonagricultural value-added deflator depends negatively on that of real nonagricultural value added (equation 5), which in turn is a positive function of the export growth rate (equation 4).

22. See the references cited previously, particularly Westphal, "The Republic of Korea's Experience," pp. 363–76.

23. The coefficient of the export term in the equation for real nonagricultural value added is nearly equal to the average ratio of exports to nonagricultural value added over the sample period. In turn, the significance of the money supply variable in the same equation may be traced to its serving as a proxy for lagged investment, which is suggested by equations 13a and 13b.

24. The authors are simply wrong in suggesting that the responsiveness of exports to incentives and relative prices is both irrelevant and unknown. Previous research by, among others, Charles R. Frank, Jr., Kwang Suk Kim, and Larry E. Westphal, *Foreign Trade Regimes and Economic Development: South Korea* (National Bureau of Economic Research, 1975), pp. 83–86, demonstrated the fallacy in thinking that exports are simply determined by export targets, the role of which is far more subtle than is suggested by the authors (see Westphal, "The Republic of Korea's Experience," p. 376).

omitting domestic prices. Theory suggests that imports are responsive to the landed price of imports relative to domestic prices, not simply to the former; and there is strong evidence to confirm that this is so in Korea's case.[25] More generally, the model does not reflect the Korean economy's open character—the principal reason that inflation is of concern to Korean policy makers.

To conclude, Norton and Rhee emphasize that their model should be judged by its "goodness of fit," which is indeed quite good, particularly in terms of rates of change. I would argue that greatest weight must be given to whether the model embodies the important underlying structural relationships among true policy instruments and oher variables, as suggested both by theory and by an understanding of the economy's structure and functioning. In this respect, the model is sorely deficient. In turn, the tests according to which the authors find some of these relationships insignificant are unconvincing because of their poor specification, as for example in the use of the ratio of imports to GDP as an index of import liberalization. Models recently developed by Kwack and Mered and by van Wijnbergen[26] clearly show that at least some of the salient features discussed above are significant. These models, for example, confirm the authors' suggestion that monetary expansion is not exogenous, as they have modeled it. But a good deal more work yet remains before the dynamics of Korea's inflation will be as thoroughly and confidently understood as are the workings of its real economy.

Discussion

Lawrence Krause (Brookings Institution) commended Roger Norton and Seung Rhee for an innovative modeling effort but agreed with Larry Westphal that the model should not be taken seriously for policy purposes. Krause emphasized the role of imitation of Japan's historical path in the formation of Korean export and growth expectations and noted that

25. See, for example, Frank, Kim, and Westphal, *Foreign Trade Regimes,* pp. 140–42.

26. Sung Y. Kwack, and Michael Mered, "A Model of the Economic Policy Effects and External Influences on the Korean Economy," SRI/WEFA World Economic Program working paper, unnumbered (Washington, D.C.: SRI International, 1980); and S. van Wijnbergen, "A Macroeconomic Model of South Korea," Development Research Center working paper, unnumbered (Washington, D.C.: World Bank, 1980).

following higher oil prices, Korea decided not to sacrifice growth for stability. *Tony Albrecht* (U.S. State Department) expressed concern about growing income distribution problems and their political repercussions, including the possible need to subsidize low-income groups. *Robert Emery* (Federal Reserve Board) felt the model told little about the real stabilization alternatives. He agreed with Norton and Rhee that minor changes in monetary policy would have little effect but queried the effects of a major change. He questioned the study's seeming conclusion that devaluation would help little, given the successful experience after the December 1974 devaluation.

Roger Norton replied that exports are the real limit to growth and that there are limits (including the world market) to how fast they can grow. In choosing a fast growth response to the oil shock, Korea was gambling that there would be an upturn in the world economy in 1976; they were right. Norton recognized that the model emphasized goodness of fit and indicated his intention to give greater emphasis to policy in future specifications of the model. He noted that current (as opposed to lagged) money supply did not prove statistically significant. More generally, Norton emphasized that monetary policy had amounted to accommodating the increase in real transactions demand caused by growth.

To Westphal's criticism that the import equations should have included domestic price, Norton replied that because other equations of the system relate the exchange rate to domestic price its influence is present indirectly in the exchange rate variable included in the import equations. Norton emphasized that, contrary to Westphal's comment, the study does consider export incentives and relative prices to be relevant to the determination of exports, but because this relationship has not yet been measured satisfactorily the model relies instead on exogenously specified levels of exports. Although agreeing with Westphal's point that export credit affected the growth of money supply and therefore inflation, at least in the 1970s, Norton indicated that with preferred loans for exports constituting only 6 percent of domestic credit this factor could hardly have been dominant. Norton also rejected Westphal's criticism that another important source of inflation was neglected by the model: sectoral imbalance and rising relative agricultural prices. He cited sectoral GDP deflators showing no such rise, and noted the lack of statistical significance of agricultural price variables in explaining inflation.

CHAPTER THIRTEEN

IS/LM in the Tropics:
Diagrammatics of the New Structuralist
Macro Critique

LANCE TAYLOR

THERE IS growing consensus that orthodox IMF-style stabilization policies do not work well when administered to semi-industrialized countries, the usual victims of inflationary balance-of-payments disease. Assessments of past stabilization efforts point to this conclusion, and new macrotheory is being developed to explain why. This chapter expounds that theory in terms of familiar IS/LM (investment-saving, money demand–money supply) graphs. The ideas are deformed by the routine formulation, but enough should come through to show what they are about. The thrust is "structuralist" in the classic sense, that is, inflation and balance-of-payments problems are part and parcel of underdevelopment and do not easily melt away. As discussed at the end of the chapter, ameliorative policies may exist but must be applied within the existing economic structure. First, one must be clear about structure; thereafter, one can ponder interventions for improvement.

In outline form, the argument begins with a review of financial, production, and commodity market arrangements in the economy whose characteristics are to be worked out. The next section is devoted to algebraic formulations of the key relationships, and the third and fourth sections to derivation of IS and LM curves, respectively, describing the economy in the short term. Then comparative statics of the standard stabilization policies—devaluation, monetary contraction, and fiscal restraint—are presented. As it turns out, under many circumstances these policies are stagflationary, leading to output contraction and inflationary spurts, and a taxonomy of macroresponse patterns is presented to indicate when the bite from each policy is likely to be worst. In a digression,

465

the IS side of the analysis is extended from a one-sector to a two-sector framework to deal with food price inflation problems characteristic of many poor economies. Growth and inflation are described over the medium term in the basic model, and various monetarist modifications are discussed, with suggestions why they lead policy astray. Finally, viable policy options are examined.[1]

Economic Structure

Successful macroeconomics requires clear assumptions about institutions, since policy conclusions flow therefrom. We deal with a semi-industrialized economy, open to foreign trade but without financial breadth. Since comparative statics is the main theoretical tool, we also assume that the economy is not dramatically removed from equilibrium (that is, no hyperinflations, extreme foreign trade shocks, or egregious past economic mismanagement can be considered). The "short term" used here is a period of a quarter or so, during which the money wage and the stock of capital are fixed, but prices have time to clear markets and adjust to changes in other variables. Major areas of economic activity differ in their characteristics from those that Northern economists usually assume.

1. With fixed capital stocks, commodity production in the short term requires labor and raw materials. Labor use is determined from demand, with adjustments in the money wage to inflation and growth reflecting labor supply response (or worker-capitalist conflict) in periods of a year or more. The cost of raw materials (treated for simplicity as reducible to imports) is determined by world prices and exchange rate, which vary in the same time frame as the money wage. There is ongoing inflation, and the nominal interest rate is high. Moreover, interest rate changes affect prices and output in the short term, since firms are dependent on borrowing to finance working capital (wage and raw material bills) and to pass along

---

1. The presentation here is mostly verbal and graphical. For a more analytical formulation, see Lance Taylor, "IS/LM in the Tropics: Mechanics of the New Structuralist Macro Critique" (Massachusetts Institute of Technology, May 1979). Complementary models are given by Daniel M. Schydlowsky, "Containing the Costs of Stabilization in Semi-Industrialized LDCs: A Marshallian Approach" (Boston University, January 1979), and Michael Bruno, "Stabilization and Stagflation in a Semi-Industrialized Economy," in Rudiger Dornbusch and Jacob A. Frenkel, eds., *International Economic Policy: Theory and Evidence* (Johns Hopkins University Press, 1979).

their financial costs. The nominal rate, rather than the real interest rate, pushes prices, precisely because of the fixed exchange rate and money wage.

2. The only primary assets in the financial system are central bank monetary liabilities (the money base) and the physical capital stock, there being no market for government bonds. Private wealth can be held as money or loans to firms. Together with bank loans (regulated by the authorities), the private loans add up to the total capital supply. Demand and supply schedules for capital determine the interest rate, which varies to clear the loan market in the short term. Private loan supply may rise with the interest rate, from the usual substitution response. But private loan supply also may fall if interest rate increases bid up the price level and the nominal value of capital stock enough to increase money demand and "squeeze out" private loans. This wrong-signed wealth effect can cause macroinstability and is most likely to create problems when the interest elasticity for money demand is low and the ratio of physical capital stock to wealth is high. The latter condition is symptomatic of semi-industrialized countries, where primary wealth in the form of government securities does not exist and a long history of inflation has taught people to keep their money balances down.

3. Because of the weak financial markets, firms are highly dependent on retained earnings for savings supply. The institutions that channel short-term private saving into long-term investment finance (insurance companies, the stock market, pension funds) are not active, because in an inflationary environment with imperfect market information, it is very risky to lend for long periods. Banks concentrate on financing working capital and leave investment finance to companies already there. On the supply side, most people are poor and have scant reason to trust the few savings institutions that exist. As a consequence, personal savings are low, both on average and at the margin. Government and foreign savings supplies fluctuate with the conjuncture, perhaps in unexpected ways (the balance-of-payments deficit—or foreign savings—may *rise* with devaluation, to take one common case). Retained earnings are the only flexible, secure savings supply, and for that reason the savings share from capital income will be high.

4. Investment response to changes in output and the real interest rate will differ from country to country. In some economies (Brazil and South Korea, perhaps), investment may respond rapidly enough to financial signals to give a positively sloped IS curve in the output/interest rate plane.

Under such an investment regime, contractionary monetary policies will follow the IS curve down, causing reductions in both production and the interest rate. Since interest costs are a component of price, inflation may drop off as well. In another, perhaps more likely case, investment responses to output change will be weak, leading to a downward-sloping IS curve. Monetary contraction now reduces output and raises interest rates. Price increases follow, and the policy is stagflationary in the short term. Such differences in investment response can be expected in any kind of economy, but their significance is magnified by the impact of interest rates on prices in many developing countries.

5. Imports are mostly noncompetitive intermediates and, as such, enter into prime cost. An increase in the import price (from devaluation or the world market) is inflationary because it will be passed along in final output price. At the same time, the increased import outlay may lead to an increase in the trade deficit measured in domestic currency, and potential savings will go up. The resultant output contraction coupled with rising prices marks another instance in which orthodox policy can go awry.

6. Available savings depend on the income distribution, rising with the profit share. As a consequence, progrowth and anti-inflation policies may be founded on a slow increase (relative to the rate of price inflation) of the money wage. Such slowdowns in money wage growth are usually possible only under sufficiently repressive regimes. Respect for institutional reality requires that a macromodel include a theory of wage dynamics, which can deal with changes in the political rules from time to time. One such approach is adopted later in this chapter.

7. Finally, inflation is often sparked by sectoral imbalances—a price-wage spiral kicked off by lagging agricultural supply is a classic case in point. We will discuss briefly how the macromodel can be extended to take this possibility into account.

To summarize, these institutional considerations suggest a Keynesian model, but one that differs from the textbook models in several ways. The most important are

—The impact of interest rate changes on the aggregate price level, with further repercussions throughout the macrosystem;

—differences in how stabilization policy works under stable ("Keynesian") and output-responsive ("Fisherian") investment demand;

—explicit consideration of whether devaluation stimulates economic activity, depending on import intensity and export response;

—consideration of whether the sensitivity of the price level to the interest rate may reverse the usual dampening effect of interest rate increases on money demand;

—recognition that the rapidity of money wage responses to inflation is determined politically and strongly influences possibilities for medium-term growth; and

—consideration of the possibility that inflation may be touched off by lagging supply in some sectors, especially nontraded goods and food.

The details of these revisions to the usual macromodel appear naturally in the formal structure, which follows.

Structure in Equation Form

Production Sector

Recent formulations of production theory typically begin with a cost function, as is done here.[2] The three inputs are labor, capital, and intermediates, with the last consolidated through the interindustry structure into imports. (The intermediate import share of GNP typically amounts to 25 percent or so in semi-industrialized developing countries.) Their respective unit costs are: labor, $(1 + i)w;$ imports, $(1 + i)eP_0;$ and capital, $rP;$ where w is the wage rate, e is the exchange rate, P_0 is the border price of imports, r is the profit rate, and P is the price of output. The costs of the current inputs—labor and imports—are multiplied by an interest factor $(1 + i)$ since they are used in the production process well before the final sale. Especially in an inflationary environment where interest rates are high, the financial cost of this working capital has to be taken into account. If most processes are completed within the short term, the *nominal* interest rate i measures working capital costs. Producers lay out $(1 + i) \times$ (working advances) at the beginning of the short period and collect back only the equivalent of the advances in sales at the end. The interest rate i thus measures financial costs. If input prices were indexed over the short term to the price level, they would go up by time of sale, making the real interest rate the appropriate cost indicator. But the assumption of fixed short-term money wages and import costs is correct un-

2. For a good textbook presentation of cost-based production theory, see Hal R. Varian, *Microeconomic Analysis* (W. W. Norton, 1978).

der an institutionalized inflation in which adjustments are widely spaced (typically once a year).[3]

Under constant returns and competitive assumptions (maintained here for simplicity) the short-term cost function will take the form

(1) $$P = F[(1 + i)w, (1 + i)eP_0, rP],$$

so that any changes in cost are assumed to be passed along rapidly into the output price P.

Besides this cost function, competition means that the usual marginal productivity conditions apply. By a result known as "Shephard's lemma," these conditions can be derived by differentiation of cost function 1. For example, demand for capital is given by

(2) $$K/X = \partial F/\partial(rP),$$

where K is the capital stock and X is the level of output (calculated gross of intermediate inputs as in equation 4 below). But if capital is fixed and fully utilized subject to substitution possibilities in the short term, equation 2 states capital costs rP are determined as a quasi-rent on K by output X. Hence substituting equation 2 into equation 1 gives a new cost function:

(3) $$P = P[(1 + i)w, (1 + i)eP_0, (X/K)].$$

Here, costs and the price level will rise with output under decreasing returns to capacity in the short term. In other words, a rising aggregate supply curve can be postulated, with price level determined by output and variable input costs.

These equations have two corollaries, used later. First, equation 2 says

3. For more on these points, see Andre Lara-Resende, "Inflation, Growth and Oligopolistic Pricing in a Semi-Industrialized Economy: The Case of Brazil" (Ph.D. dissertation, Massachusetts Institute of Technology, 1979). Lara-Resende also presents evidence to the effect that working capital costs may run as high as 10 percent of industrial sales in Brazil, as opposed to 1 or 2 percent in the United States. Similar estimates for Argentina are presented by Domingo F. Cavallo, "Stagflationary Effects of Monetarist Stabilization Policies" (Ph.D. dissertation, Harvard University, 1977). Cavallo's work stimulated the recent emphasis on importance of working capital costs. However, as Lara-Resende points out, the insight is an old one, although largely confined to the "underworld" of North Atlantic macroeconomic thought except in very recent work such as Ray C. Fair, "Inflation and Unemployment in a Macroeconometric Model," in *After the Phillips Curve: Persistence of High Inflation and High Unemployment,* Conference Series, 19 (Boston, Mass.: Federal Reserve Bank, June 1978).

that the profit rate (as well as the price level) rises with output, a result used in discussing investment demand. Second, the interest factor $(1 + i)$ in equation 3 multiplies all variable costs. As a consequence, an increase in i will have no effect on resource allocation but will simply be passed along in price. The elasticity of P with respect to i is $i/(1 + i)$ from the functional form of the financial cost markup. This result is used in discussing the shape of the LM curve later in this chapter.[4]

With constant returns, the cost of output is exhausted by input costs (including imports) according to the equation

$$(4) \qquad PX = (1 + i)(wN + eP_0mX) + rPK,$$

in which N is the level of employment and m is the intermediate import/output coefficient, assumed constant for simplicity. This equation describes factor payments in the economy. To trace these around to determine demand, the first step is determination of disposable income by an equation such as

$$(5) \qquad PY = (1 - s_F)rPK + wN + i(wN + eP_0mX) - PT.$$

Here, firms retain a fraction s_F of total profits rPK to finance investment. Other income flows are the wage bill wN and interest payments that accrue to the owners of banks. A lump sum tax (value PT) is taken by the government from income flows.

Assume that personal consumption is given by

$$(6) \qquad PC = (1 - s)PY.$$

Substitution of equations 5 and 6 into the commodity market balance equation,

$$(7) \qquad PX = PC + PI + PG + PE,$$

(I being investment, G government consumption, and E exports) and some algebra give the saving-investment balance as

$$(8) \qquad \begin{aligned} PI = & [s_F + s(1 - s_F)]rPK + s[wN + i(wN + eP_0mX) \\ & - \tau PX] + (\tau - \gamma)PX \\ & + [eP_0mX - H(eP_E/P)X], \end{aligned}$$

---

4. The independence of output from financial charges depends on our competitive, constant returns assumptions. With decreasing returns and/or monopoly power on the part of firms, rising interest rates would reduce output as well as drive up prices. For more on this supply effect, see Bruno, "Stabilization and Stagflation."

where $\tau = T/X$, the tax rate relative to output; $\gamma = G/X$, government consumption relative to output and the function $H(ep_E/P)$ shows how the export share E/X rises in response to a fall in the price of domestic commodities abroad (P/e) relative to the price of foreign similars (P_E). The right-hand side of equation 8 states that investment is financed by corporate saving, private saving, government fiscal surplus, and the balance-of-payments deficit, respectively.

Investment Theory

As discussed more fully below, firms face a nominal borrowing cost i, or a real cost j given by

$$(9) \qquad\qquad\qquad j = i - \pi,$$

where π is the expected inflation rate. On the other hand, the real return to capital is the marginal product r. Investors presumably weigh returns versus cost in determining how much to spend. Along lines suggested by Tobin,[5] a plausible investment function will have capital formation increasing with the profit rate r and declining with the real interest rate j. But, as already noted, r will rise along with output X. Hence write investment demand as

$$(10) \qquad\qquad\qquad PI = \phi[r(X), j]PK.$$

Rapidly responding investors might even make the Irving Fisher arbitrage condition $r(X) = j$ apply, but such agility in an underdeveloped financial market seems unlikely to be displayed. If it were, the Fisher condition (a positively sloped line in the (X, i) plane) would replace the savings-investment identity 8. This more Keynesian formulation adheres to reality and, with substitution from 10, can be restated as

$$(11) \qquad\qquad\qquad \phi(X, j) = s_k r + \mu(X/K),$$

with

$$s_k = s_F(1 - s),$$

and

$$\mu = s[1 - (eP_0/P)m - \tau] + (\tau - \gamma) + [(eP_0/P)m - H(eP_E/P)].$$

5. James Tobin, "Money, Capital and Other Stores of Value," *American Economic Review*, vol. 51 (May 1961, *Papers and Proceedings, 1960*), pp. 26–37.

From equation 10, $\phi(r, j)$ is the rate of growth of capital stock. Equation 11 shows that the growth rate is the sum of savings per unit profits ($s_k r$) and other savings flows per unit of capital stock ($\mu(X/K)$).

To focus on determination of equilibrium, restate 11 as an excess demand equation for output, ED_X:

(12) $\qquad ED_X(X, i) = \phi(X, i - \pi) - s_k r(X) - \mu(X/K).$

The level of production is supposed to vary rapidly in the short term to assure $ED_X = 0$. Stability will be more readily attained if the partial derivative of ED_X with respect to X is negative. Perusal of equation 12 shows that this condition holds when an increase in X generates more additional real saving than investment, a response pattern usually postulated in the short term. However, both recent theory and empirical evidence suggest that savings effects do not always dominate investment effects. As is discussed below, the macroeconomy reacts differently to stabilization attempts, depending on whether or not the usual hypothesis applies.[6]

Financial Structure

The relevant balance sheets for the model's financial structure appear in table 13-1.[7] The key balances are those of the commercial banks and

---

6. Since $\partial ED_X/\partial i < 0$, the condition $ED_X = 0$ defines a negatively sloped line in the (X, i) plane if $\partial ED_X/\partial X < 0$. This is the usual downward sloping IS curve in which an increase in X generates an excess of saving over investment and i must fall to stimulate investment and bring commodity market equilibrium back. However, as shown above, rapid investment arbitrage gives the condition $r(X) = i - \pi$, a positively sloped relationship between X and i. One need not be a fanatical Fisherian to believe that IS may sometimes slope up. See, for example, the econometrics in Nathaniel H. Leff and Kazuo Sato, "LDC Macroeconomics: Short-Run Growth, Instability and External Dependency" (Columbia Business School and the State University of New York at Buffalo, 1979). The fact that savings versus investment behavior crucially affects macroresponse is noted sporadically in the literature but not emphasized enough. Useful reminders are given by Amartya K. Sen, "Neo-Classical and Neo-Keynesian Theories of Distribution," *Economic Record,* vol. 39 (March 1963), pp. 54–64, and William Darity, Jr., "Essays on Growth, Distribution and Development (Ph.D. dissertation, Massachusetts Institute of Technology, 1978).

7. The following discussion is based squarely on Sweder van Wijnbergen, "Credit Policy, Inflation, and Growth in LDC's" (Ph.D. dissertation, Massachusetts Institute of Technology, 1980), which gives an elegant analytical treatment of many of the issues discussed informally here. The work of van Wijnbergen in turn follows from the papers of Bruno and Cavallo cited above.

Table 13-1. *Balance Sheets for Major Economic Agents*

Assets		Liabilities	
Central bank			
Foreign reserves	q_F	Reserves for deposits	q
Domestic reserves	q_D		
Commercial banks			
Reserves for deposits	q	Deposits from private sector	Q_P
Loans to firms	L_B	Deposits from firms	Q_F
Firms			
Deposits	Q_F	Loans from banks	L_B
Capital stock	PK	Loans from private sector	L_P
Private sector			
Deposits in banks	Q_P	Wealth	R
Loans to firms	L_P		

of firms. The latter presumably finance their holdings of fixed and working capital by borrowing from the public and from banks. Bank lending to firms (L_B) is regulated by the monetary authorities, through either credit limits or reserve requirements (which amount to the same thing if free reserves are negligible in an inflationary environment).

Loans from the public to firms depend on the interest rate, assumed to vary rapidly to clear the market for loans.[8] Since there is no serious market for equity and prudent investors find government bonds too unreliable, the public's only options for holding wealth are loans to firms and money. Again for simplicity, money is assumed to be held only as deposits; the demand function is

$$(13) \qquad\qquad Q_P = \psi(i)(q + PK).$$

A fraction of ψ of total wealth R,

$$(14) \qquad\qquad R = q + PK,$$

is held by the public in the form of money. That fraction declines as the rate of interest paid by firms goes up.

---

8. Authors such as Bruno, "Stabilization and Stagflation," assume that regulated bank loans carry a controlled interest rate i_0, while a freely varying curb rate clears the nonbank money market. Mostly to keep the disposable income accounts simple, assume that bank loans are issued at the market rate as well. In effect, banks vary compensating balance requirements and similar hidden charges to keep up with what other lenders charge at any time.

Firms demand loans to finance their physical capital PK and also working balances. As discussed above, the latter are advance payments for current production inputs. But since one firm's input is another's product (and payments to workers turn immediately into some firm's sales), in totality the money required for advance payments has to be held as net balances of firms throughout the system. That is why working capital is treated as deposits held with commercial banks in the quantity Q_F. Needless to say, these balances can always be put to other uses. They serve, for example, as liquid assets when the political situation makes firm managers see a need to indulge in capital flight. But under normal circumstances, firm deposits will correspond to aggregate working capital requirements for the wage bill and intermediate import costs,

$$(15) \qquad Q_F = wN + eP_0mX.$$

Equation 15 is a demand function for working capital. But since Q_F is held with commercial banks, the banks' consolidated balance sheet sets the supply of working capital equal to $q + L_B - Q_P$, bank assets less deposit liabilities to the public. After substitution from equations 13 and 14, the excess demand function for working capital becomes

$$(16) \qquad ED_i = wN + eP_0mX - (1 - \psi)q + \psi PK - L_B.$$

The interest rate varies to regulate the public's demand for money. But since an increase in money demand can come only with a fall in loans to firms, changes in i also drive ED_i to zero (under stability assumptions) in the short term.[9]

Savings-Investment Balance: Keynesian and Fisherian Investment Demand, and Contractionary Devaluation Effects

The usual story about the IS curve makes excess demand for commodities independent of the price level, and the latter unresponsive to the interest rate. One diagrammatic presentation appears in figure 13-1. The horizontal line gives the level of the interest rate i at which (for a given

9. If working capital is suppressed for the moment, equation 16 becomes $ED_i = \psi(i)(q + PK) - q$, that is, excess demand for money is the public's demand less the money supply. The story about working capital puts transaction demands together with the public's portfolio balance monetary tastes.

Figure 13-1. *The Usual IS Model: Effects of an Increase in Output on the Interest Rate (i) and Price Level (P)*

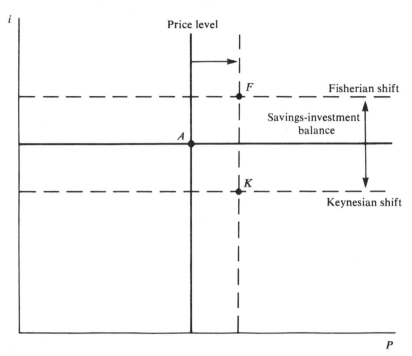

level of output X) excess demand for commodities ED_X in equation 12 is equal to zero. The vertical line gives the price level P corresponding to the given output X along the aggregate supply curve.

Now consider the effect of an increase in X. The price level will go up if there are increasing costs in the short term, shifting the price line to the right. However, the savings-investment balance may shift either way, as shown in the following two cases.

1. In a Keynesian analysis, investment demand is not very responsive to an increase in output. On the other hand, savings will go up if the aggregate marginal propensity to consume from current income is less than one. As discussed in footnote 6, potential savings will rise more than investment, and the interest rate must fall to stimulate investment and restore savings-investment balance overall. As figure 13-1 shows, the increase in output is accompanied at the new equilibrium K by a lower interest rate and a higher price level.

2. The other possibility, of course, is that investment demand responds

Figure 13-2. *The IS Model When the Price Level Depends on the Interest Rate*

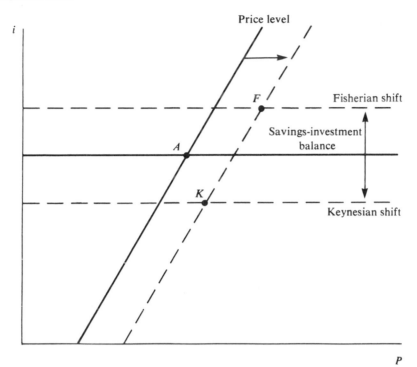

strongly to an increase in the profit rate and (with decreasing returns) to output as well. An increase in X will lead to a potential excess of investment over savings, and the interest rate must rise to choke the former off. This is the Fisherian shift shown in figure 13-1. At the new equilibrium F, both interest rate and price level rise as output goes up.

To extend this reasoning to a semi-industrialized economy, two additional complications must be brought into play. First, since finance of working capital enters into cost, the price level rises with the interest rate, or the price line is not vertical, but angled up. Figure 13-2 shows the impacts of an output increase when this dependence of price on interest rate is taken into account. As before, a Fisherian investment response leads to an increase in both the interest rate and the price level at point F. With a Keynesian response, the interest rate falls, but the price level can shift either way. In particular, the price may fall because interest charges have gone down or may rise when output goes up.

Figure 13-3. *The IS Model When Devaluation Improves the Trade*
Deficit in Domestic Prices or a Price Increase Makes the Deficit Grow[a]

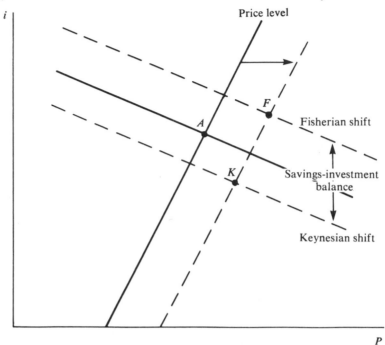

a. The resultant increase in savings must be balanced in macroequilibrium by a falling interest rate.
which stimulates investment demand.

The second complication is a dependence of the savings-investment
balance on the price level. One source of savings in a semi-industrialized
country (in practice, usually a large one) is the trade deficit on current
account. From the definition of parameter μ in equation 11, the real
deficit in domestic prices depends on price level P. For a given output level
X and exchange rate e, an increase in P will reduce real imports $(eP_0/P)mX$. If the foreign export price P_E is fixed, a rising P will also reduce
exports $H(eP_E/P)X$. Which of these two trade responses dominates is
unclear.

A clue is provided by the usual supposition that devaluation (an increase in the exchange rate e) will cause the real trade deficit in terms of
domestic product, $(eP_0/P)mX - H(eP_E/P)X$, to fall. Contrariwise, an
increase in P will cause the real deficit to go up. But since an increasing
deficit is a source of savings, the interest rate must fall as P rises to stim-

ulate investment demand and restore macroequilibrium. Hence the savings-investment line in the (P, i) plane will slope down. In figure 13-3 an output increase generates a rising price level in the Fisherian case. However, the interest rate may shift either way. The interest rate always falls with the Keynesian savings-investment response, but the price change can be of either sign. Prices will go up if the response of net saving to trade balance effects is relatively weak.

The final case to be considered is one in which exports do not respond strongly to devaluation, or the real trade gap widens when the exchange rate is adjusted up.[10] A price increase has the opposite-signed impact, namely, a reduction in the deficit and a fall in ex ante savings. Since investment must fall in equilibrium, the savings-investment line in the (P, i) plane slopes up. A Fisherian investment response would lead to both interest rate and price increases when output rises and to a potentially unstable system. The Keynesian case (in figure 13-4) is potentially stable, but even here a price increase seems likely to accompany growing output, especially if the wrong-signed savings response is relatively weak. All in all, there is a strong inflationary bias in the semi-industrialized macroscheme.

In summary, an increase in output has differing effects on the interest rate and price level, depending on which configuration of savings-investment and devaluation responses occurs. Some order can be imposed by transferring all this information to a single graph relating output X with the interest rate i *or* the price level P. Either of the latter variables can be used in the graphical analysis, since they are related monotonically through the cost function 3. The traditional IS/LM story, of course, is told in the (X, i) plane. But since the main interest here is inflation, in a break with tradition, these diagrams illustrate trade-offs between X and P.

10. This nonstandard result from exchange rate increases was labelled "contractionary devaluation" by Paul Krugman and Lance Taylor, "Contractionary Effects of Devaluation," *Journal of International Economics*, vol. 8 (November 1978), pp. 445–56. The name comes from the observation that if the interest rate is pegged, then the widening trade gap accompanying devaluation will stimulate potential savings and lead via Keynesian mechanisms to a production drop. Carlos Diaz-Alejandro, *Exchange Rate Devaluation in a Semi-Industrialized Economy: The Experience of Argentina* (MIT Press, 1965), is an early English-language source in which empirical support of this phenomenon appears. Diaz-Alejandro's study, Krugman and Taylor's "Contractionary Effects," and Schydlowsky's "Containing the Costs" cite other empirical studies as well. A well-known study is Richard N. Cooper, "An Assessment of Currency Devaluation in Developing Countries," in Gustav Ranis, ed., *Government and Economic Development* (Yale University Press, 1971).

Figure 13-4. *The Effects on Price Level and Interest Rate of an Output Increase in the Contractionary Devaluation Case*[a]

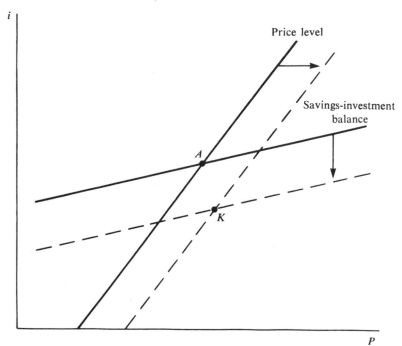

a. Only the Keynesian savings-investment response is potentially stable.

The corresponding interest rate movements can easily be recovered from equation 3.

The "normal" case is a negative relationship between output and price, such as occurs in figure 13-3, when there are no price effects on saving through the trade balance and Keynesian demand effects (perhaps reinforced by supply effects as in footnote 4) are strong. However, with more responsive Fisherian investors, a positive relationship can easily emerge. This possibility is indicated by the counterclockwise rotation of the IS curve in figure 13-5. Monetary contraction generates a leftward move along IS, as shown below. Output will fall, but the price response will differ depending on which investment specification applies. Orthodoxy is Fisherian if it assumes that monetary contraction immediately cuts prices. The higher wisdom is to recognize that monetary restraint will cut back on output and may make the price level shift either way.

Finally, considering contractionary devaluation, the stronger the contractionary effects are, the steeper the savings-investment line in figure

Figure 13-5. *The IS Curve in the (X, P) Plane under Different Assumptions about Savings-Investment Response and the Impacts of Devaluation*

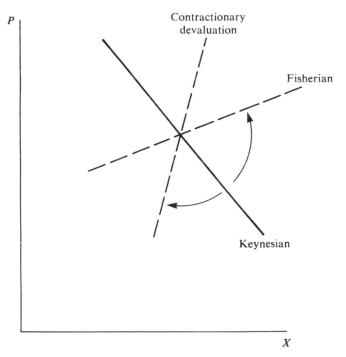

13-4 will be. Ignore the shifting price line in the figure for a moment and assume that "effects become stronger" so that the savings-investment line rises in slope. A given output increase will be associated with more negative price changes until the slopes of the two lines coincide, with price increases declining from positive infinity thereafter. Including the shift in the price line complicates this story but does not change its general lines. For that reason, stronger contractionary devaluation effects can be viewed as rotating that IS schedule in figure 13-5 clockwise, until it finally assumes a steep positive slope.

The Market for Loans: Substitution and Wealth Effects in Interest Rate Response

In this section, diagrams in the (*P*, *i*) plane are used to derive an LM curve. The cost function 3 still applies (giving a positively sloped rela-

Figure 13-6. *Determination of the LM Curve in Response to Output Shifts*[a]

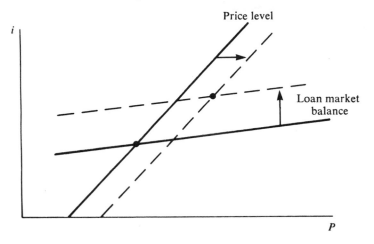

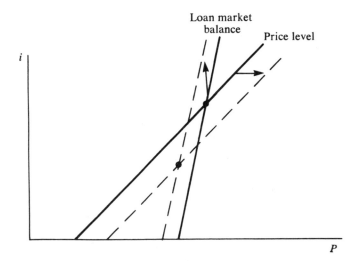

a. In the upper panel the portfolio response to interest rate changes is relatively strong; in the lower panel the response is weak.

tionship between P and i), but now the excess demand function for loans (equation 16) must be taken into account. Note there that a price increase will drive up excess demand via the term ψPK on the right-hand side—a wealth effect in loan demand. To compensate, the interest rate must rise, inducing a portfolio substitution response against money and in favor of loans. As a consequence, equation 16 generates a positively sloped line in the (P, i) plane. For a given P the line shifts upward in response to an increase in working capital demand.

The diagrammatic analysis appears in figure 13-6. Two cases are possible—the price line is steeper (upper figure) or shallower (lower figure) than the loan market balance line. In the first case, an increase in output generates a rise in the price level and interest rate, while in the second case price level and interest rate fall.

The economics behind these responses becomes clear when one recalls that the elasticity of price with respect to interest rate from the cost function 3 is $i/(l + i)$. The elasticity along the loan market excess demand function 16 is $-\psi^*/(PK/R)$, where ψ^* stands for the elasticity of the money demand function $\psi(i)$. In the excess demand elasticity the term PK/R will be close to one and nearly constant, since in an economy with poorly elaborated financial markets, physical capital is by far the dominant component of nominal wealth $R = q + PK$.[11] Comparison of the two elasticities shows that the loan market response of price to interest rate will be less than the cost function response when $-\psi^*$ is less than $i/(l + i)$. Such is the situation shown in the lower diagram of figure 13-6.

It is difficult to say a priori how the elasticity $-\psi^*$ changes with respect to $i/(l + i)$ as the interest rate varies over a range. The answer depends on the functional form of the money demand function $\psi(i)$, a bit of knowledge that is difficult to obtain. The widely used semilog function $\psi(i) = ae^{-bi}$ can give rise to the LM curve shown in figure 13-7.

When the interest rate and price level are low (relative to the money wage and exchange rate), LM, derived from the lower diagram in figure 13-6, has a negative slope. At higher prices and interest rates, the curve takes on its more familiar upward cant. And when the price level is independent of the interest rate, LM always slopes up.

11. The importance of a high "real asset ratio" (taxa de imobilização) such as PK/R in leading to an inflationary bias in financial markets was pointed out by the Brazilian author Ignacio Rangel, *A Inflação Brasileira* (Rio de Janeiro: Tempo Brasileiro, 1963). His model has been neatly formalized by Francisco L. Lopes, "Teoria e Politica de Inflação Brasileira: Uma Revisão Critica da Literatura" (Rio de Janeiro: Pontifical Catholic University, 1978).

Figure 13-7. *Comparative Statics of the LM Curve*[a]

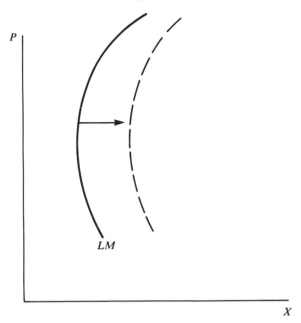

a. The shift is due to an increase in the money supply.

Comparative Statics

The IS and LM curves can illustrate a number of structuralist findings about the impact of policy moves. The analysis in this section is short term in the usual Keynesian sense, that is, the capital stock and the main elements in prime cost (the money wage and import prices) stay fixed. Also this section will not deal with rates of inflation or output growth but rather with how much the *level* of prices or output may shift. In terms of calendar time, such an approach is relevant for assessing policy impacts over the first few quarters—longer-term perspectives are developed below.

Routine stability analysis shows that the economy will maintain short-term equilibrium if the IS curve cuts the LM curve from the left on either its positively or negatively sloped branch. Since monetary expansion shifts the LM curve to the right, as was shown previously, its impact is unambiguous: output goes up and prices fall (see figure 13-8A). An in-

Figure 13-8. *Impacts of Policy Changes in the Keynesian IS Case*

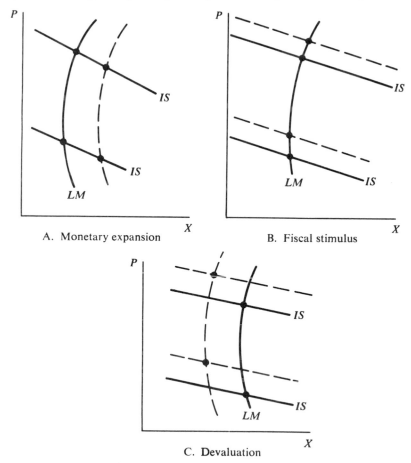

A. Monetary expansion   B. Fiscal stimulus

C. Devaluation

crease in the money supply (q) or bank loans to firms (L_B) reduces interest rates and costs—hence the price decrease. To maintain equilibrium
in the commodity market with dominant savings effects, output must rise.

The policy interest in this story comes when it is told in reverse, as has
been done by a number of younger structuralist economists.[12] Figure 13-
8A shows that monetary restraint will shift LM to the left and lead to

12. See Cavallo, "Stagflationary Effects" on Argentina, and also Samuel Morley,
"Inflation and Stagnation in Brazil," *Economic Development and Cultural Change*,
vol. 19 (January 1971), pp. 184–203.

stagflation—the price level rises and output falls off. The next section will show that the lower profit rate associated with reduced output leads to lower growth and in the long term to reduced demand for money, or excess demand for loans. As a consequence, a lower growth rate of money will ultimately lead to a rightward shift of LM and a downward shift in IS due to more slowly growing wage demands and lower inflationary expectations. Permanent monetary restraint causes *both* the growth rate *and* the inflation rate to fall, but the inflation rate has to have an upward excursion en route.

Figure 13-8B shows what happens with fiscal stimulus. An increase in the government deficit reduces potential savings, raises excess demand for investment, and, to maintain equilibrium output, rises while IS shifts up. On the upward-sloping branch of LM, fiscal expansion then leads to both price and output increases, the standard case. However, when the interest rate elasticity of money demand is weak (or when the real asset ratio PK/R is high), the fiscal stimulus will lead to high prices and *reduced* profit rates and growth. Because of the special characteristics of underdeveloped financial markets, a standard policy fails to have the expected effects.

Finally, figure 13-8C illustrates the short-term impacts of devaluation. Both IS and LM shifts lead to price increases. The LM shift (along IS) would also reduce output, but the effect on X of the IS shift depends on which branch of the LM curve applies. If, however, LM is rather steep, a reduced output level from the overall maneuver seems likely to result. Devaluation is another policy that is stagflationary in the short term. Whether an increase in the nominal exchange rate improves the current account is unclear—imports will decrease because of reduced output, but price increases will dampen the improvement in the real exchange rate (e/P), and the export response may even be perverse.

The conclusion is that the stabilization tools normally applied—monetary restraint, fiscal control, and devaluation—all have stagflationary impacts to a greater or lesser extent. Moreover, their efficacy in improving the balance of payments may also be small. The other configurations of the IS curve will show if prospects are any more favorable there.

First, take the Fisherian case, in which investment demand responds strongly to profit and interest rate shifts. In effect, savings determines investment in this specification, and purely Keynesian economic responses are suppressed. The model properly refers to a buoyant economy in full

Figure 13-9. *Impacts of Policy Changes in the Fisherian IS Case*

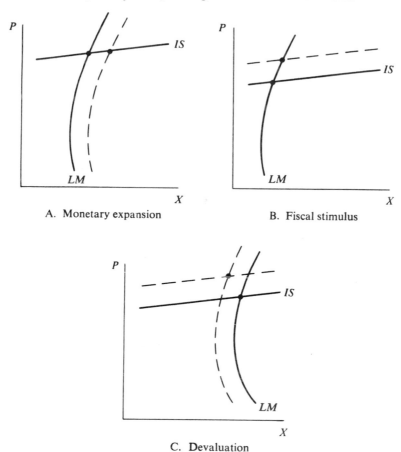

A. Monetary expansion   B. Fiscal stimulus

C. Devaluation

capacity growth and, not surprisingly, has been adopted by a number of Brazilian economists over the years.[13]

For stability, the upward-sloping IS curve has to cut LM from the

---

13. Fisherian models in which investment responds strongly to shifts in available savings and aggregate demand are used by Rangel, *A Inflação Brasileira,* and Lopes, "Teoria e Politica." The same assumption is used in a growth model discussed more thoroughly below by Eliana A. Cardoso, "Inflation, Growth and the Real Exchange Rate: Essays on Economic History in Brazil" (Ph.D. dissertation, Massachusetts Institute of Technology, 1979). Perhaps not surprisingly, the stagflation model of figure 13-8 is more properly of Argentines and Chileans, or Brazilians when their growth rate is down.

left—investment response cannot be "too strong" and lead to a more shallow LM than IS. Moreover, any intersection of IS with the negatively sloped branch of LM is not stable. The unstable lower branch when there is elastic investment demand shows how Rangel's suggestion—that a high real asset ratio leads to inflation and high interest rates—works itself out.

Figure 13-9A illustrates the comparative statics of monetary expansion. Both prices and output go up. Monetary restraint will lower the price level but will bring down output as well. Moreover, as the LM curve slides down the IS curve during the deflation, prices and interest rates might fall far enough to weaken substitution effects and to bring the wrong-signed wealth effect on money demand into play. In this case, the economy would become unstable, and further policies aimed at reducing inflation would abort. Again, responsive investors and a high real asset ratio put a lower bound on how far inflation can be reduced.

Figure 13-9B shows that fiscal expansion leads to higher prices and output—the same result as before. Finally, with a steep LM curve, devaluation is likely to be stagflationary in figure 13-9C. All in all, the policy prospects under Fisherian conditions are more favorable than in the normal case (with its sluggish investment response), but how widely they apply is a moot point.

The final case is contractionary devaluation, illustrated in figure 13-10. Recall from figure 13-5 that the IS curve here is likely to be quite steep, since it results from a clockwise rotation from the normal case. Indeed, the stability condition is that IS cuts the upward-sloping branch of the LM curve from below. Any intersection with the negatively sloped branch is unstable.

Figure 13-10A shows that monetary expansion reduces prices, by easing off on interest rate pressures, but slightly reduces output and the rate of growth. Monetary restraint, on the other hand, would lead to sharp price increases. Output would also rise, pushed up by reduced potential savings resulting from the improvement in the balance of payments caused by the lower value of the real exchange rate (e/P).

Fiscal stimulus raises prices and the profit rate in figure 13-10B, while devaluation will be stagflationary (higher price level, lower output) with a steep IS curve in figure 13-10C. On the other hand, devaluation would improve the balance of payments in this case. The export response to shifts in the real exchange rate is weak by hypothesis, but the reduction in output will make raw material imports fall. With near constant exports and falling imports, the trade balance in world prices should improve.

Figure 13-10. *Impacts of Policy Changes in the Contractionary Devaluation IS Case*

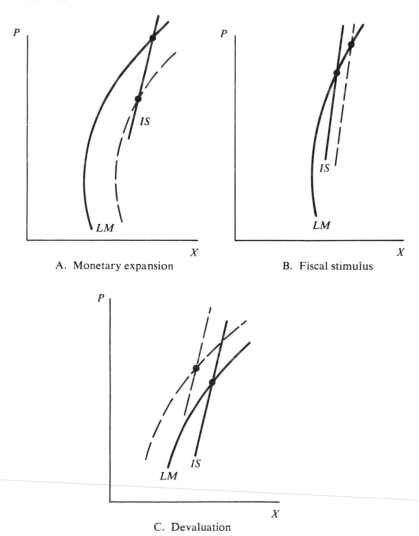

A. Monetary expansion

B. Fiscal stimulus

C. Devaluation

However, because *P* goes up, the trade balance change in terms of domestic prices is of uncertain sign. The longer-term impacts through changes in the growth rate of money base would also differ from case to case. Finally, note that in the short term there is merit in coupling devaluation with monetary ease. The inflationary impact of the exchange rate increase would be offset by monetary policy, and appropriate juxta-

Table 13-2. *Impacts of Stabilization Policies Under Various Regimes*[a]

	Keynesian		Fisherian		Contractionary devaluation	
Policy	*Output*	*Price*	*Output*	*Price*	*Output*	*Price*
Monetary restraint	−	+	−	−	+	+
Fiscal restraint	−(?)	−	−	−	−	−
Devaluation	−(?)	+	−(?)	+(?)	−(?)	+(?)

a. Question marks indicate the most probable signs, given the configuration of the curves.

position of the instruments could, within limits, lead to improvements in both the current account and growth.

Table 13-2 summarizes this section, showing how the usual stabilization policies affect output and price in the short term (question marks indicate the most probable signs, given the configuration of the curves). Fiscal restraint will reduce both variables under all policy regimes—a leftward shift along the positively sloped branch of the LM curve gives this result. The effects of monetary restriction are harder to predict. Monetary restriction is stagflationary under Keynesian investment demand conditions and can give both inflation and output expansion when devaluation has contractionary IS effects. Only under Fisherian investment conditions do the normally expected price and output decreases ensue.

Finally, depending on the shape of the LM curve, devaluation may be stagflationary in all cases. Devaluation's impact on the balance of payments (in either world or domestic prices) is unclear. However, even if export response is weak, the output contraction might usually be expected to make the world price balance-of-payments deficit improve.

A Complication: Inflationary Pressures from Nontraded Goods

Further comparative statics exercises could be pursued, for example, policy mix questions of the type mentioned above. But to extend the analysis, it is more appropriate to ask how the model can deal with issues of inflation and growth. Preparatory to that, however, we look briefly at the comparative statics of price pressures from sectors whose products are not fully open to international trade. Agriculture is a classic case, if only because developing countries lack adequate port facilities and transport infrastructure to handle even hundreds of thousands of tons of imported wheat. Other nontradables (or near nontradables) such as cement can also cause inflationary bottlenecks in the short term. Price varies (perhaps illegally) to clear markets for such commodities, and that is presumably the case here. By contrast, Keynesian adjustments apply in the rest of the economy, with supply varying to meet demand. To keep life tolerably simple, Fisherian investment responses and contractionary devaluations are assumed totally away.

Figure 13-11 gives a four-quadrant diagram for the sort of model we have in mind.[14] Price in the A-sector ("agriculture") is measured on the horizontal axis running left from the origin. For given supply conditions, income in the sector will be a rising function of its price (Z). Consequently, demand for N-sector ("industrial") products from the A-sector will rise with Z, as shown in the northwest quadrant. At the same time, real savings generated by the A-sector will also increase in the southwest.

The northeast quadrant is a standard Keynesian cross for the N-sector. Demand comes from autonomous expenditures and the A-sector (both are lumped on the upper vertical axis) and also from N-sector output X according to the marginal propensity to consume. The intersection with the forty-five degree line determines X for a given A-sector price Z.

The model is closed in the southeast quadrant, which shows savings "required" from the A-sector, that is, autonomous expenditure less savings generated from the N-sector. The required A-sector saving is a declining function of X and must equal savings produced by that sector in the southwest.

An initial equilibrium is shown at Z_0 and X_0. Assume a bad harvest so that agricultural supply drops. For a given Z, both consumption demand and savings from the A-sector will be less, and the curves in the northwest

---

14. Models similar to the present one have been worked out by a number of authors, although the diagram seems to be new. The classic structuralist paper is by Osvaldo Sunkel, "Inflation in Chile: An Unorthodox Approach," *International Economic Papers*, no. 10 (1960), pp. 107–31. Comparative statics of figure 13-11 are developed by Graciela Chichilnisky and Lance Taylor, "Agriculture and the Rest of the Economy: Macro Connections and Policy Restraints," *American Journal of Agricultural Economics*, vol. 62 (May 1980), pp. 303–09. The same model is independently extended in the direction of Sunkel by incorporating an inflation theory (along the same lines as in this chapter's section on long-term trade-offs) by Eliana A. Cardoso, "Food Supply and Inflation," *Journal of Development Economics*, forthcoming.

Figure 13-11. *A Two-Sector Model*[a]

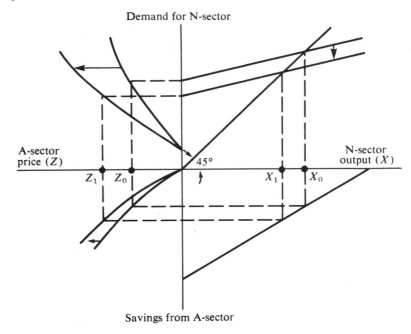

Demand for N-sector

A-sector price (Z)   45°   N-sector output (X)

Z_1 Z_0 X_1 X_0

Savings from A-sector

a. In this model, price varies to clear the market in the A-sector (agriculture) while output responds to demand in the N-sector (industry). A downward shift in the A-sector supply function leads both to less real saving and to less demand for the N-sector commodity for a given A-sector price (Z). The outcome is an increase in price from Z_0 to Z_1 and a fall in N-sector output from X_0 to X_1.

and the southwest will shift out. N-sector consumption demand will fall, leading to a decrease in X and an increment in agricultural savings required. The price will rise from Z_0 to Z_1 to determine a new equilibrium, and N-sector output will fall from X_0 to X_1. The adjustment mechanism is a shift down in the consumption function in the northeast.

The sort of supply shock shown in figure 13-11 can easily set off a burst of inflation, if money wages respond to the rising agricultural price, and drive up N-sector costs in turn. A sequence of shocks can keep inflation going if, for example, population growth runs ahead of the growth rate of agricultural supply. One can deal with such stories formally, but in this chapter they would take us too far afield. Rather, this study looks at wage-price dynamics in the N-sector only, but bear in mind that the sorts of complications discussed in this section often arise. Even if sharp sectoral price increases are not observed, they may be latent just because policy makers are holding down aggregate demand.

Long-Term Trade-offs among Inflation, Income Distribution, and Growth

To analyze growth in the long term, it is necessary to add hypotheses about dynamics to the IS/LM system described earlier. There are three main equations restated here for convenience. The cost function, given in equation 3, is

$$P = P[(1 + i)w, (1 + i)eP_0, (X/K)].$$

The IS equation for commodity market clearing is

$$(17) \quad \phi[r(X), i - \pi] - s_k r(X) - \{s[1 - (eP_0/P)m - \tau]$$
$$+ (\tau - \gamma) + [(eP_0/P)m - H(eP_E/P)]\}(X/K) = 0,$$

and finally, the LM equation for loan market is

$$(18) \qquad wN + eP_0 mX - [1 - \psi(i)]q + \psi(i)PK - L_B = 0.$$

These equations are supposed to hold in the short term, with equalities assured by rapid variation of employment (the cost function), output (IS) and interest rate (LM). They act as constraints on all variables entering the growth of the system. The formal discussion here concentrates on growth in a closed economy (although some thoughts about how the system behaves when it is opened to trade appear at the end of this section).

The key dynamic variables are the expected inflation rate (π), the growth rate of the money wage (w'), and the capital stock growth rate (K').[15] It seems most realistic to assume adaptive expectation for inflation,

$$(19) \qquad\qquad d\pi/dt = \epsilon(P' - \pi).$$

The expected rate π is adjusted for discrepancies from the actual inflation rate P' according to a response coefficient ϵ (which usually takes a value of around one-half when estimated from annual data).

Two hypotheses naturally present themselves regarding wage growth. The first is that because of surplus labor conditions, the expected real wage stays constant, or $w' = \pi$. However, one should recognize that income distribution mechanisms in a semi-industrialized, inflationary economy are complex. Inflation is the outcome of conflicting claims to product, with different social classes having the upper hand at different times.

15. The "prime" notation just introduced signifies growth rates, for example, $w' = (dw/dt)/w$.

Such conflict is most realistically modeled in disequilibrium terms, as by Lara-Resende.[16] For present purposes, however, it is better to stick with a simple differential equation version of wage response. This equation follows Cardoso[17] in postulating that changes in the growth rate of the money wage (dw'/dt) are given by

(20) $$dw'/dt = \lambda\pi + \eta(K' - K_0') - w'.$$

According to this specification, the bargaining process limits money wage increases to a fraction (λ) of expected inflation in the short term. The parameter λ has substantial political content and will be lower as the state is able or willing to take the side of profit recipients and hold down wage increases by bringing its police-military apparatus to bear. (Think of the different political situations in Brazil in 1964 and 1979, or perhaps in Chile in 1973 and fifteen years thence.) Higher wage growth will be permitted when the capital stock growth rate (and, as will be seen shortly, the profit rate) is high relative to some standard level K_0'. Under these hypotheses, what might be called "warranted" wage growth is $\lambda\pi + \eta(K' - K_0')$. Equation 20 states that if the actual growth of money wages falls below the warranted rate, that growth will speed up. A politically naive argument often advanced by monetarist economists is that $\lambda = 1$. In this case, money wages will grow at a constant rate ($dw'/dt = 0$) only when the capital stock is growing at K_0', its "natural rate."

Capital stock growth is limited by savings, from the IS equation. Dropping foreign trade variables from equation 17 allows the capital growth rate to be written as

(21) $$K' = s_k r + [s(1 - \tau) + (\tau - \gamma)](X/K).$$

Growth is higher as the profit rate goes up and also depends, from the terms in brackets, on personal and government savings shares.

Global stability analysis of differential equations 19 through 21 subject to equations 3, 17, and 18 is too daunting a task to undertake here. Even verification of local stability around a steady growth path requires a fair bit of bashing away with Routh-Hurwitz conditions. From these, one set of sufficient conditions for local stability around a steady state is that (1) the IS/LM short-term system is stable with respect to changes in the interest rate, output, and employment; (2) the wage response parameter λ in equation 20 is not greater than one, so that money wages do not over-react to price increases; and (3) the parameters of the IS/LM system are

16. Lara-Resende, "Inflation, Growth and Pricing."
17. Cardoso, "Inflation, Growth and Exchange Rate."

such that money wage increases do not lead to output increases in the short term.

These are only illustrative conditions; in particular, the second and/or third conditions can be relaxed if parameters for adaptive expectations (ε in equation 19) or wage responses to growth (η in 20) are small. What one has to rule out is an explosive price-wage-employment spiral, which could lead to a cumulative inflationary process. Hyperinflation (or its near misses) is of substantial policy interest, but it is not analyzed here. Rather, the focus is on steady states, to point out the conflicts among growth, distribution, and inflation that arise even when the economy is well behaved.

In steady state, the conditions $dK'/dt = dw'/dt = d\pi/dt = 0$ will apply. How the variables in the IS/LM system are determined along a steady growth path is the next problem to be solved.

First, from equation 21, note that if capital stock growth K' is constant, then the profit rate r and the output-capital ratio X/K must be constant also. Also from equation 19, expectations are realized, or $P' = \pi$. But since the growth rate is also equal to investment demand, $K' = \phi(r, i - \pi)$, the interest rate i must also be constant. With all these constants inserted into the cost function 3, there can only be price inflation if the wage is growing equally fast, $w' = P'$. Hence the real wage stays constant along a steady state.

Now consider the LM curve. Growth in money supply will influence the inflation rate here. To keep to essentials, assume that the government fixes the ratio of bank loans to base money,

$$(22) \qquad\qquad L_B = \xi q;$$

thus the credit multiplier is set. Also observe that without foreign trade, money growth is given by

$$(23) \qquad\qquad dq/dt = (\gamma - \tau)PX,$$

or the fiscal deficit is completely monetized. If one puts these conditions into a differential version of the LM equation 18 to get a money growth versus inflation equation, the result turns out to be

$$(24) \qquad\qquad P' = M' - K',$$

in which

$$M' = \frac{r(1 + i)(1 - \psi)(1 + \xi)(\gamma - \tau)}{r\alpha_N + (1 + i)\alpha_K},$$

and α_N and α_K are the wage and profit shares, respectively, in value added.

In equation 24, parameter M' stands for the effect of money growth on price inflation through the LM equation. Parameter M' is displayed in full to show that to a degree, monetary expansion can be regulated by the authorities who control spending and tax parameters (γ and τ) and also the credit multiplier through the loan-base money ratio ξ. But M' is also endogenous insofar as the profit rate r, the interest rate i, and the variables they affect can adjust. Without entering into details, it serves the purpose here to assume that the authorities do have enough control to determine M'. If that is the case, then equation 24 shows that for a given rate of monetary expansion, higher capital stock growth is associated with lower inflation, with a trade-off parameter equal to one.[18]

To get another relationship between growth and inflation in steady state, consider wage response. When money wage growth w' is constant, equation 20 shows that $w' = \lambda P' + \eta(K' - K_0')$. Combining the condition with a constant real wage ($w' = P'$) gives

$$(25) \qquad\qquad (1 - \lambda)P' = \eta(K' - K_0').$$

Assume that there is some wage control, so that $\lambda < 1$. Then the steady state equilibrium is determined as in figure 13-12.

The first thing to note about this figure is that the wage equation imposes a *positive* long-term relationship between inflation and growth. An increase in money supply growth M' will shift up the IS/LM line, leading to increases in both K' and P'. During the transition, inflation will accelerate above its new long-term value, causing a falling real wage from equation 20. The real wage reduction shifts income toward profits, generating the saving required to support the new higher rate of growth. The long-term trade-off will not exist when $\lambda = 1$ and the economy grows at its natural rate K_0'. The politics of recent stabilization efforts in a number of semi-industrialized countries belies the likelihood of immediate wage response to the inflation rate.

The other major point to observe is that a reduction in the parameter λ, which represents workers' ability to protect their income claims against inflation, will reduce the slope of the wage line in figure 13-12. As a consequence, a given rate of money supply growth will be consistent with lower inflation and faster output growth. Stabilization programs in de-

18. The unitary long-term price and quantity elasticities for money demand arise from the $\psi(i)PK$ term in equation 18, which states that equal percentage increments in P and K generate the same percentage growth in demand. Dependence of the demand function ψ on X would change the size but not the sign of the inflation versus growth trade-off in equation 24.

Figure 13-12. *Long-Term Trade-offs between Inflation and the Growth Rate of Capital Stock*

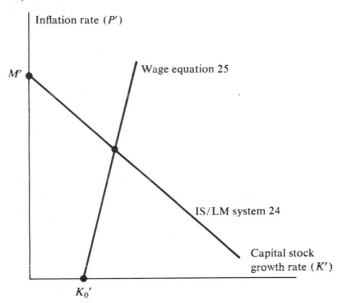

veloping countries often feature both monetary contraction and wage restraint. Figure 13-12 illustrates why. Both inflation and growth targets are easier to achieve as long as λ is reduced. Only the workers and the poor have to pay for the "miracles" that orthodox policy occasionally engineers.

Finally, note that much of this reasoning carries over into open economy models, where the price level, wage, and exchange rate must all grow equally rapidly in steady state, $P' = w' = e'$. With the addition of a dynamic equation like equation 20 to describe how policy makers set the exchange rate, a number of stories about inflation and the balance of payments can be told. For details, Cardoso's work is the best source.[19]

Monetarist Approaches

The purpose of this chapter is to sketch a version of the Keynesian model that applies to semi-industrialized countries. The task is straightforward (though tedious) because Keynes and the structuralists claim

19. Cardoso, "Inflation, Growth and Exchange Rate," essay 5.

much common ground. Trying to bring monetarism into the picture is more difficult because fewer common assumptions are shared between the rival camps. Nonetheless, the effort is worth making, since monetarist arguments often buttress orthodox policy prescriptions in developing countries.

Insofar as policy is concerned, monetarist recommendations follow from zealous application of Walras' law that the sum of excess demands in all markets should be zero at all times. Suppose that this is true, and suppose further that the cost function and IS and LM curves exhaust all existing markets. Then the implicit approach here of permitting potential excess demands (for labor, commodities, and loans) in all three markets is wrong. That is, if one knows two of the excess demands, one should know the third from Walras' law. More narrowly, if prices equal costs, then an excess demand in, say, the money market "determines" as its mirror image an excess supply for commodities. Only the money market need be considered to understand everything that is going on.

The Keynesians' traditional escape from this problem is to postulate some background adjustment process that enables Walras' law to be satisfied while there are simultaneous, independent excess demands in IS and LM. Numerous possibilities exist. An extra "market" can be imagined to clear the sum of excess demands, for example, unintended inventory change in the multiplier story or the traditional "bonds." Or extra agents may enter—foreigners who buy and sell in the export commodity market and the monetary authorities who clear the exchange market against them. The Keynesian view is that it is perfectly possible for an asset market (for example, money) to clear while a flow market (for example, commodities) does not. By contrast, monetarists think that stock excess demands call forth corresponding flow excess supplies by Walras' law. This approach to policy amounts to postulating an excess demand or supply of money and asking where its spillovers to the rest of the economy will land. The usual targets are the commodity market and the balance of payments, both of which are taken up in turn.[20]

20. The best theoretical treatment of the issues raised here is Duncan K. Foley, "On Two Specifications of Asset Equilibrium in Macroeconomic Models," *Journal of Political Economy,* vol. 93 (April 1975), pp. 303–24. Policy-relevant discussions are given by Lopes, "Teoria e Politica," and Shafiqul Islam, "Reflections on the Monetary Approach to the Balance of Payments" (Harvard University, May 1979).

The commodity market spillover was emphasized in the "gradualist versus shock treatment" debate in Brazil in the 1960s. A closed economy was correctly assumed in which an excess demand for money was to lead via Walras' law to an excess supply of goods. Moreover, the public would allegedly respond only slowly to excess money demand, gradually increasing their liquidity by buying less. As a consequence, prices would decelerate slowly, even though "goods chased money" in an active way.

The creation via monetary restriction of a large excess money demand is a shock treatment. By the Walras' law story there will be unintended stock accumulation, and output will rapidly drop off. Slowly declining inflation means that the recession lasts a long time. For that reason, a "gradualist" policy of less abrupt monetary restraint amounts to a better cure.

That gradualism embodies a good deal of common sense cannot be denied. Nonetheless, gradualism will be reinterpreted here in a Keynesian frame where responses along IS as well as LM determine outcome. The simultaneous decline of price and output that the gradualists postulate clearly labels them as Fisherians in the scheme presented here—figure 13-9A captures their mechanism quite well. But then questions arise: Is the economy really Fisherian so that both prices and production immediately drop off? If the economy is Keynesian (in the sense of this presentation) and if monetary restraint will cause stagflation instead, the whole gradualist approach to stabilization gets off on the wrong foot.

How does the cost function enter the story? If money wages continue to grow fast, then so will prices unless output quite brusquely falls. Contrariwise, the postulated price reduction requires a smaller output recession if money wage growth slows down. This employment versus income distribution conflict comes up in any stabilization effort, but monetarists ignore it by concentrating only on the politically immaculate market for funds.

Are there other stabilization policies? Quite clearly, fiscal and expenditure-switching policies of the type mentioned earlier have been left out.

What about the balance of payments? In most countries, spillovers of excess money demand to foreign trade may be substantial. This topic is taken up next.

The introduction of balance of payments into the monetarist schema makes the Walras' law game harder to play—it is now necessary to trace through the impacts of demand for money on price, domestic commodities, and foreign trade. The science of detecting spillovers underlies the "financial programming" exercises routinely undertaken by the IMF.[21]

Typically, financial programming starts from an unvarying output projection, called "full employment" when monetarists write models down. Then a price projection is made, based on a cost function more or less like equation 3. In an inflationary situation, a stabilization program wants a slower rate of price increase from this year to next than has been the case in the past. If profit rates are maintained (to keep up savings), inflation control requires a reduction in the real wage. In wage cutting, financial programmers have learned the lesson of figure 13-12 all too well.

With price and output projections (and some assumptions about credit multipliers), one can calculate demand for money base. Of course, the two sources of base are a fiscal deficit and a balance-of-payments surplus. If the former is cut, then by the accounting logic underlying the whole system, the foreign surplus has to go up. If need be, the increase will be helped along by simultaneous devaluation and dismantlement of trade barriers, to reap efficiency gains by "getting the prices right."

From a structuralist point of view, this procedure has a number of weak points. Certainly, a list would include the following points (some already mentioned above).

1. The whole exercise leaves out the IS curve. The interest rate is implicitly fixed in the money demand projection, and commodity production is determined ad hoc. Whether the output level is consistent with savings and investment propensities of different functional economic classes (with changing real incomes) is never spelled out. In this sense, financial programming does not embody a consistent macroprojection, so that it often fails.

2. This lack of consistency shows up in the kinds of policies chosen. An earlier section explained that it is quite likely that both devaluation and monetary contraction will cause stagflation under semi-industrialized

---

21. There are no succinct references explaining what financial programming is all about. The model is essentially that of J. J. Polak, "Monetary Analysis of Income Formation and Payments Problems," *IMF Staff Papers,* vol. 6 (November 1957), pp. 1–50, or Alexander K. Swoboda, "Monetary Approaches to Balance-of-Payments Theory," in E. Claassen and P. Salin, eds., *Recent Issues in International Monetary Economics* (Amsterdam: North-Holland, 1976), but there is no denying that in some IMF stabilization exercises a good deal of non-model-based economic sophistication is brought to bear. Some feel for the approach appears in E. Walter Robichek, "Financial Programming Exercises of the International Monetary Fund in Latin America" (Washington, D.C.: IMF Institute, International Monetary Fund, 1975).

macroconstraints. By leaving the possibility of an output reduction out of their models, financial programmers cannot deal with this natural consequence of the policies they commend. They implicitly tax the poor twice, by real wage reductions and employment declines. In fact, figure 13-12 shows that financial programmers may even tax the poor again, if the wage repression/monetary restraint policy reduces the long-term rate of growth.

3. Finally, the brusque short-term stabilizations administered by international agencies leave out even the monetarist wisdom of gradualism, not to mention prospects for long-term institutional change. The macro-situation in poor countries *is* difficult; the narrow limits to acceptable policy make any conjuncture terribly tight. Policies that may loosen some of the restrictions are taken up next.

Possibilities for the Medium Term

How can the bottlenecks be widened? There are no magic wands in economics, and sensible policy begins by recognizing that fact. Gradualism in a general sense has much to recommend it, since one gains little by pushing hard. Moreover, the results described in earlier sections on short-term policy and on the long term serve as reminders that orthodoxy runs a severe risk of making a bad situation worse.

What options are there, then? One favored by many authors is export promotion. The benefits are clear—generation of foreign exchange and reduction of the potential contractionary impact of a glut of foreign savings through the trade gap. Export promotion can most easily be achieved through targeted policies—drawbacks, special credit provisions, crawling pegs, and dual exchange rates. These policies run afoul of international organization ideologies, and potential exporting countries have suffered therefrom. More institutional tolerance from the IMF and GATT would be a fine thing. But such tolerance would require an improbable degree of acquiesence from the developed countries, which to a large extent manipulate the international agencies to further the new, soft imperialism of the North.

Even if Northern jobs and capital were not threatened by developing country exports, they may not always be the best policy for the South. Special export promotion policies pursued too far can lead to efficiency losses—a little understood trade-off exists between growth benefits and productivity costs of such programs. More seriously, it is clear that export promotion can only add to growth in the long term if exports add to national savings. But that achievement may require income concentration in the export sector of a most visible and unpleasant kind. Extreme social inequality stands out in some of the "success cases." Is that the way other countries want to go?

The export promotion option is one of a larger class of programs concentrating on the side of supply. Another is modernization of the agricultural and other nontraded sectors, to reduce the severity of inflationary shocks of the type illustrated in figure 13-11. These policies have to be designed to fit the situation at hand—not just economic in terms of factor intensities and interindustry linkages, but social problems as well. This is not wholly an ideological matter; serious planners may contemplate land reform in one valley and subsidize the landlords in the next. The point is that social relationships within the mode of production condition patterns of economic response. The patterns will not change unless their structural correlates also change.

A third set of policies focuses on income distribution and savings within the country. The growth-inflation synergy of figure 13-12 is dampened, for example, if workers and, by extension, the poor save more. Creation of appropriate financial institutions may further this end, as well as perhaps reduce the impact of interest rate changes on price by making working capital easier to obtain. More generally, the goal is to widen control over the means of production, to make subordinate capitalism's income inequalities less capitalistic. One route to this end is social democratic—open the economy, promote exports, use economic incentives to push or pull people into sectors where their productivity will be high. Another route is more leftist and directed—close the economy, run production from the center, and force the income distribution toward equality via supply control and rationing.

There are countries now following both paths, and by their own standards they are doing reasonably well. Stabilization policies enter their schemes in various fashions, but in one way or another these countries avoid the fiscal stringency/credit contraction/devaluation/wage repression packages so beloved of orthodoxy and the IMF. A reformist would hope that Northern economic practitioners such as those at the IMF could be taught to enforce less draconian measures when internal mismanagement or external mischance brings them down upon some developing economy. If they do not learn soon, then well-justified political resentment on the part of Southern countries which find their growth and internal equity sacrificed to Northern economic conceits could lead to the end of the present international economic system. Even reformists might not regret that end.

Comments by Kemal Dervis

In my view, the basic message of Lance Taylor's paper is that the short term cannot and should not be ignored and that in the short term, things may not be as they seem. The argument has a strong traditional Keynesian flavor: in the short term, one can get something for nothing, and implicitly, in the long term, we are all dead. Thus "an increase in the money supply reduces interest rates and costs—hence the price (level) decrease. To maintain equilibrium in the commodity market with dominant savings effects, output must rise." Not only is monetary restraint bad for inflation but the argument also holds in reverse—monetary expansion can beat inflation—in the short term! The key relationship that leads to this perverse link between quantity of money and price level is the cost function that includes nominal interest as part of prime cost. In fact, there are other factors in semi-industrialized as well as industrialized countries that can lead to such a perverse relationship, including monopolistic price formation rules in the urban industrial sector or the direct impact of credit on output through its effect on bankruptcies and strikes. The basic point is that supply and demand *both* determine price. A policy that tries to restrict demand, and ends up reducing supply by even more than it reduces demand, will be inflationary. And in the short term, supply may depend rather critically on the volume of credit, more so in developing countries than in advanced industrialized economies.

While these points are quite true and while IMF-type stabilization packages are built on an underlying model that minimizes the role of the supply side of the economy, one cannot argue, and indeed Taylor does not argue, that the kind of perverse relationships stressed within a short-term framework are still relevant and important in a longer-term perspective. The problem is that while one cannot ignore the short term, one cannot ignore the long term either. As many countries have found, some at the cost of great violence and tragedy, populist policies that do not recognize the link between money growth and price growth, or between the real exchange rate and trade performance, result in total economic and political collapse. The reverse is, of course, also true: governments that embark on orthodox stabilization programs that might well reestab-

Figure 13-13. *Alternative Adjustment Paths under Economic Stabilization*

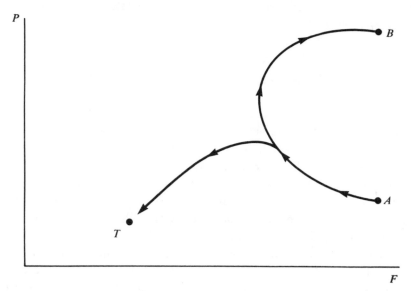

lish equilibrium after two years of extreme hardship may not survive the first year. Indeed, the whole effort may break down because the short-term costs are simply too high. These political considerations explain why there appears to be such a distasteful link between "successful" stabilization and political repression.

Clearly, the aim should be to generate a feasible (politically and economically) transition from an unsustainable disequilibrium to some kind of sustainable and desirable new configuration of key magnitudes.

Methodologically, the analysis of transition path requires a dynamic model that can focus explicitly on the *relative speeds of adjustments* of the important policy and target variables. The problem is illustrated in figure 13-13.

The objective in figure 13-13 is to get from A to the vicinity of T. Point F on the horizontal axis measures magnitude of net foreign resources, and point P on the vertical axis measures inflation rate. One can think of a dynamic model of the form

$$\dot{P}/P = f(M, R, X),$$

$$\dot{F}/F = g(M, R, X),$$

and $M \in S_M$, $R \in S_R$, $X \in S_X$, where M, R, and X stand for monetary policy, exchange rate policy, and fiscal policy (public sector price policy, for example) and S_M, S_R, and S_X restrict the paths of various policy variables to feasible sets determined not only by strictly economic considerations but also by the political and institutional context. The problem, then, is to choose the time paths of M, R, and X to get from A to T and minimize a cost function with arguments such as unemployment, social unrest, and foreign debt. An optimal path could be of the form AT in figure 13-13. But by miscalculating either the short-term economic mechanisms at work or the feasible sets constraining policy choice, one may well end up at point B, having for example, triggered off a series of monopolistic wage and price increases and exacerbated the struggle for relative shares by a large devaluation at the time, say, of a bad harvest or a few months before a crucial election. To build such a dynamic framework of analysis is, of course, much easier said than done. But the real problems are dynamic and concern relative adjustment speeds and political constraints. Current dissatisfaction with the theory and practice of stabilization programs will persist until more knowledge is gained about dynamic adjustment processes and until economic analysis is integrated with a constructive analysis of political constraints and feasibilities. This achievement is impossible within the comparative static IS/LM format.

I would like to conclude with two more specific comments. The distinction between devaluation from a position of open (foreign financed) deficit and a devaluation from a suppressed deficit managed by across-the-board import rationing is crucial in evaluating any particular stabilization package. There is, for example, no import cost-push effect from a devaluation that is premium absorbing. On the contrary, the user cost of imports and close substitutes may actually fall after such a devaluation, particularly if it is accompanied by increased foreign resource transfers. In this context it is worth stressing that resistance to devaluation may not always, or only, come from the working class or the left but may come even more strongly from the interest groups that benefit from large import premia and quantity rationing. Turkey in 1978 and 1979 provided the spectacle of a left-of-center populist government fiercely resisting exchange rate adjustments while huge rents were earned by a small group of traders and the distribution of income deteriorated rapidly. At no time were there bigger fortunes made overnight.

Finally, specific supply bottlenecks and constraints from the nontradable sectors may indeed be very important and cause continuous stagflationary problems, making efforts at stabilization policy and balance-of-payments management even more difficult. But here the answer may lie not in macroeconomic policy but in action at the microeconomic and/or institutional level. When macroeconomic policy is made difficult or impossible by microeconomic structure and institutional constraints, it may be time to widen "the narrow limits of the possible" by actions other than macroeconomic policy. Of course, these actions should encompass much more than the perennial "get the prices right." It is not a coincidence, for example, that some of the success stories of the last decades occurred in countries that had benefited from quite radical land reforms. I am thus in agreement with what I take to be Taylor's basic argument that there is much more to successful policy than cutting credit and devaluing and that the state of the art should not allow overconfidence by the IMF or others in any particular prescription. Every case is different and requires in-depth, specific analysis. Simple rules applied indiscriminately on the basis of minimal analysis will not do.

Discussion

Peter Clark (Federal Reserve Board) argued that Taylor's study failed to demonstrate its central hypothesis that standard policies should be discarded and that gradualism is preferable to shock treatment. The model is one of comparative statics, yet a dynamic model showing adjustment over time is essential to knowing the effects of policies over the longer term, the proper time horizon for a stabilization program. Thus Taylor's conclusion that monetary restraint raises inflation is a short-term result that would probably be reversed over a period of, say, two years. Clark pointed out that Taylor's study can have the absurd policy implications that in the face of inflation and balance-of-payments deficit, the country should expand the money supply rapidly and revalue. Clark called for additional research into the best time path for stabilization, and into the key parameters and economic relations relevant for stabilization programs. *David Overton* (Central Intelligence Agency) stated that the model's characteristics and data requirements made it applicable to only a few countries.

Lance Taylor accepted that the model was not necessarily generally applicable. He expressed concern about the emphasis in the comments on the longer term, arguing that policy is made quarter by quarter. He agreed on the need to pursue the time path analysis Dervis suggested. Defending the use of comparative statics and the steady state, he averred that these are the tools available and that in between is a wasteland.

Conference Participants

with their affiliations at the time of the conference

James Adams *World Bank*

Montek S. Ahluwalia *Ministry of Finance, Government
of India*

Tony Albrecht *U.S. State Department*

Arne Anderson *American University*

Joel Bergsman *World Bank*

Stanley W. Black *Vanderbilt University*

Hollis B. Chenery *World Bank*

Peter Clark *Federal Reserve Board*

William R. Cline (conference cochairman) *Brookings Institution*

Margaret E. Crahan *Woodstock Theological Seminary,
Georgetown University*

Jorge del Canto *International Monetary Fund (retired)*

Sidney Dell *Centre on Transnational Corporations,
United Nations*

Kemal Dervis *World Bank*

Carlos Diaz-Alejandro *Yale University*

Robert Emery *Federal Reserve Board*

Albert Fishlow *Yale University*

Alejandro Foxley *Corporación de Investigaciones Económicas
para Latinoamerica (Chile)*

Irving S. Friedman *First Boston Corporation*

Stephen E. Guisinger *University of Texas*

Arnold C. Harberger *University of Chicago*

G. K. Helleiner *University of Toronto*

H. Robert Heller *Bank of America*

John Holsen *World Bank*

Abraham Katz *U.S. Commerce Department*

Lawrence B. Krause *Brookings Institution*

Anne O. Krueger *University of Minnesota*
Danny Leipziger *U.S. State Department*
Frank J. Lysy *Johns Hopkins University*
Ronald I. McKinnon *Stanford University*
Constantine Michalopoulos *U.S. Agency for International*
    Development
Arnold Nachmanoff *U.S. Treasury Department*
Roger D. Norton *University of New Mexico*
Stephen O'Brien *World Bank*
David Overton *Central Intelligence Agency*
Gustav F. Papane *Boston University*
Robert Pelikan *U.S. Treasury Department*
Seung Yoon Rhee *Korea Development Institute*
Sherman Robinson *World Bank*
Joanne Salop *International Monetary Fund*
Daniel M. Schydlowsky *Boston University*
Marilyn Seiber *U.S. Commerce Department*
Robert Slighton *Chase Manhattan Bank*
Ernest Stern *World Bank*
Jack Sweeney *U.S. Treasury Department*
Lance Taylor *Massachusetts Institute of Technology*
Saúl Trejo Reyes *Office of the President, Mexico*
Henry Wallich *Federal Reserve Board*
James H. Weaver *American University*
Richard Weinert *Leslie, Weinert & Co., Inc.*
Sidney Weintraub (conference cochairman) *Lyndon B. Johnson*
    School of Public Affairs, University of Texas
Larry E. Westphal *World Bank*
Joseph Winder *U.S. Treasury Department*

Approximately 125 participants attended the conference, which included a dinner
address by Anthony M. Solomon, Under Secretary for Monetary Affairs, U.S. Department of the Treasury. This list includes only authors of papers, discussants, and
other participants whose contributions are reported in this volume.

Index

Abramowitz, M., 209n
Abusada-Salah, Roberto, 327
Adams, James, 374
Africa, 1–2, 33, 52
Aggregate demand, 126–27, 134–35, 316–17, 326–34
Aghevli, Bijan B., 52, 416n
Agriculture: crop failure, 60–61; favorable harvests, 104; Mexico, 273; modernization, 502; Pakistan, 376, 381; production fluctuations, 50; South Korea, 459–60; supply shocks, 490–92; Tanzania, 340, 352, 358, 360, 362–64
Ahluwalia, Montek S., 161n
Akrasanee, Narongchai, 110n
Albrecht, Tony, 463
Alexander, Sidney, 226
Aliber, R. Z., 216n
Alliance for Progress, 140
Altimir, Oscar, 274
Ando, Albert, 46n
Arellano, J., 220n
Argentina: food production decline, 60n; stabilization policies, 199n, 204. *See also* Latin America, stabilization policies
Aronson, Jonathan D., 3n
Arrow, Kenneth, 209n
Asheshov, Nicolas, 308n
Asia, inflation reduction, 1–2, 33, 60
Assets: concentration, 127, 211–15; indexation, 53
Auguiano Roch, Eugenio, 276
Avery, Robert B., 62n, 73n

Bacha, Edmar, 205n
Baer, Werner, 227n
Balance-of-payments deficits: ability to control, 31; financing of, 96–97, 354; Mexico, 280–83; overview, *1970s,* 2–3, 80; Pakistan, 375, 378–80; as response

to excess demand, 95–96; stabilization effect on, 124; Tanzania, 345; and world trade volume, 57, 59, 171–75, 185–86
Balassa, Bela, 111n, 273n
Baldwin, Robert, 90n
Ball, R. J., 48n, 410n
Bangladesh: destabilizing food subsidies, 61n; expansionary stabilization, 233, 404; negative growth rate, 403; ratio of debt to export earnings, 239
Banks. *See* Commercial banks
Baraona, P., 205n
Barro, R. J., 209n, 414n
Barua, Luis, 306
Behrman, Jere R., 46n, 92n
Beim, David O., 305n
Belliveau, Nancy, 306n
Bergsman, Joel, 270, 273–74
Bhagwati, Jagdish N., 106n, 141, 150n, 218n
Bhalla, Surjit S., 35n, 50, 60
Bhutto, Zulfikar Ali, 382, 389
Bias of trade regimes. *See* Trade regimes
Black, Stanley W., 43n, 81
Blair, Calvin P., 281n
Blue, Richard, 335n
Bolivia. *See* Latin America, stabilization policies
Borrowing, in stabilization plans, 112–13
Bortolani, Sergio, 51n
Bottleneck inflation, 193, 310, 491, 505; and "excess demand," 326–34; export promotion to relieve, 501
Bravo Aguilera, Luis, 277n
Brazil, 3; bypassing of IMF, 139, 140; crawling-peg exchange rate, 135, 141, 146; exchange controls, 37, 133; expansionary stabilization, 35, 42, 134, 136; public debt service ratio, 240; removal of export taxes, 110; stabiliza-

tion policies, 38, 92, 104, 205. *See also*
Latin America, stabilization policies
Brimmer, Andrew F., 51n
Brown, Gilbert T., 458n
Brunner, K., 410n
Bruno, Michael, 152n, 211, 217, 393,
466n, 471n, 474n
Bueno, Gerardo M., 273n, 274n, 277n
Burns, T., 410n
Business cycle, worldwide, *1970s,* 53–55,
62

Calmfors, L., 216n
Campos, Roberto, 194n
Canitrot, A., 195n, 199n, 211n
Capital flow: and crawling-peg exchange
rate, 36, 135, 141–42, 146; interna-
tional mobility of, 33, 128–33; sterili-
zation, 36–37, 46, 49–50, 59–60
Capital formation: devaluation effect on,
167–68; Southern Cone weakness, 128
Cardoso, Eliana A., 487n, 491n, 494
Carvalho, Jose, 110n
Cashew nuts, price changes, 441–43
Cavallo, Domingo F., 211, 470n, 485n
Chenery, Hollis B., 274n
Chernow, Ron, 310n
Chichilnisky, Graciela, 491n
Chile, 368; food production decline, 60n;
guarantee deposit requirements, 109;
public debt service ratio, 240; results
of stabilization policies, 92, 199n,
201–04. *See also* Latin America, sta-
bilization policies
China, 368
Chu, Ke-Young, 53
Cizauskas, Albert C., 75
Claasen, E., 500n
Clark, Peter, 506
Cline, William R., 1n, 32n, 33n, 35n,
36n, 44n, 50n, 62n, 66n
Coffee, production fluctuations, 343, 345.
Cole, David C., 458n
Collier, D., 196n
Colombia: crawling-peg exchange rate,
135, 141, 146; stabilization experience, 32–33, 102, 134, 136
Commercial banks: activities during stabilization period, 247–50; attitudes toward lending, 255; developmental
role, 6, 251–53, 265–66; evolution of
lending to developing countries, 235–
40; expectation of debt servicing, 254;
external financing, 240–42, 255–56,
266–67; funds recycling, 3; IMF relationship, 243–50, 253–54, 267–68; in-

fluence on developing countries, 253;
in Jamaica, 263–65; lending policies,
243–47; overlending, 40–41; over-
view, 18–19, 268–70; in Peru, 260–63,
305–06, 309–10, 333; in Turkey, 259–
60; and U.S. loans, 3; in Zaire, 256–
59
Compensatory Finance Facility, IMF,
51, 72, 78
Connors, T. A., 245n
Convertible Turkish Lira Deposit
(CTLD), 259–60
Cooper, Richard N., 101n, 149n, 150,
154, 156, 383, 479n
Copper, 303
Cortés, H., 216n, 218n
Cost-push inflation, 213
Cotton, 341–43
Crahan, Margaret E., 232–33
Crawling-peg exchange rate, 36, 135,
141–42, 146
Credit controls, 397–98
Credit extension: expansion, 51–53; re-
duction, 107–08
Creditworthiness, 62–63
Cuba, 368
Currency devaluation. *See* Devaluation;
Devaluation models
Current account deficits: financing of,
59; selected years, 2–3, 80. *See also*
Balance-of-payments deficits
Czechoslovakia, 364

D'Arista, Jane, 3n
Darity, William, Jr., 473n
Davis, Jeffrey M., 61
Debt restructuring: Jamaica, 263–65;
need for international refinancing fa-
cility, 325; Peru, 260–63, 325; role in
stabilization programs, 106, 110, 249;
Turkey, 259–60; Zaire, 256–59
Debt service: bank expectation of, 254;
priority list, 242; ratios, 238–40
Debt, term, 235–40
Deficit financing: as accelerating infla-
tion, 51–52; foreign lending and aid,
96; Mexico, 278; strategy for, 59
Deficits. *See* Balance-of-payments defi-
cits; Current account deficits
del Canto, Jorge, 333
Dell, Sidney, 4n, 32n, 45n, 81n, 146,
325n, 333, 354
Demand for exports, 171–75, 185–86
Denmark, 137
Destabilization. *See* Stabilization prob-
lems

Devaluation: alternative consequences of, 152–54; as contractionary, 34, 150–52, 154–56, 215–19, 384–87; as expansionary, 149–50, 216, 383; under Fisherian and Keynesian investment conditions, 484–90; as inflationary, 96, 355, 383; liberalizing effect, 98–100; Mexico, 271; Pakistan, 382–87; Peru, 305, 307; and savings-investment responses, 478–81; Tanzania, 351, 355

Devaluation models: combination of stabilizing policies, 174–75; effect on output levels, 161–63; equations used, 158–61; with 5 percent devaluation, 179–81, 183–85; with 5 percent increase in world export prices, 185–86; five-sector model, 175–79; increase in export demand, 169–72, 186–87; one-sector model, 156–58, 163; overview, 13–16; Pakistan, 384–87; reduction in investment demand, 172–73; with 10 percent devaluation, 165–69, 187–88; validity of, 188–89, 226–27, 229–30

Developing countries: creditworthiness, 62–63, 255; destabilizing, conditions, 1–3; GDP growth rates, 3–4; and IMF, 6. *See also* specific countries and issues

Diamand, M., 192, 222n

Diaz-Alejandro, Carlos F., 93, 102, 106n, 150, 154, 218n, 479n

Domestic growth. *See* Gross domestic product; Growth

Dornbusch, Rudiger, 216n, 393n, 466n

Droughts, 358, 381

Echeverría, Luis, 272, 274–78, 280, 283, 284, 296

Eckaus, Richard S., 151, 183n

Eckstein, Otto, 213n

Economic growth. *See* Gross domestic product; Growth

Economic instability. *See* Stabilization problems

Economic models: discriminant analysis of stabilization problems, 62–71, 73–77; LINK model, 48–49. *See also* Devaluation models; South Korean stabilization model; Structuralism, IS/LM model

Economic stabilization: conditions necessitating, 1–4; early action, 33; elimination of inflation, 250–51; expectation of success, 32–33, 91, 101–02; expenditure reduction policies criticized, 354; feasibility of objectives, 102–03; foreign borrowing, 112–13; foreign loans and aid, 113–14; gradual versus abrupt change, 111–12; granting of trade preferences to developing countries, 114, 171, 186–87, 189, 501–02; macromonetary components, 107–08; monetarist theory, 194; orthodox policies criticized, 310–12, 465; policy assessments criticized, 114–17, 141–42; political constraints, 39–40, 47, 225; populist theories, 120–22, 195–96; preexisting conditions, 103–06; responsibility of individual country, 6–7, 72–73, 81; short-term costs, 100–01, 110–11; socialist theory, 354–55; structuralist theory, 34–35, 192–94, 465; success criteria, 106–07; trade and exchange rate components, 108–10; typical program, 122–23, 149; unpredictable factors, 39. *See also* specific countries and issues

Egypt, 4, 61n

Eisenbeis, Robert A., 62n, 73n

Elasticity of exports. *See* Devaluation models

Emery, Robert, 463

Escobedo, Gilberto, 278n

Exchange rate: adjustment to domestic inflation, 46, 50, 53; crawling-peg, 36, 135, 141–42, 146; fixed, floating, 43; and growth, 89; as monetary function, 84; policies, 108–09; realignments, 43; sliding-peg, 84–86, 93–95, 103

Expansionary stabilization: as policy alternative, 35–36, 133–38; in selected countries, 233, 404; structuralist model, 493–97

Expectation: of inflation, 120–21, 206–08, 323; of successful stabilization, 32–33, 91, 101–02

Export demand: increase in, 124–25, 171–75, 185–86; promotion by developed countries, 114, 117, 186–87, 189, 501–02

Export earnings: and external debt, 239; world trade volume changes, 46–50, 53–57, 59, 61

Export promotion: growth under, 88–89; market restrictions, 448; to relieve bottleneck inflation, 501; South Korea, 441, 443–44. *See also* Trade regimes

Fair, Ray C., 470n

Felix, David, 274n

Feltenstein, Andrew, 53

Ferrer, A., 199n
Ffrench-Davis, R., 195n
Financial markets: liberalization, 129–30, 137–38, 145; segmentation, 211–15
Finland, 137
Fiscal policy: effect on stabilization plan, 52–53, 104; income distributional effects, 219–21; in Pakistan, 387–93; restraint under Fisherian and Keynesian investment conditions, 484–90; standard stabilization policies, 107–08; in Tanzania, 356
Fisherian investment demand. *See* Structuralism, IS/LM model
Fishlow, Albert, 104n, 205n
FitzGerald, Edmund V. K., 276n, 277, 294
Foley, Duncan K., 498n
Foreign banks. *See* Commercial banks
Foxley, Alejandro, 198n, 199n, 202n, 215n, 220n
Frank, Charles R., Jr., 62n, 66n, 461n, 462n
Frenkel, Jacob A., 393n, 466n
Frenkel, Robert, 199n, 206n, 211n, 289n
Friedman, Irving S., 237n
Fues, Thomas, 354

Galbis, Vincente, 129n
Galleguillos, S., 205n
Garcia, Adalberto R., 274n
Ghana, 5, 60n
Glezakos, Constantine, 61n
Global economy, 43–45
González, L., 199n, 204n
Gordon, David, 283n
Green, Reginald, 341n, 346n, 347n, 349n, 352n, 353n, 358n
Griffin, K., 194n
Gross domestic product (GDP): and export growth, 443–44; and external debt, 239; Mexico, 272–73; and monetary restraint, 445–49; Pakistan, 375, 378–79; Tanzania, 338–40; worldwide decline, 3–4
Grossman, H., 209n
Gross national product (GNP), 144, 368–69
Growth: economic stabilization and, 7; effect of inflation, 89, 92; and trade regime bias, 90–91; under various trade regimes, 86–89
Guisinger, Stephen, 387n
Gurley, John, 368
Guyana, 368

Hachette, D., 199n
Haddad, Claudio, 110n
Harberger, Arnold C., 218n, 410, 415n, 445, 449
Hemphill, William L., 49n
Herring, Richard, 46n
Hirschman, A., 192, 196n
Holsen, John, 332–33
Hungary, 364
Hyperinflation, 125

IMF. *See* International Monetary Fund
Import liberalization. *See* Trade regimes
Import licensing: as alternative to devaluation, 382–83; premiums defined, 97; system revision, 109
Import substitution: growth problems, 87–88, 144, 280; and resource allotion, 90–91; and stabilization, 105–06. *See also* Trade regimes
Income distribution: after devaluation, 154–55; and economic stabilization, 7, 37–39; Mexico, 274–75; neoclassical theory, 157–58, 169; Peru, 317–21; regressive outcome, 127; Tanzania, 353, 372–74
Indexation of exchange rate. *See* Sliding-peg exchange rate
India, 33, 60n, 61n, 239, 405
Indonesia, 60n, 61n, 233, 404
Inflation: acceleration in *1970s*, 1–2, 33, 60; costs of, 89; and crawling-peg exchange rate, 36, 135, 141–42, 146; and deficit financing, 51–52; exchange rate adjustment, 46, 50, 53, 95–96; expectation of, 120–21, 206–08, 323; and exports, 443–44; and growth, 89; interest rates, 51–53; monetarist theory, 194; and monetary restraint, 34, 445–49; Pakistan, 375, 377–78; reducing, 10–13, 31, 92, 102–03, 125–27, 250–51; South Korea, 410–11, 457–60; structuralist theory, 192–94, 465; supply relationship to, 399–406; suppression by fixed exchange rate, 95–96; trade regime policy, 93–100
Interest rate adjustments, 51–53, 108, 355
Interim Committee, IMF, 44
International Development Association, 371
International Finance Corporation, 362
International Monetary Fund (IMF): Compensatory Finance Facility, 51, 72, 78; extended facility, 286; Interim Committee, 44; Jamaica agreement,

263–65; Mexico agreement, 285–89; oil facility, 78; Peru agreement, 262–63, 306–09; and private banks, 138–41, 243–47, 248–50, 253–54, 267–68; provision of balance-of-payments support, 253; revision of loan conditions, 5–6, 41–42; and stabilization programs, 4–5, 324–26; Tanzania agreement, 351, 369–72, 374; Turkey agreement, 260; World Bank meetings, 44; Zaire agreement, 256–59

Investment: devaluation, 167–69, 179–81, 183–85; Keynesian theory, 167, 177–78

Investment-savings (IS) balance. *See* Structuralism, IS/LM model

Islam, Shafiqul, 498n

Israel, 92

Jamaica, 263–65, 368

Jameson, Kenneth P., 368n

Japan, 448

Johnson, Harry G., 186, 226

Johnson, Omotunde, 5n

Jud, Gustav D., 53n, 73n

Katz, Abraham, 295–96

Kenya, 240

Kerstenetsky, Isaac, 227n

Keynesian economics: orthodox stabilization policies, 497–501. *See also* Structuralism, IS/LM model

Keynes, J. M., 167, 177

Khan, Mohsin S., 52

Kim, Chuk Kyo, 409n

Kim, Kwang Suk, 461n, 462n

Kim, Mahn Je, 409n

Kirkpatrick, C. H., 193n

Korea. *See* South Korea; South Korean stabilization model

Krause, Lawrence B., 35n, 270, 462–63

Kritz, E., 204n

Krueger, Anne O., 50n, 59n, 110n, 119n, 141, 387n, 458n

Krugman, Paul, 150, 154, 217, 479n

Kuczynski, Pedro Pablo, 299n

Kwack, Sung Y., 462

Laidler, David, 410n, 415n

Lara-Resende, Andre, 470n, 494, 497

Lary, Hal B., 110n

Latin America, stabilization policies: asymmetric wage and price policy, 206–09, 211; deficit financing, 52; dependence on authoritarian government, 197, 224–25, 228–29; devaluation, 215–19; employment and income distribution, 199–205; expansionary stabilization, 133–38; financial market segmentation, 211–15; financial policies for trade liberalization, 141–47; fiscal policy, 219–21; inflation, 1–2, 33; interdependency of adjustment mechanisms, 221–22, 228–29; international short-term capital mobility, 128–33; monetarist, 194–95; monetarist-structuralist blend, 196–98; overview, 16–18, 502–03; populist, 120–22, 195–96; results of, 124–28; structuralist, 195; supply disinflationary shocks, 222–24; typical elements of, 122–23, 198–99; underutilization of IMF credit, 138–41; utility of structuralist-monetarist debate, 227–28, 230–32. *See also* specific countries

Lawrence, Roger, 4n, 32n, 81n, 354n

Leff, Nathaniel H., 473n

Leijonhufvud, A., 208n, 209n

Leipziger, Danny M., 44n, 62n, 189, 233, 289n, 325n

Lemgruber, Antonio C., 35n

Leontief, Wassily, 47n

Levhari, David, 414n

Lewis, W. Arthur, 48n, 156, 227

Liberalization of trade regime. *See* Trade regimes

LINK model, 48–49

Liquidity, international, 43

Loaeza, Soledad, 271n

Loan market (LM) curve. *See* Structuralism, IS/LM model

Lofchie, Michael, 345, 362–64, 368

Lopes, Francisco L., 483n, 487n, 498n

López Portillo, José, 271–72, 289–90, 296

Lyman, Princeton N., 458n

Lysy, Frank J., 157n, 158n, 161n, 176n, 179

McKinnon, Ronald I., 51n, 142n, 393

McNamara, Robert S., 42n

Macroeconomic fluctuations. *See* Stabilization problems

Malaysia, 33. *See also* Devaluation models

Malinvaud, E., 209n

Manila Conference, UNCTAD, *1979*, 44

Manufacturing: Mexico, 273–74; Pakistan, 376–77

Markets: asymmetric treatment of, 206–09, 211; under different trade regimes,

84–86, 95; restrictions on export expansion, 448. *See also* Financial markets

Marquez, Javier, 284

Marston, Richard, 46n

Martin, R., 218n

Martirena-Mantel, Ana Maria, 130n

Mason, Edward S., 458n

Meltzer, A. H., 410n

Mered, Michael, 462

Mexico, 3; assessment of Echeverría administration, 292–96; destabilization, *1971–76*, 20, 276–84; destabilizing trends, *1950–70*, 19–20, 273–76; devaluation, 271; food production decline, 60n; GDP growth, *1950–78*, 272–73; IMF agreement, 285–89; Investment Program for Rural Development, 280; public debt service ratio, 239; stabilization program, 20–21, 271–72, 284–85, 289–92

Michaely, Michael, 90n

Michalopoulos, Constantine, 116

Middle East, 1–2, 33

Millan, Patricio, 327

Models: discriminant analysis of stabilization problems, 62–71, 73–77; LINK model, 48–49. *See also* Devaluation models; South Korean stabilization model; Structuralism, IS/LM model

Modigliani, Franco, 192n, 222n

Monetarist theory: on inflation and stabilization, 194; in Latin America, 194–95, 197–99; structuralist-monetarist debate, 227–28, 231–32. *See also* Structuralism, IS/LM model

Monetary policy: asymmetric sterilization of reserves, 46, 49–50, 59–60; expansion, South Korean model, 444–49; impact on stabilization plan, 52–53, 104; inflationary aspects of restraint, 34; in Pakistan, 393–98; restraint under Fisherian and Keynesian investment conditions, 484–90; standard policies, 107–08

Monson, Terry, 110n

Mookerjee, S., 245n

Morales Bermudez, Francisco, 305

Moreya, Manuel, 307

Morley, Samuel, 485n

Mtei, Ndugu E. I. M., 352n, 356n

Muellbaner, H., 208n, 209n

Murray, David, 61

Musgrove, Philip, 320n

Myrdal, Gunnar, 186

Nachmanoff, Arnold, 189

National Bureau of Economic Research, 10, 114

New International Economic Order, 44

Nigeria, 60n

Nixson, F. I., 193n

North-South dialogue, 44

Norton, Roger, 463

Notaro, J., 199n, 204n

Nyerere, Julius, 336, 337, 347n, 361, 363

O'Brien, Stephen, 374

O'Donnell, Guillermo, 120n, 196n, 289n

Oil facility, IMF, 78

Oil prices: destabilizing aspect of increases in, 59, 71, 115, 303; increases, *1974*, 43; model of economic shock factors, 439–42

Oil revenues: Mexico, 288; Peru, 302, 322

Okun, Arthur M., 222n, 223n

Oligopolies, 209

Overton, David, 506

Pakistan: balance-of-trade deficits, 375, 378–80; destabilizing food subsidies, 61n; devaluation as inflationary, 382–87; development, *1950–70*, 25, 376–77; exogenous economic shocks, 379–82; fiscal policy, 387–93; GDP growth fluctuations, 375, 378–79; inflation, 33, 375, 377–78; monetary policy, 393–98; stabilization policies, 25–26, 39, 398–404

Papanek, Gustav F., 146, 233

Paris Club, 256–58

Park, Yung Chul, 51n, 409n

Parkin, J., 194n

Parkin, M., 193n

Patinkin, Don, 414n

Pelikan, Robert, 268–69

Perry, George L., 222n, 223n

Peru, 2, 4, 32, 194; assessment of stabilization program, 310–12, 321–22; debt restructuring, 260–63, 325; devaluation, 305, 307; economic failure, 21–22, 297–301; economic prospects, 322–24; excess demand, 22–23, 316–17, 326–34; exogenous economic shocks, 301–05; exports, 302–03; IMF agreement, 262–63, 306–09; IMF involvement, 324–25; income distributional effects of stabilization, 317–21; military deficit spending, 303–04; and private banks, 305–06, 309–

10, 333; structuralist theory, 312–16, 325–26

Petroleum. *See* Oil prices; Oil revenues

Philippines, 33, 60n

Piazza, Walter, 306

Pinto, A., 193n

Polak, J. J., 245n, 500n

Poland, 364

Political constraints on stabilization strategy, 39–40, 47, 225

Populist economic theories, 120–22, 195–96

Portes, R., 208n, 209n

Prebisch, Raul, 186

Prices: adjustment effect on employment and income distribution, 206–09, 211; controls, removal of, 104–05; domestic subsidies, 61–62; level, determination of, 84; worldwide changes, 302–03, 441–43

Private banks. *See* Commercial banks

Quantitative restrictions, 87, 90, 97–100, 142. *See also* Trade regimes

Rama, Ruth, 273n

Ramos, Joseph, 121n, 207n, 208n

Rangel, Ignacio, 483n, 487n, 488

Ranis, Gustav, 101n, 149n, 274n, 479n

Recession: *1970s* characterized, 43; result of reduced inflation, 92

Reichmann, Thomas M., 5n, 107, 119n, 245n

Reserves, sterilization of, 36–37, 46, 49–50, 59–60

Resources: optimum allocation, 86–87; reallocation, 90–91

Rimez, M., 199n

Robichek, E. Walter, 500n

Robinson, Sherman, 188–89

Roció R. de Villareal, Norma, 277n

Rodriguez, Carlos A., 130n, 416n

Roemer, Michael, 365n

Ruete, Silva, 307

Rwegasira, Delfin, 341n

Salant, Walter S., 35n

Salinas Arizpe, Orel Javier, 247n

Salin, P., 500n

Salop, Joanne, 5n, 189

Sato, Kazuo, 473n

Savings-investment balance. *See* Structuralism, IS/LM model

Savings, sources of, 355

Schydlowsky, Daniel M., 116, 298n, 311, 312n, 316, 327n, 330n, 466n, 479n

Seiber, Marilyn, 269

Sen, Amartya K., 473n

Sheahan, John, 298n, 300n, 306n, 311, 321n

Sheehey, Edmund J., 50n

Shivji, Issa G., 358n

Simulations. *See* Models

Sisal, 441–43

Sjaastad, L., 216n, 218n

Sliding-peg exchange rate: alternative market interactions under, 84–86, 95; formulas for, 93; preferable to fixed rate, 93–94; role in stabilization plan, 103

Slighton, Robert, 269

Socialist economies, 354–55. *See also* Tanzania; Tanzanian stabilization program

Sohmen, Egon, 100n

Solís, Leopoldo, 278n

Southern Cone. *See* Latin America, stabilization policies; specific countries

South Korea: current account deficit financing, 96n; destabilizing food subsidies, 61n; inflation reduction, 33, 92; interest rate reform, 108; quantitative restrictions, 98n

South Korean stabilization model: consumption function, 410; equations used, 411–25; export growth policy simulation, 441, 443–44; focus of model, 407, 409–11; model utility, 457–63; monetary policy simulation, 444–47; oil price increase simulation, 439–42; overview, 26–28; policy implications, 447–49; sample period performance, 425–38

Sri Lanka, 33, 60n, 61n, 368

Srinivasan, T. N., 106n

Stabilization. *See* Economic stabilization

Stabilization problems: asymmetric sterilization of reserves, 36–37, 46, 49–50, 59–60; discriminant analysis of, 62–71, 73–77, fluctuation causes, 46–47, 60–62; inflation, 60; internal and external factors, 6–7, 71–73, 77–81; overview, 8–10, 31–32; statistical analysis, 62–71, 73–77; transmission mechanisms for disturbances, 47–53; world trade volume changes, 53–57, 59

Stallings, Barbara, 298n, 306n, 311

Stepan, A., 205n

Sterilization of capital inflows, 36–37, 46, 49–50, 59–60

Stern, Ernest, 81

Stillson, Richard T., 5n, 107, 119, 245n

Structuralism, IS/LM model: devaluation, 478–81; differences from Keynesian model, 468–69; equations used, 469–75; expansionary stabilization policies, 493–97; inflationary pressure from nontraded goods, two-sector model, 490–92; IS curve, derivations, 475–81; LM curve, derivation, 481–84; monetarist theories, 497–501; overview, 28–31, 505–06; policy alternatives, 501–03; semi-industrialized countries, 466–68; standard stabilization policies, 484–90; timing of adjustment policies, 503–05

Structuralist theory: criticism of standard stabilization policies, 310–12; empirical tests of, Peru, 312–16, 325–26; on inflation and stabilization, 34–35, 192–94, 465; in Latin America, 195, 197–99; structuralist-monetarist debate, 227–28, 231–32

Subsidies, 61–62, 319–21

Sudan, 2

Sunkel, Osvaldo, 193n, 194n, 491n

Sweeney, Jack, 333

Swoboda, Alexander K., 500n

Taiwan, 33, 448, 459

Tanzania: balance of payments, 345; components of import increases, 340–41; food subsidies, 61n; fluctuations in exports, 341–43, 345; GDP components, 338–40; GNP growth, 368–69; socialist orientation, 336–37, 339; socioeconomic data, 335–36. *See also* Agriculture

Tanzanian stabilization program: centrist critique, 358–62; critiques summarized, 24, 354–55, 367–69; economic status after implementation, 352–54, 374; effects and costs of, 348, 353; government policies, *1970–71*, 346; government policies, *1974–75*, 23–24, 346–52, 355–57; IMF agreement, 351; income distribution, 353, 372–74; leftist critique, 357–58; rightist critique, 362–67; split with IMF, 369–72, 374; World Bank, 351–52, 359–62, 371–72

Tanzi, Vito, 52

Taxation, 38, 220–21

Taylor, Lance, 116, 150, 154, 205n, 217, 310–11, 383, 409n, 414, 466n, 479n, 491n

Tea, 441–43

Term debt: amounts and components, 235–40; definition, 235n

Thailand, 33, 60n, 239, 240

Thorp, Rosemary, 194, 298n, 300n, 311, 312n

Tidrick, Gene M., 365n

Tobacco, 441–43

Tobin, James, 167, 213n, 472

Trade regimes: alteration of, 90–91, 102–03; alternative market interactions, 84–86, 95; bias of, 10–13, 87; favorable trade movements, 104; financing of payments deficit, 95–97; growth conditions under, 86–89; import liberalization, 143–44, 323; and increased imports, 92; liberalization, 97–100, 109–10, 141–47; policy objectives, 84; resource allocation after alteration of, 90–91; responses to inflation, 93–95

Trejo Reyes, Saúl, 274n, 290

Turkey, 2, 92, 105, 505; current account deficit financing, 96n; debt restructuring, 259–60

Unemployment, 127, 201, 274

Urquidi, Victor L., 280n

Uruguay, stabilization policies, 204–05. *See also* Latin America, stabilization policies

Van Arkadie, Brian, 341n

Van Wijnbergen, Sweder, 462, 473n

Varian, Hal R., 469n

Villareal, René, 277n

Vogel, R. C., 410n, 416n, 445, 449

Waelbroek, J., 48n

Wages: adjustment, 206–09, 211; increases, 53; rates after devaluation, 155–56

Wallace, Robert Bruce, 273n

Wallich, Henry C., 137n, 269–70

Walras' law, 498

Weaver, James H., 335n

Webb, Richard C., 299n, 318n

Weinert, Richard S., 309n, 333

Wells, J. R., 220n

Westphal, Larry E., 458n, 461n, 462n

Wicht, Juan J., 298n, 311, 312n, 316, 327n, 330n

Wilber, Charles K., 368n

Williams, David, 365n

Williamson, J., 142n

Winder, Joseph, 116

Witteveen, H. Johannes, 245n

World Bank: IMF meetings, 44; lending policies, 6, 42, 253; Tanzania agreement, 351–52, 359–62, 371–72
World trade volume. *See* Export demand; Export earnings

Yugoslavia, 239, 364, 365

Zaire, 2, 239, 256–59
Zambia, 2
Zis, G., 193n